Theories of Learning

Theories of Learning:

Traditional Perspectives/Contemporary Developments

Leland C. Swenson
Loyola Marymount University

Wadsworth Publishing Company
Belmont, California
A Division of Wadsworth, Inc.

Psychology Editor: Kenneth King
Production Editor: Carolyn Tanner
Designer: Robert Hu
Copy Editor: Victoria Nelson
Technical Illustrator: Evanell Towne

ACKNOWLEDGMENTS

Excerpts in Chapters 4 and 9 reprinted with permission of Macmillan Publishing Company, Inc., from *Science and Human Behavior* by B. F. Skinner. Copyright © 1953 by Macmillan Publishing Company, Inc.
Excerpts in Chapter 5 from E. M. Standing, *Maria Montessori: Her Life and Work* (Fresno: Academic Press Guild, 1959). Reprinted by permission.
Excerpts in Chapter 9 from Werner K. Honig, *Operant Behavior: Areas of Research and Application*, © 1966, pp. 426–427. Reprinted by permission of Prentice-Hall, Inc., Englewood Cliffs, New Jersey.

Printed in the United States of America
1 2 3 4 5 6 7 8 9 10—84 83 82 81 80

Library of Congress Cataloging in Publication Data

Swenson, Leland.
  Theories of learning.

  Includes bibliographical references and indexes.
  1. Learning, Psychology of.   2.   Conditioned
response.   I.   Title.
BF318.S93   153.1'5   79-15139
ISBN 0-534-00698-1

Table of Contents

Table of Contents

The completion of most major projects in our lives have a history and this learning textbook is no exception. When I began teaching courses in learning psychology at Occidental College in Los Angeles I was faced with a problem. I was unable to find a single text that covered most of the topics I thought essential to an adequate exposure to this very important area of psychology. My response was to order a variety of supplemental books. This response created a new problem—that of students being reluctant to buy and read multiple texts. This forced me to begin writing and distributing short supplemental handouts. Later in my current teaching position at Loyola Marymount University I continued to write and revise these supplements until I had finally replaced all but one of the supplementary texts. By 1975 my supplements had developed into the rough draft of a complete learning text manuscript. Discovering this, various publishers' representatives suggested submitting this manuscript to their publishing houses. The initial feedback was sufficiently encouraging to goad me into serious writing and revising.

My goals were to create a text that combined a historical perspective on the development of major learning theories, a sound exposure to major principles of learning, and information about how learning principles and theories were being applied in the real world, with student-oriented writing and a multitude of examples. I wanted to expose students to both animal and human research and to the process by which early discoveries about learning evolved into the issues and principles of interest to today's psychologists and educators. I planned my language and examples to be interesting and understandable to students, hopefully without oversimplification. Most of all I wrote to communicate my excitement about the great progress being made in understanding learning and how it affects all our lives.

This text was designed to provide a solid background in the psychology of learning for students with a wide range of academic and career objectives. To make this complex subject area understandable to students with diverse interests, I incorporated many learning aids including: introductory and perspective sections for all chapters and parts of the text, mini-summaries of major points, lists of key terms, a glossary of such key terms, and comparisons of each major theory on six key points. All of these features were developed over several years of class testing and interactions with the Wadsworth editorial and peer-review personnel.

The organization of this text reflects ten years of my experiences in presenting the essential aspects of learning psychology. The first half introduces the major principles incorporated within the great theories of learning, arranged in rough chronological order. The second half builds on these theories and principles by showing how current research has forced re-evaluation of many of their major assumptions. Approaches covered in the second half of the text are arranged in the same order as the earlier versions of these approaches to facilitate comparisons and a sense of continuity. A major content innovation in this text is thorough coverage of modern cognitive theories, including the information processing paradigm. Both parts of the text provide extensive review of applications related to basic points of theory and principle to further aid the student in mastering the material.

Finally, any writing project of this scope is rarely a solo effort. I would like to gratefully acknowledge the detailed reviews provided by the following reviewers: Kenneth Basilio, Salem State College; William Hellix, San Diego State College; Peter Holland, University of Pittsburgh; Jerry Ison, Missouri Western State College; and Susan Mineka, University of Wisconsin. Additionally, I would like to thank Laurel Bartlett for her inspiration and assistance during the formative stages of this manuscript, Beverly Frazier, Nancy Clark, Patrice Miles, Sharon Geraci, and the Loyola Marymount University faculty secretaries for their help in typing, editing, and evaluating the developing text, the Wadsworth people (especially Ken King, the psychology editor) for their advice and assistance, and my students for continuing support and feedback. This book would never have been completed without the enthusiasm of my students: I hope you come to share their (and my) excitement with this text and the field of learning psychology.

Theories of Learning

Somewhere, somebody has just discovered that he really likes jazz. This seems strange to him, because he has always hated jazz. By coincidence, he is fiercely in love with someone who loves jazz and spends weekends listening to it.

Somewhere else, a student sitting at her desk has a sudden flash of insight about why psychology departments require their majors (who are enrolled in psychology to understand people) to take courses in statistics and what the relationship is between statistics and understanding people.

And finally, a teacher is giving elementary school pupils checkmarks for desirable behaviors. The children have been told that they will be able to have various treats and privileges at a later time based on the number of checks they receive, and the teacher notes with satisfaction that their behavior is getting better day by day . . .

All these events are examples of the process (or processes) that we call learning. Learning is the most important process by which we manage to change, adapt, and become (hopefully) more competent over the years. The study of how this process occurs is a special and important responsibility of the serious student of psychology. Of all the subdivisions of psychology, none has seen such widespread application, in so many places and for so many purposes, as the psychology of learning. The principles derived from the work of B. F. Skinner have led to the powerful technology of token economies, a technique which is extensively applied in schools, hospitals, prisons, and therapy settings. Parts of Piaget's theory have become common practice in modern lower-grade classrooms. In many environments and in many ways, the results of research by learning theorists on how we learn are changing lives.

Ironically, nowhere else in psychology have the positions of major theorists been so far apart and the arguments so heated as in debates among learning theorists—especially between the strict **behaviorists** and the **cognitive humanists.** Behaviorists claim that our behaviors are caused by events in our environments (stimuli), and cognitive humanists assert that we are capable of free choices; there seems little room for compromise between the two.

The arguments are heated and the stakes are high. In the application of learning principles, psychologists claim to have the technology not only to aid learning and change individual behaviors but, ultimately, through universal application, to mold the type of world in which we live. With stakes such as these, it is important for anyone involved in the study of psychology who plans to "work with people" to become familiar with the major learning theories and learning principles. To understand the assumptions, vital findings, and laws of learning of each theoretical position, moreover, you must be familiar not only with current major theories but also with their historical roots. The first half of this book provides just such a historical foundation.

Speculation about what is learned and how we learn it has a long history. Aristotle, the Greek philosopher, suggested that learning occurred because of the associations in the same times, or spaces, of things and ideas. For example: If a professor always prefaced important points by clearing her throat, you would tend to get ready to take notes whenever she showed this behavior. This **associationist** or **contiguity** explanation of learning reappears in the writings of such eighteenth- and nineteenth-century British philosophers as James Mill and John Stuart Mill (in Horton and Turnage, 1976) and continues to be influential via the principles of **classical conditioning** developed by Pavlov in Russia. In addition to assuming that learning occurs through the contiguity of sensations, the associationists assumed that the mind of the newborn human was a blank slate **(tabula rasa)** upon which experience wrote. Opposed to the associationists' **nurture** or environmental bias were the views of such philosophers as Descartes and Kant, who believed that the content and operations of the mind were largely **innately** determined. As you will see, this **nature** bias is still important, if in a weaker form, in some of the theories to be presented to you.

The purpose of this extremely brief summary of the philosophical background of investigations about learning has been to introduce some of the issues that divide learning psychologists. Let us now outline these issues. This outline will, in turn, provide us with a system for classifying the theories and theorists discussed in this book.

The Hows and Whys of Learning: Some Key Issues

The first major issue is the content of learning. Most of the philosophers who were concerned about learning assumed that the substance of what was learned was ideas or mental structures. Ideas are also called **cognitions,** and psychologists who believe that ideas are units of learning are called **cognitive learning** theorists. The student mentioned at the beginning of the chapter who had a sudden **insight** into the relationship between statistics and understanding people illustrated cognitive learning. In opposition to this viewpoint are the **connectionist** theorists, who believe that the essential unit of what is learned is a new connection between an environmental event (stimulus) and either another stimulus or a response. Since most connectionists reject the idea of examining ideas in favor of observing overt (that is, observable) behaviors, an activity that is assumed to be more objective and scientific, they are also often labeled behaviorists.

A second major issue is how the elements learned are connected. Aristotle and the British associationist philosophers previously mentioned assumed that the **contiguity,** the proximity or close association, of the elements was sufficient. The example we saw of the pairing of jazz with a distinctly pleasant stimulus (in this case, a girlfriend) was able to bring about positive feelings towards jazz. Theories of learning based on this assumption are thus labeled contiguity theories in this book. The opposing view assumes that the pleasant or unpleasant (or drive-reducing or painful) consequences of behavior determine whether something will be learned, as when a teacher, for example, is able to increase the desirable behavior of children through rewards. These theories are related to the philosophy of **hedonism,** which concerns itself with the effects of pain and pleasure on human behavior. Theories of learning which focus on the consequences of behavior are labeled **reinforcement** theories in this book. Here reinforcement is regarded as roughly like reward, but without its subjective emotional connotations.

The third major issue dividing learning theorists is the issue of nature versus nurture: that is, to what extent are innate factors responsible for learning? Behaviorist theorists retain the nurture (environmental) bias of the early associationist philosophers, while theorists with closer ties to biology tend to favor including innate or nature factors in their theories. John Watson, the first self-identified behaviorist, believed in the *tabula rasa* or blank state concept so strongly that he thought all human differences in ability and personality traits were the result of learning. Recently, the behavioristic nurture bias has been challenged by theorists who think we may inherit an inborn predisposition to learn some things more easily than others, such as fears of snakes or spiders.

To prepare you for the material to be covered in this book, Table I.1 shows you where each of the major theorists stands on these three central issues. It may be helpful for you to review Table I.1 as you finish studying each of the two parts of this book.

The opening chapters of each part of the book cover the contiguity-connectionists followed by the reinforcement connectionists, the cognitivists, theories using many biological concepts, and finally **two-factor** (a theoretical approach we will examine in greater detail), multifactor, and **eclectic*** theories. Both parts of the book then conclude with summary and integrative material.

In addition to the three great issues just discussed, some other important points of controversy bear mentioning. One of these is the question of the legitimacy of generalizing principles discovered through research on animals to human learning. Skinner has developed teaching machines for use with children based on the same principles used in building "Skinner boxes" for pigeons. The assumption that the basic laws of learning are the same for rats, pigeons, and humans has been a central assumption of most behaviorists. We will discuss the relevance of this assumption to behavioristic models of learning as well as reviewing attacks on it, both by cognitive theorists who feel that human learning is qualitatively different from animal learning, and by biologically oriented theorists who feel that the forces of evolution have led to some differences in how the laws of learning apply to different species.

Another issue that divides theorists is that of the continuity or discontinuity of the basic learning process. Most behaviorists (Guthrie is a noted exception) believe that the learning of connections is a gradual and continuous process,

---

* Eclectic means tolerant and willing to borrow ideas from a range of opposing viewpoints. For example, some **two-factor** theorists have proposed that some kinds of learning occur through the actions of contiguity factors while other kinds of learning occur through reinforcement factors.

Table 1.1 Theorists and Issues

The What of Learning

Connectionist (S-R and/or S-S Bonds Learned) ———— Neutral ———— Cognitivist (Ideas or Mental Structures Learned)

Connectionist (S-R and/or S-S Bonds Learned)		Neutral		Cognitivist (Ideas or Mental Structures Learned)
Watson	Pavlov		Tolman	gestalt theorists
Guthrie	early Mowrer		late Mowrer	Chomsky
Skinner	most neo-Skinnerians		Montesorri	Piaget
Miller and Dollard	Hull and Spence		Saltz	
Thorndike	Garcia		Luria (neo-Pavlovian)	
			Bandura	
			Pribram	
			Seilgman	

The How of Learning

Contiguity as the Mechanism ———— Neutral ———— Reinforcement as the Mechanism

Contiguity as the Mechanism	Neutral		Reinforcement as the Mechanism
Pavlov	Spence	Hull	Thorndike
Watson		Skinner	Miller and Dollard
Guthrie		neo-Skinnerians	

Involvement of Innate Factors

Nurture Bias ———— Neutral ———— Nature Bias

Nurture Bias		Neutral		Nature Bias
Watson	Pavlov	Pribram	gestalt theorists	ethologists
Guthrie	Thorndike		Montessori	
	Hull and Spence		Chomsky	
	Skinner and neo-Skinnerians		Piaget	
	Tolman		Seligman and Garcia	
	Saltz			
	functionalists			

This table shows the relative positions taken by the theorists presented in this book on three major issues. Theorists not listed under a particular issue present no clear position. S = stimulus, R = response.

with the strength of the connection gradually increasing as the number of successful trials increases. Guthrie and most cognitive theorists believe that a connection or cognition or insight can appear suddenly and at full strength at one particular moment.

Another important issue which has led to many heated discussions at psychological conventions is the issue of determinism versus free will. The extreme behaviorists see our behavior as "caused" by events in our past and present environments, but most cognitive theorists see us as being able to make real choices about our behavior. The behaviorists accuse the humanistic-cognitive theorists of being illogical and romantic and the cognitive humanist psychologists call the behaviorists manipulative and blind to the real meaning of what it is to be a human being. These differences among psychologists have more relevance than simply inciting interesting cocktail party conversations. They determine what principles get applied, by whom, and for what purposes.

Because one factor determining the influence of a given theoretical approach is the extent to which its principles can be translated into useful applications, this text will follow up the purely theoretical material in the chapters with suggestions for application and examples of applications. This material on applications should help you to gain a broader appreciation of the impact of the learning theories and a better understanding of the theories behind the applications.

On Theories and Theorists

You will discover that part of the difference among viewpoints is a matter of defining the same things in different ways. The same facts may be interpreted by different theorists in different ways. Theorists may also use the same term but define it differently. Just what does the term "reinforcement" mean? Pavlov defines it as following a learned cue (or stimulus) by a cue to which the organism is innately programmed to respond. Skinner, on the other hand, defines it as whatever increases the probability of a reoccurrence of the response which occurred just before the reinforcement event. What does the term "unlearned drive" mean? Tolman suggests that exploration is an example of such a basic need, while Watson limits basic needs to biological necessities such as food, water, and sex.

Theorists also interpret the same objective event in different ways. A rat can learn to alternate between going left and going right in a T-shaped simple maze. The cognitive theorists would maintain that the rat has a concept about the relationship of trials and directions to turn. The behaviorists retort that the rat has learned a series of internal stimulus-response connections. And so it goes . . .

Another source of difference among learning theorists is related to the personalities and prejudices of the major theorists and their willingness to defend their theories. You will find that theories are more likely to cease being taken seriously as a result of their major advocate's death than as the result of devastating experiments conducted by their foes. In general, as long as a theorist remains interested in his theory, he tends to change it to handle potentially dangerous data rather than switching to embrace the theory of a rival. As theories are modified to prevent direct contradiction by data that does not fit the theorist's original concept, they tend to lose the special clear insight of their developers and become diffuse and complex. The result of this process is that theories tend to become more and more like one another while retaining their specialized systems languages, or jargons.

If so much depends on definition and personality, why study learning theories at all, and especially why study obsolete theories? Part of the answer is that the major theories developed before 1955 dealt with the same major issues that divide the modern theorists to be presented in Part 2 of this book. For another, the early theories provide clear and consistent views of different aspects of learning and illuminate and clarify the major issues. This illumination of major issues is a very valuable tool in trying to understand the same issues concealed within the more diffuse framework of modern positions. A sound knowledge of the basic aspects of early psychological theories of learning will help to provide a perspective for the study of current theories and a unifying base on which to build knowledge about current trends and principles. In addition, the early theories provide a logical place to begin introducing major principles, since these principles were developed within these organized theoretical systems.

Theories are essentially tools to help us to understand complex events. They are simplified versions of reality which, if well designed, can predict what will happen in reality. Theories are thus models of reality, just like most model airplanes are designed to represent real airplanes. If a model airplane is enough like the real airplane it represents, some of its "behaviors," such as gliding characteristics, will predict similar actions in the real airplane. If a theory is a close enough match to the real world, predictions generated from that theory will predict real behavior of real organisms.

Most of the theories presented in Part 1 of this book are comprehensive theories that attempt to explain a wide range of behaviors. Many of the theories presented in Part 2 of this text, however, are much more limited in scope. Chomsky's theory of language learning is an example. Such miniature theories are often called models rather than theories. Use of the term "model" does not make such a miniature theory any less a theory, and the comments about the uses of theories also apply fully to models. The trend towards models about limited kinds of learning reflects the increased knowledge about learning which has resulted from continuing research. As our total knowledge increases, so does the difficulty of fitting all the different kinds of findings into one comprehensive theory. Theories have helped to promote immense creativity in research by forcing their creators to defend their own work and to discredit rival theories. The progress of psychologists trying to understand learning has often been slow, and if theorists were not motivated to defend and attack theories, much less important and useful research would have been done than is actually the case.

The data collected as a result of this intense process may eventually lead to one **unitheory** of learning. This hypothetical unitheory would be the "one" theory of learning, just as chemists have one theory of the relationships of the physical elements in the periodic table. We are a long way from that goal, however. As our science matures, the role of clearly defined and differentiated theories is diminishing. Learning is now generally conceded to be much more complex than the early theorists thought. Increasingly, psychologists are becoming eclectic and are borrowing from many viewpoints. As you go through this text, compare the theories of the first and second parts and note this process of increasing complexity. Some prominent theorists (such as Skinner) have argued for simply collecting empirical facts and avoiding premature attempts to explain underlying variables. This does not mean, however, that Skinner is unwilling to discuss theoretical issues.

The essential assumptions about man and learning that underlie the positions of the connectionist theorists as compared to the cognitive theorists are worlds apart, and these differences lead to major differences in their respective prescriptions for action. The differing assumptions influenced the basic and comprehensive laws that have been developed by each theorist; these laws in turn determined the applications suggested for use in the real world (the world lying two feet outside of the borders of all colleges and universities). To understand these all-important assumptions, it is helpful to refer back to their historical roots. Theories and theorists are not independent of historical influences.

Because the historical context was so important in influencing the work of major theorists, a short biographical statement about each of these theorists is presented in Part 1 of this book. This background should aid you in understanding why these theorists developed the assumptions that they did. Most of the trends initiated by the major early theorists are explored further in Part 2. Because Part 2 for the most part develops existing trends covering many contributors and is focused on new principles rather than theories, such biographical information is not included in the second part.

Key Terms

associationist	contiguity	nurture
behaviorist	eclectic	reinforcement
classical conditioning	hedonism	*tabula rasa*
cognition	innate	two-factor theory
cognitive humanist	insight	unitheory
cognitive learning	instrumental	
connectionist	nature	

One

The first theories we will look at in Part 1 are the connectionist theories, because the modern era of the study of learning began with Pavlov's study in Russia of contiguity conditioning and Thorndike's study in America of reinforcement(reward)-dependent conditioning. Watson and Guthrie were the first to develop American theories of contiguity conditioning. Watson not only brought the term "behaviorist" into the language of psychology but, during his last years in the academic world, popularized Pavlov's findings as well. The part begins with the contiguity theories; Chapter 1 covers Pavlov, and Chapter 2 introduces Watson and Guthrie. The reinforcement-connectionist theories are also presented in historical sequence, beginning with Thorndike and Hull in Chapter 3 and finishing with Skinner in Chapter 4. All these theories are distinguished by a common emphasis on animal learning as an analog for human learning; by a focus on the cues or stimuli present in the learning situation rather than on inner causes of behavior; and by a mechanistic flavor to their laws of learning. Both types of connectionist approaches have led to a wide range of powerful and widely used applications, some of which are reviewed in Chapter 6.

Some interesting comparisons may be made initially between Pavlov on one hand and Watson and Guthrie on the other. Pavlov's work developed from his training as a physiologist, and he is consequently more willing than his American counterparts to incorporate biological variables in his theory, including assigning a limited inherited component to learning ability. He also developed extremely intricate principles derived from a multitude of carefully controlled experiments by himself and his research associates. Neither Watson nor Guthrie had access to anything approaching Pavlov's resources for research, and both their fairly simple theories reflect their lesser research productivity. While Pavlov saw himself as a continuation of a strong tradition of objective science, Watson and Guthrie saw themselves as revolting against the "nonscientific" use of mental data gathered from verbal reports about mental events by trained subjects. In their rejection of this mentalism and their desire to make psychology an "honest science" (Pavlov once called psychology "the hope of a science"), they embraced the opposite extreme of radical behaviorism (the belief that only behavior could be used as data). Although Pavlov's principles and terminology still exert considerable influence today, Watson and Guthrie are primarily of importance because of their tremendous influence in moving American psychology in the direction of behaviorism. By the 1930s, the behavioristic banner was slipping into the hands of the reinforcement-connectionists.

Although the duration of the dominance of contiguity theorists in the United States was relatively short, reinforcement-connectionist theories date back to the publication in 1898 of Thorndike's dissertation on cats' escape strategies from puzzle boxes. Then, in the 1940s and early 1950s, Hull (and his follower and modifier Spence) produced the most elaborate and specific (in terms of predictions) theories developed to that time within American psychology. Finally, Skinner has challenged non-behavioristic views of learning from his early work in the 1930s to the present. He is one of the most dominant and active advocates within any branch of psychology. These theories, with their emphasis on behavior as determined by the reinforcing consequences of the environment, were (and, in Skinner's case, are) widely accepted and applied and just as widely attacked as representing an affront to the dignity of man. In view of the behaviorists' goals of predicting and controlling human behavior, some of the anxieties motivating those attackers might be justified if one is opposed to prediction and control!

Chapter 5 explores the theories of some of the attackers of behaviorism. This chapter examines cognitive alternatives to conditioning theories; one is American and the others are European transplants.

First, Tolman's "purposive behaviorism" (in which cognitive elements such as "cognitive maps" replace stimulus-response bonds as the "what" of learning) illustrates that there can be bridges between American behaviorisms and the cognitive viewpoint. Then the gestalt learning theories of Köhler, Koffka, Wertheimer, and Lewin are introduced to show a purer cognitive approach. Reflecting their German backgrounds, these theorists named their approach after the German word *Gestalt,* which means a form, shape, or figure. An emphasis on whole structures is indicative of the gestalt theorists' view that learning and perception are more than the sum of environmental stimuli—the organism's internal world must also be explored.

Next, the cognitive-biological theory of Maria Montessori is summarized. The work of Maria Montessori lies outside the mainstream of psychology, yet it has been widely applied and is of considerable importance to the psychology student interested in the field of early childhood education. Her sensory-motor maturational theory, developed in the slums of Italy, prefigures Piaget, and today a worldwide network of schools applies her principles in educating young children. Finally, some trends relevant to current cognitive theories are introduced. Chapter 6 reviews some applications derived from the theories covered up to this point.

Chapter 7 discusses theories which incorporate multiple factors instead of trying to explain all learning as occurring by a single process. First, the theory of Miller and Dollard, which attempts to integrate a neo-Hullian drive-reduction theory with principles of Freud, is reviewed. Then the various stages of Mowrer's theory are presented, showing the evolution of his thinking from neo-Hullian to cognitive. Finally, that loose collection of theorists often referred to as the "functionalist school" is discussed. Characterized by a pragmatic, integrative, and eclectic orientation, this school specialized in the study of verbal learning.

Part 1 concludes with a general summary and integration. As you read this part, try to fix the relationship of the historical progression of theories to the developing trends to be presented in the second half of the book. The historical progression was meant to provide a sense of perspective to aid you in understanding how science, assumptions, research, and the beliefs of particular historical periods interacted in the development of knowledge about this most vital business of learning.

1

Basic Principles and Background of Pavlovian Conditioning

The type of learning called classical or Pavlovian conditioning was first system-atically explored by Ivan Pavlov in the Soviet Union. Because Pavlov's work has contributed many currently useful insights about learning as well as much of behaviorist jargon, we will spend considerable time in this chapter in going over the main points of Pavlov's findings and theoretical speculations. Since many of Pavlov's ideas reappear in subsequent theories, it is important for you to be-come very familiar with his major ideas.

Many points of similarity occur between Russian psychology and the psy-chology that developed in the United States. Both emphasized environmental factors rather than genetic (innate) factors in behavior, and both may have done so because of similar sociopolitical beliefs about the improvability of man. Both the American Horatio Alger legend and the dream of the "New Soviet Man" demanded optimistic learning theories supporting the plausibility of remolding man in better and more successful forms. In its extreme expression, this position led to statements like those of the American John Watson, who claimed that he could take any well-formed infant and make anything of him that anyone would want, or the Soviet suppression of modern genetic theories in favor of the theory of acquired characteristics proposed by Lamarck and Lysenko. In the United States, this environmentalist bias insured the growth of a healthy behavioristic school of psychology, progressing from Thorndike and Watson on to Hull and Skinner and the modern proponents of behavior modification. In the Soviet Union, the congruence between Pavlov's emphasis on environmental influences in changing people and the Marxist-Leninist philosophy of man as improvable ensured at least intermittent government support for Pavlov's research. This support in turn made possible his tremendous research productivity and his discovery of most of the important principles of contiguity-based learning.

Ivan Petrovich Pavlov (1849–1936)

Pavlov's father was a Russian Orthodox priest in a poor parish who imparted to his son a love of learning in lieu of material possessions. Because of his back-ground, Pavlov was able to obtain a certificate of poverty that qualified him for a scholarship to the University of St. Petersburg, where he earned a degree in natural science. He worked at a series of laboratory posts in physiology, win-ning acclaim and a gold medal for his research but little money. When he married in 1881, he was so poor that his wife remained living with her family to save money. In the course of his work, he found time to earn a medical degree, and in 1890 was appointed professor of pharmacology. He organized and directed the department of physiology in the Institute of Experimental Medicine (Babkin, 1949). It was in this post that he developed the surgical techniques that were to serve him well when he began his study of learning. In 1904, he received the Nobel Prize for his work in digestion. In this work he noted that a sham-fed dog secreted stomach acid when food was introduced in its mouth, even though a tube inserted through an opening in the throat prevented the food from reaching the stomach. Furthermore, he noted, saliva was secreted to the sight of food as well as to the food itself. These "psychic secretions" (Asratyan, 1953) were to provide the basis for his second distinguished career—this time in the study of learning.

Pavlov's background in physiology and the official Soviet emphasis on the improvability of men through exposure to Marxist society (Cole and Cole, 1971) produced in his theorizing a combination of an optimistic philosophy related (sometimes loosely) to precise measurement of physiological functions. This outlook was reflected in the official Soviet definition of human psychology as the study of consciousness (rather than of behavior, as it was defined by the American behaviorists). Of course, consciousness and all other mental phenomena were viewed as dependent upon and originating in the functioning of the neurons of the brain. Since mental activity is totally a product of the brain, thinking in humans is seen as the same as behavior in lower animals. That is, human mental activity is viewed as a reaction to environmental stimuli in the same sense that the knee jerk **reflex** is a reaction to the stretching of a tendon, or a dog's barking may be a reflex triggered by the intrusion of a stranger. Thus, Pavlov saw all behavior as reflexive and assumed that the same basic laws described both human and animal behavior.

Pavlov's approach of taking complex actions (such as thinking) and trying to explain them by the same laws governing less complex actions (such as reflexes) is called the **reductionistic** approach. This approach is also the one followed by many American connectionist (conditioning) theorists.

Classical Conditioning

The first type of learning to be subjected to intense scientific investigation is today called **classical, respondent,** or **Pavlovian conditioning.** The basic phenomena of contiguity-based learning were also described by Twitmyer as early as 1904 at a meeting of psychologists in the United States. Twitmyer, however, was ignored. Speaking in 1903, Pavlov was the first to bring the phenomena to the attention of the scientific community (see Hall, 1976).

The prototypical Pavlovian experiment goes something like this: A dog stands on a platform in a restraining harness. Meat powder is placed in his mouth and he salivates. This salivation is an inherited reflex. Next, a bell is sounded just before the meat powder is put in the dog's mouth. This procedure is repeated several times. Then the bell is sounded and no meat powder is applied. The dog, however, still salivates. This salivation to the bell is what

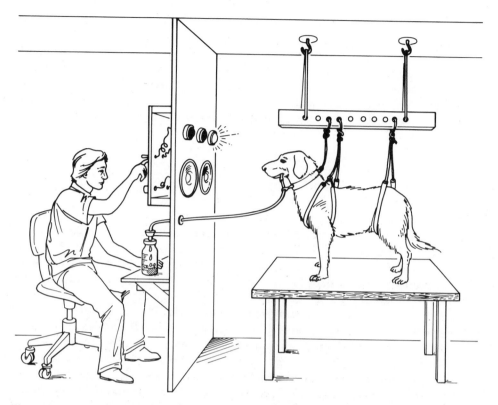

Figure 1.1   A typical Pavlovian experimental situation. A wall prevents the dog from becoming distracted by the experimenter or from receiving uncontrolled cues from him. The dog is restrained in a harness. The tube leading from the dog's mouth collects saliva, which drips into a measuring flask on the experimenter's side of the wall. The experimenter can manipulate the wires controlling lights and sound-generating devices set in the wall between the two halves of the chamber.

Pavlov first called "psychic secretions" (see Figure 1.1). The dog is said to have been conditioned to salivate to the bell. Essentially, this conditioning occurs as the result of the close association between two cues: one either innately effective or previously learned, and the other a new cue. The first cue is called the **unconditioned stimulus (US),** and the new cue is called the **conditioned stimulus (CS).**

Before any conditioning has taken place, the animal responds to the US with an appropriate reflex. This is why classical conditioning is sometimes called respondent conditioning. The reason a given US always **elicits** a particular reflex is assumed to be that the part of the **cerebral cortex** activated by the US is physically connected by nerve fibers to the part of the brain controlling the reflex. Because no conditioning is required to make the reflex appear in response to the US, this reflex is called the **unconditioned reflex (UR).** In the original Russian it was called the **unconditional reflex** to signify that no conditions of prior learning were required. Unfortunately, in early translations of Pavlov's work, this term was mistranslated and we are now stuck with the term "unconditioned." Pavlov assumed that the result of the repeated associations of the US and CS was the formation of new connections in the brain. With time, the connection between the two stimuli becomes so strong that the CS elicits the reflex almost as if it were the US. Since the production of the reflex by the CS is conditioned upon repeated associations of the two cues, this reflex (or response) is called the **conditioned** or **conditional reflex (CR).** Thus, the basic paradigm of classical conditioning looks like this:

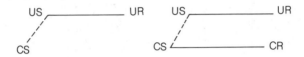

Usually, the response elicited at first by the CS is identical to that elicited by the US. With repeated trials, it may become more perfunctory than the UR (Hall, 1976). Pavlov (1960)* found that with many trials, often fewer drops of saliva were secreted to the CS than to the US. Pavlov saw the role of a CS as a signal to the dog to expect the US. Thus, the CR is, in a sense, a reflex of getting ready to respond to the US. As a "getting-ready" response, it does not need to be as strong as the UR. This has adaptive significance because it enables an animal to respond efficiently to its environment. Pavlov saw the function of the conditioning process as closely linked to biological adaptation. Complex animals need to respond to changing environments. Thus, it is not possible for them to inherit reflexes that would anticipate every environmental situation. Nature has solved this problem by having evolved a mechanism to connect new environmental cues (CSs) to the appropriate responses. This conditioning mechanism gives higher organisms greater flexibility in dealing with their environments and makes them more likely to survive changing conditions. To respond to the outside world, any organism must detect and respond to signals for action from that outside world. Pavlov called this system of stimuli or environmental cues (such as the meat powder or the bell) the **first signal system.**

Classical conditioning is a type of learning which occurs when a new cue (CS) is paired with a cue (US) which has the property of eliciting a reflex (UR). After the pairing, the CS also acquires the property of eliciting a reflex (CR) that is more or less similar to the UR.

Reflexes: The Physiological Basis for Classical Conditioning

Basic to an understanding of classical conditioning is some knowledge of what Pavlov meant by unconditioned and conditioned reflexes. Pavlov wrote:

Three hundred years ago Descartes evolved the idea of the reflex. Starting from the assumption that animals behaved simply as machines, he regarded every

---

* Pavlov (1960) refers to the 1960 Dover edition of lectures delivered by Pavlov in 1924. These first appeared in English in an Oxford University Press edition published in 1927.

activity of the organism as a *necessary* reaction to some external stimulus, the connection between the stimulus and the response being made through a definite nervous path; and this connection, he stated, was the fundamental purpose of the nervous structures in the animal body. [Pavlov, 1960, p. 4]

The essential point is that reflexes are predetermined reactions to stimuli. This deterministic viewpoint has permeated most subsequent connectionist theories of learning. Unconditioned reflexes are usually assumed to be "prewired" in the brain during brain maturation in ways determined by the genes. The brain is innately programmed to recognize the appropriate cues, which trigger the expression of prewired reflexes. In an actual experimental situation, it may be impossible to determine if a given reflex is of the prewired type or the result of prior learning.

Reflexes may be classified in order of complexity. The simplest would be those requiring only a sensory and a motor neuron, such as the knee jerk or tendon reflex elicited by the rubber hammers of doctors during physical examinations. Beginning at this level, reflexes can be classified as those of the spinal cord, the lower brain, and finally the outer layer of the highest part of our brain, called the cerebral cortex. Reflexes of the cerebral cortex may be simple, such as the salivation of the dog to meat powder, or complex, such as feeling a desire to imitate the actions of others in a mob (the "militant enthusiasm" described by Lorenz, 1963). Complex reflexes are often labeled instincts. Pavlov (1960) considered "instincts" to be only complex chains of reflexes in which the whole chain could be released by a single cue and all reflexes in the chain appeared in an innately determined order. There are many complex reflexes shown by higher organisms. Two examples are: the pattern of struggling in response to physical restraint (Pavlov's "freedom reflex"), and the movements of a human newborn infant which aid her in finding her mother's nipple (the "rooting reflex").

Because of Pavlov's background in physiology, he saw his investigations of complex and conditioned reflexes as a continuation of his investigations of the physiology of digestion—except that he was now investigating the physiology of the cerebral cortex! During conditioning, the cerebral cortex was assumed to be altered so that the portion of the cortex (called a "cortical analyzer" by Pavlov) that "noticed" the CS became a physical part of the US-UR connection. When the new connection was completed, the process of conditioning was complete.

It is not enough, however, for a complex organism to learn to respond to new cues that signal food or sex or safety. Sometimes an animal needs to recognize cues that tell it to stop a pattern of responding in order to survive. Therefore, Pavlov also investigated what he called **inhibitory (−) reflexes,** which are those reflexes that act to stop other reflexive activity. As he classified all reflexes as either inhibitory or **excitatory (+)** in nature, he also classified all stimuli as acting usually to elicit either inhibitory or excitatory reflexes.

The basic units of responding in Pavlov's theory are reflexes, which are elicited by stimuli. These can be innate or learned, simple or complex, and can either elicit actions or stop ongoing actions.

Inhibition

Pavlov considered the process of inhibition to be as important as that of excitation. He distinguished two basic types of inhibition: (1) **external inhibition** and (2) **internal inhibition.**

External inhibition   External inhibition can be illustrated by the important type of unlearned reflex with inhibitory components called the **orienting reflex** (OR) or the "what-is-it" reflex. In animals, this is also sometimes called the "freezing" reflex. You have noticed how people hearing a new sound will stop all motion, except to turn their heads to localize the sound. Even in humans, this action is stereotyped, often unconscious, and involves very consistent changes in brain activity (Grossman, 1973). Any stimulus which arouses the OR will stop all ongoing activity and interfere with the continuation of previous conditioning. This in turn sets the stage for the occurrence of new conditioning.

For conditioning to occur, the subject must be paying attention. We do not, however, give our attention to everything in our environment. If we did, we would be overloaded with trivial stimulation. Pavlov suggested that our brains have independent cortical analyzers for all the major senses and that these analyzers decide which stimuli we should attend to. When the analyzers decide to pay attention, we freeze, our muscles become taut, our brain waves become fast, and we produce increased adrenalin. The stimuli which trigger this innate response are of the following types:

1. Very loud stimuli, such as a sudden backfire or a tired student's head hitting the desk.
2. Very soft stimuli, such as the classroom getting very, very quiet as your head falls towards the desk.
3. Novel stimuli, such as a new person joining a small party, or stimuli likely to lead to rewards or negative consequences. This implies that the cortical analyzers somehow recognize all your familiar stimuli as well as the cues associated with consequences. Thus, the analyzers are assumed to function as stimulus filters to prevent your paying active attention to stimuli that are familiar but inconsequential, such as lecture material that you have already learned will not be covered on exams.

In addition, any stimulus which is stronger than the CSs or USs being studied may act as an external inhibitor. The savory aroma of a pizza may act as an external inhibitor. The sudden smell of the pizza may disrupt your studying, or an uncouth student's voice in the hall outside of a laboratory room may disrupt the conditioning of a rat. A special case of this type of external inhibition occurs when the US is given before a well-established CS. If you have a piece of pizza in your mouth (the US for the UR of salivation), you will no longer respond with further increases in salivation to merely the sight of pizza, which would otherwise be a CS for increased salivation.

Internal inhibition   Pavlov assumed that the cortical analyzers somehow distinguished novel and/or important stimuli from familiar unimportant stimuli. This internal process results in the inhibition of attention responses (the OR) to familiar unimportant cues. This process is called **habituation.** The inhibitory effects of habituation can in turn be inhibited by the occurrence of a mild inhibitory stimulus in the environment. This last process is called **disinhibition.** Pavlov has described an experiment in which a dog was trained to salivate to the appearance of a rotating object (the CS). Then this response was inhibited. When the dog was transferred to a new experimental room, the effect of the "new room cues" was temporarily to inhibit the inhibition, and the dog again salivated to the sight of rotating figures (Pavlov, 1960). The "new room cues" (novel cues) in this example operated as external inhibitors and probably elicited the OR.

Inhibition may also be transferred to new stimuli by conditioning. In this type of conditioned inhibition, something which was formerly a weak CS or US for an excitatory reflex may come to inhibit that reflex if paired frequently with a strong inhibitory US. This changing of the response elicited by a given CS is also called **counterconditioning.** After many months of working in a pizza parlor, even the word "pizza" may become an inhibiting CS. After months of shrill complaint associated with sexual activity, the sight of the partner's nude body may only elicit the conditioned inhibitory response of impotence or frigidity.

The movie *A Clockwork Orange,* directed by Stanley Kubrick, vividly illustrated the process of inhibitory conditioning. The main character is a spoiled youth whose main joys are brutality and Beethoven. Finally, "Little Alex" is betrayed by his fellow juvenile thugs and imprisoned. Given a choice between continued prison life and a "scientific program," Little Alex chooses the treatment program. Treatment consists of dosing him with a drug that makes him feel nauseous and as if he "wishes to die" (the US). His eyes are then clamped open and, before the drug's effects begin, a program of films about atrocities, rapes, and other violent acts is begun, which he hugely enjoys. Gradually his enjoyment turns to panic as the drug's effects become apparent. With repeated sessions, acts or scenes of sex or violence are counterconditioned to become excitatory CSs for the CRs of nausea and fear, which inhibit aggressive and sexual reflexes and (presumably) thoughts.

To demonstrate the success of their program, the "therapists" lead Little Alex out onto a stage in front of a large audience. A half-nude girl approaches and Little Alex approaches her with intent to molest. He is immediately seized with the CRs of nausea and dread and falls to the stage. By the end of the demonstration, her mere approach is enough to make him turn away and the audience applauds. Soon his very urges towards sex and violence become inhibited. What were once very excitatory cues have now become powerful inhibitory cues! As a final cruelty (or act of justice), the program administrators played Beethoven during the conditioning process. As a result, Little Alex is no longer able to stand the sound of what had formerly been his one nonpathological source of comfort.

Conditioned inhibition may also occur following discrimination training. When one tone is paired with food and another tone is never paired with food, any cues associated with the nonreinforced cue may also acquire conditioned inhibitory properties. This process is called "differential inhibition," and may be the way we learn to focus on the specific things that are adaptive for us. Some people may never reinforce us, and eventually we perceive them as surrounded by "bad vibrations," which may be conditioned inhibitory cues.

Another type of internal inhibition is extinction (the loss of the power of the CS to elicit the CR as the result of several trials without the presence of the US). Examples include loss of salivation to the sight of ice cream after working in an ice cream parlor or loss of physiological arousal to nudity after a frustrating summer at a nude beach. The probable USs would be ice cream in the mouth and tactile stimulation in your erogenous zones, respectively. This will be discussed further in the next part.

A final note on inhibition is appropriate here. Pavlov (1960) suggested that the brain processes responsible for the types of inhibition discussed so far are identical to those responsible for sleep. In fact, he thought that conditioned inhibition is caused by local areas of the brain entering into a sleeplike state and that the inhibition of a person's will when in a hypnotic trance represents partial sleep. As we have seen, inhibitory conditioning involves the active process of interfering with the elicitation of some reflexes. It is hard to see how such effects could be produced by the same process responsible for turning off parts of the brain in sleep. Pavlov's process of internal inhibition may be derived from nothing more than observations of the absence of excitation. In other words, Pavlov evokes the process of inhibition to account for most phenomena which do not seem to fit the laws of excitatory phenomena.

Inhibitory reflexes are of two basic types: (1) those elicited by external cues which can be effective without learning (external inhibition), and (2) those requiring some sort of learning process (internal inhibition).

The Stages of Conditioning and Extinction

As previously mentioned, the orienting reflex plays a vital role in conditioning. Learning cannot occur unless you first pay attention to the CS and US and then settle down to the business of being conditioned. Therefore, the first stage in the conditioning process is the elicitation and habituation of the OR. After this has occurred, and with several additional pairings of the CS and US, the CS becomes capable of eliciting the reflex (now called the CR). If the CS is presented several times in succession without being followed by the US, the CR vanishes. This process is called experimental **extinction.** This does not mean, however, that the subject has forgotten the CS-US relationship or that it is restored to its preconditioning state. If the extinction trials are followed by a rest period, upon the next presentation of the CS it will again be effective in eliciting the CR, although usually not as strongly as before. This phenomenon is called **spontaneous recovery.** If the CS is still not followed by a US, the spontaneously recovered CR will usually reextinguish quickly.

In general, classical conditioning extinguishes rapidly. There are ways to compensate for the lack of durability of such learning, however. Pavlov (1960) notes that after several conditioning and extinction sessions have been given on successive days, extinction usually is slower. In general, anything which reduces the organism's ability to predict when the US (the reinforcer, in Pavlovian literature) will not follow the CS makes the conditioning more resistant to extinction.

The strength of the conditioning may also depend upon the intensity of the original US. The stronger the US is, the more likely the learning will be resistant to extinction. Very strong USs, for instance a dog biting you, may result in durable, one-trial learning. When this is a negative emotional experience, it is called a traumatic experience. Behavior therapists (in Kanfer and Phillips, 1970) have suggested that this type of classical conditioning may be responsible for many **phobias,** or unreasonably strong aversions that have been over-generalized.

Pleasant or not, the conditioning that results from very strong USs is often highly resistant to extinction. Such learning may persist for a patient's entire life. A person who first confronted a dog in the company of his hysterical mother may never again get close enough to any dog to discover that dogs are far less fearsome than he was conditioned to believe. Yet another way to increase the durability of conditioning is to pair the same CS with multiple USs. For example, money is paired with food, meeting social and stimulus needs, and social approval. If you are confronted with a situation in which no restaurants are open to allow you to exchange your money for food, you do not feel significantly less emotionally attached to your money. Of course, if you had foreign currency which you could neither spend nor exchange, its conditioned positive value for you would probably extinguish with time and repeated extinction trials. Such a CS, which is a signal for many reinforcers, has been labeled by the Skinnerians as a **generalized secondary** (or **conditioned**) **reinforcer.**

For conditioning to occur, the OR must first be elicited and then habituated. Presentation of a CS alone (experimental extinction) results in its ceasing to elicit a CR. Following a rest period, however, the CS will spontaneously re-cover some of its power to elicit the CR.

Discrimination and Generalization

In addition to learning to respond to new signals from the environment, the organism must learn to distinguish the cues which should signal different re-flexes. This process is usually labeled **discrimination,** although Pavlov preferred the term **differentiation.** Pavlov attempted to explain this learning process in terms of cortical functioning. He thought repeated trials with a CS triggered a physiological process in which excitation was concentrated at the site in the brain aroused by that CS. If these conditioning trials were randomly alternated with trials in which another cue was presented that was never reinforced by the US, this nonreinforced cue would become a signal not to respond. Presentation of the nonreinforced cue was supposed to build up an inhibitory potential in its cortical analyzer, so eventually the reflex would occur only following the CS, and never after the unreinforced cue (Pavlov, 1960).

In the process of conditioning, a CR will come to be evoked by stimuli similar in some dimension to the original CS. For instance, if someone you love always says, "Hey, you," in a soft voice (the CS) before doing something (the

US) which always makes you blush (the UR), eventually you will blush to the words "Hey, you." If they then substitute the words "Hello, you," you may then blush to those words, too, but not quite so much. Other words that are more different from the original CS will evoke a weaker "conditioned blushing reflex." This phenomenon is important in allowing the organism to respond to a range of cues which may be signaling the same US as the training CS. This process is called stimulus **generalization,** and Pavlov explains it as a process of **irradiation** (spreading from the focal point excited by the original CS) of excitation within the cortex. Since stimuli most similar to the CS are processed in places in the cortex near the site excited by the CS, those stimuli receive the most irradiated excitation and are the most likely to have enough excitatory potential to result in responses. Not only is excitation generalized, but also the inhibition built up during extinction generalizes through the irradiation of inhibition from the inhibitory CS in the cortex (Pavlov, 1960).

Discrimination and generalization are two opposing processes. Discrimination is distinguishing CSs from other cues. Generalization is a tendency to respond to cues which are similar to a CS, almost as if they were the CS.

The Basic Types of Conditioning

The general process of classical conditioning has been described previously. Several types of classical conditioning, however, have been distinguished on the basis of the experimental procedures used to produce them.

Primary conditioning   Sam (the CS) always stumbles over your feet, causing pain (the US), which is innately connected to the aggression response (the UR). After several such incidents, you feel angry whenever Sam gets near your feet. If Sam enrolls in Arthur Murray's tantalizing tango class and is allowed to walk near enough to your feet to demonstrate that he is no longer the heavy-heeled marauder, extinction will take place. If he is so overjoyed by your recovery from your "Sam-phobia" that he dances around (a novel cue), you may show disinhibition or recovery of the conditioned aggression response. If the aggression response is extinguished and subsequently Sam vanishes from your life, a return of aggression, coinciding with the return of Sam, represents spontaneous recovery.

Another example of primary conditioning might be experiencing stomach "rumbles" when you view a clock whose hands indicate that it is dinner time. Schacter (1971) found that obese people tend to eat more than thin people and experience stomach contractions when shown a clock whose hands had been moved from the real time (say, 10 A.M.) to noon. The sight of the clock (the CS) must have preceded whatever internal physiological states (USs) normally triggered feelings of hunger many times, before the clock alone became an effective CS.

Any cue (which can be an environmental cue, a physiological state which is detectable, or thoughts in humans) which has a strong prewired or innate bond with a UR (which is usually a smooth or visceral muscle response or a thought in humans) can be a US. This combination can be paired with almost any discriminable cue inside or outside of the organism to serve as a CS. Pavlov (1960), however, stated that the aftereffects of external cues usually persisted for minutes at most, while the aftereffects of visceral and odor cues might last days. Thus, all cues may not be equally conditionable. He also noted that many cues elicited both motor and secretory reflexes rather than operating in a simple fashion to elicit one particular reflex. In general, CSs to which the subjects were originally indifferent were found to condition most easily.

Primary conditioning procedures in which the CS is presented just before the onset of the US have been the most commonly employed procedures and usually are most effective in producing conditioning. These are called delayed procedures, and half-second CS-US intervals seem generally most effective. These procedures are distinguished from procedures in which the CS and US are presented simultaneously, which are usually less effective (Hall, 1976).

Defense conditioning   A special type or primary conditioning procedure must now be examined. This is the paradigm explored by Bekhterev, a contemporary rival of Pavlov's. In this method, the CS (usually a tone) was followed by an electric shock to the forepaw of a dog. At first, only the shock (the US) elicited the UR of a flexion response of the paw. Eventually the dog would withdraw the forepaw to the tone alone (in Tarpy, 1975). Because leg flexion to the tone would protect the dog from experiencing subsequent shocks such a defense conditioning shares aspects of both classical and reinforcement conditioning.

Second-order conditioning   When the US is a cue that was formerly a CS, rather than being innately connected to an UR as in primary conditioning, the conditioning is called **second-order conditioning.** If meat in your mouth (which is the US for the reflex of salivation) is preceded by the smell of cooking (the CS), then the smell of cooking may eventually be enough to elicit the CR of the salivation. If the cue of turning on the stove then always precedes the smell of cooking, the sound of a stove igniting may eventually trigger salivation. In general, the CRs to a second-order CS are weaker than the CRs to a primary CS. Another example might be the touch of another person on your skin (the US) eliciting the reflex of arousal (the UR). The person is the CS; with enough trials, his or her presence alone may trigger an arousal reflex. If the person is paired reliably with a special song even in the absence (or it would not be secondary conditioning) of any touches, the song may act as a secondary CS for the arousal CR (that is what makes the song so special). Later, the song will elicit the response even if the person is no longer in your life.

A note of caution is necessary here. If several cues are present at the same time, they are all potential primary CSs and none of them should be considered a secondary CS. In our example, if you had heard the song while the person was touching you, the conditioning would be direct, and both the person and the song would be primary CSs.

Even higher-order conditioning is possible, although the CRs may be weaker. Pavlov (1960) reported an experiment in which shock to the front paw (US) of a dog was paired with tactile stimulation of the hind paw (CS). Tactile stimulation of the hind paw was then paired with the sound of bubbling water (the second-order CS). Finally, the water sound was paired with a tone of 760 Hz, which became a third-order CS. Higher-order conditioning tends to extinguish easily and be difficult to produce. Pairing a second-order CS with multiple primary CSs (as our generalized secondary reinforcers), however, makes a stronger bond.

Backward conditioning   In this paradigm, the CS *follows* the US rather than serving as a signal for its arrival. An example would be putting meat in your mouth (the US) and hearing your mother say, "Yum" (the CS). If this CS gained the power to elicit salivation (the CR), then conditioning would have occurred which had no signal or biologically useful function.

In fact, because such conditioning serves no warning or signaling function, its existence was in doubt for many years. Pavlov (1960) first said such learning was impossible and later reversed this negative stance (in Hall, 1976). Although many researchers have claimed to have demonstrated that **backward conditioning** (also known as **pseudoconditioning**) does occur, many others have been unable to replicate these results (in Hall, 1976). Hall concluded that because a control procedure using cues other than the "CS-to-be" was not used in many of the affirmative studies, it is difficult to determine if backward conditioning does in fact occur. The reason why the random presentation of new cues is so important as an experimental control procedure is because of a phenomenon called **sensitization**. The sequence of presentation of the cues in backward conditioning is shown as follows.

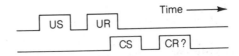

Sensitization is a general state of arousal which occurs after exposure to a strong US, such as a shock or a bright light. When an organism is sensitized, it may be so nervous that it will respond to any cue presented to it. If you present only one cue (which you hope will become a CS) the subject will respond to that cue—not because it is conditioned but because it is sensitized. If you had presented a random order of novel cues, it would have responded to all of them also. A human example of sensitization would be the tendency to jump at every small noise just after being almost hit by an automobile while trying to walk across the street. Sensitization must always be controlled for in attempts to demonstrate classical conditioning.

Trace conditioning   Pavlov assumed that the presentation of a CS made a physiological modification of the cerebral cortex in the form of a neural trace or area of altered activity. The term **trace conditioning** is derived from the assumption that such traces could initiate reflexes some time after the CS had been presented. The assumption of such traces was necessary to account for conditioning which deviated from the normal procedure of giving the CS about .5 seconds before the US—since with delays between CS presentation and US presentation, there could be no overlap between the cortex's responses to the cues. In trace conditioning, therefore, the bond is between the trace of the CS and the area of the cortex excited by the US. Pavlov distinguished between short trace conditioning, where the time delay between CS and US was under 1 minute, and long trace conditioning, where the delay was over 1 minute.

For example, a tactile stimulus is presented (the CS); after 30 seconds, a weak acid is injected in the mouth (the US), producing the alimentary defense reaction of salivation (the UR). After several trials (Pavlov, 1960), the subject begins to salivate following the application of the touch and continues to salivate for about 40 seconds (or until the US would have been applied and dissolved). With more trials, the subject does not salivate when the CS is applied, but after about 30 seconds (or when the US would have been applied) begins a 10-second bout of salivation. Trace conditioning also illustrates a type of internal inhibition called the "inhibition of delay." This is the process by which the CR is only given at the time at which the US would have been given, rather than during the entire interval between the CS and the appropriate time. An example might be waking up frequently the first few nights when you have an early job or class, until you become conditioned to the new time interval and wake up only just before the alarm clock gladdens your heart with its merry buzzing. You have conditioned an inhibition of your waking until just before the US (the alarm).

Temporal conditioning   The following example illustrates this type of conditioning.

> A dog is placed in the stand and given food regularly every 30th minute. In the control experiment any one feeding after the first few is omitted, and it is found that despite the omission a secretion of saliva with a corresponding alimentary motor reaction is produced at about the 30th minute, but it may be one or two minutes late. In the interval there is not the least sign of any alimentary reaction, especially if the routine has been repeated a good number of times. When we come to seek an interpretation of these results, it seems pretty evident that the duration of time has acquired the properties of a conditioned stimulus. [Pavlov, 1960, p. 41]

The next example should be more familiar to many of you. Again it illustrates that in **temporal conditioning,** time itself is the CS. You have the misfortune to have to take an 8:00 A.M. class. Every morning at 7:30 A.M., your sleep is rudely shattered by the insistent braying of your alarm clock (the US) which immediately elicits the UR of automatic (visceral) nervous system and behavioral arousal (the OR) from your comfortable sleeping state. After many days of being awakened at the same time, you may begin to wake up *before* the alarm shatters your dreams. This "conditioned" awakening depends upon a specific time interval somehow acquiring the properties of a CS.

Although it is still not clear how an interval of time can become a CS, it is possible that changes in blood sugar throughout the night may be the real CS and that we possess "biological clocks" in the brain. It is now known that humans do have internal clocks which can be modified with time. When the world does not match our internal CSs for eating and sleeping after a long jet plane trip, we may feel extremely disoriented until our internal clocks are reconditioned to our outside environment.

Several types of conditioning procedures have been distinguished. These are: (1) primary conditioning, (2) defense conditioning, (3) second-order conditioning, (4) backward conditioning, (5) trace conditioning, and (6) temporal conditioning.

Effects of Combinations of Excitatory and Inhibitory Stimuli

The effects of combining CSs may not always be obvious from the individual properties of the cues. If several weak +CSs* are added, they may summate to produce a CR even though they are individually too weak (perhaps because of prior extinction) to elicit any responses. An example might be combining food odors and the nearness of lunchtime to produce a CR of salivation.

If many +CSs and −CSs† are alternated, the resistance to extinction of the CRs to the +CSs will increase. This is somewhat like alternating conditioning with extinction several times to produce a more durable trace. If the cues responsible for salivation are alternated with fear cues which produce dry mouth, the conditioned cues for salivation will remain effective even in the prolonged absence of the USs for salivation.

It is also possible to present +CSs and −CSs simultaneously. This combination of cues (a new compound stimulus) may have effects different from either component. These effects may be quite complicated. A combination of food odors and the time cue of 10:00 A.M. may be inhibitory (inhibition of delay creating the conditioned inhibition of salivation), unless a strong distraction results in disinhibition, in which case the new combination may elicit copious salivation. If the brain alpha rhythm is conditioned to a tone (to produce conditioned relaxation) and a new cue to relax is then given, the alpha rhythm will vanish.

Other effects of combined + and − influences   If very strong or extraordinary excitatory (+) and inhibitory (−) stimuli are combined, a **conditioned neurosis** may result. This may be demonstrated in various ways. Pavlov trained dogs to respond to circles and not to respond (inhibition) to ellipses. He then made the two figures more and more like each other. When the dogs were unable to discriminate the figures (the + and − cues were combined) and the dogs were in conflict, the normally calm animals became extremely upset. When they were returned to problems that they had formerly found extremely easy, they refused to pay attention to them, urinated, and became difficult to handle. Pavlov assumed that the cause was the clashing of excitatory and inhibitory processes in the brain, which produced a disconnected response conditioned to

---

* +CS = a CS that elicits an excitatory response or reflex.
† −CS = a CS which blocks excitatory reflexes (such as salivation) and elicits a defensive reflex. These are usually cues which signal the occurrence of aversive events.

the confusing stimulus. With repeated trials, these disconnected responses were assumed to generalize (spread) to anything similar to the test stimulus, which prevented responses, other than the disconnected maladaptive responses, being given even to readily discriminable circles and ellipses (Pavlov, 1960).

Because Pavlov saw the processes of inhibition and excitation as producing fields of activity or suppression in the cortex of the cerebrum, he suggested that these fields might produce field effects similar to physical electrical fields. One of the effects he described was **induction,** wherein prolonged activity of one sign causes a "bounce-back" or afterimage of the opposite sign after a period of time. He used the example of the sudden burst of frenetic (+) activity often seen in small sleepy children, after they have been increasingly drowsy just before going to bed and/or sleep. Another example might be the sudden fit of depression that often follows euphoria, as when someone feels depressed following the excitement of a graduation ceremony.

When more than one CS is presented simultaneously, this compound stimulus may have properties different from those of its components. Combinations of strong stimuli sometimes produce a conditioned neurosis.

From Laboratory to Real Life

Verbal behavior and other complex reflexes   You may protest at this point that humans often think before behaving, and that in any case human behavior is more complex than simple stimulus-response connections. Pavlov, however, explained that verbal thoughts and overt speech constituted a **second signal system** which operated much like the environmental cue or first signal system. He even hypothesized that a thought resulting from another thought was as much a predetermined CR as any alimentary response (although he was never quite sure). Just as the taste of a steak elicits a salivary response (does this apply to vegetarians?), so does a conversation about juicy, tender, savory steaks or even thoughts of luscious thick steaks smothered in mushrooms. Hence in humans (and probably only in humans), the meanings of words become conditioned to a variety of USs in the environment and gain the power to elicit reflexes. We have not only a second signal system (verbal cues) but also a second reflex system (words and thoughts). The basic rules and operations, however, are assumed to be the same for both systems. Although Pavlov recognized that it was sometimes difficult trying to explain complex human behavior in terms of the principles derived from research on dogs, he felt that further exploration of the laws of conditioning would make such explanations possible.

It would be the height of presumption to regard these first steps in elucidating the physiology of the cortex as solving the intricate problems of the higher psychic activities in man, when in fact at the present state of our work no detailed application of its results to man is permissible.

Nevertheless, inasmuch as the higher nervous activity exhibited by the cortex rests, undoubtedly on the same foundation in man as in higher animals, some very general and tentative inferences can even now be drawn from the latter to the former. In the future it may confidently be expected that a full and detailed knowledge of at least the elementary facts of this activity will be obtained as regards both normal and pathological states. [Pavlov, 1960, p. 365]

With a spirit both hopeful and humble, Pavlov attempted to generalize his findings to man. He considered habits acquired through training and education to be nothing but long chains of conditioned reflexes. Such associations, once learned, could be automatically elicited by appropriate CSs, even against our wills. For example, consider the great difficulty encountered in trying to get rid of superfluous movements in skiing, gymnastics, or other skilled complex acts. As further proof of the reflex chain theory of complex skills, Pavlov cites the example of trying to stop midway in the process of tying your shoe, waiting, and then resuming the chain. Because each act is the CS for the next act, the wait causes the cortical representation of that CS to decay, making the resumption of shoe tying awkward. Although such an explanation is appealing, Pavlov never specified the underlying UR from which the chain of CRs was supposedly derived.

Pavlov also suggested that such reflex chains could be inhibited by adding extra stimuli (which would, of course, elicit the OR). Further examples might be the disorientation experienced when you attempt to break a long-established routine, as going to school or work the same way each day, or the difficulty of resuming the routine CRs of studying (as page turning, underlining, and similar acts, in which each CR serves both as CR and as CS for the next routine action) when your involvement in this activity is interrupted. As opposed to the smooth, efficient action of habit, the conscious control of study is laborious and slow. Of course, the danger exists that late in a study session you may find yourself emitting the "reading chain reflex" without understanding or memorizing any of those pages inspected by your weary eyes. Pavlov also discovered that as CSs of the weak and monotonous variety habituate, they become CSs for that profound cortical inhibition known as sleep. Hence your fatigue in reading may be the result of the repetition of the inhibiting CSs of non-understandable and irrelevant facts. In this context, becoming bored in lecture is a function of your not making the material important to you, and falling asleep in class may be a reflexive response to the monotonous CSs emitted by the professor rather than either real fatigue or malice on your part.

Conditioning and Abnormal Behavior

Pavlov applied his theories to abnormal behavior as well as to theories of education. He considered neurosis and psychosis to be different only in the amount of disturbed cortex involved. Neurosis, he believed, is the result of functional disturbances. For example, traumas are the result of exposure to very strong stimuli which overload the nervous system and cause irradiation of excitation or inhibition of areas of the cortex responsible for normal behavior. This causes anxiety to be elicited by too wide a range of CSs, as when one bad experience with dogs generalizes to a pathological fear (phobia) of all dogs.

Pavlov suggested that another cause of neurosis is the inability to express emotions. This, he hypothesized, leads to abnormal levels of inhibition or depression. This concept is of course very similar to Freud's theory of neurosis, which assumed that blocking of id-produced (instinctual energies or drives) emotional expression by the super-ego or conscience (which Pavlov might see as reflexive second signal system activity) could cause neurotic behavior.

Neurosis could also result from an unusual clashing of excitatory and inhibitory processes in the cortex as the end products of conflicts. This theory later appears in Western psychology in the learning approach to psychopathology propounded by Dollard and Miller (see Chapter 7). Pavlov predicted that the result of such conflicts in persons with strong nervous systems would be a state like hypochondria (an exaggerated concern with bodily symptoms of "illness"), typified by alternating high levels of activity and subsequent exhaustion. Persons with weaker nervous systems (or more dominated by inhibition) were predicted to be more prone to agitated and nonuseful activity, as their inhibitory processes were disrupted by the surging back and forth of alternating waves of tendencies towards excitation and inhibition.

Pavlov assumed that most severe mental illnesses were the result of the destruction of large areas of the cortex, which unhinged the balance between excitatory and inhibitory areas. Catatonic psychotics were seen as having weakened nervous systems that allowed any stimulus to induce motor inhibitions. Pavlov suggested giving weak and monotonous CSs related to the CSs involved in clashing of + and − cues or traumatic experiences. He predicted that such weak presentations would eventually reciprocally inhibit the CSs responsible for the abnormal behavior. This is, of course, the basis for Wolpe's **reciprocal inhibition** method of treatment. In the form of systematic desensitization (discussed in Chapter 6), it is a major tool of clinical behavioral modification. Pavlov assumed that the treatment he advocated led to a state of cortical inhibition or a physiological state of the brain conducive to *not* responding in the former pathological manner. Conversely, cortical inhibition which prevented good behaviors (as in unreasonable fears) would also be pathological. Even courage and cowardice were explained in terms of cortical inhibition:

> Developing these conceptions further we are bound to regard the obsession of fear, and different phobias as natural symptoms of inhibition in a pathological and weakened nervous system. There are of course, certain forms of fear and cowardice, as for instance flight and panic, and certain postures of servility, which apparently do not conform with the idea of an underlying inhibitory process, having a much more active aspect. These types must, of course, be subjected to experimental analysis, but it is perhaps not impermissible to regard them provisionally as developing in co-operation with, and as a result of, inhibition of the cortex. [Pavlov, 1960, p. 410]

Pavlov's Positions on Major Issues

Nature/nurture   Pavlov believed that many complex reflexes, including the reflex to escape restraints (the freedom reflex), the reflex of self-defense (Pavlov, 1960), and the orienting reflex, are innate. In addition, he postulated innate differences in the capacity to form conditioned traces, depending upon the type of nervous system inherited. He suggested that some individuals of any species inherit nervous systems dominated by inhibition and others inherit nervous systems dominated by excitation. Individuals with inhibitory dominance could learn inhibitions more easily than positive responses, and vice versa. These inherited factors, however, only served to bias the effects of the more important environmental shapers of behavior.

The how of learning   The primary basis for the formation of new bonds is the reinforcement of a CS by a subsequent US. If the inhibitory effects of fatigue are avoided, the strength of the bond is a function of the number of "reinforced" trials. Drive, however, can set the stage for learning. Conditioning of the salivary response cannot occur unless the UR is possible. If the animal is not hungry, then the UR is not possible and no learning can occur. Actual learning, of course, is solely a matter of contiguity-association factors.

The what of learning   The unit of learning which Pavlov discussed in most detail was the formation of new connections in the cerebral cortices between the centers excited by a new cue (CS) and those controlling responses. This new connecting first involves the formation of a bond between an US and the CS. In the case of complex new responses, connections have to be made between the simple reflexes participating in the new response. In any case, the unit is bonds between stimuli and stimuli, between stimuli and responses, and between responses. When the responses involved are highly complex, the behavior unit can be large or molar. When a simple glandular response is conditioned, the unit can be very small or molecular.

Other issues   In most of the animal studies he reported (Pavlov, 1960), learning, as measured by the increasing power of the CS to elicit the CR, is gradual. This would suggest a mechanism of the gradual strengthening of bonds among the S and R elements. In human learning, however, simple CS-CR relationships may be learned in a single trial. Pavlov had no use for the concepts of understanding and insight, so his explanation of the phenomena took two forms: First, man can signal himself via the second signal system of thought and language and hence perform the equivalent of internally conditioning traces. In addition, Pavlov's conception of reflex was so broad that he was willing to extend concepts, such as utilization of knowledge or acquired connections in new situations, to animals. "This is the characteristic associationist view of understanding: the utilization of past experience through some kind of transfer" (Hilgard and Bower, 1975, p. 86).

Pavlov was, of course, willing to generalize the learning laws derived from animal research to human behavior, and he saw behavior as environmentally determined, with the qualification that human speech could function as part of an interior environment.

Chapter Perspective

Almost any type of stimulation in the environment (including a stimulus's getting softer or dimmer) can serve as a CS, which introduces a problem in determining precisely the relationship between a controlled CS and the conditioning.

In the United States, the difficulty of controlling extra CSs limited explorations into classical conditioning. In the Soviet Union, Pavlov's prestige prompted a "keen and public-spirited Moscow businessman" (Pavlov, 1960, p. 20) to donate the funds to build Pavlov's elaborate laboratory in Petrograd as an adjunct to the Institute of Experimental Medicine. This laboratory contained chambers to separate the experimental animals and the scientists, with every chamber insulated against outside noise and light. In addition, the entire building was surrounded by a moat to dampen the vibrations of trucks passing outside.

To illustrate the problem, imagine a situation in which the sound of a metronome is used as the CS to be applied just before application of meat powder to the mouth of a dog. After a while, the sound of the metronome becomes effective in eliciting salivation. After more time, the dog may begin to salivate to the approach of the experimenter, who has now also become a CS. The animal may even begin to salivate when brought into the room and fastened in the harness. The harness is necessary to prevent the animal from finding its own CSs or indulging in competing responses and to permit accurate measurement of desired responses.

It is bad enough that the dog might salivate to the appearance of the white lab coat of the experimenter. What makes the problem even more complicated is that it is difficult to interpret how the coat produces its effect. Was salivation to the lab coat conditioned simultaneously with the metronome? Or was the lab coat conditioned to the metronome, which was conditioned to the meat powder, which would thus be a case of second-order conditioning? Given the physiologist's tradition of precision (salivation was measured drop by drop and times recorded), such problems became critical to an accurate interpretation of results. Pavlov and his coworkers responded by developing automated methods of stimulus presentation and response measurement that were ingenious and accurate. Until Professor Skinner's elegantly simple "Skinner box," the Soviet behavioral technology was the most advanced in the world.

It is perhaps indicative of Pavlov's careful approach to objective research that none of the major laws of classical conditioning systematized by him have been shown to be false—and this when the work was essentially completed by 1926. Compare this to the rise and fall of a myriad of American learning theories. But even though the empirical findings of Pavlov and his many coworkers have withstood the test of time, his theoretical foundations have proven to be of little utility.

This is particularly true of his attempts to explain complex behavior in terms of brain states. For example, Pavlov suggested that consciousness might consist of states of general cortical excitation. Unconscious learning, he speculated, might be the result of a local synthesizing area in an excitatory state becoming surrounded by states of inhibition. This would cause learning in that area to be isolated from consciousness or to be unconscious. When the surrounding areas again became excited, the subconsciously formed association would enter the field of consciousness as a link seeming to have arisen spontaneously. He felt that his experimental procedures would eventually demonstrate the existence of such localized foci of excitation.

As such hypotheses illustrate, Pavlov's theory, which was designed to explain the effects of his learning laws, was often based upon speculations about unobservable events. Although his laws of learning remain useful in predicting behavior occurring as the result of application of his experimental procedures, his theory often neither explains nor predicts. Failures in predicting the occurrence of a given response are explained away as the animal's drowsiness or domination by inhibition. The appearance of unpredicted responses is explained as the result of slight alterations of the environment which must have elicited the OR or disinhibited previously inhibited responses. To be fair to Pavlov, the post hoc (after-the-fact) quality of his efforts to explain complicated phenomena such as complex habits and consciousness was partly the result of the pressures put on most well-known scientists to explain and integrate their results. In Pavlov's case, these pressures resulted in his theory's going far beyond the facts gathered from his carefully executed experiments. Consequently, his laws of learning and his experimental procedures have continued to be influential, while his theory is today considered primarily of historical interest.

One beneficial effect of Pavlov's willingness to speculate about mind and complex behavior has been the continued investigation of such phenomena within a tradition of rigorous experimentation in the Soviet Union. Pavlov's open-minded attitude towards the existence of complex cognitive events was not mirrored in the theories of the American learning theorists Watson and Guthrie to be reviewed in the next chapter. These theorists were radical in their repudiation of such ideas as "mind," and their efforts to be objective resulted both in the development of a rigorous experimental tradition and a rejection of the investigation of cognitive phenomena.

Key Terms

backward conditioning

cerebral cortex

classical conditioning

conditioned neurosis

conditioned (conditional) response (reflex) (CR)

conditioned stimulus (CS)

discrimination (differentiation)

disinhibition

elicit

excitatory (+) reflex

external inhibition

extinction

first signal system

generalization (irradiation)

generalized secondary (conditioned) reinforcer

habituation

induction

inhibitory (−) reflex

internal inhibition

orienting reflex (OR)

Pavlovian conditioning

phobia

pseudoconditioning

reciprocal inhibition

reductionistic

reflex

respondent conditioning

second signal system

second-order conditioning

sensitization

spontaneous recovery

temporal conditioning

trace conditioning

unconditioned (unconditional) response (reflex) (UR)

unconditioned (unconditional) stimulus (US)

Annotated Bibliography

The one outstanding source for those students wishing to read what Pavlov actually said about learning is the 1927 English translation of lectures delivered by Pavlov in the spring of 1924 to an audience of medical men and biologists at the military medical academy in Petrograd. This book, *Conditioned reflexes* (New York: Dover, 1960), is available in paperback and also includes Pavlov's revisions of some of the material presented in those lectures in the later chapters. Students interested in Pavlov's life and early Soviet psychology should read B. Babkin, *Pavlov, A biography* (Chicago: University of Chicago Press, 1949).

2

American Approaches to Contiguity Conditioning: Watson and Guthrie

Pavlov's theory was not the only contiguity approach to learning theory. In the United States, first John Watson and then Edwin Guthrie also believed that the "how" of learning new connections was related to the association of cues, and they developed theories based on this assumption that habits are formed as the result of rote repetition. By explaining complex learning phenomena in terms of a very few basic laws, Watson and Guthrie made substantial contributions to the historical development of the psychology of learning, as we will also see by a brief summary of a theory derived from their tradition (Estes's statistical learning theory).

The mechanical formation of habits through association is the core of the contiguity theories of Watson and Guthrie. The appeal of such contiguity theories may lie in their apparent simplicity and their freedom from residual contamination by concepts such as reward, which usually imply something about the internal reactions of the "rewarded" organism.

American psychology had an opportunity to develop its own contiguity theories following Twitmyer's presentation of his results on the conditioning of the knee jerk reflex at a meeting of the American Psychological Association in 1904. The indifferent reception accorded Twitmyer's work (Hall, 1976) meant that such an opportunity laid dormant until the pioneering work of John Watson had a major impact with his 1913 publication of a "behaviorist manifesto." Watson was largely responsible for elevating the idea that conditioning occurred because of contiguity mechanisms into a dominant learning theory approach. After Watson left academic psychology, this approach continued to be highly influential in the 1930s and early 1950s, because of the work of Guthrie and then his follower Estes.

John Broadus Watson (1878–1958)

Few psychologists have had such a great impact on the field in so short a time as John Watson. From his introduction of the term "behaviorist" into the general psychological vocabulary in 1913 in his behaviorist manifesto ("Psychology as the Behaviorist Views It," 1913) to his abrupt resignation from Johns Hopkins University, Watson dominated American learning theory. He received his degree from the University of Chicago in 1903, a time when the University of

Chicago was dominated by a philosophy called "functionalism," which was a blend of evolutionary theory and a belief in mind as the major concept for understanding human beings. Watson revolted against both of these aspects of functionalism. He also attacked the more sophisticated mentalism advocated by Titchener, and labeled by him as introspectionist. Titchener demanded that psychologists study their own thoughts (introspect) and use the resulting reports of thoughts as their major source of data. From the viewpoint of Watson and Guthrie (and of most other behaviorists as well), the problem with accepting as data reports of self-observation of mental events was that such data were always private. That is, there was no way for a second observer to check the accuracy of the first observer's report. Hence, there was no way to resolve disagreements among observers.

In 1903, Watson published a major study correlating the learning ability of rats with the degree of insulation of their nerve fibers (Bolles, 1975), and his research was always to focus on animals and children. With his rejection of mentalism and his advocacy of a comparative approach to research, Watson became the spokesman of those psychologists espousing a mechanistic, objective, environmentalist, and scientific-sounding viewpoint.

Behavior as the Yardstick of Learning

Watson argued that discoveries in physics and the natural sciences had resulted from one factor only: the careful measurement of objective, physical phenomena. A basic tenet of the older and more successful sciences was that for an observation to become accepted as data for science, it must in principle be repeatable. Thus, every scientist measuring the expansion of gas under conditions of reduced pressure would arrive at similar computations, assuming that they took their measurements in the same way, and so on. Watson suggested that mental phenomena simply could not meet these criteria for objective data. Without objective data, psychology could never become a true science. Therefore, in the interest of developing a science of psychology, measurements of mind must be abandoned. Behavior, on the other hand, could be quantified and measured objectively. Several observers watching a rat run a maze would arrive at similar calculations of its running speed; hence, behavior provided true, scientifically acceptable data.

Watson also believed that behavior was the product of the brain and must follow similar principles in mammals having somewhat similar brains. For both rat and man, the basic unit of learning was the habit, and the habit was acquired as the result of the strengthening of a neural link between a stimulus and a response. By the publication of his 1914 book, *Behavior: An Introduction to Comparative Psychology,* Watson had gone so far as to deny the existence of mind and all mentalistic phenomena. Feelings, images, thought, and all such experiences he considered to be nothing more than small motions of, say, the muscles of the throat and voice box for thought. So Watson, in a sense, made up his windpipe that he had no mind! He was the extreme peripheral connectionist; that is, he felt stimuli were connected with peripheral muscle responses rather than with central thoughts in the brain.

Although such extreme positions were rejected in psychology after Watson left the field, some experimental support is available for the idea of muscle potentials occurring at the time thoughts are experienced. McGuigan (1973) found that when a psychotic patient thought he was hearing voices, simultaneous muscle-action potentials were measurable in his throat! Many recent Russian researchers (O'Connor, 1966) see muscle movement as part of early thought. Such a position also appears in extreme form in many current "pop therapies," such as Rolfing, which maintains that negative emotional experiences are "remembered" in patterns of muscle tension and that the thoughts which accompanied the unfortunate events will be brought back by deep massage of the tense muscle groups (Keen, 1970).

For Watson, learning of skills was a matter of linking muscular responses. These links then formed the objective events that intervened between environmental stimuli and responses. Thus, the reason a rat was able to run a maze correctly after many trials was that it had acquired a pattern of muscular responses corresponding to the various turns, stops, and places to run forward in the maze. Bolles (1975) reports a conversation with an acquaintance of Watson's which might explain Watson's reliance on kinesthetic (muscle position sense) cues. When H. Langfeld asked Watson how he could deny the subjective experience of dreaming, Watson had asked, "What is a dream?" Watson himself may have lacked visual imagery, or the ability to remember dreams, leading him to suggest that muscle sensations are the basis for thought and memory. It is, of course, ironic that Watson, in his desire to avoid unobservable mentalistic concepts, was forced to speculate on the role of a type of inner behavior which, in his time, was equally unavailable to direct observation.

Watson was much impressed by the conditioning model developed by Bekhterev which stressed use of USs such as shock to elicit skeletal muscle responses. Bekhterev's philosophy was as adamant in its rejection of mind as Watson's. In 1914, Watson was elected president of the American Psychological Association and reported on the reality of classical (Russian) conditioning in his presidential address. The work of Bekhterev and later Pavlov (Watson, 1916) strongly influenced his attempts to explain the mechanisms of habit formation.

How Do We Learn? Watson's Answer

First, Watson considered all learning as conditioning of habits. Second, he thought that only two basic laws are necessary to describe the conditions under which bonds would form between stimuli and responses. His first law states that the strength of a bond depended upon the number of pairings (associations) of stimulus and response (the **law of frequency**). The second law states that the response occurring just after a given stimulus is most likely to be paired with that stimulus (the **law of recency**). Successful conditioning resulted from frequent pairings of cues, or responses and cues. The pairing, moreover, would be most effective if both were presented near the same time. While Watson encountered some failures in his attempts to replicate Russian research, he did succeed in conditioning both increased heart rate and leg withdrawal to a tone presented before shock. In his writings, however, Watson made no distinction between the types of responses. This simplistic approach to theory building continued to characterize Watson's work (in marked contrast to the elaborate detail presented by Pavlov).

Watson's early theory rested on two laws of learning, the laws of frequency and recency. The strength of a given S-R bond, he believed, is dependent upon both types of effects.

A Contiguity Explanation of the Effects of Apparent Reinforcement

Watson dismissed the effects of reinforcement (in particular, his rival Thorndike's "law of effect") by stating that a successful act becomes both the most recent and the most frequent response. Therefore, reward as an explanatory concept is superfluous. For example, a cat trying to escape from a puzzle box emits a variety of responses. One of these responses finally allows the cat to escape from the puzzle box and the cues associated with that box. Only the successful response is paired with ending the cat's exposure to the puzzle box cues, and so this response is always the one most recently paired with those cues once the trial has ended. Because a cat who has successfully escaped a puzzle box is no longer exposed to the puzzle box cues (at least not until the next learning trial), the connection between those cues and the successful response is protected from interference. All the connections between puzzle box cues and earlier responses, on the other hand, are interfered with by following responses (which become the most recent responses until they, in turn, are followed by later responses). Since at least all reasonably smart cats eventually emit a successful response and escape, the successful response is always the last one emitted in the presence of the box and it rapidly becomes most strongly connected to the puzzle box cues. This results in the successful responses becoming increasingly probable in the presence of those cues; thus, this response also becomes more frequent than any other response. As it becomes most frequent, this response becomes so strongly connected with being in a puzzle box that the cat will immediately emit this response as soon as it is placed in the box. As you can see, this explanation of the cat's demonstrated ability to improve as a puzzle box escape artist is based entirely on frequency-recency considerations rather than satisfaction or drive reduction.

In the final years of his academic career, Watson appeared to realize the inadequacies of his simple model. In a book published in 1919, he downplayed the role of frequency as a major explanatory concept and moved more in the direction of the physiological and behavioral concepts originated by Bekhterev and Pavlov (Hill, 1971). By the time of his famous experiment with little Albert, conducted with his student Rayner (Watson and Rayner, 1920), Watson was ready to explain most behavior in the carefully worked-out language of classical conditioning.

The Case of "Little Albert"

In this experiment with a healthy nine-month-old boy, Albert, who was enrolled at a day-care center, a white rat was used as the CS (thereby uniting Watson's favorite subjects) which originally elicited Albert's orienting reflex and reaching.* When Albert reached for the rat, the US of a sound made by hitting an iron rail with a hammer (see Figure 2.1) was sounded, provoking the startle reflex and crying (the UR). After six trials, the sight of the rat alone (the CS) was enough to elicit crying and avoidance. This effect generalized to white rabbits, dogs, and animal furs. While Watson and Rayner discussed several conditioning procedures to remove the conditioned phobia, the removal of Albert from the center by his mother prevented any of them from being tested. At the end of the article, Watson suggested:

> The Freudians twenty years from now, unless their hypotheses change, when they come to analyze Albert's fear of a seal skin coat—assuming that he comes to analysis at that age—will probably tease from him the recital of a dream which upon their analysis will show that Albert at three years of age attempted to play with the pubic hair of the mother and was scolded violently for it. (We are by no means denying that this might in some other case condition it.) If the analyst has sufficiently prepared Albert to accept such a dream when found as an explanation of his avoiding tendencies, and if the analyst has the authority and personality to put it over, Albert may be fully convinced that the dream was a true revealer of the factors which brought about the fear. [Watson and Rayner, 1920, p. 14]

Watson's Positions on Major Issues

Nature/nurture   Watson's emphatic commitment to radical environmentalism is shown in the following passage:

> Give me a dozen healthy infants, well-formed, and my own specified world to bring them up in and I'll guarantee to take any one at random and train him to become any type of specialist I might select—doctor, lawyer, artist, merchant-chief and, yes, even beggar-man and thief, regardless of his talents, penchants, tendencies, abilities, vocations, and the race of his ancestors. [Watson, 1924, p. 82]

The how of learning   Watson first believed that the principles of frequency and recency are sufficient to explain conditioning. Because a successful act is both most frequent and most recent, it becomes the most likely to be repeated in similar circumstances. He felt the satisfier and annoyer system of Thorndike (see Chapter 3) to be contaminated by residual subjectivity. In later formulations, he adopted the Pavlovian position (Hilgard and Bower, 1975).

The what of learning   According to Watson, bonds between observable stimuli and observable or potentially observable responses are the unit of learning. What is learned was a habit or a conditioned reflex consisting of linked muscle responses.

Continuity/noncontinuity, use of animal data, and determinism   Learning occurs through an accumulation of habit strength. Apparent demonstrations of

---

* One reason Watson may have preferred infants and rats as subjects was their inability to introduce verbal contamination into the testing situation. One assumes that adults would persist in claiming they had images and thoughts and that their verbal responses would offend Watson's need for objectivity.

Figure 2.1   Watson sneaking up on unsuspecting "little Albert," who is happily playing with a white rat. In Watson's hand is a hammer which he is about to strike upon a suspended steel bar "four feet long and ¾ inch in diameter," thereby beginning the process of making "little Albert" the first human with an experimental neurosis in the form of a phobic fear of white furry objects. Watson's assistant, Rosalie Rayner, is distracting "little Albert" from Watson's approach.

insight reflect nothing but very rapid accumulations of habit strength or the end result of tiny intention movements, creating movement-produced stimuli that elicit the final sudden overt response. Thus, learning is always continuous. According to Watson, data collected from animals applies to human behavior, and behavior is determined by the environment.

Perspective

In the case of "little Albert," Watson has provided a model for how a fear might be acquired. Although he suggested a treatment for removing the fear, he did not have an opportunity to apply it. This was first done by Mary Cover Jones (1924), a student who worked with Watson after he left Johns Hopkins. She compared several methods, including Watson's proposed plan for direct conditioning of the fear stimulus to a positive stimulus. Using food as the positive stimulus, she was able to remove a fear of rabbits by gradually moving the rabbit closer and closer to her subject while he ate. Eventually, her subject had overcome his "rabbit phobia" to such an extent that he was able to handle the animal. Prefiguring Bandura's (Chapter 9) technique of modeling, she was also successful in removing such fears by a social imitation technique in which a fearless subject handled the animal in the presence of the subject suffering from the fear.

By producing a phobia (extreme fear) of white furry objects in little Albert through classical conditioning, Watson and Rayner were able to demonstrate that the laws of learning can also account for at least some forms of pathological behavior.

One reason that Watson was not the first to use techniques that we today call behavioral modification was that he was forced to leave the halls of academia in 1920 because of his affair with his laboratory assistant, Rosalie Rayner. For this affair he may have suffered less than the field of psychology did. He divorced his wife, married Rosalie, went to work for an advertising agency (J. Walter Thompson), and became wealthy. He published one major book in 1924 and left his mark on the public with his slogan, "Lucky Strike Green has gone to war"—referring to the change in color of Lucky Strike cigarette packages from green to white to save green dye for the war effort in World War II (Schultz, 1969). One assumes that this slogan was an attempt to condition smoking Lucky Strikes through contiguity of the brand name to patriotic expressions. With Watson out of academic psychology, the defense of the contiguity perspective in learning theory fell into the capable hands of Edwin Guthrie. Guthrie's theory was developed in more detail than Watson's, and his ideas were more influential in shaping the future development of learning theory.

Edwin R. Guthrie (1886–1959)

Originally trained as a philosopher, Guthrie became a psychologist when he was convinced that the experimental method might be used to approach many of the traditional problems concerning the nature of man. He was strongly influenced by the argument of the philosopher Singer that many of the problems of the mind could be translated into behavior (Guthrie, 1959), and he became a behaviorist. His first text in 1921 was largely Watsonian in tone. Simple behavior was a matter of simple S-R connections, and complex behavior was a multitude of simple S-R connections. Like Watson, he saw the brain as a *tabula rasa* and minimized innate organization and motivational principles (Bolles, 1975). Also like Watson, Guthrie used the word "conditioning" to cover almost all forms of learning, and he maximized the role of environmental factors in shaping the nature of an adult human. By 1935, however, he had moved from a restatement of an orthodox Watsonian position to the development of an equally mechanistic but highly individual theory of learning.

A Single Law of Learning

In contrast to the highly complex system developed by Pavlov or Watson's two-law system of learning (frequency and recency), Guthrie produced the ultimate in simplicity in theory building: a theory with a single law describing the necessary and sufficient conditions for learning, which he labeled the **law of contiguity.** No lists of laws, no rewards, only stimuli and movements bonded into combinations, as follows: "A combination of stimuli which has accompanied a movement will on its reoccurrence tend to be followed by that movement" (Guthrie, 1935, p. 26). To further the impression of exaggerated simplicity, the law had only one additional postulate: "A stimulus pattern gains its full associative strength on the basis of its first pairing with a response" (Guthrie, 1942, p. 30). Guthrie suggested not only that the principle of recency alone is enough to account for learning but also that all learning is **one-trial learning.** Thus, whatever was done last in the presence of a given stimulus combination will be done again when the stimulus combination next occurs.

Guthrie proposed a theory of learning with two basic principles: (1) things which occur together will tend to be associated (the law of contiguity), and (2) all such associations occur in a single trial.

Though to advocate so simple a theory might at first inspection appear unwise, Guthrie was able to defend his work against a wide range of objections without adding further laws, and on a logical rather than experimental basis. For example, we know that most learning appears to be acquired gradually rather than in the abrupt "one-trial" fashion specified by Guthrie's "one-trial learning" postulate. Guthrie, however, evaded this objection by redefining "stimulus." A situation may seem like a single cue, but in reality it is composed of a mass of stimuli that changes from moment to moment. Millions of nerve fibers carry information reporting on a world which alters as the organism moves about. The kinesthetic feedback on muscle condition is a function of millions of receptors reporting millions of small movements within muscle groups. Hence, what seems a single response is in reality a mass of responses, and what seems a single stimulus is a myriad of stimuli. Each of these elements can be combined with each other, and it is these tiny bonds that are formed in single trials. In each trial, many of these small responses are bonded to many of the stimuli. The gradual acquisition curve we see is the ultimate result of the gradual increase in appropriate bonds and the gradual elimination of inappropriate bonds. Thus, Guthrie would say that improvement in an act refers to the outcome of learning rather than to the process of learning. Errors are learning that does not fit with mastery of the final act, and learning is the process by which all cues are eventually bonded to acceptable behavior. Improvement, therefore, equals the learning of more and more correct movements. Examples might be skills (which are the same as acts, according to Guthrie) such as touch typing, in which more and more correct key strikes (movements) gradually take over from an initial pattern of inaccurate and awkward attempts to strike the correct keys without looking at them.

Furthermore, when you type highly practiced words, each letter of the word is accompanied by specific muscle sensations (**movement-produced stimuli**) which signal you that it is time to strike the next letter. The next move after a specific movement-produced stimulus is the response which has become (through contiguity) conditioned to it. This response in turn produces new cues which are conditioned to the next response, and so on. For example, it is difficult not to type the letter *u* just after typing the letter *q* because of the frequent association of these two letters in the *qu* sequence. This chaining of cues produced by your own movements to further muscle movements is a major factor in linking the separate movements into the completed act. Movement-produced stimuli linked to incorrect movements do not get conditioned to further typing responses because you pause and emit other behaviors, such as erasing the error. Only typing movements that are acceptable to you lead to stimuli that in turn get linked to further typing. Self-generated stimuli were a key part of Guthrie's theory, and this type of mediating mechanism was used in the theories which came after Guthrie.

Another objection to Guthrie's theory is that animals fail to learn to respond unless they are rewarded or escape aversive consequences (such as shock) for doing so. Guthrie defends his theory that "contiguity is the only mechanism of learning" by explaining that reward is a source of stimuli which serves to relate other groups of cues. In addition, reward protects a collection of S-R bonds from "unlearning" by making them the last things to happen just before the reward changes the stimulus situation (Guthrie and Horton, 1946). This is the same mechanism used in Watson's theory.

Drives and their reduction through appropriate actions are also seen as not necessary for learning to occur. This is in marked contrast to Hull's reinforcement theory, to be presented in the next chapter. Drives, however, are seen as often contributing to learning. This is because most drives serve as sources of **maintaining stimuli.** You know that when you are hungry, you may experience stomach contractions and enhanced sensitivity to food-related stimuli. The stimuli associated with a drive state are seen as providing a unifying element to the series of stimuli and responses which lead to the final elimination of the stimuli associated with that drive state. The cues accompanying hunger become linked to a set of S-R bonds which connect cues and movements that have led in the past to food rewards. The food rewards stop the hunger cues and thus interrupt the combination of maintaining stimuli and movement-produced stimuli. The rat presses the bar in the Skinner box when hungry because the last thing he did when he was hungry in that situation was to press the bar. Getting the food reduces the hunger cues so that the stimulus situation faced by the rat becomes different and is no longer the one bonded to bar pressing. Therefore, the satiated rat stops pressing. Essentially, the role of reward is to protect those responses made just before the reward from being connected to responses other than those producing the reward (Hilgard and Bower, 1975). Experimental extinction results in a reduction in rates of formerly rewarded responses because the subject is no longer exposed to the changes in stimuli associated with drive reduction. This results in new responses now being produced in the presence of the cues that were originally linked to movements that led to reward. Without reinforcement to protect the sequence of responses that once had been rewarded, increasing numbers of the new competing responses are linked to situational cues, and the formerly rewarded sequence gradually vanishes. This is called **associative inhibition,** and it is also the basis for forgetting. Forgetting occurs because of interference, which appears in the form of new, competing learning.

Guthrie, like Tolman (in Chapter 5), believed that drive states produce **anticipatory responses.** These anticipatory states consist of states of actual muscular readiness to do the behavior formerly emitted in the presence of the reward which reduced the drive state in the past (Guthrie, 1935). These states are physical—they are not the cognitions of Tolman's theory. The Guthrie position on reward can be summarized as a position of "stimulus change as reward," with internal stimuli and responses (acting as stimuli) being changed by reward.

If the effect of reward is to remove the animal from a situation and hence to preserve the bonds that were formed in that situation, how did Guthrie explain the effects of punishment? Again, he stated that the animal repeats what it has done last in a situation. The aversive stimuli act to produce general tension and restlessness as well as movement that eventually removes the subject from the pain. Guthrie said the animal learns to repeat its actions leading up to the pain, as well as those occurring just after the punishment (Guthrie, 1935). This led to his prediction of the following results, which seem to go against common sense: Rats were trained to run in a long alley. When they almost reached the goal box, their hind paws were shocked. After this experience, the rats responded to the cue of an alley, in which they previously jumped forward at its end (because of the shock to their rear paws) by running forward faster when they again started up that alley. This result seems to contradict the commonsense prediction that the rats would become afraid to run toward the end of the alley where they had been shocked. Thus, punishment is effective or not effective, from the punisher's point of view, depending upon what it causes the punished organism to do. Punishment is effective only when it results in a new response to the old cues. Punishment changes unwanted habits when it elicits new behavior incompatible with the punished behavior. Again, learning is the result of a change in stimulus conditions. Movements conditioned to aversive stimuli (which are the source of maintaining stimuli) are those that get the subject away from the stimuli or the stimuli away from the subject (Guthrie, 1935).

Guthrie explained phenomena such as the effects of reward and drive states, and their reduction, punishment, and experimental extinction in terms of contiguity principles related to changes in stimulus conditions rather than in terms of reinforcement.

Applications

The results just discussed are congruent with Guthrie's general suggestions on punishment. Guthrie stated that for punishment to be effective, it must cause competing responses to occur in the presence of cues for the unwanted behavior. As an example, Guthrie (1935) suggested the following treatment for a child who comes home from school and fails to hang up his coat: The child should be told to put his coat on again and should then be sent back outside to repeat the entire sequence leading into the house. Upon the child's reentry, he must hang up the coat. Thus, the cues associated with the entry should be bonded to the response of hanging up the coat. In this example, as in the applications to follow, the emphasis is on connecting specific stimuli with specific responses. The punishment of going outside again works because the child is then forced to connect the new behavior of hanging up the coat with the stimuli (those associated with the house and the muscle movements involved in entering the house) that were formerly paired with not hanging up the coat. This also illustrates another feature of Guthrie's theory: Because connections are between specific stimuli and specific responses, transfer of training would be expected to occur only to the extent that old stimuli are present in the new situations. In the example of the child and the coat, it would be expected that "coat hanging-up" might not occur if the child were entering someone else's house.

Such a method of breaking a bad habit is an example of Guthrie's **incompatible response method.** Guthrie also suggested two other methods for breaking habits, the **fatigue method** and the **threshold method.** The fatigue method consists of allowing an unwanted act to be repeated until it fatigues and "not responding" becomes associated with the cues that formerly elicited the unwanted response. An example would be the breaking of a bucking bronco by having the rider remain on his back until the horse is too exhausted to buck. The stimuli associated with the rider are now assumed to be connected to the responses of "not bucking." Ayllon (1963) successfully used a related method (which he called the method of stimulus satiation) to eliminate towel hoarding by an institutionalized psychotic woman. Instead of retrieving the ward's supply of towels from the woman's room, a nurse would enter her room at random intervals throughout the day and hand her a towel without comment. The woman would hoard the towels handed to her. By the end of the third week of treatment, she was being given an average of 60 towels daily. When the number of towels kept in her room reached the 625 mark, the patient began taking them out. Before this treatment, the average number of towels found in her room had been 20. After treatment, only an average of 1.5 towels were to be found.

The third (threshold) method involves introducing the cues which normally elicit the unwanted behavior at such low intensity that no such behavior occurs. During this time, other responses become associated with these cues. Gradually, then, the intensity of the stimulus is increased, taking care that it is below the "threshold" of the unwanted response. Eventually, the subject can be exposed to the full intensity of what had been cues for the undesired behavior without emitting that behavior. For instance, a bronco could also be broken by first putting a very light blanket on his back, then gradually adding more blankets and a saddle, and finally adding the rider. While the natural response to the weight of the rider would have been to buck, the weight of a light blanket would not be a strong enough cue to elicit bucking. As the horse gradually gets "used to" the cues of weight on his back, even the stimulus of the rider will be associated with "not bucking." This method is very similar to the technique of systematic desensitization, which is an important clinical tool of behaviorally oriented therapists. In this technique (discussed in detail in Chapter 6), a hierarchy of fear cues is presented (beginning with very weak fear cues) in the presence of cues for the incompatible response of relaxing. Guthrie (1938) suggested that the threshold method is a common feature of everyday human interactions. For example, a mother wishing to send her daughter to an expensive school might begin by casually mentioning it to her husband. Initially, discussion about the school is kept at a level that is low keyed enough to not provoke a negative reaction. When the issue is finally raised in a direct manner, the father is used to the idea and no violent reaction over the anticipated expenses occurs. In comparing his three methods, Guthrie concluded that all of them involve finding the cues which elicit the unwanted habit and then making sure that these cues become stimuli for competing responses. All methods are seen as having equivalent results (Guthrie, 1938).

Guthrie proposed three methods for eliminating bad habits, all based on his central assumption that behavior is controlled by stimuli. These are the methods of: (1) incompatible response, (2) fatigue, and (3) threshold.

Guthrie's Positions on Major Issues

Nature/nurture   Guthrie, like Watson, was a strong environmentalist:

> When a man hammers his thumb we do not explain his dancing movements and vocalization in terms of an aroused "ego" or aroused "libido," nor do we say that his activities are an expression of the self-preservation instinct. It is simply that men who hammer their thumbs usually become very active for a time . . . The problem of motives arises when it is necessary to explain how behavior becomes directed to certain ends, and this is a problem of learning . . . [Guthrie, 1938, p. 96]

In this example, the behavior is seen as environmentally dependent rather than due to instincts or inherited motives. The direction of behavior is explicitly defined as the result of learning in the environment.

The how of learning   Guthrie was the purest of the contiguity theorists:

> We shall have a much better insight into the uses of punishment and reward if we analyze their effects in terms of association and realize that punishment is effective only through its association . . . [Guthrie, 1952, p. 132]

The what of learning   The association of individual muscle movements with individual stimuli is the basic unit of learning. Complex habits represent the net sum of many of these basic units.

Continuity/noncontinuity, use of animal data, and determinism   Learning always takes place on the first pairing of a single stimulus and a single response. Skills are built up slowly, however. Guthrie explained:

> Learning occurs normally in one associative episode. . . . A skill is not a simple habit, but a large collection of habits that achieve a certain result in many and varied circumstances. [Guthrie, 1942, p. 59]

Guthrie was a typical behaviorist in feeling free to generalize animal data to humans, and he saw behavior as determined by events in the environment.

Perspective

Central to Guthrie's theory was the following idea: Because we tend to repeat movements when reexposed to the cues associated with those movements in the past, environments with unchanging cues should produce stereotyped movements. Guthrie and Horton (1946) photographed the responses of cats escaping from puzzle boxes and found that each cat did indeed develop a stereotyped pattern of escape movements.

Guthrie would argue that the reason these responses are stereotyped is that only the last response (the successful one) the cat made before escaping the box was protected from interference. A direct test of the assumption that the last response made in a situation is the only one conditioned to the cues associated with that situation was performed by Voeks (1948). She found that 56 of her 57 human subjects working at punchboard and raised-relief finger mazes performed in ways consistent with the prediction that the last response made would be the one made again when the subject was confronted with the same puzzle. This was true even though other responses had been made more frequently. Voeks (1954) also tested Guthrie's prediction that stimulus-response connections were made in all-or-none fashion, using the human eye-blink response. Half of the subjects gave conditioned eyelid responses on every trial after their first CR, and few errors were made by the other subjects. This showed that, at least for most subjects, the CRs were acquired in a single trial, just as Guthrie predicted.

Another central assumption of Guthrie's theory is that reward in the form of drive reduction is not essential for learning to occur. This assumption has been supported by a study conducted by Sheffield and Roby (1950) in which rats learned to lick a water tube for a nonnutritive sweet stimulus (saccharine solution). As saccharin has no caloric value, no biological hunger drive is reduced and stimulus factors alone seem to account for the learning.

In retrospect, Guthrie made four important lasting contributions: The first contribution was forcing psychologists to examine more extensively than before the role of stimuli in determining behavior and learning. The second was extending the lifetime of the contiguity perspective and showing a need for a reexamination of the role of reinforcement by studies of the type just described, forcing the reinforcement-connectionists into more sophisticated theorizing. The third was the development of the concept of movement-produced stimuli. This concept has been incorporated in modified form into both Hull's and Skinner's explanations of how a chain of behavior can be held together until the organism is finally in position to make the terminal response. The fourth follows from the probabilistic nature of Guthrie's theory. Because Guthrie saw learning as occurring through the "collisions" of cues that happened to be in contiguity to each other, he felt that the outcome of any given learning trial is partly due to chance and hence cannot be precisely predicted. What can be predicted is the average outcome of many trials, and in this sense Guthrie's theory is a statistical theory. This made his theory an ideal starting point for the development of a mathematical model of conditioning. As we shall see in Part 2, mathematical-computer model approaches to learning have become increasingly important through the information-processing school of learning theories. Because Guthrie's ideas lent themselves to quantification by William Kaye Estes, Guthrie's influence has been extended to more modern approaches to learning. You may now wish to take a brief view of Estes's statistical version of Guthrie's theory.

OPTIONAL SECTION

William Kaye Estes (1919–   )

Even though William Kaye Estes obtained his Ph.D. in 1943 from the University of Minnesota with Skinner as his thesis director, his theory was primarily influenced by the ideas of Guthrie. Estes became a professor at Rockefeller University in 1968 and has continued to develop his theory (Sahakian, 1976). In using several of the key concepts of Guthrie's theory in the construction of his own **stimulus sampling theory,** Estes had to make several specific assumptions. We will now review the core assumptions of Estes's model and see how they lead to predictions of basic learning phenomena. As you will see, Guthrie's theory, when developed and "pinned down" to specifics, is much more complex than it appears on first reading.

Assumption 1   All learning situations are composed of a large but finite number of stimulus elements. All the stimuli physically present for any one learning trial are labeled S. Stimuli can be inside (as in the case of movement-produced stimuli) or outside the organism.

Assumption 2   All responses are classified as either "right" (labeled A_1) or "wrong" (labeled A_2). When Estes referred to responses, he was talking about acts in Guthrie's terms, not small muscle movements (Hill, 1977).

Assumption 3   All elements in S become conditioned (or attached) to either A_1 or A_2. That is, all cues become associated through contiguity with either "right" (leading to a successfully completed act) or "wrong" (not leading to a successfully completed act) responses.

Assumption 4   The learner only actually experiences a small proportion of the elements (cues) in S on any given trial. Attention is limited.

Assumption 5   The proportion of elements sampled per trial out of all the stimuli potentially available is a constant labeled *theta* (θ). The sample of cues noticed by the learner on any given trial is assumed to return to S after that trial. In other words, just because you notice a group of particular cues on a given trial doesn't mean that you will notice all of those cues on the next trial. The cues you notice on a trial are an independent sample of all the cues you could have noticed, and each sample of cues is independent of previous samples.

Assumption 6   If an A_1 response ends a trial, the group of cues sampled is conditioned through contiguity to A_1. When the cues are returned to S, they remain attached to A_1 (the "right" response). Therefore, the more successful (A_1) trials that occur, the higher the proportion of the elements in S that are conditioned to A_1. The more cues in S that are attached to A_1, the higher the probability of A_1 cues being sampled in a given trial; hence the higher the probability of future A_1 responses. This increase in the probability of making a correct response as a function of the number of "successful" trials is what Estes labeled learning.

Assumption 7   The probability of a correct response on any given trial is predicted on the basis of the proportions of elements conditioned to A_1 and to A_2 ("wrong responses"). If the proportion of the total cues (elements) in S conditioned to A_1 is 75 percent, then the probability of an A_1 response is .75. These probabilities shift as successful trials condition elements to A_1 and unsuccessful trials condition elements to A_2. The state of the learning system continues to change until either almost all of the elements become conditioned to A_1 (completed learning) or to A_2 (extinction). As learning progresses, the number of elements available to become newly conditioned to A_1 declines. Thus, this model predicts a negatively accelerated learning curve. That is, learning is usually rapid at first, but considerable time is required for the last errors to stop occurring (in Hergenhahn, 1976).

Estes's theory can account for many of the basic phenomena of learning. As we have discussed, learning is seen as increased A_1-cue bonds. Since during extinction the trial usually ends with the subject's doing something other than A_1, the cues gradually become reconditioned to A_2 responses. Generalization is handled in a manner very similar to Thorndike's treatment of it. New situations are seen as having elements in common with situations in which conditioning has previously occurred. The extent of generalization is dependent upon the number of stimulus elements the two situations have in common (Estes, 1959). With additional assumptions, many additional phenomena of learning can be predicted or described.

The brief discussion of Estes's mathematical extension of Guthrie's theory should be sufficient to introduce you to the basic logic of trying to make learning theory more precise through application of numerical concepts. As a graduate student, the author was once assigned the job of predicting various learning outcomes when given specific values of the proportion of cues attached to correct responses (A_1, and so on). Carrying out the calculations required by Estes's formulas gave a value for the number of trials to learning at the 90 percent accuracy level and for other quantities that can be derived from the data we collected in studies of real rats.

Although Estes's theory uses a minimum number of variables and derives these more from classical statistical theory than from biology, the second theory in the next chapter (Hull) represents a more ambitious approach to the quantification of learning theory. Estes's model is limited in scope, but Hull attempts to predict the full range of learning phenomena. Hull also uses many more variables and relates them to general events occurring within his learning organisms. One reason Estes was able to limit the number of variables in his theory is because, by focusing on stimuli and their relationships, he had less need for speculation about internal states. This made it easier for him to retain Guthrie's emphasis on explaining learning through a few basic principles. For the reinforcement theorists (to be reviewed in the next chapter), motivational variables as well as environmental events must be considered. This factor complicates their theories, compared to contiguity theories.

Chapter Perspective

John Watson introduced the term "behaviorism" and the contiguity connectionist viewpoint into American psychology. Before leaving academic psychology, he abandoned his laws of frequency and recency in favor of the laws of classical conditioning developed by Pavlov. His concept of muscle-produced cues and the development of an American contiguity conditioning school of psychology were continued by Guthrie. Guthrie reduced Watson's two laws of learning to one—the law of contiguity and a postulate which stated that bonds between individual stimuli and responses were formed in one trial. Guthrie also further developed Watson's concept of muscle movement cues into his theory of movement-produced stimuli. Because Guthrie's theory was probabilistic, Estes* was able to transform it into a mathematical-statistical theory which prefigured modern information-processing theories and thus extended Guthrie's influence into the present.

Key Terms

anticipatory response	law of contiguity	movement-produced stimuli
associative inhibition	law of frequency	
fatigue method	law of recency	one-trial learning
incompatible response method	maintaining stimuli	stimulus sampling theory
		threshold method

Annotated Bibliography

An excellent cross-section of Watson's thought is presented in *Behaviorism* (New York: Norton, 1924), while the student wanting to savor a brief introduction to Watson's amusing writing style would find it profitable to read the famous "little Albert" article by Watson and Rosalie Rayner, "Conditioned emotional reactions" (*Journal of Experimental Psychology*, 1920, 3, 1–14).

Guthrie's views are well presented in his *The psychology of learning* (New York: Harper & Row, 1935). Estes's "neo-Guthrie" theory is explained well in his article, "The statistical approach to learning theory," in S. Koch, ed., *Psychology: A study of a science*, vol. 2 (New York: McGraw-Hill, 1959). Excellent biographical material on most of the learning theorists covered in your text is to be found in D. P. Schultz, *A history of modern psychology* (New York: Academic Press, 1969).

---

* Estes has recently returned to the development of his statistical learning theory, making liberal use of computer technology. He hopes that his work will point the way, by slow degrees, to the development of the kind of precise general learning theory that Hull envisioned (Estes, 1976).

3

Learning through Reinforcement: Thorndike and Hull

In this chapter we will explore the major principles developed by two theorists who saw connections between stimuli and responses as resulting from reinforcement mechanisms. Notice how these theorists altered their principles to handle potentially disconfirming results of other researchers' experiments as well as how the various laws were used to try to predict new behavior.

The theorists presented in the preceding chapter all believed that learning was a matter of the contiguity of stimuli and responses. This view was used in defense of teaching through rote repetition. The consequences of a response to the behaving organism were seen as important only if they served to change a stimulus situation. In contrast, the theorists presented in this chapter and in Chapter 4 all believed that the consequences of a response were much more important for producing learning than contiguity alone was. Pleasant consequences were seen as providing optimal conditions for the formation of a bond between a stimulus and a response. These theories took direct issue with the idea that "practice makes perfect." Teachers were directed to focus on the reinforcing aspect of school situations rather than on rote repetition.

Because reinforcement plays such an important part in these theories, let us examine the meaning of this concept. Although all the theorists we are going to discuss used the concept in slightly different ways, they all considered it to be somewhat like the popular notion of a reward. This is a very different meaning of reinforcement from that used by Pavlov. For Pavlov, reinforcement was seen as the confirmation of a CS by a subsequent US. Pavlov's concept refers to a relationship between signals or stimuli rather than to an effect of the responses emitted by the organism. You should thus be careful to distinguish between these two meanings of the term.

The first theory we will examine is that of Edward Lee Thorndike. From the time of the publication in 1898 of his dissertation on cats' escaping from puzzle boxes until the late 1930s, Thorndike had a strong influence on most learning theorists in America. Although Pavlov made no acknowledgment of Watson's theory, he was specific in pointing out the critical and germinal role of Thorndike's ideas and contributions to research.

. . . the American School of Psychologists—already interested in the comparative study of psychology—evinced a disposition to subject the highest nervous activities of animals to experimental analysis under various specially devised conditions. We may fairly regard the treatise by Thorndike, *The Animal Intelligence* (1898), as the starting point for systematic investigations of this kind. [Pavlov, 1960, p. 6]

The gestalt theorists to be reviewed in Chapter 5 gained the attention of the American psychological establishment largely through their attacks on Thorndike.

Thorndike was able to gain acceptance for a **mechanistic,** experimentally oriented approach to the study of learning as a replacement for **mentalism** (the use of assumed "mind" or mental events to explain behavior) without the excesses of Watson's theory. He made the S-R bond, rather than thought, the focus of learning. Thorndike's early work with cats marked the beginning of an American tradition of investigating the basic principles of learning, using animal surrogates to learn basic facts which were then assumed to generalize to human behavior. Both Hull and Skinner (to be presented in Chapter 4) also used rats and pigeons almost interchangeably with human subjects in developing their major principles. They also retained the behavioristic and mechanistic bias of Thorndike's work. Their approaches to developing learning theories, however, were as opposite as they could be.

Hull tried to develop theories in the pattern of the physical sciences, but after his death most American learning theorists began to turn away from such efforts. American psychology had begun with the philosophical theorizing of William James, who, as the teacher of Thorndike, had seen his former pupil turn psychology into a science characterized by direct observation of behavior and experimentation (Hilgard and Bower, 1975). Hull's intention was to be the Newton* of learning theory, and to develop a calculus of behavior through application of the principles of both formal logic and the experimental method.

In spite of many years of dedicated and careful work by Hull and his followers, this effort failed. Hull's failure to develop a theory of learning of the precision of Newton's theory of motion was not due to lack of effort or of inspiration, nor was the project intrinsically foolish. Rather, it was the complexity of the learning process, as revealed by Hull's work, that defeated him. In retrospect, one of Hull's greatest contributions may have been in demonstrating that the subject matter of the learning psychologist is fundamentally much more complicated than the phenomena investigated by Newton and the physics of his time.

Following the collapse of Hullian efforts to develop a unitheory of learning, learning psychologists retreated either into developing limited models about specific types of learning phenomena or into the stricter empirical approach of focusing on observable S-R relationships, as advocated by the Skinnerians. Hull's influence, however, continued to be felt through the work of his many talented students, who have collectively provided the major behavioristic alternatives to the Skinnerian approach. Some, like Spence, paralleled Skinner in accepting contiguity as the mechanism for learning conditioned reinforcers and

---

* Sir Isaac Newton (1642–1727) was an English physicist and philosopher. He is best known for mathematical expressions of his laws of gravity and motion.

reinforcement as the mechanism for learning overt responses. Others, like Miller, extended the drive-reduction assumptions of Hull into new areas (in Miller's case, into imitation).

Edward L. Thorndike (1874–1949)

Before Thorndike, most conceptions about animal behavior were dominated either by the assumption that animals reasoned much like human beings, or explanations in terms of instinctual mechanisms. Thorndike openly despised giving animals human characteristics (anthropomorphic projections) and sought to explain animal learning as the result of simple events and principles. He publicly presented this mechanistic replacement for animal reason with the publication of his doctoral dissertation reporting the methods by which cats solved puzzle box problems (Thorndike, 1898; see Figure 3.1). After observing the patterns of learning to escape from the boxes demonstrated by his five felines, Thorndike stated that animal learning is a matter of the gradual "stamping-in" of stimulus-response bonds through **trial and error.** If Thorndike had stopped with providing a mechanistic theory of animal learning, his impact would have been minor. Thorndike, however, saw nothing in his observations to convince him that human learning was in any way qualitatively different from animal learning. With this position, Thorndike directly opposed the dualistic doctrine which declared human learning to be insightful or an act of getting the "idea," while beasts were like machines controlled by their instincts. He also opposed the doctrine of animal reason (Bolles, 1975).

By adapting to the field of learning Darwin's conception of a continuity between men and beasts, Thorndike introduced the assumption now known as **equipotentiality** into American psychology. This concept is based on the belief that the laws of learning are independent of the types of stimuli used, of the responses studied, and of the species to which the laws are applied. These assumptions provided the rationale for the use of animal subjects in the study of the laws of learning, and Thorndike was the first to use animals for this purpose. Animal subjects have the important advantages* of usually being available when needed and of not being able to express their objections to shock and food deprivation procedures. More critically, if the study of the behavior of animals can tell us about the laws governing human learning, then animal behavior (and human also), which can be measured more objectively than human thinking, becomes the appropriate subject matter of psychology. Thorndike prefigured the practices of modern behavioral modifiers (see Chapters 6 and 10) by his willingness to generalize from cat studies to human applications.

Thorndike thought that learning is usually a matter of the automatic strengthening of S-R bonds as a result of a trial-and-error experience. He assumed that the laws governing such learning are the same for animals and humans.

---

* Advantages, we must note, only from the point of view of the experimenter.

Figure 3.1   A puzzled cat in one of Thorndike's puzzle boxes. Pressing the lever just behind the cat pulls the chain which opens the door, allowing the frustrated feline to escape.

How Learning Occurs:
Thorndike's Early Theory

Thorndike's theory remained essentially unchanged from 1898 to the early 1930s. The core of this theory was three major laws: The first was the **law of effect,** which stated that "responses just prior to a satisfying state of affairs are more likely to be repeated" and "responses just prior to an annoying state of affairs are more likely not to be repeated" (Thorndike, 1913, p. 2). Animals were viewed as tending to try to maintain satisfying states of affairs and not to maintain annoying states of affairs. Hence, in spite of the subjective tone of the words "annoy" and "satisfy," Thorndike defined these terms by the animal's behavior, without recourse to mentalistic concepts. Satisfiers "stamped" responses in and annoyers "stamped" them out (Lefrancois, 1972). These "stampings" he saw as direct, mechanical, and not requiring consciousness of the learning or awareness of the learning. Learning he therefore defined in terms of S-R bonds that are gradually "stamped" into the brain. The completed bonds then function much like inherited connections (instincts and reflexes). This definition is very similar to Pavlov's neurological speculations.

Thorndike's second law was the **law of readiness,** which was stated in terms of hypothetical neural units. This law stated that satisfaction or annoyance depends upon the state of the behaving organism. When a conduction unit of neurons is ready, then conduction is satisfying. When the conduction unit is unready, then conduction is annoying. When the conduction unit is ready and no conduction occurs, then the organism would be frustrated or annoyed. In a sense, this was much like the expectancy principles advocated by the cognitive theorists, to be discussed in Chapter 5.

His third law was the **law of exercise** and represented a concession to a contiguity interpretation of learning. Thorndike stated that use of connections acts to strengthen the connections and disuse acts to weaken them. The "use" principle primarily explains repetitive habits such as motor skills and memory of poems. The "disuse" principle explains forgetting in general. While admitting that contiguity factors could influence S-R bonds, Thorndike criticized using this principle without including the law of effect (Hilgard and Bower, 1975). Thorndike took exception to the idea that drill alone can produce learning!

In Thorndike's theory, learning occurs when: (1) a response leads to satisfaction or the avoidance of annoyance (law of effect), (2) the organism is ready to respond (law of readiness), and (3) this learning is enhanced by practice (law of exercise).

Thorndike also proposed five minor laws, as follows:

1. The **law of multiple response:** This law states that when a learner faces a problem and the first response does not produce a satisfying state of affairs, the learner will try other responses. This working through a hierarchy of possible solutions is the essence of trial-and-error learning. Success, of course, stamps in the successful response. A person locating lost keys on top of a desk after rummaging through his/her entire home will look on top of the desk when the keys are lost again.

2. The **law of set** or **attitude:** Learning does not exist independently of the state of the behaving organism. If you are feeling depressed, you may give up without finding a solution. Set is also seen as culturally determined predispositions to behave in specific ways. If a person's cultural reference group has taught that the best response to a frustrating situation is stoic indifference, that person when frustrated will behave very differently from the person whose group stresses aggressive reactions to frustration.

3. The **law of prepotency of elements:** This is the ability shown by the learner to respond only to the relevant aspects of a situation. It is like the modern Russian (see Chapter 8) analysis of the second signal system as the means by which man can signal himself to restrict attention to what is most likely to be important in solving a problem. It is also like the expectancies discussed in the chapter on cognitive learning theories (Chapter 7).

4. The **law of response by analogy** refers to the ability of humans to react to a novel situation with the responses learned in a familiar situation. This suggests that responses can be transferred across situations. Thorndike also says that the degree of transfer is a function of the similarity of the two situations (in Lefrancois, 1972). An example might be the transfer of balancing and steering skills from riding a bicycle to riding a motorcycle. This concept is akin to a generalization of response tactics, or response strategies.

5. The **law of associative shifting:** This law refers to a transfer of stimulus control from one cue to another. As such, it is much like classical conditioning. The first cue is like the US and the second like the CS. The power of the first cue to control the response, however, is shifted to the second cue by gradually altering the first cue until it becomes the second cue. Thorndike maintained that classical conditioning was a special case of associative shifting (in Hilgard and Bower, 1975). A procedure of this type is used in producing errorless learning by shifting cue control from an easy cue dimension to a more difficult one (see the discussion of errorless learning or fading in Chapter 9).

How Learning Occurs:
Thorndike's Later Revisions

Thorndike made several important modifications in his theory after 1931. The first of these was his repudiation of the law of exercise. Thorndike had never been comfortable with the idea that practice alone could strengthen response tendencies. In 1932, Trowbridge and Cason reported a series of studies by Thorndike in which practice alone failed to produce learning. These studies consisted of having blindfolded subjects attempt to draw a 4-inch line with and without feedback about their accuracy. Without feedback, there was no improvement in accuracy, even following 12 days of practice. This author, however, has used the experiment as an exercise in beginning experimental psychology courses and has found that while Thorndike's basic results are still obtained, the opportunity to watch a subject with feedback allows the watcher later to show some improvement without feedback. Thorndike would of course explain this result as implicit rehearsal of the connection leading to an internal "confirming reaction" or satisfier (Hilgard and Bower, 1975). It should be clear by this time that the durability of Thorndike's theory was partly due to his flexibility and willingness to borrow concepts, which prevented his theory's early obsolescence.

Another modification of the early theory involved a reduction of the role of punishment from that of a direct weakener of bonds equal in power to reward, to an indirect influence which might lead an animal to change its responses when confronted with an annoyer. Thorndike collected various types of evidence, including testimonials, about the relative efficacy of reward and punishment from biographies (Hilgard and Bower, 1975). As will be seen, this deemphasis of punishment in learning is similar to the minor role assigned punishment by Skinner. Thorndike's revised law of effect, with its deemphasis on annoyers, is called the **truncated law of effect.**

Thorndike was aware of the attacks on his ideas by the gestalt theorists. In concession to their research findings, he added an organizational principle to his theory (in Hill, 1971). This principle of **belongingness** states that a connection between two units or ideas can be established more easily when the two units or ideas are perceived as belonging together. In human learning, this principle was used to account for the closer connection between the ideas "David, student" than the ideas "student, beginning" in the sentence: "David is an eager but not experienced student, beginning in psychology." This, in spite of the fact that "beginning" is closer in time and space to "student" than to "David." Thorndike also used the principle of belongingness to explain the subject's perceptions of the contingencies related to reward and punishment. If a student saw a failing grade as due to her personality and not to her work, then the contingency would not "belong" to the work and her work behavior would not change. Ardent feminists, seeing the calculated use of the pronoun "her," might see the pronoun as "belonging" with the mention of failure and might consequently experience the sentence as an annoyer. Other persons, not seeing a relationship between "her" and "failing grade," would experience no emotional reaction.

Thorndike made a third modification that was a direct provocation to the gestalt view of seeing stimulus-response relationships as wholes. The modification was to state that S-R relationships were polarized or unidimensional. This principle would predict that if one learned to translate Japanese into English, one would be unable to translate English into Japanese with equal skill.

Another of his innovations was a principle titled the "spread of effect." This principle stated that the influence of a satisfying state of affairs acts not only on the connections to which it belongs, but on temporarily adjacent connections, both before and following the "satisfying connection" (Hilgard and Bower, 1975). This effect can be thought of as generalization of reward. Thorndike evoked this principle to demonstrate the mechanistic nature of the strengthening of bonds. An example might be developing a liking for a dull sociology course which was taken at the same time as a highly rewarding course in psychology, in which one learned a great deal, earned an "A," and was constantly amused. Another example might be liking the persons sitting near you in the psychology class. Thorndike saw this effect as taking place without awareness. Today, most theorists would explain these examples by the principles of simple Pavlovian conditioning.

Applications

Thorndike was not interested only in theoretical issues. He presented numerous suggestions for the application of his theory to the schoolroom. He pointed out three major areas that should receive the teacher's attention. These were: judging the difficulty with which the teacher would be able to apply satisfiers and annoyers to bonds to be formed or broken, identifying the bonds to be formed or broken, and identifying relevant satisfiers and annoyers. As we will see in Chapter 10, these areas are major concerns of modern contingency managers using the operant or Skinnerian model of learning.

Thorndike was also concerned with the motivational aspects of the classroom, and he recognized the importance of the pupils' attitudes towards learning. He listed five factors which he felt educators should be aware of to improve learning (Thorndike, 1913):

1. The pupil's interest in the work
2. The pupil's interest in improvement in performance
3. The significance of the lesson for some goal of the pupil

4. The pupil's awareness that a need could be satisfied by learning the lesson
5. The pupil's concentration span or attentiveness to the work

Many of Thorndike's suggestions for teachers came from his mechanistic orientation. He believed that **transfer** was always specific and never general, and that therefore a pupil should make some connections which would be common to life situations to be faced after schooling ended. When transfer occurs between two situations that appear different, Thorndike believed that some of the stimuli of the two situations must appear in both (Hilgard and Bower, 1975). This was known as his "identical elements of transfer" theory (similar to Guthrie's and Estes's explanations of generalization). This theory led him to advocate the training of specific skills which could be used in occupational settings rather than in general education. The general principle governing transfer of learning to new situations was that of "associative shifting," which was discussed earlier.

Thorndike made many suggestions for improving teaching. These included paying attention to motivation factors and making what was taught as similar as possible to the skills which pupils would need after graduation.

Thorndike's Positions on Major Issues

Nature/nurture   Thorndike was a strong environmentalist who was also willing to incorporate concepts from biologists, such as adaptation to the environment. He saw differences in intelligence as quantitative and involving inherited differences in the number of bonds available for "selecting and connecting."

The how of learning   Although Thorndike's early theory included the contiguity principle of the law of exercise, he later dropped this law. Throughout his career, he maintained that the consequences of behavior (whether it led to satisfiers, annoyers, or no consequences) are more important in predicting learning than the relationships of stimuli and responses.

The what of learning   Thorndike was willing to admit the existence of thought and the possible mediating role of ideas (as in rewarding yourself by thinking, "Okay, I got it right!"), but he did not think that the basic unit of learning can be anything other than S-R bonds. In the formation of these bonds, he believed, the organism's expectancies can alter which stimuli are selected for connecting, but he did not view thoughts and awareness as necessary for learning.

Continuity/noncontinuity and other issues   Thorndike emphasized that bonds are slowly "stamped in" or connected in a continuous manner. He admitted, however, that apparently insightful (noncontinuous) puzzle solutions can result if the organism selected new combinations of previously "stamped-in" connections, or through the mechanism of "response by analogy" (one of the minor laws). He felt that such insightful-appearing behavior is extremely rare in animals and can be explained even in humans in terms of habits and analogies. Thorndike pioneered the use of animals to explore the basic laws of learning and through this made behavior a central concern of psychology. He was an extremely strong determinist and had no use for such mentalistic concepts as "free will."

Perspective

Thorndike introduced a theory of learning based on the mechanical "selecting and connecting" of stimuli and responses. He made animal research and the study of behavior the business of psychologists and, based on his early observations of the escape behavior of cats from puzzle boxes, he concluded that learning is essentially "trial and error," with the satisfaction of success acting to "stamp in" S-R connections. Compared to the radical behaviorists, he was extremely flexible. As an example, in 1929 he added a fundamental new principle, belongingness, as a concession to the research findings of the gestalt cognitive theorists. He was highly interested in applications of his theory, especially in the area of teaching, and he served for many years on the staff of Columbia's Teachers College. In his educational theorizing, he stressed drill, if tied to motivational variables, and the learning of habits. Throughout, he remained a mechanistic S-R theorist who felt concepts such as "understanding" to be hocus pocus. His work has influenced most learning theories, both those of his era and more modern theories. Along with his other germinal contributions, he first made the reinforcement approach to learning a strong contender to contiguity and cognitive theories.

Clark L. Hull (1884–1952)

Raised in rural Michigan, Hull in 1905 began the study of mathematics and engineering (Hill, 1971) at tiny Alma College. During the two years he spent there, Hull was reported to have shown particular interest in applications of the logical principles of Euclidean geometry to the development of theories. This method of starting with assumptions and progressing to testable theorems was later incorporated into his theory of learning. Striken with poliomyelitis at the age of 24, he resumed his studies three years later at the University of Michigan, where he concentrated on the study of psychology. He received his Ph.D. from the University of Wisconsin in 1918. In 1928, he published a book on aptitude testing after teaching a course in that subject at the University of Wisconsin. In 1929, he accepted a position at the Institute of Psychology at Yale University, where he remained until his death (Sahakian, 1976). In 1933, he published a book entitled *Hypnosis and Suggestibility*. As the head of the group studying the place of learning in human affairs at Yale, Hull was able to develop his theories of learning, generate immense amounts of research, and conduct a weekly seminar whose members included Neal Miller, O. H. Mowrer, John Dollard, and Kenneth Spence. Contributions by this group to learning theory will be explored in this chapter and in Chapter 7.

Hull was greatly impressed by the English translation of Pavlov's *Conditioned Reflexes* (Pavlov, 1960). Initially, he accepted Pavlovian explanations of learning based on contiguity as well as the mechanistic, behavioristic orientations of both Pavlov and Watson. Two important events, however, motivated him to develop a theory that differed greatly from those of Watson and Pavlov. First, he was influenced by the work of the cognitive learning theorists. Hull had published a paper on concept formation in 1920, in which he took the purposes and insights of Tolman and the gestalt theorists (see Chapter 6) much more seriously than Watson, who saw fit to deny cognitive phenomena. His first papers on learning (Bolles, 1975) were attempts to explain purposiveness in behavior by Pavlovian S-R associations. The second major event influencing Hull was the revised "law of effect" theory presented by Thorndike in the early 1930s. Hull wrote a long analytical review of one of Thorndike's new books (Hull, 1935) in which he accepted and adopted Thorndike's emphasis on reinforcement, rather than contiguity, as the primary factor in learning. Also influenced by Darwin's theory, Hull saw learning as a means for organisms to adapt to their environments in order to survive. Therefore, his theory was designed to show how organisms' bodily needs (drives) interacted with the environment in the learning process.

The Structure of Hull's Theory

To his desire to develop a theory of learning incorporating motivation variables and to explain the complex phenomena of the cognitive theorists in simple, connectionist terms, Hull added a desire to develop a psychological theory in the mathematical-logical form of Newton's theory in physics. Hull believed that psychology could best progress by starting with specific assumptions about the relationships between stimuli and responses. These assumptions or **postulates** were to be based on experimental evidence, however scanty, and in turn to be used as the basis for deriving (deducing) testable **theorems** or laws of behavior. These deductions or theorems were to be stated in terms of concrete, observable behavior. If the theorems were not supported by experimental research, the postulates were to be modified until they resulted in satisfactory deductions. This emphasis on formal principles of theory construction indicates that Hull's mathematical and engineering training at Alma College produced a lasting influence, one which led him into methods of theory construction quite unlike those of his predecessors in psychology. His early training may also have been responsible for his attempts to state his laws of behavior as precise mathematical equations. These equations were developed by observing stimulus conditions **(independent variables)** and responses **(dependent variables)** and then attempting to find values for the inferred mediating or intervening variables congruent with the data. Essentially, the process was one of fitting curves to the values until a set of constants or values for the mediating variables would successfully predict the known response variables from the measured stimulus conditions.

Hull called his system "molar behaviorism" because his units of "what-was-learned" are whole (large-unit or **molar**) habits rather than bonds between tiny **(molecular)** muscle movements (as in Guthrie's theory) and individual stimuli. The system is rigorous in that his inferred constructs are not hypothetical neural circuits or aroused areas within the brain, as in Pavlov's theory.

Rather, his internal mediating variables are processes assumed to account for the relationships between externally observable independent and dependent variables, not requiring the **surplus meaning** of hypothesized neurological entities. His **intervening variables** have their effects at two stages: The first, internal stage involves the organism's reactions to the independent variables, and the second, internal stage is that of the organism's tendencies to make responses.

Hull retained this basic four-stage theory of behavior—with independent, dependent, and two stages of internal variables—from its first full presentation in *Principles of Behavior* (Hull, 1943) to his posthumously published second volume, *A Behavior System* (Hull, 1952), in spite of many revisions in the 1952 book. The intervening variables of the 1943 postulate system will now be presented. The 1952 revisions of the system of intervening variables will be discussed in a later section of this chapter.

Hull developed a theory of learning based on the principles of formal logic. This theory incorporates equations relating intervening variables within organisms to stimulus conditions (independent variables) and behavior (dependent variables). The units of learning are molar habits.

Major Intervening Variables

Drive   **Drive (D)** is an aroused state of an organism caused either by lack of some needed substance or by painful stimulation. It has both the specific stimulus properties which Guthrie labeled "maintaining stimuli," and a generalized energizer function. This latter property predicts that a hungry animal who is also thirsty will run faster for a food reward than an animal who is only hungry, because the hungry and thirsty animal has two sources of generalized arousal. In the absence of prior learning, the arousal component of a drive causes the animal under high-drive conditions to emit need-terminating behaviors. Either these behaviors will lead to the reduction of the drive state or the animal may die. Behaviors leading to drive reduction become connected both to the internal stimuli associated with a specific drive state and to environmental stimuli associated with drive reduction. These connections between stimuli and responses are called habits. The strength of these habits is assumed to increase on every trial on which drive reduction occurs. Succeeding trials add progressively less to the strength of the S-R bond, a phenomenon which is called the principle of **declining returns.** This principle is illustrated in Figure 3.2.

Habit Strength   **Habit strength (S^HR)** is the strength of the bond connecting a stimulus with a response. Habits represent permanent connections which can increase but never decrease in strength, and form the basis of long-term learning. Postulate 4 states that:

> Habit strength increases when receptor and effector activities occur in close temporal contiguity, provided their approximately contiguous occurrence is associated with primary or secondary reinforcement. [Hull, 1943, p. 178]

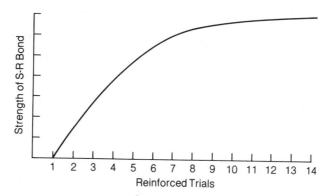

Figure 3.2   The hypothetical strength of the S-R bond goes up most rapidly on the first few trials and then goes up less with each succeeding trial. The amount of increment contributed by each succeeding trial approaches, but never reaches, zero.

When Hull developed his equations depicting the variables responsible for developing a tendency to emit a specific response in the presence of a specific cue, he assumed $S^H R$ always to be in a multiplicative relationship to D. Thus, either zero $S^H R$ (no previous connecting of a stimulus and a response) or zero D would prevent a particular stimulus from eliciting a particular response. Hull's (1943, p. 253) postulate 7 is summarized by Hilgard and Bower (1975): "Habit strength is sensitized into reaction potential by primary drives active at a given time."

Reaction potential   **Reaction potential ($S^E R$)** refers to the total tendency to make a given learned response to a given stimulus at a specific point in time. As we just saw, both experience with the response in conjunction with a particular stimulus ($S^H R$) and a motivated state (D) are necessary for values of $S^E R$ other than zero (since zero times anything equals zero). In the 1943 postulate system, $S^E R$ was also seen as being influenced by other intervening variables. We will now examine some of these variables.

Reactive inhibition   Responding (whether reinforced or not) requires muscular effort, and such effort leads to fatigue, which is a function of the amount of effort. Fatigue acts to inhibit further responding and causes the buildup of **reactive inhibition (I_R).** Reactive inhibition is specific to particular responses and spontaneously dissipates as a function of time after responding ceases. I_R is one of the causes of extinction, and its dissipation is seen as explaining the spontaneous recovery of responses that appeared to have been extinguished, after a rest period. Similarly, performance of well-learned habits may improve after rest periods. This is called the **reminiscence effect** (in Hergenhahn, 1976). I_R was also used to explain the results of experiments such as those by Hilgard and Marquis (1935), who found performance to be superior when learning trials were separated by rest periods rather than all given at once (massed trials). With distributed trials, the I_R has more chance to dissipate. I_R must be subtracted from D × $S^H R$ before the equation can be used to predict tendencies to respond.

Conditioned inhibition   Like I_R, **conditioned inhibition ($S^I R$)** was hypothesized to subtract from the strength of the tendency for a response to be emitted.
Unlike I_R, however, $S^I R$ was assumed to be specific to a particular stimulus and a
particular response. Hull (1943) suggested that prolonged responding, reinforced or not, would eventually be painful (resulting in the buildup of I_R). To
stop responding would be to reduce the drive to avoid this pain and would be
reinforcing. This tendency to stop responding would be conditioned to any cues
or stimulus traces "which chanced to be present" at the time the organism
reduced the drive to avoid the pain and/or fatigue occasioned by prolonged
responding. Thus, the tendency not to respond is as much a learned habit as $S^H R$
and, like $S^H R$, it builds up with each response. Why, then, does the organism
normally only stop responding when not reinforced? Hull would answer that
during reinforced trials, $S^E R$ (the total excitatory potential) also builds up, and
this overcomes the effects of the buildup of $S^I R$. During extinction, there is no
drive reduction to build up $S^E R$ and hence the combined influences of $S^I R$ and
I_R eventually become greater than that of $S^E R$, and responding stops. Thus, Hull
explained $S^I R$ as a conditioned cause of extinction, similar to Pavlov's explanation of extinction, which stated that conditioned inhibition built up as a result
of S-R links not being confirmed through the following of a CS by a US. Hull's
conceptualizations of I_R and $S^I R$ lead to some paradoxical predictions. For example, since $S^H R$ gradually builds up more and more slowly (the principle of
declining returns) and each trial leads to some $S^I R$, continued practice should
eventually lead to performance decreases (Gleitman, Nachmias, and Neisser,
1954). This suggests that Hull's inhibitory postulates are perhaps one of the
weakest parts of his theory.

The tendency of extinction to become faster over several separate extinction
sessions can now be explained. I_R builds up within each session and dissipates
between sessions, leading to spontaneous recovery. $S^I R$, however, builds up in a
continuing fashion as a function of total trials and hence has a greater inhibitory
effect with each succeeding extinction session. If a person quits after several
unsuccessful attempts at a task, this would be interpreted as due to the buildup
of I_R. Quitting would reduce the aversive effects of fatigue and other sources of
I_R and would reinforce the buildup of $S^I R$. This would lead to a reluctance to
begin the task later, even though I_R has dissipated.

Oscillation function   Although Hull had some success in predicting the behavior of groups of animals, he found that his dependent variables varied
widely over individual animals, and even from trial to trial in a single animal.
He was holding the independent variables, such as hours of deprivation, constant. Since these independent variables were supposed to determine the intervening variables, and they, in turn, to account for the dependent variables, wide
individual variation presented a serious problem. To handle this problem, Hull
postulated the existence of a "fudge factor," an **oscillation function** or $S^O R$. He
suggested that the threshold of response emission varies randomly over time as a
function of the animal's condition (Bolles, 1975). Response indeterminancy ($S^O R$)
was subtracted from the other determinants of response strength, and its

amount was assumed to follow a normal curve pattern. Thus, when S^OR is very large, even strong D and S^HR may not lead to a response. When S^OR is very small, even weak response tendencies may go over the threshold value needed to produce an overt behavior. As with other functions described by the normal curve, very large and very small values of S^OR are much less likely than medial values.

S^OR was also used to explain which of two equally strong competing incompatible responses will be expressed in a given situation. When S^OR_1 is less than S^OR_2 for two equal reaction potentials, the lower S^OR_1 will allow its reaction potential to be expressed as a response (Hill, 1971).

A quick summary   As we have seen, S^ER refers to the total tendency to make a given response to a given stimulus. It is the final product of all the other intervening variables, as shown in the formula:

$$S^ER = [D \times S^HR - (I_R + S^IR)] - S^OR$$

If it is over the necessary threshold value, then behavior will occur. The amount that S^ER is over the threshold for the expression of a particular response will determine the strength of that response or the total values of the dependent variable measures (response frequency, response amplitude, and so on). The level of the threshold for a given reaction is called S^LR.

In Hull's theory, drive (D) is multiplied by habit strength (S^HR). Both these variables must exist at levels above zero to generate a tendency towards a given response. Inhibition generated by fatiguelike factors (I_R) plus conditioned inhibition (S^IR) are subtracted from the result of that multiplication. Random oscillations in readiness to respond (S^OR) must also be subtracted to yield the final potential for responding (S^ER).

Let us now look at an example of a motivated behavior in Hullian terms. Suppose we were hungry in the middle of our class day (high D). This high D will both make us restless through its generalized arousal effect and make us aware that our need is for food instead of water, and so on. Let us suppose that in past times, being hungry under similar circumstances, we were able to obtain candy from a hallway dispenser so that the cues of hungry plus being at school were bonded to the response of operating the machine. Thus, we formed a habit (S^HR) of machine operation in the presence of the cues of hunger and being at school. The last time we tried to get candy, however, the machine had failed to work in spite of two dimes and three kicks. This experience of nonreinforcement would have built up a tendency not to use the machine, or S^IR. In addition, suppose that the machine is difficult to operate and we have been asked by our classmates to get some candy for them. Increasing the number of machine-operating responses, even if rewarded, will build up something like fatigue (I_R), which will tend to inhibit further responding following several effortful attempts to make the machine work properly. Of course, this reactive inhibition, because it dissipates over time, will have little or no effect if we are hungry again the next day. The rewarding effects of reducing fatigue by stopping will generate a more permanent type of conditioned inhibition (S^IR), which would be learning the habit of not trying to operate this particular machine. There might also be a generalization of inhibition which would make us less likely to operate machines which are similar to the uncooperative machine of our experience. Even with low levels of tendencies not to respond (S^IR), high drive (D) related to food deprivation, and a well-learned habit (S^HR), we might "simply not feel in the mood to use the machine" on a given day. When this inhibitory oscillation effect is high (S^OR), the impulse or action tendency (S^ER) to operate the machine may not be strong enough to impel us out of our seats and into the hall where the machine is located. Conversely, if S^OR is very low, the tendency to operate the machine may go over our threshold for responding (S_LR) even when we do not feel especially hungry.

Hull's explanation of behavioral chaining   Hull's postulate on reinforcement presented two corollaries.* The first stated that neutral stimuli repeatedly and consistently associated with the onset of a drive reduction acquire the power to elicit the internal cues associated with that drive. Since these cues make the organism likely to emit the habits that have been related to that drive, the formerly neutral stimuli now serve to create a condition of secondary or conditioned drive. The second corollary stated that formerly neutral receptor impulses (stimuli attended to by the organism) which occur repeatedly and consistently in conjunction with the reduction of either a primary or secondary drive (secondary or primary reinforcing states of affairs) become secondary reinforcers. As you can see, Hull did not discriminate clearly between the conditions necessary to create secondary drives and those making stimuli effective as conditioned (secondary) reinforcers. This confounding of learned reinforcer and learned drive properties of stimuli was carried over into Hull's explanation of how organisms come to perform a series of responses which ultimately leads to the reduction of a primary drive such as hunger.

Let us further examine Hull's ideas about secondary reinforcement and secondary drive. Hull assumed primary reinforcement to be the result of a reduction in a drive state—in our example, the drive state of hunger. Hull realized that although responses made during eating (chewing, salivating, swallowing, and so on) and the food itself constitute a powerfully reinforcing state of affairs, they do not result in an instantaneous reduction of a hunger drive. Why, then, do the responses of eating (**goal responses** or R_Gs) and the stimuli associated with them (**goal stimuli** or S_Gs) serve as reinforcers? Hull (1943) suggested that the Pavlovian process of second-order conditioning could provide an explanation for food and eating as reinforcers. Since cues generated by eating (S_Gs) are followed shortly by the altered stimulus condition of a reduced hunger drive which elicits the unconditioned or primary reinforcing response, the S_Gs be-

---

* This postulate and the two corollaries were presented formally in the 1952 postulate system. The same assumptions, with minor (for our purposes) variations, were presented in a more informal way in the 1943 system as part of Hull's general discussion of secondary reinforcement.

come second-order or conditioned reinforcing cues which elicit a "response" of secondary reinforcement.

How, then, do we account for organisms having the motivation necessary to learn long chains of preparatory responses which would eventually result in food becoming available for eating? Hull thought that organisms beginning a chain of behaviors which would finally result in eating (or any other consummatory response) would tend to make little responses similar to those made during actual eating. Thus, Hull would predict that the organisms involved in obtaining food would be salivating, chewing, and swallowing at low intensity while making the initial responses in a complex chain of behavior that would result in food. Because these anticipatory responses were like the responses made in the presence of the actual goal of food (R_Gs) but "littler," Hull called them little goal responses, or r_Gs. Since the r_Gs were assumed to have only a fraction of the intensity of responses made to actual goals (R_Gs), he also called them **fractional anticipatory goal reactions**. Like R_Gs, the r_Gs generate stimuli, which Hull named s_Gs, or $r_G =$ **generated stimuli**. Just as the stimuli (S_Gs) produced by goal reactions become secondary or conditioned reinforcers through their associations with primary reinforcement, the s_Gs just before the final goal reaction (the R_G) also become conditioned reinforcers through being paired with the S_Gs. These s_Gs would reinforce the r_Gs and other responses occurring just prior to the R_G. In turn, s_Gs further removed from the goal stimuli and responses would become conditioned reinforcers through their associations with the more primary s_Gs. The process was one of developing a chain of reinforcers in which drive reduction is the unconditioned reinforcer, the S_G is the secondary reinforcer, the first s_G is a third-order reinforcer, the second s_G is a fourth-order conditioned reinforcer, and so on. This chain of stimuli was assumed to function much like Guthrie's movement-produced stimuli in integrating a chain of responses (both overt responses, like working to gain access to food, and the covert r_Gs) and in reinforcing the occurrence of each behavioral link in the chain.

This model can account for the reinforcement of the chain of responses, but what about the problem of accounting for the student's motivation to begin the chain? Remember Hull's first corollary to his postulate concerning reinforcement. This corollary stated that formerly neutral stimuli associated with a drive and its reduction will develop the power to trigger secondary or conditioned drives. Thus, the first s_G in the chain acquires drive properties from being associated with the goal stimuli (S_Gs), which derived their drive properties from being paired with the hunger drive's reduction. The s_Gs both provide the motivation for overt responses such as bar-pressing to obtain food, going to the feeding mechanism to obtain food, and so on, and reinforce both the r_Gs triggered by the drive state and the overt responses. The r_Gs, as you remember, generate the s_Gs, and the "glue" holding the entire chain of behaviors together is the passing down the chain of the effects of the final drive reduction or primary reinforcing state of affairs.

Because the r_Gs are similar to the actual goal reactions (R_Gs), they are strengthened by generalization every time the R_G is strengthened by drive reduction. Since the r_G or r_Gs closest to the primary goal would be learned first, they would be more closely associated with the effect of "generalization of drive reduction," making them stronger components of habits than anticipatory (or antedating) responses further removed in time from the goal. This suggests that false choices near a goal would be eliminated before false choices distant from a goal. Hull also predicted that this effect causes the attracting power of a goal to increase as the animal nears attainment, because the closer r_Gs have stronger secondary reinforcement properties. This led Hull to make predictions concerning the relationship of goal attractiveness and distance from the goal, using his concept of gradient of reinforcement, very similar to those made by Lewin (Chapter 6) and Miller and Dollard (Chapter 7). This model would predict that organisms engaged in obtaining food would become more eager (more highly motivated) the closer they came to being able to eat the food. Also, habits close to eating food (such as grabbing the bits of food from the feeder) would be learned more strongly than initial responses, such as bar-pressing to trigger a feeder mechanism, because they have been reinforced by the stronger conditioned reinforcers closer to the final drive reduction.

Why did Hull add complex derived mechanisms such as r_G-s_G chains? One answer is that by the 1940s, a variety of facts about learning had been discovered that could not be explained by just the intervening variables. Primarily, these were demonstrations by the cognitive theorists that knowledge of external independent variables such as reinforced (assumed to be drive-reducing) trials was sometimes insufficient in predicting and explaining the progress of the learning process. The r_G-s_G concept provided Hull with a mediating mechanism much like Pavlov's second signal system or Guthrie's movement-produced stimuli. This mechanism was useful in explaining learning which was not immediately revealed in performance. Examples of such hidden or latent learning will be presented in Chapter 5 (cognitive theories). The r_G-s_G mechanism can be used both to describe the chaining of external events (such as series of external cues and overt responses) and chaining occurring primarily within the organism (which is similar to Guthrie's theory). Today Hull's model of internal mediation is still important as a major alternative to Skinner's theory of chaining of stimuli and responses (Hergenhahn, 1976).

Some problems with the r_G-s_G concept include researchers' failure to find anticipatory chewing, salivation, and other responses (reviewed in Hilgard and Bower, 1975), and Hull's confounding of the drive and conditioned reinforcer properties of s_Gs. Nonetheless, Hull made ingenious use of the r_G-s_G concept in many ways, including his development of the notion of the habit-family hierarchy.

Hull speculated that organisms emit fractional responses similar to those emitted in the presence of a goal (such as food) when in a drive state. These fractional r_Gs generate internal cues (s_Gs) which acquire both secondary drive and conditioned reinforcer properties. The r_G-s_G concept was evoked to explain learning chains of responses leading to goals.

Habit-family hierarchies   The **habit-family hierarchy** is a principle at the derived or intermediate level in the same sense that the principle of "generalization of drive reduction" was derived from more primary principles related to drive and habit. Hull used intermediate-level principles much like first-order principles to predict dependent variables and to generate further deductions, such as the principle that gradients of reinforcement operate as a function of distance from a goal. Similarly, the "habit-family hierarchy," which predicts the time at which shifting from one habit to another will occur in a problem-solving situation, is deduced from more basic principles. The habit-family hierarchy principle is, in turn, the basis for further deductions.

A common observation is that we do not always obtain a given goal in the same way. From food getting to sexual satisfaction, we tend to learn alternative ways of moving from a starting point to the satisfaction of a given need. These alternative habits make up a "family" of similar responses which are inferred to be integrated by a common mechanism. This mechanism is the fractional antedating (anticipatory) goal reaction (r_G), which leads to the goal stimulus (S_G) to which all behaviors are conditioned. The degree to which each response forms a connection with S_G is determined by the gradients of reinforcement. For example, long routes through a maze, which are more remote from reinforcement (food), form weaker bonds than short routes. The result of this process is that easy and quick methods to obtain drive reduction are favored and less efficient responses appear only when the more efficient ones are blocked. This order of preferred alternative habits is the habit-family hierarchy. Hull further deduced (Hilgard and Bower, 1975) that if one member of a habit-family hierarchy is reinforced in a completely new situation, other members of that family (by association) will gain in reactive potential and may in the future be evoked by that situation. This deduction of response equivalence in new situations offered Hull a means to explain non-trial-and-error, or insight, learning.

An example of this principle might be a student's writing a paper. When a particular thought is blocked, the student goes to a similar one with the next highest associative value. Similarly, if students are unsure of a particular alternative on a multiple choice exam, they may select the answer with the next highest associative value, despite the second answer's lesser pairing with the original information.

Hull suggested that alternate sets of habits related to reaching a particular goal are arranged in a habit-family hierarchy. If the solution highest in this hierarchy is ineffectual in a given situation, the next most probable response chain would be emitted, and so on.

Changes in the Theory from 1943 to 1952

Hull made several changes in the theory presented in 1943 when he wrote *A Behavior System* (1952). One type of change was the addition of several new intervening variables. The two most important of these were **K**, or **incentive motivation**, and **V**, or **stimulus intensity dynamism**.

Hull added the variable of K (K stands for Kenneth Spence, who was one of Hull's coworkers [Sahakian, 1976]) as a result of a classic study by Crespi (1942). Crespi measured the running speed of three groups of rats receiving different numbers of food pellets in the goal box. It was found that running speed was directly related to the number of pellets given. This result could have been explained as a function of greater amounts of reinforcement leading to a stronger habit through increased drive reduction, which manifested itself in faster running. The second part of this experiment, however, produced results that could not be so easily explained in terms of drive (D) and habit strength ($S^H R$).

In the second part of the experiment, Crespi gave all three groups of rats the same number of pellets formerly given to the middle group. Under these conditions, rats who had formerly received a small amount of food very rapidly increased their running speed, while those who had formerly received a large amount of food equally rapidly decreased their running speed. Since these shifts were much more rapid than the original learning of the running response, Crespi concluded that amount of drive reduction alone cannot account for learning, but it instead affects performance through some type of motivational factor. This motivational variable, which is related to the organism's experience of the amount of food encountered on the previous trial, was labeled K, or incentive motivation, by Hull. Hull thought that K is a function of the intensity of r_G (the fractional anticipatory goal response) which would be greater when the greater drive reduction produced by a larger reward generalizes down the response chain. Greater r_Gs would produce stronger s_Gs, which, of course, both induce secondary drive and have secondary reinforcing (drive-reducing?) properties. Thus, greater K was assumed to result in stronger stimuli conditions, which leads to faster running.

K was postulated to multiply with D and $S^H R$ to produce $S^E R$. It should be noted that the effect of K is on the excitatory potential ($S^E R$) and not on the strength of the $S^H R$ bond. Hull would use K to explain a person's spending more effort preparing a meal if he were working with particularly desirable foods, or someone's expending more effort in trying to date the more attractive of two possible dating choices.

V, or the intensity of the evoking stimulus, was a variable invented by Hull to explain greater response rates with stronger stimuli. V, like K, was assumed to multiply with D and $S^H R$ to produce $S^E R$. A greater tendency to seek food after being exposed to a strong odor of a desirable food compared to exposure to a weak odor of the same food might be an example of the effects of V. As these and other intervening variables were added to explain potentially disconfirming results, Hull's system became capable of explaining a wider range of data, at the cost of becoming increasingly unwieldy. The basic outline of Hull's variable system in simplified form is shown in Figure 3.3. This figure outlines the relationships of the variables, including V and K.

Another important change was in the nature of D. The 1943 theory had defined primary (as opposed to secondary or conditioned) reinforcement as dependent upon a reduction in the strength of D. The revised theory (Hull, 1952) defined reinforcement as a process either of the reduction in the stimuli pro-

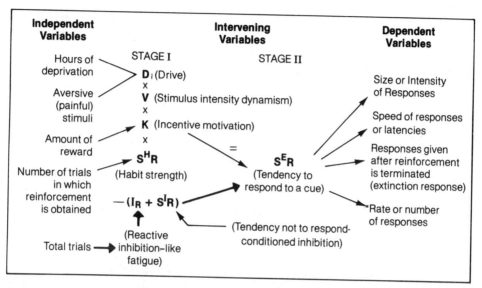

Figure 3.3   The basic form of Hull's system. The independent variables influence first-stage intervening variables, which determine the value of second-stage intervening variables, whose effects will be measured from dependent variable measures. A plus or minus sign means that the effects of a particular intervening variable should be added or subtracted from other intervening variables in predicting the final tendency to respond. An "×" sign means that the variables so connected must be multiplied by each other.

duced by a drive or of a decrease in the strength of the anticipatory goal stimuli (s_G), produced by "little r_G," the fractional anticipatory goal response. In addition, the amount of drive reduction occurring on each trial was no longer postulated to influence habit strength. Instead, only the number of trials in which drive reduction occurred was considered. Amount of drive reduction per trial is of course dependent upon the magnitude of the reward received by the animal on the previous trial (K or incentive motivation being greater with greater rewards).

In his 1952 work, Hull remains a behaviorist only in the sense that he assumed that his intervening variables had properties like those measurable from overt behaviors. Most major principles from 1943 he revised to conform with new information.

Hull made several important changes in his theory between 1943 and 1952. These included adding the intervening variables of incentive motivation (K) and stimulus intensity dynamism (V) and revising the definition of reinforcement from the result of a reduction in drive strength to the result of a reduction in the intensity of the stimuli associated with a drive (either primary or conditioned).

Hull's theory was also modified by the efforts of his followers and students. Miller's neo-Hullian theory will be reviewed in Chapter 7. Spence produced a revision of Hull's theory which follows Hull's method of theory construction very closely. This revised theory illustrates the process by which the followers of major theorists change those theories to make them more flexible and move them towards the mainstream of learning theories. We will now review some of Spence's contributions to the Hullian tradition.

Spence's Contributions to Hullian Theory

Spence is perhaps the best known of the neo-Hullians and the most closely identified with the Hullian approach, characterized by the derivation of intervening variables which are organized into equations designed to predict response variables. Spence's work helped shape Hull's 1943 theory, and Spence's later suggestions can be seen in some of the changes in Hull's 1952 theory. Spence wrote the foreword to the 1952 volume, and in 1956 was still working within the Hullian tradition (Sahakian, 1976).

Like Hull, Spence attempted to reduce the complex phenomena described by the cognitive theorists to basic mechanisms. This reductionistic emphasis can be seen in two classic papers (Spence, 1936, 1937) in which Pavlovian principles of conditioning, extinction, and stimulus generalization were used to explain both discrimination and "relational" or transpositional learning. Essentially, Spence argued, when a stimulus is reinforced, it builds up an excitatory tendency, while an inhibitory potential builds up around unrewarded stimuli, thus producing discrimination learning. Both these excitatory and inhibitory tendencies have generalization gradients (this whole argument is very similar to Pavlov's theory presented in Chapter 1). If an animal is trained to choose the larger of two circles and then is tested with a new pair of circles in which the smaller circle is now the same size as the formerly rewarded circle, the animal will usually choose the new, larger circle and ignore the formerly rewarded circle. Cognitive theorists claimed that such results prove the animal learned the "idea" of larger. Spence demurred, cleverly demonstrating that the Hullian approach could handle such results as follows: Assume that both of the original circles produce generalized reaction tendencies—one excitatory and the other inhibitory. Tendencies to emit or inhibit responding form generalization gradients, with the tendencies being directly proportional to the extent to which new circles are similar to the original circles in size (the organism would show maximal excitatory and inhibitory tendencies to the original rewarded and unrewarded circles, respectively, with lesser tendencies to new circles very similar to these in size and still lesser tendencies to more dissimilar circles). Further assume that the inhibitory generalization gradient of the unrewarded circle overlaps that of the rewarded circle. As a final assumption, assume that the generalization of excitation associated with the rewarded circle leads to a tendency to respond to circles still larger than the formerly rewarded circle. Then, if the sum of the inhibitory and excitatory potentials for the formerly rewarded circle was less than the generalized excitement for the new larger circle, the animal would choose the larger circle. The hypothesized relationships of the generalization gradients are shown in Figure 3.4 (Hilgard and Bower, 1975).

Spence was also instrumental in persuading Hull to adopt the incentive motivation construct, or K. Even though Hull's 1943 theory was based on habit

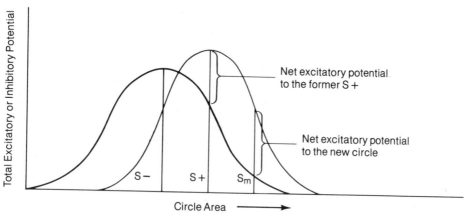

Figure 3.4 The hypothetical generalization gradients for inhibitory (dark line) and excit-atory (dotted line) tendencies for the formerly unrewarded circle(S−), the formerly rewarded circle (S+), and net excitatory charge for the new circle (S_n). The inhibitory potential is shaded.

and drive as the determiners of response tendencies, Spence postulated that an incentive or "eagerness for the goal" variable was involved in control of perfor-mance. Spence was also the first to relate K to the fractional anticipatory goal-response (r_G) variable, which was seen as the classically conditioned response causing the animal's excitement at an early point in a long instrumental re-sponse chain. In postulating his K variable, Spence moved away from Hull's drive reduction position stated in the 1943 theory and incorporated contiguity as an important element in the development of a conditioned response. In Spence's words:

> The habit strength (H) of the instrumental response, it is important to note, is assumed to be a function of the number of occurrences of the response (N_R) in the situation and to be quite independent of the occurrence or non-occurrence of a reinforcer. Thus, if the response occurs there will be an increment in H regard-less of whether a reinforcer does or does not result. This assumption, it is apparent, makes this formulation a contiguity and not a reinforcement theory. And yet the theory, as is clearly evident, implies that the excitatory strength (E) of the response in such instrumental learning situations does depend upon the occurrence and properties of the reinforcer. [Spence, 1960, p. 96]

This change from Hull's position meant that the basic equation for the tendency to respond must be different. Spence's formula became

$$S^E R = (D + K) \times S^H R - I_N$$

as compared to Hull's

$$S^E R = D \times K \times S^H R - I_R$$

Thus, for Spence, the presence of either an incentive or a drive state could lead to the performance of a response. For Hull, both drive and incentive were necessary. Another difference in Spence's equation (Sahakian, 1976) was the new inhibitory variable of I_N, which was a frustration variable resulting from non-reinforcement rather than Hull's fatigue-like I_R. I_N required previously reinforced trials to occur and could also be built up from delays in reinforcement.

Spence's changes in Hull's theory put Spence in the position of a contiguity theorist on learning, a reinforcement theorist on performance, and an almost Tolman-like cognitive theorist on anticipation and frustration. This movement towards a more eclectic theoretical base was typical of most of the neo-Hullians. By making his changes, Spence extended the viability of the Hullian approach after Hull's death.

Hull's Positions on Major Issues

Nature/nurture   Hull accepted the assumption that there are some inborn tendencies to respond in specific ways to drive states (Bolles, 1975) and Darwin's ideas about the importance of adaptive mechanisms. In spite of this, his theory is strongly biased towards seeing learning through environmental influences as more important than innate factors.

The how of learning   Hull was adamant in his later theories in insisting that no learning could occur without reinforcement. The critical variable in learning, he held, is the number of reinforcing trials. Reinforcement is a process of drive reduction (1943) or of a reduction in the intensity of stimuli associated with a drive (1952).

The what of learning   Although Hull was a connectionist, he did not see the basic unit of learning as that of connecting tiny muscular twitches to stimuli. Hull was a "molar" behaviorist; his basic unit of learning was the complex habit.

Hull never discussed cognition directly, but he did attempt to explain complex "insight" learning by his "pure stimulus acts," or r_G and s_G variables, which provide a type of anticipation mechanism. The habit-family hierarchy offers an explanation for using past experience in new situations without direct trial and error. In spite of these complex variables, Hull was as mechanistic as Thorndike and as connectionist as any behaviorist.

Continuity/noncontinuity, use of animal data, and determinism   Hull saw habit strength as building up gradually as a function of the number of reinforced trials. He freely used data from animal studies, and he saw behavior as determined by environmental events and the state of his intervening variables within the organism. Near the end of his life, he voiced some reservations about some of his laws derived "from the study of hungry rats" being fully applicable to human behavior (in Bolles, 1975).

Perspective

Hull began his work with a strong background in human research. His original plan had been to write three major books on learning: a volume on primary principles, a volume on individual nonsocial behavior, and a concluding volume on social or group behavior and applications (Sahakian, 1976). As we have mentioned, Hull died shortly before the second volume was published. With his death went the hope of the application of his principles to complex human problems in the rigorous experimental manner characterizing the development of his principles. Oddly, for a psychologist who had initially concentrated on human research, Hull tested his 1943 theory mainly on rats. In contrast to Thorndike, who spent much of his career suggesting uses for his principles in schools, Hull died before he felt his theory had been completed to a level appropriate to the advocacy of extensive human applications. On a molar level of explanation, however, Hull's constructs have some value in explaining complex phenomena such as insight. When he tried to predict specific quantitatively measured outcomes for individual organisms, it became apparent that his system was generalizable for only a few types of rat experiments. In his attempts to measure precisely units of motivation ("mots"), and habits ("habs") on a centigrade scale, he lost sight of the larger task of general learning theory development and application (Hilgard and Bower, 1975). Too many parameters had to be measured, and too much arbitrary assignment of values to the intervening variables was necessary.

While many of Hull's constructs, such as "little r_G-s_G" and the habit-family hierarchy, have continued to be useful, other key principles have not survived the test of experimental analysis. The findings by Sheffield and Roby (1950) that rats would work for saccharin (a sweet nonnutritive substance) even though no drive reduction resulted struck at the heart of the concept of all reinforcement as dependent upon reduction in the cues associated with a drive. Hull countered, however, by suggesting that because sweet tastes had in the past been associated with drive reduction, sweet taste could have become a s_G which, through its secondary reinforcing properties, reduced hunger tension cues for a brief period (Hull, 1952).

Perhaps Hull's theory must be evaluated on terms other than considerations of accuracy and generalizability. Perhaps it might better be evaluated in terms of its influence on the thinking of other learning theorists. Hilgard and Bower (1975) report that in the *Journal of Experimental Psychology* and the *Journal of Comparative and Physiological Psychology* in the years between 1941 and 1950, 70 percent of all studies in the area of learning and motivation referred to Hull's books and papers. Many of the dominant figures in the field of learning, including Miller, Mowrer, Amsel, Spence, and Hilgard, were either Hull's students or associated with him at Yale (Sahakian, 1976). No one else in the history of learning theorists has stimulated so much research and so much productive theorizing!

Chapter Perspective

Today, the work of Thorndike is of interest primarily for its influence on the development of more recent theories, and the work of Hull can be interpreted as a grand, if somewhat futile, blind alley in the history of trying to understand learning. The work of the theorist to be reviewed in the next chapter (Skinner) is current, controversial, and compelling. Skinner incorporates an environmentalism almost as radical as Watson's, an ingenuity in developing experimental apparatus perhaps exceeding Pavlov's, a propensity for suggesting applications as great as Thorndike's, and a commitment to research as great as Hull's.

Key Terms

belongingness

conditioned inhibition (S^IR)

dependent variable

declining returns

drive (D)

equipotentiality

excitatory potential (S^ER)

fractional anticipatory goal reaction (r_G)

goal response (R_G)

goal stimulus (S_G)

habit-family hierarchy

habit strength (S^HR)

incentive motivation (K)

independent variable

intervening variable

law of associative shifting

law of effect

law of exercise

law of multiple response

law of prepotency of elements

law of readiness

law of response by analogy

law of set (attitude)

mechanistic

mentalism

molar

molecular

oscillation function (S^OR)

postulate

r_G-generated stimulus (s_G)

reactive inhibition (I_R)

reminiscence effect

stimulus intensity dynamism (V)

surplus meaning

theorem

transfer

trial and error

truncated law of effect

Annotated Bibliography

Although ideally one needs to read several of these theorists' works to cover the changes in their thinking, the following sources should be helpful: (1) E. L. Thorndike, *Educational psychology: The psychology of learning,* vol. 2 (New York: Teachers College, 1913). (2) C. L. Hull, *A behavior system: An introduction to behavior theory concerning the individual organism* (New Haven, Conn.: Yale University Press, 1952), somewhat hard reading but no more so than any other of Hull's writings; (3) W. F. Hill, *Learning; A survey of psychological interpretations,* 3rd ed. (New York: Thomas Y. Crowell Company, 1977), a good secondary source that is easier reading than the previously cited primary sources.

4

Skinner: Reinforcement or Operant Conditioning

Today, Skinner's operant theory of learning has become to reinforcement theory what Pavlov's work was to contiguity approaches—a blueprint of learning expressed as experimentally verified laws which provide the basis for a wide range of practical applications. You will read about Skinner's experimental methods, his incorporation of classical conditioning principles into his theory, his basic principles, and his critical work on the effects of different patterns of giving reinforcements. Just as most of the basic terms and principles Pavlov developed remain important to understanding subsequent connectionist theories, so are Skinner's principles essential to understanding the current approaches to reinforcement theory to be presented in Part 2 of the text. Especially, you should understand the effects of the four basic types of schedules of reinforcement on both rewarded performance and on performance during extinction. The control of behavior by rewarding or reinforcing circumstances, the patterning of rewards to influence the frequency and intensity of responses, make up the major emphasis of Skinner's theory about learning.

Burrhus Frederic Skinner (1904–   )

Brought up in Susquehanna, Pennsylvania in a close, devoutly religious family, Skinner earned his B.A. in English at nearby Hamilton College. He went on to write short stories that earned the praise of the poet Robert Frost and moved to Greenwich Village, an artists' area of New York City. Six months later, Skinner determined that the ideas expressed in his writing were trivial compared to the ideas of Pavlov in *Conditioned Reflexes* (1960) and of John Watson, as discussed by Bertrand Russell. Deciding his writing was nothing but "pencil craft," he went back to college (Harris, 1971). He was admitted into Harvard, studied under psychology's foremost historian, Edwin Boring, submitted a thesis on reflexes, and was granted a Ph.D. in 1931. He began teaching at Minnesota, moved up to the chairmanship and professor rank at Indiana in 1945, and in 1948 returned to Harvard and never left (Sahakian, 1976).

In 1938, Skinner published a book on the empirical descriptive laws of learning as observed in rats and pigeons (*The Behavior of Organisms*). In 1948, he extended these laws to the behavior of persons and societies in his novel *Walden Two* (written in seven weeks). He presented his principles in a more scholarly format in *Science and Human Behavior* (1953). Although the basic laws remain essentially unchanged from that time, he has extended their application in *The Technology of Teaching* (1968) and has explored the theory of his "nontheory" in *Contingencies of Reinforcement, A Theoretical Analysis* (1969). In 1971, he clarified his essential philosophical assumptions with *Beyond Freedom and Dignity* and summarized his work and replied to his critics with *About Behaviorism* in 1974. In a sense, he completed the process of beginning with general laws, progressing to prediction of individual behavior, and finishing with a wide range of human applications which Hull had tried and been unable to finish. Skinner then went on to explore the philosophical implications of his theory.

Skinner has been consistent in his dislike of inner causes (such as motives, ego states, habit strength, and so on), and today argues about and applies his ideas with intensity and clear prose. He used his invention of the air crib (a temperature-controlled enclosed crib) in raising his daughter and, through application of operant learning principles to his own behavior, has maintained his own enormous writing productivity (Harris, 1971).

Skinner was influenced towards painstaking experimentation by Pavlov and was introduced to radical behaviorism by Watson. He believes in science as a set of attitudes which facilitate observation and experimentation (instead of accepting the ideas of so-called authorities). This philosophical stance carries over into his strong emphasis on objectivity and the acceptance of experimental data, even when it is contrary to one's own wishes. His atheism is part of his general rejection of seeing causation as the result of unobservable inner forces. Instead, he has committed himself to trying to determine forces in the environment which control behavior. Skinner does not deny that inner forces may sometimes control behavior or that the tendency of all sciences to seek inner causes has sometimes had useful results. Rather, he has sought to avoid such theorizing himself, on the grounds that unobservable events may tempt the scientist to assign properties and functions without adequate justification. He notes: "The motion of a rolling stone was once attributed to its vis viva [roughly, life force] . . . " (Skinner, 1953, p. 27).

In his advocacy of an objective scientific methodology, Skinner was following Watson's rejection of inner agents and directly attacking Hull's (and others') approaches of trying to predict and understand behavior on the basis of inferred internal processes. He deviated from the views of Watson, however, in his willingness to accept thought and other private behaviors as sources of data, insofar as they are revealed through verbal and other objective responses. In this respect, his views are not in conflict with the phenomenological approach of trying to understand inner behavior by asking subjects about their experiences (Day, 1969). It was only inner causes that Skinner avoided investigating or theorizing about, on the grounds that the ultimate cause of inner behavior could be traced to environmental influences.

This rationale for his "black box" or "empty organism" approach to the study of behavior was directly opposed to the practice of speculating about hypothetical constructs or intervening variables within organisms. One of the reasons Skinner decided to focus on environmental rather than on inner events was the richness of information available for a scientific analysis of the determinants of behavior. This type of information included both variables present in the organism's immediate environment and variables related to the organism's history. Skinner felt that these types of independent variables could be investigated using the usual tools of science. He conceded that such variables might influence behavior in subtle ways but believed that no adequate account of behavior could be possible without investigating them. His goal was to develop a method of analyzing the function of environmental events in determining and predicting the behavior of organisms.

Skinner's method of investigating the external variables controlling behavior was what he called a causal or functional analysis. His dependent variables were the effects of these external variables or the changes in behavior caused by them. His goal, through this method of analysis, was the prediction and control of the dependent (behavioral) variables. For Skinner, the laws of behavior are the cause-and-effect relationships between his independent variables (external environmental events) and his response (dependent) variables. He believed that a synthesis of these laws in quantitative terms yields a comprehensive picture of organisms as behaving systems. This approach to theory building was very different from that of Hull and others, which postulated that causation also involved the internal mediating variables assumed to exist within organisms. Skinner had no need for variables such as drive and incentive motivation because he saw speculation about such variables as simply unnecessary to a science with the goals of predicting and controlling behavior.

Skinner's Approach to the Contiguity/Reinforcement Issue

Although Skinner was radical in seeking causation in the environment, he was flexible in his position on the hows of learning. He was very familiar with Pavlov's research and with the principles of classical conditioning. Rather than rejecting a contiguity mechanism of the type described by Pavlov, he postulated that two distinct types of learning exist. In the first or Pavlovian type, a previously neutral stimulus acquires the power to elicit a response which was originally elicited by another stimulus. The change occurs when the neutral stimulus is followed or "reinforced" by the US. Skinner saw this type of conditioning as important in modifying visceral (gut) and other primitive responses of smooth muscle and glands. Since these primitive response systems are so important in emotion and motivation, Skinner made this type of conditioning (classical conditioning) the means by which new stimuli could come to elicit emotional or motivational states. This was incorporated into his theory as the basis for the power of **secondary** or **conditioned reinforcement.** His use of association principles in explaining secondary reinforcement is very similar to the approach taken by Spence and makes Skinner's theory of learning a two-factor theory. In spite of his reluctance to postulate unobservable inner events as causing behavior, Skinner explained working for delayed reinforcement or completing long response chains in terms of inner responses leading towards a goal and generating stimuli which became classically conditioned to primary reinforcers. For humans, such inner cues and responses "are certain verbal consequences supplied by the man itself . . ." (Skinner, 1953, p. 77). Conditioned reinforcers paired with more than one primary reinforcer he labeled generalized reinforcers, more powerful than any conditioned reinforcers tied to only one type of deprivation state.

> . . . if a conditioned reinforcer has been paired with reinforcers appropriate to many conditions, at least one appropriate state of deprivation is more likely to prevail upon a later occasion. A response is therefore more likely to occur. When we reinforce with money, for example, our subsequent control is relatively independent of momentary deprivations. . . . We are automatically reinforced, apart from any particular deprivation, when we successfully control the physical world. This may explain our tendency to engage in skilled crafts, in artistic creation, and in such sports as bowling, billiards, and tennis. [Skinner, 1953, p. 77]

Thus, Skinner uses a contiguity principle to provide a powerful explanatory device for behaviors which seem unrelated to immediate reinforcement.

Skinner saw classically conditioned responses as elicited by environmental cues in an automatic fashion. Hence, this type of conditioning he also labeled respondent or **type S** (stimulus-type) **conditioning.** According to Skinner, "the responses and attitudes evoked by pretty girls, babies, and pleasant scenes may be transferred to trade names, products, pictures of products, and so on" (1953, p. 57). (Herein lies the explanation of John Watson's success at advertising with his "Lucky Strike green has gone to war.")

While paying due respect to Pavlov's methodology and principles, Skinner saw respondent or type S conditioning as of limited interest. His primary concern was with overt behavior that had an effect on the surrounding world. In this type of behavior, the consequences of the behavior "feed back" into the organism and may modify the probability that the behavior which produced the consequences will be repeated. When a consequence acts to increase the probability of the reoccurrence of a response, it is said to act as a **reinforcer** and the act of delivering that consequence is called **reinforcement.** In Skinner's theory, a reinforcer is anything that increases the probability of the reoccurrence of a response; his definition is made entirely in terms of behavioral operations and does not involve internal entities such as drive or motivation. This type of conditioning is called **operant conditioning** because the organism operates on its environment, or **instrumental conditioning** because the responses are instrumental in bringing about a consequence. Operant conditioning differs from respondent (classical) conditioning in that most responses are not considered to be elicited by stimuli. From Skinner's point of view, the alleged "stimulus" for an operant is simply not observable in most cases. Operant behavior is thus considered to be spontaneously **emitted** by the behaving organism. This approach avoids attempting to identify ambiguous stimulus events. Recall the difficulties, discussed in Chapter 1, encountered by Pavlov in creating research conditions under which he could be reasonably confident about the "true" CSs and USs.

An operant may, however, and often does, acquire a relationship to a particular stimulus, and its occurrence may even be partly controlled by that stimulus. In these cases the stimulus is called a **discriminative stimulus (S_D or S+);** this stimulus serves to signal the organism when reinforcement for the emission of a specific operant is highly probable. Since the S_D is now the signal for the occasion for the operant behavior, the operant is referred to as a **discriminated operant.** The stimulus, however, does not elicit the appearance of the response, as in the case of a Pavlovian reflex. S_Ds serve to guide behavior; and will be further discussed in a later section on fixed ratio schedules and response chains. They are also the basis of discrimination learning when combined with stimuli (S− or S_Δ), which signal that emission of an operant has a low probability of being reinforced. Such S_Δ signal functions are developed by a prior history of nonreinforcement in the presence of these stimuli. The strength of the operant is independent of these excitatory and inhibitory stimuli. That is, the discriminative stimuli only signal the organism when to emit the operant.

The emphasis on responses led to the labeling of operant conditioning as **type R** (response) **conditioning.** The "R" can also be remembered through its association with Skinner's emphasis on reinforcement. Consistent with Skinner's emphasis on "R" events is the distinction he makes between reinforcement in Pavlov's theory and his own:

> Pavlov himself called all events which strengthened behavior "reinforcement" and all the resulting changes "conditioning." In the Pavlovian experiment, however, a reinforcer is paired with a *stimulus;* whereas in operant behavior it is contingent upon a *response.* [Skinner, 1953, p. 65]

Skinner acknowledged the importance of both Pavlovian (respondent or type S) conditioning, in which stimuli elicited responses, and type R (operant or instrumental) conditioning, in which responses are spontaneously emitted. Stimuli in type R conditioning (upon which Skinner focused his efforts) may act as discriminative stimuli (S_Ds) that tell the organism where and when to expect reinforcement.

Skinner and the Generalizability of the Laws of Learning

While not denying the possibility that inherited factors may influence the responses of organisms to reveal typical differences in behavior among species, Skinner maintains that in a laboratory setting, such species differences are minimized. If the organism will respond to the stimuli provided, to operate the experimental apparatus easily, and, if the reinforcers are indeed reinforcing:

> The data then show an extraordinary uniformity over a wide range of species. For example, the processes of extinction, discrimination, and generalization, and the performances generated by various schedules of reinforcement are reassuringly similar. [Skinner, 1969, p. 190]

In other words, the laws of learning discovered in the controlled environment of the laboratory are generalizable from pigeons and rats to men. In the interests of providing just such a controlled laboratory environment, Skinner invented that most useful tool of animal research, the **Skinner box.***

The Skinner Box

Like Pavlov, Skinner contributed not only a theory but a methodology. The Skinner box is relatively cheap and easily used, and we shall examine its operation in some detail. The Skinner box evolved gradually in response to Skinner's assumptions about behavior, and the type of data it produced in turn shaped the type of theory Skinner emitted. Skinner's methodology is based on the assumption that the principle of equipotentiality is usually valid in controlled laboratory settings. Therefore, if under these conditions the laws governing the selected responses are the same laws in any higher species, then the response selected for study should be as simple as possible, freely and rapidly repeatable, and easily observed and recorded.

Any single movement by an organism is a response. A class of movements or a specified behavior type that meets a previously stated criterion (such as pressing a bar or paddle in a Skinner box with enough force to trigger an electric microswitch) is called an **operant.** The frequency and pattern of the occurrence of the operants are measured. Other possible dependent variables, such as response intensity or duration, are not measured. The Skinner box provides an environment in which the subject may emit a response which can be measured as a standardized operant. Much of Skinner's theory was developed using as data the rates at which pigeons pecked stimulus keys (paddles) and rats pressed lever bars. Remember that only behavior sufficiently vigorous to close the contacts of the microswitches (thereby permitting the electrical activation of reinforcement-delivering and/or response-counting devices) qualifies as operants. By counting only operants, the Skinner box eliminates observers' subjective judgments of what to count as a criterion response. Not only does the Skinner box provide an environment in which simple, freely produced, and objectively measured behavior is emitted, it also provides a means for precisely controlling the consequences of the operants. The box is wired so that closing the contacts of the microswitch automatically triggers a device that dispenses a precisely measured amount of a substance that has been found effective in controlling the behavior of similar organisms under similar conditions of deprivation. Thus, the chance of reinforcing behavior other than the operant is greatly reduced. The Skinner box therefore yields precise data about the relationships between the history of the organism (previous training and deprivation levels) and the control exerted by the reinforcer on the rates with which the operant is emitted—all this with no need for discussing internal states! A generalized drawing of a Skinner box and a data-recording machine or cumulative recorder is shown in Figure 4.1.

The addition of the cumulative recorder to the Skinner box makes a powerful combination. By marking the occurrence of environmental events, their effects can be read directly from the record of rates of operant emissions. Since one motor moves the pen horizontally as a function of time and the stepping motor

---

* The term "Skinner box" was not invented by Skinner, who, according to Harris (1971), loathes the term. An alternative (and clumsy) designation would be "operant test chamber."

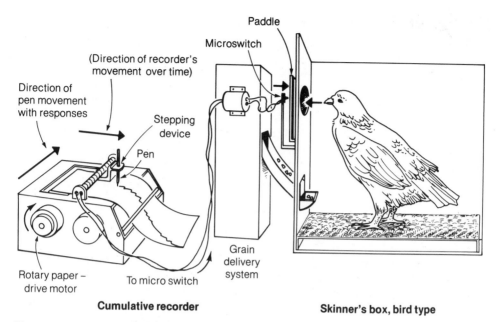

Paddle
Microswitch
(Direction of recorder's movement over time)
Direction of pen movement with responses
Stepping device
Pen
Rotary paper – drive motor
To micro switch
Grain delivery system

Cumulative recorder

Skinner's box, bird type

Figure 4.1   *A Skinner-type operant test chamber for pigeons. The paddle or pecking switch is called the "operandum." Its operation is defined as the organism's operants. Cue lights signaling the pigeon that pecking will be followed by reinforcement are called "discriminanda." The cumulative recorder adds responses as a function of time. Low response rates produce almost horizontal lines; high response rates produce very steep lines, since each response moves the pen in a vertical direction. Some cumulative recorders also mark reinforcements. (Technically, the cumulative recorder adds operants. All operants are responses, but not all responses are operants. Most authors, however, use the terms interchangeably for the sake of convenience. That response tendency applies to this author as well.)*

or solenoid moves the pen upward for every operant emitted, cumulative records can only go up. This is different from an ordinary graph of responses as a function of time, in which declines in response rates are indicated by lower points. Almost all graphs reproduced in Skinnerian-oriented journals are cumulative records. (These have the added advantage that the author can use the record made by the cumulative recorder to show the data instead of drawing a graph—a reinforcement for these authors!)

Major Principles

Working with these relatively simple but precise tools, Skinner has developed a number of laws of considerable power in predicting and controlling an extremely wide range of behaviors in a number of organisms, including humans.

Shaping   Skinner maintains that "operant conditioning shapes behavior as a sculptor shapes a lump of clay."

> Although at some point the sculptor seems to have produced an entirely novel object, we can always follow the process back to the original undifferentiated lump, and we can make the successive stages by which we return to this condition as small as we wish. [Skinner, 1953, p. 91]

If a reinforcement is only something which increases the probability of the occurrence of a given operant, then there would not seem to be any obvious manner by which totally novel responses could be added to the organism's repertoire of operants. Skinner avoids this problem by defining an operant as a class of movements. In the process of **shaping,** only those movements in the direction of the desired new behavior are reinforced. When the response topology (physical characteristics of the response) shifts so that most movements are of the type of what was formerly the extreme response, a new extreme response in the desired direction is selected to be reinforced. This process of **successive approximation** continues until the desired novel behavior is being emitted. Even responses often considered innate by those without experience in the field of animal learning, such as bar-pressing by rats, must usually be shaped. This process starts with reinforcing the rat for sticking its head in the food hopper by manually triggering the pellet dispenser whenever the rat's head approaches the hopper. This also classically conditions the US of food to the CS of the sounds of dispenser operation. When this "head in hopper" operant is being emitted at a high rate, only head movements in the direction of the bar are reinforced. When the rat is moving towards the bar regularly, only touches of the bar are reinforced. Finally, only the desired operant—pressing the bar with sufficient force to close the microswitch and automatically trigger the dispenser—is reinforced. This author has spent over three hours trying to shape this small bit of behavior in especially slow rats. The experience helped shape his behavior in the direction of using increased deprivation and more efficient shaping techniques. It did not increase his emission of seeking rats to shape!

Generalization   Shaping depends upon the organism's tendency not to make exactly the same response every time nor to emit only the precise responses that were followed by reinforcement. This tendency for a "family" of similar responses to be emitted illustrates the principle of **response generalization.** The corresponding tendency of stimuli similar to the original discriminative stimulus to influence the organism's tendency to respond similarly is called stimulus generalization. Skinner's analysis of generalization is similar to that of Pavlov and Hull. Both primary and secondary, or mediated (such as verbal), generalization are recognized, and generalization is viewed as the basis for the transfer of learning from one situation to a new situation.

A key concept in Skinner's system is shaping, or the method of successive approximation, which involves reinforcing responses which tend in the direction of the desired final response. Shaping depends upon response generalization, or the tendency of responses to vary from trial to trial.

Five easy contingencies   Reinforcers may be divided into two classes. One class consists of those events which organisms seek to experience again (recognizing that a particular event may affect different organisms in different ways), labeled **positive reinforcers.** The other class consists of those events that we try to avoid or escape, called **aversive stimuli.** If you look at Table 4.1, you will notice that circumstances or rules can be arranged so that either type of rein-

Table 4.1 Reinforcers, Contingencies, and Experimental Paradigms

| Type of Reinforcer | Contingency | | |
	Reinforcer Presented	Reinforcer Removed	Reinforcer Noncontingent upon Responses
Positive Reinforcer	Positive reinforcement (response rates increase)	Punishment or extinction (response rates decrease)	Superstitious conditioning (response rates increase)
Aversive Stimulus	Punishment (response rates decrease)	Negative reinforcement (response rates increase)	Superstitious conditioning (response rates can increase or decrease)

This table shows the combinations of two classes of reinforcers and three associated contingencies with the technical name of each combination.

forcer can be associated with either an increase or a decrease in the probability of a particular behavior's emission. The rules governing the relationship between responses and reinforcement are called **contingencies.** Either of these classes of reinforcers may be presented, contingent upon the emission of an operant, or they may be removed, contingent upon emission of a specified operant. Both may also occur without being related to an organism's responses, which together constitutes the fifth contingency. The five distinct combinations of types of reinforcers and presentation/removal contingencies are shown in Table 4.1.

Table 4.1 shows several things. One is that **negative reinforcement** is not the same thing as **punishment.** Negative reinforcement is the reinforcement received when responses are emitted which terminate unpleasant events. An example would be a man, calling up a girlfriend, who hears a male voice answer the phone. If he terminates the unexpected and aversive stimulus of the male voice by hanging up the phone, the feeling of relief experienced upon the cessation of that voice should make him more likely to emit "hanging-up" responses if the circumstances were repeated. Another example would be having attendance at traffic school count towards removal of a speeding ticket from your record. You may emit many behaviors to get rid of the aversive stimulus of the speeding ticket. Punishment, on the other hand, involves "getting hit" with an aversive consequence (or having a positive reinforcer taken away) when you emit a specific behavior, and it is experienced as unpleasant. The presentation of a speeding ticket by a policeman, contingent upon your speeding behavior, or being sentenced to traffic school, are examples of punishment. The effects of punishment are highly variable and depend upon the intensity of the aversive stimulus and upon your previous history of exposure to such aversive stimuli.*

---

* Many Skinnerians use the term "negative reinforcer" interchangeably with "aversive stimulus." This term is used to refer only to a type of stimulus and not to a contingency (such as either punishment or negative reinforcement). Because of the possible confusion between negative reinforcer and negative reinforcement, only the terms "aversive consequence" and "aversive stimulus" will be used in this text.

Punishment will be discussed in more detail in Chapter 9. In general, Skinner (1953) is opposed to the use of punishment contingencies on the grounds that they are ineffectual and likely to have undesirable side effects, such as inhibiting wanted behaviors.

Another relationship shown in Table 4.1 is that reinforcers which are not presented contingent upon the occurrence of a particular response may still come to control behavior. This effect was named **superstitious conditioning** by Skinner (1953), who suggested that many human behaviors which seem irrational may have been conditioned by this process. It must be remembered that while reinforcers may be noncontingent from the viewpoint of an outside observer, the responding organism does not know this. If a behavior is emitted just before the occurrence of a reinforcer, this behavior is followed by the reinforcer and its reoccurrence becomes more probable. Higher rates of emission of any response result in more coincidental pairings with the reinforcer. Thus, a cycle is initiated and the behavior may become very frequent. In Skinner's original studies of this phenomenon (1948), reinforcers were presented to pigeons at specified intervals throughout several long experimental sessions. Although the reinforcement was not contingent upon any particular response, early coincidences between particular behaviors and reinforcement resulted in the pigeons' eventually becoming "trapped" into emitting ritualistic, stereotyped chains of responses at high rates. These included behaviors such as hopping from one foot to the other and bowing and scraping.

Skinner distinguishes five types of rules governing the contingencies between responses and reinforcers: (1) Giving a reinforcement for a response is positive reinforcement, (2) giving a noncontingent reinforcement produces superstitious conditioning, (3) giving an aversive stimulus or (4) removing a positive reinforcer contingent upon a response is punishment, and (5) the removal of an aversive stimulus contingent upon the emission of a response is negative reinforcement.

Superstitious conditioning illustrates Skinner's view that the effects of reinforcers are "blind" with regard to the ultimate welfare of the organism (Skinner, 1969). The occurrence of any behavior is seen as predictable by observing the environmental consequences of that behavior, without regard to the intentions of an experimenter or the organism's knowledge about the true relationship between its behavior and reinforcers. An example of superstitious conditioning might be the gambler who takes a rabbit's foot to the racetrack on the day he wins the daily double. The probability of his bringing the rabbit's foot to the racetrack in the future may increase dramatically.

Extinction in operant conditioning describes a situation in which the original contingency between a response and a reinforcer is terminated. Thus, the response no longer results in the occurrence of the reinforcer. Although the specific effects of this process depend upon the original schedule of presentation of the reinforcer, the general effect is an initial increase in the force and variability of the responses being extinguished. Most humans show this effect when a coin-operated machine stubbornly refuses to reinforce the operant of feeding it money. A person who has just lost* a love affair may show both increased vigor and ingenuity in attempting to elicit personal reinforcers from the lost love before such responses cease.

Schedules of Reinforcement: Skinner's Most Important Contribution

Skinner spent most of his experimental efforts in researching and describing details of the effects of giving positive reinforcers. This procedure is, of course, called positive reinforcement and it is much like the popular conception of reward. Although Hull and Spence had focused on the effects of changing the amount (K) of positive reinforcement, Skinner concentrated upon manipulating the manner (called the **schedule of reinforcement**) in which the reinforcement was presented. So detailed was this analysis, and so powerful were the effects delineated, that it may be Skinner's greatest contribution to our understanding of the variables affecting learning.

> The schedule of reinforcement is the rule followed by the environment—in an experiment, by the apparatus—in determining which among the many occurrences of a response will be reinforced. [Reynolds, 1975, pp. 65–66]

Most of our discussion to this point has dealt with contingencies as all-or-none events. That is, the behavior was followed by the reinforcer or it was not. In the real world, however, reinforcement is often a sometime thing. If reinforcement of every response were required to maintain a given operant, most of our behavior, and especially the examples of superstitious behaviors previously presented, would have extinguished. This sometime reinforcement of a behavior is called **intermittent reinforcement** as opposed to **continuous reinforcement, or CRF.**

The environment may link reinforcers to responses either by the number of responses emitted or by the occurrence of the response within a specified time interval. These schedules are labeled **ratio** and **interval schedules,** respectively, and may be fixed (predictable by the organism) or variable (probabilistic). These terms will be explained further as each type of simple schedule is discussed. Because of the profound influence schedules exert upon behavior, it is important that you become familiar with the characteristic effects of each type of schedule.

The rate with which an organism emits an operant can usually be controlled more precisely by manipulating the schedule of reinforcement than by varying other variables such as amount of reward. Skinner maintains that behavior which has been attributed to drive states, expectations, or thought processes can often be related to particular schedules of reinforcement. This is, of course, consistent with Skinner's view that causation can most often be determined by investigating environmental influences.

---

* When love affairs go sour, the individuals involved usually take on the roles of one who wants out of the relationship (the "winner") and one who is hurt, lonely, and wishes to prolong the relationship (the "loser"). The "loser" becomes an aversive stimulus for the "winner," and the "winner" becomes more desirable, or a stronger reinforcer, for the "loser."

Fixed ratio schedules, homogeneous response chains   The CRF schedule, or continuous schedule of reinforcement, is a special case of a **fixed ratio (FR) schedule,** with the ratio one response to one reinforcer. This would be written as an FR-1 schedule. Characteristics of performance on this schedule are: rapid acquisition of the response, rapid **satiation** and a slowing of the initially high response rates, and rapid extinction once the reinforcer is terminated. (This last characteristic is called "low resistance to extinction.") As ratios grow larger, the satiation effect diminishes and resistance to extinction increases. If an organism is shifted too suddenly from a low ratio to a high ratio schedule, it will not emit enough responses to get from one reinforcement to the next before extinction occurs. This is said to result from **straining the schedule** and, of course, should be avoided. An example might be students dropping a course after the instructor increased the number of required papers halfway through the semester.

With small ratios, up to an FR-10 for the rat and an FR-50 for the pigeon (Reynolds, 1975), performance rates tend to be high and stable. Sometimes the animal will continue responding even as the reinforcers are delivered. The author has seen some rats continue to press with one leg on the lever until the food tray is filled before they finally eat the pellets. If ratios are gradually made very high (up to 2000 for the pigeon), a new pattern appears. While response rates continue to be high, there is usually a **post-reinforcement pause,** or a short period of zero responding, which is followed by an abrupt resumption of the high rate of responding. This is like a student who has just finished one term paper and finds it difficult to start a second paper, and the pause might be due to fatigue building up, much like Hull's I_R. This "fatigue" (Skinner's term is abulia) vanishes, however, when the organism is shifted to working on another schedule.

In the FR schedule, reinforcement is determined by the emission of the final operant of the specified number of operants required for each reinforcement delivered. Thus, in an FR-10 schedule the tenth response is the only one directly reinforced. How, then, does the subject come to emit the nine earlier responses? As mentioned earlier, Skinner's analysis of the mechanisms connecting essential preparatory responses to the directly reinforced final response is somewhat like Hull's r_G-s_G formulation. Skinner (1953) argues that most operants are composed of a sequence of movements in which the directly reinforced terminal movement provides feedback stimuli (both external and internal) that acquire conditioned reinforcer properties. The organism learns that the response preceding the directly reinforced response signals the availability of the final response, which has become a secondary reinforcer. Hence, the "$n - 1$" response serves as a discriminative stimulus (S_D) to emit the final response (tenth response in our FR-10 example). Because the ninth response is reinforced by the tenth response, the ninth response acquires conditioned reinforcer properties which reinforce the occurrence of the eighth response. The eighth response becomes a S_D for response 9, which is a conditioned reinforcer, and this process continues as the eighth response becomes a S_D, and so on. The conditioned reinforcing properties of responses further from the primary reinforcement are successively weaker because they are further from the primary reinforcement. This sequence of movements is called a **response chain.** When most of the movements are similar, as in a FR schedule, it is called a homogeneous response chain. The first link in any chain has only discriminative stimulus properties, while the final link (which may be eating the reinforcer) has only reinforcement properties. Because the conditioned reinforcer and discriminative properties of the links overlap, the chain is held together (Reynolds, 1975).

Not only does this model of complex behaviors as response chains allow Skinner to explain complex behaviors in terms of a few experimentally demonstrated laws, it also predicts the procedures necessary for "building in" complex behaviors. By beginning with the response producing or leading to primary reinforcement and adding new links to the chain, most of the amazing feats of trained animal acts can be produced (Hilgard and Bower, 1975).

The FR schedule is the schedule of piecework. When this author was a high school student in rural Michigan, he and some of his friends decided to earn some summer money by picking cherries. Cherry picking paid 65 cents per lug. A lug was a box about 4 inches high and 20 by 30 inches to the sides. It held many, many cherries. Essentially, they were working on a FR-thousands-of-cherries schedule to receive even the conditioned reinforcer of a full lug, which, of course, was a discriminative stimulus for picking up an empty lug and resuming picking. The postsecondary reinforcement pauses were very long indeed (an example of abulia), and he remembers experiencing a very real sense of being reinforced when looking down at each newly filled lug. This very "lean" schedule resulted in his group's emitting a great number of cherry-picking responses for what turned out to be about 35 dollars per week. When their money-deprivation state was reduced slightly, very rapid satiation occurred in the third week of work.

Fixed interval schedules   **Fixed interval (FI) schedules** are deterministic, as are FR schedules. FI schedules are arranged by using a clock; reinforcement is provided for the first response, which occurs after the lapse of a fixed interval of time measured from the original discriminative stimulus or from the last reinforcement. A schedule in which reinforcement is available as soon as the organism responds following a 2-minute time interval would be written as a FI-2' schedule. Like the FR schedule, the FI schedule produces a very lawful and orderly type of behavior.

Compared to the FR schedule, the FI schedule produces a low rate of responding. This rate depends upon the length of the time interval, with response rates decreasing as the length of the interval increases. The pattern of responses is also very different from that on the FR schedule. Following each reinforcement, there is a pause in responding, followed by a gradual acceleration of response rates. This pause and acceleration is called the **fixed interval scallop.** It is seen in records, made over the academic term, of the studying rates of students and in the pecking patterns of pigeons. The resistance to extinction produced by "long" FI schedules is much less than that produced by "long" FR schedules. This phenomenon illustrates Skinner's point that extinction can be better predicted by the history of the organism's experience with schedules than by the number of previously reinforced trials.

Since the response rates are low with long FI schedules, more of the trials (responses) are followed by reinforcement. But if the total number of possible reinforcers to be earned may be the same for long FI and long FR schedules, why is the response rate so high for the FR and so low for the FI schedules? An operant analysis of the components of the response chains for each type of schedule helps explain this phenomenon. Earlier, we discussed the component responses of a FR-10 chain as if each response leading up to the tenth and reinforced response was a fixed link in the chain. Our choice of independent responses as the links was arbitrary, however. We could have looked at each muscle movement making up each total pecking or pressing operant as a link, producing a chain with a great many links, or we could have dissected the chain into three or four large units. Whatever our unit of analysis, each link would have had both the S_D function (except the last link) and the conditioned reinforcer function (except the first link). Looking at the links as including the time intervals between operants (called **interresponse times** or **IRTs**), the following explanation of the differing response rates can be made. With FR schedules, the more responses emitted per unit time, the more reinforcement may be earned by the behaving organism. When responses are close together, IRTs are short, and since these bursts of responses are more likely to be associated with reinforcement, then the short IRTs are more likely to become conditioned secondary reinforcers than long IRTs. In a long FI schedule, most bursts of responses, other than those coming just before the end of the specified interval, are not reinforced. Hence, short IRTs tend to be extinguished early in the interval and long IRTs are more likely to be reinforced since only one reinforcement occurs during the interval. Through this selective reinforcement of long IRTs during most of the interval, the FI performance tends to become slower over time (Reynolds, 1975). Like Spence's explanation of relational learning, this is a good example of the behaviorists' goal of explaining complex phenomena in terms of basic principles.

Other examples of FI schedules include the behavior of workers whose foreman only inspects them at regular intervals and students' preparations for leaving a classroom as the end of the class hour approaches. As in our IRT analysis, bursts of such responses that occur early in the hour are not reinforced and tend to be extinguished. Thus, the well-known tendency of many students to procrastinate until just before assignment deadlines may reflect extinction of short IRTs early in the interval instead of laziness.

Variable interval schedules   FI schedules have two major defects from the standpoint of behavioral management. The first is their low resistance to extinction. The second is that response rates shift from the low levels found in the beginning of the interval to high levels near the end of the interval. If we make the time-based reinforcement probabilistic (variable) rather than fixed, the organism never knows exactly when it should be responding. Thus, temporal discrimination vanishes, resulting in high resistance to extinction. Extinction is slow and very gradual. This **variable interval (VI) schedule** produces a moderate, steady rate of responding. The moderate response rate is a function of the reinforcement of long IRTs.

"Many sorts of social or personal reinforcement are supplied on what is essentially a variable interval basis, and extraordinarily persistent behavior is sometimes set up" (Skinner, 1953, p. 102). An example would be trying to call someone who is hardly ever home. The rate of making calls may start high, but as it becomes apparent that very frequent calling is laborious (has a high response cost) and does not substantially increase the probability of making contact, the rate will decline. However low the "mature" rate is, the calling behavior may persist for weeks.

Like the FR and FI schedules that we have examined previously, the VI schedule is written in a shorthand form. Since the time after which a response must be emitted to obtain an available reinforcement is variable, the number attached to the VI represents the mean time interval, or the sum of all possible lengths of time intervals divided by the number of such intervals. When the frustrated phone caller of the example just given is trying to call someone who is in hearing distance of his or her phone only an average of once an hour, we would write the schedule as VI-1 hour.

Variable ratio schedules   The last of the simple schedules of reinforcement is the "gambler" or **variable ratio (VR) schedule.** Since any response in this schedule might be the one to be followed by reinforcement, the post-reinforcement pauses typical of high-ratio FR schedules rarely appear, and the VR schedule produces extremely high resistance to extinction. This schedule is so powerful that not only is the rate extremely high, but also if the ratio is gradually extended, considerations of response cost (abulia) become irrelevant. A good example would be the tourist who plays the slot machines at Las Vegas. The practice of professional gamblers in letting the "mark" win several times early in the gambling session illustrates a gradual shaping of a long VR ratio. The "mark" may continue gambling even on a very lean ratio of wins. The fly fisherman whose success is partly a function of the number of casting responses would be another example of the power of the VR schedule.

Like the VI schedule, the VR schedule is specified in terms of the mean number of responses per reinforcement, so that when, on the average, every tenth response is followed by reinforcement, the schedule would be written as a VR-10. So powerful is this schedule that pigeons will work for fewer food calories than they burn up in responding, to the point of working themselves to death. The gambler and the fly fisherman may also show a resistance to extinction verging on fanaticism!

The "gambler's fallacy" of believing that the next response after a string of losses will be lucky (be reinforced) illustrates the VR characteristic that every response is a potentially reinforcement-producing act. Even though the person playing the slot machine is almost certain to lose in the long run, the total number of wins will be higher the faster the responses are emitted. I have seen gamblers in Las Vegas playing several slot machines at once and pumping money into the machines as fast as their arms could make the responses!

Figure 4.2 shows characteristic cumulative records of performance on all of the schedules which we have presented to this point. This figure shows representative response rates both during stable reinforced sessions and during extinction. Note that response rates are highest with ratio schedules and lowest with interval schedules.

Four basic types of rules or schedules specify how the delivery of reinforcers is related to responses. These are the fixed and variable schedules based on time considerations (fixed interval and variable interval) and the fixed ratio and variable ratio schedules based on the number of responses required per reinforcement.

Even though the results of analyzing behavior in terms of the effects of the four simple schedules are impressive, we must note that it is rare for the behavior of an organism in a natural environment to be controlled by only one schedule of reinforcement. For this reason, Skinner and the Skinnerians have examined the effects of more complicated relationships between reinforcements and responses. Analysis of these more complex schedules may suggest various precise applications for the control of behavior. Skinner suggests:

> Thus gambling devices could be "improved"—from the point of view of the proprieter—by introducing devices which would pay off on a variable-interval basis, but only when the rate of play is exceptionally high. [Skinner, 1953, pp. 105–106]

Skinner goes on to suggest that such use of complex schedules promoting high response rates could be extended to industry and salesmanship by making bonuses or incentive wages contingent upon them. He recognizes the moral issues raised by such manipulations of behavior but concludes that schedules of reinforcement can be designed not only to raise worker productivity but also to increase the motivation and happiness of workers.

It is possible that much of human behavior under natural conditions can be explained in terms of complex scheduling variables and that the experimental analysis of such schedule effects may help us to understand many types of human behaviors. We turn now to a discussion of some of these more advanced schedules.

Multiple schedules of reinforcement   A **multiple schedule** consists of two or more independent schedules presented successively to the subject, with each schedule signaled by a specific discriminative stimulus. An example might be working for two bosses, given that one boss does not care how much work you do as long as you sit at your desk all day long (a FI-1 day schedule) and the other boss insists that you produce a specific number of units of work regardless of when you do them (a FR schedule). High rates of work will only appear in the presence of the second boss. Usually the rates of responding on such multiple

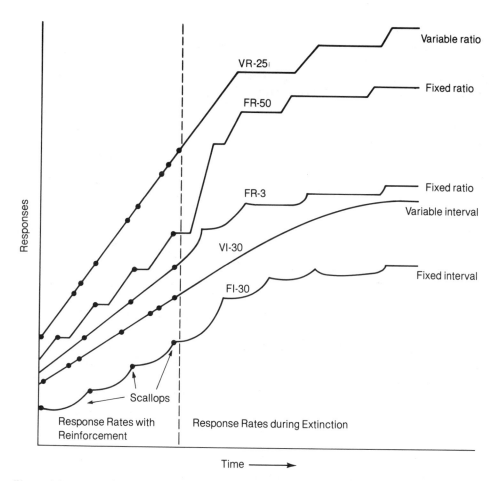

Figure 4.2   An idealized summary of cumulative recorder records of responding during a period of reinforcement availability and after reinforcement is terminated (extinction contingency) with five simple schedules. Presentation of reinforcers is indicated by dots. Steep lines indicate high rates of responding and flat lines indicate zero rates of responding. Remember that the pen of a cumulative recorder moves to the right continuously with time and moves upward every time the organism emits an operant.

schedules are primarily determined by the characteristics of the component schedules, although some interaction effects may occur (Reynolds, 1975).

Interlocking schedules   There are two types of **interlocking schedules, ascending** and **descending.** In both of these types, the number of responses required for reinforcement changes as a function of time since the last reinforcement, respectively increasing or decreasing. An example of the ascending or increasing type is the reading rates required for children to receive a specific grade. The child advancing from the second to the third grade is expected to read more for a passing grade than he was in the second grade. This schedule may be very dangerous if the child fails to progress to meet the new criterion. The child may perform at the level that formerly brought reinforcement; with the criterion set at a higher level, however, that performance is graded as failing and the child is not reinforced. This experience of failure may lead to an early extinction of the child's study behavior, and shaping towards becoming a "dropout" may begin. In this schedule, obtaining reinforcement becomes progressively harder.

An example of a descending or decreasing interlocking schedule would be a classroom in which the teacher becomes tired of trying to motivate students to meet a high criterion and lowers it. In this schedule, the student who waits the longest before submitting work will have to do the least work for a specified grade.

Differential reinforcement schedules   The contingencies for delivery of reinforcement can be specified in terms of particular patterns of responding rather than by criteria of time or number of responses. Schedules that deliver reinforcement only for specific patterns of responding are called **differential schedules.** There are three commonly used schedules of this type. The first two such schedules require responding at either very high, or fairly low, rates. The schedule which requires very rapid responding for reinforcement to be available is called the **differential reinforcement of high rates (DRH) schedule** (Reynolds, 1975). This is the "beat-the-clock" schedule; only very high levels of responding are reinforced. An example might be trying to talk to a person who talks constantly through all your pauses. Unless you talk without interruptions between your sentences, you will not be allowed to talk at all. Essentially, the DRH schedule is like a FR schedule, except that with the DRH schedule only short IRTs are reinforced.

The second type of rate criterion schedule is the **differential reinforcement of low levels** or **DRL** (or DRLL or drl) **schedule.** This schedule has been studied extensively, and its properties are known in detail (Reynolds, 1975). In this schedule, IRTs over a specified length are reinforced. The usual pattern of behavior in the acquisition of a stable DRL performance is for the subject to emit the specified operant, be reinforced, emit a burst of additional responses which are not reinforced because the IRTs are too short, to extinguish partially, and finally to be reinforced when a stray response occurs because of spontaneous recovery. Early performance is characterized by oscillations in response rate until the subject settles down to responding at a steady, slow rate.

An example of this type of schedule control might be herbivores who wait until grass in an area of meadow has regrown before returning to graze there, or a unionized worker who was required not to perform more than a minimal number of work responses in order to earn the approval of his shop steward and his fellow workers.

In the latter example there was no upper limit on the length of the work-response IRTs. In a real factory, however, there would usually be an upper as well as a lower limit on the lengths of reinforced IRTs. In our example, the worker who did almost no work would also fail to win the reinforcing approval of his fellows. The imposition of an upper limit on the acceptable IRTs is called a **limited hold.** Its effect is to control with even greater precision the rate of responding within specified limits. Many job situations provide such examples of DRL with limited hold schedule control. Such work environments would not be expected to be characterized by high productivity.

The third type of differential schedule is the **differential reinforcement of other responses (DRO) schedule.** It makes reinforcement contingent upon the emission of behaviors other than specified undesired behaviors. This is an extremely useful schedule in controlling the disruptive behaviors of disturbed and/or retarded children. Repp and Deitz (1974) have reported the successful use of DRO schedules, combined with other procedures, in reducing the aggressive and self-injurious behavior of institutionalized retarded children. As an example, one of their procedures involved giving the children tokens for every 15 minutes they were active without emitting either aggressive or self-injurious behaviors.

Concurrent schedules of reinforcement   **Concurrent schedules** independently reinforce two or more types of responses according to the demands of two or more independent schedules at the same instant in time. In the real world, our behavior is always under the concurrent control of many different schedules and many different reinforcement systems. Usually, the organism will attend to whichever schedule is currently yielding the highest rate of reinforcement. An example would be the relative rates of talking to friends and studying for tests. Because talking to friends is normally moderately reinforcing on a FR or VR basis, this will be the schedule controlling much of students' behavior early in the academic term. As test days approach (a FI component), the rate of study behavior increases and begins to compete successfully with talking to friends. The night before the exam, the student may lock the door and attend exclusively to the FI schedule. Study behavior would show the characteristic FI scallop if charted, except that the early rates of responding are even lower than normal and the final surge in responding even higher than expected because of competition with the FR or VR schedule controlling friendly conversation. Cramming may be better predicted by such scheduling variables than by inner causes such as laziness, and inability to do work early may reflect schedule competition more than the aversive qualities of the work. Of course, for study behavior to be an example of a pure FI schedule, the operant to be emitted before the end of the interval is the entire amount of studying required for adequate preparation. Skinner (1969) has noted that a specific operant can be of any size or contain many individual responses.

Skinner has not confined his analysis of the effects of schedules of reinforcement to simple schedules; he has also described various types of complex schedules. These include: (1) multiple schedules, (2) ascending and descending interlocking schedules, (3) differential schedules (of high and low rates of responding and of "other" behaviors), and (4) concurrent schedules.

Skinner's Extension of His Laws to
Complex Human Behavior

The complexities of the human condition have proved no deterrent to Skinner's willingness to explain human behavior in terms of his basic S-R laws and to propose applications based on this analysis. Since the applications will be discussed in detail in Chapters 6 and 10, they will only be mentioned here. These applications include the improvement and advocacy of teaching machines, the invention of the "vanishing" or fading method of writing and memorizing (also discussed in Chapter 9), and providing a prototype for social systems based on reinforcement principles. This prototype was first popularized in Skinner's novel, *Walden Two* (1948). Its descendants include a Walden-Two-type commune in Virginia (Kinkade, 1973) and the token economy applications discussed in Chapter 10. Of immediate theoretical interest is his attempt to extend his principles to explain language learning.

In the view of behaviorists, verbal behavior consists of "responses" under stimulus control and having stimulus consequences. Verbal labels and responses can be used as S_Ds for our own and others' behaviors as when we shout, "Stop!" They can be used to provide S_Ds signaling reinforcement for ourselves (as when I say to myself that I can eat lunch after finishing writing this section) or for others (as in telling someone what they must do to be reinforced). They can be used to reward others directly, as in saying, "You did excellent work on that paper." Also, chains of cue-producing responses are selected and used to solve problems and to learn S-R relationships (Hilgard and Bower, 1975).

In Chapter 1 we saw that Pavlov attempted to extend his theory about conditioned reflexes to apply to human language and thought by postulating the existence of a second signal system operating by laws similar to those applying to the first signal system (that of environmental cues). Skinner has also extended his theory to account for language and thought in much more detail than Pavlov. Pavlov thought that linguistic behavior is elicited by cues (either verbal or nonverbal), but Skinner sees language behavior as a type of operant behavior which follows the same laws as other operant behavior. In Skinner's theory, stimuli serve the function of signaling when a particular verbal/thinking response is likely to be reinforced; hence, there is no fixed relationship between a particular verbal response and a particular discriminative stimulus. The relationship is rather one of probabilities, and if several different verbal responses have in the past been followed by reinforcement in the presence of a particular S_D, the occurrence of that S_D may result in the emission of any of the equivalent responses. Thus, Skinner's theory is better suited to account for the flexibility of actual language. Just because several verbal responses may be given in the presence of a particular S_D, however, does not mean that the environment does not exert any control over which response will be used. Other features of the environment and your past experiences within your own verbal community*

---

* The term "verbal community" as used by Skinner refers to your sources of language experience and includes those you talk to, what you read, and what you see in media or hear on the radio. A given verbal community shares a similar interpretation of slang expressions and idiomatic phrases that may not be shared by a different social group. Your verbal community provides a reference for understanding apparently ambiguous verbal expressions.

will exert influences which are often subtle and complex. This complexity is at least hinted at in the following brief discussion of some central ideas of Skinner's linguistic theory as presented in his book *Verbal Behavior* (1957). Here he divides verbal behavior into several classes or responses, of which the most important may be **tacts, mands,** and **texts.**

Tacts roughly correspond to labels for things and states, and as such are usually nouns and their modifiers. Skinner defines tacts as verbal behaviors which make "con*tact*" with the physical world either as environmental cues ("It's a final exam") or stimuli related to internal states ("I feel angry"). Tacts tend to be emitted in the presence of a specific S_D regardless of the speaker's state of deprivation or exposure to aversive stimuli (a final exam is still a final exam, regardless of your experiencing yourself as feeling happy or angry about having to take it). Thus, they serve to allow you to reflect environmental circumstances independently of your condition at that time. Skinner suggests that tacts are established by consistent reinforcement in the presence of one S_D by many different reinforcers, or by generalized reinforcers (such as verbal praise, as when a child points to a dog and says, "Dog," and her parents respond, "Right! It's a dog."). In the real world, many tacts are contaminated by emotional connotations (such as the moral dimensions of the word "reward"), but Skinner feels that pure tacts can be found in scientific jargon (such as the term "reinforcement").

Skinner does not believe that tacts are conditioned stimuli which stand as representatives of the thing or situation labeled. Rather, tacts signal occasions in which you would be likely to experience a particular object or situation. Whether or not a listener reacts to a given tact (such as a cook saying, "Dinner!") depends upon other discriminative stimuli and the listener's past experience with the relationship of that cook's saying that tact with eating food. For example, when the author's mother would say, "Dinner!" this announcement was usually followed by a wait of at least five minutes before the food was actually ready to eat, and the author adjusted his "coming-to-the-table" behavior accordingly. In a similar way, control of the cook's tendency to emit the tact, "Dinner!" is more than a reflexive response to finished food. Other S_Ds, such as the activities of the persons who are to eat the food and their proximity to the table, may share in the control of the tact.

The term "mand" is derived from the root of such words as de*mand* and com*mand* (Skinner, 1957). Mands are characterized by unique relationships between the form of the verbal response and the reinforcement characteristically received in a given verbal community. Thus, mands specify the expected reinforcement, as when someone states, "Pass the butter, please." "Pass the butter, please" specifies an action ("pass") and the ultimate reinforcer ("butter"). Although the mand function of "Pass the butter, please" may seem apparent from the words used, Skinner notes that just the presence of butter is insufficient to control the emission of such a phrase. The emission of mands is also controlled by conditions of deprivation (the person must be hungry to request butter or any other food, in most cases) and aversive stimuli (perhaps the cook would be offended if you failed to request butter for his rolls). In this example, it should be noted, Skinner acknowledges the controlling functions of such inner conditions as states of hunger. The ultimate causation of such conditions, however, he views as involving environmental events such as deprivation or satiation.

The probability of the occurrence of a mand is also controlled by past experiences with a listener (do they seem likely to reinforce a given verbal mand?) as well as the reinforcing practices of a given verbal community (will they pass butter only if you say please?). What Skinner seeks to explain is the total verbal episode. This would also include the speaker's reinforcing the butter passer by saying, "Thank you," which might be reinforced, in turn, by the butter passer's saying, "You are welcome." These last polite verbal operants occur because their use in the past has set the occasion for other reinforcers or has terminated aversive states (as when a child is scolded until she or he says "Please" and "Thank you"). As can be seen, Skinner does not suggest that specific words function mechanically, but rather that a speaker has learned that certain classes of verbal responses are likely to be followed by reinforcement.

Texts are verbal stimuli which come to control verbal behavior. They are usually visual (such as pictures, printed words, characters, and so on) but can be tactile (as in Braille). Textual behavior illustrates the basic process which Skinner believes underlies all verbal behavior. Teachers and parents supply generalized conditioned reinforcers (such as verbal praise) when a child makes certain required vocal responses to other cues (such as marks on a page). If the child responds, "Girl," to the marks *girl* on the page, and not otherwise, he receives approval. The reinforcers for the teacher are money and the approval of peers, parents, and principals. The reinforcer for the verbal community is related to the advantages of having another literate member of that community (Skinner, 1957). Skinner also considers that reading generates automatic reinforcement, as when a story arouses emotional reflexes or gives the reading person information which she or he has previously experienced as likely to lead to other reinforcers. A scientist may read an article because it will give him or her the information to upset the theory of a rival (although Skinner acknowledges that the reinforcing effects of inflicting injury upon another can not be explained within his theory of verbal behavior). He suggests that such emotion-related reinforcing effects may depend upon Pavlovian conditioning mechanisms.

Skinner has developed a theory of verbal learning and language behavior based on his operant learning model in which responses are made because they are likely to set the occasion for reinforcement. Three important forms of verbal behavior are: (1) tacting (labeling), (2) manding (requesting), and (3) texting (roughly, reading).

Although Skinner's views on the functions and learning of language have been tremendously influential in shaping modern social learning theories (see Mischel, 1973), they have come under serious attack from more cognitively oriented psychologists.

The most critical of these attackers has been the linguist Noam Chomsky (1971). According to Chomsky, the vast number of possible verbal S-R relationships prevents a behavioristic analysis on any meaningful level. Either the explanations must be so simplified as to be trivial or so unwieldy as to be useless.

Worse, looking at sentence structure on the basis of stimulus characteristics usually leads to absurd results, since the meaning of a verbal utterance may have more to do with the context of use, the grammatical structure, and what the speaker thinks the person hearing the sentence already knows. Chomsky's cognitive/linguistic model of language acquisition and use will be explored in Chapter 11.

As a result of these criticisms, Skinner has recently made his theory of language acquisition and use more complex. Contingencies related to the "verbal community," to expectancies about reinforcement, to self-reinforcement, and to abstract meanings acting as stimuli or responses have been incorporated in his theory (Skinner, 1974). When discussing how abstract concepts can be viewed as if they were objectively viewed environmental stimuli, he writes:

> There is no point in asking how a person can "know the abstract entity called redness." The contingencies explain the behavior, and we need not be disturbed because it is impossible to discover the referent in any single instance. [Skinner, 1974, p. 94]

This example of Skinner's attempts to come to terms with the cognitive critics illustrates a possible weakness in his avowedly "atheoretical theory." When he attempts to explain events that are not visible in the environment in terms of environmental effects, his theory deviates from the behaviorist goal of accepting only objectively measured behaviors as data.

Skinner's Positions on Major Issues

Nature/nurture   Skinner views the reflexes involved in type S (Pavlovian or classical) conditioning as innate. He recognizes innate differences in learning rates among species and individuals within species. He also acknowledges that phylogenetic (evolutionary) contingencies might selectively "reinforce" the occurrence of particular genetic patterns conducive to easy or difficult learning of particular behaviors. If an animal inherited the neural mechanisms conducive to making specific types of associations and thereby was more likely to survive and leave offspring, then the frequency with which the genes responsible for that neural mechanism would increase, much like responses followed by reinforcers, becomes more probable. This would happen in different ways in different species, and, at least in terms of predicting the organism's behavior in its natural environment, would reduce the applicability of the principle of equipotentiality.

Notwithstanding, Skinner's focus is on environmental determinants of behavior. Even though he has moved away from the radical environmentalist position characterized by such theorists as Watson, he still maintains that human language, human aggression, human social behavior, and human problem solving are all learned primarily through operant conditioning (Skinner, 1969).

The how of learning   Skinner states that something like Thorndike's early law of exercise or pure contiguity may account for Pavlovian or type S conditioning of responses mediated by the autonomic nervous system. Operant or type R conditioning, however, is assumed to be the mechanism of learning adaptive skeletal muscle responses. Operant learning is learning through reinforcement. Although Skinner states that both types of conditioning processes occur, his emphasis on operant conditioning qualifies his nominally two-factor theory as a reinforcement theory. In Skinner's model of operant learning, a response must be spontaneously emitted and this emission followed by a reinforcing event for conditioning to occur. Unlike Hull's early theory, Skinner's theory does not tie reinforcement to drive reduction or other postulated internal events. In accordance with Skinner's preference towards specifying his laws only in terms of stimuli and responses, reinforcement is operationally defined as any event which increases the probability of the reoccurrence of a response emitted just prior to the reinforcing event.

The what of learning   Except for type S conditioning, which is involved in learning conditioned reinforcers, organisms learn to activate appropriate operants in the presence of specific (but often unobserved) discriminative stimuli at rates controlled by schedules. The units of learning are either S-R relationships or tendencies to emit behaviors. Skinner avoids speculating about internal variables and purposely leaves the internal unit of learning undefined.

Continuity/noncontinuity, use of animal data, and determinism   Learning, in Skinner's theory, is usually a gradual (continuous) process, except in the few cases in which one powerful reinforcing trial may form the connection. Skinner is highly deterministic and sees behaviors as determined by environmental events, except in those few cases (very few in humans) where internal, instinctual determinants may lead to responding. Skinner generalizes freely from animal data collected under controlled laboratory conditions to human behavior.

Chapter Perspective
Chomsky is not the only formidable critic Skinner has faced. Miller (1969) and the psychologists investigating biofeedback (Chapters 6 and 10) have demonstrated that responses mediated by the autonomic nervous system can be conditioned by a reinforcement process. This erodes one of Skinner's distinctions between classical and operant conditioning. In Chapter 12 we will see some examples of situations under laboratory conditions that call into question Skinner's practice of freely exchanging animal and human data. Cook (1963) has criticized the Skinnerians' generalization of pigeon data to the design of teaching machines for children. Because pigeons are required to demonstrate overt learning, teaching machines are constructed to demand overt responses. Cook has presented data showing that students who are not required to respond and be reinforced do better than those that are. In Chapter 9, Bandura's research on observational learning seems to show that the learning of operant behavior may not require reinforcement. Bandura maintains that reinforcement is critical for performance—not learning. Skinner's position on the effects of punishment seems, in retrospect, to be more the product of kindly impulses on his part than of extensive research. Solomon (1964) and Azrin and others (see Chapter 9) have demonstrated extremely effective control of behavior with carefully planned punishment contingencies.

Although the neo-Hullians moved increasingly in the direction of becoming eclectic and accepting cognitive variables, Skinner has remained as a relatively radical behaviorist. The author once heard him speak in Royce Auditorium at the University of California at Los Angeles.* A young woman asked him if he ever felt himself to be free to make choices in ways other than those determined by environmental contingencies. He replied, "Sometimes I have those feelings, but I know that they are an illusion. I know that this sounds like a contradiction, but I live with that contradiction and so can you" (Skinner, 1973). Many neo-Skinnerians, such as Mischel and Bandura, have taken operant principles and used them in combination with cognitive variables (see Chapter 9). Skinner, however, adamantly continues to restrict himself to empirical relationships between stimuli and responses, or to internal entities that are assumed to follow the same laws as external stimuli and responses.

Skinner is not unused to professional isolation. He stood apart from the Hullian mainstream and founded the *Journal of the Experimental Analysis of Behavior* which, together with the *Journal of Applied Behavior Analysis*, serve as "house organs" for Skinnerian research.

The methods of operant research concentrate on changes in behaviors within subjects rather than on comparisons among groups and focus on description rather than on statistical analysis. These are markedly different from the types of learning methods commonly reported in the *Journal of Experimental Psychology*. Many researchers working within Skinner's model have continued to make interesting and applicable discoveries, as we shall see in Chapters 9 and 10.

Of all the theorists discussed to this point, Skinner has had the widest impact outside the field of psychology. Increasingly, workers in education and mental health areas use the techniques discovered or described by Skinner and his followers regardless of their agreement with Skinner's theories. In lucid and provocative books, Skinner continues to respond effectively to his many critics.

The question for the future becomes: Will Skinner's basic position as the defender of the environmentalistic, connectionistic, reductionistic, behaviorist position survive his own death? Will the "defects" in his system cited by Chomsky and other critics eventually lead to its collapse without Skinner's powerful prose to serve in its defense? Or will a new radical behaviorist come to dominate the field of learning as Thorndike, Pavlov, Watson, Hull, and Skinner have dominated it? Perhaps the answer lies in a tendency Skinner shares with Hull. As in Hull's case, Skinner's experimental analysis and theoretical constructions are strongest in describing relatively simple forms of behavior. Like Hull, Skinner applies his laws in a looser and ad hoc fashion to complex behavior.

---

* At this lecture he was asked why he had not replied directly to Chomsky's criticisms. He replied that he was too busy writing and teaching to bother with a futile debate on theoretical issues. He then confessed that his first exposure to reading Chomsky had occurred in the past few months, when one of his students had insisted that he do so. (Perhaps he had hoped that by not responding to Chomsky, he could facilitate the extinction of Chomsky's critical responses.) When he read Chomsky's criticisms, he said, he felt that Chomsky had seriously misrepresented and oversimplified his views.

These extensions, which most depend upon their creator to defend them, seem most vulnerable to cognitive criticisms.

Key Terms

aversive stimulus	emit	reinforcement
ascending interlocking schedule	extinction	reinforcer
	fixed interval (FI) scallop	response chain
concurrent schedule	fixed interval (FI) schedule	response generalization
contingency	fixed ratio (FR) schedule	satiation
continuous reinforcement (CRF)	instrumental conditioning	schedule of reinforcement
descending interlocking schedule	interlocking schedule	secondary (conditioned) reinforcement
	intermittent reinforcement	
differential reinforcement schedule	interresponse time (IRT)	shaping
	interval schedule	Skinner box
differential reinforcement of high rates (DRH) schedule	limited hold	straining the schedule
	mand	successive approximation
differential reinforcement of low levels (DRL) schedule	multiple schedule	superstitious conditioning
	negative reinforcement	tact
differential reinforcement of other responses (DRO) schedule	operant	text
	operant conditioning	type R conditioning
differential schedule	positive reinforcer	type S conditioning
discriminated operant	post-reinforcement pause	variable interval (VI) schedule
discriminative stimulus (S_D or S+)	punishment	variable ratio (VR) schedule
	ratio schedule	

Annotated Bibliography

Skinner writes very well, and there is a great consistency, almost to the point of redundancy, evident in his numerous books and articles. For a good representative sample, I would recommend the following: (1) *Walden two* (New York: Macmillan, 1948), a novel which illustrates Skinner's philosophy that behavior is controlled by the environment; (2) "How to teach animals" (*Scientific American*, December 1951, 185, 26–29), an excellent short article about the use of shaping and reinforcement; (3) *Science and human behavior* (New York: Macmillan, 1953), a comprehensive treatment of classical as well as operant conditioning in which Skinner's eloquent contempt for "hidden" inner processes comes through loud and clear; (4) *About behaviorism* (New York: Alfred A. Knopf, 1974), Skinner's most recent summary of operant learning principles and the philosophy of a fairly radical behaviorism in which he responds to criticisms of his theories.

5

Cognitive Alternatives

In this chapter we will examine several approaches to understanding learning that are unified by two assumptions: (1) ideas or cognitions are the "what" of learning, and (2) the most important type of learning is discontinuous and sudden. A central feature of most cognitive theories is the discontinuous change in behavior through active internal processing, usually called insight. This type of sudden learning is dramatically different from the gradual improvement (continuous learning) most commonly found in conditioning. Another example of insight learning comes from the author's own research: When he was a graduate student, he tried to teach three white-necked ravens to discriminate by number. The birds were required to open one of two doors displaying plastic cards with either two symbols or one symbol mounted on them. The side on which the rewarded two symbols appeared was randomized over trials and the sizes of the symbols were varied so that the single symbol was greater in area than the two symbols on one fourth of the trials. The results of many weeks of training are shown in Figure 5.1 (Swenson, 1970).

As can be seen, two of the ravens showed some gradual and continuous learning which, when analyzed, was found to have been related to a tendency always to respond to the cues having the greater area (which were the double symbols on 75 percent of the trials). Only Schwartz seems to have really learned a number concept (which generalized readily to a wide range of novel stimuli). As you can see, he did so suddenly, after many sessions of almost random responding. This concept learning is the learning of most interest to cognitive theorists.

The approaches to be presented in this chapter differ in one critical aspect from all theories which have been presented in earlier chapters. In a sense, they represent rebellions against the limitations of the mechanistic connectionist models. Cognitive theories focus on the active characteristics of the organism rather than on behavior that is seen as inflexibly linked to the types of stimulation encountered. This focus on an active rather than an environmentally determined organism is closer to our own subjective experiences of how we learn. The dry precision of the mechanistic, molecular (S-R or S-S) theories is bewildering to lay people and unsatisfying to many psychologists. It is this compatibility with lay perceptions of mental events and avoidance of machinelike analogies which has provided the impetus for the cognitive counterattack against behaviorism. Behavioristic models tend to become overly complex when they try to

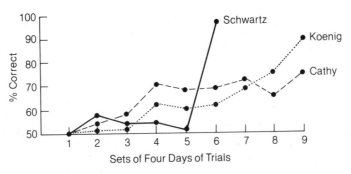

Figure 5.1   Percent correct responses by four-day blocks of trials.

confront the issues raised by cognitive theorists who, conversely, are able to handle such problems as latent (hidden) learning and partial reinforcement effects with simple elegance.

How do cognitive theories differ from most conditioning theories? For one thing, they focus on molar* behavior, or behavior analyzed in large, common-sense units, such as skills and purposes, rather than on habits or the muscle twitches of the molecular behaviorists. Their emphasis on the organism's ability to make choices further reinforces their tendency to see the basic units of learn-ing as molar—as skills, purposes, plans, changes in life spaces, and strategies. These learned molar units in turn imply that the basic orientation of behavior has much more to do with goals than with completing specific chains of muscu-lar responses. Behavior is viewed as difficult to predict without first investigat-ing the individual phenomenal world of the behaving organism in order to understand just what those goals might be. So the cognitive approach not only sees higher animals as thinking (to the horror of the staunch antimentalist S-S or S-R theorist) but also as too individualistic to allow predictions of their behavior from observation of only the immediate sources of stimuli or rewards.

The first theory we will examine represents a bridge between the cognitive and behavioristic poles. For this reason its proponent Tolman is often labeled a cognitive behaviorist. He is, in fact, a cognitive theorist in the sense that his basic units of learning are expectancies and other cognitive constructs, and a behaviorist in his rejection of the methodology of introspectionism, his atten-tion to environmental influences, and his reliance on rat experimentation to test key aspects of his theory.

The second theory is gestalt learning theory and the variant developed by Lewin. This theory incorporates the principles of organization discovered by the gestalt school of perceptual research in Europe and concentrates on subjective, phenomenological experience rather than simply on objective stimuli. One of the key strengths of this approach has been to demonstrate the degree to which the expectancies of humans can distort the perception of apparently "objective" stimuli.

---

* Hull's molar behaviorism must be distinguished from the molecular behaviorisms of Watson and Guthrie.

The third theory belongs to Maria Montessori. Although this theory was developed apart from the mainstream of academic psychology and has been studied primarily in courses on education, many of its key concepts have a curiously modern ring. The basic units of learning are ideas and combinations of ideas, which qualifies the theory as cognitive. The ideas, however, may be learned either through strict repetition of stimuli, as in contiguity behavioristic models, or through the active focusing of attention, as in other cognitive models. Although her emphasis on the training of sensory abilities is unusual, Montessori's recognition of maturation effects prefigures both Tolman and Piaget (whose cognitive-maturational theory will be covered in Chapter 11).

The chapter concludes with a brief discussion of developing trends in non-connectionist theories. The emphasis on the active organism put the focus back inside the organism rather than on environmental events. This in turn led to efforts to develop models of these internal processes which substituted complex internal mechanisms for the simple S-R mechanisms of the behaviorists. We have already briefly reviewed part of Estes's statistical stimulus sampling model in Chapter 2. Estes, however, was not the first theorist to attempt to develop analogs of learning based on the powerful tools of mathematical and engineering principles. The publication of Norbert Wiener's book *Cybernetics* in 1948 opened the expanding field of theories which combined cognitivism and mechanisms of learning. Wiener's general theory relating the behaviors of complex self-correcting machines to those of organisms through the principle of feedback was followed by electronically controlled machines that appeared to learn, and these in turn by computer analogs of complex learning processes. This finally developed into models of learning in organisms which postulated computerlike processes. These models are now known as **information-processing theories.**

Edward Chace Tolman (1886–1959)

Tolman, the foremost critic of Watson's "muscle twitchism" (in Sahakian, 1976), was granted his Ph.D. in 1915 from Skinner's alma mater, Harvard. Except for three years of teaching at Northwestern University, he spent most of his academic career at the University of California at Berkeley, until his resignation in protest against pressure to sign a loyalty oath in 1950. He then taught from 1950 to 1953 at the University of Chicago and at Harvard. He acknowledged many sources for his ideas, including his Harvard professor, Edwin Holt, as well as Kurt Lewin and his student researchers at Berkeley (where he founded the rat laboratory). He dedicated a book published in 1932 to the white rat. In 1922, Tolman announced his "purposive behaviorism" approach to learning (Hill, 1971) and continued to develop this unique approach throughout his long academic career. His task was difficult. He wished to preserve the objectivity of the behaviorist movement by rejecting the introspectionist method. He also wanted to concentrate on measurable external stimuli and responses without embracing the brittle excesses of the Watsonian movement. While adopting the behaviorist practice of using animal models to test generalized learning principles, Tolman differed from connectionist behaviorists in two critical ways.

First, he avoided the prevailing practice of treating hypothesized internal entities (as Guthrie's movement-produced stimuli) as hypothetical constructs or physical realities which would be discovered in time. Instead, he referred to his units of cognitions and the like as intervening variables, or pure abstractions, rather than as (possible) neurological mechanisms. This both allowed his theory to escape the fate of Pavlov's premature neurologizing and let him explain very complex phenomena in easily understood terms.

Second, while retaining the behavioristic emphasis on experience with external stimuli as the primary cause of learning, Tolman rejected the bonding of stimuli, or stimuli and responses, in favor of cognitions of various types as the basic units of the most important type of learning.

> For a purposive behaviorism, behavior, as we have seen, is purposive, cognitive, and molar, i.e., "gestalted." Purposive behaviorism is a molar, not a molecular, behaviorism, but it is nonetheless a behaviorism. Stimuli and responses and the behavior-determinants of responses are all that it finds to study . . .
> [Tolman, 1967, p. 418]

These cognitions have been called variously **cognitive maps,** knowledge, expectancies, and **sign-gestalts,** and they differ from S-R bonds in being more flexible and less bound to the physical properties of stimuli. They imply learning of many aspects of a situation and not just a knowledge of "if I do this, then that will happen." Although it is an S-S theory in terms of seeing **signs** (stimuli) as connected to **significates** (meanings), Tolman's theory differs from Pavlov's S-S (or CS-US) stimulus substitution theory. Tolman's second "S" is an internal "expectation." Cues elicit responses in Pavlov's theory, but Tolman's rats may or may not respond to an expectancy. In fact, there is no provision in the concept of an "expectation" to ensure that Tolman's rats would have to respond at all. As some of his critics have commented, Tolman's rats might be expected to remain "muddled in thought," rather than responding to signs. Tolman wrote of cognitions as allowing the organism not only to approach a rewarded goal but also to know what reward to expect and the general location of the goal. Tolman, however, never tried to second-guess the "true" mental state of his subjects and preferred descriptions on the order of: "The rat comes to behave *as if* it expects food when it sees the sign cues" (Bolles, 1975, p. 84).

Tolman developed a purposive behaviorism based on learning the relationship between environmental stimuli (signs) and internal cognitions or expectancies (significates, sign-gestalts, cognitive maps).

Major Principles

Tolman's work was characterized by a readable style and considerable variation over the years. Principles and concepts were added, dropped, and added again as Tolman responded to the attacks of his critics and to his own cognitions. The following four principles are seen by Bolles (1975), Hilgard and Bower (1975), and Hill (1971) as central to the theory:

1. Behavior is **purposive** or goal directed. This means that rather than making a response because of specific stimuli which have been associated with that response in the past, an organism goes to a particular place because it expects a specific outcome.

2. The knowledge of an organism is organized into a cognitive map of the environment rather than being a simple listing of local stimulus-response pairs. Learning is primarily the perceptual learning of signs.

> The brain is far more like a map control room than it is like an old-fashioned telephone exchange. The stimuli, which are allowed in, are not connected by just simple one-to-one switches to the outgoing response. Rather the incoming impulses are usually worked over and elaborated in the central control room into a tentative cognitivelike map of the environment. [Tolman, 1948, p. 192]

3. Selective preference for short or easy means to a goal, as opposed to long or difficult means, is a basic factor of behavior. This is known as Tolman's principle of least effort, and it is congruent with his preference for organisms who actively decide to go to goals that they can find by using their cognitive maps instead of organisms who are blindly led by habits composed of S-R links. This is a principle which says that being lazy is natural!

4. Molar behavior is docile, plastic, and modifiable. This principle says that behavior which can be changed to meet new circumstances is docile behavior. **Docile** as used by Tolman means teachable rather than fixed, passive, or stereotyped. Near the end of his career, Tolman admitted that the type of reflexes described by Watson and Pavlov might exist, suggesting that these stereotyped reflexes could be validly investigated at a molecular level. However, he parallels Skinner (see Chapter 4) in classifying Pavlovian reflexes as more primitive than other types of learning and of less importance in the organism's normal functioning.

Tolman had four major principles: (1) behavior is purposive, (2) learning is organized into internal cognitive maps, (3) organisms seek to obtain goals by the least difficult method, and (4) molar behavior is plastic or flexible.

Tolman was willing to learn from other theorists and made many attempts to reconcile his data on cognitive learning with the data of his theoretical opponents. One such attempt was to acknowledge the validity of his rivals' observations by developing a model of six distinct types of learning. In this system, his molar learning is one type of learning; classical and operant conditioning of various types may fit into other categories. The six types of learning postulated by Tolman (1949) ranged from his primary type of cognitive learning to learning biases, drive discriminations, and contiguity learning of sequences of small muscle movements in skill acts (as in sports). Tolman sidesteps the problem of how to explain examples of the types of learning postulated by Skinner, Guthrie, and others by including them in his system as minor and specialized types.

Experimental Evidence Supporting the Major Principles

A classic study supporting the concept of behavior as purposive was reported by Tinklepaugh in 1928. In this experiment, a monkey was trained to locate bananas hidden under one of two cups after a short delay. This it was able to do. During the delay period and unknown to the monkey, the banana was replaced by lettuce (a less preferred food). When the monkey turned over the correct cup and saw the lettuce, it was reported to have expressed surprise and rage and to have engaged in searching behavior as if looking for the missing banana. In Tolman's terms, the sign (correct cup) was connected to the significate (expectancy of finding a banana); the monkey's reaction was due to having this expectancy unreinforced, since the lettuce would have been almost as effective in reducing the monkey's hunger drive.

The issue of learning as constructing cognitive maps, in contrast to most behaviorists' view of learning as connecting S-R or S-S bonds, was the impetus for several ingenious experiments. Krechevsky (1932) used a four-unit maze with light versus dark and left versus right cues to study choice behavior in rats. He found that his subjects tended to adopt systematic modes of responding which they would "try out" for several trials before switching to a new systematic pattern. This was very different from the type of random trial-and-error learning observed by Thorndike. For example, a rat might begin with a "turn right" hypothesis for eight trials and then switch suddenly to alternating right and left turns before finally solving the problem by consistently going towards the cue of darkness. Krechevsky noted that abandonment of incorrect "hypotheses" was abrupt, as if the rats had gotten information from trying out the incorrect hypothesis, which then led them to try something new. Their abrupt changes of strategy were interpreted as evidence for discontinuous or insightful learning.

In Tolman's view, the hypotheses observed by Krechevsky acted as provisional expectancies. Reinforcement of a particular hypothesis served the function of information confirming that hypothesis. This interpretation suggests Tolman's general views regarding the role of reinforcement in learning. Drives act, he believed, to arouse states of tension, which are then expressed as demands for particular goal objects, which in turn lead to activities which are guided by expectancies. Motivations created by drive states guide the organism to notice particular stimuli (selective perception) and to acquire knowledge about these perceptual events. This acquisition of perceptual knowledge he saw as the basic mechanism of place learning. Goal objects (reinforcers) then act to confirm the expectancies related to cues associated with places. Thus, the role of reinforcement is not to produce learning directly but rather to guide perception and to make patterns of responding more likely in the presence of particular perceptual events (stimuli). Nonreinforcement is a signal to abandon provisional but incorrect hypotheses based on attention to irrelevant cues. Since a whole hypothesis about what to do is disconfirmed by nonreinforcement, shifts will tend to be abrupt and final solutions sudden and apparently "insightful."

This view of the confirmation-information function of reinforcement was also used by Tolman in explaining the **partial reinforcement effect** in extinction. If a response is rewarded only 33 percent of the time, the organism will not be able to form a clear expectancy of when reward is connected to that response. During extinction, the organism will continue to respond longer (because of uncertainty about the contingencies) than if the response were reinforced 100 percent of the time. With 100 percent reinforcement, the organism expects re-

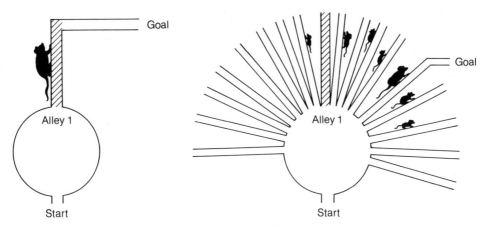

Figure 5.2   A multiple alley problem of the type used by Tolman et al. (1946a). The apparatus on the left is the training design. The drawing on the right shows the apparatus in the testing mode. The most frequent paths followed by the rats are shown by the relative sizes of the rats in the drawing.

wards for every response and rapidly ceases responding when this expectancy is thwarted.

Expectancies are related to places or cognitive maps. A test of the cognitive map hypothesis was reported by Tolman, Ritchie, and Kalish (1946a) when they trained rats to reach a goal via an indirect route. Then 18 alleys were added and the original path was blocked. S-R theory would predict that the most responses (alley entries) would be in those alleys adjacent to the blocked alley because of stimulus generalization effects. Most entries, however, were in the alley aiming most directly at the food rather than in those adjacent to the formerly reinforced alley. The type of experimental apparatus used in this study is shown in Figure 5.2. The size of the rats in the drawing is proportional to the number of entries into each alley. It must be noted that the mazes used were open at the top, allowing the rats to guide themselves by cues outside of the mazes (such as the position of the lights in the room). Such extramaze cues would seem to facilitate place learning.

Another principle illustrated by this study is Tolman's principle of least effort. Most of the rats took the alley offering the shortest path to reward. An example from the author's experience is that many rats first bar-press in ways as laborious as pushing the bar with their heads and bodies. With time, some of them can be observed pushing rapidly with one paw while their heads remain in the food magazine. Yet another principle supported is that of the docility of molar behavior. Having once learned where the goal is located, rats respond to the blockage of their accustomed path by emitting the totally new set of responses involved in going by the new, more direct route to the goal. Finally, this study illustrates the phenomenon of **latent learning.** Even though the rats had never previously been reinforced for emitting the responses involved in going up the shorter alleys, presumably the information they had learned about their

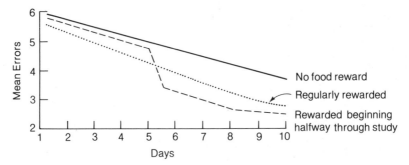

Figure 5.3   Performance in a maze of rats never rewarded, rats rewarded halfway through the experiment, and rats always receiving food in the goal box. Note that the group given food halfway through the experiment showed an abrupt change in performance—from the level of the never-rewarded group to the level of the always-rewarded group—even though they had only received half as many rewarded trials.

location (perhaps from the extramaze cues) was available once sufficient incentive was provided for them to show that learning in performance.

Another study illustrating the phenomena of latent learning, docility, and place learning was a maze experiment conducted by Tolman and Honzik (1930). In this well-known experiment, rats were allowed to explore a complex maze for a period of several days without reward. After deprivation and an opportunity to eat once in the goal box, they showed a sudden improvement in performance, bringing them to the performance level of rats who had always been rewarded in the goal box. Another group of rats having no reward at all displayed little improvement in performance. The interpretation of this experiment is that all rats learned the maze, but the group which first had exploration only, followed by deprivation and reward, was goaded by drive and reward into demonstrating the latent learning in performance. This rapid utilization of old cognitions acquired during exploration to achieve the new goal of food is, of course, a prime example of the docility of such cognitions. The data showing that the rats given food midway through the experiment were able to find the goal quickly shows that they had learned its location. This can be interpreted as evidence for place learning rather than for learning of a connection between responses leading to a goal and cues associated with drive reduction. The basic data of this experiment in simplified form are shown in Figure 5.3.

This study created serious problems for other learning theories. Guthrie's theory could not explain these results because doors between the multiple T-shaped units of the maze were set to prevent the rat from retracing his path. Therefore, the final responses made which let the animals out of the maze were the same for all groups and all groups should have improved at the same rate. Hull's 1943 theory could handle the difference between the groups after the first few days of training on the basis of differential drive reduction. The no-food groups could be said to improve slightly because of the slight reduction in aversive drives generated through the experience of bumping into the locked (incorrect) doors between sections of the maze by eliminating errors. The rewarded group improved more because the reduction in aversive drive occasioned by eliminating wrong choices was augmented by food-produced drive reduction. This version of Hull's theory, however, was not able to explain why the sudden change from no food to reward should produce such a sudden improvement in performance. Instead, the 1943 theory would predict that the group changed to food reward should show the same rate of learning as the always-fed group because both groups would be receiving equal drive reduction. These results may have also (along with research such as Crespi's) been instrumental in inducing Hull to add the incentive motivation variable (K) in his 1952 theory. This version of Hull's theory would predict that the slight reduction in drive produced by avoiding locked doors was sufficient to build up habit strength (S^HR). The addition of reward greatly increased K, and since the total tendency to respond (S^ER) is the result of multiplying drive (D) by S^HR by K, increased K would yield higher S^ER and superior performance. Tolman, of course, explained these results as support for the idea that all groups had learned cognitive maps of the maze, the reward thus serving to generate expectancies which guided the activities of the rats towards rapid running of the maze with few errors.

Although the Tolman and Honzik study supported Tolman's view that rats learning mazes acquired knowledge about the maze rather than a series of S-R connections, more direct evidence against the learning of a fixed sequence of muscle movements was provided by a study conducted by MacFarlane (1930). He trained rats to swim a maze that was filled with water, then drained the maze. In spite of the totally different pattern of muscle responses required (running versus swimming), the rats showed no increase in errors. It must be noted that the stimuli associated with local regions of the maze were also altered from wet-cold to dry-warm, and so on, and yet the animals seemed to have no trouble in locating the goal box. This again suggests place learning rather than response learning.

Place learning was directly compared to response learning in a study performed by Tolman, Ritchie, and Kalish (1946b). Rats were either required to go to a particular goal box no matter which part of a cross-shaped maze they started in or always to turn in a particular direction as the food was moved to different goal boxes. They found that all eight of their place-learning rats learned the problem within eight trials, while five of the response-learning rats still had not mastered the problem after 72 trials.

Tolman (1939) has even reported direct observations which seem to show that rats might think. Rats outside a choice-point showed considerable hesitation and made small movements towards each choice (the "muddled in thought" quip comes to mind). Tolman characterizes the "vicarious trial-and-error" behavior as external evidence that rats' choosing behavior is dominated by perceptual-cognitive processes.

Tolman's Positions on Major Issues

Nature/nurture   Tolman stated that innate differences can influence the ability to learn and even suggested that some constitutional factors may make the learning of specific types of relationships easier than others. This, of course, contradicts the equipotentiality postulate to which Skinner and other connectionist theorists have implicitly subscribed. The equipotentiality postulate says that learning laws apply equally over tasks as varied as bar pressing and language learning, and that the laws are independent of particular responses, stimuli, and reinforcers.

The how of learning   Tolman saw contiguity factors exerted through practice as the major influence in connecting environmental signs with internal cognitions or expectancies, but only when the signs "belonged" together. His criterion for belonging was very like that explored by the gestalt theorists, to be discussed in the next section of this chapter.

His view that association is the basis of learning did not mean, however, that reinforcement is not important in affecting performance. In this belief he was in agreement with Spence. He saw the role of deprivation as one of energizing previously learned cognitions so that they begin to play a function of guiding the organism towards a goal previously linked with reward. In addition, rewards serve to confirm or emphasize signs and to strengthen their related expectancies (Hilgard and Bower, 1975). Tolman tends to emphasize the nature side more than most behaviorists but stresses the nurture side more than the gestalt theorists and Maria Montessori.

The what of learning   In spite of many similarities to behavioristic theories, Tolman's theory does not consider the S-R bond as the unit of learning. What is learned is the bonding of signs (stimuli) to cognitive units of large or molar type (expectancies, significates).

Continuity/noncontinuity, use of animal data, and determinism   Tolman agreed with Guthrie and the gestalt theorists, claiming that learning can occur in a single trial. Guthrie, of course, claimed that all learned bonds are formed in one trial. Tolman, however, also saw practice as gradually or continuously affecting (usually by increasing) the strength of a given expectancy which had been learned in one trial. This practice effect was not seen as the cause of the initial selection of a (correct) response, which was assumed to reflect the organism's initial expectancies.

Tolman differed from most other cognitive theorists in being willing and able to use data collected from rat experiments in challenging the views of the strict behaviorists. In spite of seeing his organisms as responding on the basis of complex internal active processes, he still seemed to see behavior as determined by these internal mechanisms rather than coming down strongly on the side of "free will." Thus, his views on determinism seem to fall somewhere in between those of the behaviorists and the cognitive humanists.

Perspective

Tolman was the only major cognitive theorist who demonstrated a credible performance in conducting creative and appropriate rat research. Perhaps for this reason alone, the "behaviorist" at the end of "purposive" is appropriate. Tolman began with a broad eclectic theory which grew broader and more eclectic over the years as the concepts of his rivals were digested and incorporated. In general, he was stronger when engaged in a penetrating critique of weaknesses in the connectionist/behavioristic position than in formulating a coherent postulate system of his own. His gift of clever experimental design forced the S-R theorists into ever more complex theorizing (Hull is a clear example; see Chapter 3) in their efforts to explain the phenomena he so skillfully demonstrated.

In the end, any recognizable form of his theory failed to survive his retirement, in spite of attempts by MacCorquodale and Meehl (1954) to pull it together into a strict, Hull-type system of postulates and theorems.

Nonetheless, bits and parts of Tolman's theory appear in various modern theories. Garcia's demonstrations that organisms are prepared by their heredity to learn some types of cues more easily than others (see Chapter 12) may be compatible with Tolman's formulation of field cognition or learning biases.

Perhaps the greatest of Tolman's contributions was to make cognitive approaches respectable again and, with grace and creative experimentation, to fight against the charges of mentalism raised by the strict behaviorists against cognitive viewpoints. The respect earned by Tolman and Tolman's followers for their extensive experimental efforts facilitated the acceptance of the more radical cognitivism of the gestalt psychologists. This, in turn, opened the gates of academic psychology to a serious consideration of the modern cognitive theories of Bruner, Piaget, Chomsky, Saltz, and information-processing theories by such researchers as Donald Norman (Chapter 11).

Gestalt Learning Theory: Wertheimer, Köhler, Koffka, and Lewin

At the same time that Watson was initiating the reaction in America to the introspective structuralism of Titchener, Max Wertheimer (1880–1943), Wolfgang Köhler (1887–1967), Jurt Koffka (1887–1941), and Kurt Lewin (1890–1947) were coordinating a similar reaction against the introspectionism of Wundt (Titchener's teacher). All of them spent part of their graduate careers at the University of Berlin; for this reason, they are sometimes referred to as the Berlin group. Wertheimer, Köhler, and Koffka met at Frankfort-on-the-Main and coordinated their ideas closely. Wertheimer, Köhler, and Lewin all held academic posts at the University of Berlin, although Lewin's version of gestalt theory is different enough from that of the three other gestaltists to warrant a separate treatment following the discussion of their mainstream gestalt theory.

Origins of the Gestalt Movement

In 1910, while on a vacation trip, Wertheimer became interested in the **phi phenomenon.** With Köhler and Koffka serving as subjects and experimental colleagues, Wertheimer conducted a series of experiments that were to serve as the basis for the founding of a new school of psychology. The phi phenomenon is the illusion of a single moving light that appears when two (or more) lights are quickly and successively turned on and off. This illusion of apparent motion is, of course, the basis for the apparent movement of many illuminated advertising signs and for motion pictures. The importance of the phi phenomenon is that it shows that the whole of our visual experience cannot always be predicted from a knowledge of individual stimulus events. The reason this occurs, the gestalt psychologists reasoned, is because organisms organize their sensory inputs. Therefore, to understand perception (which is the input for learning), we need to study not only stimuli in the environment but also the principles of organization within the organism. Understanding perception (and, by extension, learning and memory) could only come about through studying perceptual wholes and not by analyzing individual stimuli—to dissect is to distort!

In 1912, one year before the publication of Watson's *Psychology as the Behaviorist Sees It,* Max Wertheimer published his account of the phi phenomenon, *Experimental Studies on the Seeing of Motion,* in which he challenged Wundt's structuralist psychology (in Sahakian, 1976). The focus of this German rebellion, however, was not against seeing consciousness as a legitimate area for psychological investigation, as in Watson's manifesto. Rather, it was directed against the introspectionists' search for the atoms of consciousness. This concern for undivided wholes is reflected in the name **gestalt** psychology (*Gestalt* is a German word meaning whole, pattern, form, or configuration). The battle cry was: "The whole is more than the sum of its parts!" Wertheimer finally fled Nazi Germany and continued to promote the gestalt viewpoint in the United States, ending his career at the New School for Social Research in New York City.

Not many years after the appearance of Wertheimer's pivotal monograph, his colleague Wolfgang Köhler was interned during World War I on Tenerife Island of the Canary Island chain off the coast of Africa. In the four years he was forced to remain on the island, he occupied his time in the productive endeavor of conducting a series of studies on learning and problem solving in apes (chimpanzees). He also studied problem solving in chickens (four years is a long time to stay on an isolated island). As you would expect, chickens differed in problem solving from chimps. For example, in the detour problem, the animal could see a reward through a window but was required to go outside the room, down a hall, and around the outside of the building to get the reward. Chickens had great difficulty solving such problems, but apes did so with ease (Köhler, 1925). Köhler noted that his apes either solved a problem or they did not. Their early efforts did not seem to lead to partial learning of a solution. When they did reach a solution, there was usually a sudden change in their behavior, as if they had "come to see" how the elements of a problem fit together. From these observations, Köhler deduced a major tenet of gestalt doctrine. Insight (sudden or discontinuous learning), not gradual (continuous) trial and error, was the most important mode of learning in higher organisms, given that the organism had perceptual access to the elements necessary to solve the problem. The trial-and-error solutions of the puzzle box problems by Thorndike's cats (see Chapter 3) were explained away as the results of the restricted environment of the puzzle box, which prevented the cats from seeing all the cues related to escaping successfully.

Köhler described other examples of detour behavior (which requires the organism to stop fixating on a goal, to see the goal in relationship to the whole problem situation, and then to move away from the goal in order to obtain the means by which it may finally successfully obtain that goal) and related it to insight in his apes. For example, Sultan (described by Köhler as his brightest chimp) was confronted with a banana hanging from the ceiling of his cage and a pole lying on the floor of the cage at some distance from the banana. At first, Sultan (like most of Köhler's apes) made several unsuccessful attempts to obtain the banana by leaping for it. When this strategy failed, he sat quietly, looking around. Finally, he began to play with the stick and then used the pole to knock the banana down. Note that he had to leave the banana to get the stick (detour behavior) and that the final solution was sudden (insightful). Sultan demonstrated a similar sudden solution when confronted with the more difficult two-stick problem. Again, a period of unsuccessful efforts (trying to knock the banana down, first with one stick and then with the other) was followed by suspended motor activity as Sultan looked over the entire situation. Following this, he went up to the sticks, fitted them together to make one long pole, and obtained the banana. Such sudden insights following presumed introspection have been named "Aha!" experiences.

Sultan excelled in solving other types of problems requiring him to use something in his environment as a tool to reach bananas. He was the only one of Köhler's chimps that spontaneously placed a box under a banana in order to reach it. Six other chimps mastered this problem after they had been shown the solution, through having the box placed under the banana by Köhler. Just watching Sultan was not enough to provoke a solution. Chimps who watched Sultan would leap off the box towards the banana, but they failed to move the box underneath the lure. Once seven chimps had mastered the single box problem, Köhler made the problem more difficult by setting the banana so high that two boxes had to be stacked on top of each other to reach it. The apes did show insight-type solutions of the basic idea of stacking boxes, but only through gradual trial-and-error learning did they begin to make stable structures. One chimp, named Grande, even mastered a four-box problem. Once the idea of stacking boxes had been achieved, little additional time was required for the apes to demonstrate the ability to make more elaborate structures. The apes even mastered combination problems, which required them to stack boxes and then to use a pole to knock down the banana (Köhler, 1925).

Köhler maintained that insight learning was essentially pure cognitive learning based on perceptual processes. The apes were held literally to use "inner sight" in solving the problems. Even slow progress involved a series of small insights rather than the mechanical process of S-R bonding which Thorndike thought explained trial-and-error learning.

Köhler observed sudden or insightful learning in chimpanzees that seemed to show that his subjects perceptually reorganized the elements of a problem rather than blindly learning correct responses. Detour behavior, in which the chimps temporarily moved away from a goal if that was necessary to solve a problem, also occurred. This behavior showed that their responses were not mechanically connected to goal stimuli.

Figure 5.4   Either the two faces stand out as figure or the vase stands out as figure. Which you see as figure is decided in your brain as an active process and is not part of the ambiguous stimulus's essential eliciting properties.

Publication of the English translation of Köhler's research (*The Mentality of Apes,* 1925) and visits to America by the other gestalt theorists brought the new theory vividly to the attention of American psychologists. In the United States, the gestalt theorists formed a dynamic nucleus of opposition to the excesses of the prevailing behavioristic orientation of American academic psychology. Koffka had begun to introduce gestalt ideas in the United States in a series of lectures given at Cornell University in the 1924–1925 academic year, and Köhler continued the introduction as visiting professor at Clark University during 1925–1926. Köhler left Germany in 1934 to escape the Nazi tide and taught at Swarthmore College until his retirement in 1958. He continued his research activities after retirement, in several academic settings, until his death in 1967 (in Sahakian, 1976).

The Laws of Organization for Learning, Memory, and Perception

The core of the argument raised by the gestaltists against the connectionists' analysis of behavior is that behavior cannot be understood as simply the sum of its component parts or as the product of the stimuli present at a given time. Rather, aspects of a situation having relationships to each other are interpreted and perceived as gestalts or wholes. For gestalt theorists, learning is a function of how the organism structures the problem situation rather than merely the stimuli present. This can be seen in the ambiguous drawing in Figure 5.4. Either you see the vase or you see the faces. By shifting your internal mode of organization, you can shift to seeing one **figure** (the meaningful part of the drawing) at one moment and the other figure at the next moment. The part of the drawing which serves only to outline the figure is the background, or the **ground** in gestalt terms. Learning then becomes a matter of "seeing" the correct stimulus patterns, or seeing information as figure, rather than losing it in ground.

In this sense, Köhler's apes were presented with perceptual problems. The ease or difficulty of these problems depended upon their ability to organize what they saw into a figure congruent with solving the problem. If they literally

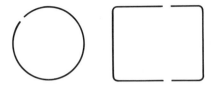

Figure 5.5   Incomplete figures are usually seen as wholes. Two half rectangles are seen as a rectangle. Such incomplete figures are often remembered as wholes, illustrating the law of closure.

"saw" the situation correctly, they had "in-sight." Koffka (1935) wrote that the laws of perception proposed by Wertheimer described how organisms organize the stimuli and memories available to them in a learning situation and therefore should also be considered as laws of learning. Wertheimer's major laws or principles of active internal organization follow.

There is one overriding principle of **Prägnanz,** or "good" form, which states that whatever is perceived will take the best possible form. A physical example of the principle of *Prägnanz* is the tendency of a soap film when lightly distorted to return to a perfect spherical shape as soon as the distorting influence is removed. In general, "good" form is the simplest form possible. The type of "good" form assumed in a particular instance is governed by four additional principles.

1. *Closure:* Closed areas are more readily perceived as units. Things which are not quite closed, or finished, will often be seen and remembered as closed. An example is shown in Figure 5.5. A tendency to want to complete an unfinished problem is also seen as an example of the **closure** principle (the Zeigarnik effect discussed under Lewin).

2. *Proximity:* Units that are close in space or time are perceived as wholes. Köhler's apes required the **proximity** of sticks and bananas before being able to use the sticks to reach the bananas. In speaking, we think of our words as each being a distinct unit, although a visual sonograph tracing may show that the physical sounds occur continuously (more continuously in some people than in others). Proximity could be used to explain why close contiguity of a CS to a US is most advantageous for most types of Pavlovian conditioning. Through the process of being presented together, the CS and the US become equivalent in their power to elicit their reflex (the UR or CR). A gestalt view might be that the CS and the US through their proximity become seen as a whole, and so the CS part of that whole alone comes to elicit the reflex.

3. *Continuity* (also *common direction*): Elements or points are experienced as grouped together if some appear to continue or complete a meaningful series or sequence. This principle is seen as applying to situations in which a rule for extrapolation can be applied, as in letter, design, or number completion tasks. Kaswan (1957) presented subjects with pairs of geometric figures in which the second member of the pair either demonstrated good **continuity** or lack of continuity. Subjects were then shown the first member of the pair and asked to draw the second member. As expected, learning

Good Continuity   Noncontinuity

Figure 5.6   *Examples of pairs of geometric figures showing good continuity and bad continuity.*

and recall of the pairs with good continuity was superior. Examples of good and bad continuity are shown in Figure 5.6.

4. *Similarity:* Stimuli that show **similarities** tend to be noticed and remembered as a grouping if this effect is not overridden by proximity. An example would be understanding and remembering what one person is saying in the midst of a noisy party. The author recalls reading a newspaper article reporting that the best format for freeway signs was using either all capital or all lower-case letters.

A major principle of perception and learning is *Prägnanz*, or good form. This principle says that memories and perceptions are altered to take on a clearer, and usually simpler, form. Four subprinciples which predict how this tends to occur are: (1) closure, (2) proximity, (3) continuity, and (4) similarity. All of these are active internal processes.

As perception is an active process and the world is experienced by each person as a function of his or her own type of activity, so is memory an active process. Rather than remembering the world as it actually happened, we remember it through the filters of gestalt influences on our engrams, or long-term memories.

For something to be remembered easily and naturally (other than through the process of laborious stamping in of rote memories), it must be integrated into a cognitive unit, or "understood." Wertheimer (1959) has summarized and reported a series of studies in which "understanding"-type learning was faster and more generalizable than rote solutions to problems. Examples include having children discover their own methods of estimating the area of a parallelogram rather than simply forcing them to memorize a formula. "Understanding"-type solutions were found to generalize to new, irregular figures.

Artificial techniques for "chunking" new information into previously existing cognitive units are one kind of memory-aiding device. An example of such a device for better learning is a specially created additional association for memorizing, say, the phone number 649-2771 through the (seemingly more) complex sentence of "six forty-niners found two lucky numbers in one." To make learning easier, gestalt theory has pointed out that material must be assimilated either through "understanding" or through integration with previously learned material.

Kurt Lewin's Version of Gestalt Theory

One facet of gestalt theories is that all environments are seen as combinations of ground (background) and figure (what you pay attention to). Lewin took this part of gestalt theory and made it a central factor in his system. In addition, he shifted from the traditional gestalt emphasis on perception, learning, and thinking to focusing on goals, motivational factors, and tension systems. In this way, he was much closer to Tolman than were the other gestalt theorists.

Lewin stresses the phenomenological or personal aspects of each human's environment as inferred from observing the person's behavior. This is called the individual's **life space.** The life space includes a person's goals, which are diagrammed with plus signs to indicate **positive valence,** and the things the person desires to avoid, which are diagrammed with minus signs to indicate **negative valence.** Aspects of a person's life such as fears or environmental restrictions which prevent access to goals are signified by lines or barriers. The thickness of the lines indicates the strengths of the factors blocking access to goals.

Lewin represented these goals, situations to avoid, valences, and barriers in diagrams drawn in accordance with the principles (Lewin, 1936) of **topology,** or the geometry of boundaries between regions. For such a geometry (often called rubber-sheet geometry), the shapes and areas of regions are irrelevant. Forces acting on persons and barriers between persons and their goals are crucial to understanding their perception of their life space.

The topological regions indicate the paths available to a person. To answer the question of which paths would be followed, Lewin added **vectors** to his system. Vectors are forces operating in specific directions and with specific amounts of force. In Lewin's diagrams, they are represented by arrows. The direction of the arrows indicates the direction of a person's approach and avoidance tendencies, and the length of the arrows is intended to be proportional to the strength of the forces acting on the person. An example of a Lewin-type representation of a life space is shown in Figure 5.7.

Lewin's theory and the prediction of learning   The representation made of anyone's assumed life space by themselves or by psychologists is the result of behavioral observations, and both the behavior observed and the subsequent life spaces depicted do change as the result of learning. Lewin delineated four basic types of learning. The first involves changes in the basic structure of the life space. This type of cognitive restructuring can involve making the life space more complex by differentiating unstructured areas, as might be shown if you were to divide up the region of your life space representing psychology into areas representing key ideas from different learning theories. It can also involve restructuring of previously learned cognitions, as when you correct misconceptions or when you make realistic discriminations between reasonable career goals and unlikely ones. The second type of learning involves motivational changes, which in Lewin's system would be represented by changes in valence or changes in the direction and force of vectors. The third type of learning involves changes in where you see yourself in relation to regions of the life space, as when you accept new ideologies or patterns of group identification.

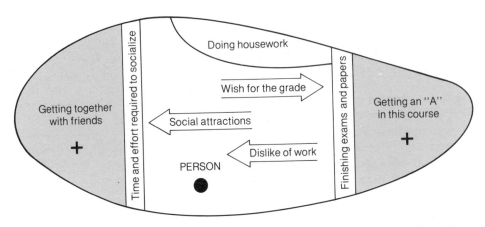

Figure 5.7   A topological diagram of a student's life space. At present, the student is in conflict. The student would like to get good grades as well as to see friends, but the barrier of finishing course work separates the student from the goal of good grades. There are both positive and negative forces (vectors) acting on the barrier. Since the only force operating on socializing is positive, the student is most likely to find the time to socialize. Both goals have a positive valence.

Finally, learning new motor skills (physical coordination) extends your ability to overcome some types of barriers in the life space (Lewin, 1942).

Lewin's focus on the life spaces of individual persons, however, instead of on the development of generally applicable laws of learning precluded his system from being of much use in predicting future learning. The theory is much more useful for post hoc description than for prediction. Still, in a clinical situation with adequate time to determine the life space of a particular client, knowledge of the client's life space might be of use in predicting approach/avoidance conflicts and the like. Lewin's effort to map out those situations having attractant and avoidant effects on the person's behavior parallels the **experimental analysis of behavior** used by operantly oriented psychologists to determine the reinforcers affecting the behavior of their subjects.

Even though Lewin's own work does not offer a precise basis for predicting learning, that is not true of a contribution made by one of his students, Bluma Zeigarnik (1927), who worked with him when he was a professor at the University of Berlin. Bluma Zeigarnik carried out an important series of experiments on Lewin's tension theory (which assumes that behaviors result from internal tensions in the life space rather than from habits). She found that unfinished tasks (which are presumed to be active vectors in the life space) were remembered approximately twice as well as completed tasks. She assumed that the recall of unfinished tasks remained high because at the time of report there still existed an unsatisfied quasineed (remember Lewin's emphasis on motivational factors) which generated a desire to remember and to finish the task. "Unfinished" is, of course, relative to the individual's perceptions of what constitutes satisfactory completion and can be determined by obtaining information from the subject about his/her life space. The pedagogical value of this **Zeigarnik effect** is that leaving students hanging or wanting more at the end of a day's lesson should facilitate better learning (through better memory and more motivation to continue with learning-related tasks). The motivation to continue reading episodes of comic strip stories in the daily paper may reflect the Zeigarnik effect, as would your memory of the previous day's episode.

Lewin developed a version of gestalt theory based on the analysis of each individual's life space. Such a theory is best suited to explain motivational factors, and it can also account for individual differences in what is learned and how this changes behavior. One of Lewin's students found that uncompleted tasks have motivation properties and tend to lead to better learning (the Zeigarnik effect).

Gestalt Positions on Major Issues

Nature/nurture   Because they considered principles to be primarily innately determined and universal, and because they recognized individual differences in capacity, the gestalt psychologists saw learning as much more affected by biological substrates than either behavioristic or Tolmanian psychologists. Acceptance of inherited factors, it must be noted, is much more common among European theorists than American academic psychologists.*

The how of learning   Gestalt theorists took a position on the contiguity/reinforcement issue very similar to that taken by Tolman. Associated elements are combined through an active process by the organism into cognitive units. Only those things attended to (the figure or gestalt), however, will be available for processing. Reward and punishment can act to shift attention and hence what can be learned. Drives energize organisms, placing them in situations where rewards or punishments will act to confirm or disconfirm attempted solutions of problems. The efficacy of practice (creating contiguity) depends upon active processes, the gestalt principles. These principles were developed further and stressed more by the gestaltists than the active processes of Tolman's theory were by Tolman and his followers.

The what of learning   The content of what is learned is molar. Perceptions, cognitions, expectancies—all are large-scale units rather than bonds relating individual stimuli and responses. Further, the gestalt theorists would insist that the whole of what is learned is more than the sum of S-R bonds. Lewin's unit of learning was nothing less than a change in the person's entire life space.

---

* This author has often speculated on the effect of myth and folklore on underlying assumptions about people. In Europe, inherited titles were accepted, while menials aspired to very little. European folklore insists that the baby prince raised by peasants remains a prince. Placed in a princely environment, he will display the appropriate princely behaviors. American folklore or myth teaches that the social class of your parents is much less important than what you do. With sufficient hard work, any person can become almost anything. Is it possible that the strong environmentalism of Watson or Skinner resulted from an early conditioning of attitudes through exposure to the Horatio Alger story?

Continuity/noncontinuity, use of animal data, and determinism　　Although the gestalt theorists recognized that learning can occur gradually through a rote process, they characterized this process of learning as inefficient and the resulting learning as situationbound, stupid, and rigid. Gestalt emphasis was on insight and understanding, which are usually discontinuous and sudden processes.

Although Köhler used data from apes, most of the gestalt data was derived from human experimentation. The gestalt attitude was that to understand human behavior, one should study humans. In seeing organisms as making active choices, their position was nondeterministic. In regarding these choices, however, as influenced by perceptions which reflect the effects of current stimulation, as modified by the inherited brain mechanisms responsible for the gestalt principles of organization, the gestaltists had a deterministic element in their theory.

Perspective and Applications

In general, psychologists and others of the humanistic persuasion have found gestalt approaches enormously attractive. Conversely, the more "hard boiled" of the academic psychologists have resisted all cognitive approaches in favor of quantitative and molecular theorizing. The gestalt psychologists have been accused of relying too heavily on individual description and of avoiding clear, systematic development of their principles. Although they described principles such as similarity, it is difficult to determine when and how much each principle will affect perception and learning. This loose aspect of gestalt theory makes it difficult to predict individual behavior precisely from the general laws, and many gestalt "predictions" allow room for ad hoc or after-the-experiment interpretations of the results.

Consequently, it is in those behavioral science areas where tight theorizing is not as greatly stressed that the major impact of applied gestalt theories has taken place. These areas include the use of the **discovery learning** technique in elementary schools, which emphasizes the child's arriving at her or his own understanding rather than simply having rules "stamped in" in the Guthrian or Thorndikian mode (Hill, 1971), and in gestalt therapy. Gestalt therapy (greatly popularized by the late Fritz Perls) adopted Lewin's concept of breaking through barriers, developing new social learning by a process in which neurotically stupid conditioned responses were acted out and finally understood, and closure of painful memories of uncompleted interactions and experiences was achieved. By making better gestalts of a person's memories, the destructive motivational (Zeigarnik) effects of events experienced as incomplete were to be reduced or eliminated. This process will be further discussed in Chapter 6. A fairly pure Lewinian influence can still be detected in a wide range of principles of sensitivity/encounter group operation.

Both the principles of perceptual organization and the need to put the organism back into the S-R formulation are now widely accepted within mainstream American psychology. The effects of internal biases on learning and memory are also accepted by all but the most hard-line behaviorists. The early simplistic behaviorist theories have been broadened and made more sophisticated in order to handle phenomena such as insight within an associationist framework. For more than thirty years, gestalt psychology has defended cognitive alternatives to behaviorism. Current cognitive approaches, as well as the so-called "third force," or humanistic movement, owe a large debt to the gestalt research that demonstrated inadequacies in simple mechanistic S-S and S-R models. At this point, gestalt theory has succeeded in having its major principles accepted within psychology but during the process has gradually faded away as a distinct movement. This demise of the gestalt movement was related to the deaths of Wertheimer, Koffka, Köhler, and Lewin—not to experimental repudiation.

Maria Montessori (1865–1952): A Biocognitive Sensory-Motor Theory

Origins of the Montessori Method

Maria Montessori was the first woman to earn a medical degree from the University of Rome. As a result of the sexism rampant in Italian society of that time, she was not allowed to practice medicine in the hospitals and turned to working with feeble-minded children. In this job, her keen skills of observation and her scientific training enabled her to develop effective methods for increasing the responsiveness of the children to the point where many of them were reported to be functioning normally. It was during this work that the main points of her theory and many of her ingenious devices for promoting sensory-motor development originated. In 1907, she set up a school (the Casa dé Bambini) located in a tenement building in Rome, where she was to apply and refine her theory for many years. During this time, she continued her observational research, which she considered to be in the tradition of biology, comparing it to the techniques of the French naturalist, Fabre.

> Fabre did not take his insects into his study and experiment with them there. Rather he left them free in the environment most suited to them; and—without letting his presence in any way interfere with their natural functions and mode of living—patiently observed them until they revealed to him their marvelous secrets. [in Standing, 1959, p. 4]

In 1912, her first book in English, outlining the major points of her theory, was published, provoking a positive response from educators (Standing, 1959). It appears, however, to have been ignored by academic psychologists. Adoption of her procedures was at first widespread. By 1916, there were 200 authorized Montessori schools in the United States (Spock and Hathaway, 1968). The number of Montessori schools was reduced as Dewey's less restrictive "functional approach to education" became popular between the world wars, but it is presently increasing again.

Montessori's Maturational Model of Children's Learning

Dr. Montessori was concerned with the whole child. She provided activities that dealt with the child's diet, exercise, mental health, and intellectual and social development. Her goal was "scientific pedagogy."

Our aim in education in general is two-fold, biological and social. From the biological side we wish to help the natural development of the individual, from the social standpoint it is our aim to prepare the individual for the environment. [Montessori, 1912, p. 215]

To reach this goal, Montessori said that the school situation must permit the free natural manifestations of the child's behavior. She believed in **sensitive periods** for the development of different cognitive abilities, and that interference by adults with a child's natural tendencies to learn the things appropriate to his or her particular stage of development during these sensitive periods would cause enduring deficits. This view of maturational changes determining what can be and will be learned at different stages of the child's development led Montessori to postulate that the teaching procedures which were applicable for adults were not appropriate for children's immature nervous systems. Several of these sensitive periods are described. From around one and a half to five years old, the child is especially susceptible to learning language. The following message illustrates the Montessori position on sensitive periods very well:

So great is the child's capacity for words at this stage that he can pick up two or three languages at the same time without any special effort. Never again will he be able to learn the pronunciation of a language perfectly nor with such ease. It would seem that children have such a void within them, waiting to be filled with words, that at this stage, they sometimes make up an extra nonsense language of their own to satisfy it. [Standing, 1959, p. 38]

The concept of an innate readiness to learn language will also be further discussed in the section on Chomsky in Chapter 11, and sensitive periods in general in the section on imprinting in Chapter 12.

Other major stages are a stage for learning written words from five to six and a half years, and a stage for learning grammar which follows the sensitive period for written word learning. These free natural tendencies to learn different skills during different sensitive periods seem to be innate drives to learn specific things and perform certain types of behavior.

Another of Maria Montessori's basic principles was that liberty is activity and that you achieve discipline through liberty. The composition of her schools include an open-air space in which the children are free to come and go and to work at any activity they desire. To preserve the liberty of the child, the teacher in a Montessori school has to assume a new role. The teacher is a passive observer who must be sure to avoid arresting the child's spontaneous movements. The teacher's purpose is to lead the child toward independence.

Maria Montessori believed that children's nervous systems are prepared to learn certain types of things during each of several sensitive periods, or maturational stages. She also thought that children can best learn these things if the teacher assumes a passive role and allows the children to choose their own learning activities.

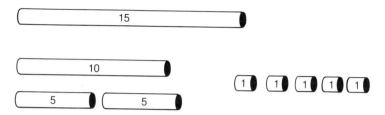

Figure 5.8   Counting rods. The rods are usually of different colors. In this example, the two "5" rods are placed together below the "10" rod, showing the child that ten divided by two is five or that two fives make up ten. The rods allow the child a visual check on number relationships. The child could also see that five "1s" and a "10" equal the "15" rod. The rods allow the children to develop a perceptual understanding of arithmetic.

The Didactic Materials

The teacher, or directress (as Montessori calls her), has the difficult position of trying to direct the child from the concrete to the abstract, from sensations to ideas and on to the association of ideas, without interfering with the child's liberty. The method the teacher uses is to isolate "inner attention" and focus it upon the child's perceptions. The first part of this task, the development of attention, is produced by the inherent structures of the educational materials or **didactic materials** developed by Montessori in response to particular teaching problems. The use of "self-teaching" tasks, games, and teaching aids is perhaps the most unique aspect of this system. These materials were developed by the empirical method of trying out a wide range of materials on children, noting which led to measurable performance gains in skills such as writing, and then retaining only the most successful of the materials (Montessori, 1912).

The didactic materials embody the principles of Montessori's ideas of learning. First, to preserve the child's sense of liberty and independence, the materials are autoeducational. That is, they contain within themselves the control of errors through providing the child with feedback on the success of his or her efforts. They are thus self-correcting, and the child doing something wrong knows it without the intervention of the directress. The only legitimate point at which the directress should interfere is when the child uses the didactic materials in a way in which it cannot be effective in having its autoeducational effect. Thus, a child using counting rods as hammers would be corrected and shown how to use the rods to learn number relationships (Figure 5.8).

The didactic materials are not only autoeducational but also intrinsically reinforcing. Only those materials that were played with spontaneously by her original test groups of children were retained for testing of their self-teaching properties. In the sense that the child can work with the didactic materials at her or his own pace and that they provide immediate feedback with high levels of positive reinforcement, the didactic materials are similar to teaching machines (see Chapter 6). External rewards were explicitly rejected by Montessori, who believed that the success and achievement felt by the child were sufficient reward.

Montessori stresses the notion that competence and epistemic motives exist from the start of life, and the mere presence of appropriate activities will arouse them without the need of extraneous reinforcers for learning. The child always succeeds because he is allowed to move at his own pace. [Kohlberg, 1968, p. 112]

These materials are adapted to cause the child to exercise the senses and form a graded sequence. "The education of the senses has, as its aim, the refinement of the differential perception of stimuli by means of repeated exercises" (Montessori, 1912, p. 173). This goal of training sensory abilities as a prerequisite to learning is why the Montessori theory is here labeled a sensory-motor theory. One sort of instructive matter, for example, a series of blocks with solid geometric forms, educates the eye to the differential perception of dimensions. The first property of the material, however, is that it attracts the spontaneous attention of the child.

Each didactic material trains a specific sensory modality. As a child approaches the material, his attention is developed, which in turn allows mental activity to develop. This focus on attention is, of course, also found in Russian psychology (see Chapter 8) and in the theories of Tolman and the gestalt school presented in this chapter.

Another aspect of the didactic materials is that they create a "prepared environment" which:

is designed to help the child achieve a sense of himself, self-mastery and mastery of his environment through the successful execution and repetition of apparently simple tasks which are nonetheless linked to the cultural expectations the child faces in the context of his total development. [Rambusch, 1962, p. 71]

It is important that Montessori believed the school must be prepared, in the sense that each toy is in its place from day to day. She felt that it is critical for children to have this type of order presented to them. For a very young child, learning operates best in an environment filled with familiar stimuli, to which new activities and associations may be added. This means starting from order. Order, to the young child, means finding things in the same place, being able to count on repetition and ritual. Clutter distracts attention from the autoeducational function of the didactic materials. From this external order, the child may develop an internal order of coherent cognitions and learn to govern impulses. Internal order facilitates concentration on learning.

Montessori believed that the child's response repertoire did not emerge automatically as a function of brain development. Instead, she believed that early cognitive experience was important for later development. In particular, the senses must be trained because of their importance in the child's informational interactions with the environment (Hunt in Montessori, 1964). The didactic materials used in sensory training were designed to be used in an ordered sequence, which was intended to teach children the basic skills they would need for the subsequent learning of reading and writing.

After all this preparation in areas related to reading and writing, the teaching of concrete abilities begins. In the teaching of reading and writing, Montessori's technique of graded stimuli is used to a large extent. This procedure, related to the fading or vanishing technique advocated by Skinner for classroom use, is discussed in Chapters 6 and 10. The following description will illustrate this technique. In the Montessori class, writing is broken down into its component parts. The child learns writing through a gradual acquisition of small muscle control in a procedure similar to some suggested by Guthrie (see Chapter 2). The instructive materials for writing (which comes before reading) are large intaglio letters in a metal form. The child can use his fingers to trace the letters of the alphabet. With a progression of sensory tasks, the teacher serves her major role in the teaching of reading and writing.

> She aims to bring each new sensory experience to the child with a minimum number of words and movements, thus confining his attention to the central fact of the experience. [Ward, 1913, p. 83]

The didactic materials for reading consist of slips of paper or cards which have clear, large script; words or phrases are written on these slips. Initially, the teacher presents the most familiar words to the children. As words are learned, familiar cards are presented first, gradually working up to the least familiar words. In this way the child learns to associate language with the printed word. In the "keyword" procedure, the process progresses from easy, extreme stimuli to difficult, less visually arresting stimuli.

The most unique feature of the Montessori method is the use of self-teaching and self-reinforcing educational materials (didactic materials). Graded series of these materials were designed to teach specific sensory skills for each of the sensitive periods of a child's maturation.

Research on the Effectiveness of the Montessori Method

A virtue of psychology as a discipline is its commitment to testing ideas by experimentation. This is not so true of the field of education.

In spite of the limited cooperation of Montessori teachers, there has developed a body of empirical research on the effectiveness of application of the Montessori method. Laosa and McNichols (1975) summarize some of this research and conclude that Montessori schools are somewhat effective in raising general intelligence as measured by IQ tests such as the *Stanford-Binet*. Their effectiveness was greater when perceptual-conceptual and perceptual-motor tasks were given, which suggests task-specific effects of the didactic materials. Kohlberg (1968) has found Montessori preschool training to be effective in increasing the attention span of low-income children; the correlation between increased attention span and increased IQ was .65. Because many of the Montessori tasks are designed to help the children concentrate, the modest IQ test gains reported earlier may reflect better visual and auditory concentration on IQ test tasks. Kohlberg failed to find any relationship between Montessori schooling and ability to perform logical tasks. He interpreted his results as throwing into doubt Montessori's contention that cognitive operations rested directly on sensory experience.

Some research on the effect of Montessori training on creativity has shown gains in creativity, and other research has found declines. This may reflect methodological problems, including inadequate control groups, lack of cooperation from Montessori officials, and differences in the extent to which Montessori's ideas are implemented in the official schools certified by the Montessori family compared to the nonofficial schools based loosely upon her philosophy.

Montessori's Positions on Major Issues

Nature/nurture   Montessori's discussion of "instinctual needs," capacity differences, and maturational limitations on learning all make her theory the most nature-biased of the theories covered in this text thus far. In her writings she often made reference to biological concepts such as sensitive periods, and she considered her methods those of naturalistic observation. She believed, however, that the development of intelligence is not fixed by heredity.

The how of learning   Although Montessori's excitement over insight learning might lead one to suppose that she would seek to reduce the amount of rote activity in her classrooms, quite the opposite is the case. Montessori believed that repetition or temporal contiguity was a necessity for the child's learning behavior to proceed normally. This did not mean that she advocated rote education, but that she believed that the repetitive character of behavior spontaneously emitted by the child is associated with the development of emerging mental abilities which will later burst forth in an "explosion," or insight experience. Most connectionists' efforts to explain noncontinuous learning have relied upon similar formulations of the gradual development of simple small learnings (or S-R/S-S bonds for the behaviorists) until there is a sudden, observable change in performance, labeled an "insight." Montessori, however, viewed repetitious functions very differently from the behaviorists. She believed that repetition allowed the maturation of developing cognitive abilities and served the child's innate need for duplication and predictability through redundancy in its environment. Montessori saw repetition as leading to the "polarization of attention" and aiding in the child's concentration on its task. Her emphasis on attentional mechanisms was somewhat similar to that of the gestalt theorists.

The need for repetition is served by collective activities, such as marching around the room (Montessori, 1912), and by allowing a child to do the movements intrinsic in a given toy as often as desired. The child, she believed, will stop and move on to the next toy as soon as there is satisfaction with achievement on the first.

The what of learning   Montessori did not believe that external reinforcers are necessary for learning; her unique position on contiguity was discussed in the previous section. Although Montessori, like the other cognitive theorists reviewed, discusses the gradual acquisition of small muscular movements, she was more interested in the noncontinuous learning of ideas and understanding. Montessori (Standing, 1959) discusses "explosions" in which the child suddenly shows a spontaneous leap of the "mind" to a new and higher level. At these times, the child's intellect discovers in a "flash" some new law or relationship, bringing a moment of sudden joy. The description of such moments has much in common with Köhler's description of the ape, Sultan, showing insight behavior.

Perspective

Unlike many others interested in the learning of children, Maria Montessori was totally committed to putting her ideas into practice. In common with many other theories whose applications were popularized (such as Freud's), her theories have a distinct ideological and dogmatic orientation. To some extent, this is the fault of some of her overzealous followers, who, in their desire to protect the insights of the *dottoressa,* have resisted innovation and experimental tests of the various aspects of the theories. Maria Montessori herself was less dogmatic. She (1912) tells a story of how she once visited a Montessori classroom and proposed an improvement in a procedure she observed. The teacher, who did not recognize her, exclaimed: "Maria Montessori would never allow any changes in her perfect system!" Whereupon Dr. Montessori revealed her true identity and discussed the virtues of a more open attitude.

Given that the theory of learning and development proposed by Montessori has had such a powerful influence on education, why has it been ignored by academic psychology as a serious learning theory? Many humanistically oriented psychologists (who are more likely to be teaching developmental psychology than learning) send their students to observe in Montessori classrooms. Piaget was also introduced to American academic psychology by developmental psychologists. However, the resistance to outside experimenters conducting research in Montessori schools, the emotional prose of many of her chroniclers (see the example that follows), and isolation of her advocates within schools of education apart from learning theorists within departments of psychology have all contributed to the exclusion of her theory from serious consideration in most psychology courses about learning.

> The Montessori method is not a closed system, discovered once and for all, henceforth to be applied unchangingly. It is continually growing like a living thing, growing in depth, richness, and variety.
>
> This applies not only with respect to the wide application of its principles, but also with regard to the depth of those principles themselves. The more one studies them, the more one finds in them to study. The reason for this is twofold. In the first place, the principles, based on the profound and secret forces of life, are as limitless as life itself; and secondly, on account of the extraordinary genius of the founder of the system. [Standing, 1959, p. 6]

In addition, the profound environmentalist bias of early American behaviorists tended to reject any formulations as biologically or instinctually oriented as Montessori's theory. While her writing is no less systematic than that of the gestalt theorists, she was not a psychologist, she did not come to the United States to live and defend her theory, and (most important), she did not engage in the "duel-by-experiment" testing of her theory. This latter is an intrinsic part of the process by which a theorist is supposed to act upon his or her aspirations to scientific rigor.

Through the acceptance of Piaget (who does not consider himself a psychologist, either), however, maturational factors in learning have become newly respectable. This author predicts that Montessori's model will gain increased attention in psychology.

Norbert Wiener's *Cybernetics:* A Possible Gateway to Tomorrow

Although all the theories presented in this chapter have focused on active internal processes rather than on environmental contingencies of stimuli and responses, none has provided concrete models of how such inner processes might function. In the next few pages, you will see an approach which attempts to objectify these inner processes. Cybernetics uses the powerful system languages of engineering and mathematics, as well as machine and computer models of possible internal learning processes, to simulate possible active processes taking place within real organisms. These theories appear near the end of the early history of learning theories (pre-1955) and have had a great deal of impact on some of the approaches to be reported in Part 2 of this book.

The term **cybernetics** was first used in its modern form by Norbert Wiener (1948) to refer to the study of control mechanisms or self-governing systems (Apter, 1970). The word is derived from the Greek word *Kybernetike,* which means roughly "steersmanship," and was used by Plato in *The Republic* to refer to the science of piloting ships. Since it is concerned with devices that keep such operations as the course of a sailing ship within appropriate limits through monitoring the effects of their own actions, cybernetics is also called **feedback** theory. The computer simulation of learning and behavior has, to a large extent, emerged as part of this new and exciting discipline of cybernetics (Apter, 1970).

There are two types of feedback processes. The first is **negative feedback,** involving adjustments in a **homeostatic** system that tends to keep it in a steady state by compensating for deflections from that state. An example is a thermostat and a furnace. When the temperature falls from the preset desired (homeostatic optimum) point, the thermostat turns the furnace on until the temperature rises enough to shut off the thermostat. The temperature in the room is the input or stimulus, and the activity of the furnace is the output or the response of the system. The feedback is called negative because it produces a response in the opposite direction to changes in the stimulus of falling or rising room temperatures. Such systems are also called servomechanisms, and cybernetics is an attempt to apply their principles to problems in psychology and related fields. Such systems are prototypes for all adaptive systems in that they adapt to changes in their environments to try to maintain homeostatic equilibrium (Wiener, 1948).

Cybernetics and the concept of negative feedback can be applied to simple behavioral processes such as the execution of skilled acts of the type of reaching for a glass of beer. When the progress of the hands deviates from a path which will intercept the glass, inputs from the eyes and the muscles warn the person that a mistake is being made (assuming they are sober enough to notice), and corrections will be applied. The same principles of negative feedback can be applied to complex, purposive, goal-directed behaviors of the type described by Tolman. If you are with a date and your behaviors begin to produce negative reactions in your partner, you will (if sensitive to the information or inputs produced by the partner in response to your actions) alter your behavior until the partner's negative reactions cease. A system may control its behavior, using negative feedback, not only to maintain a state it is already in, but to attempt to achieve some state it has not yet been in. If you are driving to pick up your date by a particular time, you not only need to watch that your car does not leave the road, but also that you arrive at your destination on time. This is accomplished by watching cues to your locations at various times and checking your watch in order to adjust your speed appropriately. Such examples illustrate behavior actively governed not only by present cues but also by expectancies (cognitive maps?).

As mentioned earlier, there are two types of feedback process. The second type is called **positive feedback,** which amplifies deviations in performance from the original homeostatic levels. An example might be responding to increased success in dating by expending more effort in dating to increase your success still more. This is much like the increases in behavior related to reinforcement described by the operant reinforcement theorists.

The feedback model represents a middle position between connectionist and cognitive theory. Like connectionist theory, it is concerned with fairly mechanistic processes related to stimuli and responses. In this case the stimuli are the inputs, the responses are the outputs, and the individual is the system. Learning is the changes in behavior occasioned by either negative or positive feedback, which provide the stimuli to control responses. Feedback theory, however, is concerned with the ways in which purposive behaviors are maintained by flexible control systems that are responsive to events in the environment and internal expectancies.

Like Lewin's theory about purposeful behavior, cybernetics is less a theory of learning than a new descriptive language. Topics as diverse as trying to reduce hunger drives through operant responses to approaching incentives with positive valences and following the paths in Lewinian life spaces can all be treated within the cybernetic framework. This system language emphasizes the continuous control of sequences of behavior, thus attending to the fine detail of molecular analysis, combined with the flexible, purposeful view of molar analysis of the cognitive theorists (Wiener, 1948).

Wiener was the first to use the term "cybernetics" to refer to the study of mechanisms controlling functions of organisms and machines. Much of this control is effected either by positive and negative feedback or by the system's responding to the consequences of its actions by increasing or decreasing those actions respectively.

Machine and Computer Analogs of Learning

Walter (1953) produced an electronic machine, one version of which was named *Machina docilis* (the teachable machine), which would ride about on its wheels,

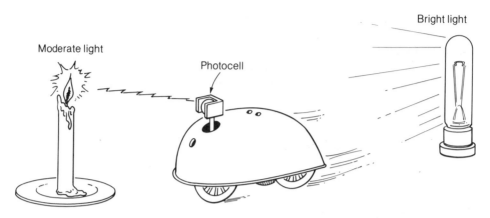

Figure 5.9   A general representation of a Walter's learning machine. The head is attached to the front wheel of the tricycle wheels and turns the machine in the direction it is "looking" with the photocell in the head. The body shell is loosely attached to the inner mechanisms. When obstructed, the photocell functions as an oscillator, causing the machine to advance and retreat until the obstacle blocking the shell has been dislodged or the machine has moved around it (after Walter, 1953).

approaching lights of moderate intensity and moving away from very bright lights (see Figure 5.9). It could be "conditioned" to approach a whistle that had been paired with the turning on of a "reinforcing light" (which allowed its photocells to recharge its batteries) and could show both forgetting and extinction of this response. It would avoid obstacles, show avoidance of stimuli with kicks, and all this with no complex electronic brain. Models such as this demonstrate that many of the phenomena of learning *could* be produced by fairly simple mechanisms in the brain as well as by fairly simple electronic devices.

Estes's model of learning has been tested with computers, and computer analogies of complex cognitive processes have been developed (summarized in Feigenbaum and Feldman, 1963). It must be remembered that these systems have been created to test certain assumptions about how organisms might learn by programming the principles the theorist thinks could apply to organisms into the computer. If the machine generates results like those obtained by research with real organisms, then the assumptions at least remain viable analogies of learning in organisms. Machine learning, however, does not prove that organisms learn in exactly the same ways.

Wiener's Positions on Major Issues and Perspective

It is awkward to try to pin down the cybernetic-machine-computer theorists on their positions on the kinds of issues dividing more conventional approaches to learning. What can one say about instincts in a machine? Only that a machine or computer program can be constructed to simulate either instincts or environmental control. As to the whats and hows of learning, the whats are alterations in the way the electronics and storage systems function, and the hows are a matter of electrical engineering and skill at programming. "Learning" in such systems may be either continuous or discontinuous, at the discretion of the designer (or, in different situations, both). Being willing to make generalizations from artificial creations to learning in animals, humans, or both seems to imply at least a limited acceptance of the principle of equipotentiality, dependent upon the degree to which the creators of the machines assume that the processes of their creation simulate the processes in actual organisms. Since such systems are deliberately designed, determinism is obviously built in. What this says about determinism in organic creatures is unclear. The usefulness of such approaches in helping us to understand learning processes in humans and animals may only be judged by the extent to which predictions of the behaviors of such artificial systems predict behavior in real organisms. Even then, such congruence may only reflect the fact that different processes may yield similar results. At this point, it is too early to determine whether the approaches sampled in this section of this chapter point to the wave of the future or whether they are only another attempt to generalize the prestige of the physical sciences to psychology by adopting their terminology.

Chapter Perspective

The approaches of this chapter represent a major challenge to the behaviorists' assumption that behavior could be understood by focusing on events in the environment. By turning their analysis inward to the hidden world of the organism's perceptions of the world, they both increased our knowledge about such possible internal mechanisms and forced the behaviorists into abandoning overly simplistic mechanistic views of learning. As we shall see in Part 2 of this book, this position has forced the entire field of learning to become more cognitively oriented. Behavioristic and cognitive approaches still differ greatly, however, and this will be shown clearly in the applications of both approaches, to be discussed in the next chapter.

Key Terms

closure	ground	positive valence
cognitive map	homeostatic	*Prägnanz*
continuity	information-processing theories	proximity
cybernetics		purposive
didactic materials	latent learning	sign
discovery learning	life space	sign-gestalt
docile	negative feedback	significate
experimental analysis of behavior	negative valence	sensitive period
feedback	partial reinforcement effect	similarity
figure	phi phenomenon	topology
gestalt	positive feedback	vector
		Zeigarnik effect

Annotated Bibliography

A classic article illustrating the main points of Tolman's theory is "Cognitive Maps in Rats and Men" (*Psychological Review*, 1948, 55, 189–208). For a readable broad introduction to the gestalt theorists, I would recommend W. S. Sahakian, *Introduction to the psychology of learning* (Chicago: Rand McNally, 1976), which has some nice photographs of cognitive chimpanzees piling boxes to reach bananas. A good basic introduction to the life and principles of Maria Montessori is J. McV. Hunt, *Maria Montessori; The Montessori method* (New York: Schocken Books, 1964). A somewhat emotional but very readable approach to her work is E. M. Standing, *Maria Montessori, Her life and work* (Fresno, Ca.: Academy Guild Press, 1959). For those students interested in provocative books, I suggest N. Wiener, *Cybernetics* (New York: John Wiley & Sons, 1948) for the machine approach to behavior.

6

The Payoff: Applications of Selected Learning Theories

Theories have two general kinds of uses. The first is to explain a range of phenomena in order to integrate related data and to suggest directions for new research. This use is often mainly of interest to scientists. The second is to suggest applications for the real world. This second use is of far more interest to the public at large, who would like to see some practical benefit result from the tax dollars expended on research grants. To a large extent, nonscientists judge the worth of theories (perhaps unfairly) by their utility as a source of ways to improve the lot of humankind. Applications of theoretical principles in psychology tend to be of two types: those directed towards improving learning in school situations and those directed towards the elimination of maladaptive behaviors. Some applications, such as those for reducing disruptive behaviors of school children, may serve both purposes.

Many suggestions for applications have already been mentioned in the five previous chapters. Learning theories have been so productive in generating applications, however, that additional coverage seems warranted. This chapter will review some selected applications developed from theoretical principles originating prior to the 1960s. Later innovations will be the subject of Chapter 10, in the second part of this text.

If theories were to be judged solely by the diversity of their uses, then early applications developed from the behavioristic-connectionist approaches (such as Pavlov's) would support the dominance of these theories over cognitive theories. This chapter opens with the extension of Pavlovian principles to making the process of childbirth less frightening and painful. The history of efforts to use these applications of contiguity conditioning in modified form in the Western world—specifically, to a problem of maladaptive behavior (fear in childbirth)—will then be reviewed, followed by a brief summary of efforts to use the principles of classical conditioning in the treatment of other types of maladaptive fears—the neurotic phobias treated by clinical psychologists. Next, applications of reinforcement principles as developed by Skinner for the training of animals and small children and students will be presented. Finally, the chapter concludes with a treatment for fears and conflicts developed from the gestalt cognitive tradition. This gestalt therapy has currently earned a wide following among nonbehaviorist clinical psychologists and other mental health professionals.

All these applications should reinforce the view that the study of learning is important for more than purely academic reasons. Psychology's claims to greater usefulness are likely to be made on the basis of the kinds of applications presented in this chapter and following chapters. For any of you going into either education or the mental health professions, an understanding of how applications follow theoretical principles is a valuable sort of learning, indeed. As you will see, it is from the study of learning that most of psychology's useful contributions to society are likely to originate. As you read this material, try to relate each application to the basic learning principles previously presented. Let us now examine some applications.

Extension of Pavlovian Principles to the Process of Childbirth

As you will read in Chapter 8, one area of advancement in the study of classical conditioning since the death of Pavlov has been in gaining a greater understanding of the workings of the second signal system (thoughts and words) in man. Not only can verbal cues serve as traditional CSs (as when you tell someone to "turn right"), but also meaning can be conditioned **(semantic conditioning).** In addition, research originating in the Soviet Union has shown that the functions of the internal organs and circulatory system can be conditioned using either words or conventional physical CSs as cues. This procedure, combining an external CS to elicit an internal reflex or response, is called **extero-interoceptive** conditioning. An example might be pairing the word "red" with shock (a US which raises blood pressure). Eventually, "red" will become a CS and elicit the CR of raised blood pressure. Nonverbal CSs, such as touches, tones, or lights, can also be used.

Russian scientists' attempts to explain pain in childbirth illustrate a combination of findings in the areas of verbal or semantic conditioning and extero-interoceptive conditioning. For example, Chertok (1959) reports an experiment in which a tube containing water heated to 63° C (which was experienced as painfully hot) was applied to the skin and elicited vasoconstriction. This US was preceded by the sound of a bell, which later elicited the CR of vasoconstriction and the experience of pain. Still later, the words "I ring" were sufficient to elicit these CRs.

Thus, words can evoke painful internal states in accordance with Pavlov's interpretation of second signal functions.

> "Speech," Pavlov wrote, "is a real conditioning stimulus, just the same as other stimuli common to men and animals: but it also is quite unique. No qualitative nor quantitative comparison can be made between them. Speech, on account of the life experiences of the adult man, is linked with all the internal or external excitation impinging the cortex—it is their signal, and it replaces them." [Chertok, 1959, p. 102]

This suggests that the association of verbal CSs, which elicit fear CRs with cues originating in uterine functions, could produce second-order conditioning fear. This second signal system interaction with the uterus was assumed to be cortically controlled. Some of Pavlov's followers were able to demonstrate conditioned reflexes of the uterus and interpreted these results to mean that the cerebral cortex has a functional relationship with the uterus and its receptors and muscles (Chertok, 1959).

This view of the role of the cortex in controlling uterine functions and pain originating from these functions led to the development of hypnosuggestive methods for verbal obstetrical analgesia. You will recall from the discussion of inhibition in Chapter 1 that Pavlov thought hypnosis was the result of localized cortical inhibition. The researchers assumed that the excitatory reactions to verbal stimuli presented by a hypnotist caused an inhibitory counterreaction, or negative induction effect. Work on hypnosuggestive methods, while continued from 1926 to 1951, was based on the idea that pain associated with childbirth was cortically mediated through the second signal system. Some Russian researchers, however, attacked this theory, suggesting instead that the pains of childbirth were "mixed pains," having both semantic (second signal system or thought) and visceral components. This meant that not all the pain of childbirth could be attributed to the mother's conditioned fears about childbirth. Unconditioned pain reactions arising from uterine receptors also had to be dealt with.

Because of this and other problems, a conference was held on obstetrical analgesia in Leningrad in 1951. Although the question of the source of birth pains continued to be debated, Velvovski's method of preventing birth pains through psychological means (psychoprophylaxis) was accepted. The procedures of the psychoprophylactic method were subsequently published as the state-approved method of childbirth in the Soviet Union. By the 1956 conference on verbal analgesia in Kiev, both theory and procedures had become fairly standardized. These procedures were designed to deal with conditioned pain cues by preventing verbal or thought stimuli from eliciting pain reactions (prophylactic action). Therapeutic actions directed towards the elimination of unconditioned pain were designed to create prolonged cortical excitation, which was thought then to induce inhibitory actions on the cortical pain analyzers. The "excitatory" effects of verbal suggestions designed to create a belief that childbirth was not necessarily painful were seen as directly resulting in inhibition of pain. Consistent with the Pavlovian view that second signal system stimuli operated through a classical conditioning mechanism, teaching and suggestion were extensively used in each of the five principal stages of the psychoprophylactic method.

First, the mother-to-be was given a physical and psychological examination by a physician. Her medical problems and type of nervous system (dominated by excitation or inhibition) were noted in order to individualize the conditioning procedures.

Second, she was taught about the physiology of birth and why birth can and should be painless. Educated mothers were given lectures on Pavlov's theory as it applied to the birth process.

Third, she was coached in what stimulation to expect when giving birth and how to note and time contractions. The attempt was to prevent the association of fear-eliciting second signal system cues with the stimuli caused by labor contractions.

Fourth, she was taught several pain-reducing procedures, including techniques assumed to create the prolonged states of cortical excitation conducive to inductive inhibition of pain and techniques for the voluntary control of uterine muscles.

Fifth, she was educated in what to expect and do during each stage of the labor process. She was also given lectures on the joys of motherhood and placed in contact with other women who had successfully used the psychoprophylactic method during childbirth, in order to "consolidate second signal system conditioning of a positive nature."

Chertok (1959) cites a wide range of benefits of the psychoprophylactic method, including a reduction in average labor time of two hours for first-time mothers compared to mothers having drug-assisted births. Forceps deliveries were decreased from 12.7 percent to 8.6 percent and stillbirths from 2.1 percent to .6 percent. Although these results seem to support the view that the psychoprophylactic method is effective, its success in extending the range of Pavlovian conditioning principles seems less clear. To what extent the method represents a rigorous application of classical conditioning, rather than an enthusiastic application of Pavlovian terminology, may be difficult to determine.

The Read Method

Grantly Dick Read was an English physician. Around 1914, his obstetric work in the poor district of Whitechapel in the East End of London led him to the revelation that women who expected to have painful deliveries had painful deliveries, while women who expected no pain had none. From this work, he concluded that fear caused tension in uterine muscles, which caused resistance at the outlet of the womb. Resistance and tension, in turn,

> give rise to real pain, because the uterus is supplied with organs which record pain set up by excessive tension. Therefore, fear, pain and tension are the three evils which are not normal to the natural design, but which have been introduced in the course of civilization by the ignorance of those who have been concerned with attendance at childbirth. [in Chertok, 1959, p. 54]

To reduce the effects of fear, pain, and tension, he prescribed reading material of a nonfear-arousing nature that explained the basic stages of birth and the physiological processes involved. He also prescribed diets, exercise, and **Jacobson relaxation** (Jacobson, 1938) techniques. He banned anxious mothers and mother-in-laws! He claimed that exercise and relaxation would minimize fatigue and tension as sources of stimuli for conditioned fear responses.

Dr. Grantly Read made a great contribution by questioning a mechanical medical tradition which viewed women in childbirth as "sick," needing help "to get over it" by being given numbing chemicals from a team who knew "best" how a woman's body worked. His emphasis on glorious spiritual experiences, however, did little to prepare his patients, other than cognitively, to face childbirth unafraid, exercised, and relaxed when the uterus did send pain impulses to the brain. The primary problem with the Read method was an inadequate knowledge of birth physiology. His theory of the actions of the fear/pain/

increased fear/increased pain loop remains a useful concept in trying to reduce learned sources of pain during childbirth.

The Lamaze Method

In 1951, the year of the Leningrad conference on applications of Pavlovian principles to obstetrics, a French physician, Dr. Fernand Lamaze, attended that conference and visited several hospitals where the psychoprophylactic method was being applied. Impressed by what he observed, he took the method back to France in a modified form. His modifications included using the method of "neuromuscular education" (similar to Jacobson exercises) in place of the Pavlovian hypnotic methods (Chertok, 1959), and preparing or training the expectant mothers in group sessions rather than individually.

Within a few years of the Leningrad conference, a version of his method incorporating aspects of the Read theory became popular in the United States, and an English translation of *Painless Childbirth: Psychoprophylactic Method* appeared in 1970. It is reported that over 90 percent of the mothers prepared by the "Lamaze method" experience childbirth without requiring major anesthesia.*

In contrast to the Russian psychoprophylactic method (in which teaching is individually conducted by physicians), expectant mothers (and expectant fathers, if possible) are conditioned, or educated during weekly sessions by teachers who are usually nurses or Lamaze midwives ("montrices"). Group process and group exercises are stressed. Positive socialization begins with learning never to say "labor pain" (the words used are "labor contraction") and reading glowing testimonials of former students. Such a procedure is consistent with Pavlovian thinking about conditioning of the meaning of words such as "labor" that must acquire a new second signal system semantic (meaning) context.

The **Lamaze method** is based upon a Pavlovian analysis of the causes of unconditioned pain. Such pain is thought to come mainly from two sources—fatigue of uterine muscles, which causes cramping, and premature efforts by the mother to push the baby's head against an undilated cervix. This was assumed to cause bruising, swelling, and pain. To combat fatigue, a system of graduated breathing was developed, designed to ensure that uterine muscles would not go into painful cramps for lack of oxygen. All participants were trained in conditioned control of deep muscle relaxation using verbal cues. Husbands were specially trained in the giving of the CSs for relaxation between labor contractions. This allowed all muscles to rest and interfered with the development of the cycle of increasing pain and fear. If the hospital balked at allowing the husband in the delivery room, as many still do, a Lamaze-trained midwife would deliver the CSs for relaxation and the "effleurage."†

---

* Much of this material is taken from notes collected by myself when I attended a Lamaze training course in 1969.

† The "effleurage" is a soft massage of the skin above the abdominal muscles. It has an unconditioned pain-reducing effect—presumably because messages are sent to tactile analyzers in the cortex which compete with the pain messages that would otherwise be received by these regions of the cortex. Pavlov thought that strong and evenly matched excitatory and inhibitory stimuli would lead to a conditioned neurosis but that strong inhibitory influences paired with weaker excitatory influences would cause the excitatory stimuli to become conditioned inhibitors.

The use of midwives and husbands to coach the mother during delivery and the use of trained midwives rather than physicians to administer the lessons have now been adopted in many clinics in the Soviet Union. As in the American and French versions of the method, use of midwives as teachers has made psychoprophylactic training available to more expectant mothers. Chertok (1959) states that too often physicians were too busy or lacked interest in supervising preparation of the mothers-to-be.

The women were trained in the specialized breathing techniques mentioned earlier. These were graduated to ensure sufficient oxygen without hyperventilation (common in panic) early in the labor, and were fast and violent during the transition between early labor and actual delivery of the infant. The "forced panting" of the transition period inhibited attention to the USs for pushing and allowed the mother-to-be to hold back on the pushing response until fully ready to deliver.

Many women report that pain stimuli during childbirth are inhibited by this means and that they feel euphoric. Normally this method is not recommended in cases of breech (backwards) orientation of the fetus, but the author read reports in his class of women who had such complete control of uterine contractions that, after their doctors had determined the embryo to be in the breech position, they were able to move the embryo into the normal birth position. Surely this method represents an achievement in the development of a behavioral alternative to chemical and surgical procedures!

Pavlovian principles have been extended successfully in reducing pain associated with childbirth. These methods assume that much of the pain is conditioned pain and that this conditioning involves verbal CSs (semantic conditioning). Treatment uses both verbal and nonverbal cues to inhibit the effects of both this conditioned pain and unconditioned pain. Even uterine functioning is reported to be changed by these techniques.

Applications of Classical Conditioning in Clinical Psychology

Although applications of classical conditioning to the process of childbirth are both important and interesting, they are not procedures used by many psychologists. The technique that will now be described is a major therapeutic tool of behaviorally oriented clinical psychologists.

Systematic Desensitization

Let us return to Dr. Watson and Dr. Rayner and the case of the much-mentioned "little Albert." Although the sudden reappearance of little Albert's mother prevented the good behaviorists from undoing the conditioned neurosis they had induced, they did manage to develop a treatment plan which went something like this: The child would be put in a high chair with nicely flavored morsels to absorb his attention. As he began to eat, a rat would be quietly placed in a far corner of the room; gradually, the rat would move closer. At the moment the child's attention seemed divided between the rat and the ingestion of the food, the approach of the rodent was to be slowed down until eating resumed with its former vigor. If all went according to plan, the child would eventually be able to eat with one hand while petting the reluctant rat with the other.

The method involves **counterconditioning,** and it was directly derived from Pavlov. The theory went as follows: Eating inhibits the cortical representations of defense reactions or disinhibits positive responses inhibited by fear. This occurs because eating, salivation, and other functions utilize the response pathways needed for the physiological responses of fear (the CR) to the CS (the rat). Part of this competition would be between the parasympathetic branch of the visceral nervous system activated in eating and the sympathetic branch activated in fear. With numerous pairings of the rat with the pleasant sensations of eating, the rat should become a conditioned stimulus for food and might even elicit salivation! This would of course make the rat a conditioned inhibitor of fear and restore Albert to his natural heritage as a lover of small, furry things. The paradigm looks like this:

1. Rat(CS)—Fear(CR)
2. Food(US)—Eating(UR)
   Rat—/(inhibited by eating)
3. Rat(CS)—Eating(CR)

Though Watson and Rayner never got the chance to apply their proposal, Mary Cover Jones (1924) did successfully treat **phobic avoidances** using such counterconditioning procedures (as we mentioned in Chapter 2).

After this, little formal interest seemed to be taken in the principles of counterconditioning until Wolpe (1958) published the results of his research on methods of eliminating phobias (*Psychotherapy by Reciprocal Inhibition*). Wolpe began with research on cats. One group heard a buzzer followed by a painful electric shock. The other group first was presented with several trials in which the buzzer was paired first with eating and then with the shock. Pavlov (1960) had suggested that the conflict created by a situation in which an animal could not distinguish between the CS signaling a positive event (food) and the CS signaling an aversive event (shock) could create an experimental neurosis. Wolpe, however, found that both his nonconflict and conflict groups of cats showed equal fear responses; in both groups, anxiety about shock acted to inhibit eating. Wolpe reasoned that if conflict was not the essential condition for the development of phobic avoidances, perhaps conflict could be turned to therapeutic advantage. If strong fear was effective in inhibiting relatively weaker urges to eat, perhaps strong urges to eat could reciprocally inhibit weak fear urges. He tested this idea of reciprocal inhibition, that is, the relationship between his food-related CSs and his shock-associated CSs, by giving his cats food in cages that were very dissimilar to the cages in which they had been shocked. He found that under circumstances in which the CSs conditioned to shock were minimized, eating occurred. He then moved his cats through a series of cages that were more and more like the cages in which they had been shocked while continuing to feed them. Finally, the cats would eat in their home (shock-related) cages, whereupon Wolpe began to pair the buzzer at low intensity with food. Eventually, the cats would continue to eat in their home cages even when the buzzer was sounded at full intensity, showing that their conditioned fear responses had been successfully inhibited. From this research, he developed a series of techniques in which various responses incompatible with fear were paired with weak fear cues. These included relaxation, assertive behavior, and sexual behavior. Training subjects to display assertive behaviors in situations which would otherwise elicit fear is called assertion training and is widely used today in women's consciousness-raising groups. Use of sexual arousal as the excitatory response to inhibit sex-related anxieties, a technique widely used in sex therapies, will be discussed in Chapter 8. Of all of Wolpe's procedures based on the principle of reciprocal inhibition, however, using relaxation to oppose fear is by far the most widely applied.

This procedure, called **systematic desensitization,** goes as follows. First, the client is trained in deep progressive muscle relaxation by the Jacobson technique (Jacobson, 1938). In this procedure, various muscle groups are tensed and relaxed upon the therapist's command so that the client learns to discriminate the sensations of the different degrees of tension. Gradually, the client becomes capable of progressively tensing and relaxing any or all of the striated muscles to such an extent that she or he offers no resistance to someone's moving any given relaxed limb. The client is then requested to describe a hierarchy of potentially fear-inducing situations related to her/his phobia, going from the least frightening possible situation to the most frightening. Once this is done, the client is shown the least frightening situation (or, if the **covert desensitization*** technique is used, she or he is asked to imagine it) while being given verbal cues by the therapist to relax. The relaxation is intended to function as a CR which reciprocally inhibits the fear CR elicited by the fear CSs. If the client is able to remain relaxed, he or she is exposed to the next most terrifying situation, and so on. As the client remains relaxed for each situation, he or she is advanced gradually until the most terrifying situation in the hierarchy can be faced. If at any time a step in the sequence proves too extreme and the client admits to experiencing fear responses which, if prolonged, would inhibit the relaxation response, the sequence is "backed up" until he or she no longer experiences the fear. Eventually, the client is able to face the real world situations that once aroused such debilitating anxiety without being troubled by the maladaptive fear.

Wolpe considers three sets of variables as vital in successful countercondi-tioning. First, it is necessary to select an anxiety-neutralizing stimulus capable of inducing a competing condition of sufficient strength to inhibit the fear CR. Relaxation is, of course, a direct opposite of fear. Second, the aversive cues are presented, beginning with the weakest forms so that any emotional responses that occur can be easily extinguished. The arousal potential of more aversive

---

* Today, most behavior therapists use the covert desensitization technique for reasons of prac-ticality. Most psychotherapists would rather not be bothered with keeping collections of snakes, spiders, and rats in their offices, not to mention the problems in providing clients with graded sets of heights, and so on. If one believes Pavlov's description of the second signal system's function, mental images should be just as effective as real (first system) environmental cues.

situations is supposedly progressively reduced by generalization of anxiety extinction from preceding weaker items. The construction of such hierarchies must be done very carefully to avoid too-extreme gaps between items (which would result in the undesirable elicitation of fear). Usually, subjects are first asked to generate a list of fear-arousing situations and then asked to rate them on a 100-point "subjective unit of discomfort scale" (SUDS). Finally, the timing of the presentation of the anxiety-reducing cues and the cues eliciting fear must be considered. Generally, the CSs for fear are presented (or the client is asked to imagine them) just before the client is asked to relax. It is considered important that the CSs which once elicited fear become strongly conditioned to the cues for relaxation through a close contiguity relationship. The prompt presentation of the relaxation cues also minimizes the time in which a fear reflex can be evidenced.

The theoretical base of systematic desensitization   Wolpe originally presented his method in terms of Hull's theory and tried to explain classical conditioning as involving drive reduction and fatigue (I_R) as the basis for extinction of fears (Bandura, 1969). Today, systematic desensitization is usually explained in orthodox Pavlovian terms. There is still considerable disagreement about the basic mechanisms involved, however. Bellack and Herson (1977) note that four processes have been proposed: (1) reciprocal inhibition as originally proposed by Wolpe (1958), (2) habituation, which is a type of internal inhibition in which the brain learns to ignore cues that are not associated with USs or consequences, (3) counterconditioning, which would be the long-term effect of reciprocal inhibition and would involve what had once been a CS for fear becoming a CS for relaxation, and (4) extinction, which might be a long-term effect of habituation. Wolpe postulated that the mechanisms were reciprocal inhibition and counterconditioning. Bellack and Herson (1977), however, note that the CSs which formerly were fear eliciting do not usually come to elicit relaxation, as predicted by the antagonistic response, counterconditioning theory.

There is also some doubt about Wolpe's theory that inhibitory tendencies generalize from weak items in the hierarchy to stronger fear cues. Using a descending hierarchy, Krapfl (1967) found that ultimate fear reduction was as complete as with the traditional hierarchy, which begins with weak items and ascends to more fear-eliciting items. Bandura (1969), however, has pointed out that such descending orders may cause clients considerable initial distress that may result in an early termination of therapy. As we will see in Chapter 8, newer forced extinction methods do not all use Wolpe's type of hierarchies. In general, Wolpe-type hierarchies which minimize fear elicitation seem to be more effective than descending or random hierarchies.

The role of the antagonistic response of relaxation is also unclear. Schubot (1966) found that deep muscle relaxation was only necessary with extremely phobic subjects. Rachman (1968) found such relaxation training to be helpful but not necessary. Paul (1969), however, found greater decreases in several measures of sympathetic nervous system arousal (the fight/flight branch of the partly automatic nervous system that is highly involved in visceral and vascular responses of fear) in subjects receiving deep muscle relaxation than in subjects told to relax or given hypnotic suggestions to relax. Again, the conclusion seems to be that relaxation training is beneficial, if not essential, to phobia elimination.

Wolpe thought that systematic desensitization operated as an automatic conditioning process, but he also advocated instructing clients in the theory of reciprocal inhibition (in Bellack and Herson, 1977), which may have generated cognitive expectancy effects. Woy and Efran (1972) found that self-perceptions of improvement were better in groups having positive expectancies but did not find these groups to vary on measures of sympathetic nervous system arousal. Persely and Leventhal (1972) found that clients with positive expectancies did better but obtained significant improvement in subjects without positive expectancies. These results seem to show that although cognitive factors increase the effectiveness of systematic desensitization, they are not necessary for reducing fear. This supports the view that the process involves automatic, unconscious conditioning mechanisms.

How effective and efficient is systematic desensitization?   A broad range of problems may be treated with systematic desensitization. Some of the types of phobias reported to have been successfully treated are: fear of heights, fear of driving, a variety of fears of animals, test anxiety, fear of flying, fear of water, fear of going to school, fear of rejection by others, fear of authority figures, fear of injections, fear of crowds, fear of public speaking, fear of physical injury (is it wise to treat such a fear?), and even fear of death (Rimm and Masters, 1974)!

Advocates of systematic desensitization often make comparisons of its efficiency with that of psychoanalysis. In contrast to the years of therapy required in psychoanalysis, Paul (1969) claims that the median number of sessions involving actual desensitization ranges from 16 to 23, depending upon the therapist and the intensity of the phobia. This could represent considerable savings of time and money for the client. Such savings are useless, however, if the treatment is not effective. How well do the results of systematic desensitization compare with those from other modes of psychotherapy?

Wolpe (1958) has published data showing a success rate of 90 percent with 210 clients treated with systematic desensitization, as opposed to an average success rate of 60 percent for clients treated by insight therapies such as psychoanalysis. Breger and McGaugh (1967) point out that such glowing reports must be interpreted with caution. Wolpe's role as a leader in the field of behavioral modification may have biased his perceptions, the treatment may only be effective for a limited subclass of the client population, and individuals who did not experience relief may have dropped out of therapy. The first controlled study, published by Lang and Lazovik (1963), tested systematic desensitization against a no-treatment control group. Many more of the treated subjects became symptom free from their snake phobias, and a six-month followup showed the difference had increased over these months (an incubation effect). Lang, Lazovik, and Reynolds (1965) improved on that design by repeating the study using a "pseudotherapy group" to control for **placebo effects** (improvements shown by clients either because of attention from therapists or because of clients' beliefs that they are being helped). Again, snake phobias were more effectively removed by systematic desensitization. Paul conducted a study comparing systematic desensitization to insight therapy in removing fears of public speaking (1966), using five weekly sessions for each condition. Though it can be argued that five sessions is not enough time to expect the subtle processes of insight therapy to be effective, the fact that positive results were obtained using the systematic desensitization procedure in that short period would seem to support the behavioral methods advocates' claims of efficiency. After six weeks, all of Paul's subjects were rechecked. Not only were the systematic desensitization subjects the most symptom free, but no evidence of **symptom substitution** could be found. This result is important because it has been the claim of analytic therapists that systematic desensitization represented a method capable of changing only the surface manifestations of deeper pathologies. With time, therefore, new symptoms should "substitute" for those removed. These results support the behaviorists' focus on direct observation as opposed to believing authorities and their theories.

A more recent major study has found similar evidence for the superiority of behavioral approaches to psychopathology in general. Sloane and colleagues (1975) compared groups receiving behavior therapy, dynamic psychotherapy (as in insight/psychoanalytic therapy), and minimal contact. Their subjects were matched over groups by severity of disturbance but not by specific symptoms. All therapy was carried out by experienced therapists and all clients were clinic patients. The most common treatment given the behavior therapy group was systematic desensitization, but other treatments were also used (such as assertion training). Over 80 percent of the behavior therapy clients improved on target behaviors compared to 48 percent of minimal contact clients. In terms of ratings of overall adjustment, 93 percent of the behavior therapy clients improved, compared to 77 percent of psychotherapy and control subjects. Improvement with psychotherapy was limited to fairly verbal clients, but behavioral approaches worked with most types of clients. Although these results do not directly show the superiority of systematic desensitization over conventional psychotherapy (because of confounding by the use of other behavioral approaches), they do suggest such superiority.

Even though its theoretical foundations are still debated, Wolpe's technique of systematic desensitization has generally been found to be effective. This technique uses the association of cues for relaxation with weak cues for fear, arranged in an ascending hierarchy, for counterconditioning fear.

Applications of Skinner's Reinforcement Theory

While applications of classical conditioning principles have dominated most early intrusions of learning theory into psychotherapy, reinforcement theories have been the most frequently applied in the field of education. Most of these applications have either been developed directly by Skinner or are heavily indebted to his theory. Three such areas of application will be reviewed. Let us start with the training of animals.* The first step is to select something that your subject wants, such as food. Skinner notes, however, that it is very difficult to give food at the precise second that a desirable behavior occurs. Therefore, you must use a conditioned reinforcer. Skinner suggests sounding a toy clicker (cricket) and tossing a scrap of food. Eventually, the clicker becomes a CS for food receiving behaviors, and the animal will go to the place where food has been received as soon as the clicker sounds. Begin by reinforcing any behavior that could be part of your final desired behavior. Sound the clicker precisely when your selected behavior occurs. Gradually become more and more fussy about which behaviors to reinforce. Reinforce only those which bring the animal closer to your behavioral goal. This is, of course, the process of shaping or successive approximation. Remember to give food after each click of your "cricket." After a fairly simple behavior is shaped, such as having a dog touch its nose to a door knob, you will find it easier to train more complex behaviors, such as having the dog execute simple dance steps. Again, the process involves shaping the behavior slowly by rewarding only the actions that are progressively closer to your final desired target behavior.

This procedure illustrates several Skinnerian principles. For learning to occur, the organism must be active and must emit responses (or you would have nothing to reinforce). Your sense of timing must be exquisite, for if you delay your reinforcement, you might accidentally reinforce an undesired behavior. To make it easier to deliver reinforcement at the right moment, a conditioned reinforcer serves as a useful **bridging stimulus** between response and primary reinforcement. All of these principles have been applied in Skinner's designs for **teaching machines** to be used by children. Let us now examine Skinnerian teaching machines as a second application of his operant learning theory.

Skinner's procedures for shaping new behaviors in any higher organism begin with classically conditioning a bridging stimulus (or secondary reinforcer) to your primary reinforcer (usually food, for animals). Give this conditioned reinforcer (and sometimes the primary reinforcer) every time your subject makes a response which progressively comes closer to your target behavior.

Teaching Machines and Programmed Learning

The largest number of people touched by the technology of operant learning theories have been school children. Although early predictions that teachers would be replaced by teaching machines and computers have not been realized, teaching machines, **programmed learning,** and contingency management concepts are widely disseminated and their technologies widely used. Of all the types of applications, the one which is probably most familiar to the public at large is the teaching machine. Although the first patent for a teaching machine

---

* "Any available animal—a cat, a dog, a pigeon, a mouse, a parrot, a chicken, a pig—will do. (Children or other members of your family may also be available, but it is suggested that you save them . . .)" (Skinner, 1951, p. 1).

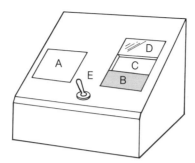

Figure 6.1   A stylized drawing of a Skinnerian-type teaching machine. A is the window where the steps of the program are displayed; B is the opening that allows the learner to write his answer; and C is the glassed-over window for the learner to read his answer after he has pulled the lever (E) to open the shutter over the correct answer (D).

was issued 110 years ago (Holland, 1960), the modern form of the teaching machine was developed by Skinner and represents a direct extension of his ideas about learning. Three of the most important principles of Skinnerian learning theory are: (1) reinforcement should be immediate, (2) behavior is learned only when it is emitted and reinforced, and (3) complex behaviors can only be created by the process of gradual shaping of responses closer and closer to the behavioral objective. The teaching machine is only a means to ensure that these principles are applied.

Essentially, a teaching machine of the Skinnerian type consists of a window to display items of educational material. Usually this material has one or more words missing. Sometimes a short question follows the informational statement. In any case, the student has been instructed to respond by writing the answer in an answer space which is usually to the right of the statement window. The learner then pulls a lever which opens a small shutter revealing the correct answer as his answer is moved under glass where it can be compared with the correct answer. After comparing his answer with the correct answer, the student moves a lever to indicate whether or not his answer was correct. If it was not, he repeats the item after the complete program is finished. If his answer matched the displayed answer, he or she moves on to the next step of the program. Figure 6.1 shows a teaching machine. All machines do not look just like this, but all have the same basic elements. As can be seen, the role of the machine is to be sure that reinforcement (seeing the correct answer and, hopefully, discovering that your answer matches it) is immediate, and to force you to emit an overt writing response which can then be reinforced. The application of the third principle of shaping complex learning responses through gradual changes in behavior is the function of the program displayed by the machine. This program is usually printed on a long roll of paper which is unwound as the program advances and rewound on a take-up roll. The construction of effective programs is itself a difficult and technical matter.

An effective program must begin at the level of the learner's existing skills and then present more advanced material. This makes it difficult to design programs for classrooms in which previous knowledge of the material presented varies widely. The size of the steps of the program is critical also. If the steps are too small, bright learners may get bored. If they are too large, the number of errors will increase and extinction of using the machine may occur. Holland (1960) suggests "pre-testing" programs to eliminate items responsible for too many errors. Each program must be tailored to a particular target population. The responses of program users must be allowed to shape the program writing efforts of the program designer.

Programmed materials may be used as "teaching machines without the machines," or programmed texts. Many of these require students to cover a column of correct answers with a piece of paper while writing their answers. The piece of paper is then moved so that a student's answer may be compared with the correct answer. The effectiveness of this method depends heavily on the integrity of the student, and it has been most widely used on the college level.

The type of programs used in teaching machines and in most programmed texts presents the material as a gradual sequence of items, progressing from easy to more complex or more difficult. This **linear program** approach, however, suffers from the deficit of not being able to be individualized for the different needs of multiple users. An alternative approach is that of the **branching program.** Such a program may begin with pretests to determine the learner's beginning level of competency. Based on the patterns of the learner's errors, he or she is directed to the specified sections of the programmed text covering review material. When learners are able to pass tests over the review material, they are advanced back into the next step of the main program (Crowder and Martin, 1961). Not only does such a program allow learners to advance at their own pace, as in linear programs, but faster learners may skip simple material and slower learners are provided more review and explanatory material. The major disadvantage of such material is that many students become impatient with flipping back and forth through the book.

A fourth principle, which is applied in carefully constructed programmed materials, is that of **fading** "prompts" or leading cues (Holland, 1960). In the first few frames, all but the word requested as an answer would be displayed. In later frames, prompting words or some letters of prompting words would be progressively eliminated. A student advancing through the program should be able to continue to give correct answers with less and less help until finally his or her memory becomes complete, with no aid from the program.

Teaching machines and other versions of programmed learning have been used at every level of instruction. Although most such applications cover the learning of core material, Holland and Matthews (1963) have used teaching machines to teach speech sound discriminations. Such widespread use opens the question of the effectiveness of such methods. After reviewing 36 studies comparing programmed instruction to traditional instruction, Schramm (1964) found no difference in 18 of the studies. In 17 studies, the programmed approach was superior; the traditional approach was superior in one study. The author has used a comparison of programmed and traditional textbook material as a "cookbook" experiment in his experimental psychology courses and has usually found no differences in retention and errors. In any case, programmed material does not seem to be inferior. The approach would seem appropriate when well-programmed materials are available and when such materials can provide for individualization of instruction beyond that provided by student-teacher interactions. Because teaching machines elicit such high rates of responses and feedback, they should be particularly useful in shaping attention in pupils who may be deficient in this area.

Operant learning principles are applied through teaching machines, which require pupils to respond to programmed material. The machines give almost immediate reinforcement for correct responses. Programs can also be used in texts in either linear format (as in Skinner's teaching machines) or in branching format.

Factors working against more widespread use of teaching machines include the costs of the machines, the difficulty in obtaining specialized programs, and teacher and community resistance to applying "rat" psychology to children. Attention to teaching machines and programmed instruction seems to have peaked in the mid-1960s. An inspection of the tables of contents of issues of the *Journal of Applied Behavior Analysis* after 1972 reveals that almost no current research is reported on programmed learning and teaching machines. Most attention is being paid to the various facets of contingency management, an area of classroom applications of operant learning principles that we will review in Chapter 10.

The third area of application makes more use of Skinner's general assumptions about causality in the environment than it does of any particular principle or procedure. This application to the college classroom makes use of Skinner's techniques for analyzing the contingencies in the environment and modifying them to promote more adaptive behaviors (in this case, study behaviors).

The College Classroom

Because most of the experts on operant learning theory have been academic psychologists employed by colleges and universities, it is natural that we have attempted to apply our own ideas to our classrooms. At some point, every professor becomes curious about whether the theories taught actually work. In a sense, the motivation for learning theorists to apply their principles to their own teaching is a reflection of the limits of their tolerance for the purely abstract. Because they may find their cherished theories to be irrelevant, such testing of ideas may precipitate a crisis of the self. As many students are themselves perpetually involved in such crises about the relevance of their courses, this common plight may aid communication.

An early attempt at applying reinforcement principles to college teaching was made by Ljungberg Fox (1962) who applied the experimental analysis of behavior to implementing the Robinson studying technique, which was developed in 1946 to increase the efficiency of study procedures. Of all the elements necessary for a student to learn, his or her study habits are most critical. The most brilliant lectures or the most concerned professors notwithstanding, a student who does not study will probably fail. Conversely, if students study arduously, they may learn from the most boring and incompetent of instructors.

The first step in trying to increase the efficiency of study is the experimental analysis of study behavior. Fox began by having five students note their activities throughout the day. Times and situations associated with both study behaviors and social behaviors were noted. Once this had been done, the students were counseled to set aside a modest amount of time each day to study each subject in a place which was unlikely to provide S_Ds (discriminative stimuli) for socializing. The students were instructed that if they began to daydream or to experience discomfort (which would become associated with the place of study), they were to complete one easy problem or one page of text material. Then they were to leave immediately, even if their interest in study had been renewed. On the next day, all students were questioned to make sure the instructions had been followed. After this, the number of pages of work to be completed before taking a break (a reinforcer) was gradually increased until one hour per day per subject was filled with concentrated study. This gradual shaping of working on leaner ratio schedules was designed to prevent schedule strain. The program was originally applied for each student's most difficult course. It was expanded to cover their other courses, with a week's successful practice of this method on prior courses required before each new course was brought under the plan. Each course was studied in a different location, on the theory that each environment would become a specific S_D for studying that particular subject. Assignments were broken up into blocks of four or five pages each, and all students were told that they could leave the study area only after the completion of one or more of these blocks of pages. This strategy was to have the completion of each block act as a reinforcer and to put study behavior on a ratio schedule. The number of pages per block was set low enough not to "strain" the schedule. Gradually increasing the number of blocks completed served to shape study behaviors. Association of the study rooms with completed assignments was assumed to cause the room stimuli to become conditioned reinforcers.

Once this stage of the project was successfully implemented, students were introduced to the **SQ3R method.** "S" (survey) refers to skimming the boldface and italicized headings in a chapter to obtain an overall picture or schemata of the material. "Q" indicates that the student should formulate questions about the material from the survey. The first "R" of the 3R stands for reading the material with the goal of answering the questions raised during the "Q" phase. The second "R" stands for reciting or outlining the material with the book closed, to emit active responses. (This is much like answering the questions presented in the frames of programmed material.) The final "R" stands for reviewing the material by checking the outline against the book or rereading the material to check for errors of omission and commission. Each of these steps was implemented separately, and the next stage was not begun until the previous one had been mastered.

All five students in the pilot project continued using these techniques for the two academic quarters of the study. All increased their grade point averages by at least one full grade point, and four were able to do this without studying on weekends. The fifth student required two hours of study on Saturday (Fox, 1962).

The operant approach to study behavior stresses an experimental analysis of study behavior and designing study programs to reduce interference from cues for competing behaviors while maximizing reinforcement for discrete segments of completed study behavior.

The applications presented so far illustrate an engineering approach to dealing with problem behaviors or creating new behaviors. These approaches put the locus of control out in the environment, in the relationships of stimuli and reinforcers. The next approach to therapy to be examined reverses this procedure. The gestalt therapist sees cognitive events happening within the client's head as more important than stimuli or reinforcers, and the mode of change as the facilitation of a restructuring of the client's cognitions. The therapeutic role of the gestalt therapist, however, is no less active than that of his or her behaviorist counterpart and, in a sense, he or she is no less manipulative. He or she simply manipulates the focus of attention and thought processes of the client rather than the client's external stimuli or reinforcement contingencies.

Gestalt Principles Applied

We have already mentioned Wertheimer's (1959) application of gestalt principles to childhood education, in which he advocated solving problems by "understanding" rather than rote memory. He believed in productive thinking, letting the child see an entire situation rather than trying to analyze its parts or having to memorize formulas. Wertheimer's emphasis on "discovery learning" and seeing situations as wholes is paralleled by the gestalt holistic (dealing with wholes) approach to dealing with psychopathology.

Kurt Goldstein took the gestalt viewpoint and extended it to treating brain-damaged soldiers. In this work, he discovered that neurological damage to a local region of the brain did not leave the victim completely helpless but rather that other regions of the brain could be taught to compensate for the functions lost with the injury. Thus, the person tries to function as a whole, a gestalt, and not as a fragmented entity. Goldstein (1963) contended that each person has a basic drive to try to function as a whole again, and this drive he called the drive for **self-actualization.** This drive for self-actualization, or making a good (beautiful) gestalt out of one's life and memories, is a central feature of the gestalt therapy we will discuss next. Self-actualization is a basic source of motivation or tension that drives healthy people towards making a healthy whole (good gestalt) of their lives. The tendency towards striving to maintain homeostatic equilibrium (keeping their lives as they are now) was seen as pathological. Therefore, the focus of gestalt therapy has not been on making mentally ill persons "normal" but rather on making "fairly normal" persons healthy: "Therapy is too good to be limited to the sick" (in Polster and Polster, 1973).

A basic assumption of gestalt therapy is that much human maladaptive behavior and unhappiness comes about because of faulty learning. In this, they are in agreement with the connectionists. The nature of this faulty learning, however, is regarded very differently by the two schools of thought. Rather than believing that the environment presents contingencies conducive to maladaptive behavior, the gestalt therapist sees the problem as one of a person's faulty perceptions. If the perceptions of "reality" are faulty, the personality structure or life space that is built up with experience brings unhappiness and/or neurosis to the client. Therefore, the task of the therapist is to aid the client in organizing her or his life space in more appropriate ways. Learning, for the Lewinian gestaltists, means a change in the life space.

Faulty learning can occur in several ways. Two examples of these ways demonstrate inadequate differentiation of the person's real self (figure) from others involved in their life space. In the first example, a person accepts the values of significant others (such as parents) uncritically. These "alien values" are called **introjects.** Since the introjects are not the products of the person's own unique experiences about what works best for him, they may lead to responses that are not adaptive to the "here and now," the person's immediate environment. Ground (others' values) has traded places with what should be figure (the person's authentic values). The gestalt therapist tries first to aid such clients in discriminating or differentiating introjects from values derived from clients' own learning experiences with the external environment. Second, the therapist aids clients in either not responding to the introjects or in "owning them" as integrated parts of the person's own values. A second example of inadequate figure-ground differentiation occurs when a client acts as if others shared his own feelings and values **(projection).** In this case, the client attributes his values and motives (figure) to others, whose real values and motives thus remain as ground and can not be experienced by the client. This faulty perception of others' values and motives also results in disfunctional response tendencies. Again, gestalt therapy is directed towards helping the client to perceive and respond on the basis of accurate information, which is possible only when the client ignores inappropriate ground and focuses on appropriate figure.

Another source of faulty learning comes about through a failure to discriminate when a process is finished. Processes experienced as unfinished create tension systems (vectors) in the life space (Zeigarnik effect) and may drive a person into repeating neurotic patterns (such as repeating the same destructive patterns in relationship after relationship). Therapy consists of trying to help the client to achieve closure. The way in which this is done reflects the gestalt belief that persons respond to their phenomenological realities, in which environmental cues are organized in accordance with the gestalt principles, rather than responding directly to unprocessed external cues.

Because learning and memory are seen as dynamic processes occurring in active organisms, not mechanistically driven by particular environmental circumstances, the therapist is able to engage these active processes in the "here and now" rather than trying to understand a history or recondition bad habits by manipulating the environment. In the gestalt view, the only reality a person has is his life space, or his perceptions of the world and of himself. To achieve closure, therefore, the gestalt therapist has the client "reenact" the unfinished business. Since the reactions of the participants in the client's personal drama have importance only as the client perceives them as having occurred, the client is asked to act out the roles of the various actors in his situation. This may take the form of moving to another seat and playing the role of the girlfriend who had recently terminated a relationship. The client will speak to his recently vacated chair in the way he thinks the late girlfriend would have spoken to him if she had been able to express her feelings directly. He will then move back to his original seat and express his feelings (usually anger or grief) and reply to her. These exchanges often help the client learn that the relationship is really over, which involves changing his perception of the situation to that effect. The session may end with the client's displaying his learning of a better (or at least a more realistic) gestalt by "telling her chair" goodbye and finishing his grief work through crying. He has moved towards *Prägnanz,* or good form, in his gestalt about the situation by learning that he can give up unrealistic hopes of a resumption of the relationship, and his Zeigarnik effect tension should be gone or reduced through his having achieved closure. The reason this is supposed to work is because the life space lies inside the person's head rather than in what the environment has done to him. Symbolic cues can lead to reorganizations of how he sees the world just as effectively as cues originating outside of the therapy session. Part of his learning (or change in how his life space is structured) is reducing the terminated relationship to ground rather than ineffectively and inappropriately trying to keep it as figure in his life. Since learning in gestalt terms is perceptual restructuring (either of cues from the environment, such as no longer hearing her detached voice on the phone as secretly being a cue for him to persist in trying to reestablish the relationship, or of his internal cognitions), such learning can occur suddenly. Such a sudden "insight" is as exciting in a therapy session as it must have been for Wertheimer in explaining the phi phenomenon.

Once the person's gestalt about the world is more congruent with the actual contingencies in the environment, he feels better or more healthy since the drive towards *Prägnanz* or good form (self-actualization of her or his life) is innate and its satisfaction is experienced as rewarding. Insights are therefore often felt as **peak experiences,** or moments of great joy and/or relief. Persons who have formed "good gestalts" about their feelings and their world are then able to act out of an integrated life space, or be "authentic," rather than acting from neurotic tensions and phony (unintegrated) motives. By experiencing (perceiving) the world appropriately rather than trying to explain away inconsistencies—Fritz Perls (1972) once called intellect the whore of intelligence*—they are able to avoid neurotic stupidities caused by faulty perceptions and to deal effectively with their lives. The gestalt therapy session is designed to facilitate direct experience of the life space through the symbolic role playing of unfinished business and through helping clients to perceive when they are "stuck" in a neurotic pattern resulting from a faulty perception of themselves and their circumstances. The therapist tries to prevent clients from talking "about" their conflicts

---

* Meaning that our intellectual explanations of things often serve as a cheap substitute for experiencing the world realistically and that intellectualizations interfere with truly intelligent (effective) behavior.

rather than experiencing them. Having clients act out the parts of their resistances to better perceptions helps them to identify and overcome barriers in their life spaces. As with Wertheimer's discovery learning (productive thinking), the stress is on understanding in an active, experiencing (rather than purely verbal or intellectual) way. This is like the behavioristic approaches to therapy in its emphasis on active engagement of problem behaviors, but it differs in promoting understanding rather than externally imposed treatments such as systematic desensitization.

Because the gestalt theorists see memory as a dynamic process, like perception and learning itself, a side benefit of the therapy sessions may be the reforming of memories into better-integrated gestalts. The type of reforming that may occur also follows gestalt principles.

Gestalt therapy is one of the leading schools of therapy derived from cognitive learning theory. It is a blend of classical gestalt theory, Lewin's innovations concerned with life spaces and tension systems and the ideas of Fritz Perls (Polster and Polster, 1973). It stresses perceptual (seeing your world as different) and cognitive (interpreting events differently to make your whole life a better gestalt) reorganization.

Chapter Perspective

We have reviewed several applications of learning theories. Although more recent innovations employ principles derived from more current research, all the applications covered in this chapter continue to be widely employed, with considerable evidence for their effectiveness. Systematic desensitization and gestalt therapy continue to be extremely popular and useful therapeutic approaches, illustrating that research and theory in the area of learning can change lives for the better.

The theories behind these applications, characterized by consistent viewpoints about the principles governing learning, are strongly identified with a few major theorists. As such, they have a certain narrowness of scope in terms of the range of their theoretical constructs. The theories to be covered in the next chapter tend to be more eclectic, more diffuse, and, at least potentially, more flexible.

Key Terms

branching program	introject	projection
bridging stimulus	Jacobson relaxation	psychoprophylaxis
counterconditioning	Lamaze method	self-actualization
covert desensitization	linear program	semantic conditioning
extero-interoceptive conditioning	peak experience	SQ3R method
	phobic avoidance	systematic desensitization
fading (vanishing)	placebo effect	symptom substitution
gestalt therapy	programmed learning	teaching machine

Annotated Bibliography

The best book on the subject of applying psychological principles to childbirth I have found is L. Chertok, *Psychosomatic methods in painless childbirth; History, theory, and practice* (New York: Pergamon Press, 1959). For those interested in teaching machines, my recommendation is J. G. Holland's "Teaching machines: An application of principles from the laboratory" (*Journal of the Experimental Analysis of Behavior,* 1960, 9, 65–78). For general Skinnerian applications to training dogs and children, read Skinner's "How to teach animals" (*Scientific American,* 1951, 185, 26–29). For the early theory and practice of systematic desensitization, skim J. Wolpe, *Psychotherapy by reciprocal inhibition* (Stanford, Ca.: Stanford University Press, 1958), and for a recent comprehensive treatment of systematic desensitization, read A. S. Bellack and M. Herson, *Systematic desensitization* (Baltimore, Md.: Williams & Wilkins, 1977). Finally, an excellent introduction to gestalt therapy can be found in E. Polster and M. Polster, *Gestalt therapy integrated, Contours of therapy and practice* (New York: Brunner/Mazel, 1973). On the negative side, a provocative critique of clinical approaches based on learning theory is L. Breger and J. L. McGaugh, "Critique and reformulation of 'learning theory' approaches to psychotherapy and neurosis" (*Psychological Bulletin,* 1965, 63, 338–358).

7

Multifactor and Eclectic Approaches

Most of the theories previously summarized in this part of the book possess a common trait—that of seeing a single set of laws as governing all forms of learning. Conflicts between theories, for the most part, resulted from interpreting the available data from mutually exclusive viewpoints. Each side's research was oriented towards disproving particular predictions made by theorists in the enemy's camp. It is small wonder that one can be left with a feeling that all laws of learning have exceptions which destroy the most careful attempts to summarize the mechanisms of learning. Pavlov's theories possess the virtues of careful research and intricate development. The reinforcement theorists share commonsense intuitions about the effects of rewards and aversive events. Conversely, the cognitive theorists appeal to our need to reject oversimplified mechanistic views of learning, although their theories are heavily dependent upon guesses about unobservable inner events. In the midst of these somewhat gloomy musings, one clear ray of hope emerges. As has been discussed, Guthrie was a more sophisticated behaviorist than Watson, and both Hull and Skinner's theories were better able to handle a wider range of data than those of their predecessors.

Spence built on Hull's work, as did Miller and Dollard as well as Mowrer. All their theories were able to incorporate the wide range of phenomena first introduced by the cognitive theorists by adding new, more flexible principles. All developed multifactor models in which different types of learning processes were evoked to account for learning in different types of situations. These theories all evolved out of the Hullian tradition. Not all learning psychologists and learning research, however, were organized around tightly delineated schools of thought dominated by influential major theorists. Parallel with the development of the major theories, a pragmatic and eclectic orientation, often labeled **functionalism,** continued to appeal to those psychologists who had reservations about the major theories advanced so far. Functionalism dates back to the turn of the century and, like behaviorism and gestalt psychology, was a reaction to the rigid structuralism of Wundt and Titchener. While the structuralists sought to understand the structural anatomy of mind through using the introspectionist technique and the behaviorists rejected the whole concept of mind as mentalistic and unscientific, the functionalists focused on the role of mind in the adaptation of organisms to their environments.

This chapter will briefly explore several approaches to learning that share a common flexibility. First, the neo-Hullian theories of Miller and Dollard and of

Mowrer will illustrate how connectionism evolved in the direction of cognitive theories. Second, a sampling of functionalist contributions will show how the field of learning has advanced through approaches not closely identified with the great theories. Finally, Harlow's concept of the learning set, which suggests that the ability to show "insight" is acquired through previous trial-and-error experience, is briefly summarized as a contribution to the study of learning in the functionalist tradition.

In reading this material, try to see how some of the major principles added by these theorists have increased the explanatory power of the principles covered in previous chapters. In particular, note how two-factor approaches are helpful in understanding avoidance learning and conflict, how functionalist approaches help in understanding transfer of learning from one situation to another, and how Harlow's work provides a bridge between connectionist and cognitive theories.

Two-Factor Principles, Neo-Hullian Approaches

In Chapter 3, we examined the theories of Hull and the foremost neo-Hullian, Spence. The theories of Miller and Dollard and of Mowrer, to be presented in this chapter, represent other neo-Hullian approaches to learning. Like Spence, they modified the Hullian theory in many ways and broadened the range of types of variables postulated. This increase in the variety of variables they accomplished by suggesting that learning involves two distinct stages. For both these theories, sign or stimulus learning was seen as one type of learning and response or solution learning as a second type. The theorists, however, disagreed on the mechanisms for the learning of signs. Miller and Dollard suggested that cues are learned through a drive-reduction mechanism. Mowrer believed that cue or sign learning occurs through contiguity mechanisms. Both theories agree that response learning involves drive reduction. Miller and Dollard take a position much like Thorndike's in their insistence upon reinforcement as the basis for all learning, and this single principle makes their theory less of a two-factor theory than Mowrer's. Because Mowrer's early theory classified all learning into Pavlovian and operant types, it qualified as a two-factor theory in the same way that Skinner's did. Mowrer, however, investigated both types of learning, which Skinner did not. By the final revision of his theory, Mowrer had moved to a cognitive position very similar to that of Tolman (Chapter 5).

Miller and Dollard proposed a model of imitative behavior which anticipated Bandura's theory of modeling (Chapter 9) and incorporated an analysis of the functions of feedback much like that in Wiener's cybernetics (Chapter 5). They also developed a model for the acquisition of fear as a learned drive that has been useful in explaining the resistance to extinction of neurotic phobic avoidances.

Neal F. Miller (1909–   ) and John Dollard (1900–   )

Neal Miller received his doctorate in psychology from Yale University in 1935, spent a year in Austria at the Vienna Psychoanalytic Institute, and returned in

1936 to the Yale Institute of Human Relations, where he was associated with both Hull and John Dollard. His research background was in learning and he became a full professor at Yale in 1950. In 1966, he joined the faculty at The Rockefeller University. His areas of theory and research interest range from a neo-Hullian postulate system, which predicts conflict behavior, through imitative learning, anxiety as an acquired drive, feedback and cybernetics, **learning sets** (learning strategies), and early demonstrations of biofeedback. He is best known for his collaboration with John Dollard in developing a neo-Hullian learning theory which translated Freud into Hullian terms and covered anxiety, social, and imitative behavior.

John Dollard received his doctorate in sociology from the University of Chicago in 1931. He studied at the Berlin Psychoanalytic Institute for a year before beginning his long association with Hull, Miller, and the Yale University Institute of Human Relations. In collaboration with Miller, he wrote three books dealing with their approach to learning. The social learning theory they developed comprises a synthesis of Hullian behavior theory, Freudian psychoanalysis, and culture theory. This theory extended Hull's basic ideas in a cognitive direction by stressing **higher mental processes** rather than habit formation (in Sahakian, 1976). In their collaboration, Miller contributed the operational definitions of terms and use of animal data. Dollard provided most explanations of group behaviors and the majority of the suggestions for applications.

Although the strong influence of Hull can be seen in their work—Miller and Dollard proposed sets of formal postulates dealing with the relationships of avoidance and approach tendencies and conflict—for the most part this theory was loosely constructed and worded in lay language. This is in marked contrast to the complex and idiosyncratic system languages of Hull and Spence. Neither Miller and Dollard nor Mowrer attempted to make highly specific quantitative predictions in the Hullian tradition, but they were all oriented toward explanation of real world phenomena and toward real world applications. With time, the Hullian influence in these theories diminished to the point of becoming almost unrecognizable.

Primary Principles of the Miller and Dollard Theory

Four fundamental concepts are central to this theory: **drive, cue, response,** and **reward.** All learning was seen as involving these four elements in this sequence. Let us now examine the properties of each of these elements of the theory.

Drive   A drive has both arousal and stimulus properties. In this, Miller and Dollard agree in their analysis with Hull. Any strong source of stimulation that arouses the organism, however, is considered a drive. Thus, drives originating from outside, such as the response to a painful wound, are no less effective in impelling behavior than the more traditional drives of hunger, food, and sex that originate internally. Drives such as anger are the result of the stimuli produced by our physiological responses to the originating stimuli. As long as the strong stimulation persists, the organism remains active. When the stimulus/

drive is reduced, activity decreases. Miller and Dollard postulate two classes of drives: primary drives, which are innate (such as hunger, fatigue, pain, and so on), and secondary drives, which are learned through association with the reduction in strength of the cues associated with a primary drive. Miller and Dollard postulated that fear in the presence of specific stimuli operates as an acquired drive—one of their most significant contributions. A learned motivation to avoid a fear stimulus is as much a drive as pain avoidance or hunger. The fear cue has as much arousal function as low blood sugar (which arouses the hunger drive).

All learning, according to Miller and Dollard, depends upon the reduction in the arousal produced by a drive stimulus. As arousal decreases, however, the stimulation of the drive is reduced; reinforcement ceases to be effective and learning becomes impossible.

> The drive must inevitably be lower after the reinforcement so that unless something is done to increase it, it will eventually be reduced to zero, at which point further reinforcement is impossible. [Dollard and Miller, 1950, p. 40]

Cue   Stimuli that are too weak to have drive properties may determine when, where, and how responses will be made. Distinctive cues function much like Skinner's discriminative stimuli (S_Ds) if they do not have drive properties. Even cues that have drive properties may also have guidance functions. The specific directing functions of most of the cues in our environments must be learned through having these cues occur in the presence of drive/stimuli reduction. The guidance functions of cues associated with drives are presumed to act much like Guthrie's maintaining stimuli.

Response   Behavior involves responses to certain cues in the presence of drive stimuli. Drive stimuli arouse responses which are guided by the cues.

> If the first response is not rewarded, this creates a dilemma in which the extinction of successive non-rewarded responses leads to so-called random behavior. If some one response is followed by reward, the connection between the stimulus pattern and this response is strengthened, so that the next time that the same drive and other cues are present, this response is more likely to occur. [Miller and Dollard, 1941, p. 36]

Thus, responding must occur for learning to result. Responses may also be the source of stimuli, as in Hull's r_G creating s_G. As mentioned in the discussion on drive, "learnable drives are strong stimuli produced by responses" (Miller, 1951, p. 439).

Reward   For Miller and Dollard, reinforcement is anything that decreases the intensity of a strong stimulus for the organism. In contrast to Skinner, who defined reinforcement by its effects on the probability of the reoccurrence of a response, their focus is on drive reduction, much as in Hull's theory. Miller and Dollard, however, have broadened the range of what can be reduced by redefining drive as any strong stimulus. Reward acts to strengthen connections between responses and cues.

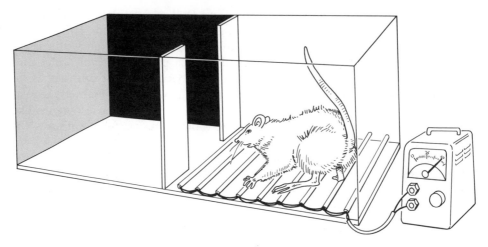

Figure 7.1a   The rat is shocked in the white chamber, which elicits the unconditioned fear drive as a response to pain cues. The rat becomes very active, which is seen as a sign of fear, and eventually escapes the shock by running into the black chamber.

The interactions of these four basic elements can be seen in Miller's experimental analysis of how the drive of fear is acquired (Figure 7.1). In the classic experiment (Miller, 1948), white rats were placed in a box with a white chamber and a black chamber. They were shocked in the white chamber and allowed to escape into the black chamber. To demonstrate that a learned drive of fear had been produced to the cue of the white box, Miller and Dollard terminated the shocks and installed an exercise wheel that would open the door (which had just been closed) between the chambers. The rats quickly learned the response of turning the wheel, which allowed them to escape into the black box. Since the rats were making responses that were followed by a reduction in the cues associated with the white chamber as the rats escaped that chamber, their escape constituted a reward and strengthened the cue-response bonds. Because the fear stimuli had drive properties, Miller was able to demonstrate the learning of the response of bar pressing for the reward of escaping from the white box cues. He concluded that "the acquirable drive motivating the learning of the new response of turning the wheel was fear and that a reduction in the strength of this fear was the reinforcing agent" (Miller, 1948, p. 97).

The acquisition of the original conditioned fear drive in the white chamber may have been facilitated by changes in the throbbing, shock-produced pain when the animals made responses that momentarily reduced the intensity of the pain drive. Moving away from the white chamber would cause the unconditioned fear/anxiety drive to be reduced, since this would reduce the intensity of the shock and hence the pain experienced. The association of reductions in the unconditioned fear-of-pain drive with the act of moving away from "white

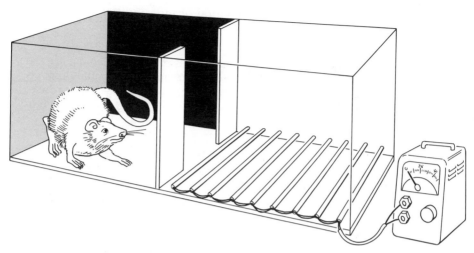

Figure 7.1b   *Even though the shock in the white chamber is turned off, the rat avoids entering that chamber, showing that the cue of "white chamber" elicits anxiety. Since going away from the white chamber should reduce the conditioned anxiety, the rat is assumed to have learned a fear drive.*

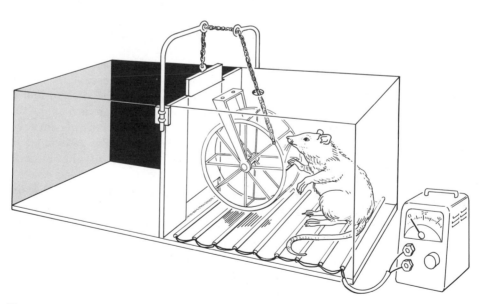

Figure 7.1c   *As evidence that a learned fear drive to the white chamber has been learned, even with the shock turned off the rat will learn the response of turning the wheel which raises the gate and lets the rat escape. Escape reduces the fear drive and rewards the new response (Miller, 1948).*

chamber cues" would result in the acquisition of the conditioned fear drive to avoid the white chamber.

Miller and Dollard stated that all behavior involves four basic elements, in the following sequence: Drives (which have both arousal and stimulus properties) in the presence of cues (which are stimuli having guiding, but not drive, properties) set the occasion for responses, which reduce drive stimulus intensity. This reduction constitutes reward.

Fear, anxiety, and neurosis: The connection to psychoanalysis   As was noted earlier, both Miller and Dollard had psychoanalytic training, and their theory was influenced by psychoanalytic concepts. This is shown most clearly in their second book, *Personality and Psychotherapy* (1950), in which they discussed the learning of personality characteristics, particularly the learning and unlearning of neurotic behavior. They provided three diagnostic criteria for labeling a person neurotic: He is miserable because of his unresolved conflicts (their theory of conflicts will be presented soon), he is stupid in not being able to resolve his conflicts, and he has observable symptoms. All these characteristics are acquired by learning and, in particular, by learned drives of fear. These learned fear drives are "the basis of the conflict, the source of the misery, and the cause of the stupidity" (Hill, 1977). Fear drives were assumed to be learned in the same way that the rat placed in the box with white and black chambers learned to become afraid of the white chamber in which it had at one time been shocked.

Dollard's influence may be seen in the extension of their four-stage model of learning to human phobias. The phobic-to-be has a traumatic experience, or witnesses someone else having a traumatic experience (more on imitation phenomena presently), but escapes from the situation. This causes the cues associated with the situation to develop drive properties, because escape from them is rewarding. The response of escaping is also linked to the discriminative function of the cues. In the future, exposure to these cues, such as a snake to a person with a snake phobia, arouses the learned drive of fear. If the person could pet the snake without being bitten, the learned drive and the associated response of escape would both extinguish. By the definition of phobia as an unreasonable avoidance tendency, however, the phobic person instead reacts to the drive of fear in the presence of the cue of snake with the response of escape, which rewards or strengthens the bonds between snake and escape. It must be noted that both Skinner and Mowrer would interpret the snake's coming to have strong conditioned reinforcer properties as a classically conditioned component in a sequence which terminates with the operant response of escape.

If a person bitten by a snake, or seeing someone bitten by a snake, or hearing of someone bitten by a snake (Miller and Dollard accepted language as a source of cues), were only to become phobic about that particular species of snake or about snakes looking like that snake, the avoidance behavior would generate few problems. Miller and Dollard, however, postulated that rewards for making a specific pattern of responses (in this case, escape responses) in the presence of any cues associated with the offending snake strengthens avoidance of that particular type of snake as well as the tendency to avoid not only other types of snakes but, in extreme cases, things shaped like snakes (review your Freud on penis fear) and environments where snakes might be found, such as forests and mountains. Miller and Dollard saw the tendency for such generalization to occur as innate ("innate stimulus generalization," Miller and Dollard, 1941) and the degree of generalization as becoming less as the new cues are less similar to the original cues conditioned to the fear drive. This they called the **gradient of generalization.** Fear then becomes neurotic partly as a function of the extent to which the gradient of generalization is too flat (which means that the fear response overgeneralizes to inappropriate cues). The stupidity of the neurotic is maintained because avoidance reduces the fear drive by removing the neurotic from the source of the cues that elicit the fear drive. The neurotic is miserable because such an overgeneralized fear drive conflicts with his effective functioning.

A learned fear drive, as the source of phobic avoidance responses, produces severe enough conflicts with normal living. The situation is even worse when the fear drive is learned to the cues associated with a pattern of behavior which would normally be adaptive. What of the little girl who is punished for being "unladylike" when she behaves in an assertive manner? Such a child may acquire a learned fear of assertive behavior that will be a great handicap when she becomes an adult in a world which increasingly expects females to behave in competent ways and to express their needs. If, as an adult, she tries to solve this conflict by entering into love relationships in which she can be dependent and allow the male to make decisions for her, she may find that such a solution interferes with her growth and achievement and her image of herself as a person in her own right.

How, then, would Miller and Dollard propose treating such a source of neurotic misery? Essentially, their psychotherapy would consist of persuading the conflicted client to make weakly assertive responses in a therapeutic environment in which she was sure she would not be punished for these responses. Gradually, she would be encouraged to make more and more assertive responses, first in therapy and finally out in the real world. Such a method has much in common with systematic desensitization. Just as Lewin's ideas had much to do with the development of modern sensitivity/encounter groups, these therapeutic suggestions of Miller and Dollard underlie the behavioristic approach of **assertion training,** used frequently as part of consciousness-raising experiences in women's movement groups. Therapeutic approaches to more conventional phobias would be conducted along similar lines designed to promote extinction of the inappropriate fear drives, or at least to reduce "neurotically stupid" overgeneralization of the cues which elicit learned fear drives.

Miller and Dollard suggested that neurotic behavior (such as phobias) can often be explained as representing learned inappropriate fear drives. Showing how such learning can fit their "drive-cue-response-reward" model, they proposed psychotherapeutic techniques based on their learning theory.

Imitation   Dollard's background in sociology may have helped him in explaining a variety of complex social situations, including imitative behavior, by the four-stage model of learning. Essentially, Miller and Dollard (1941) saw most human learning as taking place either by a process of trial and error or by copying (imitation). Since successful copying of the behavior of others is usually faster in reducing drives than trial-and-error learning, a general tendency to imitate is reinforced. This results in much of human behavior being learned from observing the responses of others rather than through trial-and-error learning. This, in turn, explains the tendency of people to behave similarly in group situations—even in ways they would never behave if acting alone. They postulate that this tendency to imitate is a learned drive acquired through making a response similar to that emitted by a nearby person when our subject is aroused by a drive. The imitative response is only learned if it leads to a reduction of the drive, which is the reward. Not only is the specific imitative response made more probable, but the tendency to make responses like those of persons around you also increases. Because a child often observes older people (who have had more time in which to acquire successful responses) make responses, and because the child's responses that imitate the successful older people have more chance of reducing drives than responses originating within the child, the imitative response tendency becomes very strong.

As the foregoing suggests, it must not be assumed that this tendency is nonspecific. Miller and Dollard conducted experiments in which they demonstrated that models who were rewarded were more likely to be imitated. Since the child subjects were also more likely to be rewarded when they imitated successful models, they rapidly came to imitate in the presence of some cues and not others. This tendency was also observed to generalize to models similar to successful models. Summarizing the results of their studies of imitation, Miller and Dollard concluded:

> There seem to be at least four classes of persons who are imitated by others. They are: (1) superiors in an age-grade hierarchy, (2) superiors in a hierarchy of social status, (3) superiors in an intelligence ranking system, and (4) superior technicians in any field. [1941, p. 183]

Social phenomena such as lynch mobs were seen as examples of imitative tendencies operating in an inappropriate fashion and producing destructive behaviors which would not be aroused by the drive states of the participants if they had been acting as individuals (Miller and Dollard, 1941). By adding the concept of imitation, Miller and Dollard moved closer to the cognitive theorists and anticipated Bandura's examination of modeling from a Skinnerian viewpoint, which we will review in Chapter 9. Although the analysis of imitation shows the influence of Dollard, the next area of discussion illustrates Miller's Hullian background.

The theory of imitation developed by Miller and Dollard stated that imitation is learned through drive reduction because imitating successful models makes the imitator more likely to be successful. The objects of imitation are persons likely to be successful. Imitation is not a nonspecific behavior.

Conflict behavior   Miller developed a series of postulates predicting the results of different types of conflict situations and went on to conduct an admirable series of experiments. This miniature model* was used to provide a learning theory explanation of Freudian concepts, such as choosing a "displaced love object" (Hilgard and Bower, 1975).† Freud's concept of anxiety was treated as a learned "fear drive" responsible for avoidance tendencies, and so on. The basic postulates were summarized by Miller (1959) for approach-avoidance conflicts or conflicts in which the person both fears and desires to approach a goal.

1. Increasing the motivation to go near a goal should cause the subject to go nearer to that goal, which will result in stronger fear. For example, if a student is afraid of a professor and receives a note from her telling him to come to her office because she is considering raising the student's expected grade, the student would be more likely to approach her office than if he had not received that note. As he gets closer than he would have without the note, however, he would also become more afraid.

2. Decreasing the overall strength of avoidance motivation should cause the subject to go nearer the goal. At this nearer point, fear will be greater than at more distance from the goal. If the student in the example just presented is told by his friends that the professor is really not so intimidating, he is likely to approach closer to her office, but as he does, his fear will be greater than if he had stayed farther away.

3. If a closer approach to a goal is produced by raising the gradient of approach, fear should be greater than if the same closer approach had been produced by lowering the gradient of avoidance. In our example, increasing the incentives to see the professor does not automatically reduce the student's fear of her.

4. No matter how a closer approach is facilitated, getting closer to the goal should increase fear. In the examples presented with postulates 1 and 2, the end result was always increased fear.

5. Once the goal is reached, additions to the strength of approach motivation should not add to fear. Further reductions in the strength of avoidance tendencies, however, should produce additional reductions in fear experienced. Once the student is actually in the presence of the professor, he is as afraid of her as he will ever be; higher incentives to remain in her presence will not make him more afraid. If she is pleasant to him, this will reduce his need to leave her office and make him less fearful.

6. The strength of avoidance increases more rapidly with nearness than does that of approach, or the gradient of avoidance is steeper than the gradient of approach. If this were not true, there would be no tendency to begin to approach a goal with mixed good and bad attributes, and there would be no point at which the more steeply rising gradient of avoidance meets the gradient of approach, causing you to experience conflict and indecision in your behavior. Miller predicts that you may stay immobilized at the points where the two gradients cross.

---

* A miniature model is one which focuses on a specific type of situation rather than attempting to be a general theory.

† Choosing a "displaced love object" follows from Freud's ideas about "displacement behavior." A person may resolve his ambivalence (conflict) about a choice of love object (such as his mother) by choosing as the goal of his courtship a person "subconsciously" representing his mother.

7. If you are in conflict about either approaching or retreating, the tendency with the higher gradient at the goal will determine your final response. In other words, if the student feels he really has to talk to the professor and that this is more important than anything negative that might happen in their interaction, he will approach her and talk to her.

There are other postulates, but the foregoing serve to present the flavor of this attempt to extend learning theory into explaining conflict. Most important, it must be noted that the **gradient of avoidance** is steeper than the **gradient of approach.** This postulate, labeled 6 in our list, explains the tendency to think we want something and to approach it, only to find as we get closer that we become increasingly anxious. An example might be going up to an attractive member of the opposite sex whom we have not yet met. At a distance, striking up a conversation seems plausible and inviting. Up close, most of us become increasingly shy and unsure unless reassured by a smile or acknowledgment from the other person.

From these postulates, Miller and Dollard developed a model predicting behavior in the four types of conflict situations: **approach-approach, approach-avoidance, avoidance-avoidance,** and perhaps the most common real world type, **double approach-avoidance.** This type is shown in Figure 7.2. An example of a double approach-avoidance conflict might be the conflict experienced by a student torn between the goal of being more active socially and the goal of raising grades through increased study time. As the student prepares to study, he fears losing social contacts, and as he prepares to socialize, the fear of doing poorly in school becomes more pronounced. Miller and Dollard used this model in explaining to their patients where the conflict lay, and in trying to design extinction procedures for acquired fear drives. Because Miller and Dollard thought that the source of conflicts could be the dynamic internal events postulated by Freud, they were criticized by many behaviorists (in Breger and McGaugh, 1967).

Miller developed a postulate system related to his four types of conflict. Approach-approach and avoidance-avoidance conflicts were supposed to be resolved quickly, while single approach-avoidance conflict was supposed to lead to immobilization at the choice point. Double approach-avoidance conflicts were supposed to lead to oscillations between the two goals.

Other contributions   Miller has continued to be active in a range of research activities. In 1941, he modified his S-R position by adding the element of feedback. Feedback is the mechanism by which the organism checks its own responses against an internal model and modifies them if necessary. With DiCara (1970), he demonstrated the operant control (feedback was provided) of internal processes such as heart rate. This was interpreted as a major blow to the Skinnerian two-factor position that visceral responses can only be classically conditioned. Although some aspects of his work on operant control of the viscera (providing the animal with feedback and punishing undesired responses) have not been replicated (Shapiro, 1977), the excitement and research engendered by

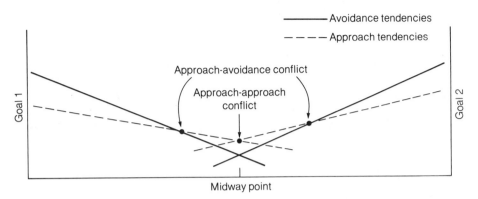

Figure 7.2   The gradients of approach and avoidance in a "double approach-avoidance conflict situation." Fear is assumed to increase with the strength of avoidance tendencies. In approach-approach conflict, movement towards either goal ends the conflict. Points of approach-avoidance conflicts should represent the points of closest approach to the goals under normal conditions. Whichever line is higher at a given distance from the goal predicts whether the subject will approach (approach gradient higher) or avoid (avoidance gradient higher).

this report still qualifies it as germinal to the present biofeedback movements (see Chapter 10).

Dollard's and Miller's Positions on Major Issues

Nature/nurture   Dollard and Miller are strong environmentalists. They do not deny, however, that some of the physiological mechanisms of motivation and learning may be innate. The physiological changes associated with the emotion of anxiety, such as sympathetic nervous system arousal, are postulated to be innate responses to fear (the motivation to avoid something). Generalization, from a cue which elicits the fear drive to similar cues, is also assumed to be innate.

The how of learning   Dollard and Miller are the strongest reinforcement theorists of those reviewed in this book. According to them, all learning requires reward from drive reduction. All learning also requires a drive in the presence of cues followed by a response that reduces the drive, thus rewarding the response.

The what of learning   The variety of types of things that can be learned is very great in this theory, ranging from tendencies to imitate to the drive of fear. Most things that are learned are treated as molar units but are assumed to consist of connections between stimuli and responses. Connection is used in a very loose sense, and many of the things that are learned sound much like cognitions.

Continuity/noncontinuity, use of animal data, and determinism   Trial-and-error learning may be gradual and continuous. Once the learned drive to imitate has been gradually acquired, imitative responses may appear discontinuous and sudden. Following Harlow's analysis of "learning to think" in the learning of strategies or learning sets in rhesus monkeys (Harlow, 1949), Miller (in Koch, 1959) saw the acquisition of basic problem-solving responses and familiarity with the cues of the problem situation as gradual; once these were learned, problem solutions would be of the discontinuous or insight type.

Miller and Dollard developed many of their key concepts, such as their model of the learning of fear drives, from work with rats. If they are determinist in their views, the determinants are complex indeed, including cues, thoughts, social situations, and feedback factors.

Perspective

While Neal Miller continues to make important contributions to the field of learning, the extension of Hullian principles to Freudian theory has had much less impact on therapeutic practice than the Pavlovian and Skinnerian applications to be discussed in Chapter 10. Miller's and Dollard's model of conflict and their analysis of fear as a learned drive strongly influenced Wolpe and other behavioral modifiers of the Pavlovian school and are still widely accepted. More recently, Miller (Bolles, 1975) has backed off from his drive-reduction theory of fear-drive acquisition. His original theory was two-factor in postulating that both stimuli (which may be drives) and responses must be learned and one-factor in not postulating two sets of learning laws to explain the learning of his two types of elements. In any case, Miller's and Dollard's greatest contribution has been to liberalize S-R learning theory and to extend it into the areas of conflict, psychopathology, and social learning.

O. Hobart Mowrer (1907–   )

If you feel that it has been difficult learning the basic principles proposed by so many learning theorists, be grateful that they were not all like Mowrer. At different times in his career he proposed three distinct theories. Like Miller and Dollard, Mowrer was associated with Hull at Yale. He received his Ph.D. in psychology from Johns Hopkins and was at Yale from 1936 to 1940. He has taught at Harvard and, from 1948, has been teaching at the University of Illinois. He began his theorizing in the Hullian tradition of relating learning to drive-reduction mechanisms. In the middle, he was like Skinner in having two sets of laws to explain two types of learning. In his final theory, he was a modified two-factor theorist in postulating that while there were two types of reinforcement (reward and punishment), there was only one type of learning law. Mowrer's most significant contributions were contained in his two-factor theories.

The Two-Factor Theories
The first two-factor theory   Mowrer defined two-factor theory as follows:

> Basically the two-factor, or two-process, hypothesis holds that *habits* are learned
> on the basis of the reinforcement provided by reward, or drive reduction, and
> that *fears* are learned (conditioned) on the basis of contiguous occurrence of a

signal and punishment, in the sense of drive induction. Pavlov had held that *all* learning is a matter of conditioning or stimulus contiguity, while Thorndike and Hull had stressed habit formation on the basis of reward. Two-factor theorists, by contrast, have held that it is not here a matter of either-or but of *both:* both sign learning (conditioning) and solution learning (habit formation). [Mowrer, 1956, p. 114]

As mentioned in the preceding section, this two-factor approach is easily applicable to avoidance learning. **Sign learning** begins in this way: Cues (signs) associated with an aversive stimulus become CSs for that unconditional cue. Eventually, the CSs come to elicit the physiological responses formerly attached to the US. Since these internal responses are experienced as unpleasant, the subject will try not to experience them. He **learns** the **solution** of escaping from the CSs (signs) that elicit internal fear responses, which reduces his fear drive (in Miller's and Dollard's terms) and thus avoids potentially aversive USs. If he learns to avoid the USs through an active response, this solution is labeled, appropriately enough, **active avoidance.** If he experiences the aversive US and gets away from it, this is labeled **escape.** Remaining still and not approaching the potential location of an aversive US is called **passive avoidance.** Finally, if a specific response is associated with aversive USs and these USs can be avoided by not repeating that response, then the situation is described as **punishment.** Punishment requires that presentation of the aversive US be contingent upon the occurrence of that specified response. Any of these kinds of learning can result in an increase in the probability of avoiding and escaping responses, in Skinnerian terms; or in states of affairs that switch from annoying to satisfying, in Thorndike's terminology; or in reducing the intensity of the stimuli associated with the pain drive, in Hull's 1952 theory and Spence.

Although Skinner had acknowledged that two types of learning might exist and Miller and Dollard had presented a model of learning in which fear was learned first, followed by responses (their two-stage or "two-factor" model), Mowrer was the first to analyze the interactions between the types of learning or stages of learning. This approach, we will see, is useful in attempting to explain punishment and avoidance learning. Remember that the internal physiological responses to a shock are probably the same, regardless of whether the shock occurs as the result of the subject's emitting a particular response (punishment) or whether the shock follows frequenting a particular location which could have been avoided. The behavior which results in these two cases, however, is quite different.

If the fear-arousing stimulus is external to the organism, behavior will be reinforced if it carries the organism away from the stimulus; and if the fear-arousing stimulus is internal, i.e., response-produced, the organism will be relieved, rewarded, reinforced for discontinuing the behavior which is responsible for such stimulation. In the one case, the organism may be said to be motivated to "get out of harm's way"; in the other case, to "avoid trouble." In both instances, however, the resulting behavior is fear-prompted and is reinforced by fear reduction. [Mowrer, 1956, p. 116]

The first case presented by Mowrer is, of course, the avoidance paradigm, and the second is the punishment paradigm. Because the "solution" of avoidance or inhibition of responding, respectively, prevents the conditioned fear signs (CSs) from extinguishing in the absence of shock (the original US), the conditioned fear drive may persist for years after the original classical conditioning that produced the fear of the CSs. Thus, the "solution learning," or operant component of the situation, protects the classically conditioned component from being extinguished (Konorski, 1948). The responses of avoidance or escape prevent the organism from discovering that there isn't any more shock. Fear, in Mowrer's model, is the expectancy that there will be shock if the subject does not get away from the cues that once were paired with shock. This model provides an explanation of the remarkable persistence of learning created by traumatic events and/or of phobic responses. As we will see in Part 2 of this text, however, this model of the persistence of avoidance responses has recently been severely criticized.

For example, let us say that you were once humiliated by someone you had thought was your friend. The experience was traumatic and the stinging verbal cues emitted by your attacker (the USs for the purpose of this example) became connected to the appearance and voice of the attacker (the CSs). A few days later, you see the person at a distance and decide to discuss the distressing interaction. As you get closer (a case of the avoidance gradient being steeper than the approach gradient), your stomach begins to knot and your pulse to race (the CR). This conditioned fear drive gets so unpleasant that you walk by the person at a distance without talking. As the person gets farther away, your conditioned discomfort decreases, reinforcing the avoidance response. The person has become a sign for discomfort, which presents you with a problem. Your solution for the problem is avoiding the signs. It may be that the explanation of the attack on you was that your former friend had just had a terrible day and was quite unlike himself. Without confronting the person, however, extinction of the conditioned property of his being a CS for a fear response can never occur. The implications for interpersonal relationships are obvious.

Mowrer's first two-factor theory stated that signs are cues classically conditioned to reinforcing or aversive events which elicit emotional expectancies (hope and fear, respectively), and solutions (responses) are operantly conditioned. Signs (CSs) related to phobias are protected from extinction because avoidance solutions (reinforced by reductions in anxiety) prevent the discovery that the aversive US will not follow the CS.

The final two-factor theory   Mowrer's two-factor theory has gradually been modified to reduce the difference between what is learned in each of the stages. In his final version, he pointed out that solution learning has many of the same characteristics as sign learning. Why not, Mowrer asks, consider that the subject's internal responses following a solution may be signs of hope (Mowrer, 1956)? Thus, the sensations of hope become bonded through a contiguity rela-

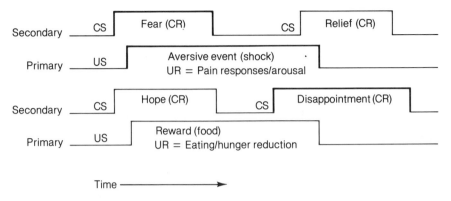

Figure 7.3   Relationships of primary (unlearned) reinforcement and responses and secondary (conditioned) reinforcement and responses to aversive and rewarding events. Note that cues associated with the onset of an aversive event and the termination of rewarding events are related to incremental reinforcement. Cues conditioned to onset of reward and termination of aversive USs are related to decremental reinforcement. Primary aversive USs lead to incremental reinforcement, and primary reward USs lead to decremental reinforcement. The heavier black lines indicate situations which increase drive (incremental reinforcement).

tionship with specified responses. In this later theory, all learning becomes sign learning, and Mowrer moves closer to the cognitive camp. Extinction becomes counterconditioning in which either a fear is not confirmed and provides relief, or a hope that is not confirmed provides disappointment. Even the learning of motor skills, such as riding a bicycle, involves feelings of doing it correctly (pride) or doing it poorly (frustration). These feelings have marked cognitive components related to the expectancies of the would-be rider. This allowance for expectancies makes Mowrer's final theory much like Tolman's, even to the point of seeing the learning of what are essentially cognitive units as taking place through a process of conditioning.

The incremental-decremental model of reinforcers   One other significant contribution of Mowrer's to learning theory deserves mention. He provided a classification system for reinforcers congruent with his modified two-factor theory. One type of reinforcement, which he called **incremental reinforcement,** involves increases in drives as in responding to pain cues. The signs (CSs) signaling the danger of exposure to aversive cues are those of fear, while the signs signaling that rewarding and/or safe conditions are about to end are those of disappointment. The second type of reinforcement is **decremental reinforcement,** in which drive intensity is reduced, as when food eaten reduces a hunger drive. Rewards are decremental reinforcers, and the signs associated with expectancies about rewards are those of hope. Relief is the sign that a CS associated with danger is about to end, which results in reduced arousal and thus is also a decremental reinforcer (Mowrer, 1956). The relationships of the signs (which are internal conditioned responses) to primary reinforcement of both aversive (shock) and reward (food) types are shown in Figure 7.3.

In Mowrer's second two-factor theory, all learning is sign (cue) learning, which is related to expectancies about reinforcement. The theory remains two-factor, however, in that signs which increase drive (fear and disappointment) lead to incremental reinforcement, and signs which reduce drive (hope and relief) lead to decremental reinforcement.

Mowrer's Positions on Major Issues

Nature/nurture   Mowrer held that primary drives, and such things as fear as an innate response to pain, are genetically determined. All other drives, cues, and responses are learned.

The how of learning   Mowrer began from the orthodox Hullian position of explaining learning through drive-reduction (reinforcement) mechanisms. He then moved to a two-factor learning theory in which signs (CSs) are learned through contiguity, and solutions (responses) are learned through reinforcement. In his final theory, all learning is sign learning, but dependent upon feedback or confirmation. Thus, all learning involves reinforcement, but this reinforcement can involve drive reduction (reward) or drive onset, as with punishment. In the latter case, in which reinforcement was taken to mean the confirmation of signs signaling the onset of an aversive condition, the meaning is very close to Pavlov's definition of reinforcement, which was based upon contiguity. In having two distinct types of reinforcement, Mowrer's theory retained two-factor characteristics.

The what of learning   In his first theory, the units of learning were the usual Hullian habits. When he moved to a two-factor position, the units of learning became either bonds between cues (signs) and drives, or between drive reduction and responses. In his final theory, Mowrer postulated that all learning was the learning of signs or cognitions of the Tolmanian expectancy type. In this theory, he still referred to the learning of "habits," but such "habits" he saw as no different from the learning of secondary reinforcement. That is, both of these involve the conditioning of fear decrement or "hope" to particular stimuli (in Sahakian, 1976). Mowrer seems to be a connectionist of sorts, but the nature of his connections has become extremely vague and general.

Continuity/noncontinuity, use of animal data, and determinism   The progression of Mowrer's views on learning seems to range from that of a typical Hullian connectionist who viewed learning as a continuous process of habit or bond formation to a mechanistic cognitivist who accepted both continuous and discontinuous learning. Writing in 1960 (in Sahakian, 1976), he described how organisms scan their environment for cues related to emotional states and how insightful learning follows confirmatory feedback. Both the orientation and the language of this last position seem close to the cybernetics of Norbert Wiener and the information-processing approach to learning. As part of this theoretical evolution, Mowrer began by using animal data extensively and ended by accepting primarily human and machine language concepts. Although his theorizing retains a deterministic flavor, he has now accepted the complex internal mechanisms of the information-processing-oriented cognitive theorists.

Perspective

The changes in Mowrer's theory reflect the changes taking place through much of learning theory. Beginning with the connection of habits and stimuli, Mowrer gradually shifted more and more towards accepting first cognitive and then cybernetic theory concepts. On his way, he contributed many useful ideas on the relationship between types of reinforcement and emotions and ways of explaining and classifying avoidance and escape behavior. In his shift towards incorporating more cognitive variables, he paralleled most of the neo-Hullians, as well as some of Skinner's followers (especially Bandura, who is discussed in Chapter 9). His work shows how theorists who attempt to protect their ideas from disconfirmation by new data often see these theories become progressively less specific and less precise, stating predictions that would not be generated by any other similar theory.

Although the work of Miller and Dollard and that of Mowrer illustrates changes in theories beginning from a unified theoretical position, not all learning theorists were ever identified with such a coherent viewpoint. The contributions of various such researchers, collectively identified as functionalists, will now be briefly reviewed. Our review will cover only selected areas of their research, chosen to illustrate their approach.

Functionalism: A Position for All Reasons

Although functionalism never became a coherent school of psychology like the theories examined earlier in this part, and although there is no functionalist theory per se, several themes identify psychologists and theoretical positions within the functionalist tradition: First, the functionalists were empiricists and highly productive in experimental work. Any method, however, from introspectionism to animal research, was permissible. Second, coupled with this tolerance of methodological divergence was a tolerance of commonsense ideas and commonsense terminology such as "mind" and "meaning."

Third, at least early in the movement, most functionalists were concerned about practical applications of their research. This close tie between theory and application reached a peak with John Dewey's development of a laboratory school at the University of Chicago in 1896 (CRM, 1973). The findings of this school in the area of techniques for motivating pupils culminated in the progressive education movement which swept American public schools during the 1930s. These schools organized their curricula around teaching academic subjects through activities related to occupations such as sewing, carpentry, cooking, and so on. This stress on the child's interests, as opposed to learning by rote, can also be seen in Thorndike's comments on educational applications, as reviewed in Chapter 3.

Fourth, functionalists tended to avoid discontinuities such as instinct versus learning or insight versus trial-and-error learning. Tolman, while identified with the cognitive theory position, refused to insist that all learning was cognitive in nature. As discussed in Chapter 5, Tolman identified six distinct types of learning, stating: "Conflicting theories of learning may each be correct for some different kind of learning" (Tolman, 1949, p. 144). He identified two of his types of learning as involving connections and fitting Hull's model of drive reduction, while a third type involved the connecting of movements by a contiguity mechanism as postulated by Guthrie. This eclectic tolerance is very much in the functionalist tradition, and it also illustrates the difficulty in identifying precisely who is, and who is not, a functionalist. Thorndike may be considered to belong to both the functionalist and behaviorist camps. Even the arch-behaviorist Skinner, in his acceptance of classical conditioning as well as operant conditioning, in his interest in the functional analysis of behavior, and in applications, shows functionalist characteristics.

This avoidance of discontinuities or dichotomies led the functionalists to accept the **empirical law of effect** without having to reject contiguity and/or cognitive factors in learning. The empirical (or weak) law of effect incorporates data such as those produced by Thorndike (1931), showing that in some circumstances reward may be necessary for learning, as well as evidence that changes in behavior (performance) may depend upon reinforcement without insisting that "effect" is the sole mechanism of learning. The general approach was to investigate what type of conditions would produce each kind of learning and to conceptualize each type of learning as extremes or as points on a common continuum (Hilgard and Bower, 1975). The researchers would seek out pure examples of each learning type and try to determine the whys and wheres of the example's occurrence.

Fifth, functionalism is very much psychology in the American tradition. It was not as tolerant on the nature/nurture issue as on most other issues and was marked by a strong environmentalist bias. Practical, pragmatic, commonsense approaches were stressed. All types of learning problems were investigated, and all types of experimental subjects were used.

With time, however, there came to be an increased emphasis on verbal learning as the most appropriate medium for studying the functioning mind and on the "transfer of training" problem as the most related to the practical problems of education and industrial training. This focusing of emphasis moved the functionalists closer to the cognitive position and away from its early close relationship with behaviorism. As will be discussed in Chapter 11, the modern cognitive-verbal learning theory proposed by Eli Saltz is a descendant of the functionalist tradition in concentrating on the verbal learning mode of experimental inquiry and on transfer phenomena.

The Transfer of Training Problem in Verbal Learning

The transfer of training problem refers to the question of how best to have training in one situation apply to, or transfer to, another situation. This is, of course, the basic problem of education—how to make what is learned in school transfer over to increased abilities in the outside world. In the same spirit that led the behaviorists to hope that laws of learning gleaned from rat experiments

Table 7.1 Time Relationships of Retroactive and
Proactive Inhibition

Retroactive Inhibition

Learn Task A ⟶ Learn Task B ⟶ Test recall of task A
$\qquad\qquad\qquad$ (Interference with
$\qquad\qquad\qquad$ recall of task A)

Proactive Inhibition

Learn Task A ⟶ Learn Task B ⟶ Test recall of task B
(Interference with
learning and recall
of task B)

---

would generalize to humans, the functionalists hoped that what was learned from verbal-learning studies would apply to human learning and transfer in general.

Verbal learning research methodology stresses two techniques: the **paired-associate procedure** and **serial learning.** In the paired-associate method, the subjects, when given one word of a pair, are required to respond with the other word. In serial learning, which dates back to Ebbinghaus and the late 1800s, the subject must learn an entire list of words or nonsense syllables. With these procedures, the shapes of serial position curves (early and late words are learned first), the superiority of distributed practice (rest periods between blocks of trials) versus massed practice (no rest periods) in most situations, the effects of inserting a known word in a list (it facilitates learning the words before and after it), and many other relationships were discovered. Much of our basic knowledge of memory, interference effects, and forgetting derive from this work. To illustrate the process followed by the functionalists, let us now turn to the history of the investigation of memory.

A basic tenet of functionalist thought (remembering that within this diffuse movement not all functionalists would accept such a tenet) is that nothing is ever really forgotten. Rather, newly learned material interferes with the recall of previously learned material. This backward interference is called **retroactive inhibition**[*] and is a type of **negative transfer** effect. Old memories may also interfere with the learning of new material. This forward association, called **proactive inhibition,** is also a negative transfer effect. Retroactive inhibition is illustrated through the A (first learning), B (new material), A (testing of retention of the first learning) paradigm. Proactive inhibition is shown in the B (old learning), A (new learning to be measured) paradigm (see Table 7.1). Note that as in cognitive theories, learning and performance (in this case, recall) are seen as separate, since the material interfered with is not forgotten.

An example of retroactive inhibition would be memorizing the phone number of a potential "date" on one day, then meeting someone with a similar

---

[*] Or retroactive interference. The general effect is considered to be that of interference by an inhibitory process.

phone number on the following day and memorizing that number. When you later try to remember the phone number of the first person, you may end up with a number somewhere between the two phone numbers. An example of proactive inhibition would be having trouble learning Spence's equations for predicting the strength of tendencies to respond because of interference from Hull's formulas which you had learned previously. When asked to give Spence's equation, you might give Hull's or a combination instead.

Jenkins and Dallenbach (1924) were able to support strongly the theory of "forgetting" as interference. One group of their subjects learned a list of ten nonsense syllables and was asked to recall them after eight hours. Other groups were asked to recall the syllables after from one to eight hours of sleep. It was found that the subjects with no sleep (those learning the list in the morning) had forgotten over half of the syllables. There was about 10 percent forgetting during each of the first two hours of sleep and none after that. The authors suggest that activities during waking interfere with the recall of the syllables. This is, of course, the retroactive inhibition paradigm. McGeoch (1929) found that much of this retroactive inhibition could be prevented if the subjects practiced the list after mastering it, or **overlearned** it. These results suggest that extensive studying followed by some sleep before a major examination might better facilitate test performance on the following day than cramming through the night and up to the time of the examination.

Most verbal learning studies support the view that interference rather than true forgetting is responsible for apparent memory loss. Old learning that interferes with forming new memories is proactive inhibition (interference). New learning that interferes with recall of old learning is retroactive inhibition (interference).

Once the functionalists had suggested some tentative "laws" about interference, they began conducting experiments to investigate more subtle relationships. Osgood (1949) discovered that the similarity of the cues used during the original training sessions to cues presented during testing was not sufficient to predict the type and extent of interference effects. The similarity of the responses required during training and testing and the interaction of cue and response similarity also needed to be considered. To summarize the complex relationships of cue and response similarities, he developed a model based on a three-dimensional surface in which width represented stimulus characteristics, length represented response characteristics, and height above and below a zero reference plane indicated the direction of transfer, positive or negative (see Figure 7.4). Looking at this figure, find the place on the rear upper edge where similar stimuli intersect with identical responses. Since this is above the dotted line representing the plane of zero transfer (or generalization), **positive transfer** and **retroactive facilitation** (recall of old memories being enhanced) should occur. Reacting in the same way to stop signs of different shapes might be an example. If identical or very similar stimuli are presented and the subject is required to make antagonistic responses (lower right front edge of figure), the model pre-

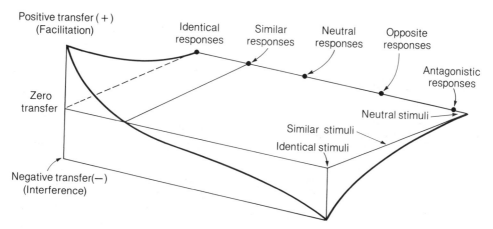

Figure 7.4   *A simplified version of Osgood's transfer and retroactive surface. The top line represents the extent to which the responses involved in transfer are alike. The line to the right shows how similar the stimuli involved in transfer are to each other. The vertical line on the left represents the type (positive or negative) of transfer of training or facilitation versus interference in recall. To predict the type of transfer or facilitation/interference with recall, find out how similar the cues were between the two training situations. Then do the same for the responses required in the old and new situation. Locate these points on the stimulus line and the response line, respectively, and find the point on the curved thick line where they would meet.*

dicts that high amounts of negative transfer, or retroactive interference, would occur. For example, if a person who is first trained by his parents to always "turn the other cheek" when confronted with rudeness later takes a course in assertion training in which he learns to make assertive responses to the same situations that formerly elicited "meek" behavior, his previous types of responses will be antagonistic to the more recent assertive response. In this case, the cues which now are supposed to elicit assertive responses are the same or similar to those that formerly elicited "meekness." This will result in a negative transfer between previous learning and the results of the assertiveness training. Previous learning that interferes with the new learning produces proactive interference; new learning that interferes with remembering the early patterns of responding produces retroactive interference. Finally, the figure predicts that combining identical training and test condition stimuli with identical response requirements (read above the lower lefthand edge) will maximize positive transfer. Because providing extra practice of the same responses to the same cues is nothing but overlearning, this is indeed true.

The effects of similarity variables based on entire lists of words on proactive interference were also investigated. Underwood (1949) found that proactive inhibition increases with the similarity of the two lists and with the degree of prior learning of the first list. This latter finding is simply the greater interference produced by well-known material, as when a person fluent in Spanish encounters difficulty in learning French. Contrasted with the effects of time on retroactive inhibition (it increases), proactive inhibition decreased with more time between learning A and learning B.

Bilodeau and Schlosberg (1952) found that it is not only the similarity of the words in the lists that affects interference. When the interpolated material (the B in the A-B-A paradigm of retroactive inhibition) was learned in different rooms and with the subject's assuming different postures, the retroactive inhibition effects decreased by almost 50 percent. Nor is it enough to know the similarity of the cues in the lists and the testing conditions. Slamecka (1960) found that the "meaning similarity" of prose passages was more related to extent of interference effects than the physical similarity of the constituent words of the passages. This finding, that the basic unit of learning may be a "meaning," is, of course, congruent with the beliefs of the cognitive theorists as well as with those of the neo-Pavlovian Russian theorists to be discussed in Chapter 8. Further evidence against the Skinnerian or Hullian explanation, which states that a series of words acts as an S-R chain, was provided by Young (1962), who found that serial position effects depend more on the position of a word in a series than on the stimulus characteristics of the words surrounding it. Interference seems to occur in units larger than individual words. Keppel, Postman, and Zavortink (1968) even found that the total list learning experience of the subjects made a difference. When student subjects had to learn many lists, proactive inhibition effects were minimal on the first set of lists and maximal on the last set. They interpreted proactive inhibition as mixed recall or confusion, and noted that it increases as the time after the learning of both lists increased. These complications illustrate the process of functionalist investigation of a problem and their trend towards ever more complex laws.

However complex, the laws of interference have been found to apply in similar ways to meaningful as well as to nonsense information. This suggests that meaning and insight may lie on a common dimension (or continuum) with trial-and-error and rote learning. In a sense, meaning and insight (phenomena of positive transfer) are implicit, internal responses subject to the same laws as explicit trial-and-error responses. This view would probably be shared by Pavlov, Hull, and Spence, except that they would see the constituent words of a thought rather than meaning units as the units to which the laws apply.

Although the discussion just concluded about the functionalist study of the problem of transfer may appear highly abstract, the principles discovered may be applicable to real world situations such as the design of flight simulators to be used to train airline pilots. In this case, Osgood's surface would predict that positive transfer would be maximal if the flight simulator was as similar as possible to an actual airplane and the responses required were also very similar.

Factors influencing the extent and direction (positive represents facilitation; negative, interference) of transfer include the similarities of old and new cues and responses and their interactions, the meaning of the cues, the contexts in which learning occurs, and the similarity of whole lists of words.

Functionalist Positions on Major Issues

Because functionalism is such a diverse school of thought, no clear generalizations can be safely made except to state that most functionalists were eclectic in their approach and inclined towards environmentalism. Most also made minimal use of animal data. One exception is Harry Harlow, who, by developing a model of learning in which trial-and-error learning is placed on a theoretical continuum with insight learning and by taking a strong environmentalist view, should qualify as a functionalist. We may now briefly summarize Harlow's monkey studies on the relationship of trial-and-error learning to insight learning.

Harry F. Harlow (1905–)

Harlow received his education from Stanford University, earning his Ph.D. in 1930. Most of his academic career was spent at the University of Wisconsin, where he directed the primate center for many years, trained a generation of talented primatologists, and conducted an extensive and significant series of research projects using rhesus monkeys as subjects. He is currently in semiretirement in Arizona but maintains many of his professional involvements. Harlow is perhaps best known for his studies of factors related to the early development of emotional attachments in monkeys, including the famous "wire and cloth" mother surrogate experiments (summarized in Harlow, *Learning to Love,* 1971). He has conducted other equally significant research on learning in monkeys, however. Harlow fits into the functionalist tradition in his concern with the continuum relating gradual learning and insight, with the mechanisms underlying transfer of training, and with a very environmentalist approach to learning.

By focusing on changes in problem-solving behavior in monkeys (who are more likely than rats to learn like human beings), Harlow has documented the phenomenon of "learning to learn," or learning sets. Harlow observed that monkeys given discrimination problems in object quality initially solve them by trial and error, as predicted by Thorndike and most behaviorists. After being given many series of similar problems, however, the monkeys began to show rapid, "insightful" solutions. Harlow (1949) suggests that such "insightful" solutions do not represent the type of sudden perceptual reordering of the problem-related environment postulated by the gestalt theorists. Rather, the monkeys have learned more than a set of individual habits from their long exposure to a particular type of problem. What they have learned is how to learn efficiently (a plan for approaching a particular type of problem). This learning how to learn is a learning set, and it consists of the animal's acquiring the insight necessary to transfer the ability established in learning previous problems to another situation which requires solving. Learning of learning sets transforms the organism from one dominated by slow and inefficient trial-and-error processes to one that adapts by utilizing hypotheses and insight. Thus, for Harlow, trial-and-error learning and insightful learning are ends of a common continuum unified by progressive amounts of experience. Insight is not an innate ability but rather one acquired through experience with the environment. In forming the ability to show insightful learning (acquiring a learning set), the number of series of problems is the determining factor. You may recall the study reported at the beginning of Chapter 5 in which one of the author's ravens learned to discriminate by number. Although this initial ability to discriminate stimulus cards showing one figure from those showing two figures took many trials to acquire, subsequent acquiring of successful discriminations of numbers up to five was very rapid, a circumstance that seemed to show that the raven had acquired a set for discriminating by number.

For Harlow, learning sets represent a process by which a shift occurs from conditioning to reasoning. As in Montessori's theory, insight is a process that depends (in a lawful way) on previous experience and which develops gradually from that experience. Transfer of training, for Harlow, is the transfer of this "learned insight," which is a problem-to-problem process, rather than the transfer of the actual training of a specific skill. Viewed in this way, the insight demonstrated by Köhler's chimpanzees was the end result of skills gradually acquired through playing with the sticks, boxes, and so forth, leading the animals to form learning sets related to the use of objects to reach bananas.

Harlow has conducted research on monkeys which shows that apparently insightful behavior in problem solving is the result of a gradual process (which begins with conditioning, or trial-and-error learning) and represents acquisition of learning sets, or learning how to learn.

Harlow (1959) has suggested that subjects formed learning sets because they learned what not to do. Thus, the inhibition of tendencies to make systematic errors was postulated to be the process underlying the formation of learning sets. This hypothesis stemmed from Harlow's observation that initial errors seemed to reflect incorrect hypotheses. The idea that animals' early errors during apparent trial-and-error learning reflect systematic biases was discussed in Chapter 5.

Perspective

Functionalism represents a convergence point. Spence was more eclectic than Hull, and Bandura (to be discussed in Chapter 9) is more eclectic than Skinner. By moving away from commitment to tightly defined schools, the functionalist is able to evaluate all schools objectively and these evaluations have resulted in forcing many theorists towards the common ground. Yet even with these successes, functionalism has not produced a unitheory. For one thing, the tendency to develop more and more elaborate laws concerning less and less has resulted in isolated miniature models which are difficult to apply in the real world. This failure to fulfill the promise of producing functional practical applications has been the result of overly complex miniature models (though the functionalists would retort that the complexity of their models reflects the complexity of the real world) and a lack of a unifying, coherent schemata.

Development of the overall unifying schemata to give organization to the limited-area laws of the functionalist is needed to move us onwards towards unitheory. Along with bringing meaning variables back into good repute within the experimentalist community, the functionalists may have prefigured the final complex nature of our hypothetical unitheory which explains and predicts all types of learning.

As we shall see in Part 2 of this book, most of the major laws of the theorists presented in Part 1 have been retained, even if modified and supplemented by new laws, and in many cases have been applied to meaning variables. The theoretical approaches presented in Part 1 have not succeeded in eliminating one another, in spite of considerable research and argument directed towards that goal. For example, verbal learning paired-associate tasks include contiguity variables (words close in time or space to each other), reinforcement variables (the satisfaction of recalling a pair correctly), and cognitive variables (associations of the words and mnemonic devices). The varying interpretations derived from distinct theories may tell us more of a theorist's viewpoint than of the total picture of how we learn. In the end, the eclecticism of the functionalist may seem to demonstrate less lack of commitment and more wisdom.

Chapter Perspective

The impacts of each of the theoretical positions covered in this chapter have already been discussed in the perspective after each section. The point to be made about two-factor and eclectic approaches is that the theorists involved have, in general, been more willing to stay open to a range of possibilities about the processes involved in learning than most orthodox defenders of the major theories. Consequently, the theorists covered in this chapter have explored topics barely discussed by the major theorists and have offered alternate explanations to topics covered in depth in the writings of the major theorists. Because the alternate explanations reflect their writers' tendencies to borrow what they felt most valuable from more than one major theory, the multifactor theories are often more congruent with the actual complexity of learning, hence better predictors of the eventual nature of unitheory.

Key Terms

active avoidance

approach-approach conflict

approach-avoidance conflict

assertion training

avoidance-avoidance conflict

decremental reinforcement

double approach-avoidance conflict

drive, cue, response, reward

empirical law of effect

escape

functionalism

gradient of approach

gradient of avoidance

gradient of generalization

higher mental processes

incremental reinforcement

learning set

negative transfer

overlearning

paired-associate procedure

passive avoidance

positive transfer

proactive inhibition

punishment

retroactive facilitation

retroactive inhibition

serial learning

sign learning

solution learning

Annotated Bibliography

The approach of Miller and Dollard is shown in N. E. Miller "Studies of fear as an acquired drive: 1. Fear as motivation and fear-reduction as reinforcement in the learning of new responses" (*Journal of Experimental Psychology*, 1948, 38, 89–101), and N. E. Miller and J. Dollard, *Social learning and imitation* (New Haven, Conn.: Yale University Press, 1941). Mowrer's theory and its changes are presented in his article, "Two-factor learning theory reconsidered, with special reference to secondary reinforcement and the concept of habit" (*Psychological Review*, 1956, 63, 114–128). The literature on functionalists' approaches to verbal learning is too vast to suggest other than the influential article by Osgood, "The similarity paradox in human learning: A resolution" (*Psychological Review*, 1949, 56, 132–143). Harlow's work on learning sets can be sampled fairly painlessly in H. F. Harlow, "The formation of learning sets" (*Psychological Review*, 1949, 56, 51–65).

We will first review the contributions and important principles contributed by each of the major theorists covered in this part. Then we will take an overall look at the evolution of learning theories and try to project the trends that will be covered in the second part of this book.

Contiguity Theorists

Pavlov was the first to investigate systematically the laws of association learning or classical conditioning. He suggested that most behavior is reflexive in nature (that is, dependent upon brain mechanisms rather than upon "free will") and that these reflexes may be elicited either by prewired stimuli, the USs or unconditioned stimuli, or by stimuli which have been repeatedly associated with the USs, the CSs or condition(al)ed stimuli. The process by which the CS comes to serve as the signal for the probable appearance of the US is called conditioning. The response to the CS is called the conditional (or conditioned) reflex or response. These CRs are at first identical to the reflexes elicited by prewired stimuli (the URs), but gradually the CR usually becomes less vigorous.

If the CS is presented several times without the reinforcement of the US, eventually it becomes ineffectual in eliciting the CR, or extinction takes place. After a rest period, the CS may again have the power to elicit a CR, which represents spontaneous recovery. A strongly established CS resists extinction and may serve as a stimulus to pair with a new CS to establish a second-order conditioning, which is a weaker connection than that between the original US and the first CS. Extinction is a type of inhibitory process which stops responses from occurring. Another type of inhibitory process is the orienting reflex (OR), or the "What is it?" reflex that stops all conditioning. Almost any stimulus may be a CS if it is not stronger than the US. Even time intervals may be CSs in temporal or trace conditioning. A clashing of inhibition and excitation or other conflict may produce a conditioned neurosis. Environmental cues are considered the first signal system; human thoughts and words, the second signal system. When an organism distinguishes between two stimuli, the process is called discrimination; when a CR is emitted to a stimulus which has never been conditioned but which seems like the CS, the process is called generalization. These terms and principles described by Pavlov appeared in almost all the learning theories covered in this part. This is why the most important ones are listed here so that you can check and be sure you understand each of them.

Watson's primary contribution was to focus the attention of American psychology on the behavioristic approach. Although he first explained learning by the associationist principles of frequency and recency, Watson later simply adopted Pavlov's principles and was instrumental in introducing Pavlov to American psychology. He also originated the concept that muscle responses act as or generate stimuli, which was further developed by Guthrie as the concept of movement-produced stimuli. Guthrie reduced Watson's original two-principle theory to one basic law of learning, the law of contiguity, with one additional postulate. This postulate stated that the bonding of each stimulus to an individual muscle movement occurred in only one trial. Since a complete act (such as learning to ride a bicycle) is a collection of many muscle movements, it is a matter of probability (related to how many "correct" movements get bonded to the appropriate stimuli in how much time) when an entire act can be learned. This probabilistic feature of Guthrie's theory was used by Estes in developing his statistical stimulus-sampling theory which prefigured many modern mathematical theories.

Reinforcement Theorists

Beginning with Thorndike, the idea that behavior is controlled by its consequences has had a powerful impact on American learning theories. At the beginning of this century, Thorndike's was the dominant American learning theory. After a period of dominance by Watson's and Guthrie's contiguity theories, first Hull's and then Skinner's theory established the ascendance of the reinforcement position. Although they came to use many of the terms first suggested by Pavlov,* the reinforcement theorists extended the power and scope of the conditioning model. Thorndike and Hull came to develop models in which all learning was explained by rewarding or punishing behaviors (one-factor theories). Spence and Skinner admitted that some types of learning might occur through contiguity but concentrated on learning through reinforcement (two-factor theories).

The reinforcement theories presented here were based on data derived from extensive experimental labors with animal subjects, and all assumed that the truth of the principle of equipotentiality justified the generalization of laws discovered through experiments on animals to human behavior. All were strongly mechanistic. Complex human and animal behavior was seen as determined by environmental contingencies and the lawful relationships between stimuli and responses. All these theorists attempted to mold psychology on the model of the natural and physical sciences and strongly opposed explaining behavior in terms of variables of the mind. All their theories were most successful in predicting simple behaviors of the sort that could be produced in controlled laboratory settings. All were less successful in applying similar precision to their explanations of complex behavior. Both Hull and Skinner saw many of their followers lose much of their purity as behaviorists and adopt many of the concepts advocated by the cognitive theorists.

Thorndike, the earliest of the reinforcement theorists, stated his theory most loosely and in terms closest to those used in everyday conversation. Hull attempted to design a formal theory employing the logical model proposed by Euclid and used by Newton. Hull deduced testable theorems from postulates and attempted to discover the numerical relationships among stimuli, intervening variables, and responses. Although he assiduously pursued the goal of precise quantitative prediction of behavior, Hull did not reach this goal except for some limited types of rat behavior under laboratory conditions. In his very precision, Hull exposed his equations to experimental disproof. This procedure, however, may be preferable to Thorndike's type of theory, which is so loosely formulated that any sort of result of an experimental test may be claimed to fit it.

---

* Hilgard and Bower (1975) report that 31 of the terms in Kimble's 1961 learning text's glossary are described as originating with Pavlov; 21 others are attributed to all other conditioning theorists combined.

Skinner, who claimed to be atheoretical, did avoid postulating the range of internal variables characteristic of Hull's theory. In attempting to explain complex human behaviors, however, Skinner invented such entities as S_D — secondary reinforcer chains, which sometimes share the same unobservable qualities that he criticized in the theories of others. As with Hull's, Skinner's model is most precise in predicting simple behaviors under controlled conditions. Skinner today is the dominant voice in American learning theory, if not in American psychology. By restricting himself to a theory which is based primarily on empirical descriptions of the relationships between the environment and behavior, Skinner has developed laws that have stood up to most experimental tests and that are being widely applied.

The apparent contradiction between Skinner's avowedly atheoretical position and his theory must be explained. He is against theory as an attempt to construct models of what happens inside organisms, as in Hullian or cognitive theories. He is not against descriptive theory, nor even against a Hull-type theory, if the level of knowledge about behavior has reached a point to justify such an approach. His generalization of his basic principles to humans' verbal and social behaviors might be interpreted as signifying that he now believes that the data base is available to begin the process of theorizing about mediating variables. The criticisms of Skinner's higher-level theory of language acquisition by Chomsky and others suggest that the safer course for Skinner might have been to continue to limit his efforts to the development of descriptive laws through a strict empirical process.

Skinner dealt with the contiguity versus reinforcement issue by recognizing both types of learning. He saw each, however, as applying to the learning of different types of relationships and did not explore the interrelationships of the two basic types of conditioning (type S and type R), except insofar as type S conditioning was responsible for the formation of conditioned reinforcers.

Thorndike's most important contribution was his law of effect. Thorndike influenced most other learning theories and was one of the first such theorists to apply his ideas to the field of education. Hull contributed a sophisticated model of mediational processes (r_G-S_G) which today is a major connectionist contender to Skinner's model of mediational (internal) processes. Although his attempt to construct a precise, mathematically expressed general theory of learning failed, Hull inspired numerous talented followers and great research productivity.

Skinner contributed the following principles: (1) shaping, or the method of successive approximations, (2) a precise analysis of the effects of varying different modes of delivering reinforcements (the schedules of reinforcement), (3) the discriminative stimulus model of response chaining and discrimination, (4) the ideas of superstitious conditioning and negative reinforcement (as opposed to punishment), and many more. Like Pavlov, he contributed to experimental methodology (the apparatus today called the Skinner box) and extended his technological skills into developing the most commonly used type of teaching machine.

Cognitive Theorists

Most of the cognitive theorists were strongly opposed to the mechanistic-connectionist viewpoint of the theorists summarized to this point. An exception was Tolman, who combined a connectionist view of the "how" of learning with a cognitive view of the "what" of learning. Tolman participated in research demonstrating the naive behaviorist dogma that learning was always reflected in behavior (performance) was not always true. In showing the existence of latent learning (learning which does not become apparent in performance until after suitable reinforcing conditions are provided) and learning of places (cognitive maps were presumed to be the units of learning), rather than habits formed of linked previously emitted responses connected to stimuli, Tolman forced the behaviorists into more complex theorizing. Tolman also demonstrated that events existing outside the physical environment, such as the organism's expectancies, could influence behavior.

The gestalt theorists contributed further to the cognitive view of the organism as an active organizing entity rather than as a passive respondent to the stimuli present in the environment. By extending the gestalt laws about the organization of perceptual events into the field of learning, the gestalt theorists set the stage for what is now known as the human information-processing approach to the field of learning. They also stimulated interest in discovering the mechanisms of the complex internal processes they described, which has contributed to the extension of cybernetic principles (first developed by Norbert Wiener) to learning. Basic gestalt principles included the idea that attention is focused on limited aspects of a stimulus situation (called figure as opposed to noncentral or ground) rather than being a process of indiscriminate sampling of available stimuli. They suggested that organisms reorganize perceptions, learning, and memory according to the principle of *Prägnanz,* which means good form or good gestalt. This, with the principle of closure (the tendency to finish uncompleted figures or uncompleted processes), is an integral part of gestalt therapy, which is becoming a major contender to behavior therapy. The motivational powers of uncompleted processes were named after their discoverer as the Zeigarnik effect.

Maria Montessori, like the gestalt theorists, incorporated innate factors in her theory—in particular, ideas about the development of sensory processes. She saw cognitive development progressing through sensitive periods, or periods of time in which a child's brain was predisposed to learn certain things more easily than other times. Like Skinner, she also contributed to the physical technology of teaching through her inventions of didactic materials, or self-teaching classroom aids.

Multifactor and Eclectic Theorists

The work of the major theorists has been augmented and extended into new areas by the neo-Hullians (Spence, Miller and Dollard, and Mowrer). Miller and Dollard made significant contributions in designating four types of conflict, in theories of imitative processes, and in attempts to extend learning principles into psychoanalysis. Mowrer's theory illustrates the evolution of much of learning theory in the direction of incorporating more cognitive variables, although this tendency can be seen in the other neo-Hullians' theories as well. He contributed a decremental (as in fear drives) versus incremental (as in reward) classification system for types of reinforcing situations and tied these to related emotional states much like Tolman's expectancies.

The loosely organized school of psychologists labeled the functionalist school made significant contributions in the areas of verbal learning and the transfer of training, showing both retroactive (acting backwards on previous learning) and proactive (acting forward on new learning) interference and facilitation effects. Like the neo-Hullians, they began by explaining their phenomena in S-R associationist terms and later incorporated meaning (cognitive) variables. Harlow developed the concept of the learning set, or learning how to learn over series of related problems.

Part Perspective

In following the sequence of theories presented in Part 1 of the text, you may be struck with the extent of progress that has been made in articulating the principles for different types of learning and in developing increasingly sophisticated methods for exploring learning. Given the crude experimental methods of turn-of-the-century psychology, it seems entirely appropriate that the most successful theories (in terms of their influence within psychology as a field) were originally based on the rejection of mentalism and cognition. Behavior is easier to measure objectively than inner mental activity, and animals do provide a convenient means to study behavior. Stimuli can be at least approximately controlled and overt responses related to those controlled stimuli. Even investigations of learning based on the S-R mechanisms of the connectionists required the significant advances in experimental technology exemplified in the equipment and procedures developed by Pavlov, Thorndike, and Skinner. With these methodologies, the basic principles explaining rather simple and automatic types of learning were discovered and are still generally accepted. Of course, as we shall see in the work of Rescorla reviewed in the next chapter, the apparent simplicity of classical conditioning as compared to cognitive learning may be illusory. The work of Tolman and the gestalt theorists opened the doors again to investigating the phenomena derided by the early radical behaviorists as "mentalistic." With the advent of powerful computers, the cognitive theorists may have as powerful investigative tools for their types of learning as Pavlov's apparatus and the Skinner box have been for the conditioning types of learning.

It is true that even though the early theories and theorists have not decisively settled the great issues mentioned in the introduction to this book, they have generated the research which has led to the elimination of many simplistic dogmas. This process has brought greater tolerance in its wake. It may be true that both contiguity and reinforcement can serve as the mechanisms for different types of conditioning; it may also be true that we are capable of learning either mechanistic habits or complex cognitions. Most theorists would agree that any model of learning must somehow account for internal mediating mechanisms within organisms rather than trying to predict behavior (except under the most highly controlled of conditions with lower organisms) entirely from a knowledge of the cues available in the environment. The processes investigated today are more complex, and the tools for investigating them have often shown a parallel increase in complexity. Not only are some sort of mediating mechanisms generally accepted (although they may be represented as duplicating the laws of conditioning developed with external cues and responses, as in Pavlov's, Guthrie's, Hull's, and Skinner's theories), but also even Skinner (1974) accepts some innate factors in behavior. This was a position (nature bias) articulated very early by Maria Montessori and the gestalt theorists and developed today by the "preparedness dimension" theorists who will be reviewed in Chapter 12. The use of animals in research continues, but with new awareness of the limits on the generalizability of such data to humans. There is also increased use of higher animals (which originated with Köhler's studies on apes) in investigating higher types of learning. Only on the issue of absolute determinism is there no movement towards resolution, and perhaps this problem will have to be left to the philosophers.

Two

In Part 1, the great themes, theorists, and theories of psychology's early history were introduced, discussed, and compared. We saw that the four types of approaches reviewed (contiguity-connectionist, reinforcement-connectionist, cognitive, and biological-cognitive) varied widely in their basic assumptions and in their positions on the great controversies. From that seething caldron of controversy, several coherent trends seemed to emerge. Research begat complexity in theories as their developers modified them rather than abandoned them. An increasing acceptance of cognitive variables by many theorists (especially the neo-Hullians such as Spence and Mowrer) was a consistent trend. And, finally, there seemed to be a move towards recognizing some principles as valid laws describing at least simple conditioning, as well as toward eclectic and model or "microtheory" approaches.

Different sets of learning principles seemed to fit different types of learning. Classical conditioning principles best described the formation of bonds between cues and internal states (motivations, emotions, visceral responses), and this learning operated through the simple mechanism of contiguity. Operant learning, or the shaping of response tendencies, seemed to be a function of the automatic "strengthening" properties of reinforcement. As an apparent sign of increased tolerance correlated with the growing maturity of learning theory as a part of a developing science of psychology, several connectionists (Skinner, Spence, Mowrer) accepted both types of conditioning mechanisms in their two-process theories. Some more complex types of learning, such as latent learning in rats and verbal learning in humans, did not always lend themselves easily to connectionist explanations, and in these cases the explanations offered by cognitive theorists seemed more reasonable. Many theorists combined an acceptance of active processing by the organism (expectancies, incentive motivation, frustrative inhibition, and so on) with an acknowledgment that automatic connectionist-type learning might also exist (Tolman, Mowrer, and some of the functionalists). All of this seemed to signify that the "battle of theories" was almost over and that what remained was to specify precisely where each set of laws of learning could best be applied. It appeared likely that the emerging unitheory would probably explain acquired motives and emotions through contiguity principles, acquired skeletal-muscle responses through reinforcement mechanisms, and complex learning through cognitive learning—all very eclectic and with the loose ends tied up at last.

Unfortunately, as we will see in Part 2, there is no peace in the land of learning theories. The basic foundations of assumptions about the mechanisms of conditioning are being attacked by both cognitively oriented and biologically oriented researchers. Paradoxically, while the real world applications derived from the connectionist approaches are becoming ever more refined and more effective, we have less and less idea of how they work. In spite of decades of defending the strong environmentalism implicit in the doctrine of equipotentiality, more and more learning theorists have turned to the investigation of long-neglected topics, such as instinctual influences on behavior and the effects of selective evolution on what can be learned by a given species. In this part, you should note with satisfaction (or anxiety) that many new principles have been discovered and that our knowledge of learning is becoming more complex and more complete (recognizing that one student's complexity is another's confusion). As we learn more and more about the learning process(es), the early dream of having one simple set of laws describe all forms of learning seems, in retrospect, naive at best. Even classical conditioning may be both more complex than was once thought and more influenced by cognitive variables. Perhaps when unitheory is finally realized, it will be so complex and so subtle that only the super-computer of the future will be able to comprehend it in its entirety.

The "state of the art" of learning theory today is strange indeed. Paradoxically, we know too much and too little. Suspended between the simplistic theories of the past and the eventual integration of conflicting viewpoints and research that should take place in the future, the present is a time for absorbing masses of data and rethinking basic premises. Let us now preview the material to be covered in this part as a prelude to sharing the excitement of new discovery and new ways of thinking about learning. The basic format, in terms of the sequence of topics, is similar to the first part. We will again begin with classical conditioning; next, examine operant instrumental conditioning and its extensive theory of application; then sample trends in cognitive theories; and finally, review biologically oriented approaches to the study of learning. Because so many theorists' and researchers' contributions will be covered, no biographical data nor review of each theorist/researcher's position on the six major issues discussed in Part 1 will be presented. The focus instead will be on presenting new principles and new ways of conceptualizing various types of learning.

Chapter 8 first focuses on Soviet post-Pavlovian developments in classical conditioning, which have extended the scope of this paradigm (pairing of CSs with USs) down to the viscera and up to conditioning of meaning in humans. Then, under American contributions, researchers have added new principles while calling into doubt previous assumptions about contiguity as the basic process responsible for the organism's coming to respond to the CS almost as if it were the US. Some of this research has found that awareness plays a much larger role in forming these associations than had formerly been suspected. Finally, the chapter presents recent innovations in applying classical conditioning to real world problems.

Chapter 9 brings us up to date on developments in the field of instrumental or operant learning. First, the contributions of neo-Hullian theorists are reviewed, followed by the contributions of neo-Skinnerian researchers. Three types of neo-Skinnerian approaches are distinguished: (1) those fairly close to Skinner's ideas, (2) those focusing on the use of aversive control of behavior, and (3) social learning theory, which combines behaviorist and cognitive principles. Where appropriate, key articles suggesting reformulations of the basic assumptions about instrumental or operant learning are reviewed. As you will see, the authors of these articles have suggested that instrumental learning is more closely related to the biological principle of selective evolution than had formerly been thought.

Chapter 10.begins with·a discussion of how to apply operant learning theory in a wide range of real world settings. The principles of operant learning, and of applying operant learning, are illustrated with a sampling of applications in a wide range of environments. Finally, the chapter reviews recent developments in the theory and applications of biofeedback.

Chapter 11 brings us up to date in developments in cognitive theories of learning. Four very different approaches are summarized: (1) Eli Saltz's concept-growth theory, which is closely related to the functionalist approach to learning, (2) Noam Chomsky's psycholinguistic theory of language learning, (3) Jean Piaget's cognitive-developmental theory, and (4) Donald Norman's information-processing theory of learning, which is closely related to cybernetics and physiological theories of learning.

Chapter 12 begins with a review of trends in "looking inside the black box of the brain." We will see how many approaches to exploring the neurophysiology of learning have been integrated into Karl Pribram's theory, which is also related at many points to information-processing theory. You will see how the detailed exploration of brain mechanisms in learning has provided support for cognitive interpretations of learning mechanisms. The second half of Chapter 12 covers research supporting a renewed need to consider innate mechanisms in learning. This research has reopened the nature/nurture question by demonstrating the importance of instinct and instinctually biased learning in predicting the behavior of individual species.

Part 2 and the text conclude with a summary and evaluation of the contributions of current approaches to understanding learning. Finally, some tentative suggestions are put forward for the development of an integrative approach to learning in general, based on the author's appraisal of current theoretical trends and the results of recent research.

In your study of this material, it is important for you to keep in mind the historical roots of each of the four types of learning theories reviewed. In particular, you must try to understand the relationship of new principles and theories about the processes underlying learning to previously presented principles and theories. Learning theories have evolved in a logical manner through the efforts of many researchers. By trying to understand this evolution as a "gestalt," you will find it easier to incorporate new material with what you have already learned. Psychology (and related disciplines) is well on the road to understanding how learning "works"; by your careful study of this material, you can participate in this process. May your experience in sharing these discoveries be an exciting one!

8

Advances in Classical Conditioning: Soviet and American

The classical conditioning of a maladaptive physiological response involves many complex elements not directly predicted by the principles of classical conditioning discussed in Chapter 1. The nature of such complexities will be the subject of this chapter. In reading this material and the following section on American contributions, it is important to compare the innovations presented with Pavlov's original principles and theory. You should try to understand the significance of each new phenomenon presented and be able to define the new terms.

Classical conditioning, or the **Pavlovian paradigm** (set of procedures), was presented first because historically it has been considered a simple form of learning, it has been extensively researched early in the history of learning theories, and it has contributed much of the vocabulary and principles used in other learning theories. As conceptualized in the mid-1950s, classical conditioning consisted of procedures by which CSs were presented (usually) in close contiguity to USs; this contiguity was assumed to form the bond between the two types of cues. The CSs were then assumed to elicit either an inhibitory response (CS−) or an excitatory or active response (CS+), which was usually a response of some system (such as the cardiovascular system, the viscera, or the salivary glands) mainly controlled by the **autonomic nervous system.** The process of experimental extinction was assumed to reflect the changing of a CS+ to a CS− (or vice versa)* through lack of reinforcement of the bond between the CS and the US. The experimental procedure for such bond weakening is to give CS-only trials. This was contrasted with instrumental (or operant) conditioning procedures, which were assumed to bond stimuli to responses or to increase the probability of the emission of a response through the process of following the response with a reinforcer (which was an event that would be subjectively labeled as either pleasant or unpleasant). Extinction was assumed to follow elimination of the **contingency** between the response and the reinforcer. The responses conditioned were usually bodily acts (skeletal muscle movements) controlled by the **central nervous system** (brain and spinal cord).

As we shall see, research using the Pavlovian paradigm did not stop with

---

* Or simply restoring the former CS to the status of a neutral cue through a process which inhibits its ability to elicit the CR.

Pavlov's death, and such research has expanded the scope of Pavlov's theory by adding important new principles. If this research had only added new principles to Pavlov's theory, the clear distinction between the two basic types of conditioning just summarized would still provide you with a useful conceptual guide to understanding conditioning in general. As research using the Pavlovian paradigm has progressed both in the Soviet Union and in the United States, however, it has become apparent that both the responses studied and the processes underlying them are much more complex than suggested by Pavlov or Skinner. This complexity has introduced doubts about some of the underlying distinctions between classical conditioning and instrumental learning and the basic mechanisms for both types of learning. The complexity (or confusion, depending upon your point of view) which has resulted from basic research using the Pavlovian paradigm has had important implications for the use of classical conditioning procedures in psychotherapy. Some of the innovations in behavior modification procedures of the classical conditioning type will be reviewed, as well as new conceptions of how these procedures should be used and reinterpretations of what conditioning therapy actually accomplishes. As we will see, both in applied areas and in basic research, increased attention has been directed towards the role of cognitive variables in classical conditioning, which was long considered the most automatic and least cognitive type of learning process. Let us begin the process of examining the evolution of Pavlov's theory by reviewing innovations originating within the orthodox Pavlovian tradition.

Soviet Psychology since Pavlov: Advances in Expanding the Scope of the Pavlovian Paradigm

Although the behavioristic approach and the verbal-cognitive approach to understanding learning are seen as opposing views in the United States, the study of verbal and cognitive aspects of human behavior in the Soviet Union has taken place within the theoretical bounds of the Pavlovian conditioning model. This seemingly unlikely combination has been strongly influenced by two unique sets of events in the history of Russian psychology. First, Pavlov never had to contend with a strongly developed mentalistic school of psychology; hence, he avoided the excesses of John Watson's rejection of introspectionism. Second, the closest Soviet analog of American behaviorism (the "collective reflexology" model of reinforcement-based conditioning without consciousness, developed by Bekhterev) was rejected by the Soviet Academy of Science. This rejection was prompted by pressures to adhere to the Marxist ideal of man as active and striving rather than as passively responding and by the considerable power of the Communist party to establish priorities and guidelines for each scientific area (Leontiev in Cole and Cole, 1971).

Hence, while Watson was rejecting the use of verbal data as unreliable and subjective, Lev Semionovich Vygotskii was developing a powerful theory of the relationship of language and thought that had a strong Pavlovian flavor. The counterrevolution of the American gestalt-oriented cognitive theorists against the mechanistic constraints of the strict behaviorist model was simply unnecessary in the Soviet Union, where consciousness was always considered legitimate and important as a factor in human behavior.

Soviet psychology has changed in many ways since the death of Pavlov in 1936, and many of these changes have brought it closer to American psychology. In 1966, psychology was divorced from the philosophy faculty (school of philosophy) and recognized as a separate science (Leontiev in Cole and Cole, 1971). In the early 1970s, an Academy of Psychology was formed. It is now possible for Soviet students to major in psychology instead of taking psychology-related courses within departments of education, philosophy, and biology. Before, most psychological research was conducted by either physiological/neurological or educational institutes, resulting in use of the jargons of physics and physiology rather than a set of purely psychology-related terms. One result of the recognition of psychology as a separate science has been the relegation of research on animals and the first signal system (nonverbal) conditioning to physiologists. Thus, while American experimental psychology is still heavily committed to rat and pigeon research, Russian psychology has stopped using even the dog as an appropriate subject for psychology (O'Connor, 1966).

With the development of a separate structure, Soviet psychology has broadened its subject areas. In addition to a continued interest in conditioning phenomena, much research is being conducted in the areas of social psychology, engineering psychology, and all areas of sensation and perception, including extrasensory perception.* The work in the area of perception has been applied in developing new methods of teaching tone-deaf adults to discriminate musical notes (Leontiev in Cole and Cole, 1971). These applications involved an important modification of Pavlovian learning by focusing on feedback procedures, a development that parallels the increased attention given to feedback in Western psychology in recent years. The incorporation of feedback procedures in conditioning of humans was first introduced by Anokhin (in Cole and Cole, 1971). Following Pavlov's (1960) discoveries that not all his dogs responded the same to conditioning procedures (which he assumed to be related to the relative balances of excitatory and inhibitory processes in the cortex inherited by his subjects), the study of the interaction between individual differences and learning has become an important area of Soviet psychology.

Even with recently allowed diversity within the psychology establishment, however, the dominant theme of research in learning in the Soviet Union remains allied to Pavlovian classical conditioning. O'Connor (1966) has identified three major trends, of which two (Pavlovian conditioning of internal organs, or interoceptive conditioning, and verbal or semantic conditioning) represent

---

* This author was present at a Western Psychological Association symposium on Soviet psychology chaired by Karl Pribram of Stanford University in the spring of 1975. At this meeting, a member of the audience questioned the Soviet psychologists assembled about the book *Psychic Discoveries Behind the Iron Curtain*. The Soviet psychologists participating in the symposium denied that such breakthroughs in parapsychology had been made and claimed the authors of the book had taken seriously stories made up by these psychologists after the entire group had enjoyed an evening marked by the consumption of large quantities of vodka. Since some of these psychologists had subsequently been granted asylum in America, there would seem to be no political motivation for their denial of the reports of breakthroughs in the areas related to extrasensory perception.

post-Pavlov extensions of Pavlovian learning principles. We will now examine research on interoceptive, semantic, and verbal conditioning, in that order.

Interoceptive Conditioning

As you will recall from Chapter 1, **interoceptive conditioning** is classical conditioning in which either the CS or the US or both are delivered directly to the mucosa of some specific visceral organ (such as the stomach). There are several types of interoceptive conditioning: type 1, in which both the CS and the US are delivered to the viscera (intero-interoceptive); type 2, in which the CS is external (as a tone or light flash) and the US is delivered to the viscera (extero-interoceptive); and type 3, in which the CS is interoceptive (as the inflation of a smooth-walled stomach balloon) and the US is exteroceptive (intero-exteroceptive).

The methods of delivering the interoceptive stimulation vary. Some animal procedures have depended upon either bringing portions of the viscera to the surface via fistulas, or making it possible, by surgical means, to gain direct access to the viscera. Souces of stimulation include pressure from stomach balloons, thermal stimulation from pouring water at different temperatures into the balloons, direct irrigation with chemical stimuli, specialized apparatus to allow touching of the visceral mucosa, jets of air, and stimulation via electrodes. Only balloons and electrodes on the surfaces of balloons are normally used with human subjects.

There are many reasons for the investigation of the conditioning of the viscera. For one thing, Western psychology long considered the viscera to be inaccessible to voluntary nervous system control. The Soviet demonstrations of conditioned control of stomach contractions and other internal states prompted both Soviet and American psychologists to explore the limits of visceral conditionability. This work showed that the central nervous system is more intimately involved in the control of visceral responses than was previously thought.

Another major impetus for research into the relationship of the central nervous system and the viscera was the hope of developing medical applications. These applications included methods for dealing with such psychosomatic ailments as ulcers and asthma, and the development of what in America is called **aversion therapy** to treat alcoholics. In the latter procedure, an emetic is added to the alcohol with the hope that alcohol will become a CS for a conditioned nausea response (Anokhin in Cole and Cole, 1971). Of course, such a treatment had to be supervised by a medical doctor, as all bodily treatment is given by doctors in the Soviet Union.

It was further hoped that research on the relationships between the nervous system, the viscera, and the endocrine glands would reveal the physiological basis for fluctuations of awareness and moods, emotional mechanisms, and changes in drive levels. Although the recent Soviet research in these areas owes much to Pavlov's work on the mechanisms of stress* (Kirman in O'Connor, 1966)

---

* Pavlov investigated the types of stressful conditions that were likely to result in pathological disturbances in behavior (i.e., experimental neurosis).

and has involved psychologists, current interest there is largely concentrated in schools of medicine. This shift of academic psychologists away from physiological problems is consistent with the general movement away from the Pavlovian emphasis on physiology and animal research. The close relationship of many branches of psychology with medicine in the Soviet Union, however, and the utilitarian bias of psychology there, would seem to preclude any total withdrawal of Soviet psychologists from research on visceral conditioning—or at least from research involving the second (verbal) signal system and human subjects.

This research has had impressive results. In 1945, Airapetyantz and Bykov reported learning of a conditioned discrimination by the viscera (small intestine) in a soldier who had had a fistula connected to his middle small intestine as an aftermath of wounds suffered in the Russo-Finnish war. These researchers inserted a small rubber balloon into the intestine via the fistula and filled the balloon with either warm or cold water (their USs). The warm water was then paired with the CS of a blue light and cold water with the CS of a red light. After many conditioning trials, the subject reported warm sensations to the blue light presented alone and cold sensations to the CS of the red light presented alone. Felberbaum (1951) found that both visceral and skeletal components of uterine responding could be conditioned in dogs. Razran (1958) reported a conditioned inhibition of the rate of acid produced by the stomach. This discovery could suggest treatments for some types of peptic ulcers.

Research on extero-interoceptive conditioning, with possible implications for the treatment of psychosomatic symptoms, has also been conducted in the United States. For example, Hutton, Woods, and Makous (1970) paired a complex external CS (odor of menthol, blood sampling and an injection, placement in a different cage) with an injection of insulin (a US which produces an UR of decreased blood sugar or hypoglycemia). They found that after five conditioning trials, the CS alone produced a CR of decreased blood sugar in their rats. Hypoglycemia in humans is often accompanied by many pathological symptoms such as depression, unexplainable fatigue, irritability, and irregular heartbeat, and is thought to be related to psychological stress. These results suggest that such reactions might be conditioned responses in some people.

Such reactions (along with ulcers and many other physical symptoms) that occur in the absence of known organic causes are labeled "psychosomatic" symptoms in human patients. (It must be noted that the symptoms of both ulcer patients and the rats tested by Hutton and colleagues are physical and real—but the mechanism triggering their occurrence may be explained in terms of classical conditioning.) Since such subtle conditioning of maladaptive visceral states may be unconscious (Tarpy and Mayer, 1978), an appropriate treatment plan might include counterconditioning. Such treatment of psychosomatic symptoms has been used by Malmo (1975).

The external CSs in extero-interoceptive conditioning can be verbal cues (Pshonik in Razran, 1961). These could be the source of important psychological influences on internal physiological responses. For example, just hearing the name of someone you have learned to fear or dislike might make your heart race and your stomach "feel tied in knots."

In general, conditioning with a visceral component is difficult to obtain, but once the conditioning is completed, it is much more resistant to extinction than exteroceptive conditioning. Thus, the next time you feel your stomach lurch or heart palpitate at the sight of a person after years of separation, it may help to remember that the response can be attributed to your extinction-resistant viscera manifesting type 2 (extero-interoceptive) interoceptive conditioning! The CS is, of course, visual and external, the US is the nervous mechanisms responsible for the tightened stomach and internal sensations, and the CR is the actual stomach contractions, which are internal.

Visceral responses can be classically conditioned either by using internal CSs (intero-interoceptive conditioning) or by using external CSs (extero-interoceptive conditioning), which may be verbal cues in humans. Such conditioning, which may be a mechanism for the development of psychosomatic illness, reflects central nervous system influences over the viscera.

Semantic and Verbal Conditioning

Russian psychologists since Vygotskii have always seen consciousness and speech as legitimate subjects for research, hence as conditionable and objective as any other form of behavior. American behaviorists have concentrated their research on the conditioning of increased emission of selected types of words (such as personal pronouns) through verbal or body language reinforcements (Greenspoon, 1955). Russian psychologists, however, have conducted extensive research both on using the meaning of words as CSs for a variety of external and internal responses and on using verbal instruction to investigate the directing function of second signal system cues.

Semantic conditioning   **Semantic conditioning** is defined as the successful conditioning of a reflex to a word or sentence irrespective of the letters making up the words, the sounds of the words, or the particular words of the sentence. Thus, conditioning of the appearance of words or sounds of words does not constitute semantic conditioning. Semantic conditioning is conditioning of the meaning (semantic content) of the word or words.

In America, many behaviorists, including Skinner and Watson, claimed that words act as conventional stimuli and that they are learned through conditioning that attaches or bonds them to specific responses of either a verbal or motor behavior type. Vygotskii and Luria, however, as well as the American cognitive theorists, suggested that the basic unit of learning is a thought, or cognition, and not a connection of the stimulus aspects of language with responses.

Semantic conditioning methodology permitted a direct comparison of these claims. The basic technique is illustrated in an early study by Gregory Razran (1939). Even though Razran conducted his research in the United States, he was a leading worker in the Pavlovian tradition, as well as the source of many of the English translations of Russian research which have familiarized American psychologists with trends in Russian learning theory. The response studied was salivation, as measured by weighing cotton rolls held under the tongues of the three college students participating in the study. The USs were chewing gum, lollipops, and sandwiches that elicited generous salivation (the UR). During the eating period, the CS words were flashed 15 times each. The subjects were then given 8 minutes of CS words alone to determine the extent of conditioning. Saliva was collected for 1-minute periods following each CS word. Following this, a series of five test sessions was given to check for transfer to synonyms (same meanings as the CS words) and homonyms (words with similar sound characteristics as the CS words but with different meanings).

Not only did the subjects salivate to the CS words, they also salivated to the synonyms and homonyms. Generalization was greater to the synonyms (59 percent as much saliva was generated to these words as to the CS words, compared to 37 percent of CS word saliva elicited by the homonyms), showing that semantic (meaning) content of the words was conditioned to a greater extent than visual-auditory characteristics were. Shvarts (in Rahmani, 1973) found the relative conditionability of synonyms and homonyms to be a function of the number of conditioning trials. As the number of trials increased, conditioned responses to the homonyms decreased and CRs to the synonyms (meanings) increased. She also found that administration of chloral hydrate (which depresses cortical activity) abolished synonym-elicited CRs, while homonyms continued to be effective CSs. This result suggests that "meaning" or semantic conditioning is dependent upon higher cortical functions than the presumably more primitive "physical resemblance" homonym conditioning, which is mediated by lower brain areas that are more resistant to the effects of the drug.

Other studies have extended these results. Luria and Vinogradova (in Razran, 1961) conducted an interesting disproof of strict stimulus-response theories of verbal conditioning. Electric shock was paired with specific words. The shock acted as a US for the UR of vasoconstriction of finger blood vessels and the vasodilation of blood vessels of the head. Semantically related words were found to be more effective in eliciting the CRs (finger vasoconstriction and head vessel dilation) than words sounding like the CS word but having different meanings. When a transfer word was also reinforced with shock, the class of words intermediate in meaning between the original CS and the new CS (the transfer word) became effective in eliciting the CRs. This generalization of meaning effect was weaker than the responses to the two reinforced CSs. When a word had a double meaning, with one meaning related to the conditioned word and one meaning not related to the CS, the word elicited a CR when it was used in a sentence where it had the same meaning as the original CS. When a sentence was used in which the word had a different meaning from the CS, only very weak transfer or generalization effects could be seen. This showed that meaning is more conditionable than the simple stimulus dimensions of a word; hence, most verbal learning is not a connection between an environmental stimulus and a response made by the subject. These results are an elegant antidote to the anticognitive biases seen in many of the strict stimulus-response formulations of American psychologists.

Although the Russian semantic conditioning research would seem to support the theoretical position of American cognitive theorists on the issue of the basic unit of language learning (meanings), the Russian researchers also maintained that this meaning of words (the second signal system) is an objective and observable phenomenon. Thus, Pavlov was correct in maintaining that most of the basic laws of conditioning apply to both signal systems. One important difference is that second signal system conditioning often occurs with one trial, while one-trial learning is rarer with first signal system cues. Even interoceptive systems thought to be beyond nervous system control (such as blood clotting) have been found to be influenced by semantic factors (Razran, 1961).

There are some limits in seeing all languages as always dominated by semantic factors. Luria (in Cole and Cole, 1971) has reported that conditioning based on meaning is found in school-age and older children and adults. Very young children show transfer based on first signal system characteristics (physical dimensions as appearance and sound) of words; moderately retarded older children show transfer based on meaning and phonetographic (sound similarity) factors; and very retarded children manifest only phonetographic conditioning. Even with adults, fatigue and alcohol reduce **semantic transfer** and increase conditioning by physical dimensions (Slobin in O'Connor, 1966). Thus, fatigue and alcohol make adults learn more like small children. The Russians have also conducted extensive research on the "directing" function of speech. Luria states:

> Thus he becomes capable of *actively modifying the environment that influences him*; by using speech for himself, he alters the relative strength of the stimuli acting upon him, and *adapts his behavior to the influences thus modified.* [1961, p. 20]

The major dividing point between the mechanical responding of animals and the active mental life of humans is the unique ability of humans to use verbal cues from other humans and from their own brains, to redirect the orienting reflex and hence the occurrence and content of learning. Man is the animal that can signal himself!

Luria has worked out a developmental sequence for the second signal system which is somewhat parallel to the sequence for the development of semantic conditioning (in Cole and Cole, 1971). From birth to 18 months of age, a child responds only to first signal system cues; from 18 months to 42 months, only to excitatory commands from adults. From three and a half to around four and a half years of age, the child responds to the stimulus aspects of words emitted from adults and is able to follow all sorts of commands. Responses to semantic aspects of speech become noted between four and a half and five and a half years of age, and the child is now able to take general instructions and reword them internally. Difficult instructions are repeated aloud, but easy ones do not require overt speech by the child. Older children become able to formulate verbal instructions for themselves to guide their behavior independently of direct environmental cues. Luria's view differs from Piaget's in that even "egocentric" speech is seen as communicative; that is, the child's speaking to himself is serving the function of the child's communicating directions to himself. Luria has suggested a progression from overt speech to subvocal speech to pure "inner or semantic" language as the child matures (in O'Connor, 1966).

As we saw in the section on Watson's theory in Chapter 2, there has been some recent support for the idea that subvocal movements may be involved in language functions. Garskaya (1975), however, has demonstrated that although even many adults may show electrical potentials from tongue muscles (electromyographic or EMG potentials), these potentials may be reduced through biofeedback or reinforcement training. The subjects actually decreased their problem-solving times after decreasing the muscle involvement in their thinking. These results are of interest in suggesting that even though speaking to himself may aid a child in developing language functioning, such subvocal speech is detrimental in the adult. They also illustrate that operant conditioning is being done in the Soviet Union today. Luria's emphasis on the inner control of behavior is similar to that of such American cognitive theorists as Tolman, and it is directly opposed to the viewpoint of early radical stimulus-response behaviorists. While the implications of Russian research seem to support cognitive theorists, however, their methodology is decidedly behavioristic.

When words are used as CSs, both stimulus characteristics of the original words and meaning characteristics are conditioned. Conditioning of meaning is called semantic conditioning, and the relative strength of this type of conditioning increases with age, with number of trials, and in the absence of drugs that interfere with higher cortical functions.

Verbal conditioning   A common verbal conditioning procedure would be to use a tone as the CS, verbal instruction to press a bulb as the US, and bulb-pressing as the response. Many American psychologists might question calling the results of this procedure "conditioning" in the usual sense. American cognitive theorists would interpret the results as showing rather that the subject had gained an understanding that when the tone sounded, he was to press the bulb. The Soviet psychologists would retort that except for the speed of conditioning, the second signal system obeys most of the same laws as the first signal system. Hence, "understanding" the relationship between the tone and the instruction to press the bulb is as much an example of conditioning as any canine salivation to a tone which had been presented before meat powder. In humans, responses mediated by the autonomic nervous system (such as increased heart rates) can be conditioned to verbal stimuli. Luria maintains that such conditioning in humans, like conditioning in animals, is subject to the **rule of force,** which states that the strongest component of a complex stimulus decides what response will be made and when. When humans are presented with complex stimuli which include verbal cues, the conditioned responses can often be elicited by verbal cues combined with nonverbal cues different from those present in the original complex conditional stimulus. Thus, a person may have a conditioned emotional reaction to a stranger having the same name as someone who once presented our person with an aversive situation, in spite of the stranger's differences in physical appearance and other features.

This rule also illustrates Luria's contention that for most humans, second signal system cues are stronger than other types of signals and determine the response. Since speech directs attention immediately to the relevant stimuli, it is hardly surprising that human conditioning involving the second signal system is so rapid (Luria, 1961). In explaining the gestalt phenomenon of figure-ground reversals with ambiguous figures (such as the example in Chapter 5), Luria also evokes the theory that internal second signal system cues (thought) direct the orienting reflex.

Consistent with Luria's view that the directive function of the second signal system becomes internalized as the child becomes older, laboratory procedures using overt verbal cues were found to be most effective with children and ineffectual with teenagers. Children below nine years of age did not show good generalization between second signal system cues and first signal system cues (the tone). The best results were with children between the ages of nine and thirteen, and the best transfer was from the first signal system to the second signal system. These results may be interpreted as meaning that younger children fail to translate between signal systems easily, and that older teenagers and adults find the game so simple that they play it erratically. That is, adults are responding to more complex self-generated signals and are not being directed by the experimenter's instructions. The pattern of allowing behavior to be directed by external signals is seen as more primitive, in the sense that it is more influenced by inherited mechanisms and more like animal learning. Luria (in Cole and Cole, 1971) has experimental evidence supporting this view. He found identical twins around five years old tended to learn the same words from word lists and to remember them equally well, while nonidentical twins (different genetic patterns) showed less twin-twin similarity in learning patterns. When older children (who were assumed to be more controlled by socially mediated second signal system mechanisms) were tested, however, there was less evidence for genetic-relatedness factors in learning patterns; adult identical twins showed learning patterns unrelated to genetic closeness. This shows a maturational trend away from responding to the physical characteristics of words in a way determined by inherited mechanisms and a trend towards responding predominantly to learned semantic factors in verbal conditioning.

The use of verbal cues in a Pavlovian paradigm is called verbal conditioning. The rule of force predicts that such cues will be more decisive in determining CRs than other components of complex CSs. The influence of verbal cues in relationship to first signal system cues increases as a function of age and learning.

American Contributions to Classical Conditioning Theory

As we saw in the preceding section, Russian learning theory has evolved in ways that are very similar to American learning theory. Two points of marked congruence have been the incorporation of more cognitive variables (as in semantic conditioning) and increased complexity of the general theory of Pavlovian conditioning. As in America, the Russian connectionist approach has been a rich source of principles that could be applied in a wide variety of situations. Not all evolution of the theory of Pavlovian conditioning has taken place in the

Soviet Union, however. The originally simple Pavlovian paradigm has been expanded and reinterpreted through the efforts of many American researchers. American learning theorists have developed an alternative method for estimating the strength of the association between a CS and an US, have identified new Pavlovian phenomena, and have suggested new explanations of the basic mechanisms underlying the conditioning produced through use of the Pavlovian procedures (Pavlovian paradigm). The net result of this work has been to suggest that the effects of the Pavlovian procedures are more complex than was once thought. We will begin this section of the chapter with a description of several phenomena investigated by American researchers. These have expanded the scope of the Pavlovian view of learning. First, the phenomenon of autoshaping will be presented, which illustrates that Pavlovian principles may apply to responses similar to those shaped through operant conditioning. Then, the conditioned suppression, or conditioned emotional response, paradigm will be presented; it has provided a useful alternative to conventional methods of measuring the strength of the CS-US association. Then, what seems to be a case of "pure" contiguity learning (sensory preconditioning) will be presented, followed by work on the interrelationships between the components of compound CSs (overshadowing and blocking). Finally, suggestions for reconsidering the mechanisms of classical conditioning will be presented, beginning with Rescorla's predictiveness hypothesis, followed by Seligman's learned helplessness model, and concluding with a discussion of the role of mediating variables in classical conditioning. A section on recent applications of classical conditioning in therapeutic settings will conclude the chapter.

Pavlovian Phenomena Discovered by American Researchers

Autoshaping   A recently discovered Pavlovian phenomenon is **autoshaping.** Until this "automatic shaping" response was described by Brown and Jenkins (1968), it was thought that conditioned pecking of a key by pigeons was a response acquired through instrumental learning principles. These authors reported that food-deprived pigeons could be trained to peck a lighted response key if the key were simply illuminated for a few seconds before food delivery. Fewer than 100 lighted key (the CS) and food (the US) pairings were necessary to develop high response rates. Since "voluntary" skeletal muscle responses were involved (which are most often associated with instrumental conditioning), these results were somewhat paradoxical.

What leads most authors (such as Tarpy and Mayer, 1978) to label this type of learning "Pavlovian conditioning" is that food delivery was independent of the birds' responses (every time the key was lighted, food delivery followed). Wasserman (1973) has noted that when the US is presented before the CS (the usually ineffectual backward conditioning paradigm), no autoshaping occurred. Jenkins and Moore (1973) photographed pigeons' pecking with both food and water CSs and found that the CRs elicited resembled natural eating and drinking URs, respectively.

Atnip (1977) demonstrated the phenomenon in rats and found acquisition of bar-pressing to be faster than with conventional operant shaping methods of reinforcing successive approximations of pressing. Because the responses involved are so different from those usually studied with classical conditioning, some authors have tried to explain the phenomenon in terms of operant principles. Davol, Steinhauer, and Lee (1977) suggest that pecking may generalize from a lighted food hopper to the lighted key.

Autoshaping is the phenomenon in which responses, such as key-pecking by pigeons, seem to be acquired as CRs to CSs, such as lighted response keys, when these CSs are followed by USs, such as food. Although such "self-shaping" seems to follow Pavlovian laws, the type of response is that normally considered to be learned by operant principles.

The conditioned emotional response, a measurement technique   In most of the experiments by Pavlov and his successors (both Russian and American), the success of a conditioning procedure was demonstrated by presenting the subject with the CS in the absence of the US. This "CS-only trial" technique was thought to provide a direct estimate of the strength of a CS-US bond through measuring the intensity of the CR. This method, however, suffers from one major drawback. Presentation of a CS without a subsequent US (reinforcement, in Pavlovian terms) is also the experimental extinction paradigm in Pavlovian conditioning. Therefore, the CR may become weaker over a series of CS-only trials, and a spurious indication of the strength of the CS-US bond will be obtained. Estes and Skinner (1941) developed an alternative indirect method of estimating the strength of the CS-US association which they called the **conditioned suppression, or conditioned emotional response (CER)**, method.

The original experiment went like this: A rat was placed in a Skinner box and shaped to press the lever for food reinforcement. The mechanism connecting the lever to the food delivery system was programmed so that lever-pressing yielded food only once every 4 minutes (a FI-4 minute schedule), which caused hungry rats to press the lever at a steady rate. After this, 1-hour experimental sessions were given in which a tone was sounded for 3 minutes at a time; at the termination of each tone, the rat received a brief, unavoidable shock. The food reinforcement schedule remained in effect at all times and was independent of the tone-shock sequence. After a number of sessions, the rats were observed to have greatly reduced their rate of bar-pressing every time the tone was on. This conditioned suppression lasted until the end of the shock that concluded each tone-shock sequence. Following shock, the rats resumed their normal response rates until the next tone (the CS for the US of the shock) began. Thus, the extent to which bar-pressing is suppressed during CS presentation, relative to non-CS/US time periods (sometimes calculated as a suppression ratio), is assumed to reflect the strength of the CS-US bond. Estes and Skinner also observed signs of emotionality or anxiety in their rats (such as defecation, squealing, freezing) when the tone was sounded. They concluded that such reactions to the CS were conditioned emotional CRs, hence the term "conditioned emotional responses" (CER). CERs usually include changes in responses mediated by the autonomic nervous system. The CERs are assumed to mediate the changes in instrumental response rates.

Various refinements of the CER procedure have been made since the Estes-Skinner experiment. These include giving the tone-shock training in an enclosure different from the Skinner box, in which lever-pressing rates are measured (to reduce generalized suppression of lever-pressing), and developing the previously mentioned suppression ratio method of calculating the effects of the CS (reviewed in Hall, 1976). In any case, as we shall see, this procedure, utilizing a combination of operant conditioning (lever-pressing) and classical conditioning (tone or some other CS and shock), has been widely used in investigations of phenomena related to classical conditioning.

One line of research that has employed the CER paradigm is the investigation of the most effective CS-US intervals for strongest conditioning. In contrast to much of the early literature, which reported that conditioning was always strongest when the US followed the CS by about .5 seconds, more recent reports have noted maximal conditioning intervals to vary for different types of CRs, with the longest being 13 seconds. The optimal CS-US interval seems to be a function of the type of CR elicited, with autonomic (involuntary) CRs tending towards most effective conditioning with longer intervals (reviewed in Tarpy and Mayer, 1978).

Another line of research in which later (but not the original) researchers used the CER paradigm has been the investigation of the phenomenon of **sensory preconditioning.** We will now turn to a discussion of this phenomenon, which resembles (but is not identical to) Pavlovian conditioning, because of its theoretical implications in trying to answer the question of the "what of learning" in classical conditioning.

An alternative way of measuring the strength of a CS-US association is provided by the conditioned emotional response (CER), or conditioned suppression, procedure, which measures decrements in instrumental response rates in the presence of a CS which had previously been paired with an aversive US, relative to response rates without that CS.

Sensory preconditioning   The phenomenon of sensory preconditioning was first discovered by Brogden (1939), who used a modified Bekhterev defensive reflex conditioning procedure. Eight dogs were given 200 pairings of a light and bell. The animals were then exposed to a Bekhterev-type procedure in which one of the cues served as a CS signaling a shock US, which elicited a foot withdrawal UR. Following the conditioning training, the other cue was found to be effective in eliciting the leg flexion response—in spite of never having been paired with shock! The sensory preconditioning phenomenon has since been replicated by many researchers using a variety of classical and instrumental conditioning procedures (Hall, 1976, reviews 18 studies replicating Brogden's basic findings).

An example of a study of sensory preconditioning, using a combination of classical conditioning and instrumental conditioning (the CER procedure), is a study done by Prewitt (1967). In phase 1 of this study, four groups of rats were given pairings of a tone and a light, with individual groups receiving 1, 4, 16, and 64 pairings. A control group received no such pairings. For half of the experimental animals, the tone was presented first; for the other half, the light was presented first (one cue being followed by the other potential CS rather than by an US, as in regular Pavlovian conditioning). In phase 2, all the rats received normal Pavlovian conditioning in which the cue, which had been presented first in the previous pairings, was the CS and a mild shock was the US. Finally, the subjects were deprived of water and given access to a drinking tube containing sugar water. While they were emitting the instrumental responses, the cue which had been given second during phase 1 (and not paired with shock in phase 2) was presented for 10 seconds at a time, at about 1-minute intervals. Prewitt found that rats that had received no "prepairings" of the two cues showed no conditioned suppression of their drinking responses in the presence of the cue that had not been a CS. Rats receiving one and four "prepairings" of tone and light in phase 1 of the experiment showed some suppression of drinking (licking) responses to the cue which had not been paired with the shock US during phase 2. Maximal suppression ratios were obtained from rats having 16 and 64 pairings of tone and light, with about one third as many licks being counted during CS-on time periods as in CS-off time periods (a suppression ratio of about .33).

Sensory preconditioning may also occur between cues which subsequently signal reinforcement in the operant sense (S_Ds or discriminative stimuli). This may occur when two cues are paired repeatedly without either being followed by reinforcing consequences (such as food reward). If a response is then reinforced in the presence of one of these stimuli, the other cue will also be found to have some power as a S_D (although discriminative control is not as pronounced as with the reinforced S_D). Reynolds (1975) states that such transfer of control has been demonstrated not to involve normal generalization, as the initial bond was formed through pure association. The concept of sensory preconditioning agrees with the view which states that learning can occur by association, but the performance of a response is contingent upon reinforcement.

Sensory preconditioning presents some interesting theoretical problems. The most important of these is trying to determine the nature of what gets learned in the process. Is it a pure S-S bond in the absence of reinforcement, in either the classical conditioning (confirmation of a CS by a US) or instrumental/operant sense (following the learning by a reinforcing event), or is some type of internal mediating response attached to both cues? Noting that many of the same principles which apply to classical conditioning also apply to sensory preconditioning, Hall (1976) nonetheless concludes that the evidence for internal USs and URs to the paired cues is equivocal. He suggests that perhaps we should think that the brain mediates consistent relationships in the environment rather than seeking unobservable responses in every type of learning situation.

Finally, Russian researchers have also investigated sensory preconditioning. Koltsova (in Rahmani, 1973) noted that associations can be formed between "indifferent CSs" without Pavlovian reinforcement. She suggested that such associations were formed because the first cue of the pair was functionally a CS that becomes conditioned to the second cue's acting as a weak US, which elicits the orienting reflex. She reported that when a light is followed by a sudden sound for several trials, a child will show an orienting reflex in the direction of the sound source even when no sound is presented. She suggested that the initial pairing of the two cues caused them to become a compound stimulus. This is why the subsequent conditioning of the first cue to a strong US gives the second cue the power to elicit a CR related to the UR elicited by the strong US. The subject is actually responding to one component of a compound stimulus as if both components had been presented. The relationship between components of a compound stimulus and how they may be changed by conditioning is our next topic.

Sensory preconditioning is an interesting phenomenon which closely resembles classical conditioning. Two cues are paired (usually for several trials), and one of them is then used as a CS and paired with a US. Following this conditioning of the first cue, the second cue is found to have acquired the power to elicit the CR.

Overshadowing and blocking   In the real world outside laboratory conditions, most classical conditioning probably occurs to compound stimuli. Within the laboratory, much research effort has been expended on determining the relative roles of the components of compound stimuli. In general, it has been found that dynamic or intermittent stimuli, such as flashing lights or beeping, are more "salient" (have a greater power to elicit a CR) than "static" cues, when both types are part of a compound stimulus. When the two components of a compound stimulus are very different in their relative salience, the strongest component of the compound will be found to control responding almost totally following conditioning in which the compound stimulus is the CS. That is, the CR will appear when either the whole compound or the stronger component is presented, but not (or only very weakly) when the weaker component is presented. This greater power of the stronger or more salient component is predicted by Pavlov's rule of force, which was discussed earlier in the context of Luria's work on verbal conditioning in humans. As we noted then, verbal cues tend to be more salient than nonverbal cues in human conditioning. In such a case, the verbal cue overshadows the effects of nonverbal components of a compound stimulus. Bolles (1975) notes that the general phenomenon of the stronger component of a compound stimulus that interferes with the CR-eliciting properties of the weaker component has been demonstrated repeatedly by American psychologists. This phenomenon is labeled **overshadowing** in the United States. The power of a cue to overshadow other components of a compound stimulus can also be acquired through a conditioning procedure. This conditioned overshadowing, or **blocking phenomenon,** was reported by Kamin in 1969.

Kamin used a modified CER procedure to demonstrate blocking. As in the usual CER paradigm, rats were first trained in lever-pressing for food and then exposed to a light (the CS) that was followed by unavoidable shock (the US) for eight trials, which produced conditioned suppression of bar-pressing. The next phase of the study, however, involved a new experimental manipulation. Half of the rats were then given presentations of a compound stimulus consisting of the light and a tone. The remaining rats received eight trials in which a tone was the CS paired with the shock US. Finally, all animals were tested for suppression (with the independent food contingency remaining in force), with both tone and light CSs presented separately before the US. Those animals having first light and then tone paired with the shock demonstrated suppression of the instrumental bar-pressing responses to either cue. The rats given the combination stimulus during the second phase of the experiment showed strong suppression of bar-pressing to the light, but no suppression to the tone. Kamin suggested that because the association of the light with shock was so strong, it blocked any effects of presenting the light in combination with an additional stimulus (the tone); the effects of the light, in other words, overshadowed the effects of the tone. In the second group, the tone alone was presented with the shock and was able to develop its own conditioned association.

Rescorla and Wagner (1972) have suggested a formula which predicts that when maximal conditioning is already present with a given CS, there is no more "conditionability" left, or nothing new can be associated with the US-CS combination. Essentially, Rescorla and Wagner would explain Kamin's results by saying that the animal is already deriving maximal information from the first CS and ignores additional cues (such as the tone) that give it no additional ability to predict when the shock will occur. Rescorla's model of explaining classical conditioning in terms of prediction variables will now be examined.

When one component of a compound stimulus is much stronger or more salient than another component for a particular CR, the stronger component when presented alone will be effective in eliciting the CR and the weaker component may become ineffectual or be overshadowed. The blocking phenomenon occurs when one component becomes more salient through previous conditioning.

Reinterpretations of Classical Conditioning Mechanisms

Rescorla's predictiveness hypothesis   Pavlov wrote about the signal functions of both USs and CSs. As a signal for the elicitation of either an unconditional or conditioned reflex, these cues would seem to provide the organism with predictive information. Most interpretations of the mechanism for connecting CSs to USs, however, have stressed that the strength of the resulting bond was purely a function of number of pairings and the extent of their contiguity. This stress on contiguity rather than signal mechanisms may partly reflect the fact that Pavlov's work was largely introduced to American psychology through the efforts of John Watson, who, as you should remember, was a strict contiguity theorist. Recently, this contiguity mechanism has been strongly challenged by Rescorla.

While still a graduate student, Rescorla began his research using a

Pavlovian fear-conditioning paradigm somewhat similar to Bekhterev's procedure to condition defense reflexes. His goal was to test the orthodox Pavlovian idea—that mere contiguity of a CS with an US was sufficient to produce an association between them—against his own informational theory. Rescorla thought that perhaps CS-US associations were acquired because CSs provided information to the subject about whatever event followed it in time (the US in the forward classical conditioning paradigm). Thus, excitatory conditioning occurred because the CS allowed the subject to predict when the US would occur, and inhibitory conditioning (as in extinction) occurred because the CS allowed the subject to predict that no US would be presented. Rescorla predicted that if a CS was presented randomly with a US, it would sometimes be followed by the US and sometimes preceded by the US. In this case, the CS would be uncorrelated with the US and would not predict the occurrence of the US. If CS-US associations were the result of the organism's recognizing the contingency between the CS and the US, "truly random" CS-US relationships should result in no conditioning, even though the stimuli were sometimes in close contiguity to each other. To test his **predictiveness hypothesis,** Rescorla used a modified CER procedure to measure the strength of conditioning when the CS predicted the occurrence of the US, when the CS predicted the absence of the US, and when the CS gave no information about when the US would occur. In the first of his critical series of studies, Rescorla (1966) trained three groups of mongrel dogs in Sidman avoidance. This paradigm, which will be discussed further in Chapter 9, essentially consists of training subjects to emit an instrumental response (such as lever-pressing) before the end of a time interval to delay the onset of a shock. Lever-pressing resets the clock controlling the shock, so high rates of pressing can delay shock onset indefinitely. Rescorla required his dogs to jump a hurdle (the instrumental response) that separated the half of the shuttle box (see Figure 8.1) where shock was delivered for a particular trial to get to the safe side. On the next trial, the dogs were required to jump back to the other side, and so forth. As opposed to normal CER procedures, in which the strength of conditioning is shown by suppression of food-getting responses, excitatory conditioning in Rescorla's procedure would be shown by increases in avoidance behavior (jumping rates).

After three days of Sidman avoidance training, the subjects were given Pavlovian fear conditioning (using unavoidable shock as the US) in three different ways. One group of dogs (positive prediction group) received only those shocks programmed to occur 30 seconds after the time of the tone CS onset. The second group (negative prediction group) received no unavoidable shocks within 30 seconds following the onset of the tone. Rescorla's prediction was that this group would show conditioned inhibition of the jumping response. The third group was the control, and for these subjects both the shock and the tone were presented on a random interval schedule designed to insure that no consistent relationship (contingency) existed between CS and US. The number of times the CS was presented just before the US was the same in this control group and in the positive prediction group.

As we noted in Chapter 1, it is important in classical conditioning studies to

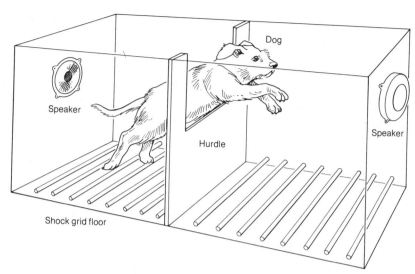

Figure 8.1   A shuttle box of the type used in Rescorla's experiment. During Sidman avoidance training, the dog learned the response of jumping over the hurdle within 30 seconds of the time that the tone was sounded over the speakers, thus avoiding the shock delivered by the grid floor.

guard against the possibility of pseudoconditioning, or sensitization. This can result from a strong US that makes the subject more ready to respond to any stimulation (which would fool the researcher into thinking he or she had observed a CR). The most common way to guard against this possibility is to have a control group in which the "CS" never precedes the US, under the assumption that any responses elicited by this "CS" would be the result of sensitization. Rescorla has argued that such a control procedure is inadequate because such a "CS" gives the subject information that the US will not follow it; hence, it should function as an inhibitory CS. Thus, Rescorla's negative prediction group was analogous to the conventional control group. The performance of this group was to be compared to his "truly random" control group, in which the CS did not predict when the US would occur. From this viewpoint, demonstrations of the nonoccurrence of a CR with a conventional control group would reflect inhibitory processes rather than an adequate control for sensitization. Only the nonoccurrence of a CR from "truly random" control subjects would adequately demonstrate that sensitization to the US did not occur.

The performance of the "truly random" control group is also important as a test of Rescorla's contention that the informational or contingency relationship of a CS to a US, not contiguity factors, is the vital variable in determining conditioning. Since the US did follow the CS in this control group about half the time (the CS did sometimes have a contiguity relationship with the US), evidence that the "CS" in this case had become effective in eliciting a CR could show learning through contiguity, as well as sensitization. If, however, contiguity was the mechanism of classical conditioning, the negative prediction group would not show any signs of inhibitory conditioning. You can see that Rescorla's hypothesis demands that the "truly random" control group should show no conditioning and that signs of inhibitory conditioning should be found for the negative prediction group.

After Rescorla had exposed his three groups to the three types of Pavlovian conditioning procedures, he alternated days of Sidman avoidance training with days of Pavlovian conditioning procedures. This was continued until day 13, when a single test session was given with the tone CS superimposed upon the Sidman avoidance schedule (much as the CS is superimposed on the food reward schedule in a conventional CER paradigm). Rescorla found no changes in jumping rates in his control subjects (which is assumed to reflect the absence of conditioning, just as an absence of suppression reflects no conditioning in a conventional CER procedure), as predicted by his contingency versus contiguity view of the mechanism of classical conditioning. The positive prediction group showed an abrupt increase in their rates of avoidance behaviors, and the negative prediction group showed an equally abrupt decrease in such behaviors. Rescorla explained that these results showed that the extent to which the CS signaled the occurrence of the US determined the extent to which the fear CR and increased instrumental responses occurred. For the dogs in the negative prediction group, the CS seemed to have become a CS−, or a conditioned inhibitory stimulus. Thus, it acted to inhibit both the fear CR and the instrumental avoidance response—this in spite of the fact that all three groups had received almost equal exposure to the CS and the US. This phenomenon led Rescorla to the conclusion that the contingency relationships of the CS and the US were more important in predicting classical conditioning than contiguity factors were.

Rescorla followed up these results in 1967 in an important review paper written with Solomon (whose grant funds had supported the research reported in 1966). This paper attacked Hull's classically conditioned r_G-S_G model of mediational chains leading to goals on the grounds that: (1) such anticipatory fractional antedating goal responses were usually not found when the appropriate measuring procedures were available to look for them, and (2) such a complex mediating mechanism was simply unnecessary. It is more reasonable, they stated, to assume that the subject has expectancies concerning goals and rewards, and that it responds to cues which it has learned predict their proximity in time or space. It is this predictive function of CSs which accounts for the effects of the Pavlovian experimental procedure on both the normal classical conditioning and on instrumental goal-directed behavior. Further support for the contingency hypothesis was provided when Rescorla (1968) demonstrated that animals receiving more pairings of a CS and shock which were not related by a contingency showed less fear in the presence of the CS than animals that had received fewer shocks, when those shocks were predicted by the CS.

Several other researchers have reported findings supporting Rescorla's views. For example, Whitehead, Lurie, and Blackwell (1976) used a "truly random" control group of human subjects to control for US sensitization in a study of conditioned blood pressure decreases. In accordance with the predictiveness hypothesis, subjects in this control group showed no conditioned drop in blood pressure during CS-only trials, in spite of previous randomly occurring CS-US pairings. Biferno and Dawson (1977, 1978) have reported that conditioning of most aspects of the galvanic skin response (GSR) in college students occurred only after their subjects became aware of the contingencies between the CS and the USs (loud noise or shock). Brickman and Schneiderman (1977) found no conditioning in the rabbits of their "truly random" control group, using brain stimulation as the US and a tone as the CS. Conditioning was rapid in their positive prediction group. Taken together, these results (and many others that could have been cited) show that Rescorla's hypothesis has strong experimental support. As we shall see, however, there are negative research findings. Problems of interpretation also occur when studies such as those by Biferno and Dawson are cited in support of Rescorla's theory. While Rescorla states that his subjects predict US onset, he does not speculate about active, aware cognitive mechanisms of the type that seem to be operative for Biferno and Dawson subjects. Thus, the degree to which the expectancies of those subjects illustrate the conditioning mechanisms postulated by Rescorla depends upon how one interprets Rescorla's idea that the organism gets information about a US from CSs. Let us now turn to some criticisms of Rescorla's work.

Rescorla postulated a predictiveness hypothesis which states that the mechanism of classical conditioning is related to the contingency relationship between CSs and USs rather than to contiguity variables. He suggested that an adequate "truly random" control group in which the occurrence of the CS gives no information about the US should produce no conditioning, while traditional "CS = no US" control groups should produce inhibitory conditioning.

Furedy and Schiffmann (1973) reviewed a series of their studies in which they conditioned human GSR reactions. They used both "truly random" and negative prediction control groups, and, contrary to Rescorla's hypothesis, found no evidence that responding was inhibited in the negative prediction groups when compared to the performance of the "truly random" control groups. Since Rescorla indirectly evaluated the conditioning of his CRs (internal emotional states related to fear and assumed to be largely mediated by the autonomic nervous system) by their effects on rates of performance of an instrumental response, it could be argued that these different results are artifacts of his modified CER procedure. As we have seen, however, other researchers who directly measured internal physiological CRs have obtained results supporting Rescorla.

Prokasy (1977), who also reviewed Rescorla's work and the evidence related to it, has concluded that additional factors, such as differential habituation rates (nonconditioned decrements in responsiveness to cues) between experimental and control groups in GSR studies, preclude an unequivocal decision about Rescorla's hypothesis. He suggests that it is still possible logically to defend the contiguity mechanism theory for some types of classical conditioning. Perhaps, he says, we should consider classical conditioning (the Pavlovian experimental paradigm) as a set of experimental operations which specify the relationship between two or more stimuli, and which may result in a variety of processes. A more unequivocal rejection of Rescorla's ideas as well as an alternative explanation of his results (and of classical conditioning in general) has been stated by Seligman. We will now turn to a discussion of his views.

Seligman—unpredictability and learned helplessness   Martin E. P. Seligman has been one of the more prolific contributors to modern learning theory. Among his contributions (another will be discussed in Chapter 12) is an interesting view of the differences between classical conditioning and instrumental learning, which leads to a reevaluation of Rescorla's results, and a theory of learned helplessness. In Seligman's view, instrumental learning is only that type of learning characterized by voluntary responses which are modified by reward and/or punishment. Pavlovian conditioning, on the other hand, is concerned only with responses that are not voluntary. In the CER paradigm, for example, a tone CS is followed by a shock US, which elicits a pain UR. With time, the tone gains the power to elicit anticipatory conditioned responses, such as increased sweating and increased heart rate. The subject, however, is shocked regardless of whether he sweats or not. What defines a Pavlovian experiment is precisely helplessness. No response, conditioned or otherwise, can prevent the subject from being exposed to the CS or, in classical conditioning, the US (Seligman, 1975). These involuntary reactions, in turn, mediate the conditioned suppression obtained with most CER paradigms.

Seligman distinguishes various ways in which CSs can be paired with USs. In explicit pairings (even intermittent ones), the CS predicts the occurrence of the US. In explicit unpairings (as in Rescorla's negative prediction group), the CS reliably predicts the nonoccurrence of the US. If, in either case, the organism can use this information to do something about the US, then the outcome is dependent upon the subject's response, and the paradigm is that of instrumental or operant conditioning. If the outcome is independent of the subject's response, then the paradigm is one of classical conditioning. When a given outcome is independent of all responses, you (or any other subject) are helpless, and that outcome is uncontrollable. Seligman postulates that the basic kinds of learning are: (1) learning that a cue (CS) predicts the occurrence or nonoccurrence of a US (or outcome); (2) learning that by doing or not doing something in the presence of the CS, you can alter the outcome (or exposure to the US), which is instrumental learning; and (3) learning that you can't do anything about the outcome.* Learning of the third kind is learning that responses are independent of outcomes; this learning is usually adaptive in nature (such as learning that no responses in the presence of the cues which signal an oncoming rainstorm can prevent that rainstorm). However, Seligman notes, sometimes the organism learns a relationship of the third kind that subsequently prevents it from learn-

---

* Classical conditioning paradigms produce learning of both the first and the third kind. In Rescorla's original research, his positive and negative prediction groups showed learning of the first kind and his "truly random control group" showed learning of the third kind.

ing a coping response (learning of the second kind, or instrumental learning). This is the paradigm for **learned helplessness.**

Seligman has applied these ideas to the development of a line of research which ultimately led him to reconceptualize Rescorla's results in terms of learned (conditioned) helplessness. Let us now look at some of Seligman's research on the conditions which create learned helplessness. An example of the basic learned helplessness experiment would be one performed by Seligman (with Maier and Overmier; in Seligman, 1975). They began by exposing dogs to a tone CS followed by shock. After considerable exposure to this Pavlovian paradigm, the dogs were put in a shuttle box like the one used in Rescorla's 1966 experiment. Normally, if a dog is put in a shuttle box and shocked, it rapidly learns to jump over the hurdle separating the compartment where shock was delivered from the safe side, thus escaping the shock. Soon the dog learns to escape the CSs associated with shock and thus may avoid the US (shock) altogether. However, the dogs tested by Seligman and colleagues first ran around frantically (like normal dogs) and then lay down and quietly whined. When a minute had passed without the dog's escaping, the shock was turned off until the next trial. Most of these dogs that had previously been exposed to the Pavlovian paradigm (learning of the third kind) never learned to escape. Seligman concluded that when an organism has experienced trauma it cannot control, its motivation to respond in the face of later trauma is lost. Even when the dogs blundered over the hurdle and escaped the shock, they seemed to have trouble perceiving and believing that the response had worked and they did not repeat the response on the next trial. Along with the lack of instrumental learning, Seligman's dogs showed emotional changes characterized by depression and anxiety. Seligman observed this learned helplessness pattern in about two thirds of his subjects and found that these helpless dogs behaved differently from nonhelpless dogs outside the test situation. After tests were over, they neither resisted the experimenter's efforts to remove them nor eagerly greeted him. Instead, they "wilted" and rolled over passively.

These results were not due to just the effect of exposure to shock. Other dogs, who were shocked in a Pavlovian harness but were able either to turn the shock off by pressing a panel with their noses or to turn it off by the passive response of remaining motionless, rapidly learned to escape in the shuttle box. Seligman concluded that these results were not caused by trauma per se or by learning "not to do something." Rather, they were the result of learning that nothing could control the trauma (that shock USs were independent of their efforts or actions). Seligman reports that such effects have been replicated in species from cockroaches to man.

In reviewing human research on the learned helplessness phenomenon, Seligman noted that these results were dependent upon a wide range of other variables, such as on instructions which created cognitive sets of being able to control or not to control outcomes, or on the personality type of the subjects. He found that "inner-directed" persons, who have a general tendency to see themselves as influencing their environments, became helpless less easily. The effects could also be produced in man and animals with a wide range of types of apparatus, and these effects generalized from shock situations to frustration situations. Helpless organisms showed reduced shock-elicited aggression and tended not to compete as much for food. Helpless college students were slower to solve difficult problems, which is similar to the effect Miller and Dollard labeled "neurotic stupidity" in their conflicted clients. The helplessness syndrome could even be created in college students by giving them insoluble problems. This suggests that Pavlov's demonstrations of "conditioned neurosis" in dogs faced with nondiscriminable excitatory and inhibitory cues may have reflected the dogs' helplessness in making correct discriminations.* It also may offer a way to predict when conflicting excitatory and inhibitory cues will lead to beneficial results (as in systematic desensitization), as opposed to conditioned neurosis. In systematic desensitization, clients learn that by relaxing, they can control the anxiety experienced in the presence of the phobia-related cues. Their expectancies about success in the treatment situation may also prevent their experiencing relaxation (inhibition) after anxiety (excitation) as conflicting. This last interpretation is highly cognitive, which agrees with Seligman's conclusions about the effects of instructions on influencing cognitive sets conducive or nonconducive to the development of helplessness.

Seligman found that helpless students did not change their ratings of the expectancy of success in problem situations as the result of either success or failure. They seemed to have learned that they could neither predict success nor create it. This was interpreted by Seligman as showing that the students had learned that there were no contingencies between the cues (CSs?) available to the students and feelings of success (USs?). This led Seligman to conclude that situations in which the subject could not predict USs from CSs were not situations in which no conditioning takes place, as postulated by Rescorla. Rather, he thought that the subjects learned that they were helpless even to predict outcomes, let alone control them. Viewed in this light, Rescorla's positive prediction dogs had learned to predict shock during Pavlovian conditioning. After learning, they could sometimes escape shock in the shuttle box training situation; they were able to show those adaptive responses in the presence of the CS which signaled shock during the critical test day. The dogs in the negative prediction group had learned when not to expect shock (learned safety), and they responded to the CS on the critical test day by reducing hurdle jumping. The dogs in the "truly random" control group, however, had learned that their responses were independent of shock (learned helplessness) and so did not alter their jumping rates on the test day. Seligman suggested (1969) that the dogs in the "truly random" control group should have been experiencing the most anxiety, or arousal, as a result of learning that they were helpless. In examining dogs given the "truly random" procedure, Seligman (1975) found evidence for ulcers and chronic fear reactions.

Seligman (1975) has proposed a general model of learned helplessness in

---

* Once the conditioned neurosis was established, Pavlov's dogs became unable to make discriminations that once were easy for them. A similar effect has been observed by Seligman (1975) in helpless dogs.

which cues provide information about contingencies (positive prediction, negative prediction, or no prediction), which then interact with the subjects' expectancies (or beliefs or learning about how helpless they are in a given type of situation). This, in turn, determines if and how they may respond. He has also proposed a general theory of how to deal with learned helplessness (and the depression which usually goes with it) in a wide range of organisms. He suggests (and has conducted research supporting this view) that prior experience with successful control can "immunize" organisms against the harmful effects of conditions that usually produce learned helplessness. He has also suggested that once learned helplessness develops, it can be reversed by forcing the subject to control outcomes successfully. For example, he was able to reverse learned helplessness in dogs by dragging them over the hurdles of a shuttle box to escape shock, although from 25 to more than 200 draggings were necessary before the animals learned to respond on their own.

Seligman has proposed that classical conditioning procedures can be distinguished from operant conditioning procedures by the fact that subjects are unable to control their exposure to CSs and USs in classical conditioning. Learned helplessness occurs when the subjects generalize their learned lack of control to situations where they could learn adaptive responses.

The issue of mediation   As Seligman's and Rescorla's work has made clear, the question of the "how" of classical conditioning is still unresolved. Rescorla thinks that subjects learn about the contingencies relating the CS to the US, and Seligman has suggested that subjects learn expectancies or beliefs. When variables such as beliefs act to influence the process of learning, they are said to mediate between stimuli and responses. Many researchers have tried to investigate the role of such mediating variables, which can be operantly conditioned skeletal muscle responses or cognitive variables. Let us now examine, in some detail, a few studies which have investigated mediating variables, to show you the methods employed and the problems involved in interpreting the results.

Whitehead, Renault, and Goldiamond attempted to address directly the problem of mediating variables. To control for cognitive mediation, the subjects were asked to think of various things, and measurements were made of stomach acid secretion during various types of thoughts suggested by the experimenters. To evaluate skeletal muscle mediation, the **electromyographic potential (EMG)** of the muscles over the stomach (diaphragm muscles) was recorded. By using a DRH (differential reinforcement of high rates) schedule with money reward in a biofeedback paradigm, they were then able to increase acid secretion threefold in three of their four subjects. When the schedule was switched to a DRO (differential reinforcement of other than high secretion) schedule, the three successful subjects were able to bring secretion rates back to baseline (pre-biofeedback) levels. The DRO schedule was much more successful than simple extinction procedures. One subject maintained the threefold increased level of secretion even after 11 days of extinction. The problem with interpreting these results as showing pure instrumental conditioning of a response mediated by the autonomic nervous system was that both striate muscle (voluntary muscle) and thought patterns were correlated with the changes in secretion rates. The authors noted that the patterns of correlations varied over subjects; within subjects, they varied over time. Whitehead and colleagues (1975) concluded that they had demonstrated true operant control of an autonomically controlled response, but that their subjects were likely to "bring into play a variety of physiological and other mechanisms that help maintain and produce the response required for the reinforcer to be delivered" (Whitehead et al., 1975, p. 155). Since subjects' verbal reports on the cognitive strategies employed were reported as inconclusive, it appears possible that the results were produced by mediating mechanisms rather than by true instrumental conditioning.

While the research on the issue of demonstrating that both instrumental and classical conditioning occur through contingency (reinforcement) mechanisms remains equivocal, what of the issue of awareness of contingencies raised by Rescorla's predictive hypothesis? Two recent studies by Biferno and Dawson on autonomic conditioning in human subjects have strongly supported the cognitive, or expectancy, aspect of the predictive hypothesis. These researchers have worked within the framework of the **psychophysiological** orientation.

"Psychophysiological observation is as old as the first young man who noted a women's blush. . . . A mental state was inferred from a well defined physiological change (increasing blood flow to the face)" (Hassett, 1978, p. 1). Psychophysiology is the science of studying the effects of manipulating behavior (its independent variables) on changes in physiological states (its dependent variables). Hassett (1978) notes that since the body usually responds as a unit, some sort of mediation is to be expected in conditioning physiological states. Thus, this discipline would be expected to be oriented to investigating the issue of mediation in classical conditioning.

In the first study reviewed, Biferno and Dawson (1977) found that classical conditioning of the first component of the skin conductance response (commonly referred to as the galvanic skin response, or GSR, by most psychologists and as the electrodermal response by psychophysiologists) occurred only after their college student subjects reported awareness of both the positive (CS+) and negative (CS−) contingencies. In all their subjects, signs of conditioning of the first component GSR appeared suddenly, consistent with the cognitive interpretation of the CSs acquiring its predictive power as a result of an insight process. Controls employed by the authors included embedding the conditioning paradigm within a masking task to delay the onset of awareness so that pre- and postaware trials could be analyzed, and using three ways for subjects to report awareness (this was to control for the possibility that the appearance of the CR was in some way an artifact of the reporting procedures). Reporting procedures used were a spring-loaded dial with seven buttons labeled with varying degrees of certainty of when the subjects expected the occurrence or omission of the US (a loud noise) as well as verbal reports of expectancies, including "why" the subjects expected the US or its omission. During extinction trials, extinction occurred only in subjects expressing their expectation that the CS would not occur. There was a potentially important complication, however. The authors also measured a second, longer-latency "second component" skin conductance response. (An important contribution of psychophysiologists and others investigating the responses normally conditioned using a Pavlovian paradigm has been to show that most such responses consist of different components which may be affected in different ways during conditioning.) For some subjects, this "second component" appeared suddenly with awareness (discontinuous or insightful learning), while for others, it appeared slowly as a function of the number of pairings of CSs and the USs. Thus, the apparent contradiction between the results of Furedy and Schiffmann (1973), which did not support the Rescorla hypothesis, and the major trend of Biferno's and Dawson's (1977) findings might be explained by suggesting that some components of the GSR are more likely to be conditioned due to contiguity factors and that others depend upon cognitive, expectancy-based mediation.

The second study by Biferno and Dawson (1978) supports the view just expressed, that the Rescorla hypothesis might hold for most autonomically controlled responses as well as for skeletal muscle responses controlled by the central nervous system. In this study, subjects were informed of the relationship between color of lights turned on for 7 seconds (one color the CS+ and another the CS−) and the US (shock occurrence or omission). Halfway through the conditioning trials, a light of a third color was turned on. Half of the subjects had previously been informed about this novel stimulus and half had not. After this light was turned on, the uninformed subjects reported greater uncertainty about the contingencies between the CS and the US. This was accompanied by a decrease in their long-latency (second component) conditioned skin conductance responses, which is congruent with Rescorla's (1966) report of a lack of conditioning in his "truly random" control group, where the dogs were presumably uncertain of the contingencies between CS and US. No such changes, however, were observed in conditioned vasomotor responses (pulse volume activity recorded from the little fingertips of the subjects' left hands). Further, the short-latency (first component) skin response increased on the first uncertainty cue trial for the uninformed subjects, showing that uncertainty itself may serve as a US for some autonomically mediated responses (perhaps as part of an orienting or arousal reflex to new information). As we noted in the discussion of Seligman's work, uncertainty by itself may be stressful and may result in learned helplessness rather than the learning expected. Stress and arousal, which have been implicated as important variables in classical conditioning in some physiological studies on animals, may operate as mediating variables.

Wilson, Simpson, DiCara, and Carroll (1977) found removal of the adrenal glands of rats (which are the glands presumed to chemically mediate anxiety or stress related responses) facilitated both simple and discriminated Pavlovian conditioning of reduced heart rates. These results support the theory that arousal-related variables may confound interpretations of Pavlovian conditioning. Further, as was mentioned in several of the studies reviewed, and as concluded by Hall (1976) in his extensive discussion of appropriate controls to use in classical conditioning experiments, what were once seen to be unitary URs and CRs may actually have several components which may be affected differentially by the Pavlovian paradigm.

We have now come to the close of this presentation of American contributions to the discovery of new phenomena and reinterpretations of Pavlovian theory. If nothing else, we hope to have shown that the end result of the research process on what was once considered a simple form of learning (classical conditioning) has been to discover how complicated this learning may actually be. Our conclusion, therefore, is that we are still waiting for a theory about the mechanisms underlying classical conditioning which is adequate to predict precisely what sort of conditioning will occur in the various situations in which the Pavlovian paradigm may be applied. This lack of an adequate theory to explain the principles governing classical conditioning has not, however, prevented significant advances in developing applications based on the Pavlovian paradigm. In some cases, as we shall see, these advances have even been related to basic research.

Recent Innovations in the Application of the Pavlovian Paradigm to Clinical Psychology

Applications of Pavlovian learning theory date back to the pioneering work of Mary Cover Jones (1924), but they were largely eclipsed by Freudian psychoanalysis and other "insight" approaches. This situation was reversed when Wolpe's technique of systematic desensitization (reviewed in Chapter 6) began to be employed in the late 1950s. Wolpe based his treatment on the Pavlovian principle of reciprocal inhibition, or counterconditioning of conditioned avoidance responses (phobias). In his view, cognitive processes were entirely secondary to subcortically (usually autonomically) mediated conditioning of the physical responses associated with anxiety. As we have seen in the work reported from Razran to Seligman, however, it has become apparent that most classical conditioning processes may be influenced by cognitive variables. As a result, some of the new techniques make allowance for variables such as semantic generalization and the predictive values of cues (in Lazarus, 1977); few behavior modifiers see their therapy as simply automatically conditioning visceral correlates of fears. Just as radical behaviorists are an almost vanished breed, so are radical behavior modifiers who believe that most phobias are acquired by direct conditioning of the type experienced by the unfortunate "little Albert" at the hands of Watson and Rayner. Rimm and colleagues (1977) investigated the origins of fears in 45 phobic female college students. Sixteen subjects could indeed recall a frightening direct experience, four became phobic after verbal instruction from significant others (such as parents), and three became fearful after seeing someone else experience a frightening event (vicarious experience). Combining subjects who first reported feeling fearful in situations not related to their phobias (nine subjects) with subjects with no recall about the origins of their fears (thirteen subjects), it can be seen that only about a third of the subjects had first become phobic as a result of a direct conditioning experience. Seven thought they had become phobic as a result of a cognitive learning event (the verbal and vicarious subjects), and about half could not relate their phobias to any specific learning event. It might be assumed that these latter subjects had acquired their fears through more abstract mediational mechanisms. As we saw in our review of the literature on the role of mediating variables, the majority of studies support the view of the importance of some type of mediating mechanism, but simple Pavlovian pairing of cues cannot be ruled out. This would suggest that the most effective behavioral modification procedures would take into account both contiguity and mediational factors.

One theorist who has done this is Peter Lang (1969), who sees phobias as potentially having three types of components: (1) verbal or symbolic acts, such as saying, "I feel afraid," or an unwillingness to push a button that triggers the appearance of a slide picture of the feared object, (2) instrumental response acts, such as approaching a feared object, and (3) a visceral or autonomically mediated component. He has developed automated procedures which act on one or more of these components (and which greatly reduce the boredom experienced by therapists when slowly presenting a list of fear cues). One advanced device* included not only a button (symbolic act) allowing the subject to control the rate of progress through a series of slides depicting objects at different levels of the systematic desensitization fear hierarchy, but also a mechanism including electrophysiological recording devices to sense the onset of visceral or sympathetic nervous system arousal. The outputs of these devices go to a computer, which resets the slide presentation of fearsome cues to a level that the client can tolerate while automatically turning on a tape-recorded voice giving instructions to relax. The effectiveness of this automated system is reported as somewhat higher than that of flesh and blood therapists, which is assumed to result from the machine's greater consistency. This work also supports the contention of Wolpe and others that their results represent true counterconditioning and not placebo or therapist effects.

Schandler and Grings (1975) have experimented with using electromyographic (EMG) biofeedback techniques to increase the depth of relaxation. When compared to the traditional progressive (Jacobson-type) relaxation procedures used in most systematic desensitization, the EMG biofeedback did produce greater decreases in heart rate and respiration rates, and these changes persisted longer than changes created by progressive relaxation. Progressive relaxation, however, was more effective in reducing psychological tension (based on verbal reports and responses to tests of anxiety) as well as frontalis (forehead) and forearm muscle tension(!). One is reminded of the results of basic research reported earlier which seem to show that skeletal muscle responses are more likely to be affected by procedures with greater cognitive- and/or contingency-based mediators. Control subjects told to "just relax" showed no changes in tension or physiological functioning.

Even though Wolpe considers the mechanism of counterconditioning to underlie the success of systematic desensitization, is it not possible that a sim-

---

* Which he called "DAD," or Device for Automated Desensitization.

pler explanation might suffice? Remember that Rescorla's dogs in the condition where the CS (CS−) predicted the nonoccurrence of the shock showed reduced avoidance behavior? The process by which an organism learns that a CS no longer signals the occurrence of an aversive US is a form of learning not to be afraid of a cue or, more technically, of classical extinction of the fear-eliciting properties of the CS. This suggests that if a phobic person could be kept in the presence of phobia-related cues with nothing bad happening to them, their fear CR would eventually extinguish without the necessity of relaxation procedures. Such **forced extinction** procedures, based on studies by Solomon and Wynne (1954) of traumatic avoidance learning in animals, have been described by Stampfl and Lewis (1967) and are offered as alternatives to systematic desensitization. The object of such procedures is to teach phobic persons that no contingency exists between the phobic cues and aversive events.

Forced extinction procedures   Stampfl and Lewis (1967) labeled their techniques **implosive therapy.** Most authors (Marx and Bunch, 1977) also call this technique **flooding.** Rimm and Masters (1974), however, distinguish these two labels as corresponding to somewhat different approaches to forcing the extinction of the phobic CR.

> In theory, and somewhat in actual procedure, implosive therapy is similar to flooding, or response-prevention techniques. . . . There are several distinct differences, however. Implosive therapy is based upon clearly specified assumptions concerning the psycho-dynamics of the individual under treatment. Earlier, we noted that childhood trauma is proposed to be the source of most avoidance behaviors.
>
> Typically, in implosive therapy, scenes of avoided behavior and stimuli are presented in a hierarchical fashion, beginning with the less anxiety-provoking items. . . . Flooding or response-prevention techniques require that images related to specific behavioral problems must be presented for sufficiently long periods of time to allow the dissipation of anxiety. [Rimm and Masters, 1974, pp. 334–335]

Flooding and implosion therapy are two similar forced extinction techniques for relief of phobias. Both involve imagining a graded series of fearful situations until the fear response has extinguished.

While the passage just quoted would seem to imply that implosive therapy rests on a Miller and Dollard type of theoretical base (combining Freud with learning theory) and flooding rests on the explanations of anxiety presented by Miller and Dollard, Mowrer, and Pavlov, what happens in both cases is forced exposure to aversive images. The goal is always to force the client to face fear- or anxiety-arousing cues until these cues become ineffectual through extinction of their conditioned reinforcer properties. In Pavlovian terms, what happens is that numerous (or lengthy) exposures to a CS for a fear CR without confirmation by the original US (the traumatic event) will lead to extinction as a result of the irradiation of inhibition building up through nonconfirmation. The original persistence of the CS may be explained through either Miller's and Dollard's or Mowrer's models of the two stages involved in fear-drive learning. Forcing the subject to confront the CS prevents him or her from escaping or avoiding, thus causing his or her exposure to extinction contingencies. There is the danger, of course, that the subjects may be so terrified that they will break down completely (which Pavlov would explain as the pathological result of a clashing of the excitation generated by the CS with the second signal system cues that the CS is harmless), or they may thwart the therapist and continue their avoidance or escape behavior.

Barrett (1969) found that implosive therapy, which interprets the fear object and extends the extinction process to "symbolically" related objects, was effective in removing symptoms in only 45 percent of the time required with systematic desensitization. The implosive therapy subjects, however, showed considerably greater variability in results than the systematic desensitization subjects. That is, while many were improved, some others were made much worse. This is, of course, understandable when you consider the amount of fear encountered in facing a dreaded situation (such as imagining having snakes crawl all over your body).

In the flooding procedure, no surplus meaning is attached to the images of feared happenings. The subject is simply exposed to those images or, in some cases, to the actual objects. The procedure is much like Guthrie's forced exposure procedure. An example might be visualizing yourself getting back on a motorcycle after an accident. You might begin with visualizing looking at the bike, then sitting on it, then driving slowly, and finally driving between lanes of stationary automobiles on the freeway during rush hour.

Flooding has been found to be quicker than systematic desensitization but less effective (Rimm and Masters, 1974). There are several conflicting studies on exactly how effective either of these methods is. Except for possible savings of time, both appear to offer greater dangers and, at best, effectiveness equal to systematic desensitization (where the gradual progression through the fear hierarchy combined with relaxation enables the subject to face the phobic cues with little anxiety). While Krapfl (in Rimm and Masters, 1974) found that many subjects were helped when hierarchies of fear cues began with the most fearsome and avoidance was prevented, dropout rates (a form of unavoidable avoidance, from the therapist's point of view) were much higher than with conventional systematic desensitization procedures.

A recent study has carefully investigated the relationship between client satisfaction and effectiveness in reducing psychological and physiological signs of phobic anxiety using both the flooding procedure and systematic desensitization (Rudestam and Bedrosian, 1977). Clients having specific phobias* rather than general anxiety in social situations showed much greater reductions in the physiological signs of arousal to the fear CSs. The social phobics showed somewhat less GSR and heart rate signs of arousal after treatment by flooding than with treatment by systematic desensitization. But although flooding was found

---

* Such as fears of snakes, dark places, water, and so on.

to be more effective in reducing the autonomically mediated component of the fears, significantly more subjects reported themselves as improved after systematic desensitization; this was most true of the specific phobics.

Not only did the self-reports of the subjects contradict the changes in the physiological signs of arousal measured, but their therapists also rated them as more improved after systematic desensitization. Clients treated by both methods, however, were rated on the average as successfully treated both by themselves and by their therapists. These results show, if nothing else, that Lang is probably correct in considering a phobic reaction to be composed of multiple elements. In a sense, this conclusion agrees with that reached in the basic research literature: What were formerly considered unitary responses to CSs have been found to be composed of several responses, not all of which respond in the same manner to a given conditioning procedure. The discrepancy between cognitive systems (beliefs about the effectiveness of treatment) and actual measured conditioning of physiological mechanisms discussed in the previous study has direct relevance to the topic we will now examine.

Aversion therapy   Even though most patients who come to a therapist do so for the purpose of gaining relief from fears and bad feelings, some clients may be treated with the therapeutic goal of inducing fears and anxieties. This is usually the case in which the client wishes (or some referring agency wishes) to stop some specific behavior deemed maladaptive. The conditioning of fear responses to the CSs associated with cigarettes, pretty little children,* overeating, and alcoholism is the goal of aversion therapy. A US (usually shock or a nausea-inducing drug, for treatment of alcoholism) is paired with the object or situation to be avoided or a graphic representation of the object or situation. Eventually, the situation acquires conditioned aversive properties and becomes capable of eliciting the fear response. Unfortunately, unless a classically conditioned response is strongly conditioned, it may extinguish quickly. Thus, an important problem faced by the aversion-conditioning therapist is the impermanence of many of the "bad habit phobias" so painfully conditioned "into" his clients. Why is it that "natural phobias" (which Rimm and colleagues, 1977, have shown to be directly, let alone traumatically, conditioned in only about a third of their subjects) are so resistant to extinction? It is at this point that the automatic S-R conditioning approach to pathological behavior is most clearly shown to be inadequate. As Rudestam and Bedrosian (1977) determined, cognitions (beliefs) and the results of measurable conditioning may not always be completely congruent. Following the trends of the basic research literature reviewed earlier in this chapter, the answer may lie in an analysis of the client's expectancies about the contingencies in the environment. Phobic clients may escape from unpleasant tasks or gain sympathy and attention (secondary gain) for their pathology. During the author's counseling practicum, he had a client who was a social worker and hated her work. She appeared at the agency where the author worked because of a phobia of small elevators (found in many of the buildings

---

* This is directed towards sex offenders, not potential parents.

she was required to visit) and of dirty people who might give her diseases (like some of her clients). She reported no direct experiences with aversive consequences of being in small elevators or of catching strange diseases. It is not hard to see, in a situation like this, how cognitive variables related to her dislike of some aspects of her job might mediate the resistance to extinction of such phobias. On the other hand, the client referred for aversive therapy usually likes doing the thing he or she is supposed to learn to fear. The expectancies of positive contingencies related to resuming the "maladaptive" behavior and CSs conditioned to those positive contingencies may conflict with fear elicitation, resulting in what appears to be rapid, Pavlovian extinction. The stimuli faced by the subject when tempted to perform the "maladaptive" behavior in the real world would be compound stimuli consisting of CSs having positive associations with the "maladaptive" behavior as well as CSs having negative associations acquired through the aversive conditioning procedure. In these situations, the strong CSs related to positive associations may overshadow weaker fear-related CSs in the compound, and the subject will behave as if the fear CR had been extinguished.

Such competing processes may be illustrated by the following example. The author was once involved as an assistant in administering aversion therapy to an alcoholic juvenile delinquent with a history of eight years of imprisonment. He was given unlimited quantities of sweet red wine in a baby bottle to which was added gradually increasing amounts of vinegar. When he at last became ill, he was cleaned up and urged to drink more until he strongly refused. Following this treatment, he remained dry for over three months. At this time a visitor to the halfway house facility smuggled a bottle of beer into the presence of our subject. Although reportedly reluctant, the subject did succumb, and from that point onward he began to drink an increasing variety of alcoholic beverages, beginning with those least like sweet red wine. Six months after treatment, he would drink anything except wine and two years after treatment he would drink anything except sweet red wine—the smell of which continued to make him nauseous. In this case it is possible that even though the odor and taste of beer may have resembled that of sweet red wine to some extent, most of the CSs associated with beer were positive ones, and only a few (perhaps second signal system cues related to alcoholic beverages in general) were associated with nausea. Therefore, the positive associations overshadowed the effects of the negative CSs present in the total stimulus situation, and he showed behavior which was misinterpreted as extinction of fear CRs to alcohol.

A more conventional treatment for alcoholics is to give them the drug apomorphine, which interacts with alcohol to create a severe nausea and stays in the body for up to two weeks. A reformed alcoholic enrolled in a seminar in alcoholism with the author told him that when his alcoholic friends felt a strong need to resume drinking, they would stop taking their apomorphine and then wait the week or two required for the drug to become ineffective. In the absence of the US (nausea), extinction of any conditioned nausea to the smell and taste of alcohol was rapid, with each succeeding drink reducing their conditioned anxiety and aversion. Raymond (1964) discusses the inadequacy of apomorphine conditioning as a sole means of treatment. He notes that the treatment is usually only effective once the patient has accepted the fact that alcohol is a serious problem in his life and he has agreed to undertake the treatment voluntarily. In this form of treatment, patients receive several daily pairings of alcohol and nausea (which is induced by the influence of apomorphine). The treatment continues for a week to ten days, within the confines of a "therapeutic community" in a treatment center. They are allowed to drink only a little, since to become drunk alleviates the nausea and allows no conditioning to occur. Before leaving treatment, patients are repeatedly warned of the hazards of alcohol and told they will now be able to live without it. After leaving treatment, if possible, provisions are made for family and/or employers to check on patients' continued consumption of the apomorphine. It should be clear from this report that effects of the aversive conditioning are supplemented by a wide range of cognitive mediators.

The selection of appropriate CSs illustrates a major problem in learning. For many years it was thought that all potential CSs were equal in conditionability (the principle of equipotentiality discussed earlier) and that the laws of learning applied equally to all situations. Pavlov (1960) considered each type of sensory experience to be processed by different cortical analyzers. This suggested that CSs which were similar to the USs would be more easily conditioned since shorter connections in the brain would be required. Lublin (1968) and Lublin and Joslyn (1968) found that the types of CSs required to produce lasting aversive conditioning varied as a function of the specific USs involved. They reported that using electric shock as the US was effective primarily through attaching anxiety responses to formerly attractive visual stimuli. If anxiety is the goal in therapy, this may be the optimal therapeutic strategy. Feldman and MacCulloch (1968) found that hardcore male homosexuals became anxious in the presence of nude or sexy males after shock therapy and reported their lives to be happier as a result (through avoidance of harassment).

There are important limitations to this approach, however. If shock is strong enough to produce long-lasting anxiety, these anxiety effects may generalize widely. "We do not wish our former smokers to have to give up their smoking friends along with their cigarettes" (Lubin, 1968, p. 78). Instead of shock, which conditions anxiety, Lublin advocates more exploration of other types of aversive stimulation. He has reported success in using the olfactory cue of stale cigarette smoke in a **negative practice paradigm*** to stop cigarette smoking without eliciting generalizable anxiety.

Another advantage of the use of a nonshock US is that such cues are more difficult for the subject to discriminate from naturally occurring cues. Mowrer (1938) reported that shock-conditioned autonomic responses in humans disappeared as soon as the electrodes were disconnected. Stale cigarette smoke is much more difficult to discriminate from ordinary cigarette smoke than shock

---

* In the negative practice paradigm, the subject is forced to indulge in the formerly enjoyed habit until it becomes aversive. In Lublin's example, subjects were required to smoke to the count of a metronome until their eyes and lungs felt as if they were burning. A few hardcore smokers seemed to thrive on this procedure, but most lost their desire to smoke.

situations are from nonshock situations. The taste of adulterated sweet red wine is also not that different from the unadulterated version of the same product. Powell and Azrin (1968) reported that 17 out of 20 subjects in an experiment involving severe shock for smoking quit being experimental subjects rather than quit smoking.

Summarizing his assumptions about effective USs, Lublin relates:

> A short while ago, pursuing my interest in aversive stimulation, I was a guest on the Joe Pyne TV show. Mr. Pyne asked this question: "If you wanted someone to hate tomatoes, I suppose you'd sock him in the face with a tomato a few times." My answer was, "No. That would be a good way to teach a person to hate me. If I wanted him to hate tomatoes, I'd feed him putrefied tomatoes every day for a week." [1968, p. 80]

Lublin (personal communication) has also suggested some ingenious ways to implement his suggestions about using CSs on the same stimulus dimensions as his USs. For example, he claimed that telling overweight people to use toilet paper instead of napkins at meals was an effective behavior modification technique.

Aversive USs such as shock and nausea-inducing substances are used in aversion therapy to condition phobias of stimuli related to maladaptive behavior, such as overdrinking.

All the therapeutic applications of classical conditioning make a fundamental assumption consistent with the views of Ivan Pavlov. This assumption is that pathological behavior is based on the same laws of learning as normal behavior and that pathological behavior, therefore, results from bad learning experiences. This view assumes that a reordering of the environment or reconditioning of disordered behavior is necessary in therapy rather than an "understanding" of Freudian dynamic processes. However, Pavlov (1960) also recognized individual differences, to the extent of describing individuals dominated by excitation and those dominated by inhibition, which is a recognition not held by all behavior modifiers.

Consistent with recent recognition of the complexity of the classical conditioning paradigm and a greater appreciation of the role of cognitive mediators in such learning, behavioral modification in the Pavlovian tradition has also moved from its strict behaviorist origins. Mahoney (1977), commenting on the growing momentum of this cognitive learning trend in psychotherapy, concludes that while the Pavlovian experimental paradigms are still useful, the formerly simple theoretical bases are now outmoded and such techniques should be used with cognitive procedures. A recent example of such a trend is the development of covert or **imaginal aversion therapy,** in which the subject internally visualizes being nauseated or shocked (the USs) after imagining the CSs to be avoided.

Applications in Sex Therapy

Although most of the techniques used in the new sex therapy have already been presented in this chapter (such as desensitization), the effectiveness and recency of the extension of Pavlovian principles to this clinical area warrants a brief survey of such procedures. In addition, many of the techniques have been adapted for "in vivo" home use by couples. "In vivo" means "in life," or in this case, actually facing anxiety-arousing situations "in the flesh" rather than covertly visualizing them in a therapist's office. Because of the very nature of sexual dysfunctions, actual practice of sexual acts with a partner is often required. Even in this liberal age, such practice in the therapist's office would raise serious questions of privacy, as well as ethical-legal issues. Let us now look at specific techniques used for specific sexual dysfunctions, as reported in Helen Singer Kaplan's book, *The New Sex Therapy* (1974).

Male Dysfunctions

Impotence   Impotence is the condition of erectile dysfunction.

> In a sense, all the causes of impotence delineated above involve faulty learning. The patient rendered impotent by Oedipal conflicts learned to fear sexual expression as a child; the unhappy husband learns to circumvent the anxiety engendered by the destructive interactions with his wife by avoidance of all sexuality. However, specific sexual phobias may also play a role in some cases of impotence. For example, some impotent men are phobic of the woman's genitals. [Kaplan, 1974, p. 261]

Kaplan suggests that the sexual reflexes are primarily controlled by excitatory centers in the spinal cord. When cues related to sexual functioning become associated with unconditional stimuli which elicit sympathetic (flight-fight system) arousal, anxiety, and inhibition of parasympathetic dominance (which is essential for penile erection), however, these sexual cues may become conditioned inhibitory stimuli. Therefore, the primary therapy for many sexual dysfunctions is disinhibiting the inhibited spinal reflexes to let sexual behavior occur "naturally." One approach is to inhibit anxiety by a negative reinforcement approach. Kaplan reports a case in which a man had a pathological fear of female genitals, leading to complete impotence. Therapy consisted of shocking the man for avoidance and terminating the shock for approach. Along with the obvious operant elements of this treatment, it was assumed that the association of female genitals (the conditioned stimuli) with the US of shock termination would eventually elicit a CR of relief and happiness. Therapy was successful.

A less dramatic and more preferred approach is to have the couple practice a series of "nondemand" pleasuring tasks at home. These are of the type first developed by Masters and Johnson. The tasks begin with gentle nongenital caresses and are followed by genital caresses but with coitus prohibited. The man is instructed to proceed sexually at his own pace and to back up to an earlier point in the program if the interactions become too threatening. He is told to pay attention to his own sensations rather than worrying about pleasing his wife, to reduce the demand characteristics of the situation and his fears about failure. Only after he obtains a reliable erection does the couple move to intercourse. Kaplan recommends that this begin with the wife above and with the man concentrating on sexual fantasies. Until the man has confidence in the staying power of his erection, intercourse does not continue to ejaculation.

This latter approach is, of course, a specialized variation of systematic desensitization, or reciprocal inhibition. Originally, cues associated with coitus are conditioned stimuli for anxiety and inhibition of the erectile reflex. As compared to the desensitization procedures used in the treatment of phobias, pleasurable stimuli related to sexual behavior are used as the counterconditioning stimuli rather than the stimuli associated with muscle relaxation. By introducing tactile stimulation in ways that are less likely to trigger the anxiety response, these cues resume their normal roles as unconditioned stimuli for the erectile and pleasure URs. Gradually, a nonfearful response to coital activity is shaped by keeping the interaction at the level where it is pleasurable and not stressful.

Premature ejaculation   In a sense, this problem is the opposite of impotence. While the problem in impotence is to disinhibit the excitatory erectile reflex, in premature ejaculation an overexcited reflex must be partially inhibited. One basic technique (the "stop-go" procedure) attempts to condition those cues formerly associated with the approach of orgasm, to inhibition of ejaculation and often partial loss of penile erection. This is done by having the male withdraw his penis from the vagina of the female as soon as he experiences those cues signaling the approach of an ejaculation. He does not reenter until both the urge and his urgency are gone. Before treatment, these warning cues were excitatory conditioned stimuli associated with the unconditioned stimuli of the "stage of inevitable orgasm." As such, they were assumed to trigger the ejaculatory reflex (which is then a conditioned reflex) prior to the time it would otherwise have occurred. Gradually, the time to ejaculation would get shorter and shorter until, in some extreme cases, it was reported to occur as soon as the penis touched the vagina. After treatment, the warning conditioned stimuli have been reconditioned to inhibition of the ejaculatory reflex. Even though this inhibition extinguishes rapidly, each "stop-go" exercise retards the course of ejaculation up to several minutes; by occasional "booster" exercises of the procedure, the man may develop almost complete control over the timing of his ejaculation.

A more drastic treatment for premature ejaculation is the Seman's technique, which depends upon the female's squeezing the penis of the male as soon as he reports an urge to ejaculate. Done with sufficient force, this squeezing not only inhibits ejaculation and reduces the erection but also pairs the urge for rapid ejaculation with a highly painful and aversive stimulus. As this aversive conditioning may generalize to the partner, many females are reluctant to use this approach.

Female Dysfunctions

Frigidity (general sexual dysfunctions)   Kaplan assumes that a female's failure to experience arousal during intercourse is the result of the association of aversive experiences (which would be inhibitory unconditioned stimuli) with sexual stimuli. These then become reconditioned to act as conditioned inhibitors of sexual reflexes. As with impotence, the primary treatment is a modification of systematic desensitization, called the "sensate focus" or pleasuring approach. In this version, the woman sets the pace; intercourse occurs only when the woman feels relaxed and aroused after noncoital stimulation. Kaplan also states that women who voluntarily hold back their orgasms may become frigid. In this case, the cues of holding back act much like the cues of inhibition of ejaculation experienced by the male trying to recondition premature ejaculation. Eventually, the stimuli formerly associated with the onset of female orgasm develop into conditioned inhibitors. If this allows the woman to control herself in an anxiety-provoking situation, a reinforcement element may be added to the development of classically conditioned inhibition. Kaplan (1974) sees many female sexual dysfunctions as resulting from involuntary overcontrol of the orgastic reflex. She also assumes that the female orgasm is easily conditioned and easily inhibited. What once started as voluntary inhibition rapidly becomes involuntary.

Vaginismus   "Vaginismus is a conditioned response which probably results from the association of pain or fear with attempts at or even fantasies of vaginal penetration. The original noxious stimulus may have been physical pain or psychological distress" (Kaplan, 1974, p. 414). The actual response is a rapid constriction of the muscles surrounding the vagina so that intercourse becomes painful and difficult or even impossible. This constriction is a normal UR of the vaginal area to pain or acute anxiety. It is only when the cues associated with sexual activity become conditioned stimuli which elicit this response as a conditioned reflex that constriction is pathological. Treatment consists of insertion of a series of graduated rubber or glass catheters, with each left in place until it can be tolerated without discomfort. The last catheter is the size of an erect penis and is often left in place overnight to facilitate the deconditioning process. The husband may be asked to insert the catheters so that his value as a conditioned cue for the vaginal spasms will be reconditioned. It is essential to proceed slowly so that the catheters do not become CSs for the vaginismus response.

To deal with phobic elements of the woman's fear of intercourse, she may also be asked to visualize successive scenes of her husband's approach, in conjunction with the Jacobson exercises, as in conventional covert desensitization. To minimize the reestablishment of the phobic reactions, initial intercourse consists of the husband's entering and remaining motionless unless otherwise signaled by his wife. Initial thrusting is slow and gentle, and thrusting to orgasm is usually deferred until the wife is able to be relaxed and unafraid. This is to prevent cues related to her husband and intercourse from being painful and hence retriggering the vaginismus reflex (Kaplan, 1974). Gentle reassuring conversation may help by adding second signal system stimuli which are incompatible with stress and fear. In many ways, this approach is similar to that taken in dealing with the fear and tension associated with childbirth.

Chapter Perspective

Several significant innovations in techniques have been developed by workers within the orthodox Pavlovian tradition. While more basic principles have been added, however, understanding of the mechanisms behind existing principles has not shown a corresponding advance except to show that what appeared to be a simple form of conditioning is actually very complex.

Many basic concepts derived from the work of Pavlov and other investigators of stimulus-type conditioning have been applied in a wide range of problems. These applications include most of the types of behavioral modification in which a one-to-one relationship with the therapist is stressed. The users of these applications typically report that such learning-theory-derived methods are significantly superior to more conventional approaches. Critics have pointed out, however, that the bridge between the rigor of the laboratory and real world application is often shaky. In many cases, only a few of the concepts or laws of learning theories are applied, and these loosely. In addition, critics have been reluctant to accept glowing reports of success from those individuals having a vested interest in said success.

Although application of stimulus-type or classical conditioning learning theory is widespread, most applications in clinical psychology have been within the traditional framework of therapist and client. Large-scale institutional settings have been more likely to use the principles of reward-based conditioning, the operant model of conditioning developed most fully by Skinner and his followers. In Chapter 10 we shall examine these applications.

Key Terms

autonomic nervous system	electromyographic potential (EMG)	negative practice paradigm
autoshaping	exteroceptive	overshadowing
aversion therapy	flooding	Pavlovian paradigm
blocking phenomenon	forced extinction	predictiveness hypothesis
central nervous system	imaginal aversion therapy	psychophysiology
conditioned emotional response (CER)	implosive therapy	rule of force
conditioned suppression	interoceptive conditioning	semantic conditioning
contingency	learned helplessness	semantic transfer
		sensory preconditioning

Annotated Bibliography

An excellent review of earlier post-Pavlovian Russian work can be found in G. Razran, "The observable unconscious and the inferable conscious in current Soviet psychophysiology: Interoceptive conditioning, semantic conditioning, and the orienting reflex" (*Psychological Review*, 1961, 54, 357–365). More current and more comprehensive glimpses of trends in Soviet psychology may be found in S. Cole and M. Cole, "Three giants of Soviet psychology, Conversations and sketches" (*Psychology Today*, March 1971, 4, 43–98) and L. Rahmani, *Soviet psychology: Philosophical, theoretical and experimental issues* (New York: International Universities Press, 1973).

Rescorla's views about classical conditioning are given in R. A. Rescorla and R. L. Solomon, "Two-process learning theory: Relationships between Pavlovian conditioning and instrumental conditioning" (*Psychological Review*, 1967, 74, 151–182) and R. A. Rescorla and A. R. Wagner, "A theory of Pavlovian conditioning: Variations in the effectiveness of reinforcement and nonreinforcement," in A. Black and W. F. Prokasy (Eds.), *Classical conditioning II: Current theory and research* (New York: Appleton-Century-Crofts, 1972), 64–99. Seligman's theory of learned helplessness and classical conditioning mechanisms is well presented in M. E. P. Seligman, *Helplessness: On depression, development, and death* (San Francisco, Ca.: W. H. Freeman, 1975). An excellent secondary source covering recent work and theory related to classical conditioning is J. F. Hall, *Classical conditioning and instrumental learning, A contemporary approach* (New York: J. B. Lippincott, 1976).

The literature on applications of classical conditioning to psychotherapy is too vast to do more than suggest a few sample readings. A very good secondary source, wide in scope, is D. C. Rimm and J. C. Masters, *Behavior therapy: Techniques and empirical findings* (New York: Academic Press, 1974). Readable and historically important is M. C. Jones, "The elimination of children's fears" (*Journal of Experimental Psychology*, 1924, 7, 382–390). An amusing article about technological innovations in behavior therapy is P. J. Lang, "The on-line computer in behavior therapy research" (*American Psychologist*, 1969, 24, 236–239). An article on recent cognitive trends in behavior therapy is A. A. Lazarus, "Has behavior therapy outlived its usefulness?" (*American Psychologist*, 1977, 32, 550–553), and behavioral techniques in sex therapy are discussed in H. S. Kaplan, *The new sex therapy: Active treatment of sexual dysfunctions* (New York: Brunner/Mazel, 1974).

9

Recent Developments in the Study of Reinforcement-Related Learning

As we saw in the last chapter, many new principles have been added to the body of knowledge about conditioning contributed by Pavlov, and several new theories about the mechanics of such learning have been suggested. There has been a parallel advance in our understanding of reinforcement and of the types of learning normally associated with reinforcement mechanisms. The effects of reinforcement, the province of operant or instrumental learning theories, are the emphasis of this chapter. Although the emphasis in the Soviet Union has been on research using the Pavlovian paradigm or some refinement of it, learning psychologists in the United States have excelled in developing principles based primarily on the reinforcement paradigm, or from procedures combining instrumental and classical conditioning procedures (as in the work of Rescorla). Two of the traditions reviewed in the first half of this text have made the greatest contributions to understanding conditioning-type learning. These are the Hullian and the Skinnerian traditions. Though, as we shall see, those theorists representing or closely identified with Skinner's basic model of behavior have been most concerned with developing applications of connectionist principles, much valuable work has been accomplished by the neo-Hullians in developing instrumental theories of learning. Following our sequence of discussing Hull and Spence before Skinner, we will briefly review some important contributions in the Hullian tradition. Then we will review three types of trends within the Skinnerian mode accompanied by key critical treatments of some of the primarily Skinnerian, or operant, school's explanations of central points about reinforcement-based learning. This, in turn, leads into Chapter 10, which reviews principles and examples of the widely used behavioral modification practices based upon the Skinnerian or neo-Skinnerian view of learning and behavior.

Let us now turn to selected developments within the neo-Hullian or instrumental learning approach to learning theory. As you will discover, these continue Hull's interest in motivational variables (for Hull, drive and incentive motivation) and are much more likely to develop models of internal processes than theories developed within the avowedly atheoretical Skinnerian mold. In reading the material presented in this chapter, you should focus on major new concepts such as the frustration hypothesis, errorless learning, modeling, and the Premack principle, as well as attempts to use new concepts in explaining phenomena such as the partial reinforcement effect. You should also become familiar with new knowledge about the effects of controlling behavior through use of aversive consequences.

Contributions to Reinforcement Theory in the Neo-Hullian Tradition

We have already reviewed the contributions made by several of Hull's students (Spence, Miller and Dollard, Mowrer). The Hullian tradition does not end there, however. Many workers, either influenced by Hull or Hull's students, have generated additional hypotheses on the nature of the reinforcement process. Many of these hypotheses are related to Spence's I_N or frustration-induced-by-nonreinforcement variable, and it is to these we shall turn first.

How Exposure to Unrewarding Experiences Influences the Effects of Reward

Frustration as a source of motivation   One of the first of these models of motivation was proposed by Amsel, a student under Spence at the University of Iowa. He saw frustration as an acquired, aversive drive which resembles pain except that, unlike pain, it is acquired as a result of the nonreinforcement of a formerly rewarded instrumental response. When reward is delayed or not forthcoming, the feeling of frustration or the emotion of anger results. Amsel classified three types of conditioning events: reward, punishment, and frustration. Frustration arises from the absence of reward when reward is expected. This primary frustration becomes conditioned to cues occurring before its elicitation (through classical conditioning processes); these conditioned cues become aversive and gain drive properties. The anticipatory frustration responses to these cues become linked with cues as a **fractional anticipatory frustration (r_F-S_F)** mechanism (like Hull's fractional anticipatory goal responses), which mediates behavior related to expected frustration. This motivates the organism to show avoidance of situations in which nonreward might be expected (Amsel, 1958). Amsel noted that the vigor of frustration-driven responses was proportional to the degree of anticipation of reward, with high degrees of anticipation producing high amounts of frustration, high drive, and vigorous behavior.

Wagner extended this model to suggest that the effects of frustration induced by nonreward and those effects induced by nontraumatic punishment may be similar. Much punishment is followed by a resumption of the punished response (which is maintained by some sort of reward), so that the punishment itself may become a cue that reward is forthcoming. If the organism then deliberately seeks the punishment (which has become a conditioned reinforcer), one would be justified in speaking of conditioned masochism. Just as the response decrements produced by some punishment situations are unstable and impermanent, so are the response decrements produced by frustration that is subsequently followed by reward. For example, the student who, by a mighty effort, gets a good grade in what initially seemed an impossibly difficult course may subsequently enroll in even more difficult courses. Wagner (1966) notes that depressant drugs which reduce the distressing emotional effects associated with frustration or punishment usually induce an increase in the frustrated or punished response. By reducing the aversive effects of the frustration or punishment, the drugs permit the conditioned reinforcement effects to act with full force.

It must be noted that in these models of the effects of frustration, the analysis of the learned drive properties of frustration is very similar to Miller's and Dollard's analysis of how fear acquires the properties of a learned drive. Most of the frustration drive models, however, suggest a contiguity mechanism (classical conditioning), while Miller and Dollard invoked a drive-reduction mechanism.

Amsel and others have postulated that the frustration which is created by lack of an expected reward may become a conditioned motivator as the result of drive reduction on subsequent trials or may lead to conditioned avoidance if subsequent trials are not rewarded. Conditioned frustration can have both stimulus and drive properties.

The partial reinforcement effect   Amsel has used his frustration variable to explain the **partial reinforcement effect (PRE),** in which occasionally rewarded responses become more resistant to extinction. Amsel proposed that the fractional anticipatory frustration experienced in the presence of the nonrewarded trials is followed by rewarded trials. Eventually, the drive properties of the frustration become conditioned to the eventual reward and add to the drive properties generated by reward. The organism learns to work in the presence of frustration-generated cues, and, when experiencing these internal stimuli during extinction, reacts to them by continuing to respond. Rats with a history of consistent reinforcement never learn to respond when frustrated; hence, the r_F generated by nonreward competes during extinction with tendencies to respond.

Capaldi developed an alternative to the frustration theory explanation of the partial reinforcement effect which he called the **sequential hypothesis.** First, he suggested that performance during extinction is a better measure of the PRE (and strength of learning in general) than acquisition measures. (It must be noted that using extinction as a measure of learning is contrary to the view that losses of performance during extinction reflect motivational decrements rather than losses of associative strength as such.) He then used this measure to compare performance following training with different types of sequences of rewarded and nonrewarded trials. He found that two major types of sequence variables influenced the magnitude of the PRE measured during extinction.

First, transitions from nonrewarded to rewarded trials produced greater PRE than transitions from rewarded to nonrewarded trials (Capaldi, 1971). This was influenced by the number of nonrewarded trials occurring before each rewarded trial and by the regularity with which a particular number of nonrewarded trials preceded reward when the number of nonrewarded trials was varied in the course of a particular experiment. Capaldi (1967) predicted that greater experience with a specific number of nonrewarded trials before rewarded trials would lead to greater PRE. He suggested the following explanation of why greater PRE resulted from nonreward to reward transitions. Assume that, following a nonrewarded trial, the animal remembers the experience of nonreward and that this produces an internal stimulus state characteristic of nonreward. When the following trial is rewarded, the stimulus characteristics resulting from the previous experience of nonreward become associated with the stimulus characteristics produced by the reward (such as reduction in hunger drive). Therefore, the stimulus characteristics of nonreward become conditioned to the instrumental response and acquire control over it. When the transition is from reward to nonreward, there is no association of cues related to nonreward with drive reduction because the nonrewarded trial is not followed by drive reduction. Therefore, the experience of nonreward does not acquire secondary drive or secondary reinforcer properties. This is why the specific sequence of nonrewarded to rewarded trials, not the total percentage of reinforced trials, is responsible for the PRE (Capaldi, 1971).

Capaldi (1958) has also conducted research on the effects of the predictability of reward from particular experiences with nonrewarded trials. He compared regular alternations of reinforced and nonreinforced trials to irregular alternations of such trials and found resistance to extinction was greater with irregular alternations. This could be explained as due to the circumstance that the rats exposed to irregular alternations had learned that any nonrewarded trial might be followed by a rewarded trial.

Capaldi's theory assumes that the rat has the memory capacity to remember sequences of reward and nonreward. He suggested that the formation of such memories (or internal stimulus states) begins on the first trial and could be modified by a single trial. That is, the rat can modify its behavior on the basis of what happened to it (reward or nonreward) on the trial just previous. This prediction of the rapid acquisition of the factors leading to the PRE is opposed to Amsel's prediction that frustration responses are acquired gradually over many trials and that frustration gradually acquires secondary drive properties through its association with subsequent reward and drive reduction. Amsel, Hug, and Surridge (1968) tried to explain away the results of studies which had supported Capaldi's notion that PRE can be acquired in a small number of trials. Noting that these studies had used multiple food pellets, they suggested that what appeared to be only one trial was, in reality, a situation in which the rat made multiple approaches to the food cup. Hence, there were really many trials for the frustration effects to develop. Going further, Amsel (1967) suggested that perhaps there were really two types of PRE: One would develop with massed trials and would be dependent upon stimulus aftereffects (since massed trials are closer in time to each other, the memory capacities that Capaldi's theory requires would be more plausible). The other would be a PRE that develops with longer intervals between trials and reflects conditioned frustration variables. Capaldi and Wargo (1963), however, have demonstrated that even with 20-minute intervals between responses, rats exposed to series of single alternations of nonrewarded trials with rewarded trials showed greater resistance to extinction than rats given rewarded and nonrewarded trials in a random order with fewer nonrewarded to rewarded transitions. This suggests that the short-term memory capacity of the rat for sequences must be at least 20 minutes. Thus, Capaldi's theory is a cognitive theory to the extent that the rat's memory of sequences and expectancies about sequences determine subsequent behavior.

A student whose questions in class are only acknowledged part of the time may become more persistant as a result, which may reflect a PRE effect. Capaldi referred to this effect as **intertrial reinforcement** and suggested that performance on each trial was regulated extensively by reinforcement associated with earlier trials. An example might be someone who goes to discos and receives several rejections before being rewarded with a desirable dance partner. With time, longer and longer intervals of rejections will have less and less effect, or the person will become increasingly persistent (and accept some ratio of bad experiences to good experiences as the normal price to be paid for the good experiences).

The PRE (partial reinforcement effect), which is the increased resistance to extinction resulting from intermittent reinforcement, created problems for early learning theories, which said response strength was a direct function of the number of reinforced trials. PRE has been explained by both frustration (Amsel) and sequence (Capaldi) variables.

The partial reinforcement effect depends on changes from a rewarded to a nonrewarded state over sequences of rewarded and nonrewarded trials. If the total elimination of reward sometimes has such a powerful effect on behavior, what would be the effect of increasing or decreasing the amount of reward after a series of trials? The answer is that increasing the amount of reward (or its desirability) sometimes increases the intensity or rate of responding, and decreasing the amount of reward (or its desirability) usually decreases the intensity and/or rate of responding. These changes in responding resulting from changes in reward situations are called contrast effects, and the organism's expectancies about reward in particular situations is called incentive motivation. Let us now examine research and theory related to these topics.

How Changing the Amount or Kind of Reward Influences Behavior

Reward contrast effects   Another effect which is nicely explained by the frustration hypothesis is the type of **contrast** effect called **negative contrast,** which takes place when either the amount or the desirability of a reward is reduced. Amsel (1958) suggested that a reduction in reward elicits a primary frustration response which interferes with the organism's previous learning. Hall (1976) has provided an extensive summary of studies on the effects of either reductions of reward or increases in reward. In most cases, a reduction in reward is followed by decreases in response rates or intensity of the responses. In the first study of this type, Crespi (1942) found that reductions in amount of reward obtained by rats running down a runway resulted in a reduction in running speed. Crespi also found a **positive contrast** effect, in which increases in the available amount of reward increased running speed. Hall (1976) notes that this latter effect has only been found by about half of the investigators testing for it; if one assumes that such an effect exists, its mechanism must be other than frustration. A plausible explanatory mechanism is that of the incentive motivation variable (K) developed by Hull (1952) and further specified by Logan (1970), whose work will be reviewed immediately following this discussion of contrast effects. It has been the author's experience, for example, that the effects of a raise in pay on work performance in most job situations is, at most, a transitory increase in the amount of work performed. Conversely, the effects of a reduction in pay or even receiving a smaller raise than was expected usually result in considerable emotional effects and reduced work output. It may be suggested that positive contrast effects are usually weaker and more transitory than negative contrast effects. A student might increase his or her rate of question asking in class if told by another member of the class that the questions were a valuable contribution; this is an example of a positive contrast effect.

Negative contrast is the effect observed when amount or desirability of reward is reduced. The effect is one of decreased response intensity or response rates. Some researchers have also found weaker positive contrast effects where increases in amount or desirability of reward leads to increases in response intensity or response rates.

A general model which could account for contrast effects might postulate that the organism's expectancies about the amount and desirability of reward influence the organism's incentive motivation.

Incentive motivation and quantitative aspects of responding   You may recall that one of the variables added by Hull in the 1952 version of his theory was K, or **incentive motivation.** Logan has refined this concept and defined it in a Tolmanian way: "Incentive motivation, the individual's expectation of reward for a given behavioral response, is to be distinguished from the goal per se. It is a pull or motivation toward a goal. The goal is reinforcing, but the principle of reinforcement is a performance principle, not a learning principle" (Logan, 1970, p. 192). This focus on expectancies is similar to that of Tolman, who demonstrated through latent learning studies that learning could occur without food reward but faster running time to the goal box appeared only after the rats had come to expect food to be there. Like Tolman, Spence, and some other theorists, Logan accepted a distinction between learning and performance. For example, a student may learn from classroom lectures but may never discuss what was learned with professor or peers. Once the incentive is made available (such as course credit to be earned by passing a test), however, the previous learning may be translated into performance.

Logan also saw incentive motivation as determining how responses were to be made. If a teacher reinforces verbose answers to essay test questions, students will couch their answers in flowery language with long discourses on the material covered. If the teacher makes clear that brevity is preferred, the same information may be written in a terse and telegraphic format. Logan refers to such situations, in which, the reward is at least partially dependent upon the nature of the response, as involving correlated reinforcement. Logan (1970) explained the decision process in conflict situations as a function of the net incentive motivation which results from subtracting expectancies about aversive events from expectancies about rewarding events. This may be seen in a study by Rachlin (1972) in which pigeons and rats were trained to key-peck or bar-press, respectively, for food reinforcement. This food reinforcement contingency remained in effect throughout the experiment. A shock mechanism was then activated so that every response would increase the level of shock delivered to the subjects (levels of shock declined between responses). All subjects continued to respond at a level lower than preshock but just sufficient to maintain a constant shock intensity. Logan would explain this "critical rate" of responding as reflecting the net incentive motivation resulting from subtracting the effects of shock from the effects of obtaining food. This type of analysis could also be extended to explain conflict behavior of the approach-avoidance type described by Miller and Dollard, without evoking the theoretical constructs of goal gradients. Logan saw incentive as distinguished from reward in three ways: (1) incentive is learned, (2) incentive is not directly proportional to differences in the amount of reward available, and (3) incentive reflects the organism's expectancies of reward rather than the actual contingencies.

Logan saw the quantitative aspects of responding as determined by net incentive motivation. Working too hard increases the negative incentive motivation occasioned by the punishing pain of fatigue. Working too slowly decreases the expectancy of the amount of reward to be obtained. Therefore, the precise type of response made or the effort expended is usually carefully tailored by the responding organism to yield the maximal net expected reward or incentive motivation. Logan's model can handle the data on the relationship of reward amount to effort expended. We have already noted that some researchers have found increases in response effort accompanying increases in reward during the course of an experiment. The incentive motivation concept would also seem to apply to the data on the effort expended by different groups of subjects experiencing differing amounts of reward. Hall (1976) has summarized 29 such studies; in all but six, effort was indeed higher for subjects in the groups receiving the higher amounts of reward (or more desirable rewards). Most of the studies did not find the aspect of reward manipulated (taste, number of pieces of food, amount by weight of reward) to be directly proportional to the increases observed with "more" reward. This supports Logan's postulate that incentive is not directly proportional to the amount of reward available. There may also be time-based factors, as when the high levels of reward obtained under large-reward-per-trial conditions lead to faster satiation (which reduces the incentive value of the reward).

Like many of the neo-Hullians reviewed in this text, Logan has provided us with a theory about some detailed aspects of instrumental responding, which, by including some cognitive variables, fits nicely with many of our intuitions about motivation and behavior. His analysis of response discrimination, which views quantitatively different behaviors as different responses, is congruent with many a student's experience of carefully gauging his or her amount of study effort to that required for an acceptable grade in each course. If you recall from Chapter 4, Skinner (and the neo-Skinnerians) found schedule variables to be better predictors of response rates, resistance to extinction, and satiation than the variables related to expectancies about type and amount of reward studied by the neo-Hullians.

While many of the neo-Hullian concepts have been useful in explaining a variety of behavioral phenomena in humans and infrahuman organisms, the Skinnerian approach, with its greater emphasis on measurable environmental determiners of behavior (such as schedules of reinforcement rather than expectancies or such mediating variables as incentive motivation), has generated more real world applications. We will now turn to an examination of developments in neo-Skinnerian theory and research.

Contributions to Reinforcement Theory in the Neo-Skinnerian Tradition

Skinner may well be the best known of living American psychologists, and researchers identified with his operant conditioning approach to learning may be the most influential and productive of any current school of learning theory. Among operant learning psychologists, at least three distinct trends can be identified: (1) extensions of Skinner's approach retaining Skinner's emphasis on positive reinforcement, (2) extensions examining the effects of aversive consequences (or the annoyers of Thorndike's first law of effect), and (3) models incorporating cognitive variables. Although the assumptions about learning held by workers operating within each of these three traditions are not entirely the same, all these offshoots of the operant learning model have generated applications identified as part of the behavioral modification movement. The behavioral modification movement's operant learning branch and its ties to operant learning theory will be discussed in Chapter 10.

Among the extensions of operant theory emphasizing the role of positive reinforcement, we will focus on the work on discrimination learning by Skinner's students, Reynolds and Terrace, and on contributions to new theories of reinforcement by Premack and by Timberlake and Allison. These researchers have developed new principles within the operant model and have suggested some modifications of Skinner's empirical laws and hypotheses about the nature of reinforcement.

The second group of theorists have been active in developing empirical laws pertaining to the effects of aversive contingencies; some of them have suggested guidelines for the development of applications using such contingencies. In doing this, they have deviated from Skinner's views. Skinner accepted Thorndike's later (truncated) law of effect, which stated that the effects of punishment were both weaker and more unpredictable than the effects of positive reinforcement. Reading Skinner's writings on the subject of aversive consequences, the author perceives that his conclusions are based on something less than extensive investigations of punishment. Skinner's arguments against the use of punishment depend heavily on pure theory and have a moralistic flavor. He spent far less time investigating the effects of aversive techniques than in conducting research on the effects of positive reinforcement. Chapter 12 of *Science and Human Behavior* (1953) is titled: "Punishment: A Questionable Technique." This chapter begins:

> The commonest technique of control in modern life is punishment. The pattern is familiar: if a man does not behave as you wish, knock him down; if a child misbehaves, spank him; if the people of a country misbehave, bomb them. Legal and police systems are based upon such punishments as fines, flogging, incarceration, and hard labor. Religious control is exerted through penances, threats of excommunication and consignment to hell-fire. . . . The fact that punishment does not permanently reduce a tendency to respond is in agreement with Freud's discovery of the surviving activity of what he called repressed wishes. [Skinner, 1953, pp. 182–184]

For Skinner to evoke the name of Freud instead of the results of controlled experiments is, to say the least, surprising.

This bias against research on the functions of aversive stimulation has been severely criticized by Solomon (1964), who blames Thorndike, Skinner, and Freud for originating "unscientific legends" about presumed inadequacies and undesirable effects of aversive control. Solomon, Sidman (1960), Azrin (1967), and others have attempted to correct this state of affairs by conducting a series of careful investigations.

The models of learning which have attempted to synthesize operant and cognitive principles are best known through the work of Albert Bandura (1969). Along with Mischel (1973) and other so-called "social learning" theorists, he has succeeded in providing a viable alternative to radical (Skinnerian) behaviorism which conforms with the experimental orientation of the behavioristic view. Social learning theory has combined aspects of Miller's and Dollard's emphasis on the importance of indirect or imitative learning, Skinner's emphasis on reinforcement, and Tolman's use of subjective expectancies as a basic unit of learning. As a form of cognitive behaviorism, social learning theory has continued the Tolmanian-functionalist tradition of combining laboratory research with "mentalist" variables. As with all behaviorisms, social learning theory, as its name implies, is focused on environmental determinants of behavior.

Contributions of Neo-Skinnerians Emphasizing Positive Reinforcement

Stimulus control of attention in discrimination learning   The first step in discriminating one cue from another is to pay attention to the relevant cue dimension. If the organism is to learn to tell red lights from green lights, it must first focus on color and not on other stimulus dimensions such as brightness or shape. Reynolds (1975) has introduced the term **superordinate stimuli** to describe the class of stimuli which serve to direct the subject's attention towards a particular property of a situation. As such, they act to focus perception. For example, when a student is told that research findings will be stressed more than theories on a test, she or he will focus on learning and discriminating salient features of research findings. Hence, superordinate stimuli are a specialized subclass of discriminative stimuli (S_Ds) which tell the organism that reward is more probable if it pays attention to particular aspects of a complex array of stimuli. They also tell the organism when a particular cue is likely to be important in a particular context (as when a specific schedule of reinforcement is likely to be in effect) so that the organism can focus on relevant rather than irrelevant S_Ds. These stimuli determine what is figure as opposed to ground as well as what types of cues can elicit the OR (orienting reflex). Pigeons can learn to respond to the shape of illuminated figures when a red cue light is on and to the color of the figures when a green cue light is on. The cue lights function as superordinate stimuli. This concept is useful in explaining why a particular stimulus may be a cue for action in one context, a conditioned reinforcer in another, and ineffectual in a third.

Cues which direct attention to the salient stimulus features of a discrimination learning situation are superordinate stimuli. They tell the organism which other stimuli to focus on.

Learning to discriminate the conditions of reinforcement   We mentioned in the previous discussion that superordinate stimuli can tell the subject when a particular schedule of reinforcement is likely to be in effect. Let us now examine material on the learning of optimal response patterns for particular conditions of reinforcement.

We have already discussed the positive and negative contrast effects created by changes in the amount of reward available for instrumental responses. There is a similar phenomenon generated by shifts in the type of reinforcement used, or of the schedules of reinforcement used (including shifts to extinction schedules), called **behavioral contrast** by operant learning theorists.

Reynolds made behavioral contrast a standard term in the operant vocabulary, although the phenomenon he described was first discovered by Pavlov and later investigated by Skinner. Behavioral contrast may best be described as a change in response rates in a direction opposite to that expected from the operation of generalization. Reynolds states:

> We have an example of generalization when a child's unruly behavior extinguishes more slowly than usual at home because it is reinforced on the playground; we have an example of behavioral contrast when the extinction of unruly behavior at home makes for increasingly frequent unruly behavior on the playground.
>
> Contrast seems to depend on the relation between the reinforcing conditions associated with the two stimuli. When the consequences of a response become less reinforcing in the presence of one stimulus, we can expect the frequency of the response to increase in the presence of another stimulus where its consequences remain reinforcing. [1975, p. 50]

The concept has been extremely important in explaining some of the effects of punishment in the real world. The responding person learns to discriminate where and from whom punishment is likely to originate. The result of this is that responses suppressed by the punishing are acted out in a safe environment. The high rate of recidivism among incarcerated felons may illustrate this principle. The antisocial responses that are suppressed by punishment in the prison environment are emitted (and often reinforced) once the former felon graduates to the streets again.

The principle of behavioral contrast can also be used to explain the effects of contrasting two schedules of reinforcement. When an organism is offered the chance to earn reinforcements on a schedule that is "richer" (more reinforcements/response) than its training schedule, the rate of responding to the new, rich schedule will be higher than for subjects beginning with that schedule. In addition, the rate of responding to the old, lean schedule will drop far below training levels. This only applies when the conditions under which each schedule is to be in effect are clearly marked by S_Ds. In general, the term "contrast" is used whenever rates of responding to two different stimuli or conditions move in opposite directions. When there is behavioral contrast between the components of complex or multiple schedules, the interaction effect of the schedules results in divergence of response rates.

Waite and Osborne (1972) were early demonstrators of this effect. Under controlled conditions, they exposed children to two types of multiple schedules. In the first case, the components of the multiple schedule were as follows: Variable interval schedules were presented successively. In these, the change from the first independent schedule to the second independent schedule was marked by a discriminative stimulus. Response rates to each schedule were equal, showing the absence of contrast effects. The second multiple schedule had a variable interval schedule as its first component and an extinction schedule (signaled by an S_Δ, as before) as its second component. As the children were exposed to alternating successive presentations of these two components, a reciprocal pattern emerged: Response rates to the variable interval component increased as response rates to the extinction schedule decreased. This divergence of response rates to the two components illustrates the phenomenon of sustained behavioral contrast, an effect which can be compared with the momentary contrast effects obtained when a subject is shifted to an extinction schedule that is not part of a multiple or complex schedule paradigm. These momentary extinction effects usually consist of short-lived increases in the rate, vigor, and variety of responses emitted (Staddon and Simmelhag, 1971).

Behavioral contrast occurs when the organism discriminates between reinforcing conditions in two or more situations (or two or more S_Ds). In contrast to generalization, response rates to the stimuli signaling reinforcement increase as responses to the cues signaling nonreinforcement decrease; in other words, response rates in the two situations "move away from each other."

Learning discriminations without errors   Although behavioral contrast illustrates one way in which organisms maximize positive effects from the environment and minimize aversive or unrewarding effects, our next topic is a procedure which eliminates unreinforced responding. This is the **errorless learning** or **fading** technique developed by Terrace.

Several early discrimination learning studies (reviewed in Hall, 1976) found that subjects (which ranged from rats to monkeys to children) given exposure to incorrect cues and making incorrect responses (unrewarded responses) in the presence of those cues learned discriminations faster than subjects only exposed to the cues signaling reward or given minimal exposure to the cues signaling nonreward (S − s). These results suggested that presentation of the S− and responding to it were important in learning simple discriminations. Therefore, Terrace's demonstration that discriminations could be learned without any incorrect responses at all has considerable theoretical importance in understanding discrimination learning.

Before Terrace's development of his errorless learning technique, it was widely believed that discrimination learning depended upon a process in which the organism made some errors and failed to obtain reinforcement following those errors. This was thought to weaken the tendency to make such responses; thus, by the process of elimination, the subject would be more likely to emit the correct response, which would then be followed by reinforcement. The reinforcement would strengthen the tendency to repeat the correct response, and, through a process of classical conditioning, cues associated with the reinforcer's occurrence would become CSs or discriminative stimuli (S_Ds). The cues associated with nonoccurrence of the reinforcer (the US) would become CS − s or, in operant terminology, S_Δs. Terrace (1963a) was able to show that errors were not an essential element in discrimination learning. Using pigeons as subjects, he demonstrated such learning in the absence of nonreinforcement of the S−. He began by lighting up the S_D pecking key, making it an inviting target for pigeon pecking,* and noted that his subjects began immediately to emit these correct responses. Terrace then gradually increased the intensity of the light behind the S− key (which had originally been completely dark), until it was as bright as the S_D key. Still the pigeons continued to peck only at the S_D key (the correct key). Thus, a completed discrimination was achieved without the element of error, which would have resulted in nonreinforced trials. Terrace describes his procedure as follows:

> Responses to S− ("errors") are not a necessary condition for the formation of an operant discrimination of color. Errors do not occur if discrimination training begins early in conditioning and if S+ and S− differ with respect to brightness, duration, and wavelength. After training starts, S−'s duration and brightness is progressively increased until S+ and S− differ only with respect to wavelength throughout training. Performance following discrimination learning without errors lacks three characteristics that are found following learning with errors. Only those birds that learned the discrimination with errors showed (1) "emotional" responses in the presence of S−, (2) an increase in the rate (or decrease in the latency) of their response to S+, and (3) occasional bursts of responses to S−. [1963a, p. 1]

---

* The tendency of the pigeons to peck at the lighted key without extensive shaping may be an example of the autoshaping phenomenon discussed in Chapter 8.

Terrace (1963b) extended this learning without errors over two dimensions in a procedure which began with a dark circle (the S−) and a bright red circle (the S_D); gradually, a green light was faded in for the S− (S_Δ). After stimulus control had been shifted from brightness to color (wavelength), a geometric shape was added to the bright red S_D. Another shape was then gradually faded into the S− and the colored lights were faded out. At the end, the subjects were making perfect shape discriminations without ever having made errors! Schusterman has replicated these results in the California sea lion (1966). (In some respects, this procedure has much in common with sensory preconditioning; color and brightness are originally paired without special contingencies for responses to color, and color is then shown to have acquired the property of being a S_D through its association with brightness as a S_D.)

Skinner has developed a version of this procedure, labeled vanishing, as an aid for teaching children to draw the letters of the alphabet. In this procedure, the children are given letters which they are to trace on sheets of paper. The paper used has been chemically treated so that errors show up as bright yellow. In addition, the concentration of the dye decreases from the top to the bottom of the page, so that at the end the children are tracing the letters without the extra feedback of the dye. Another technique presents material to be learned (usually in a programmed text) with some of the letters of the answers to questions printed in the blanks where the answers are to be written. Such prompts are gradually reduced or faded out as the program progresses (Skinner, 1968). I once conducted a research project in which fading techniques were used to teach elementary school children to discriminate symmetrical figures from nonsymmetrical ones. Unfortunately (from the perspective of developing useful educational techniques), although significant differences were found, they favored traditional discrimination training over the fading procedures (Swenson, 1969).

By designing a procedure which eliminates the aversive effects of frustration related to making errors (which are nonreinforced responses), Terrace has moved behavioral technology one step closer to Skinner's ideal of learning environments devoid of aversive failure experiences.

Terrace developed a method of errorless learning or fading which involves shifting stimulus control from a highly salient cue which always signals the availability of reinforcement to a more difficult stimulus dimension. If this is done gradually, the organism ends up always responding correctly on the more difficult problem without ever having made errors.

The effects of prior discrimination learning on generalization   Hanson (1961) found that when pigeons were trained to peck a key illuminated with a particular wavelength of light (the S_D) and not to peck the key when it was illuminated by similar higher and lower wavelengths (S_Δs), a very steep generalization gradient was found. This generalization gradient was much steeper than that obtained from pigeons in the control group that were only exposed to the S_D (reinforced cue). If only a single S_Δ was used in the discrimination training, the peak of the generalization gradient was shifted away from the S_D. This **peak shift** phenomenon was also found by Terrace (1963a), except when he used errorless learning procedures. This suggests that the organism does not develop any tendencies to avoid the potential S_Δ when it never experiences the presumably aversive event of responding to the S_Δ and not receiving reinforcement for the response. In errorless learning, therefore, the organism only learns to respond to the S_D and does not learn what not to respond to. Generalization gradients after discrimination training with one, two, and no (errorless learning or control groups) S_Δs are shown in Figure 9.1. Note that the peak of the one S_Δ group is shifted towards the left away from the single S_Δ, while the generalization gradient is flatter for the control or errorless learning group.

Prior discrimination training in which the S_D is "surrounded" by S_Δs results in a steeper generalization gradient. If the prior training involves a single S_Δ on one side of the S_D, the peak of the generalization gradient will "shift" away from that S_Δ.

Of the phenomena related to discrimination learning that we have covered in this section of the chapter, only the errorless learning technique has directly generated real world applications, although all these phenomena may have important implications for applications. The work of David Premack, the first learning researcher we will examine in the following section, has generated many useful applications. These applications, along with others derived from the operant approach to learning, will be reviewed in Chapter 10.

Reinforcement as the opportunity to respond   David Premack has contributed two important hypotheses to the psychology of learning: the **prepotent theory of reinforcement** and the **reversibility (transitivity) of reinforcement.** These concepts have been useful in formulating a definition of reinforcement that is not contradicted by experimental data and that also happens to be more specific than Skinner's definition. Breger and McGaugh (1965), criticizing Skinner for failing to provide a specific list of reinforcers, have suggested that his definition of reinforcement in terms of behavioral consequences is nothing but a circular definition (tautology). While Skinner's view, that a reinforcer is anything which can increase the probability of the reemission of a response, is in the tradition of Thorndike's statement that a satisfier is anything the organism seeks to prolong, such statements only permit the identification of a reinforcer after the behavioral event. Premack's hypotheses offer a way to predict effective reinforcers in advance, without abandoning the atheoretical-functional approach to specifying the empirical law of effect. Note that in Premack's theory (and in the modification of that theory proposed by Timberlake and Allison), reinforcers are responses (or the opportunity to emit responses) rather than things, as in more conventional views.

The prepotent theory of reinforcement allows Premack to predict which events will serve as reinforcers relative to specified instrumental behaviors. He states this theory as follows: "Any response A will reinforce any other response B, if and only if the independent rate of A is greater than that of B" (1959, p. 220). In most cases, these rates are measured using a paired baseline technique.

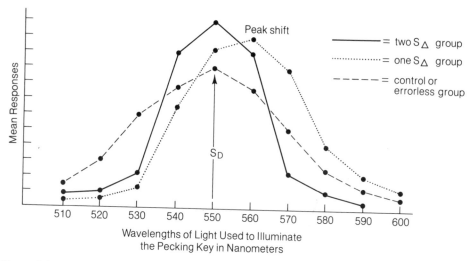

Figure 9.1 *Idealized generalization gradients for groups of pigeons trained to peck at a S$_D$ illuminated by light of 550 nanometers and also given experience with the key lighted (or another key lighted) with either two surrounding wavelengths (two S$_\Delta$ group), one other wavelength shown as 540 nanometers in this figure (one S$_\Delta$ group), or no effective S$_\Delta$ (errorless learning or control groups).*

This technique consists of simply collecting baseline data on the "free operant" rates with which two behaviors are emitted. The behavior which has the higher operant level can be used as a consequence (reinforcer) if access to it is made contingent upon the organism performing the less likely (lower operant level) response. Today this modern version of mother's method of behavioral control ("Eat your spinach and then you can have ice cream") is called the **Premack principle.**

Premack also advanced the hypothesis of reversibility (transitivity) of reinforcement. This hypothesis states that reinforcers are relational or relative to the rates with which they are emitted during baseline conditions, compared to specific alternate behaviors. Thus, a given response may on one occasion be more probable than another response and serve as a reinforcer for the second response. If conditions were to be changed to make the second response more probable than the first response, then it would be the second response which would be the reinforcer. This reversibility of reinforcement hypothesis gives rise to some surprising predictions. If Premack is correct, then licking water from a drinking tube (at least for a rat) is reinforcing because licking is a high probability response relative to other behaviors, such as bar-pressing. Given that tissue deprivation associated with thirst is not reduced immediately after drinking, and given that most organisms will emit instrumental responses to gain access to nonnutritive but tasty liquids, such a response-probability theory of reinforcement may be more effective in predicting behavior than either Skinnerian definitions of what a reinforcer is or drive-reduction definitions. For example, Premack's hypotheses predict (as would most definitions of reinforcement) that water deprivation could cause a rat to learn to run on an exercise wheel for purposes of gaining access to water. Premack, however, would also predict that by restricting access to the exercise wheel and allowing free access to drinking, a situation could be created in which "wheel-running" becomes the higher-probability response during paired-baseline measurement; hence, it should be an effective reinforcer for increased drinking (1962). Premack was able to demonstrate that rats deprived of opportunities to operate the exercise wheel would drink water to gain access to wheel-running even when they had consumed a normal day's ration of water. These results support both the prepotency hypothesis (wheel-running became the more potent or probable response when its occurrence was reduced below baseline measure levels by the wheel-running deprivation procedure) and the reversibility hypothesis (in most situations, drinking would have been the reinforcer and wheel-running the instrumental response). The Premack principle has important implications for the design of contingency management systems; in these, behaviors may be used as reinforcers rather than physical rewards (such as food or toys). Examples of contingency management-based behavior modification programs which utilize the Premack principle will now be presented.

Homme and colleagues (1963) used this principle in controlling "acting out" (screaming, running around the room) behaviors in three three-year-old subjects. After baseline measures had been made of "acting out" behaviors (high probability) and of sitting quietly in a chair and looking at the blackboard (low probability), the researchers began the procedure of waiting for the few instances in which the low-probability behavior was being emitted. They would then ring a bell and give the instruction: "Run and scream." The subjects would leap to their feet and run around the room screaming until the signal to stop was given. Within a few days, rates of "acting out" were greatly reduced and "sitting quietly and watching the blackboard" greatly increased. The authors note that they had achieved good behavioral control without the necessity of using any aversive consequences. At a later stage, the children were able to earn tokens for emitting low-probability behaviors; these tokens could be exchanged for the opportunity to engage in high-probability activities.

Todd (1972) used a covert type of Premack principle to promote the development of self-esteem in a depressed woman. The woman was instructed to write down all the positive things about herself that she could think of (a very low-probability behavior); with considerable prompting from the therapist, she was able to find six such statements. These were printed on a card that was trimmed to fit inside the cellophane wrapper of a cigarette package. Since smoking was a high-probability behavior for her, she was instructed to read one or two of the items and to think positive thoughts about herself before taking a cigarette from a pack. Within two weeks she reported feeling better than she had in years, and she had added 21 positive items to her list. You can also use the Premack principle to direct more of your time towards studying. If your first act in the morning is to brush your teeth or make a cup of coffee, try making the performance of these higher-probability behaviors contingent upon the completion of a few pages of study material (a low-probability behavior at that time of day for most of us). Premack's hypothesis (that the differential probabilities of responses determine what will be effective as a reinforcer) brings us a long way from conceptualizations of reinforcement, either as "satisfiers" or "annoyers" or as the result of drive-reduction mechanisms. It also represents an advance over the definitions of reinforcement presented by Skinner and Spence. These theorists ignore speculations about prediction in favor of a more pragmatic definition of "reinforcers" that is couched in post hoc terms (that is, some responses are emitted at higher rates following specific environmental events).

These **empirical law of effect** definitions not only fail to predict in advance which events will increase or decrease instrumental behaviors, they are also unable to handle the reversibility-of-reinforcement effects found by Premack. Premack's principle predicts the outcome of contingencies between two events previously defined as reinforcers and also predicts the failure of a satiated rat to continue working for a food "reinforcement."

Timberlake and Allison (1974) note that reinforcement is usually seen as strengthening tendencies to respond (or as driving a learning process), and that both this strengthening of learning view of reinforcement and the empirical law of effect are derived from Thorndike's original law of effect. These authors point out, however, that the strengthening process is intuitive: "The process itself is a mystery" (1974, p. 149). As we saw in our discussion of research by Rescorla and others on classical conditioning, the processes of that apparently simple learning are still unknown, are debatable, and may be multiple. Timberlake and Allison (1974) note that phenomena such as all-or-none learning, latent learning, and partial-reinforcement effects suggest the involvement of similar multiple processes in what has usually been seen as the unitary phenomenon of instrumental (or operant) learning. In their attempt to clarify the nature of reinforcement in instrumental learning, these authors review some of Premack's data and focus on an interesting anomaly.

In their 1974 study, Timberlake and Allison demonstrated that simply depriving rats of access to performing the less probable response (as defined by paired baseline measures) makes this response (which Premack defines as the instrumental response, based on his differential probability model) effective as a reinforcing contingent response. For example: rats spend more time licking tubes which give them .4 percent saccharin (a nonnutritive sweetener) under paired baseline measurement conditions than licking for .1 percent saccharin. Premack would predict that the rate of licking for .1 percent saccharin should increase if this is made the instrumental response to gain access to .4 percent saccharin. While acknowledging that this does occur, Timberlake and Allison (1974) further demonstrate that depriving the rats of the opportunity to lick for .1 percent saccharin results in their licking the .4 percent saccharin tubes for longer durations than measured during the baseline period (in other words, the .4 percent saccharin tube licking has now become the instrumental response and the .1 percent saccharin tube licking has become the reinforcing event). They therefore conclude that while the Premack theory is a significant advance over the strengthening of learning theory of reinforcement and over the empirical law of effect, it is still inadequate to explain all aspects of instrumental learning. They offer their **adaptive model** as a more adequate theory.

The adaptive model focuses on the responses* used by an organism in gaining access to consequences (which ultimately lead to situations conducive to the survival of the organsim, such as chewing food). The theory states that these responses are more likely to occur when the organism is deprived of the opportunity of access to some consequence. The consequences can be appetitive behaviors, which would normally be part of a chain of responses terminating in consummatory behavior (such as drinking), or they can be consumatory responses. Hence, reinforcement is a function of depriving the organism of the opportunity to perform a given response at baseline (or free operant) levels. Rather than predicting reinforcing properties on the basis of the differential probabilities of two responses as measured by the paired baseline procedure, the **response deprivation model** bases its predictions on the relative deprivation from those rates of responding measured during the paired baseline phase. The power of a reinforcer, so defined, is produced by the organism's conflict between its "need" to emit a response which in the past has provided access to consequences, and the lack of opportunity (induced experimentally by the response deprivation procedures) to emit that response at baseline rates. In nature, the end result of this mechanism is that the organism is placed in a position where it is likely to survive by either satisfying tissue needs (through eating, drinking, breathing, and so on) or by escaping aversive consequences (such as a bloody encounter with a predator). The adaptive value of the response deprivation mechanism may be seen in the following example: A wild cat has to catch small moving things (which are usually rodents and birds) to survive. If prey is scarce, there may be no appropriate targets to elicit the "leaping at movement" instrumental response. The response deprivation theory would predict that as the cat is deprived of the opportunity to emit leaping and catching responses, it will become more likely to engage in other behaviors (such as moving to another section of its hunting grounds) to "earn" the opportunity to indulge in leaping and catching. If such "traveling" behaviors put the cat in a place where it can emit leaping and catching responses (which should result in its catching edible prey), its chances of survival are higher than they would have been had it not emitted the "traveling" responses. In this example, "leaping at movement" is contingent upon the instrumental response of "traveling" and, in turn, the ultimate consequence (eating prey) is contingent upon "leaping at movement."

A human application of Timberlake's and Allison's (1974) response deprivation theory might be the following: Before exams, the cleaning of your house or apartment has to be put aside to permit adequate study time. As you are deprived of the opportunity to emit cleaning responses (which, while of admittedly low probability for some of us, may be related in our evolutionary history to avoidance of disease-transmitting situations), the urge to clean becomes stronger and cleaning behavior becomes more reinforcing. If you then make cleaning (which, because of deprivation, has become a reinforcer) contingent

---

* As we will see in Chapter 12, many theorists now think that responses that are closely linked to survival may either be instinctual or be partly "prewired" so that learning them is easier than learning other responses. The organism may also have an innate need to emit such responses.

upon the instrumental response of studying (which is presumably a nonde-prived response before exams), you should study harder in order to allow yourself access to some cleaning behaviors. Cleaning would then function as a reinforcer for studying responses completed! The author, who has tried this technique and found it quite effective, would like to add the following additional hypothesis to Timberlake's and Allison's response deprivation theory of reinforcement: Behaviors which you are forced to emit at levels considerably above baseline rates may become momentarily aversive. He has found this to be true in his own experience (when social pressures forced him to spend too much time in personal interactions, he began to experience socialization as aversive and the idea of getting back to work on this book as reinforcing). It might also explain the success of **forced practice** techniques in behavioral modification. For example, when a smoker is forced to smoke at levels considerably above his normal (baseline) rates, he begins to find smoking responses aversive.

Let us now turn to the subject of aversive control of behavior in general.

The Premack principle and the response deprivation model both predict that responses which you want to do (either because of a relatively high operant level or because of deprivation, respectively) can serve as reinforcers for either lower operant level or less deprived responses, respectively. Premack also suggests that the instrumental response in one situation can be the reinforcing response in another situation.

The Control of Behavior by Aversive Consequences

Punishment   Punishment has historically presented greater difficulties for learning theorists than either positive contingencies or association learning. Thorndike revised his early symmetrical view of the effects of satisfiers and annoyers to diminish the role of punishers, and Skinner spent more time in polemics against punishment than in punishment research. Part of the reason for these difficulties lies in the nature of the responses to punishment, which vary from response enhancement (through an arousal effect) to total and permanent response suppression. Much of the rest of the difficulty lies in the varied nature of the procedures that were labeled as punishment. Although negative reinforcement, or active avoidance, has been differentiated from punishment, passive avoidance and escape procedures are both considered as involving punishment. Even deliberate removals of positive reinforcers, or time-out procedures, are usually considered as punishers, although this departs from the more common format of adding a definite aversive event to the subject's environment. In addition to the subject's emitting any operant responses, such as escape or avoidance, punishment usually involves emotional or autonomic nervous system mediated responses—a sign of a classically conditioned component. In attempting to clarify these matters, it may be useful to follow a punishment situation through various stages.

The basic paradigm for contingent punishment is simple and straight-forward: a specific response, previously acquired and maintained by positive reinforcement, is followed by a noxious stimulus. . . . In fact, the same behavior is often maintained under concurrent schedules of aversive and positive control. This state of affairs, in the laboratory as in daily life, is commonly designated as conflict. [Kanfer and Phillips, 1970, p. 350]

Thus, from the beginning, the effects of punishment are the end result of an interaction between the positive consequences and the strength of the aversive event. We have already defined (Chapter 3) punishment as the addition of an aversive consequence that results in the reduction of a tendency to perform a response. As we shall see, this suppression definition, while generally useful, does not describe all types of punishment.

In general, with punishment, we are very concerned with the behavior we wish to eliminate but are less concerned with the hows of the subject's termination of the aversive events. Thus, all punishment involves a desire by the punishers to inhibit a particular response (by whatever means necessary to stop the subject from doing that which you wish it not to do), although this procedure may not always have the desired effects. For example, laziness in a student might be treated by presenting him with loud handclaps behind the head every time he is caught dawdling, as a punishment. How he forces himself to pay attention is irrelevant to the punisher, and there is always the danger he may simply look like he is paying attention without actually learning anything.

We have already mentioned that schedule variables influence the effects of positive reinforcement more than amount-of-reward variables. Intensity of the aversive stimulation, however, is highly related to the effects of punishment. Solomon (1964) has described the effects of differing strengths of aversive consequences in a parametric fashion. These results are depicted in Figure 9.2. With very weak punishment, the primary effect is arousal, resulting in a net increase in rates of the unwanted response. An example might be telling a child who is "acting out" (the current euphemism for a child's raising hell) in a mild voice to please quiet down. The extra attention may actually serve to enhance the rewards of misbehavior. If the aversive consequence is a little more severe, the effect will be a modest suppression of the desired response, followed by emission of the "lost" responses during the next punishment-free session (a case of behavioral contrast). Still more extreme punishment temporarily eliminates the unwanted behavior totally, but behavioral contrast still occurs during periods of nonpunishment. Extreme punishment eliminates the punished response for prolonged periods of time and, if traumatic enough, may result in the subject's learning (via reward mechanisms) avoidance responses (passive) which prevent extinction of the conditioned (classically) fear response produced by the punishment procedure. This is, of course, the situation described by Miller and Dollard as inducing neurotic fears in their patients.* This state is also the desired one following aversive therapy for bad habits (described in Chapter 8).

It follows from the foregoing that for punishment to be effective, it must be severe. Severity, however, is not just a function of the stimulus characteristics of

---

* Miller and Dollard actually theorized that the fear drive is learned by drive reduction.

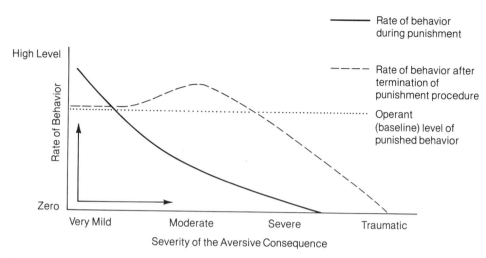

Figure 9.2   *An idealized illustration of the relationships between the subjective severity or strength of an aversive consequence and the rates of the punished behavior to be expected: before punishment (baseline or operant level), during presentation of the punishing (aversive) consequence, and after termination of the aversive consequence that was contingent upon emission of the punished response.*

the aversive stimulus. It also is dependent upon the previous history of the subject. Exposure to punishment that begins with very low intensity and gradually involves increasingly extreme aversive conditions is effective in shaping **resistance to punishment.** If a very weak aversive cue is paired with a strong positive reinforcer, the aversive cue may even become a conditioned S_D and the condition labeled "conditioned masochism" will result. If the aversive cue then becomes gradually stronger, the subject may actually seek increasing levels of punishment and experience them as pleasurable. To help other users of punishment avoid the disastrous effects of such mishandling of aversive contingencies, Azrin and Holz have provided a list of 13 suggestions to be followed in making the use of punishment effective. This list is reproduced in whole as follows:

(1) The punishing stimulus should be arranged in such a manner that no unauthorized escape is possible. (2) The punishing stimulus should be as intense as possible. (3) The frequency of punishment should be as high as possible; ideally the punishing stimulus should be given for every response. (4) The punishing stimulus should be delivered immediately after the response. (5) The punishing stimulus should not be increased gradually but introduced at maximum intensity. (6) Extended periods of punishment should be avoided, especially where low intensity of punishment is concerned, since the recovery effect may thereby occur. Where mild intensities of punishment are used, it is best to use them for only a brief period of time. (7) Great care should be taken to see that the delivery of the punishing stimulus is not differentially associated with the delivery of reinforcement. Otherwise the punishing stimulus may acquire conditioned reinforcing properties. (8) The delivery of the punishing stimulus should be made a signal or S_D that a period of extinction is in progress. (9) The degree of motivation to emit the punished response should be reduced. (10) The fre-

quency of positive reinforcement for the punished response should similarly be reduced. (11) An alternative response should be made available which will not be punished but which will produce the same or greater reinforcement as the punished response. (12) If no alternative response is available, the subject should have access to a different situation in which he obtains the same reinforcement without being punished. (13) If it is not possible to deliver the punishing stimulus itself after a response, then an effective method of punishment is still available. A conditioned stimulus may be associated with the aversive stimulus, and this conditioned stimulus may be delivered following a response to achieve conditioned punishment. [Azrin and Holz, 1966, pp. 426–427]

While such elaborate considerations for the successful use of punishment would seem excessive, the harmful consequences of poorly used punishment require they be given careful attention. Azrin (1967) has found that a wide range of animal species respond to unavoidable shock by attacking any available targets. He suggests that this **pain-aggression response** is reflexive and innate. Hutchinson and Emley (1977) have replicated this effect with squirrel monkeys in a test environment containing a rubber hose, response lever, and a water spout. Shock delivery produced preshock lever-pressing and postshock biting—attack episodes directed at the rubber hose. As a further complication, water-deprived monkeys followed biting responses with drinking behavior (from the water spout). Removing the opportunity to attack the hose increased the levels of the alternative behavior of postshock drinking. Could increased drinking of alcoholic beverages by members of a losing football team (assumed to be punished by their loss) after the game (when opportunities for socially sanctioned attack behaviors are no longer available) result from similar mechanisms? The general issue of the effects of punishment procedures on alternative (unpunished) responses will now be discussed in terms of Dunham's (1971) theory of punishment.

Dunham notes that two assumptions have traditionally been used to explain the suppressive effects of punishment. The first was Thorndike's negative law of effect, which states that annoying events weaken the S-R bonds preceding that event. Following Thorndike's rejection of this assumption in favor of the truncated law of effect (which stresses satisfiers), it has largely been discarded. The second assumption states that the decrement in the behavior suppressed by punishment is related to an increment in some alternative behavior. Most contemporary explanations of punishment suppression are elaborations of this alternative-response assumption. These elaborations may be either one-factor or two-factor theories.

Estes and Skinner have offered a one-factor approach based on the classical conditioning of the emotional events elicited by the aversive stimulus to stimuli preceding the punishment. These emotional CRs are assumed to cause suppression by competing with the punished response. Miller and Dollard have offered an instrumental learning theory of punishment-related suppression which assumes that responses associated with the termination of the aversive stimulus become more probable (through association with reductions in pain and/or fear drives) and compete with the punished response, resulting in its suppression (in Dunham, 1971).

Two-factor theory is represented by Mowrer's view, which suggests that fear is first classically conditioned to stimuli associated with the punished response and that the organism then learns instrumental responses (solutions), which are rewarded by escape from the fear-associated cues and which then elicit the feeling of relief. Dunham (1971) notes that neither the emotional processes involved in either type of theory, nor the supposed reinforcers in theories with an instrumental component, have been consistently measured. Seligman and Johnston (1973) report that animals having previously learned escape responses rarely show signs of fear in the presence of cues signaling aversive stimulation. Dunham concludes that such theories are unsatisfactory and that a wide gap exists between punishment research and punishment theories. To fill that gap, he offers a methodological approach to test the implications of existing punishment theories. He calls this approach the **multiple-response baseline procedure.**

This procedure contains elements from both traditional operant (Skinnerian) paradigms, where a single response is shaped under constraints, and the techniques of ethology (to be discussed in Chapter 12), which involve observations of multiple behaviors in a natural or seminatural setting. As an example of his approach, Dunham (1971) reviews a study conducted in his laboratory in which nine gerbils (a small desert rodent from Mongolia) were randomly assigned to three groups. Each gerbil was placed in a response chamber with food bin, drinking tube, and adding machine paper (gerbils will spend a lot of time shredding paper if allowed to do so), for daily half-hour sessions. Baseline of time spent in eating, drinking, and paper-shredding under deprivation conditions were recorded, with paper-shredding filling most of the time, followed by eating and drinking. Then group E was punished for eating, group P for paper-shredding, and group D for drinking. The new behavior of grid-biting appeared in response to shock and was also timed.

Dunham (1971) suggested that the response most frequently and immediately associated with shock onset would decrease in probability (be suppressed) and remain below its operant baseline, while the response most frequently associated with the absence of shock should increase above prepunishment baseline levels. Just as predicted, gerbils punished for eating increased the high-probability behavior of paper-shredding and subjects punished for paper-shredding showed an increase in grid-biting (both responses that were highly likely to be associated with shock offset). Of the two gerbils punished for drinking, one increased paper-shredding and the other increased grid-biting. The increase in grid-biting behavior (which always followed shock onset and therefore was associated with reductions in shock-produced drives) predicted by one-process theories did not occur. Instead, that behavior gradually declined in many subjects. The prediction derived from two-factor theories, that increases in the alternative behaviors would be directly linked to suppression of the punished response, was contradicted by the rapid onset of suppression and the gradual increase in the alternative behaviors. Dunham (1971) concluded that even though the animals were not able to reduce the shock frequency, a response which consistently followed shock from their viewpoint predicted a lower likelihood of immediately being shocked again. Thus, the process responsible for the increases in alternative responses was directly related to prediction variables (expectancies), as in Rescorla's predictiveness hypothesis. Dunham's conclusions about process put his views closer to the neo-Hullian perspective of punishment and further from the Skinnerian mainstream.

Skinner (1968) has observed that punishment may result in either overgeneralized aversiveness (as when school becomes aversive for a child who is punished in class) or in unwanted inhibition of desirable as well as undesirable behaviors. Although the technique of removing a misbehaving child from opportunities to gain reinforcement in the classroom would seem more attractive than direct use of aversive stimuli, such time-out techniques can also trigger an aggressive reaction (Azrin, Hutchinson, and Hake, 1963). Excessive use of this type of procedure in the classroom may remove the misbehaving child from exposure to educational experiences and, if used with a child who does not find the classroom positively reinforcing, it may actually shape increased "acting-out" behavior.

While the complexities of punishment (review Azrin's list quoted earlier in this section) may intimidate the would-be behavior modifier, punishment in its various forms will continue to be used for one very good reason. For all its faults, punishment is usually the fastest method for dealing with unwanted behaviors. Often the target of an unwanted behavior finds that behavior highly aversive; if escape is not possible, he may punish the offender to avoid further incidents of the behavior. When active responding prevents the occurrence of aversive events based on time considerations, the paradigm is the same as that of Sidman avoidance, which has been extensively studied in the laboratory. We will now turn from our discussion of punishment to that of other forms of aversive control, beginning with Sidman avoidance.

Punishment is a complicated paradigm that involves from the beginning a conflict between a positively reinforced response and an aversive consequence. It may produce very different results, depending upon the intensity of the aversive stimuli relative to the organism's history and on the alternative responses available. Results range from arousal to total suppression.

Avoidance learning, Sidman and signaled   Avoidance learning paradigms can be divided into two basic categories: (1) active avoidance and (2) passive avoidance. These types were briefly discussed in Chapter 7 within the context of Mowrer's theory. Active avoidance involves an instrumental response by the organism, and so it has also been labeled operant avoidance. There are two widely used operant avoidance paradigms, **Sidman avoidance** (discussed briefly in Chapter 8 in the presentations of Rescorla's and Seligman's research) and **signaled avoidance.** We will begin with a discussion of Sidman avoidance and its theoretical implications, and then move to an examination of research on signaled avoidance, also conducted by Sidman.

Sidman's first studies were done in 1953. Rats were given electric shocks at regular intervals unless they pressed a lever. Pressing the lever reset the clock controlling the shock and delayed it for 30 seconds. Failure to press the lever exposed the rats to regular shocks; pressing the lever rapidly prevented the clock from ever "timing out," which meant the rat could avoid the shocks totally. Although training the rats was time consuming, most subjects eventually responded at high stable rates. Shock-shock intervals could also be set by variable interval as well as fixed interval schedules, and high response rates were still found (Sidman and Boren, 1957). Sidman's results and his avoidance learning paradigm raise some interesting theoretical issues related to the functions of CSs in avoidance learning.

In Mowrer's two-factor theory, escape from a CS, an elicitor of conditioned fear which was supposed to be a sign for an impending aversive US, was assumed to reinforce avoidance learning. Konorski (1948) suggested that escape from fear cues acted to inhibit extinction of the fear response to the CS. Sidman (1955), however, observed that when fixed shock-shock intervals were used, the rats learned to space their responses in a way which resulted in efficient shock avoidance. Since no explicit CS was presented, such results are difficult to explain within the context of two-factor theory unless it is assumed that rats were able to use the passage of time as a CS to predict when shock was about to be presented, and responded to these temporal CSs in learning successfully to avoid the shock USs. Results such as these led Herrnstein (1969) to propose a one-factor theory of avoidance learning based on reinforcement mechanisms as an alternative to two-factor explanations of avoidance learning. According to Herrnstein, the rats matched their efforts to that needed to reduce shock frequency; they did not respond because of classically conditioned fear reactions to the CSs and reinforcement resulting from CS offset. Direct evidence supporting the matching hypothesis has been found by Boren, Sidman, and Herrnstein (1959), using a signaled avoidance paradigm which resembled Sidman avoidance except that an explicit CS (in this case, a buzzer) signaled when the US (shock) was about to occur. With this research design, they found that the rates of bar-pressing emitted by their rats were directly related to shock intensity. Further, Herrnstein and Hineline (1966) found that rats could learn avoidance responses with no warning CS at all and when bar-pressing only reduced the frequency of shocks rather than eliminating them. Contrary to Mowrer's two-factor theory, there was no offset of a warning (fear-eliciting) CS to provide reinforcement through fear reduction (escape from the CS), and therefore no instrumental CR could have moved forward in time to be energized by fear. Also, shock delivery was not always delayed by lever presses, so these responses were not always followed by a reinforcing event. These authors concluded that their subjects learned whatever responses reduced shock frequency rather than learning because of fear of a CS.

Herrnstein's matching-reinforcement theory of avoidance learning has been no more immune to criticism than Mowrer's two-factor theory. Bolles and Riley (1973) compared contingent and noncontingent shocking of freezing responses and found no effects of the punishment contingency. Random shocks inhibited freezing to the same extent as shocks contingent upon freezing. They conclude that freezing is an unconditioned response to shock not effected by programmed consequences of freezing behavior. Therefore, it is unlikely that reinforcement mechanisms function in the reactions to aversive USs used in avoidance learning. As an alternative to Mowrer's and Herrnstein's theories, they offer a more cognitive alternative. They suggest that the animal's perceptions of the situation as safe or dangerous determine when and how avoidance responses will be made. A more explicitly cognitive theory of avoidance learning has been offered by Seligman and Johnston (1973), following their review of research disconfirming both Mowrer's and Herrnstein's theories. As in Tolman's theory, expectancies (in this case, about when shock might occur) are the basic units of learning in avoidance paradigms. These expectancies are about the contingencies between responses and their outcomes; therefore, if animals have come to expect that an avoidance response will prevent shock, they will make that response with no signs of fear (since they expect to be safe following the response). As previously noted, these authors have found experienced subjects to show few signs of fear in the presence of CSs associated with shock. CSs then serve only as signs to arouse expectancies.

To finish this discussion of the role of CSs in avoidance learning, we must note that Flaherty and colleagues (1977) have reviewed the literature on both warning CSs and reinforcement factors in avoidance learning and have concluded that even though CS offset can facilitate avoidance learning in some types of avoidance learning situations, such presumably reinforcing effects are not necessary for avoidance. This suggests that even though fear reduction related to CS offset may sometimes play the role postulated by Mowrer, it is not the mechanism of avoidance learning in general. Let us now turn to a discussion of other variables involved in responding to aversive events.

Both Sidman and signaled operant avoidance procedures are modern laboratory analogs of the old "do this or else" principle. As such, they offer a way to conduct an experimental analysis of behavior into variables underlying maladaptive responses to aversive contingencies. One example of such an analysis was conducted by Sidman (1960), using a modified CER (conditioned emotional response) paradigm in which the instrumental response was bar-pressing to avoid avoidable shock, and the expected effect of unavoidable shocks would be conditioned facilitation of pressing. This is similar to Rescorla's procedure in which the shuttle-jumping response was facilitated in his positive prediction group (Chapter 8). Monkeys were trained on a Sidman avoidance schedule with a FI-20 second shock-shock schedule. After the instrumental avoidance response was learned, a clicker (CS) followed by unavoidable shock (US) was introduced. The effect of this addition was for the monkey to increase its response rates during the clicking interval. When the avoidable shocks (Sidman contingency) were terminated, leaving only the unavoidable shocks, this **conditioned facilitation** effect persisted. Sidman suggested that from the monkey's viewpoint,

> lever pressing, by which it has in the past effectively avoided shocks, seems to remain largely successful. Avoidance of shock still reinforces lever pressing, even though the relation is a spurious one. The monkey's behavior during the clicking period is nonadaptive because the rules of the environment have changed and the changes have not yet elicited appropriate response modifica-

tion. The occasional shocks only serve as false discriminative cues to keep the animal behaving in a fashion appropriate to the former circumstances. [1960, p. 66]

Such maladaptive behavior can be seen to be produced in the same lawful fashion as "normal or adaptive" behavior. Sidman suggests that such "superstitious" behavior in man and monkey results from the subject's inability to discriminate the true pattern of contingency relationships between his responses and the aversive events. Thus, the development of abnormal behavior is seen as a product of unfortunate environmental events rather than as a sign of the disintegration of an inner personality structure. It must be noted, however, that the maladaptive (since in the late stages of the experiment all shocks were unavoidable) conditioned facilitation of the pressing response eventually vanished as the monkeys learned the true state of affairs. It is characteristic of most Sidman avoidance responses that if the response cost is too high, the subject will occasionally neglect to respond. If such pauses are never punished, they will tend to become longer and more frequent. Furthermore, in the conditioned suppression paradigm (CER) discussed in Chapter 8, the subjects rarely reduced their overall levels of bar-pressing for food. Rather, they ceased pressing during the clicking interval and made up the lost responses during the nonclicking intervals. This may represent another demonstration of behavioral contrast in a punishment situation.

Active avoidance (operant avoidance) requires the subject to emit an instrumental response (such as shuttle-jumping or bar-pressing) to avoid shock. Shock is presented on a fixed or variable interval schedule in both Sidman and signaled avoidance paradigms, which differ only in that a warning CS precedes shock in signaled avoidance, while only internal cues can be CSs in Sidman avoidance.

In this chapter we have looked closely at aspects of the punishment and avoidance (active) types of aversive control paradigms. Let us now summarize some of the relationships of these types of aversive control to one another and to the escape and passive avoidance procedures defined in Chapter 7.

An overview of aversive control   As noted in Chapter 7, there are three basic paradigms for describing aversive control: escape, avoidance, and punishment. In escape, the subject experiences the aversive stimulus but subsequently gets away from it. In passive avoidance, the subject must only refrain from emitting a particular response to totally avoid experiencing the aversive US. An example would be a paroled felon who avoids specified behaviors to keep from going back to jail. Active avoidance, as we saw, requires the emission of some instrumental response either before the end of some time period (Sidman avoidance) or after a warning signal (signaled avoidance). Examples could be the felon's reporting to his or her parole officer at specified intervals or actively avoiding "bad influences" following warnings from his or her parole officer, respectively.

Punishment involves the application of an aversive consequence for the emission of a specified undesirable behavior. In contrast to escape, the subject is not able to get away from the aversive stimulus by an active response (or the punishment is not really punishment, from the viewpoint of the one punished). In contrast to avoidance, the subject cannot avoid the aversive stimulus except by not emitting the specified response. Punishment is like passive avoidance in that the subject can avoid experiencing the unpleasant stimulus by not doing some specified act. It differs from passive avoidance in that the subject, instead of not approaching CSs which warn of an aversive US, must refrain from emitting a response which is positively reinforced. Aversive stimuli used in punishment may be either events causing pain, or the removal of a specified positive contingency, or the access to emit behaviors leading to positive reinforcers (known as **time out**). An example of time out would be making a fourth-grade pupil sit facing a corner every time he is observed disrupting another child's work. It is assumed that the malcreant prefers classroom participation to corner watching. A summary of some relationships of the various types of aversive paradigms is shown in Table 9.1.

Finally, it should be repeated that the effectiveness of aversive control is highly influenced by the subject's judgment of how severe the aversive stimulus really is. This is a function both of the physical features of the aversive cue and the subject's previous history of exposures to such cues. Subjects socialized in cultures where aversive consequences are a frequent and accepted part of childhood would be less likely to be significantly influenced by levels of punishment that someone coming from a less punitive background would consider severe and a significant deterrent to antisocial behavior. An early exposure to accelerating levels of punishment might produce conditioned resistance to punishment. While the effects of aversive control are more influenced by intensity factors (taking into account the subject's past history) than positive control, and less influenced by schedule-of-reinforcement variables, schedule variables can influence the effects of aversive stimuli. McKearney (1972) found that squirrel monkeys exposed to shock in a multiple schedule paradigm (a variable interval component and a fixed ratio component) displayed conditioned suppression on the fixed ratio schedule and no suppression when shock was programmed on a variable interval schedule.

According to Sidman's research, we have noted, maladaptive behavior can be generated through aversive conditioning procedures. This raises the question of whether maladaptive behavior can also be reduced with aversive stimulation. One psychologist who thinks so is Ivar Lovaas, whose use of shock with autistic children illustrates the therapeutic use of a variety of operant aversive control procedures.

Ivar Lovaas and a shocking application of operant principles   Ivar Lovaas (in Lovaas, Schaeffer, and Simmons, 1965) lists three ways in which aversive events can be used as tools in therapy. The first approach uses punishment procedures similar to the aversion therapy approaches reviewed in Chapter 8. The second uses the negative reinforcement paradigm, in which shock is re-

Table 9.1   Paradigms of Aversive Control

Effect of Behavior	Experiences Aversive Event	If Successful, Does Not Experience Aversive Event
Increases target behavior	Escape	Active avoidance
	Conditioned facilitation (some noncontingent avoidance)	Sidman avoidance and signaled avoidance
Decreases target behavior (suppression)	Conditioned suppression or conditioned emotional responses (CER)	Passive avoidance
	Punishment and time out from positive reinforcement	

This table shows a system to classify the various paradigms of aversive control. The effects on the organism's behavior (suppression or facilitation of ongoing behavior) are noted in the first column, and the subject's experiences of the aversive event (for example, does the subject actually get shocked on most trials?) are noted in the column heads.

moved or withheld contingent upon specified behaviors (negative reinforcement was discussed in Chapter 4). The third uses conditioning S_Ds to pain reduction, with the goal of having S_Ds become conditioned positive reinforcers or signals for the absence of pain. We have seen that Dunham found that his subjects increased their rate of emitting alternative behaviors associated with shock offset, or the absence of shock. According to Lovaas's model, the effects of this third kind of aversive procedure would be an increase in positive alternative behaviors, as a paradoxical by-product of pain; this would cause persons with a "safety-predicting" cue value to become conditioned positive reinforcers. Let us now examine Lovaas's work with infantile autism and his results.

Childhood autism is often classified as a subtype of childhood psychosis. It is characterized by self-stimulatory behaviors, which may be self-destructive, and a general lack of social responsiveness. Autistic children do not respond well to traditional psychotherapy. Therefore, shock procedures were used as a last resort. In the first experiment (Lovaas et al., 1965), the children (two five year olds) were placed barefoot on a shock grid floor and escape-avoidance procedures were initiated. One of the experimenters stretched out his arms and said, "Come here." Any movement towards the experimenter terminated the shock for that trial. If the child did not move, the second experimenter pushed him in the direction of the first experimenter (which also terminated the shock). This escape phase was followed by an avoidance procedure in which shock was withheld if the child approached the experimenter within 5 seconds after the command, "Come here." Shock was also used to punish self-stimulation and/or tantrum behaviors. The verbal command "No!" was associated with shock and acquired limited effectiveness as a conditioned aversive reinforcer. It was found that not only did the children learn to come to the experimenters to avoid or escape shock, but that the verbal command "Come here" became effective in environments where shock was potentially available (the problem of subjects learning to discriminate when shock was likely to occur during aversive conditioning procedures was discussed in Chapter 8). As predicted by Lovaas, alternative behaviors did appear. Surprisingly, these included seeking the experimenters' company, showing affection, and increasing their alertness to the environment. Lovaas and colleagues (1965) commented that during successful avoidance trials the children "appeared happy." There was also limited generalization of the adult-seeking and affectionate behavior to situations outside the chock-avoidance training environment.

Lovaas tested the hypothesis that the adults who had been associated with safety from shock following avoidance trials and had hugged and fondled the children when the children approached them would become conditioned positive reinforcers. The children were taught to operate a candy dispenser which gave them both candy and a view of the experimenter's face. During extinction trials (no more candy), the photograph of the face of the experimenter (associated with shock reduction) was more effective in slowing down the rate of extinction than photographs of other faces. In addition, ward nurses reported that following the shock avoidance training, the children began, for the first time, to come to them for comfort when they were hurt in play. On the negative side, Lovaas and colleagues (1965) noted that the positive shock-produced changes in behavior were often highly situational in nature (showed limited generalization to new environments and people) and extinguished rapidly. This suggests that even though aversive operant techniques may be useful in managing autistic children, they do not "cure" autism.

Lovaas (1974), it should be noted, is deeply concerned with the ethical and practical issues surrounding the use of extreme aversive techniques such as shock. First, he recommends their use only for dealing with extreme behavior such as self-mutilation (some autistic children have literally chewed fingers off) and total lack of responsiveness to other people. In these cases, shock can inhibit destructive behavior that formerly had been reinforced by adults who had let the child have his or her own way to avoid temper tantrums or self-mutilation. Second, he recommends that therapists using aversive techniques should have a deep love for children, be patient enough to provide large doses of affection for positive behavior, and be willing gradually to shape desired behaviors that can compete with the destructive behaviors. Finally, he suggests training the parents of autistic children in operant control procedures (including aversive techniques) so that these parents can overcome their own feelings of ineffectuality and frustration to the point where they can successfully manage the behavior of their autistic children in their own homes. This involves both showing the parents how paying attention to tantrums and self-mutilation may have reinforced these behaviors and coaching the parents to "load the child up with love" for positive behavior. He teaches the parents that suppressing bizarre behavior (such as self-mutilation) through aversive control provides the opportunity to begin building up appropriate behaviors which eventually allow the child to meet his or her needs in nonpathological ways.

Using punishment and avoidance procedures with autistic children, Lovaas was able to increase their attention to people; he found that positive alternative social behaviors increased as withdrawal was suppressed. He also found that experimenters associated with shock reduction became conditioned positive reinforcers for the children.

Getting children to pay attention to adults and to find them positively reinforcing is a prerequisite for children to imitate adults. This imitation, or modeling, of adult behaviors is a primary learning mechanism in social learning theory, which will be presented next.

Social Learning Theory

As we saw in Chapter 8, the major direction of the neo-Pavlovians in the Soviet Union was away from animal research and toward cognitively oriented work on the second signal system. In Chapters 3 and 7, we examined the increased openness to cognitive variables shown by the neo-Hullians—Spence, Miller, Dollard, and Mowrer. The parallel movement within the Skinnerian tradition, now called **social learning theory,** has its foremost advocate in Albert Bandura. The social learning theory movement is parallel in some respects to Tolman's efforts to combine rigorous experimentation, a behavioristic viewpoint on the mechanisms of learning, and cognitive units of learning.

Social learning theory is distinguished by several explicit assumptions:

1. Most human behavior is learned rather than innate, and most behavior (including maladaptive behavior) is controlled by environmental influences rather than by internal forces. Therefore, positive reinforcement—the modification of behavior through alteration of its rewarding outcomes—is an important procedure in behavioral therapy (Bandura, 1967).

2. The principles and laws of operant learning developed by Skinner and the orthodox neo-Skinnerians are the laws of performance and of much human learning. The techniques used are those of operant conditioning, which was developed largely by Skinner and his colleagues at Harvard University (Bandura, 1967). Thus, Bandura's theory is identified as being of the behavioristic tradition, and applications of social learning theory, of the **behavior modification** movement.

Bandura (1977) has taken the position that the effect of reinforcement on performance is not that of an automatic shaper of human conduct. Rather, he sees humans as using information about reinforcement contingencies to regulate their behavior. Awareness plays a crucial role in this process.

3. The internal representations of learning are rarely S-R relationships. Instead, they are either images of events or secondary coded symbols summarizing and categorizing events. Therefore, while most of the mechanisms of learning are behavioristic in form, the content of learning is cognitive.

4. Although humans can learn through direct reinforcement and shaping procedures, a more efficient learning mode is observational learning. Observational learning is the basis for most things learned from other humans (hence

the label "social" learning theory), such as language and social roles and norms. This is also called **vicarious learning,** or **modeling.** Models can be humans or representations of humans, such as dolls or pictures (Bandura, 1967).

Other Skinnerians have attempted to explain imitative or modeling behavior through the following paradigm: $S^d - R - S^r$, where $S^d =$ the discriminative stimulus for modeling or the modeling stimulus, $R =$ the overt matching response performed by the observer, and $S^r =$ the reinforcement provided by some agent for imitation. This explanation is similar to that advanced by Miller and Dollard (see Chapter 7) in viewing frequency of imitation as dependent upon the level of reinforcement produced by successful copying of others' behaviors. Bandura disagrees with this paradigm for the following reasons:

> The scheme . . . does not appear applicable to observational learning where an observer does not overtly perform the model's responses in the setting in which they are exhibited, reinforcements are not administered either to the model or to the observer, and whatever responses have been thus acquired are not displayed for days, weeks, or even months. Under these conditions, which represent one of the most prevalent forms of social learning, two of the factors $(R \rightarrow S^r)$ in the three-element paradigm are absent during acquisition, and the third factor (S^d or modeling stimulus) is typically missing from the situation when the observationally learned response is first performed. [1971, p. 6]

For Bandura, modeling reflects symbolic processes that occur during exposure to the modeled activities before either the emission or the reinforcement of any imitative responses.

5. The primary effect of reinforcement is to provide the person with information about conditions likely to yield reinforcement in the future, much as in Tolman's theory. Knowledge of reward acts to provide incentive motivation, as in Hull's and Spence's theories. The person's emotional responses to this information act like Mowrer's "hope" variable in setting the stage for the performance of a response. As we will see in the next section, reinforcement affects every stage of the modeling process. Its functions are both more complex than the theories suggested by the orthodox Skinnerians and less automatic.

To summarize to this point, Bandura has adopted some of the laws and assumptions of operant learning theory. He then moves to the cognitive position in suggesting that cognitive units are learned and much learning is associational and symbolic. In suggesting that modeling is the primary learning mode for humans, Bandura attacks both the assumption that learning occurs automatically because of reinforcement and the equipotentiality assumptions held by most operant learning theorists.

Bandura divides imitative learning into four processes. These are:

1. *Attentional processes:* Before someone or something can be modeled, the subject must notice them. What is noticed is a function of previous reinforcement; specific perceptual habits are shaped by rewards received while "attending to" specific gestalts. This "attending to" may be shaped in by a

therapist. Bandura (1967) cites Lovaas's work with autistic children, in which visual attentiveness to the therapist was shaped by either avoidance of aversive consequences or food reward. This reinforcement of noticing the therapist was necessary before further conditioning could proceed. We may also attend to someone else's being reinforced, and this "vicarious" reinforcement may determine who is to be watched and modeled. Bandura (1969) has reviewed the characteristics of models who elicit attention. Models who have demonstrated high competence, "who are purported experts" or celebrities, and who possess status-conferring symbols are likely to command more attention than models deficient in these attributes. Other variables that may affect attention include: attractiveness, ethnic identification, sex, and age. Some of these may interact in complex ways. Although most studies with older primary children have found that children are likely to model same-sexed models more accurately, and that males are generally more effective models, Bartlett (1977) found that first- and second-grade children all modeled female models (adults) more accurately. Males watching male models in a movie did least well in accurately reproducing a pyramid of wooden blocks.

Modeling behavior in general, or modeling of specific types of models, may be increased by selective reinforcement (Miller and Dollard, 1941; Bandura, 1969), and beneficial change in nonbehavioristic therapy may be the result of the client's modeling of the "healthy behaviors" of the therapist (Bandura, 1967). One assumes that this latter modeling is highly reinforced. To summarize the relative effects of reinforcement and model attributes on attentional processes, Bandura states:

Indeed, incentive control of observing behavior can, in most instances, override the effects of variations in observer characteristics and model attributes. It should be noted, however, that in the present theory reinforcement variables, to the extent that they influence the acquisition process, do so principally by augmenting and sustaining attentiveness to modeling cues. [1969, pp. 137–138]

2. *Retentional processes:* These are the processes by which the modeled behavior becomes encoded as a memory by the observer. While Bandura (1969) reviews studies demonstrating what appears to be contiguity learning, he feels that either overt (which allows external reinforcement) or covert rehearsal can considerably enhance the stabilization and strengthening of acquired responses and observational learning. Reinforcement in this process acts to increase the frequency of rehearsal of modeled responses associated with rewarding outcomes. Increased rehearsal does more than just "stamp in" modeled responses. Bandura assumes that rehearsal helps reinforce modeled responses by active processes and not by sheer repetition. Rehearsal of a modeled response protects it from interference from other possible responses. Practicing a response, either overtly or covertly, lets the person doing the practice see if he or she is doing the response as much like the model as possible. This, in turn, helps the modeler focus his or her attention on the cues for modeling more intently.

Two representational systems are involved in human modeling: imaginal and verbal. The **imaginal system** is operative during exposure to modeling stimuli: Sequences of corresponding sensory images are associated on the basis of physical contiguity. Essentially, the stored images act as cognitive maps (as in Tolman's theory) to guide the observer in imitation. The **verbal system** is a symbolic system; as such, it represents coded or derived information. In suggesting that the most efficient learning involves translating action sequences into abbreviated verbal systems and grouping constituent patterns of behavior into larger integrated units, Bandura (1969) is taking a strong molar, cognitivist position.

3. *Motoric Reproduction:* This third major component of the modeling process involves the translation of the symbolic (cognitive) representations of the modeled stimuli into overt motor acts, or actually performing the modeled behavior. As the person attempts to translate his idea of what he thought he saw the model do, he checks his performance against his memory of what he saw modeled. Such motoric reproduction is like the shaping of overt behavior through reinforcement from the environment, except that in this case the reinforcers are the person's internal reinforcers arising from the feeling that he has copied the action as accurately as possible.

   Motoric reproduction and observational learning in general are limited by the extent to which component responses are already learned. It is easiest to learn from watching a professional play tennis if you already are familiar with many of the required movements and know what to look for. It is easiest to learn from a model and to reproduce his or her actions accurately when all you are required to do is to synthesize previously acquired response patterns into the new complex behavior exhibited by the model.

   Motoric reproduction is also inhibited by physical differences between the model and the person doing the modeling. This author is not going to play basketball like Wilt the Stilt, regardless of his efforts at rehearsal. Finally, situations in which it is difficult to observe the subtle movements of a model may interfere with subsequent motoric reproduction.

4. *Incentive and Motivational Processes:* The roles of reinforcement are far more complex than in Skinner's theory. Reinforcement determines what is noticed, what is modeled, what is rehearsed (which strongly influences retention), and what behavior is emitted. While Bandura does not see reinforcement as a direct learning variable, the expectancy of reward (or avoidance of aversive consequences) is necessary for a behavior to be emitted; positive incentives are required for an overt expression of matching behavior to continue to be expressed. Thus, reinforcement has both important "informational" properties for learning and direct effects on performance. Of course, the reinforcement for matching behavior may be vicarious or internal (as knowing that you performed a response correctly).

The range of situations in which modeling procedures may be used is vast. Bandura (1967) has reviewed clinical applications ranging from the use of dolls to reduce hyperaggressive reactions in children, to therapists having patients "try out" desirable behaviors modeled by the therapist. These studies, taken together with other work concerning the influence of vicarious reinforcement on aggression, contradict the Freudian view which postulates that aggressive acts are beneficially cathartic. In real life, watching violence may encourage violence. Bandura (1962) demonstrated that children who were frustrated were more likely to behave aggressively after observing a model behave in an aggressive manner. Let us now turn to the more positive side of the modeling phenomenon—its effectiveness in applied areas.

Applications of modeling   Modeling procedure has been successfully employed in two major areas. The first of these is teaching small children. A study by Martin (1975) illustrates the basic procedure. Two retarded children were exposed to daily imitation training in which the teacher or a nurse modeled and instructed each child to imitate 12 sentences containing one of six animal names. Praise was given for correct verbal imitation. Each of the sentences also contained descriptive adjectives related to the color and/or size of the animals. During probe sessions at another time of day and in a different environment, the children were asked to describe 12 pictures of animals different from those described during the modeling sessions. Not only were the children able to imitate the sentences modeled, but the adjectives used generalized to the new animals' pictures.

The second area of application has been in the clinical area. Bandura, Grusec, and Menlove (1967) treated children with dog phobias by exposing them to peer models who interacted in a progressively more fearless manner with a dog. At the end of eight 10-minute sessions held over four days, the majority of the children in the modeling treatment groups were able to approach either the original stimulus dog or another dog, feed them, and remain alone in the room with them. This study shows two important innovations over simple modeling: (1) the children were treated in groups of four, which is a more efficient approach than individual treatment of phobics, and (2) **progressive modeling** was used, which Bandura feels reduces initial fear and facilitates the speed of treatment. Progressive modeling uses a graduated series of modeled behaviors parallel to the fear stimuli hierarchies used in systematic desensitization. Group treatment may be even more effective than individual treatment. Nemetz, Craig, and Reith (1978) treated women suffering from debilitating sexual anxiety by the process of **symbolic modeling,** using videotapes. Treatment began with relaxation training, followed by the viewing of 45 videotaped vignettes depicting graduated sexual behaviors. The 16 experimental subjects were randomly assigned to either individual or group treatment. There was a trend towards greater improvement (decreases in anxiety and increases in sexual behavior) in the subjects who received the group treatment, although the individual treatment subjects also improved. The six control subjects showed a slight trend towards deterioration. While this study shows symbolic modeling to be effective, most recent attempts to reduce phobias have involved a technique usually referred to as **participant modeling.** In this procedure, the therapist demonstrates the first approach to the feared object or situation while imparting verbal information. The subjects are then asked to practice the approach (which reflects the first stage of the desensitization hierarchy). This is followed by the therapist's modeling of the next stage of the hierarchy, with the subjects again practicing overcoming their avoidance behaviors, and so on. Smith and Coleman (1977) found subjects (17 females with rat phobias) in all their treatment groups to show improvement on several measures (behavioral approach tests, fear indexes, reactions to a generalization rat). Subjects, however, who had self-directed practice following the formal participant-modeling procedure showed greater improvement than subjects who received additional therapist-directed practice (overlearning group), especially when exposed to novel rats of new breeds (with different-colored coats).

Before leaving this brief survey of variations on the modeling theme, let us briefly examine one more modeling technique, known as **self-modeling.** This technique consists of having subjects observe video recordings of themselves performing target behaviors. Using this procedure with hospitalized children, Miklich, Chida, and Danker-Brown (1977) were able to improve bed-making behaviors in their 12 subjects, without the subjects reporting any awareness of their behavior being changed or even that the purpose of the video recording was to affect them. This result is curious, considering that Michael Dawson and others (reviewed in Chapter 8) have shown awareness to be a prerequisite for most human classical conditioning (which has traditionally been considered a simpler form of learning than modeling).

Although Bandura's theory of modeling represents an interesting synthesis of concepts derived from the connectionist and cognitive learning traditions, the modeling process seems to have greater generality than just to human learning, in spite of the common view that humans use more cognitive-dominated processes in learning. Bandura (1969) has found modeling to occur in dogs and Old World primates, and Riess (1972) was even able to demonstrate a modeled acceleration of avoidance responding in rats, using a classical conditioning paradigm. **Vicarious extinction** was also demonstrated when the model rat no longer received shock (the US) after a light (the CS) and the response rates of the observer rats eventually returned to baseline levels. These demonstrations of learning without overt reinforcement again point out the inadequacies of law-of-effect-derived theories about the nature of reinforcement and learning processes. Viewed in terms of adaptive models of the nature and function of reinforcement, any social organism able to learn from watching successful behaviors emitted by other members of his or her group would be more likely to survive than an animal dependent upon individual trial and error for learning. Such an interpretation fits nicely with the adaptive model proposed by Timberlake and Allison, and we will return to the analysis of learning in terms of evolutionary variables in Chapter 12.

Bandura has proposed a theory in which the primary mode of learning in higher organisms is imitation or modeling of others in the environment who have certain characteristics, such as control of the modeler's future reinforcements. The four processes involved in modeling are: attentional, retentional, motoric reproduction, and reinforcement mechanisms. Many modeling procedures are used in therapy, including graduated modeling, participant modeling, and self-modeling.

Chapter Perspective

We have reviewed advances in neo-Hullian and three types of neo-Skinnerian theories and principles. We have seen many advances in discovering new principles and applicable techniques. Yet the search to develop a satisfactory theory about instrumental or operant learning has not yet led to a generally accepted theory of how reinforcement works, let alone what reinforcement is. If there is any dominant trend, it is towards a rejection of such simple theories of reinforcement as Thorndike's law of effect or Hull's drive-reduction mechanisms. The neo-Hullians have become increasingly willing to discuss learning in terms of having emotional and/or cognitive components, as in the treatments of frustration and incentive motivation. Only the strict Skinnerians still discuss reinforcement as a process which automatically strengthens tendencies to respond. Even they have moved to the paradigmatic approach in which reinforcement is treated as nothing more than a procedure for controlling behavior.

In moving toward increased incorporation of cognitive-predictive variables and in seeing reinforcement as primarily the result of specified types of procedures (or paradigms), the evolution of instrumental/operant learning theory has paralleled that of classical conditioning theory.

Another noticeable trend has been the incorporation of more biological variables, as in Timberlake's and Allison's (1974) adaptive model of instrumental performance. Even Skinner, who once advocated a strict environmentalist approach, has discussed parallels between the response-selecting aspects of reinforcement and natural selection (evolutionary) variables. This has forced a reexamination of the Skinnerian view of the effects of reinforcement as "blind" or unaffected by variables within the organism. The major line of evidence for the Skinnerian assumption that reinforcement is blind to the purposes of the organism is derived from the superstitious conditioning phenomenon described in Chapter 4. Skinner (1948) showed that random delivery of food to a hungry pigeon was sufficient to produce operant learning. Staddon and Simmelhag (1971) have suggested that behaviors which increase in frequency, rather than being randomly selected by the effects of reinforcement, are usually related to natural food-getting behaviors; they reflect the organism's prediction that, as time increases since the last reinforcement, reinforcement becomes more probable. These responses are assumed to operate as discriminated operants and to resemble the responses actually made to the terminal reinforcer. Hence, through stimulus substitution mechanisms, the cue properties of the responses operate like Rescorla's predictive CSs. Staddon and Simmelhag make the point that responses occurring just before the noncontingent reinforcer should be looked at as reflections of the organism's "mood" or state (such as hungry or fearful), rather than as behaviors. Therefore, the variety of responses observed by Skinner using the noncontingent reward procedure reflect various alternative behaviors associated with that particular internal state; these responses are assumed to have had adaptive value in the evolution of that particular organism.

Seligman (1975) noted that Staddon and Simmelhag reanalyzed Skinner's "superstitious pigeon" data and found the behaviors reported by Skinner to be similar to natural "food-expecting behaviors." Seligman suggests that these responses are conditioned to the schedules under which food is presented (much like the responses classically conditioned in autoshaping research to pecking keys when they are paired with food availability for hungry pigeons). As such, the behaviors are conditioned reflexes which resemble natural unconditioned species-specific responses to food under hunger conditions, not arbitrary behaviors "stamped in" by happy coincidence with food reinforcement. In Seligman's view, such "superstitious" responses are involuntary, like a dog licking his chops before dinner. Seligman further suggests that apparently "superstitious" responses are the subject's reaction to its helplessness actually to control the delivery of reinforcement. Thus Seligman explains "superstitious" behavior in terms of his model of "learned helplessness" (reviewed in Chapter 8).

Staddon and Simmelhag (1971) have also investigated the behaviors occurring just after a reinforcer has been delivered and consumed. These interim activities, presumed to reflect the organism's prediction that reinforcement is not immediately forthcoming, are thus related to other kinds of motivational states. Put simply, the organism realizes that it does not have to get ready for a food reinforcement, so it attends to other business. Dunham's (1971, 1972) observations of increased drinking behaviors following shock in gerbils and rats could also be interpreted as the animal's prediction that the postshock period is a safe time in which to emit non-shock-related instrumental behaviors. These interim activities resemble the appetitive behaviors (those ultimately leading to consumatory responses) described by the ethologists (to be reviewed in Chapter 12). Thus, Staddon and Simmelhag have begun the process of discovering common principles underlying both instinct-biased and instrumental/classical conditioning phenomena. This allows them to look at reinforcement and learning mechanisms in terms of the well-researched biological concepts of selection and variation. This may provide a basis for a final resolution of the instinct versus learning (nature/nurture) issue and a general theory of behavior.

To conclude, Staddon and Simmelhag have proposed a reevaluation of an operant phenomenon which incorporates both cognitive (predictive) and biological-evolutionary variables. As such, their work suggests a direction for relating operant phenomenon with cognitive principles (to be covered in Chapter 11) and biological principles (to be covered in Chapter 12). Before we examine these approaches, however, let us look at the impressive range of applications which have been the by-product of the operant approach to behavior in its present state.

Key Terms

adaptive model	fractional anticipatory frustration ($r_F = S_F$)	pain-aggression response
behavioral contrast		partial reinforcement effect (PRE)
behavior modification	imaginal system	
conditioned facilitation	incentive motivation	participant modeling
contrast	intertrial reinforcement	peak shift
empirical law of effect	modeling	positive contrast
errorless learning (fading)	multiple-response baseline procedure	Premack principle
forced practice	negative contrast	prepotent theory of reinforcement

progressive modeling	sequential hypothesis	time out
resistance to punishment	Sidman avoidance	verbal system
response deprivation model	signaled avoidance	vicarious extinction
reversibility (transitivity) of reinforcement	social learning theory	vicarious learning
self-modeling	superordinate stimulus	
	symbolic modeling	

Annotated Bibliography

Three representative readings related to neo-Hullian approaches to instrumental learning are: (1) A. Amsel, "The role of frustrative nonreward in noncontinuous reward situations" (*Psychological Bulletin,* 1958, 55, 102–118; (2) E. J. Capaldi, "Memory and learning: A sequential viewpoint," in W. K. Honig and P. H. James (Eds.), *Animal memory* (New York: Academic Press, 1971); and (3) F. A. Logan, *Fundamentals of learning and motivation* (Dubuque, Iowa: William C. Brown, 1970).

Neo-Skinnerian approaches to positive reinforcement and new principles are well represented by: (1) two articles by D. Premack, "Toward empirical behavioral laws: I. Positive reinforcement" *Psychological Review,* 1959, 66, 219–233, and "Reversibility of the reinforcement relation," *Science,* 1962, 136, 255–257; (2) G. S. Reynolds, *A primer of operant conditioning: Revised* (Glenview, Ill.: Scott Foresman, 1975); and (3) two articles by H. S. Terrace (*Journal of the Experimental Analysis of Behavior,* 1963, 6, 1–27 and 223–232). Key readings in the area of aversive control of behavior should include: (1) N. H. Azrin and W. C. Holtz, "Punishment," in W. K. Honig (Ed.), *Operant behavior: Areas of research and application* (New York: Appleton-Century-Crofts, 1966); (2) P. J. Dunham, "Punishment: Method and theory" (*Psychological Review,* 1971, 78, 58–70); (3) I. Lovaas, "After you hit a child, you can't just get up and leave him; You are hooked to that kid (A conversation with P. Chance)" (*Psychology Today,* January 1974, 7, 76–84); (4) M. E. P. Seligman and J. C. Johnston, "A cognitive theory of avoidance learning," in F. J. McGuigan and D. B. Lumsden (Eds.), *Contemporary approaches to conditioning and learning* (Washington, D.C.: V. H. Winston & Sons, 1973); (5) M. Sidman, "Normal sources of pathological behavior" (*Science,* 1960, 132, 61–68); and (6) R. L. Solomon, "Punishment" (*American Psychologist,* 1964, 19, 239–253). Cognitive behaviorism and modeling is presented in A. Bandura, *Social learning theory* (Englewood Cliffs, N.J.: Prentice-Hall, 1977).

For those wishing to read two provocative articles evaluating older views of instrumental learning, I would recommend J. E. Staddon and V. L. Simmelhag, "The 'superstition' experiment: A reexamination of its implications for the principles of adaptive behavior" (*Psychological Review,* 1971, 78, 3–43 and W. Timberlake and J. Allison, "Response deprivation: An empirical approach to instrumental performance" (*Psychological Review,* 1974, 81, 146–164).

Applications of Operant Learning Principles to the Real World

When most people think of behavioral modification, they think first of phobia removal through systematic desensitization or of aversive conditioning of the type popularized in the film *A Clockwork Orange*, which we described in Chapter 6. These types of behavioral modification, the first to be highly developed, continue to be important in helping people overcome problems caused by inappropriate fears or motivations. More lives, however, are currently being touched by a recently developed form of behavioral modification that is often labeled **contingency management.** Contingency management is the art and science of controlling the rules relating a person's behavior to the consequences of that behavior (reinforcements).

Although applications of classical conditioning for the most part have been confined to clinical settings in which a therapist or medical doctor works with a single client, reinforcement-based conditioning principles have been found useful in an extremely wide range of settings. These range from asthma relief in clinics to zoo programs for increasing animals' daily activity levels. The principles have been used in one-to-one counseling, in group settings, and on whole wards or natural populations of people. They have been applied by the usual professionals, such as counselors, teachers, and medical doctors, by paraprofessionals, and by individuals on themselves and/or their significant others. Because of the extreme diversity of environments and target populations affected by application of reinforcement principles of the type first systematized by Skinner, only a few general guidelines can be given. This chapter will begin by presenting these general rules for application of Skinnerian conditioning theory, after which specific types of applications and specialized rules will be given.

General Principles of Contingency Management

There are three stages to all well-done programs of contingency management, and we will explore the various events and procedures applied to each stage. The three stages are: (1) **specification,** (2) **observation,** and (3) **consequation.** Malott (1974) calls this the "SOC it to 'em!" model of contingency management.

Specification

Before designing a program for contingency management, you must first specify: (1) which behaviors you wish to work with, (2) what reinforcers you will use, and (3) how the reinforcers will be related to the occurrence of the behaviors (the contingencies).

The first step in beginning the process of contingency management is to decide what behavioral changes you wish to see occur and with whom. Programs try to change visible behaviors because changes inside of peoples' heads, such as "better life adjustment," cannot be observed. Therefore, different observers would not be able to agree when your goal had been reached. To aid in objectivity, it is a good idea to list a set of observation procedures or operations that any trained observer could follow and tell when your target behavior had occurred or not occurred. This is called the **operational definition** of your dependent variable (the target behavior). Specifying the operationally defined, desired behavioral outcomes of your program of contingency management is called stating your **behavioral objectives.** An example of a behavioral objective might be reducing a child's rate of talking back to the teacher from over twenty times per day to under two times per day. The rules for defining "talking back" should be so specific that other observers would agree with you both on when such undesired behavior had occurred and when your goal had been reached. Just because the goals, or behavioral objectives, of contingency management programs should never be stated in terms of things happening within the "target person's"* head does not mean that contingency managers do not feel that things like "better life adjustment" are unimportant; it only means that behavior alone can be measured reliably (as in having several observers agree), and that therefore the contingency manager must carefully select target behaviors which he or she assumes to be related to the inner experiences of the client or target person.

There are two other important aspects of selecting the behaviors to be modified. First, they should be within the target person's capabilities. Unrealistic selection leads to frustration and extinction on the parts of both modifiers and persons to be modified. Malott (1974) suggests a "think small" rule. By having limited objectives, the probabilities of accomplishing big are increased. Once one goal is reached, it is always possible to set up a second and more demanding goal. Demanding too much, too early, strains your schedule control. Second, you must select an appropriate beginning point for change. Normally, the most efficient strategy is to "begin where the behavior of the person to be modified is at" and reinforce small changes in the desired direction until finally your behavioral objective is reached. This is, of course, the same as saying that the desired target behaviors have been fully shaped.

The selection of reinforcers must also be carefully specified. Good reinforcers must be available to the modifier, must be reasonable in cost both in terms of money and of modifier's time, and must be easily deliverable. And, of course, they must be reinforcers in Skinner's terms. That is, they must be wanted

---

* The term "target person" is used to refer to the person whose behavior is to be modified. The undesirable emotional connotations of the word "target" are regrettable, but most alternative terms, such as "client" or "subject," do not apply in all cases, and precise and nonemotionally loaded terms, such as "person whose behavior is to be modified," are unwieldy and boring to read and write.

enough by the target person to have him or her change behaviors to get the reinforcers. What seems to be a reinforcer to you may not be a reinforcer to your target person. Praise from a teacher to a child who dislikes that teacher may actually be an aversive event rather than a reinforcer! A good way to determine what to use as reinforcers is to list all the reinforcers you might use and then have the target person specify which of these he or she would work for.

A common misconception about reinforcers is that they must be physical, such as candy or money. Many persons object to such concrete reinforcers both on grounds of tooth decay and of moral decay (the modifier is "bribing" the target person). Leaving aside the issue of whether many such critics would continue working on their own jobs without concrete reinforcers, behaviors may be as useful as concrete reinforcers in shaping desired behaviors. We explored the use of high-frequency behaviors as reinforcers in Chapter 9 in the section covering the Premack principle. Roughly stated, this principle suggests telling the target person, "If you do this low-frequency behavior that you do not seem to like to do, then (the contingency) I will let you do a high-frequency behavior that you seem to want to do a lot." Or, more concretely: "If you eat spinach, then you can emit some ice-cream-eating behaviors." Of course, the would-be modifier must make sure that he can control when the target person will be able to emit the reinforcer responses. A general rule for classroom applications is to use highly liked behaviors which require some physical supplies or accessories. Thus, not fighting might be reinforced by being allowed to play records that the teacher can lock up until the behavioral objectives are reached. Behaviors that require the cooperation of the modifier may also be used as reinforcers. The author once heard a talk in which the speaker related that being given access to a Freudian psychoanalyst was the reward for the mental patient's emitting desired behaviors in a hospital behavioral modification program. Attention from a teacher, the teacher's reading of an exciting story, or contingent praise might equally be used.

As a general rule, nonphysical reinforcers are most useful with target persons who are relatively bright, mature, and free from severe behavior problems. When these conditions are not met, some concrete reinforcers must be used. The more severe the problems, the more reliance must be placed on physical rewards.

Even when physical reinforcers must be used, it is often difficult to deliver them immediately after the desired behavior occurs (or after a specified interval elapses) without having the undesired behavior occur in between. In such cases, conditioned or secondary reinforcers may be used. These may only be a signal to the target person that he has met the behavioral criteria*; they may be marks on

---

* When animal trainers are faced with the problem of maintaining a long sequence of behavior which takes the animal out of range of the trainer and primary reinforcers (such as fish for killer whales), they use a secondary reinforcer called a "bridging gap." This is either a hand or body visual signal or an auditory cue from a clicker or whistle which has become associated with the primary reinforcer through a classical conditioning procedure. The signal is given whenever the animal successfully completes a portion of the sequence.

a blackboard or in a notebook, or they may be physical "tokens," such as poker chips. For severely retarded or disturbed target persons, physical tokens are usually necessary, and they should be large enough to discourage being eaten. Large size may also help reduce theft problems in ward settings. Tokens must be guarded as carefully as primary reinforcers, and, in the case of blackboard or notebook marks, the target persons must be prevented from cheating by erasing or adding marks. A person trying to shape his own behavior may use a golf counter to note when he reaches behavioral goals, such as not smoking during a 15-minute interval. Each press of the button on the counter is a secondary reinforcement if the person later rewards himself for specified total counts. In general, tokens or other types of conditioned reinforcers are more convenient than primary reinforcers and help to prevent satiation, which might occur through delivery of too many primary reinforcers. This phenomenon of maintaining a behavioral chain through secondary reinforcement and obtaining superior resistance to extinction and satiation involves the partial reinforcement effect. This is the same effect that maintains responding on long ratio and interval schedules. As with "lean" schedules of reinforcement, it is often necessary to begin with continuous reinforcement using primary reinforcers, gradually shaping acceptance of more and more secondary reinforcers to each primary reinforcer. Failure to shape the response to the leaner schedule gradually often results in straining the schedule, or unplanned extinction of competing responses.

A final note on the specification of reinforcers. Even though many reinforcers may be effective in maintaining high levels of desired behaviors, the reinforcers themselves may have undesirable side effects. Harlow (1953) found that rhesus monkeys given food rewards for solving mechanical puzzles subsequently solved fewer such puzzles when the food was discontinued than monkeys given the puzzles without food rewards. This raises the danger that some primary reinforcers may interfere with the operations of less powerful reinforcers (such as a love of learning), which may reflect a behavioral contrast effect (see Chapter 9). A second possible undesirable side effect of potent reinforcers is that these reinforcers may themselves evoke undesirable responses or have undesirable consequences. For example, the author has found that while juvenile delinquents could be induced to improve their room cleanup behaviors markedly by use of cigarette reinforcements, this led to a sharp rise in their rate of smoking, raising the specter that the behavior modifiers will further contribute to their health problems.

The final goal in the specification stage of a contingency management program is specification of the relationship, or contingency, between the desired behavioral outcomes and the reinforcers. Should you begin with a constant ratio of reinforcers to behaviors, or should you try to shape tolerance for leaner schedules as your program progresses? Should you use the same reinforcers throughout, or should you try to progress from primary reinforcers, such as food or toys, and powerful generalized secondary reinforcers, such as money, first to a token system, and finally to social reinforcers such as praise? Is your goal to maintain the desired behaviors indefinitely through your schedule of reinforcement; or, after your behavioral objectives have been obtained, do you hope gradually to terminate your reinforcers?

In general, the rule specifying the relationship of behavior to reinforcement should be very clearly communicated to your target persons. Because changes in your rules make the contingency unclear, they should be avoided in your initial program. Seligman (1973) has presented data suggesting that failure to perceive the relationship between behaviors and outcomes may result in the phenomena of learned helplessness, where the person ceases to try to gain reinforcements. With brighter or more mature target persons, a token or other type of secondary reinforcement system can be instituted from the beginning. The author has used such a system with college students for years, with good results. Attempts to modify it in midcourse, however, lead to confusion and often resentment. Therefore, shaping to leaner schedules, transferring control from concrete reinforcers to social reinforcers, and other attempts to reduce the **response cost** of a contingency management system to the modifier should only be made after the original behavioral objectives have been met. Signs of resentment or breakdowns in schedule control should be carefully watched for, and the modifier must be prepared to institute changes very gradually to prevent "strain." Abrupt extinction procedures are to be avoided, as they may result in increases in the behaviors specified as undesirable as well as increased variability in what may be ineffectual coping responses.

The success of attempts to change the originally specified contingencies is related to the level of your target persons. Brighter and/or better-adjusted persons have more intrinsic reward systems and more alternate sources of reward, and may tolerate changes better. Ward populations and severely retarded persons may require planned contingency management for much of their institutionalized lives. In a sense, contingency management programs may simply help such persons to be able to see the relationships between their actions and environmental consequences for the first time. Because the contingencies are specified in a simplified and exaggerated way, in deliberate programs compared to normal social environments, highly retarded or disturbed individuals may comprehend for the first time in their lives that such relationships exist. For such persons, the contingency manager's emphasis should be on immediacy and simplicity. For "normal" populations, considerations of flexibility and reduction of the efforts required by the managers may be most important. Even with sound-minded college students, however, the author has found it necessary to be highly explicit about what he expects for so many points of credit towards a specified course grade. Successful contingency management depends upon clear communications!

There is one final aspect of specifying the contingencies in a particular situation: Should only one simple contingency be used, or are multiple contingencies desirable? Often a system based only upon positive reinforcement breaks down because of competing responses. If one child gets more reinforcement from the attention of his or her peers than you can deliver for desirable behavior, then not only will you fail to control the behavior of that child, but schedules applied to other children will be disrupted. In such cases, aversive controls must be added to your system. The mildest type of these is simply to ignore the undesirable behavior in hopes that it will extinguish. If this fails, removal from the situation where positive reinforcers may be earned (time-out procedures) may be tried. If this is not sufficient, then punishment contingencies may have to be added to the positive reinforcement contingencies. Lovaas (Chance and Lovaas, 1974) has been successful in using severe physical punishment with autistic children, but in general physical punishment should be avoided. This is because it may be difficult to use such punishers at a strength which will result in lasting suppression of the undesired behaviors without producing severe side effects in the person punished and without exposing you to potential legal and ethical complications. Effective use of punishment, in general, and especially physical punishment, is a complicated task (recall the discussion of punishment in the preceding chapter), and severe physical punishment is usually forbidden in most institutional settings, such as schools.

Safer and legal punishment procedures are available, however, that are applicable in institutional settings for those situations in which aversive control is appropriate. Skinner uses the term "punishment" to describe both contingent delivery of aversive consequences and contingent nondelivery of positive reinforcers. Taking away access to desired activities or other positive reinforcers is generally both effective and less likely to cause unwanted side effects than physical punishment. Bartlett and Swenson (1975), for example, were successful in using late access to recess to control disruptive behaviors in groups of problem sixth graders. Bartlett's technique was to make undesirable responses cost positive reinforcers, an effective type of punishment procedure because it can easily be controlled by the modifier. Remember that most organisms respond to punishment with attempts at avoidance or escape; the suppression of undesired behavior will not occur until such attempts cease. The would-be user of punishment must also be alert to the possibility that desirable behaviors might also be suppressed and that punishment may trigger emotional problems in some persons.

Even with college students, some types of aversive control may be needed. The deadlines for handing in assignments, if enforced, punish "dawdling and delaying." DuNann and Fernald (1976) reported using a "doomsday" contingency: If minimal assignments were not completed by a specified date, the slow-starting students could be forced to drop the contingency-management-based course. In practice, some aversive contingencies are usually necessary whenever the modifier is under time pressures. These should be minimized and used primarily to prevent competing behaviors (such as children who disrupt classes or college students who delay completing assignments) from interfering with the effects of your primary positive reinforcement contingencies.

As a rule of thumb, brighter target persons may be exposed to as many concurrent contingencies as you and they can keep straight, as long as each contingency serves some valid purpose in helping you to reach your behavioral objectives. With disturbed or slower target persons, one positive contingency and one seldom-used punishment contingency are usually sufficient.

To design an effective contingency management plan, first define target behaviors (behavioral objectives) operationally. Note current behavior and how
to go from that behavior to the target behavior without "straining" your control. Next, specify reinforcers (primary, secondary, and aversive) and their
contingency relationships to behaviors. When aversive consequences are
necessary, emphasize the removal of positive reinforcers.

Observation

It is a general rule in conditioning that the closer in time the reinforcing event
(the US, in classical conditioning) follows the desired response (the CS, in
classical conditioning), the more effective the conditioning will be. In shaping
operant behavior, you must catch a movement in your desired direction immediately. Otherwise, you will be reinforcing a later behavior which may not help
you in completing the shaping process. Therefore, you must carefully observe in
order to deliver reinforcers at the moment when they will reinforce behaviors
related to your behavioral objectives. To do this, you must have clearly specified
what types of responses you consider examples of desired behaviors. This
specification of the rules, or operations, for measuring the occurrence of the
target behavior (your dependent variable) is, of course, the operational definition of what is considered a reinforceable response. If you fail to note instances
of desirable behaviors, such behaviors may extinguish. In a similar vein, letting
severely disruptive behaviors pass without punishment after you have established a punishment contingency reinforces "testing the limits." Most successful
programs working with severely retarded or disturbed individuals have
stressed extremely close individual observation.

While observing every desired response is the way to reach your behavioral
objectives most quickly, such an approach is impractical in environments such
as classrooms where you are dealing with several target persons simultaneously.
In classrooms, it is impossible to watch everyone every minute. Several partial
solutions have been offered for this problem. One answer is to use **time sampling.** With this approach, your observing behavior is either on a fixed or variable
interval schedule. When the planned observing time approaches, you look
around the room and quickly note what everyone is doing. If you remembered
to "think small" and do not have too many or too complicated rules for determining desirable behaviors, you should be able to note those individuals doing
desirable, undesirable, and "other" behaviors. It is very helpful to have a sheet
of paper in front of you to allow you quickly to check the appropriate categories
of behaviors for each target person by time intervals (see Figure 10.1 for an
example of a behavior recording form).

If you have access to a timing device or can glance at a wall clock or
wristwatch at regular intervals, the fixed interval "observation window" technique may be most satisfactory. If you tend to have difficulty remembering to
check the time or if your target persons learn about your fixed interval and do
most of their good behavior in the time just before you do your recording (the
fixed interval scallop), then a modified interval schedule may be a practical
alternative. In this case, you vary the times when you will observe target behav-

D = desirable   U = undesirable   N = neutral

		Sally D U N		Sam D U N		Sara D U N		Skinner D U N	
9:00 A.M.									
9:15 A.M.									
9:30 A.M.									

Totals:

Figure 10.1   A sample data sheet for recording time-sampled information from a group of people. D = desirable, U = undesirable, N = neutral.

iors around a preselected mean time value such as 10 minutes. Choosing the intervals in advance and recording them on a cassette tape machine to be played in the classroom is a good way to do this. A more detailed description of this timing tape technique is given in the appendix to this chapter. Timing tapes should only be used in situations in which the modifier is able to hear the taped cues of when to observe without allowing the sound of those recorded cues to disrupt the behaviors of the target persons.

When the taped time signal technique is impractical or impossible, you may generate a quasivariable interval schedule by attempting to check behaviors at regular intervals. If you glance at the clock and find you are a couple of minutes early, check off behaviors anyway. If you are a couple of minutes late, so much the better. In a sense, your own inconsistency can generate a desirable degree of randomness in a way which will not disrupt your modifying environment.

A last major consideration with time-sampling techniques is deciding on the frequency of the "observation windows" on the target persons' behaviors. As a rule, short intervals give more accurate information in less time but are more of a disrupting factor for you. If your main job is to observe behavior, then the response cost of short intervals will not be too aversive. If you are also required to teach or perform other functions, however, longer intervals are more practical. Short intervals are more tolerable in short-term studies or modification programs, while continuing programs reduce the need for frequent observation. Longer intervals between observations are compatible with programs of long duration, both because they take less of your time (reducing the probability of having your own schedules strained) and because sufficient data can be gathered over a long time period from widely spaced observations.

Another technique for observing behavior of persons in groups is the **focal individual** technique. In this technique, you randomly order the names of the persons to be observed. Again, printing each name on a slip of paper and putting the papers in a container is a simple randomization procedure. Do not replace names after they are drawn from the container. Write the names in order on a piece of paper and observe the target persons in that order. With this technique, only one person is observed at a given time. It is best to redraw the names for each day's observations to control for differences due to the time at which each person is observed. If this is too much work, either generate a number of lists at one time through successive drawings or rotate the names through the list so that the person observed first on one day is observed last on the next. The focal individual technique is preferable to the time-sampling technique when the behavioral objectives for the different target persons are different or where you are simultaneously sampling several behaviors and recording each of them.

However your observations are gathered, your next step is using them properly. When working with individuals who have short attention spans, you would probably have to follow up each observation of a desired behavior with either a primary (unlearned) or a secondary (conditioned) reinforcer. With individuals who have intermediate attention spans, such as normal fifth-grade school children, it may be enough of a secondary reinforcer for the child to see you make a plus mark by his name. With older normal children and normal adults who may be trying to change behaviors, the daily record may serve as a sufficient secondary reinforcer (assuming it shows progress) to maintain motivation. A record of behavior over several days is called a chart, and filling out such a chart is called **charting.** For many adults, keeping a record of their progress towards a goal, such as losing weight, may by itself allow them to emit those behaviors (such as avoiding third helpings of food) compatible with meeting their behavioral objectives. Since charting used by itself avoids the implications of bribery inherent in turning in secondary reinforcers for primary reinforcers, it would seem the program of choice for mature, well-adjusted individuals.

Backing up a program of charting behavior with other reinforcers, however, enhances the effects of such a system. Charting can also be done by target persons themselves, and will often have desirable motivational effects. The author provides charts for students to record their weekly accumulations of points and to mark cumulative point totals by weeks. Unfortunately, many students do not fill out their charts, and it is often just these students who are doing the worst in class. The author has found that backing up "chart-filling-out" behaviors on the part of students with point contingencies increases both the percentage of students filling in the charts correctly and those doing more and better-quality work (Swenson, 1975). A sample of this chart can be seen as Figure 10.2. It is filled in with the points that might be earned by an "A" student.

One advantage of charting for the modifier is that it avoids the problem of allowing your moods to color your evaluations of how well your modification program may be working. If you are feeling depressed, you may feel your program is a failure; on an "up" day, in contrast, you may feel your program is fantastic. Both of these judgments may be biased and inaccurate. Accurate observation and recording (charting) are both essential ingredients in the process of evaluating your progress towards meeting your behavioral objectives. Subjective impressions are more often inaccurate than not! Objective data may also help the teacher or counselor to demonstrate that they are meeting their behavior objectives when they meet with administrators evaluating their performance as part of an **accountability** process. Since subjective factors play such a large role in evaluating, for instance, how well a behavioral modification project is doing, the objective record of a chart is very helpful.

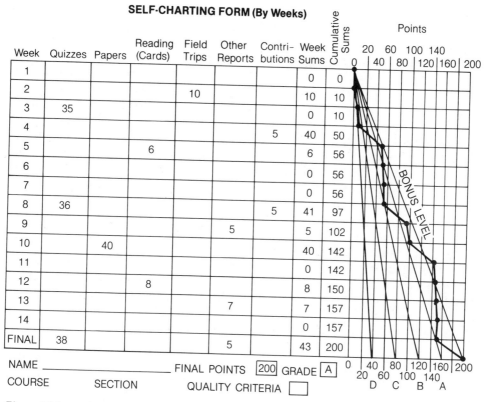

Figure 10.2   *A self-charting form as it might be filled out by an "A" student.*

Most of the discussion to this point has been on observation for the sake of accurate notation of occasions for consequation. But what about the issue of program evaluation and its relationship to objective data? Well-done charts of frequencies of target behaviors are useful, but they suffer from one serious flaw if they only chart behaviors from the beginning of the implementation of a program to its (hopefully successful) termination. This flaw is related to time-correlated changes in behaviors, which may be confused with the effects of a program. Just getting the sort of attention provided by a focused program may reinforce desired behaviors. Many children find participation in token economy programs a type of game and respond with increased interest in school. Behaviors change for reasons not readily apparent; if such changes occur during your program and are positive, who could blame you for taking credit for the changes?

One way to evaluate the precise effects of your interventions is to use the **multiple baseline procedure.** You begin by collecting data on the frequencies with which the target behaviors occur before you start your program of contingency management. This allows your subjects to get used to the observation procedures which may be themselves change behaviors. It is a time to practice observing without the necessity of also having to provide reinforcers and sharpen your original specifications. This period of time, called baseline 1, serves as a control for the effects of the contingency management program. Then you initiate your intervention ("on-contingency") time period, continue to record data until you reach the behavioral objectives or clearly have failed, and then halt your consequation while continuing to record behavioral frequencies (baseline 2). The second baseline allows evaluation of long-term effects independent of your administration of reinforcers. Multiple baseline procedures alternate baseline periods with "on-contingency" time periods several times to determine reinforcement control.

Because it is difficult to maintain the desired degree of accuracy in observations over long time periods, mechanical methods of observing behavior have been developed. An ingenious device has been developed which monitors classroom noise levels and can be set to show the minutes remaining until recess or a special treat. When noise levels go over a specified level, the clock stops running. Portable event recorders have been developed that permit the operator to indicate the occurrence of any selected behavior by pushing a button that causes a pen to make an ink line on a strip of moving paper. With five buttons and five pens, five separate behaviors can be recorded simultaneously by using all the fingers and the thumb of one hand. By holding the button down until the behavior stops, you can make a "real time" record of the duration of the behavior.

The accumulating totals of counters like those used for scoring golf also represent mechanical data collection of a simple sort. These may be used by individuals to record their own "urges to smoke or eat or do other undesirable habitual behaviors." They have the advantage of requiring less effort (push the button to record the urge) than writing down the urges. In biofeedback, the observation of the desired physiological change is always made by a machine which then tells the person producing the change how he or she is doing. By giving feedback on the formerly unobservable biological state, these machines make it possible for the person to modify physiological responses, much as seeing progress on a chart allows a person to modify more directly accessible responses. Teaching machines usually allow the learner to compare answers with the answer key after each response. This lets the learner observe directly his or her level of accuracy. As we noted for charting, knowledge (feedback) about being successful may be a powerful reinforcer.

The second stage of planning a contingency management program is specifying observation procedures, such as focal individual or time-sampling techniques. Records of observations are called charts, and charting may influence behavior. Observation is required for precise consequation of target behaviors and for program evaluation. Multiple baseline measures of behavior before, during, and after consequation aid in program evaluation.

Consequation

The last stage of the SOC model is actually delivering the consequences of the specified behaviors of the target persons according to the rules of the specified contingencies. As has been previously discussed, consequation should be immediate for best results, and this requirement increases in importance as the intelligence level or stability level of the target persons decreases. As we have also seen, a good system of secondary reinforcers can "bridge the gap" between primary reinforcers, as long as these secondary reinforcers are themselves delivered as immediately after the desired response as possible. We have seen that the degree of concreteness of secondary reinforcers that can be used effectively increases as intelligence level and/or stability-adjustment level decreases. Thus, poker chips or some other physical sign of the correct response may have to be given for every correct response with a highly retarded individual, while an adult may be able to change behaviors with only the secondary reinforcement of seeing his daily record of undesirable behaviors show decreases.

Whatever the type of reinforcers employed, however, and whatever the types of contingencies linking the target behaviors to those reinforcers, one rule applies in all cases: *Be Consistent*. This means that you must observe accurately and resist being pressured into granting unearned "bootleg" reinforcers on one hand or holding back from the deserved delivery of an aversive consequence on the other. If the target person has contracted to turn in a paper by a specified due date to prevent its being marked down (active or Sidman avoidance contingency), the penalty should never be waived. To do so would reinforce procrastination and dawdling, and shapes the behavior of the student's becoming facile in generating ever more creative excuses instead of learning to do papers on time. No responsible college professor (or teacher at any level) would wish to do such a horrible thing to a student! The responsible and humane (in the long run, anyway) course of action is, as Malott phrases it, "NOTHING IN MODERATION!" This means that your responsibility to communicate your inflexible contingencies clearly is more than a moral obligation. If the target persons do not know what you expect and if you reinforce only behavior conforming to your rules, then both you and the "modifyees" may extinguish. This does not mean that you should not listen to complaints about your program. Rather, you should think about them carefully. Later, either when you have reached your behavioral objectives or you are sadly surveying the ruins of what had once been a proud program, you should take them into account in designing subsequent plans.

Some changes in consequation should be planned for at the beginning. If you hope to have your target persons hold onto their behavioral gains after they have left your program or after you have ended your efforts, you must shape behaviors that can be reinforced by the environment or by the persons themselves. This is called shaping **functional behavior.** An example would be training a child to read. Once reading is mastered, the content of the material read will reinforce it. Once prosocial behaviors are mastered in children with emotional problems, the more positive reactions of significant others in their environments may maintain the new behaviors. Similarly, praise from their friends may maintain newly acquired "avoidance of smoking behaviors" in former smokers.

The matter of shaping functional behavior is one which has only recently been given sufficient attention by behavioral modifiers. Even today, many programs include no provisions for followups. Rightly, the critics of the behavioral modification movement have noted that even though children or ward patients may indeed behave in ways judged as more appropriate by the modifiers, these gains may vanish when the reinforcers vanish. Where continued environmental control is present, such as on a mental ward for long-term patients, such criticisms may not be very important. Even behavioral gains which must be maintained by continuing contingency management programs may make a ward much more reinforcing for both patients and staff.

Planning for the day when the target persons will leave your kindly attention, however, is vital in counseling and school settings. In counseling, shaping functional behavior may take the form of training the client to apply contingency management techniques to himself, along with other self-help skills, such as relaxation techniques. The counselor should assign to the client simple "self-help problems" and then reinforce the client for arriving at successful completions of them. If the new skills help the client obtain reinforcers on his own, they will usually be maintained, although occasional "boosters" may be needed. With school children, the most successful approach may be gradually withdrawing, or "fading out," the overt reinforcers. The modifier should observe carefully for signs of schedule strain as the schedule of reinforcement becomes leaner and leaner. Disappearance of newly acquired positive behaviors signals a need to "back up" and restore some of the programmed reinforcers.

Another criticism of contingency management programs is that they may reinforce undesirable levels of competition. Such programs, however, can also be designed to increase cooperation. Bartlett and Swenson (1975) based reinforcers for low levels of disruptive behaviors in fifth graders on the total disruptive behaviors of the members of a group of pupils seated at a particular table. The entire table's consequation was yoked together. The result was that peer pressure was exerted on unruly individuals at each table to perform well at the "good behavior game," a group contingency system first described by Barrish, Saunders, and Wolf (1969).

Another feature designed to reduce competition was having absolute criteria for reinforcement. All tables emitting less disruptive behaviors than the mean number of disruptive behaviors observed during the baseline 1 period were allowed to go to recess early. Those acting out at about baseline levels went to recess on time, and those having a greater than average number of incidents at their table went to recess late. Thus, all tables could "win the game" each time.

Such grouped consequences have several advantages. First, they are easier to administer, since group rather than individual records are required. Second, they make better use of natural peer-based social reinforcers to supplement the effects of reinforcers controlled by the modifier. With relatively "normal" target persons, such group contingencies are almost always more efficient than individual contingencies. One highly disruptive individual, however, may demoralize his or her group and disrupt an entire program. Such an individual should be exposed to individualized aversive consequences, such as time out (isolation) for extreme antisocial acts, or should be treated as a "group of one."

Grouped contingencies are, of course, limited to environments such as schools where similar goals are appropriate for several people simultaneously. Pair or family contingencies may be useful in marriage counseling.

Consistent delivery of reinforcers just after the emission of target behaviors is an essential step in effective contingency management. Because it is often difficult to deliver a primary reinforcer often enough and precisely enough, secondary reinforcers are used to bridge the gap between target behaviors and eventual primary reinforcement. The final goal of most programs is to shape functional or self-reinforcing behavior.

So far, this chapter has presented the principles of effective contingency management. Now we can turn to the wide range of situations in which such techniques are applied and how the principles previously presented are used in each of these situations. As you read through these summaries of various recent studies, look for the principles of application as well as illustrations of the principles of operant learning theory presented in Chapters 4 and 9. These examples of uses of principles, designed to help you integrate theory with application, may suggest how you can eventually design contingency management programs to aid you in your careers. These real world applications may also help you in evaluating the arguments of persons opposing and supporting the use of contingency management techniques to shape and control behavior.

OPTIONAL SECTION

Selected Examples of Operant Applications

An Introductory Smorgasbord

Proposals for the ideal living arrangements have spanned the history of western civilization from Plato's *Republic* to Skinner's *Walden Two* (1948). . . . A major problem that any experimental living arrangement must confront is that of sharing the basic work of the community. Informal accounts suggest that contemporary communes experience a breakdown in the basic housework required by the group. . . . the group could not provide its members with such potentially powerful reinforcers as a clean and neat living environment, well-prepared meals, and clean plates and silverware.

Furthermore, the withdrawal of such reinforcers could lead to an increase in aggressive interpersonal behaviors . . . [Feallock and Miller, 1976, p. 277]

A dream of any applied science of behavior has been to create the basis for a better way of life. Although Skinner's utopia, as presented in *Walden Two* (1948), has been given reality as Twin Oaks commune (Kinkade, 1973), it has not been built on the rigorous experimental basis envisioned by Skinner. Feallock and Miller have attempted to remedy this shortcoming through their work with a coed cooperative house at the University of Kansas.

A feature of the labor credit system in *Walden Two* was that the value of a given job was dependent upon its popularity. This led to desirable jobs, such as picking flowers, paying a small fraction of what was paid for sopping sewers. The Kansas house incorporates this feature, with the values of the most and least popular 10 percent of the jobs adjusted for popularity. At the beginning of their project, some of the 30 students living in the house expressed the view that a clean house was intrinsic reward enough. To test this, credits for cleaning were transferred to painting the outside of the house. At the end of the 18 days, the residents demanded the resumption of cleaning credits after serious deterioration in the cleanliness of the house had occurred. Amount of cleaning jobs completed prior to the change from a credit system was 96 percent (baseline 1). During the change, this percentage fell to 35 percent before contingencies were restored for cleaning. During the baseline 2 phase, the completion ratio again reached 96 percent. The percentages of completed painting jobs, which only paid credits during the on-contingency phase, were 3 percent (baseline 1), 99 percent (on contingency), and 0 percent (baseline 2).

A second question raised by house members concerned the necessity of making credits contingent upon the work's successfully passing the gaze of student inspectors. "Some members suggested that it would be nicer if there could be trust in the house, so that the members who agreed to do a job would not have to have their work inspected and credits awarded on the basis of that inspection" (Feallock and Miller, 1976, p. 281). Again, a simple **reversal design** was used, with the intervention phase of credits not contingent upon inspection lasting 35 days and the baseline 1 and baseline 2 phases lasting 36 and 25 days, respectively. During baseline 1, 96 percent of all cleaning jobs passed inspection. During the intervention phase, this rate had dropped below 60 percent by the final five days. During baseline 2, the rate went back up to 95 percent.

In the original plan, labor credits were convertible into rent reductions. A third question debated was the necessity of such a **backup system.** Some students argued that pride of achievements alone should be sufficient. A third experiment used a design with a middle phase in which all house members got a rent reduction irrespective of their work records. Twenty-seven of the 30 members completed less cleaning jobs; and total cleaning jobs passing inspection dropped from 94 percent to 67 percent during the "non-backup" phase.

A question arises about the feelings of the human subjects in such an experiment. Certainly the economics of a work-sharing plan of this type are favorable in comparison with dormitories that have paid cleaning and maintenance staffs (about half the cost). But what about student satisfaction? In fact, tests indicated considerably higher satisfaction for most participants. This may have resulted from other procedures built into the system. A requirement for living in the house was passing a quiz after completing a programmed self-instructional handbook on behavioral techniques. Student acceptability was further increased by having all inspectors, contingency managers, and finance managers be house members who had passed "minicourses" in these areas. The first student administrators, in turn, developed 80 self-instructional manuals and trained all subsequent peer managers. As part of student self-governance, the credit values for various tasks could be modified by majority vote. This communal house demonstrated a viable approach to group self-control procedures.

While Feallock and Miller (1976) demonstrated the utility of behavioral techniques in an environment in which the participants were involved in determining contingencies, what of less democratic institutions? Hobbs and Holt (1976) were able to improve significantly the percentages of time spent in appropriate activities by 125 adjudicated delinquent boys from around 55 percent to over 78 percent through use of a token system. Tokens were backed up by dances at a girl's training school, cigarettes, toys, candy, soft drinks, access to football and other sport events, and early release. Cost of the experiment was only $7.85 per boy per month. The authors reported that 14 months after the experiment was concluded, administrative neglect of supervision and coordination of the program, coupled with an insistence on using the system to promote behaviors such as standing straight in lines, had resulted in considerable program deterioration. The authors commented on the dilemma raised by providing the powerful tools of behavioral control to "community systems whose program interests may not all be in the best interests of the client" (Hobbs and Holt, 1976, p. 197).

One answer to the ethical issues raised by Hobbs and Holt is to give even imprisoned "offenders" more control over the contingency management process. Seymour and Stokes (1976), working with four girls confined in a maximum-security institution in Australia, were successful in increasing work behaviors and reducing disruptive behaviors for three of the girls. The girls were allowed to score their own work output, although provisions for the detection of cheating were built into the system. This self-recording procedure was successful in spite of the fact that a previous staff-directed token economy had failed. As in many other programs of this type, **token cost** (response cost) provisions were necessary to reduce competing behaviors. The girls also role-played pointing out improvements in their work to staff, or "cueing" staff. The staff (which was distinct from the experimental team) was not aware of these cues. Both cues and praise from the staff members increased in the later stages of the project. The therapist recorded the cues and delivered tokens for the girls' efforts to bring their improving work to the attention of the staff. Thus, the tokens were used to increase the rates with which the girls elicited social reinforcers.

The success of the response cost procedure used to prevent cheating in the Seymour and Stokes study is parallel to extensions into other types of group settings where it is desirable to decrease specified behaviors. Marholin and Gray (1976) were able to reduce sharply cash losses in a small business by instituting a group response cost contingency. A reversal design was used before the program was permanently instituted. Shortfalls on baseline days were around 4 percent of receipts; during "on-contingency" days, they dropped to less than 1 percent. Total fines to employees were $8.70 per person.

Not all institutions are designed to be either punitive or profit making. One such institution is marriage. Israel Goldiamond has been a pioneer in developing self-applied behavior technologies in which the professional modifier serves as coach, consultant, and evaluator. The following case illustrates his approach, applied to participants in a failing marriage.

The couple concerned had been married for almost ten years and had limited themselves to sexual relationships about twice each year. This was blamed on the husband by both parties. They were both intelligent professionals, Roman Catholics, and determined to maintain the marriage if only they could get sexual behaviors started before the wife was "driven" into extramarital affairs. It was suggested that the husband try reading *Playboy* to initiate amorous activity. He feel asleep reading it. The wife had almost extinguished on "husband-shaping" behavior:

> I don't know what reinforcements I have. The characteristic of good reinforce-ment is that it can be applied immediately and is immediately consumed. I could withhold supper, but that is not a good reinforcer, because I can't turn it off and on. I can't apply [sexual] deprivation because that's my problem. I don't know what to do. [Goldiamond, 1965, p. 857]

Part of the problem was that the husband was a rising business executive who also attended evening courses and was either too busy or too tired to make advances towards his wife. He offered to schedule his wife in his appointment book for two evenings a week. In spite of his wife's dubious attitude, charting his "wife attention" appointments was initially effective. After two weeks, however, he began to cancel these appointments and it was necessary to search for an effective backup reinforcer. Both husband and wife took personal groom-ing very seriously. She visited her beautician weekly and he, his barber. Their clothing was always freshly dry cleaned. When termination of all such affecta-tions was made the contingency for missed appointments, vanity succeeded where all else had failed.

Behavioral techniques can also be used to improve the environment. Hayes, Johnson, and Cone (1975) were able to reduce littering on the grounds of a federal youth correctional facility in spite of a lack of public spiritedness. Their method was a significant advance over previous methods, in which reinforce-ment was contingent on the amount of trash turned in, thus exposing the sub-jects to the temptation of generating new trash to supplement their reinforcers. Hayes and colleagues mention one case in which children living in a public housing project emptied trash cans into their collection sacks and collected the larger pieces of trash while leaving small pieces behind.

To avoid these problems, the experimenters surreptitiously distributed a few items of marked litter in each of the study areas on each of the on-contingency days. Unlike the previous behavioral applications for litter control, this procedure provides a variable ratio schedule of control as compared to the volume/fixed ratio schedules of "amount-based" programs. Because the marked items were coded in a way known only to the experimenters, there was no possibility of the youths' picking up only marked items. Three of the areas included in the study were "seeded" with marked items. The youths were told when marking might be done. Baseline data was collected for the three "seeded" areas before they were first marked. The average reduction in litter in the marked areas during the times when they were marked was 71.3 percent. There was actually an increase in litter in the unmarked area, which may reflect a behavioral contrast effect. Of the youths eligible to participate in this program,

25 percent did so. In addition to special privileges, such as being allowed into the camp coffee house past regular hours, a total of $14.50 was earned by all participants over the 42 days of study. This technique is interesting because of its excellent cost-effectiveness ratio, because of the absence of aversive contingencies, and because it does not require much staff time or interpersonal skills (as in convincing a juvenile delinquent that he wants to collect trash).

A variation of this system used in a forest service area (Powers, Osborne, and Anderson, 1973) paid $.25 for full bags of trash but also incorporated a lottery system which paid $20.00 to the person whose lottery ticket, accepted in lieu of cash, had been selected. This method may be superior for areas in which cheating is not a problem.

Even behaviors usually thought of as treatable only through medication have been successfully modified through contingency management. Zlutnick, Mayville, and Moffat (1975) noted that specific behaviors reliably predicted the occurrence of epileptic seizures in children. These behaviors varied from arm raising to facial grimaces. The authors hypothesized that the preseizure behaviors were part of a behavioral chain ending with the full-blown motoric, or loss-of-attention, seizure. Noting some earlier research that suggested that interruption of the behavioral chain could prevent the occurrence of the seizures, they developed aversive consequences for the preseizure behaviors. These consisted of shouting "No!" while grabbing the subjects with both hands and shaking them vigorously. For one subject, this system was supplemented by giving social and primary reinforcers contingent upon the subject's halting the preseizure behavior. During baseline 1, data was collected on the frequencies of seizures and preseizure behaviors. The interruption procedure was then instituted and remained in effect on an ongoing basis except for one day of baseline 2 (reversal) measurement. Four of the children showed significant decreases in seizure frequencies, and preseizure behaviors declined in the other three children. Seizures returned during the reversal day and decreased once the interruption procedure was reinstituted.

An advantage of the interruption procedure was that parents and teachers were able to learn it—thereby reducing the need for continued professional supervision and lowering the cost of treatment. Before the parents administered the treatments, they were each trained for 5 hours by the investigators, followed by one to three phone calls per week to monitor progress and collect data. This approach typifies the **triadic model** (therapeutic pyramid) described by Tharp and Wetzel (1969). In this model, the **change agent,** or person who actually delivers the reinforcers, is never the highly paid professional. Instead, the professional develops and implements programs and teaches techniques to nonprofessionals or paraprofessionals. Rather than acting as a therapist in the conventional sense, he or she functions as the supervisor and consultant at the top of the "therapeutic pyramid," to ensure that the mediators, or change agents, carry out instructions. Advantages of this approach include more contact time between client and change agent (change agents are usually persons normally having extensive contact with the client or target person) and a good cost-effectiveness ratio.

Although almost all the applications presented thus far have dealt with modifications of human behavior, the operant methodology was originally developed through animal research and is thus admirably suited to animal applications. A pioneer in using behavioral technology to produce practical benefits by modifying animals' behaviors is Hal Markowitz, former director of the Oregon Zoological Research Center at the Portland Zoo. Dr. Markowitz's work has important implications both for animal husbandry practices in zoos and for theories of motivation.

A major problem in zoos is that animals fed their daily ratio of food once a day become bored, inactive, and, if dominant, obese. Thus, the low-ranking animals may end up malnourished while the high-ranking animals suffer the effects of easy living without the need to work for their food. The inactivity engendered by sloth is often not distinguished from the inactivity resulting from sickness. Inactive animals frustrate the viewing public, who may resort to feeding the animals "junk food," thereby thwarting the efforts of the zoo dietitians. Dr. Markowitz tackled these problems by developing devices which could be operated by the animals to provide food. The animals, of course, had to be shaped to use these extensions of Skinner box methodology.

One example of this approach, which featured a two-stage learning problem, could be seen in the gibbon (a lesser ape) display of the Portland Zoo. First, the animals had to solve a light-dark discrimination task when the computer-controlled machine notified them, by a combination of buzzer and light cues (the discriminative stimuli, or S_Ds), that reinforcement would be available. Then they had to swing arm over arm across their cage to the second apparatus, where they pulled a lever which caused an automatic feeder to release bits of highly preferred food. In a nice extension of reinforcement principles, the initial S_D was triggered by a human's putting a dime in a slot of a box. An instruction panel explained the purpose of the apparatus. Over $3000 was collected by this box in one year, to be used for the research program.

Other interesting illustrations included training diana monkeys to perform a sequence of behaviors which resulted in the apparatus dispensing a token. The monkeys could then either spend their tokens or hoard them. Sometimes the monkeys were even observed sharing tokens! Young monkeys born after the program was initiated did not need the elaborate shaping procedures required for the adults. Instead, they successfully modeled their parents' behaviors (Markowitz, 1974). Data collection from the diana monkey and the gibbon displays was automated, and enormous quantities of information were gathered. Other products of this unusual approach to zoo displays included small wild cats (servals) that chased "flying meatballs," a bear that could trigger a fish-throwing catapult by nonaggressive growls near a hidden microphone, and a mandrill monkey who played a reaction-time game with zoo visitors for one dime a game (Markowitz, 1975a). While visiting Hal Markowitz during the fall of 1977, the author had the opportunity of losing three games in a row to the speedy baboon.

Benefits of these programs included more active and hence healthier animals, more interesting displays for the zoo-going public, an opportunity to notice illness earlier (sick animals ceased operating the apparatus), less boredom for the animals, and opportunities for research. This last advantage allowed extensive comparisons of many species' abilities on a variety of learning and simple concept-formation tasks. As the animals became more active, pathological behaviors such as infant harassment were reported to have decreased (Markowitz, Schmidt, and Moody, 1977).

Some objections, however, were raised to this program. First, it was suggested that situations such as having diana monkeys work for tokens are unnatural. Hal Markowitz defended his work in an article entitled, appropriately enough, "In Defense of Unnatural Acts Between Consenting Animals" (1975a) by pointing out that animals' behaviors in bare enclosures are not only equally unnatural, but more likely to be harmful to the animals. A second objection was that it is cruel to deprive animals of food in order to force them to operate the devices added to their environments. Markowitz countered by noting that all animals are given all the food they can eat at the end of the testing day. They rarely failed to earn all the food they wished by operating the devices and became extremely upset when the machines were disconnected for maintenance. The ostriches even ignored bins of "free" peanuts to work a machine that dispensed identical peanuts for correct responses (Markowitz, 1975b). The illustration that the animals' behaviors seemed to have more to do with deprivation of the opportunity to control effectively some aspect of their environments rather than with hunger motivation may represent a special case of the Premack principle. The animals were deprived of the opportunity to emit food-gathering behaviors; it was the opportunity to emit these behaviors (which would occur frequently in the wild) that provided most of the reinforcement. The general implication is that working for a living is, in a sense, as primary a reinforcement as drive reduction of the type discussed by Hull (Chapter 3). This is in agreement with Harlow's (1953) observation that monkeys will solve puzzles for the mere reward of being able to manipulate something as well as for food.

Some new terms introduced in these summaries of studies were: (1) token cost, or taking away tokens contingent upon unwanted behavior, (2) backup system, or a system of more primary rewards to reinforce the effects of tokens or points, (3) reversal design, another term for multiple baseline design, and (4) triadic model, or therapeutic pyramid, in which a professional trains others to be the change agents, or persons observing and consequating behavior.

Applications of Contingency Management to the Schoolroom

Most applications of contingency management principles have concentrated on the modification of overt behaviors rather than promoting the learning of academic skills. These techniques have been particularly widely used in special education. An example of this approach was the work of Cooke and Apolloni (1976) with four handicapped children enrolled in an experimental classroom. It is of interest methodologically because three other children enrolled in the classroom served as control subjects—a rarity in operant applications, where reversal or multiple baseline designs are common. During baseline 1, frequencies of smiling, sharing, positive physical contacting, verbal complimenting, and combinations of these behaviors were recorded. Each of the four behaviors was then trained in successive five-day periods. Training methods included the trainer modeling the desired behavior, as suggested by Bandura's social learning theory, praise contingent upon the specified behaviors, and direct instructions. Following each day's training session, the generalization of the trained behaviors to interactions with the untrained children was noted. Following training, followup observation of generalization was conducted over a four-week period. All trained subjects increased the frequencies with which they emitted the specified positive behaviors during the training periods, and three of them showed continuing generalized increases in the followup observations of their interactions with the untrained subjects. The three untrained subjects showed increases also, although relatively less so. These increases were explained as either the result of the untrained children's modeling of the trained children or the result of social-reciprocity effects.

The control of pupil behaviors is not limited to socially relevant behaviors. Behaviors related to cognitive functioning may also be altered. Glover and Gray (1976) were able to demonstrate behavioral control of four behaviorally defined "creative" behaviors in eight fourth- and fifth-grade children. The behaviors were (1) number of different responses assumed to reflect fluency, (2) the production of a large variety of ideas assumed to reflect flexibility, (3) the development, embellishment, or completion of an idea labeled as "elaboration," and (4) the use of ideas "that are not obvious or banal or are statistically infrequent" (Glover and Gary, 1976, p. 79). Leaving aside the subjective nature of the last category, you will note that each of the underlying internal facets of creativity has been tied to an operationally defined class of verbal dependent variables. The verbal data were generated during class hours as part of writing assignments. During on-contingency periods, points were awarded based on the frequencies of the specified behaviors; during baseline periods, the students' papers were all marked "good" and everyone was told, "You are doing very well." The responses were scored by two graduate students in educational psychology who did not know the purpose of the experiment nor the variables involved. This is called a **double-blind** procedure, as the students were also "blind" to the purposes of the researchers.

Students were also tested on the *Torrance Test of Creativity* before (pretest) and after the contingencies were put into effect. They showed a statistically significant increase in their creativity scores. This might reflect a real gain in creativity or simply learning to do more of the behaviors measured on the Torrance test. Each of the dependent variables was rewarded during one of the four experimental sessions. Each of the measures increased over baseline measures and, moreover, showed most of the increase only during the experimental session, when that particular class of verbal behaviors was subject to the point contingencies. The points gained were credited to one of the two four-child teams. The winning team was allowed to go to recess 10 minutes early and each team member received a carton of milk and some cookies. This group contingency is similar to that discussed earlier in this chapter (Bartlett and Swenson,

1975). The authors suggest that their procedures might be useful to teachers who wish to raise the frequency of creative behaviors in story writing and problem solving. A broader implication of this study is that supposedly sterile operant contingencies can be used to maximize such complex behavioral patterns as creativity. These results directly contradict some critics' contentions that behavioral modification techniques are the enemy of creativity.

Although the preceding was an example of trying to increase a somewhat unusual class of behaviors, more recent studies have addressed themselves to the problem of finding the most effective and efficient means of producing modifications of behavior in general. Hundert (1976) compared giving tokens, taking tokens away for failure to emit the target behaviors, and both giving tokens and taking tokens away. The behaviors modified were production of correct finished arithmetic problems and paying attention to the teacher and his work. There were no differences between these procedures, and all of them produced large gains in the six elementary school students. During the baseline 2 (withdrawal of token) measurement period, inattention, but not production of arithmetic problems, declined to baseline 1 levels. It may be suggested that once a competency is learned, the improved performance is likely to be self-rewarding. Not paying attention, however, may be intrinsically more reinforcing than paying attention—especially in many arithmetic classes.

Another direct comparison of the effectiveness of two methods of modifying behavior found direct reinforcement to be superior to a modeling procedure. Bondy and Erickson (1976) attempted to increase the rate of question asking by 12 retarded children. One group got points to be exchanged for food, one group had question-asking behaviors modeled by a trainer, and one group both received points and had the behaviors modeled. The modeling procedure, of the type described by Bandura (Chapter 9), had only a minimal effect. The modeling plus points group learned the fastest, but their final level of performance was no higher than the points-only group. This study supports the author's opinion that direct shaping of behavior is the superior procedure to use with retarded and disturbed individuals.

Another aspect of program effectiveness is that of the behavioral control exerted by different reinforcement parameters. Robertson, DeReus, and Drabman (1976) compared giving feedback to children about their success in emitting less disruptive behaviors with giving them either contingent or noncontingent tutoring. The tutoring of these highly disruptive and academically slow second graders was done by either fifth-grade volunteers or college students. The 18 children were divided into four groups and all children received each type of reinforcement condition at some point in the experiment. All four groups then entered a last phase of the study, during which they were again given feedback on their disruptive behavior but no tutoring. It was found that feedback alone was not significantly effective in reducing the disruptive behaviors. Performance during the final feedback phase was better than during the initial feedback-only phase. This suggests that feedback might be used as other types of reinforcers are faded out. Pupils' behavior improved during all types of tutoring. This improvement, however, was much more marked when tutoring was contingent upon reductions in disruptive behaviors. It seemed to make no difference if the tutors were college students or fifth-grade peer tutors.

This study is of interest because it suggests that availability of help from other people may be an effective reinforcement system if it is made contingent upon low rates of "acting-out" behaviors. Such an approach would seem both practical and inexpensive. A disadvantage would be the possibility that pupils most in need of special help might be denied such help by reason of their bad behavior. Since one cause of their bad behavior might be frustration with their poor academic performance, contingent tutoring might perpetuate a vicious circle in which academic frustration leads to aggressive behavior in class, which prevents tutoring and keeps academic performance low.

While it is usually considered desirable to eliminate disruptive behaviors, some behaviors are only disruptive when they occur too frequently. An example is talking out in class. Even though frequent talking out may be annoying to teachers, the thought of training silent, sullen students is no more pleasing. Rather, what is desired is to reward low levels of talking-out behavior and to have aversive events contingent upon high levels. As we noted in Chapter 9, one of the points of strength of Skinnerian theory has been the delineation of the effects of complex schedules of reinforcement. One of these schedules, you may recall, was the DRL (differential reinforcement of low levels) schedule.

Deitz (1976) examined three types of DRL procedures in behaviorally disturbed children. The first method is called the **spaced responding DRL method.** In this method, only responses separated from each other by interresponse times (IRTs) over a specified criteria are reinforced. The second method is called the **full-session DRL method.** If the total number of target responses emitted during a given time period falls below a specified number, reinforcement is delivered. This was the method used in the "good behavior game" developed by Barrish, Saunders, and Wolf (1969) and used in modified form by Bartlett and Swenson (1975). The third method is the **interval method.** If less than two talking-out responses occurred during the prescribed interval, reinforcement was delivered when the interval ended. If a second response occurred during the interval, the interval timer was reset and reinforcement was postponed. All three versions of DRL schedules reduced talking to about 15 percent of baseline rates.

As these applications demonstrate, the success of researchers presented here shows that application of operant principles is an effective approach to classroom management. The would-be contingency manager, however, must be aware that this approach is extremely literal. That is, you tend to increase the emission of all reinforced behaviors regardless of whether you actually wish to reinforce all these effects. In addition, the teacher's enthusiasm, or lack of it, may determine the success of a given project. The teacher's expectancies of success (Rosenthal effect) or the childrens' responses to the novelty of new classroom procedures (Hawthorne effect) may both confound your evaluation of the effectiveness of a contingency management procedure. Having an experimentally naive observer collect data, apply placebo treatments, such as the noncontingency tutoring used in the previous example, and use multiple baseline designs all help to reduce errors in evaluating the success of programs.

Contingency management methods are effective in educational settings. With retarded and/or highly disturbed children, direct shaping of behavior seems superior to modeling. DRL schedules provide precise control by reducing, but not eliminating, some behaviors. Double-blind procedures allow more objective evaluation of programs by eliminating observer bias.

PSI: An Application for College Classrooms

While the SQR3 method utilized by Fox (reviewed in Chapter 6) represented an extension of operant principles into the college environment, it did not provide a blueprint for a college instructor to use in developing a learning-theory-based classroom. Such a blueprint has been developed by Fred Keller. While the essentials of the "Keller Plan," or **personalized system of instruction (PSI)**, were first proposed in 1963 (Keller in Ulrich, Stachnik, and Mabry, 1966), his first report of its use to have a major impact on higher education was the pivotal paper, "Goodbye teacher . . . " (1968), which appeared in the first volume of the *Journal of Applied Behavior Analysis*.

Keller argued that the goal of education should be for students to learn all that they were capable of learning in a subject area. Conventional grading systems, however, by limiting the time available for a student to study the material, cause fast students to learn a great deal and slow students to learn much less. Keller suggested that time requirements, rather than grades, should be the variable element in higher education. Therefore, he divided his courses up into self-contained segments, or learning modules. The student was required to demonstrate mastery of the content of a particular module, as measured by a quiz, before advancing to the next module. By the end of the course (which occurred at different times for different students), all students had learned the essentials of a subject area. Since a class composed of students studying different segments made conventional lectures impractical, students studied the modular materials while alone or with the aid of tutors. The tutors, usually advanced students, gave module quizzes to those students who felt that they had mastered the content of the module.

Some psychologists have embraced the idea of replacing grades entirely with mastery criteria. Hergenhahn (1976) maintains that students in PSI classes prefer them to conventional lecture classes, and that professors using PSI usually continue to use it. Since, by the definition of mastery criteria, the student must learn the material in one module at the A or B level to progress to the next module, more students master course content in PSI classes. The self-pacing features of PSI, however, can often be detrimental to the work output of students with minimal self-motivation. Often the rate of module completion is very low early in an academic time unit. Bufford (1976) has introduced a bonus system for high rates of module completion early in the semester. He reports 2.4 modules completed per week in the bonus condition and only .96 modules completed during baseline weeks. The author, who has used such a **front-loading** bonus system in several of his partially self-paced contingency-management-based courses, has found this system to be effective in getting students off to a good start in the courses. These systems employ a differential reinforcement of high levels (DRH) schedule in modified form.

Some college administrations have been able to accommodate themselves to the indefinite time limits for course completion that self-pacing imposes. College IV of Grand Valley University in Allendale, Michigan uses only PSI. A professor who taught there for several years has reported to the author overall satisfaction with PSI in comparison to conventional "grade/lecture/fixed time limit" teaching methods. Supervising students who are completing their courses at many different times, however, can be an administrative nightmare. The author's university has a policy of tightly limiting the durations of incompletes; the PSI course in introductory psychology is modified by requiring students to finish within one semester. Because of the scheduling problems that self-pacing creates, most PSI courses reported in the current literature have only limited self-pacing and employ various techniques (such as front loading and the doomsday contingencies previously mentioned in this chapter) to speed up student progress. DuNann and Fernald (1976) used a doomsday contingency and found a significant preference for the PSI approach used in one half of an introductory psychology course to the conventional lecture approach used during the other half. Objective quiz scores were also significantly higher with PSI. The authors followed up student retention of course materials after two years (a noteworthy and rare event in the literature) and found that students with low and medium GPAs retained significantly more of the material learned during the PSI condition (DuNann and Weber, 1976). Students with high GPAs did not benefit from PSI, which is in agreement with Saltz's contention (Chapter 11) that high intelligence is related to the ability to learn under unprogrammed conditions.

Other factors which have worked against incorporation of the PSI concept in most college classrooms include the financial and ethical issues related to using advanced students as tutors and the preference of many students for lectures rather than individualized study. Giving course credit to students for being tutors raises the question of which learning experiences should legitimately count towards a degree. Paying tutors tends to raise the relative cost of PSI courses and reduces administrative enthusiasm. Many students feel entitled to lectures in return for their tuition. Some have told me that if they wanted to read text material on their own, they could have done that at home without the expense and effort of attending college. Keller's vision of the professor as contingency manager rather than teacher would seem most appealing to those professors whose lecture skills give them and their students less than adequate rates of reinforcement.

While neither the fixed academic time unit nor the lecture-and-discussion method of teaching seem likely to vanish, many college classrooms are still slated to experience the machinations of the contingency manager. Keller's pioneering work has opened the way to a variety of increasingly sophisticated applications of contingency management techniques. Miller and Weaver (1976) have progressed beyond the study guides developed by Keller and the PSI movements to programmed workbooks which use discrimination training techniques to teach complex concepts. Using **prompts** (clues) which are gradually faded out, these workbooks are reported to produce superior performance on objective tests compared to the study of conventional textbooks. The fading out of prompts is designed to reduce the aversive effects of mistakes. The idea of teaching by having the learner discriminate relevant from irrelevant examples of the concept (negative information) is derived from the operant model of concept formation.

Keller's use of students to help manage a course has also led to a variety of applications. The author once used volunteer superior students as Behavioral Technicians (Behav-a-Techs) in a project at Occidental College to improve the distribution of comments in discussion groups (Swenson, 1973). Highly vocal students (who were naive to the goals of the Behav-a-Techs) were put on a DRL (differential reinforcements of low levels) schedule, and silent students received social and nonverbal reinforcement (intense attention, smiles) for any comments. The increased rates of participation of the formerly silent students were maintained during the baseline 2 measurement period. The suppression of talking out in the highly verbal students, however, gradually dissipated with the removal of aversive consequences (inattention, foot shuffling, yawns) for talking out more than once per 10-minute time period. Student ratings of their satisfaction with the experimental discussion groups were superior to ratings of control discussion groups.

While the project just discussed was admittedly manipulative, the end result was a freer classroom environment in which control of discussion by a few students was minimized to the benefit of shyer students. The author's bias is that use of the techniques of contingency management in the college classroom is justified if such use is carefully thought out and designed with sensitivity to the needs of students rather than simply the convenience of professors. Explanations to students who have concerns about use of such techniques, of what is being done and why, may not only reduce the aversive qualities of these techniques but may also be a means to teach learning principles.

A well-known college-level application is the "personalized system of instruction" (PSI) approach, which makes grades contingent upon amount learned with unlimited time. Time constraints in many colleges have resulted in modifications, and new techniques, such as rewarding early progress with front-loading bonuses and doomsday (flunking) contingencies for laggards, have been added. Fading out of prompts has also been successful in college-level instructional materials.

Clinical Applications

As we stated in the beginning of this chapter, most applications of operant conditioning techniques in clinical psychology involved the use of token economies with large numbers of institutionalized psychotics. Hall, Baker, and Hutchinson (1977), working with chronic schizophrenic patients, compared two control groups with a token economy group. They found that the token patients decreased their outputs of three types of unwanted behaviors compared to both no-treatment controls and no-token, contingent social reinforcement controls. The patients who were most deteriorated initially were the ones who demonstrated the greatest gains. Some patients, however, increased their emissions of nontarget behaviors, which may demonstrate a paradoxical or behavioral contrast effect. The treatment was continued for 15 months. At the end of that time, the contingent social reinforcement control group had caught up with the token group. Part of the reason the token patients did not maintain their early, most improved status was reported to have been because of the attitudes and expectations of the ward nurses dispensing the tokens. Over time, the extra work entailed in noting behaviors and distributing tokens may have made the response cost of the program too high for the nurses to concentrate on maintaining it.

The maintaining of staff efficiency has been the subject of operant behavioral modification techniques. Iwata and colleagues (1976) conducted two experiments on four units of a residential facility for multiply handicapped retarded persons. Attendants in the experimental condition meeting specific performance criteria became eligible for a lottery. The prize for winning the lottery was the opportunity to choose their days off for the following week. The control condition used specified staff assignments. Attendants participated in both the conditions at different phases of the study. A multiple baseline replication showed that the lottery technique was indeed an effective way to maintain high levels of staff performance.

While the token economy is the most efficient way to modify the behaviors of large numbers of patients, primary reinforcers can be used to good advantage with individual psychotic patients. An unusual aversive reinforcer was employed by Fichter and colleagues (1976), who allowed a chronic schizophrenic patient to escape "nagging" by emission of specified target behaviors (clear speaking and placing arms and elbows on the arm rests of his chair rather than making strange gestures with them). With time, the patient learned to attend to the S_Ds for emission of the target behaviors and so was able to avoid the "nagging" entirely. During baseline 2, the clear-speaking behavior was maintained, but arm and elbow placements were not. This suggests that speaking was an example of functional behavior (behavior which creates its own reinforcements), while arm and elbow placements were maintained only by the experimental contingencies.

Although most applications of operant techniques have been concentrated in institutional settings, the modeling procedure developed by Bandura (Chapter 9) has been found useful by individual mental health workers for treating neurotic or anxious clients. Horne and Matson (1977) compared modeling, desensitization, flooding, study groups, and control groups as procedures to reduce test anxiety in college students. The modeling procedure consisted of listening to tapes of students, who expressed considerable test anxiety in the first tape, and progressively less anxiety in subsequent tapes. On the *Test Anxiety Scale,* it was found that modeling was the most effective technique, followed by desensitization, flooding, study skills, and no treatment. Measures of pulse rate showed desensitization to have produced the lowest pulse rates, and examinations of final course grades found desensitization-group students to do best, followed by modeling-group students, study-skills students, flooding-group students and controls. While these results do not clearly show modeling to be more effective than the techniques of desensitization and flooding derived from classical conditioning, they do suggest that it may be a useful addition to such techniques.

Rosenthal, Hung, and Kelley (1977) compared two types of modeling procedures. They found that when the therapist was "businesslike," as opposed to "warm," the clients were more successful in approaching feared objects and reported less fear. This type of research illustrates the process of examining the details of a procedure in an attempt to determine the most efficient and effective ways to conduct such therapies. This is a necessary and much-neglected step in making the methods of psychological intervention more precise and powerful. The biofeedback procedure, to be reviewed next, has been the subject of such a detailed examination, and this, as we shall see, has resulted in the discarding of naive hopes.

Contingency management approaches have been effective in improving behaviors of both staff and patients in mental institutions. With bright, anxious clients, modeling procedures also work well—especially if the model acts in a businesslike manner.

Biofeedback

David Shapiro, one of the pioneers in the development of biofeedback, defines biofeedback as "the application of operant conditioning methods in the control of visceral somatomotor, or central nervous system functions" (1977, p. 15). The most common procedure is to amplify the weak electrical signals associated with a body function and then to use the amplified signal to drive an auditory or visual display. Because the display tells people when they are succeeding, which most people find reinforcing, the probability of emitting similar (desired) behaviors increases.

As previously discussed, the success of the Russian psychologists in demonstrating that the autonomic nervous system controlling the viscera could be conditioned led to the efforts of Miller and DiCara (1967) to use operant conditioning procedures on behaviors controlled by the autonomic nervous system. Miller's and DiCara's demonstration of the self-regulation of what had been assumed to be automatic processes suggested a wide range of therapeutic applications of the new technologies.

A clear statement of three objectives of biofeedback research relevant to therapists can be found in the 1976–1977 Aldine annual, *Biofeedback and Self-Control*:

1. the determination of the degree to which biofeedback aids in learning increased control of physiological processes in healthy individuals, under a variety of experimental conditions that normally affects such processes (e.g., environmental stress; induced expectations; . . .)

2. the enhancement of the cure, management, or prevention of various psychological and physiological disorders through biofeedback-aided learning, including those disorders presumed to be generated by environmental stresses as well as those created by specific physiological dysfunctions (as exemplified in the cases of epilepsy and stroke)
3. the enhancement of increased awareness . . . [Kamiya et al., 1977, xv–xvi]

The potential importance of the development of behavioral technologies for controlling body states is related to the dramatic shift in disease patterns in Western countries over the past 150 years. While communicable diseases once were the leading causes of sickness, today stress-related and degenerative disorders predominate. Medical practices derived from the medical assumption that sickness is caused by specific agents, such as particular microbes or tumors, have been spectacularly successful against communicable diseases. This crisis-oriented "medical model" has been much less successful against heart diseases, ulcers, arthritis, and other stress-related diseases. Evidence is accumulating that a person's reactions to stress may be the most critical factor in these disorders. Holmes and Rahe (1967) have collected data which suggests that stress-provoking life changes are more related to a wide range of illnesses (including colds and tuberculosis) than traditional causes, such as chilling and exposure to germs. Because a person's pattern of responding to stress on a physiological level can be altered through biofeedback training, such training may become increasingly important in maintaining or regaining health. As we shall see, however, many problems still must be solved before biofeedback can reach its full potential as a means for coping with stress and hence maintaining health.

Some of the issues and problems that must be dealt with before biofeedback techniques become adequate to reduce significantly the incidence of stress-related diseases have been reviewed by Shapiro (1977) in his presidential address to the Society for Psychological Research. These include: (1) the extent to which nonbiofeedback self-control procedures such as meditation can supplement biofeedback or replace it, (2) the effects of instructions and other cognitive elements in determining the success of biofeedback procedures, (3) the maintenance of the changed behavior under stress and outside of the biofeedback training area, and (4) which techniques are effective and which are of minimal effectiveness.

Woolfolk and colleagues (1976) found meditation to be equal to progressive (Jacobson) relaxation and both to be superior to no treatment in treating insomnia. Harris and colleagues (1976) found that learning of breathing exercises (placed respiration) reduced autonomic reactivity to real and anticipated aversive events. Attention to and control of breathing is an important part of many types of meditative exercises, including Zazen (Zen) meditation. Schandler and Grings (1976) found both progressive relaxation and tactile feedback (vibrating stimulus) to be superior to the more normally employed visual or auditory feedback modes for reducing the electromyographic (EMG or electrical muscle potential) response to stress. These results suggest that further refinement of biofeedback technology is needed before it can be considered clearly superior to equipmentless methods for the treatment of general tension.

The research on the effects of instructions further shows the extent to which factors other than biofeedback can alter physiological functioning. These effects can be fairly complex. Shapiro (1977) reported that subjects instructed to alter palmar (hand) sweating were unable to do so. When they were instructed to increase heart rate, however, not only were they able to achieve as much control as subjects given feedback, but their palmar sweating also changed in consistent directions! Bouchard and Granger (1977) have reported similar results for heart rate slowing. They found no difference between subjects given instructions alone and subjects experiencing instructions in combination with feedback.

Feedback may be superfluous in control of heart rate, but the same does not seem true for blood pressure. Subjects given feedback without instructions to control blood pressure were much less effective in increasing blood pressure than subjects given instructions and feedback, but the two groups did not differ in their abilities to reduce blood pressure. Subjects given only instructions were inferior in their ability to increase blood pressure but equal in their abilities to decrease mean systolic pressure. These results both show that cognitive-verbal variables may operate to different extents with different physiological measures, and that biofeedback is not just an automatic, mechanical conditioning process.

One of the most important questions in biofeedback is the extent to which the newly trained "relaxation-related" responses can be maintained under stressful conditions. One of the early physiological responses to be modified was the EEG (electroencephalography) or brain wave response. It was found that most persons could learn to produce more alpha rhythms (8–13 Hz waves) if they were given feedback when producing such waves and that they reported feeling tranquil when producing them. Kamiya and colleagues (1977) have noted, however, that alpha may be controlled more by such factors as not looking for afterimages with closed eyes than by the electronic feedback. This suggests that producing alpha is not much different from just trying to feel relaxed. Moreover, Chisholm, DeGood, and Hartz (1977) examined subjects' abilities to stay relaxed during aversive (shock) situations in their laboratory after alpha biofeedback training. They found that although many participants could continue to produce alpha rhythms during the stress sessions, the heart rates of these participants were elevated and they reported themselves as being as tense as control subjects.

Another physiological response that has been extensively investigated in the hope of producing long-lasting relaxation states is the EMG or electromyographic response. The EMG is a measure of a muscle's readiness to constrict, and it was hoped that by reducing muscle arousal, tension (muscle tightness) headaches and general feelings of tenseness could be alleviated. Recording electrodes are usually placed over the frontalis muscle of the forehead. The frontalis has been shown to produce tension headaches when overcontracted (Epstein and Abel, 1977). However, Epstein and Abel (1977) reported that while increased EMGs in the frontalis muscle were related to increased reports of headaches, successful decreases in EMGs were often not related to decreases in headaches. Strangely enough, three of the six patients had less headaches following the biofeedback treatments and maintained these gains after 18 months. When the EMGs of the biofeedback patients were checked several months after their training, no evidence of continued self-control of muscle activity was found. Therefore, the improvements of the three patients may represent placebo effects. A placebo is an inert substance or control treatment given to subjects to make them think that they are getting treatment. Further evidence that frontalis EMG biofeedback is ineffectual in producing generalized states of relaxation has been provided by Shedivy and Kleinman (1977). They found that biofeedback-produced reductions of EMG intensity of the frontalis muscle did not generalize to EMG reductions in other muscle groups. Chesney and Shelton (1976) have even reported EMG biofeedback to be less effective than Jacobson relaxation exercises.

If both alpha and EMG biofeedback have failed to live up to the early hopes of biofeedback enthusiasts, is there any biofeedback procedure useful in producing lasting resistance to stress effects in the outside environment? Hutchings and Reinking (1976) have reported that EMG biofeedback in combination with Jacobson progressive relaxation exercises or with autogenic training (practicing feeling the hands as heavy and warm) works better than relaxation exercises used alone. Training in reducing blood pressure of essential hypertensive clients has been reported not only to result in continued lower blood pressure under stress in and out of the laboratory but also to have been related to better performance on the category test which measures cognitive functioning (Kleinman and colleagues, 1977). Shapiro (1977) has suggested combining biofeedback with systematic desensitization of probable stress-arousing situations and stimuli. He advocates having feedback training carried out in stimulating or stressful laboratory conditions to prepare the person for dealing with a stimulating and stressful outside environment. He reports success in using such an approach with the heart rate response. Many of his subjects actually learned to reduce their heart rates when anticipating and experiencing shock! To conclude this discussion of the effectiveness of biofeedback procedures in dealing with stressful situations, it seems that some treatments that were favored early in the history of biofeedback, such as alpha wave training and frontalis EMG training, do not produce sufficient lasting benefits, used alone, to justify their continued clinical use. Still being investigated are combinations of EMG training with other relaxation procedures and training of the cardiovascular responses (heart rate and blood pressure).

As the search for procedures related to general resistance to stress and tension continues, much of the most exciting research in biofeedback involves changing more specific responses. Whitehead, Renault, and Goldiamond (1975) were able to train four normal women to control their rates of stomach gastric acid secretion with combinations of visual feedback and money. When money was made contingent upon increased secretion in a differential reinforcement of high rates (DRH) schedule, secretions increased to three times that of the base rates. When the scheduling was changed to a differential reinforcement of other behaviors (DRO) schedule, secretion rates returned to baseline levels. It is of interest that other physiological parameters, such as increased EMGs, respiration rates, and heart rates, did not always change in a systematic relationship to secretion rates. As in many other studies, subjects differed in their abilities to control the selected response through biofeedback. These procedures may some day lead to biofeedback treatments for peptic and gastric ulcers.

Not only the classic psychosomatic illnesses, such as ulcers, are related to stress. The incidence of epileptic seizures is also stress related (Small, 1973). Lubar and Bahler (1976) used biofeedback to train eight severely epileptic patients to increase their output of 12–14 Hz EEG sensorimotor rhythms. This sensorimotor rhythm (SMR) is produced from the sensory-motor or central fissure area of the cerebral cortex and is assumed to inhibit motor activity. It was expected that increased SMR would inhibit the motor activity causing convulsions as well as seizures in general. Patients were also trained to inhibit theta (4–7 Hz) and epileptiform spike activity. Training consisted of three 40-minute sessions per week. Baseline measures were collected, and the half of the cortex whose output was to trigger feedback was alternated to let the EEG of the other hemisphere serve as a "within-subject control." Two patients became free of seizures for months at a time, and most of the other patients had reduced seizure incidents and reduced need for anticonvulsant medication. When patients left training to go on vacation, the numbers of reported seizures gradually increased. The authors noted that switching to noncontingent (pseudofeedback) reinforcement also led to an increase in seizures. These results suggest that biofeedback is a useful supplement to medication, especially for epilepsies with motor involvements. Just as in most behavioral modification applications, however, the gains extinguish when the program is suspended. To be fair, the muscle tone acquired through exercise also "extinguishes" when a college professor or student becomes excessively deskbound and "suspends his exercise program." The hope of finding extinction-free therapeutic methods may be a holdover from beliefs in the medical model, which assume that there exists a specific cause for each disease and that removal of this cause cures the patient.

One way to make sense of the varying effectiveness of different biofeedback methods with different stress-related disorders is to assume that the more "new" information the feedback provides to the user, the more likely the training is to be effective. Since the average person has considerable information about his general states of relaxation, simple procedures for increasing relaxation through biofeedback have been of limited effectiveness. Most ulcer or epileptic patients, however, would be assumed to be unable to discriminate physiological changes related to gastric acid secretion or output levels of sensorimotor EEG rhythms. Hence, biofeedback training would be expected to be most beneficial with such patients.

Many responses, however, are discriminable by some individuals and not by others. Kaplan (1975) has suggested that males who suffer from premature ejaculation during sexual intercourse do so because they are unable to discriminate accurately the subtle cues which distinguish the stage of sexual arousal (plateau stage) from the stage of "ejaculatory inevitability." Support for this theory has come from the work of Rosen, Shapiro, and Schwarz (1975) and Kantorowitz (1977) who succeeded in treating premature ejaculation by providing precise feedback on penile diameter, which is closely correlated to the level of sexual arousal. When provided with feedback, most subjects were able to learn to maintain arousal at the plateau stage for as long as desired. Like many sexual difficulties, this type of dysfunction may not only be caused by stress but may also precipitate additional stress in the sufferer and his cosufferers.

As the work of Rosen and colleagues (1975) and Kantorowitz (1977) demonstrates, the range of applications of operant control of internal states is wide, indeed. Sakai and Hartey (1973) were able to train male subjects first to raise their finger temperatures and later to raise the temperatures of their scrotums (testicles). In three of the five subjects, the resulting temperature rise was sufficient to kill all sperm. This experiment suggests the possibility of developing behavioral methods of birth control. (It would, of course, be essential for the male not to become slack about his daily temperature biofeedback exercises.) Recently, EMG biofeedback has been extended into the traditional medical areas of deficient neuromuscular control. Inglis, Campbell, and Donald (1976) have reviewed applications of EMG biofeedback in treating peripheral nerve muscle damage, the effects of strokes (which kill brain cells by depriving them of food and oxygen), partial paralyses, and cerebral palsy (early brain damage having a motor component). Noting that adequate control procedures to check for placebo effects are rare, they cite considerable evidence to suggest that patients can learn to gain more control over the involuntary activity of voluntary muscles. This **neuromuscular reeducation** approach has been successful in restoring function to paralyzed limbs where some neural control remains or where neural control has been reintroduced through transplanting intact nerves which had formerly controlled other muscles. Many patients were able to produce some motor unit action potentials in muscles which could not be contracted on a voluntary basis. Within a couple of hours, those patients who had at least a few intact nerve endings were producing sufficient motor unit action potentials from these surviving nerve endings to achieve large percentages of normal, voluntary muscle functioning. The various studies reported percentages of patients who benefited from such treatments from about 50 percent to over 85 percent. The basic technique also works for spastic or overconstricted muscles. Haggerty (1977) has reported on the development of miniature sensortransmitter units (disguised as ladybugs) which can be left affixed on the legs of children with cerebral palsy and send wireless data about the levels of muscle activity for prolonged time periods. This technology, which is a spinoff from the space program's need for continuous biotelemetry, could provide a means for continuous biofeedback during normal activities. This would be of special benefit in increasing the effectiveness and practicality of long-term biofeedback treatment for epilepsy and neuromuscular disorders.

Not all the possible applications of biofeedback involve treating pathological conditions. The techniques have also given rise to the dream of increasing man's abilities and altering his/her consciousness in beneficial ways. Sheer (1977) has reported that the 40-Hz fast-wave component of the EEG spectrum is related to memory consolidation. He has also reported that this response can be increased through biofeedback, opening the possibility of increasing the ability to memorize. Ormund, Quintanella, and Swenson (1978) found that while male college students initially produced higher average levels of fast-wave EEG (which is presumed to be related to active cognitive functioning), after biofeedback the female subjects were producing such waves at the highest level.

To summarize, although many of the earlier hopes for successful application of biofeedback have not been realized, the field is still developing and new and more sophisticated procedures are being developed. In addition, current research makes clear that even procedures developed from the operant or Skinnerian tradition are strongly modified by cognitive variables, although the extent to which such variables interact with the conditioning variables is not the same for all physiological measures. This advances the development of unitheory by increasing our understanding of how cognitive and connectionist factors influence each other and the types of situations in which one or the other is most important. The common observation that different persons respond to training procedures in different ways may advance our knowledge of how physiological and constitutional variables interact with learning variables.

For the future, we may expect further sophisticated use of more operant principles. The use of complex schedules by Whitehead and colleagues (1975) may be an early example of this tendency. Standard biofeedback practices will be combined with other behavioral modification techniques, including those derived from Pavlovian principles, and this may help increase our understanding of the relationship between association learning and reinforcement learning. Because of the potential for therapeutic benefit, there will be strong incentives for the development of sophisticated biofeedback devices that can be worn comfortably for long periods of time. As in the device developed from space-program biotelemetry equipment described earlier, the new devices will be in radio contact with their controlling computers and feedback displays (which might be skin vibrations). This will eliminate the wires which today clutter up biofeedback clinics and laboratories and interfere with subjects' movements. As small computers become less expensive, more work will be done on modifying patterns of several physiological processes at one time, which will be a closer analogy to our natural reactions to stress and stressors. This may eliminate the problems of lack of generalizability from laboratory to the outside world encountered in much brain wave and EMG research. As the field matures, the uncritically enthusiastic and simplistic views of biofeedback will gradually be discarded, to be replaced by real and reproducibly durable results that may nonetheless be significant and dramatic.

Biofeedback refers to providing a person with electronically amplified information about changes in physiological responses, such as blood pressure or brain waves, to allow the person to exercise voluntary control of the response. Since such control is assumed to be reinforcing, this demonstrates operant learning of inner responses. Biofeedback, which may be influenced by cognitive variables such as instructional set, has not been found to be more effective than relaxation techniques for relief of stress. It seems most beneficial when natural feedback is minimal.

Chapter Perspective

Out of the unlikely womb of the Skinner box has come a rich plethora of ways to put psychology to work in the "real" (that is, everywhere but on college campuses) world. Because the traditions of the laboratory include observance of methodological considerations which provide a basis for critical evaluations of methods, and because operant theory is straightforward enough to be reduced to formulas comprehensible to those who would develop and use applications, the methods have been widely tested. Through this testing, these methods seem to be evolving towards greater effectiveness.

Yet, ironically, for all the inventiveness of the ever-increasing hoards of operant applicators, the net effect of these applications has been to call into question the basic mechanistic assumptions of the connectionist approach to learning. The renewed legitimacy of cognitive variables bears witness to this fact. We are now faced with the paradox that the critical debate over the processes involved in classical and instrumental conditioning, together with the continued demonstrations of the success of applying operant principles, suggests that we are becoming more and more successful in using tools whose mechanisms we understand less and less. Since connectionist theory seems to be evolving towards the cognitive viewpoint, let us now examine what that cognitive viewpoint is today.

Key Terms

accountability

backup system

baselines 1 and 2

behavioral objectives

charting

change agent

consequation

contingency management

double blind

focal individual method

front loading

full-session DRL method

functional behavior

interval method

multiple baseline

neuromuscular reeducation

observation

operational definition

personalized system of instruction (PSI)

prompt

response cost

reversal design

spaced responding DRL method

specification

time sampling

token cost

triadic model

Annotated Bibliography

Because of the vast number of available sources on operant applications of learning theory, I will only recommend one book; R. Mallot, *Contingency management in education; Or I've got blisters on my soul and other equally exciting places*, rev. ed. (Kalamazoo, Mi.: Behaviordelia, 1974). This text is partly a comic book with programmed learning materials and much more. The best way to get primary access to the literature would be to scan recent issues of the following journals: (1) *Journal of Applied Behavior Analysis*, with applications to education, industry, personal habits, corrective institutions, and miscellaneous social institutions, (2) *Behavior Research and Therapy*, or *BRAT*, which focuses on clinical applications, as do (3) *Behavior Therapy*, and (4) *Journal of Behavior Therapy and Experimental Psychiatry*; for those interested in biofeedback, I strongly recommend (5) *Psychophysiology*. (Another good guide to current trends in biofeedback is the Aldine annual publication, *Biofeedback and self-control*.)

APPENDIX TO CHAPTER 10

Timing Tape Techniques for Use in Observing Behaviors

To make a timing tape to tell you when to observe behavior on a variable interval schedule, first select some reasonable length of time, such as 10 minutes, as your mean time interval. Then print a series of numbers beginning 50 percent below your mean or defining number and continuing up to 50 percent above that number. In the following 10-minute example, you would print the numbers 5 through 15 on slips of paper. Place the numbers in a container and write each number as you draw it. Replace each number before drawing the next number. Continue until the sum of the numbers (or minutes) adds up to the total time allowed for observations. You will now need a cassette recorder and a watch. Looking at your list of numbers and the watch, say, "Begin," into the microphone of the recorder (which should be recording), and time the interval of the first number on your list. When the minutes elapsed match the first number (as 6 minutes for the number 6), say, "Observe," into your microphone. Then time the interval of the second number on your list, again saying, "Observe," at the end of the interval. Continue until you have timed intervals corresponding to all the numbers on the list. A long-playing cassette used on both sides will record 2 hours of this variable interval schedule. This timing tape technique can also be used for fixed interval schedules. In this case, simply say, "Observe," at intervals corresponding to your defining number (such as 5-minute intervals for FI-5' schedule).

11

Modern Theories with a Cognitive Emphasis

The cognitive approaches we will examine in this chapter deal with the formation of concepts and how these concepts change with increasing maturity, the processes of language and memory, and selective factors in paying attention. In many ways, these topics seem both more complicated and more focused on human behavior than those of the connectionist approaches previously discussed.

As we saw in Chapters 8 and 9, many connectionist theorists have suggested modifying traditional approaches to understanding conditioning by incorporating cognitive and biological variables. The four viewpoints we will review in this chapter represent different types of cognitive approaches in a purer form. The last three of these approaches, which incorporate biological variables, are similar in some ways to recent views of instrumental learning and classical conditioning. The four viewpoints represent the following branches of the cognitive approach: (1) concept formation and verbal learning (Saltz), (2) psycholinguistics (Chomsky), (3) developmental-cognitive (Piaget), and (4) information processing (Norman).

The first section of this chapter is organized around the concept-learning theory of Eli Saltz, which represents a trend towards assimilating some aspects of behaviorism with the type of cognitive theories discussed in Chapter 5. In its eclecticism and its concentration on verbal learning, this approach is indebted to the functionalist tradition. Saltz and the other concept-learning researchers reviewed in this section are products of the American experimentalist-environmentalist bias, much as Tolman was. Their attempts to explore the interrelationships of conditioning and cognitive learning are representative of modern learning theory's "middle ground."

It is instructive to compare Saltz, who identifies himself as a cognitive theorist, with Bandura, who identifies himself as a behaviorist (and who also represents the trend towards convergence of the cognitive and behavioristic viewpoints). Bandura incorporates many cognitive variables in his theory but avoids detailed descriptions of cognitive entities. Saltz is less timid in speculating about events presumed to be happening within the heads of his subjects.

The second theoretical viewpoint, by Chomsky, also strongly rejects stimulus-response explanations of learning. He sees no need, however, to make any explorations of conditioning nor to concede any points to behaviorism.

While Saltz focuses on human verbal learning, Chomsky's system deals with linguistic (language) behavior in general and with the implications of how humans structure their communications. Like Saltz, Chomsky speculates about the structure of cognitions. Unlike Saltz, Chomsky postulates that innate and universal mechanisms determine what is to be learned and how it will be expressed. He also relates learning and behavior to the biological principle of adaptation to the environment. Chomsky has played a key role in the evolution of learning theories as the critic who focuses attention on the presumed weaknesses in the Skinnerian attempt to extend traditional S-R connectionist principles to the acquisition of language. While his academic background is in psycholinguistics rather than learning theory, his pungent (if difficult to understand) writing has served as a rallying point for cognitive theorists in their opposition to the Skinnerians.

The third theory is that of the Swiss Jean Piaget, who is also not a psychologist by training. With a Ph.D. in biology, he retained his biologist's interest in adaptive processes when he began to watch his own children. From these observations, he developed a theory that relegitimized **structuralist** and maturational variables in psychology. Because of his emphasis on developmental and maturational variables, his theory was first introduced to American psychology students as a developmental theory. It is, however, a true theory of learning which suggests that different laws of learning may apply at different maturational stages.

In its emphasis on maturation, Piaget's theory represents an extension and refinement of Maria Montessori's focus on maturational variables. In its concern with the anatomy of thinking, or cognitive structures, Piaget's theory is also structuralism, in the mode of Titchener, Lewin, Chomsky, and, to a lesser extent, Saltz. Recently, the importance of his theory to the field of learning has become increasingly recognized. When the author began work on this text in 1974, no major textbook on learning contained a chapter on Piaget. Since that time, several texts (Hilgard and Bower, 1975; Hill, 1977) have done so.

The fourth theory, by Donald Norman, represents the information-processing view of learning. Perhaps because of the identification of this view with the concepts and jargon of the rapidly advancing field of computer technology, it has become increasingly influential in recent years. While Norman sees learning as involving active internal processes (as do the other cognitive theories reviewed in this book), he explains these processes in mechanistic terms. For example, plans and strategies for learning are viewed as similar to the programs which control the operations of computers. The information-processing approach is also distinguished by its emphasis on learning as a multistage process. Selective attention is the first stage followed by several memory stages and a continuing process of incorporating learned material into existing concepts; retrieval mechanisms are the last stage.

In reading the material in this chapter, you should note the ways in which these theories differ and resemble one another. You should become familiar with major terms in the jargons of each theory and see how a term used to describe a given concept may have the same meaning as a different term used by another of these theorists to describe the same concept. Try to follow the sequence in which these theories are presented in terms of more and more incorporation of biological variables. Finally, relate each of these approaches to earlier related theories—Saltz to functionalism and Tolman; Chomsky to gestalt; Piaget to Montessori; and Norman to the short section on cybernetics in Chapter 5. Seeing the relationships among the theories presented in this chapter and previous material will aid you in understanding and learning the frameworks of these theories. Let us begin with the theory (Saltz) most related to the mainstream of academic learning psychology.

Concept-Learning Theories and the Concept-Growth Model of Eli Saltz

One characteristic shared by most connectionist theories of learning as well as by behavioristic-cognitive theories (Tolman, Bandura) is that basic laws of learning govern the behavior of all higher animals. Behaviorists' formulations of such laws were often based on animal research because the environments of animals could be precisely controlled. This allowed manipulation of selected independent variables with a minimum of interference from extraneous variables. It is true that some connectionist theorists maintained that higher organisms (including humans) might also show learning reflective of more complex processes than those presumed to account for conditioning. These theorists, however, assumed that an extensive knowledge of the laws of conditioning was necessary before complex learning could be understood. From this viewpoint, animal studies were seen as providing simple models or analogs of the basic processes of all learning which would provide the data base from which to derive the laws of complex learning. Saltz (1971) has launched a vigorous attack on this approach to understanding learning of either the conditioning or complex types.

Concepts as the Basic Unit of Learning

First, Saltz would agree with many of the researchers (Rescorla, Timberlake and Allison, and others) reviewed in Chapters 8 and 9 that the processes responsible for "simple" conditioning of either the instrumental/operant or the classical conditioning type are probably not what was once thought. In fact, they may be more complex.

Second, Saltz rejects a literal interpretation of the Pavlovian and American strict connectionist view of language as a series of internal verbal stimuli followed by internal or external verbal responses.* Defining some words as stimuli (the first word of the pair in paired-associate learning) and other words as responses (the second word of the pair) fails to predict the results of many paired-associate studies (such as those reported by Houston, 1964, and Asch, 1968) which show that either word of a pair can be given as a response to the other word. Since backward conditioning in the classical conditioning paradigm is thought to be weak or nonexistent, the demonstrations of backward associa-

---

* It must be noted that Skinner also rejects the literal stimulus-response interpretation of verbal behavior.

tions (finding that a subject given the second "US or response" word of a pair can produce the first "CS or stimulus" word) in paired-associate learning would suggest that the laws of classical conditioning do not apply to paired-associate learning. Horton and Turnage (1976) reviewed the paired-associate learning research and concluded that although backward associations are commonly reported, many studies have found such associations to be weaker than forward associations (subjects found it easier to recall the second word after presentation of the first word than the other way around). It could be suggested that the evidence for asymmetry (the second word is not as effective a stimulus as the first word) in paired-associate learning results from the fact that the relatively strong backward conditioning of the first word to the second word is weaker than the forward conditioning of the second (US or response word) to the first (CS or stimulus) word. In any case, since the classical conditioning literature provides little basis for strong backward conditioning, the view of Saltz (1971) and Asch (1968) that stimulus-response conceptions of associative learning should be abandoned in favor of seeing both words as associated with a central process or concept seems credible.

Following his review of the inadequacies of the classical conditioning paradigm in predicting the results of paired-associate learning, Saltz (1971) suggests that the common practice of beginning the study of learning with conditioning and later attempting to discuss concept formation in terms of conditioning should be reversed. His reasoning goes as follows:

> Conceptual behavior displays in a fairly clear manner the complex organization of psychological variables which is often only obliquely intersected by simpler learning situations. Thus, while this organization of variables is crucial to the simpler learning situations, these simpler learning situations may not be optimal instruments for discovering the structure of intellectual processes. [Saltz, 1971, p. 30]

Thus, for Saltz, the basic unit of learning is a concept rather than an S-R bond. Because of this emphasis, he spent considerable time developing his definition of a concept. Concepts are defined as "bounded sets of attributes." **Attributes** are discriminable stimulus characteristics of the external and internal environments experienced by the organism. Qualities such as "red" and "round" are examples of attributes. **Boundedness** is an organizational variable (like the gestalt laws) and is determined by the personal and cultural history of the human subject. This variable, which determines how we tend to group attributes within specific concepts, is related to Lewin's concept of boundaries as isolating regions of our life spaces.

The results of bounding attributes differ from individual to individual.

> A particular set of attributes may be organized by a person (or culture) as a concept so that certain instances which appear to possess these attributes can be reacted to in a similar manner. If someone cuts the attribute pie differently, he may emerge with a different set of concepts. In this sense, one concept is as "true" as another. [Saltz, 1971, p. 31]

Examples of the relative nature of concepts include the ways different languages label groups of things. In Mandarin Chinese, there is one word for wet fruits and wet nuts (as coconuts) and a different word for dry fruits and nuts. Within each group, no differentiation is made between what we call nuts and fruit (Saltz, 1971).

Because concepts represent the rules by which we divide up reality, they have implications for predicting behavior, much like the regions of Lewin's theory (at least once the observer knows what the concepts or regions are). Concepts reflect the internal units or values of the sets of **dimensions,** or continuums, to which the person pays attention. Examples of dimensions would include color, size, and interpretations of behavior (such as friendly or hostile). The dimensions we focus on in trying to decide which of our existing concepts best fits a given situation, in turn, determine how we are likely to act or the rules and strategies we will employ in deciding what responses to make in that situation. The attributes, or specific stimuli making up a dimension, may be either simple cues (such as a red light) or complex concepts in their own right. An example of an attribute that is a complex concept would be "father," as the type of person having the attributes of being male and a parent. Whatever the level of complexity of the attributes, concepts are viewed by Saltz as reflecting bounded regions in the person's cognitive space which the person reacts to as distinct entities. This neo-Lewinian definition of concept led Saltz in turn to define concept learning as the associating and bounding (seeing all attributes as part of that concept) of the set of attributes. Thus, concept learning is the assembling of attributes into a cognitive unit, or getting "the idea" that attributes belong together.

These definitions classify Saltz's theory as a pure cognitive learning theory. Not only is the unit of learning molar and cognitive (as it was for Tolman), but the method of assimilating new information is nonmechanical and nonconnectionist. This is similar to Piaget's approach, as we shall see, and opposed to the connectionists' (including Bandura and the social learning theorists) explanations of concept learning. According to the Skinnerian connectionists, concept formation is the end result of reinforcement of common or similar responses to dissimilar stimuli. Saltz, like most concept-learning theorists of the cognitive camp, totally rejects the behavioristic view that internal events involved in learning concepts follow the same rules as observable responses. Since the behaviorists' **common response,** or discrimination, **model** of concept formation so well illustrates the critical differences in the ways cognitive and connectionist theorists attempt to explain the same type of complex learning, we will now examine the common response theory and critical evidence related to it.

The two words of a pair in paired-associate learning have both stimulus and response properties and are associable in both forward and backward directions. This phenomenon has led Saltz to propose explaining conditioning phenomena in terms of concept-learning principles. Concepts are bounded (associated) sets of attributes (cues or simpler concepts) which are seen as having some qualities in common.

The Common Response Model of Concept Learning and Saltz's Critique

In the behaviorist (including social learning) view, concept learning is seen as a complex form of discrimination learning that can be explained in terms of connectionist principles. This continuity (as opposed to insight, or strategy-based noncontinuity) model assumes that a subject learns a concept by emitting the critical response to successive stimuli, sometimes correctly and sometimes incorrectly. Eventually, he learns to restrict the response to only the correct (reinforced) set of stimuli. As in other forms of discrimination learning, the role of disconfirming instances (errors, nonreinforced responses) is seen as vital by most connectionists (you may wish to review the discussion on this topic presented in Chapter 9). Most connectionist theorists assume that errors either function to extinguish the tendency to generalize responses to incorrect stimuli or result in the incorrect stimuli's becoming CSs (inhibitory stimuli) or $S_\Delta s$ (cues signaling the probable nonoccurrence of reinforcement). Since the discrimination/common response model of concept formation treats concept formation as a complex trial-and-error situation, laboratory tests are usually designed to make errors likely.

Saltz (1971) has listed three critical issues related to the behavioristic approach to concept formation which require experimental resolution: (1) how the type of "instructional set" produced by the experimental situation and the intelligence and/or maturity of the subjects relates to concept learning, (2) the degree to which reinforcement automatically leads to selection of the reinforced stimuli as opposed to the importance of awareness of the contingencies, and (3) the role of errors, or information about which stimuli do not fit within a concept (negative information). Let us now review research related to each of these issues in turn.

Strategies used by subjects as a function of experimental situations and other variables   Saltz and Hamilton (1969) found that in an experimental situation which forced the subjects to use trial-and-error concept-learning procedures, children with IQs of around 80 made no more errors on the average than children with IQs averaging 130. This suggested that tasks of the trial-and-error type force all subjects to behave in a mechanistic way. Performance of this type was found to have little relationship to other indicators of intelligent behavior (such as the subjects' IQ scores). Hence, evidence of concept learning by trial and error in a restricted laboratory setting may reflect the restrictions more than the normal hypothesis-testing behaviors of unrestricted subjects. Saltz's and Hamilton's subjects learning the trial-and-error concept-formation task showed mastery of the problem on one particular trial. This appears to contradict the common behaviorist assumption that learning is the result of the gradual strengthening of a bond (the continuity position). Because different children achieved this mastery at different times, however, the group curves showed what appeared to be a gradual increment in correct solutions over trials, which could have been misinterpreted as supporting the continuity position.

The strategies, or types of learning, of human subjects have also been shown to be a function of maturational level. Kendler and Kendler (1975) have reviewed the results of their experiments using the reversal/nonreversal shift procedure. A reversal shift is a switch to an opposite choice following nonreinforcement of a choice that had formerly been rewarded. This tendency, which develops after experiences with multiple reversals, is representative of a learning set of the type presented in Chapter 7 in the discussion of Harlow's research. As such, it shows noncontinuous or apparently "insightful" learning as opposed to associational or continuous learning. In the Kendler paradigm, reversal shifts required changing four associations of compound stimuli; nonreversal shifts required changing only two S-R associations. Therefore, S-R continuity theory would predict, nonreversal shifts should be easier. Cognitive theories, in contrast, would assume that the subjects had learned a rule which mediated between stimulus and response and that this rule would allow quick changes of responses over cue dimensions (reversal shifts). The Kendlers found that college students and children over the age of five found reversal shifts easier, and younger children and laboratory animals found nonreversal shifts easier. These results fit with Luria's observations (Chapter 8) that younger children's learning is more controlled by first signal system (environmental) cues and older children's learning is based more on internal second signal system (semantic or meaning) variables. Based on ideas such as these, Saltz has concluded that concept learning may occur in ways predicted by the common response, or behaviorist, model when the environment is restricted to promote trial-and-error learning or when the subject's maturational level or intelligence level precludes a more internal, cognitive type of concept learning. In older intelligent humans functioning naturally, however, concept formation is best described in noncontinuous hypothesis-testing terms.

The role of awareness in learning   Saltz's second critical issue—the roles of reinforcement and/or awareness—caused him to review Tolman's latent learning studies. Saltz concluded that neither reinforcement nor awareness is necessary for learning. Studies of concept attainment of the verbal learning type (such as guessing which class of words will be followed by reinforcement) have, for the most part, shown that awareness of reinforcement contingencies is necessary for an increase in operant rate of the selected words. These studies, however, did not disprove the theory that the gradual acquisition of learning (versus performance) could occur as a function of reinforcement, even without awareness of the contingencies. Silver (1967) found that by using procedures designed to minimize hypothesis testing in college students, the reinforced learning of a preference for a particular tense in conversation could be increased without the subjects' reporting awareness of their changed response patterns. After further studies, Silver, Saltz, and Modigliani (1970) concluded that learning with awareness, or by awareness, is maximized by experimental procedures promoting hypothesis testing, and that learning as an unconscious result of the effects of reinforcement is maximized by experimental procedures of the trial-and-error type. Given Saltz's and Hamilton's (1969) results showing that reinforcement-dependent learning of concepts does not correlate with IQ, it may be that non-aware learning reflects a more primitive process not representative of intelligent human behavior. In addition, Saltz and colleagues (1970) suggest that intelligent, hypothesis-testing approaches to **concept attainment** may actively interfere with the effects of "subconscious" reinforcement.

Evidence presented in Chapter 8, however, showed that awareness is an essential precondition for most types of human classical conditioning (Biferno and Dawson, 1977, 1978). Levine (1971) has demonstrated that when subjects sampled from a set of incorrect hypotheses (controlled by the experimenter), no automatic response strengthening was found, in spite of ideal conditions for reinforcement to strengthen bonds automatically. We might conclude that the balance of current evidence would seem to support the view that awareness is involved in most kinds of human learning, although unaware learning may occur in a few circumstances. Unaware learning is the type predicted by the common response model.

The role of errors in learning   Positions on the role of errors in learning do not divide on strict cognitive versus connectionist lines. Bower and Trabasso (1963), all-or-none (noncontinuity) theorists, have presented data supporting their position that learning occurs only after errors. As we saw in Chapter 9, however, Terrace (who is a connectionist) has developed a discrimination-training method (fading) in which the subject may never make responses to the incorrect cues and hence may never experience nonreinforced trials—and yet learning occurs. Freibergs and Tulvig (1961) found that human subjects first entering the laboratory had difficulty in processing negative information, or information resulting from incorrect choices. With time, as well as practice with 20 different problems, the subjects steadily gained in their ability to use information from their errors. Saltz (1971) suggests that studies showing negative inputs to be crucial reflect methodological artifacts. Further, he concludes, the fact that the subjects in Freibergs's and Tulvig's study were initially so poor in using negative information suggests that they had not had much practice using this information in the outside world. That their difficulties were not caused by the difficulty of using negative information was shown by their rapid learning of how to use this information. Therefore, the results of various laboratory studies (such as those performed by Bower and Trabasso) showing learning from errors to be an essential part of concept (and other) learning reflected the peculiar effects of those laboratory procedures. Saltz interprets this to suggest that natural concept learning is not a trial-and-error discriminative task in which nonreinforcement of incorrect responses weakens tendencies to respond to irrelevant attributes. Therefore, while Saltz admits that subjects may use negative information in the laboratory or show trial-and-error learning in such restricted environments, this does not mean that such demonstrations predict how subjects will learn concepts in the outside world. Even in the laboratory, subjects do not learn only on error trials. Levine (1966), while finding that most subjects focus on incorrect responses, reported data that seems to show that learning occurred on both error and correct trials in a hypothesis-testing task. Suppes and Schlag-Rey (1965), measuring changes in verbal classification hypotheses after correct and error trials, found changes in classifications to occur almost as often after correct responses as after errors. Hence, these results seem to support Saltz to the extent of showing that errors are not essential to concept learning, but they fail to support his contention that subjects always have initial difficulties with processing negative information.

The common response (behaviorist or continuity) model of concept formation states that concept learning is a matter of complex, unaware, trial-and-error learning in which nonreinforced errors are important. This model seems to predict best with young children and animals. Laboratory conditions may artificially increase use of information from errors, unaware learning, and use of trial-and-error strategies, which are linked to the continuity model.

Types of Concepts and Strategies for Assigning Attributes to Concepts

Saltz, like many other modern cognitive learning theorists, has described the characteristics of concepts in profuse detail. Further, he divides concepts into four basic types. Although the way each type is formed varies, all share the property that each defining attribute elicits the entire response associated with that concept.

1. A **simple concept** is a concept operationally defined by only one attribute, such as the concept "red." Apples, barns, and communists would all elicit the concept response. These concepts are tightly "bound"; once a subject identifies the concept, accuracy is very high.

2. A **conjunctive concept** is a relational concept; that is, two or more defining attributes must be present simultaneously. An example presented earlier was "father" as a combination of the attributes "male" and "parent." In the laboratory, an example would be triangular + red. Single attributes, such as a black triangle or a red circle, would not elicit the concept response.

3. A **disjunctive concept** has two subtypes, inclusive (any one of a set of attributes identifies the concept) or exclusive (any one of a set of attributes identifies the concept, except when they occur together). An example of the first type (inclusive) would be either delusions or hallucinations as defining 'schizophrenic." An example of the second type (exclusive) would be the concept of purebred animal. A purebred dog can be a beagle or a boxer, but a "beager" is not a purebred dog. This type of concept is most common in laboratory experiments.

4. A **probabilistic concept** is a concept in which specified attributes suggest the concept but do not clearly identify (define) it. Textbook-reading behavior is an attribute that is highly correlated with the concept "student." If you saw someone reading a textbook, you would be likely to classify him as someone fitting your concept of student, while he might in fact just be someone with a high tolerance for boredom who liked to read such texts for amusement. It is assumed that some attribute must exist somewhere to define the concept (in our example, it might be proof of student registration), but this definitive attribute is usually not available.

The system for classifying concepts (rules determining how subjects will respond or discriminate) proposed by Saltz is very similar to that advanced by Bruner, Goodnow, and Austin (1956) and other concept-learning theorists. Bruner and colleagues have also identified several strategies used by subjects in determining which type of concept to use. These include the **wholist strategy,** in which the subject remembers all the attributes common to correct instances and ignores other information (such as negative information) and the **partist strategy,** in which the learning focuses on one hypothesis at a time. They have also identified subtypes of these strategies which were applied when their subjects were exposed to a board with 81 stimulus cards and required to pick cards one at a time and tell if they thought each card was an example of the concept. Some subjects picked one positive card and selected subsequent cards which changed one attribute value at a time ("conservative focusing"); other subjects began with their positive card and then picked subsequent cards which changed several attribute values at once ("focus gambling"). Both these strategies were similar to the wholist strategy. Other subjects began with all possible hypotheses and eliminated incorrect ones after each following card ("simultaneous scanning"). Finally, some subjects began with one hypothesis and changed it when it failed to predict positive instances ("successive scanning"). These last two strategies were related to the partist strategy and were found to be less efficient than the focusing techniques. The main point for us to derive from this research is that different subjects used different learning strategies in varied learning situations.

Saltz (and others) have classified concepts into different types. Simple concepts are defined by a single attribute, conjunctive concepts are defined by two or more necessary attributes, disjunctive concepts are defined by multiple attributes which either are not required to appear together or must not appear together, and probabilistic concepts are suggested by attributes that do not always specify them. Subjects may use different strategies to assign attributes to concepts.

While Bruner and colleagues (1956) have identified several strategies that subjects may use to assign attributes to concepts, Saltz maintains that children begin with a single strategy, which he identifies as concept growth. Let us now examine this concept-growth model of the acquisition of concepts.

The Concept-Growth Model

Traditional discrimination models of concept formation assume that the subject begins with a category and gradually learns which instances to eliminate (note the emphasis on negative information). Saltz suggests that a child starts with a single **positive instance** (that is a dog) and gradually adds new attributes (poodles are dogs, also). Gradually, through direct experience and through hints from models and contexts, the concept "grows," or is expanded. Saltz once asked an eight-year-old boy how the child had mastered a particular concept and was told that "someone told me" (Saltz, 1971, p. 56), showing concept growth resulting from information given by adults. This "growth" model would predict that children would tend to make more errors of omission than of commission (not calling Saint Bernards dogs instead of calling cows dogs). Saltz and Sigel (1967) found that young children did tend to overdiscriminate, or use an overly restrictive criterion. Even eight-year-old children consistently refused to classify fathers who were identified as drunkards as fathers.* This absence of over-generalization is directly contradictory to the results predicted from the discrimination/common response theory of concept formation. More recently, Saltz (1973) has found additional evidence that young children form narrow concepts. When asked to classify items as clothing or not-clothing, children did not include hats, shoes, and gloves in the concept of clothing. Nelson (1974) has noted that children may either overgeneralize or undergeneralize concepts. She concludes that children's concepts are based on "core" functional relations; when new examples do confound these simple functions, undergeneralization may result. Thus, the fact that the man in Saltz's second example had doctor functions may have been responsible for the children's refusing to classify him as a father.

Saltz (1971) has reviewed studies by Jung which he interprets as supporting his concept-growth model. In these studies, subjects first learned a few pairs of words very well (which Saltz would see as learning a concept with good bound-ary strength which would be resistant to interference effects). These subjects learned new pairs of words presented successively much more easily than sub-jects presented initially with the entire list. Saltz suggests that the first small subset of pairs of words had become a conjunctive concept which was able to grow through the incorporation of new pairs of words.

The wholist strategy identified by Bruner and colleagues (1956) could also be interpreted as a concept-growth strategy. As in Saltz's model, the first positive instance is taken as the initial hypothesis, or concept. When new instances are encountered, the subject modifies the strategy to include only attributes com-mon to the new instance and the early concept. This strategy reduces the sub-ject's memory load and provides the mechanism by which whole gestalts, or things which can be incorporated into whole gestalts, are most easily remembered.

The concept-growth model states that children begin by learning simple con-cepts based on a single defining attribute. These concepts then become more general by growing through adding additional attributes (which also makes them into more complex types of concepts). The mechanism resembles Bruner's wholist strategy.

---

* While eight year olds made their classifications on moralistic grounds (being a drunkard removed a man from the category of father), five year olds used even more restrictive criteria. A man identified as a doctor was no longer classified as a father (Saltz and Sigel, 1967).

Saltz's Version of the Interference
Theory of Forgetting

Not only does Saltz see concept formation as involving a gradual growth process, he also maintains that most initial positive instances of a concept are learned in a single trial (as found by Saltz and Hamilton, 1969). While this notion sounds as contrary to our experience as it did when introduced by Guthrie, Saltz does not use Guthrie's explanation that apparently gradual learning is the result of increments in the numbers of tiny S-R bonds, each being formed in one trial. Saltz suggests that most (if not all) of our "learning" does occur on one particular trial, but most of this learning never gets beyond a temporary short-term memory stage. Competing cognitive elements (Silver, 1967) cause "forgetting" to occur almost as fast as the original learning. Therefore, the study of learning must be concerned with two types of variables:

1. Associative variables, as in Guthrie's theory, which reach their maximal strength in a single trial

2. Resistance-to-interference variables, which increase their effects slowly with time and trials

Let us now look at a simple test of this theory, which you can perform yourself. When you are given the instruction, quickly turn to the next page and glance for an instant at the capitalized word at the top of the page. Do not read anything else on that page. Then turn back to this page and count by twos to 40 slowly to yourself. Try not to have any other thoughts except the numbers and do not repeat the word on the next page. Are you ready? Turn now! Welcome back to this page. Have you finished counting? Do you remember the word? If so (and most of you will remember the word), you have demonstrated "learning" which occurred in one exposure to the word and stayed in memory in spite of your preventing yourself, with the help of the counting task, from rehearsing. Because the cues involved in such a counting task are irrelevant (and dissimilar) to the cues of reading words, Saltz assumes that this type of task also protects the memory trace from interference. This interference model of forgetting (also presented in Chapter 7 in the material on transfer effects) can account for the serial position effect, in which the words at the start of a list are learned first, followed by the words at the end, and finally by the words in the middle of the list. Saltz suggests that all the words in the list are learned with equal ease, but that words in the middle receive interference from words at both the start and end of the list. In Saltz's theory, practice does not create bonds, it reduces forgetting! Hence, learning is a short-term memory phenomenon, but "well-bounded" and interference-free memory is a long-term memory phenomenon. In reviewing the literature of studies using the paired-associate list paradigm, Saltz (1971) concluded that speed of "learning" (or developing freedom from interference, in his model) was most predictable from information about the similarity of the words making up the pairs of the list. The more similar the words, the slower the learning, which is congruent with most cognitive or functionalist models of transfer of training. Where similar stimuli control one

SERENDIPITY

response, these stimuli produce proactive inhibition of learning future words and retroactive inhibition of recall of previously learned words. Such negative transfer effects were minimal when different stimulus words could be used for a common response.

Saltz suggests that the apparent "learning" curves found in investigations of classical conditioning represent interference effects rather than gradual increments in bond strength. He cites studies by Voeks (1954, 1955, in Saltz, 1971) in which the interference of extraneous potential CSs was minimized. Under these conditions, half of Voeks's subjects showed one-trial learning of the conditioned eyeblink response, demonstrating that even classical conditioning cannot always be explained as a process of gradual increments of associations. Voeks's results are interpreted by Saltz as supporting his own idea that a study of concepts may eventually prove more useful in explaining "conditioning" than the other way around.

One reason learning often appears gradual, Saltz explains, is that concepts gradually grow in the direction of becoming more differentiated from each other. This gradual increase in concept differentiation, which is in marked contrast to the all-or-none development of associations, results in increased resistance to interference—hence, to improving levels of performance.

Saltz suggests that while stimuli and responses become associated with each other and with existing concepts in a single trial, resistance to interference develops slowly, through a process of concept differentiation, or "growing apart." Apparently, gradual learning is gradual development of resistance to forgetting, or changes from short-term memory to enduring concepts.

Integration of the Elements of a Concept

In addition to the process by which cues, concepts, and competing elements become differentiated, or acquire boundary strength in the cognitive space, another important process occurs in concept "growth." This is **integration,** or the transformation of unrelated elements into a cognitive entity. It requires that at least some differentiation has already occurred and, in turn, facilitates further differentiation. In learning reading, individual letters of the alphabet must first be differentiated from other visual stimuli before the child reacts to them in a meaningful way. Once the child knows what letters are, he or she can learn to assemble them into words or to integrate them into larger units. In this process, the child first learns the concept of the alphabet, then word concepts which are differentiated from each other, and finally sentence concepts.

Once words are learned and differentiated from each other, each word can have different attribute functions in different sentence concepts just as a given letter has different attribute functions in different word concepts. As a concept which is used as an attribute, a word has defining characteristics (its meaning) much like any simple, conjunctive, or disjunctive concept. (As an example of a word serving as a disjunctive concept, the word "read" can have a present tense meaning in one sentence concept and a past tense meaning in another sentence concept, but not both meanings in the same sentence concept.) Which defining attributes are used in a particular sentence concept depends upon the meaningfulness of each possibility in a particular linguistic context. This meaningfulness is, of course, a function of previously differentiated concepts, interpretations of what the receiver knows, and other integrated linguistic elements. Saltz speculates that "differentiation of associational groupings may involve the same principles regardless of their level of complexity or molarity" (1971, p. 270).

These factors determine how easily a new word, or a meaning of a word, will be learned. New material which can be integrated with existing concepts is, of course, most easily learned. This facilitation effect is called **mediational facilitation.** Saltz (1971) has shown that subjects presented with "nonsense words" often code them (mediate them) as sounding like or being used like well-known real words. This illustrates the principle that the mechanisms of intentional learning or seeking of meaning (actively mediated learning) are much more crucial for poorly differentiated material such as nonsense words.

Seeking meaning is another term for seeking to relate new information to existing concepts. Since existing concepts have good boundary strength, new material added to such concepts should have more resistance to forgetting (interference) than unrelated material. Thus, meaning is a mediating variable which promotes fast learning and good retention by facilitating associations. This associative model of memory fits well with what is known about memory aids, or mnemonic devices. These devices (to be discussed near the end of this chapter) represent deliberate attempts to associate new information with existing concepts. Associative techniques for aiding memory consistently yield better retention than direct reinforcement of responses or rote practice procedures. Reed and Riach (1960) found that subjects told to "associate" when confronted with a list of paired associates learned faster than subjects told to "learn the list." Making deliberate efforts to associate unrelated stimuli causes these stimuli to become integrated into concepts; this shows that "meaning" can be the result of an active, voluntary process rather than being an intrinsic property of stimuli.

Integration is the process by which previously differentiated stimuli (even seemingly unrelated ones) can be incorporated into concepts or form new concepts. Deliberate effort at associating cues can create "meaning," which aids learning and memory.

To summarize briefly, Saltz has proposed a cognitive model of learning in which the basic unit of learning is cognitive (the concept or life space region) and molar, and the mechanism of higher learning is also cognitive. He suggests that many factors and processes, such as conditioning and concept formation, are involved (sometimes in competition) in his multifactor learning model. He classified concepts into four basic types—all of which "grow" with the acquisition of new attributes, the stimulus points of attentional dimensions.

Perspective

Saltz's is not the best-known of cognitive theories, yet it presents a good sample of concepts central to verbal learning cognitive theories. His system of classification of concepts is very similar to that of Bruner, and his ideas about interference are close to the more cognitively oriented functionalists. Moreover, his ideas about the facilitative effects of associational factors in memorization appear similar to those of the information-processing theorists as well as other cognitive theorists. Other cognitive theorists have gone further in formulating the relationship between the types of concepts to be learned and the difficulty with which they are learned and in discriminating between attribute learning (learning to attend to the correct stimuli) and rule learning (knowing the rule which unites relevant attributes). Bourne (1970) has proposed a classification of rules which is very close to Saltz's classification of types of concepts. Bourne was able to show that trials to solution in a concept-learning task was a linear function of the presumed difficulty of using his various types of rules. Problems involving conjunctive rules were solved fastest, followed by problems requiring disjunctive concepts, and so on. Bourne (1974) assumed that subjects begin with conjunctive concepts, and that the extra time required for them to solve the disjunctive concept problems reflected the time required to change their original assumption.

Noam Chomsky: A Cognitive-Naturalist Model of Language Learning

Saltz made some concessions to the traditional stimulus-response connectionist viewpoints. Chomsky makes none. Some elements of Chomsky's theory and his criticisms of Skinner were introduced in Chapter 4. The following quotation will give you a fuller appreciation of Chomsky's criticisms of the Skinnerian analysis of language learning (which was the leading theory of language performance in the 1950s) as well as introducing you to Chomsky's method of attack (philosophical and abstract rather than experimental). Eloquence and logic (often so complex that it is difficult to follow) are Chomsky's strong points—not research. In this passage, Chomsky attacks Skinner's idea that a person acquires a "repertoire" of sentences (or at least of words and clauses and grammatical rules) that are likely to be emitted in the future because of having been reinforced in the past.

> But what does it mean to say that some sentence of English that I have never heard or produced belongs to my 'repertoire' but not any sentence of Chinese (so that the former has a higher 'probability')? Skinnerians, at this point in the discussion, appeal to 'similarity' or 'generalization,' always without characterizing the ways in which a new sentence is 'similar' to familiar examples or 'generalized' from them. The reason for this failure is simple. So far as is known, the relevant properties can be expressed only in terms of abstract theories describing postulated internal states of the organism, and such theories are excluded, a priori, from Skinner's 'science.' The immediate consequence is that the Skinnerian must lapse into mysticism (unexplained 'similarities' and 'generalization' of a sort that cannot be specified) as soon as the discussion touches the world of fact. [Chomsky, 1973, p. 3]

The major point Chomsky makes in this statement is that we are continually producing novel sentences (linguistic responses, if you like) which, having never been previously emitted, have never been reinforced. Principles such as generalization from similar sentences emitted in the past (and perhaps reinforced) cannot precisely predict the content or form of new sentences. If we assume, however, that language is organized by internal rules (much like the gestalt theorists thought perception, learning, and memory were organized by innate rules), and that the precise words and grammatical forms used in overt verbal behavior reflect the constraints of these rules on how one expresses meaning, then novel combinations present no problem. There are simply many lawful ways to express a given meaning; which way appears on a given occasion is only an expression of momentary influences acting upon the individual (such as his or her assumptions about what his or her audience already knows).

Like Saltz, Chomsky believes that the appropriate units of language learning are cognitive systems of knowledge and beliefs. He also sees the cognitive systems as arising in early childhood through an interplay of environmental factors. In a departure from Saltz and in general agreement with Piaget, he sees innate factors as having important interaction effects with environmental influences. Chomsky postulates the existence of "the system of **linguistic competence** that underlies behavior but that is not realized in any direct or simple way in behavior" (1968, p. 4). Competence is related to what a person knows, which is distinguished from performance, or what a person says or does. In distinguishing the product of the learning process from response measures, Chomsky is in agreement with Saltz and with most cognitive or cognitively oriented theorists. This system of linguistic competence is derived from innate organizing factors (which makes it similar to the concept of inherited intelligence) that form a sort of preexisting syntax (grammatical structure), or **natural language,** which interacts with cultural and personal environmental variables.

How Meaning Is Translated into Speech and Conscious Thought

While Chomsky's theory allows for individual differences, he also proposes that all human beings inherit a similar "language capacity" which provides a **universal grammar.** By universal grammar he means the principles that determine the forms of the **particular** (that is, actual) **grammars** used by humans; the grammars, in turn, determine the sentence structure likely to be used in a specific instance. These principles are, of course, innate organizing factors. As a result of the properties conferred by the universal grammar on all particular grammars (such as the grammar of standard American English), a person who knows a specific language has control of a grammar that can generate an infinite set of **deep structures.** The deep structure representation of a sentence (the **kernel sentence**) is the way an idea or meaning is stored in memory (Tarpy and Mayer, 1978) and is more abstract than what is actually said or thought. It expresses those grammatical functions that play a role in interpreting meanings (Chomsky, 1972) and reflects what a speaker knows about his or her situation and what he or she intends to communicate. Grammar also determines the way in which specific deep structures are mapped onto associated **surface structure sentences** (what we actually say), which provides us with a basis for phonetic interpretation. Chomsky states that the same kernel sentence, or deep structure sentence, can be expressed in any of a large number of surface structures (there are very many ways to state most ideas). It is this variability which confounds the efforts of the S-R theorist to predict which particular sentence will be spoken in a given instance. Language is not as stereotyped as conditioned reflexes.

> Honesty forces us to admit that we are as far today as Descartes was three centuries ago from understanding just what enables a human to speak in a way that is innovative, free from stimulus control, and also appropriate and coherent. This is a serious problem that the psychologist and biologist must ultimately face and that cannot be talked out of existence by invoking "habit" or conditioning or "natural selection." [Chomsky, 1968, p. 11]

Chomsky's answer to the problem posed in the passage just cited is to suggest that universal grammar contributes some general (and discoverable) properties to all particular grammars. One of these is that only a few simple rules that express rudimentary grammatical functions relate surface structures (which may be ambiguous) to deep structures (what is meant). Since we usually do understand what a person intends to communicate even when the phonetic interpretation of what he /she says is ambiguous, Chomsky states that the mind of the recipient of a communication must perform a series of **transformations** to relate what was said to an appropriate deep structure (to an understanding of what was meant). The few transformational rules (transformational grammars) can be approximated by trying to determine the operations necessary to transform a given surface structure sentence back to its deep structure form or to derive a set of surface structure sentences from a kernel sentence. Chomsky believes that the study of transformational grammars holds the key to understanding the flexibility and innovative character of language.

Let us now look at some examples of Chomsky's approach which illustrate his further point that surface structure may be misleading. For example, the sentence, "I disapprove of John's cooking," may imply either that the speaker disapproves of John's involvement in cooking in general or that the speaker has negative expectations concerning the product of John's current cooking efforts. Chomsky suggests that by transforming the grammar of the sentence by a few simple rules to approximate the possible deep structures, the ambiguity may be resolved. Thus, the sentence may be extended to become either: "I disapprove of John's cooking because cooking is women's work." or "I disapprove of John's cooking with so much garlic."

It is of interest that the one hearing the sentence usually has little difficulty determining if the objection to John's cooking was sexist or culinary. The transformations take into account what the speaker knows and what the speaker thinks the hearer knows. The ability of humans to communicate fairly clearly in spite of the ambiguity of surface structures presents a profound difficulty for the behavioristic S-R formulations, since what is actually reinforced derives its meaning from the deep structure. That is, the responses of language are more predictable from deep structure (semantic or meaning variables) than from the history of reinforcement of particular words.

Chomsky's organizing principles   Chomsky's goal was to determine a finite set of rules (organizing principles) which could be used to generate all possible correct sentences but no incorrect sentences. He developed four major types of rules (1972) to reach this goal:

1. **Phonological rules** (or morphophonemical rules), which are concerned with how sounds can be combined "legally" to form words. Examples would include changing the sounds of words through adding the *ed* sound at the end to generate the past tense form.

2. **Base rules** (or phrase structure rules), which are the rules generating deep structure syntax, or the organizational principles of syntactic units of language. Base rules specify how various parts of speech are to be assembled into sentences. Examples of these rules are:

   a. sentence = noun phrase + verb phrase

   b. noun phrase = article + noun

   c. noun phrase = noun + adjective + article

   d. verb phrase = verb + noun phrase

   e. verb phrase = verb + adjective

A sentence such as "A wise man is honest" (Chomsky, 1972, p. 29) can be generated from these rules as follows:

   a. sentence ("A wise man is honest") = noun phrase ("A wise man") + verb phrase ("is honest")

   c. noun phrase = noun ("man") + adjective ("wise") + article ("a")

   e. verb phrase = verb ("is") + adjective ("honest")

Chomsky suggests that the probable deep structure would reflect a system of two propositions, neither of which is asserted directly. The two propositions are that the man is wise and the man is honest. What makes this a system is the idea that wisdom and honesty are often found together.

3. **Transformational rules** describe how a sentence can be changed into an equivalent form which also fits the base rules (or rules of syntax). These are the rules which also apply to translations between surface and deep structures. Chomsky suggests that the deep structure of the sentence, "A wise man is honest," might be closer to "A man who is wise is honest." The rules describe permissible procedures, such as changing the order of "man" and "wise" and making "wise" part of a verb phrase rather than the original noun phrase (in order to make the two original propositions more explicit).

4. **Projection rules** are rules for determining the meaning of words which could have several meanings depending on the context in which they are used and on the meaning the speaker wishes to communicate. These would apply to ambiguous sentences such as "They are eating apples," in which eating could either be an adjective describing the type of apple or a verb.

All of these types of rules were attempts to explain the flexible and context-related aspects of human language. These aspects of language are probably the reason for the failure of early attempts at developing computer programs capable of translating one particular human language into another. The words of the sentence, "You look so nice I could eat you up," have a surface structure congruent with cannibalistic tendencies and would be so interpreted by a computer set to respond by dictionary definitions of particular words. Yet few English speakers would derive other than a meaning congruent with an expression of playful affection, in the absence of disconfirming contextual cues. Chomsky sees transformational grammars as resolving how humans understand sentences of the type just given by providing cues to the correlations of sounds (the phonemes of the surface utterance) and meaning (the deep structures).

Chomsky, like Saltz, sees his seemingly complex system (in contrast to S-R theories) as providing a simpler method of learning than the shaping and direct reinforcement or modeling proposed by the S-R theorists: In his view, the only substantive proposal to deal with the complexities of language acquisition is what he calls his "rationalist conception." This essentially consists of assuming that the human mind is innately programmed to operate in terms of a universal grammar. This grammar consists of a subsystem of rules that provides a skeletal structure for all human languages and sets limits on the range of variation of the grammars of actual human languages. He assumes that the child who learns grammar matches the "meager and degenerate" data available to him or her to the restrictions imposed by the universal grammar. By meager and degenerate he means that a child does not encounter all the information needed to construct something as subtle and complex as the grammar of most human languages from his or her early interactions with other humans. The universal grammar provides a wide range of possibilities, only a few of which are not rejected by the child's observations of how those around him speak or by others' reactions to his or her attempts at language. Rather than having to invent language from scratch, the child has only to fit the data available to him (others' speaking patterns and others' reactions to his attempts) to a fairly restricted set (specified by the universal grammar, by the base rules, and so on) of possible ways of expressing meaning and grammatical relationships.

By having innate categories and learned cognitive structures, the person is able to process seemingly ambiguous material with high accuracy. As we have said before, the attempts of behaviorists to extend their rigorously derived principles to complex behaviors such as language has both added unwanted, unmeasurable inner variables and made the theories cumbersome and ad hoc in character. Chomsky, like Saltz, has reduced the number of principles required to predict behavior by beginning with higher-order (more complex) constructs. Chomsky has also joined Luria and Piaget in using maturational variables to explain developmental changes. He suggests that maturational stages may eventually be linked to the gradual development of the full **generative grammar** of the adult human. (Generative grammar is the transformational grammar by which surface structures are generated from the deep structures.) Like Piaget, he is a structuralist and believes in innate variables in cognition.

For the future, Chomsky sees a rejection of behaviorism as not inconsistent with more recent developments. For him, as for other cognitive theorists who acknowledge innate factors:

> Speculating about the future development of the subject, it seems to me not unlikely, for the reasons I have mentioned, that learning theory will progress by establishing the innately determined set of possible hypotheses, determining the conditions of interaction that lead the mind to put forth hypotheses from this set, and fixing the conditions under which such a hypothesis is confirmed—and perhaps, under which much of the data is rejected as irrelevant for one reason or another. [Chomsky, 1968, p. 77]

Control of behavior by environmental cues is implausible because of the ambiguity of those cues and the excessive time that the shaping of behavior would take. Thus, operant principles cannot be generalized to complex human behavior, and learning theory must turn again to looking within the "black box."

Chomsky has developed a psycholinguistic theory of language acquisition and use based on the idea that all humans inherit the "species-specific" pattern of a universal grammar which determines the deep structure organizing meaning into syntax or grammar. These kernel sentences are transformed in lawful ways into surface structure, or specific human languages.

Perspective

Even though Chomsky has provided a valuable service to our understanding of learning by forcing a reevaluation of the Skinnerian interpretations of language acquisition, his theory can be attacked on two important grounds:

1. Experimental tests of the idea that surface structure sentences are the end result of a transformation from kernel sentences have provided conflicting results. Most studies have found that reaction times were longest when multiple transformations were required and shortest for sentences assumed to reflect kernel sentences directly. Other factors, however, could have produced the results interpreted as supporting Chomsky. In most studies, the kernel sentences were shorter and easier to read. It has also been found that saying, "No," for a positive sentence takes more time than saying, "Yes," while the opposite applies to negative sentences. These types of factors could have influenced the reaction time measures (reviewed in Tarpy and Mayer, 1978).

2. Connectionists working in the classical conditioning tradition have not always ignored meaning or semantic variables, as we saw in our review of the research on semantic conditioning presented in Chapter 8. Even Skinner (1969, 1974) accepts the idea that meaning can be conditioned and that the responses of the "linguistic community," as well as direct shaping and reinforcement, may influence language. Many of the concepts introduced by behaviorally oriented learning theorists have been experimentally validated. Osgood (1953) suggested that words evoke internal responses, which he called mediating responses. He postulated that these responses were subject to the laws of classical conditioning. This mediational model has been supported by research conducted by Staats, Staats, and Biggs (1958), who found

that the meanings of words could be influenced by classical conditioning procedures. The more radical behaviorism of the 1950s has largely been replaced by a behaviorism less opposed to cognitive variables; by a continued attack on obsolete radical behaviorism, Chomsky may be guilty of beating a dead horse. Ironically, by adding to the pressure on behaviorists to become more accepting of cognitive and innate variables, Chomsky may have helped the behaviorists to become capable someday of providing more adequate models of language acquisition and use.

Chomsky too has altered his views by paying more attention to meaning (semantic) variables rather than just to syntax variables. He has also increased the role of evolutionary variables of the type described by the ethologists (whose work will be presented in the next chapter) and has described language as a human form of a "species-specific" (inherited) behavior. In spite of the lack of experimental validation (or in most cases, invalidation) of many of his central concepts, he remains a dominant figure in the fields of psycholinguistics and language learning (Palermo, 1978).

The next theory to be presented shares Chomsky's concern with inherited logical structures and cognitive variables. Much of Piaget's work, however, has been experimentally validated, and he is much more specific on the hows of the acquisition of knowledge.

Jean Piaget: A Cognitive-Maturational Theory
Outline of the Cognitive Theory and Basic Principles

Experience and maturation   Much like Montessori, Piaget developed a theory of learning which combined a cognitive emphasis with maturational variables. Piaget gave Montessori credit for advancing the concept that interest and active effort go together, and that activity provided training for thought (Piaget, 1970). Both saw the role of the environment as that of providing nourishment to the child's developing brain, or, as expressed by Hilgard and Bower:

> The concept of the environment nourishing hereditary potential leads to a dual process in growth: on the one hand, native potential is realized under the influence of environment, so that *capacity to learn* is a product of this interaction; on the other hand, this capacity to learn is applied to a content of learning that owes to the environment, and to which natural ability must be subservient. In this Montessori and Piaget are in agreement. [1975, p. 342].

This realization of "native potential" depends upon the physical growth of the child's brain, and thus the sequence in which abilities unfold is as fixed as the stages of embryonic and fetal development. This is the basis for the famous "stages" of Piaget's system, which are similar to concepts such as "reading readiness." The extent to which a child realizes the innately determined potential, however, is a function of exposure to appropriate sources of stimulation at the time of the child's reaching the required level of maturation. The role of exposure, or experience, is not a purely passive one. Like Skinner, Piaget believed that an active child was a learning child. Piaget sees such activity as taking three forms:

1. *Exercise:* A type of contiguity learning that does not require reinforcement. It is seen as energized by the child rather than by environmental stimuli. Examples include the increasing efficiency, with practice, of kicking, head turning, and so on in infants.

2. *Physical experience:* A process of learning about the properties of objects, usually through manipulating them. It is the process by which the child learns that metals are usually heavier than wood or plastics, or that clay can be changed in shape. Through this process, the child gains the information needed to solve more abstract problems. Letting the child learn through unstructured, direct physical experience with the elements of a problem is the technique of "discovery learning" popularized by the gestalt theorists, and it is also similar to techniques used in Montessori schools.

3. *Logico-mathematical experience:* A higher type of learning which depends upon the special properties of the subject-object interaction, rather than the physical properties of objects, as in physical experience. This is the process by which a child develops abstract logical rules about the properties of objects. Piaget labels these rules "cognitive structures" (Phillips, 1969) and as such they form strategy rules for solving problems. They include such things as knowing that operations can be reversed and that objects (as a lump of clay) can be restored to premanipulation appearance. Other types of cognitions that are learned by children include knowledge of order effects, classification rules, and object constancy.

In addition to physical experiences with the environment, the child also learns through social interactions. Most of these social learning effects are language-mediated (as having a child's ego-centered view of the world disconfirmed by negative reactions of adults and other children). Piaget, however, sees logical operations as both "deeper" than, and arising earlier than, language.

According to Piaget, experience of three types of a child's activity interacts with the maturational sequence of brain development to produce a full realization of the child's cognitive abilities. The three types are: (1) exercise, which is self-directed and self-rewarding, (2) physical manipulation of objects, and (3) logico-mathematical experience, which is an internal abstracting process arising from the other kinds of activity.

Learning and development   Like most cognitively oriented theorists, Piaget distinguishes between behavior (what you do, such as acting or thinking) and learning. However, he also makes a distinction between learning and development. All inferences about either learning or development are made from observations of overt behavior. Thus, in Piaget's system, learning and development are both hypothetical constructs, and their distinction from each other is vital (Wadsworth, 1978). Piaget writes:

The development of knowledge is a spontaneous process tied to the whole process of embryogenesis. Embryogenesis concerns the development of the body, but is concerned as well with the development of the nervous system, and the development of mental functions. In the case of the development of knowledge in children, embryogenesis ends only in adulthood. . . .

Learning presents the opposite case. In general, learning is provoked by situations—provoked by a . . . teacher, with respect to some didactic point; or by an external situation. It is provoked, in general, as opposed to spontaneous. In addition, it is a limited process—limited to a single problem, or a single structure. [1964, pp. 7–8]

An example of knowledge, in Piaget's terms, would be the seven-year-old child's sudden realization that bending a wire does not change its length even though it looks very different. The child cannot have that realization until his or her brain is sufficiently mature, and the realization comes about spontaneously when the child manipulates wires. This knowledge provides a new cognitive structure which the child uses to understand other relationships in his or her environment. Knowledge is thus roughly the same as the kind of generalizable understanding resulting from "insightful" experiences that Köhler reported in his chimpanzees. An example of learning, on the other hand, would be the child's memorization of "two plus two equals four." The child may not understand why "two plus two equals four" or be able to generalize this rule to new combinations of numbers. He learns this rule because the teacher reinforces its memorization. Learning involves using intellectual structures in the acquisition of a skill or of specific information. Learning may involve forming memories through association or through rote practice (which can be overt in learning skilled acts, or covert in verbal learning), or it may involve learning with comprehension. Learning with comprehension involves an interaction between development (and knowledge) and learning; we will now discuss some of the mechanisms of this interaction.

Piaget distinguishes knowledge, which is spontaneous and is related to the maturing brain's becoming able to "know" some types of relationships, and learning, which is provoked by others and specific to the particular material learned. Knowledge is a generalizable understanding or a shift in a way of thinking about something.

The mechanisms by which cognitive structures grow and are altered While learning through experience is similar in Piaget's theory to the mechanisms discussed in most cognitive theories, Piaget has added a new type of more complex learning mechanism. This mechanism is that of **equilibration,** which he sees as the fundamental factor in development and necessary to coordinate maturation, physical experience of the environment, and social experience of the environment. It is an innate need for balance between the organism and its environment, as well as for balance within the organism. It is a progressive, self-regulating process and has powerful motivational properties. Equilibration is the process responsible for intellectual development at all maturational stages and is also the mechanism by which a child moves from one developmental stage to the next. Roughly, it is a dynamic shift by the child in response to situations or stimuli which disconfirm existing internal **schemata** (cognitive structures, or concepts, which filter and process incoming perceptions). Disconfirmation, or disequilibration, leaves the child in a state of imbalance and provides the motive to restructure his schemata. New schemata may provide new intellectual abilities which are qualitatively different from previous abilities. The progression of intellectual development from developmental stage to developmental stage is defined by the new schemata so acquired as a result of disequilibration and the process of equilibration (motive to restore balance).

To understand how disequilibration occurs, it is necessary to understand two additional Piagetian terms: **assimilation** ("fitting in" of new data into old schemata) and **accommodation** (the restructuring of schemata to form essentially new schemata). Assimilation is the normal process by which an individual integrates new data with previous learning. Like the gestalt theorists, Piaget sees new perceptions as occurring within a lawful preexisting framework. The child develops cognitive categories (schemata), or mental pigeonholes, in which to store new information. When something fails to fit preexisting pigeonholes, then new pigeonholes must be created. The process of altering the basic categories of thought, or of modifying some activity because of environmental demands, is accommodation, and the end result of the alteration is equilibration, which usually leads to a better adaptation to the environment. Thus, by suggesting that the processes of learning, perception, and thought all show qualitative changes as a result of the interaction between development and experience, Piaget is in disagreement (disequilibrium?) with the gestaltists' idea of fixed "laws" governing learning and other behaviors. Piaget's internal organizing principles (which are similar in many ways to the gestalt laws), or schemata, change as a function of maturation and experience into new cognitive structures, or rules for processing information. Only the **functions** (equilibration, accommodation, and assimilation) continue to operate throughout the child's development.

While Piaget rejects the idea that the cognitive categories (schemata), or mental structures, are fixed, he does maintain that the functions (basic mental processes) are not only invariant but are innately determined (Phillips, 1969). These functions interact in different ways with different sorts of experiences. For example, when children imitate, accommodation is ascendant over assimilation. The child who imitates older models is behaving in new ways which usually reflect the models' more highly developed schemata. When children play, assimilation is dominant. Piaget says children play simply to exercise responses. This has the effect of stabilizing their existing schemata, thus making them easier to recall and enhancing further learning (Wadsworth, 1978). This is similar to Saltz's idea of increasing the boundary strength of concepts through practice.

Behavior is considered to be most adaptive when these two functions are in balance, or equilibrium, but perfect balance shows gaps and inconsistencies in existing cognitive structures (disconfirmation) which produce new states of disequilibration. This is because perfect balance is balance to an existing set of circumstances; when circumstances change, the existing balanced schemata are no longer adequate. For example, the simple schema of judging the amount of liquid in glasses by their height may be perfectly adequate for the preschool child (who assimilates information about new containers into this schemata without needing to change the schema through accommodation) but inadequate in a school situation in which more precise measurement is requested by teachers.

Though the process of organization and reorganization is continuous, the results of this process are discontinuous and qualitatively different at different ages. This discontinuity forms the basis of Piaget's developmental system, in which a series of qualitatively different stages, organized into periods and subperiods, occur in the same order for all children. The periods are classified according to the highest types of schemata available to the child, and some earlier cognitive structures may persist even when a child has advanced to a higher stage. Although Piaget gives the ages at which children can be expected to be in a given stage, he recognizes that different children will advance to a given stage at somewhat different ages. Since this is intended as a text about learning, we will only summarize the stages and substages. Note that in suggesting that the basic mechanisms of information processing and learning (the schemata) change with development and experience, Piaget has suggested that a single set of learning laws is inadequate to account for the child's reactions from early infancy to early teenagehood.

Piaget identifies three critical processes or functions which are involved in learning and the acquisition of knowledge: (1) equilibration, the motive to seek balance; (2) assimilation, roughly like stimulus generalization in fitting new inputs into existing schemata (concepts, or rules for processing information); and (3) accommodation, or form new schemata (as in discrimination learning).

The Developmental System
Related to Learning*

Sensorimotor period (0–2 years)   During the first few weeks after birth, the infant responds on the basis of innate sensorimotor schemata (reflexes). The infant's first type of learning is discrimination learning; for example, the infant becomes able to discriminate a milk-producing nipple from other objects that he mouths in exercising his sucking reflex during the second stage (Wadsworth, 1978). As more sensory experiences are assimilated, old schemata become integrated into habits and perceptions through accommodation. Because the

---

* As time periods for the different stages of development vary from child to child, the ages given are averages. Transitions from stage to stage may be gradual and are assumed to be motivated by the disequilibrium process, discussed earlier, which reflects the aversive effects of disconfirmation.

infant's attention is centered on its own body and not on external objects, these reactions are called primary. Because they are endlessly repeated, they are called circular. This stage of integrating innate behavior with experience lasts from the first to the fourth month. The second stage is secondary circular reactions (four to eight months). These reactions, such as an infant's shaking a rattle to hear the sound, are repetitive and self-reinforcing. During this stage, acts become intentional, primary stage schemata are amalgamated, and the child searches for objects that are suddenly removed (object permanence).

During the third stage (eight to twelve months), the child is able to find objects hidden behind barriers and to separate ends from means. When behaviors (means) occur without ends, Piaget labels the behavior "play"; when they are related, Piaget labels the behavior "problem solving," which may be a trial-and-error process. While meaning and learning in the second stage were defined in terms of motor activity, symbolic meaning (thought, or cognitions) appears in the fourth stage. At this time the infant begins to understand causality (or contingencies between ends and means) and may wait for an adult to bring his bottle rather than continuing to scream until it is in his mouth. Although the typical one-year-old may say a few words, such as "daddy" or "mommy," these sounds are not true language but instead are instrumental responses which are reinforced by parental attention or other consequences.

Stage 5, tertiary circular reactions, extends from 12 to 18 months. True imitation (modeling) appears as a learning mechanism for accommodation, although the child continues to depend upon direct experience as his basis for assimilation. The child begins the process of **decentration,** or a reduction in **egocentricity** (the younger child is assumed to see himself as the center of the universe). Stage 6 is a period in which the child begins to apply familiar schemata to new situations, as in stage 4 (generalization of concepts), in order to modify familiar schemata to fit new situations, as in stage 5; in addition, he begins to invent new means through combinations of schemata (insight learning?). This last process is labeled by Phillips (1969) as reciprocal assimilation of schemata. In addition, object permanence now extends in time (as when a blanket is put away for a few days) rather than just when objects are hidden behind barriers, as in earlier stages. Modeling can now occur without preliminary trial-and-error behavior and after the model has vanished (as in play). Piaget's suggestion that imitative, or modeling, behavior appears in a fixed developmental sequence would seem to have important implications for Bandura's theory of modeling.

Preoperational period (2–7 years)   The **preoperational** period is characterized by the development of internalized actions that are reversible, in that the child can think of, or see, an action and then think of what would happen if that action were to be undone. During this period, the child is no longer limited to an overt S-R, or trial-and-error, type of learning but instead begins to show more and more cognitive learning. Wadsworth (1978) divides this period into the Egocentric Stage (two to four years) and the Intuitive Stage (five to seven years). During this period, the child performs mental experiments in which he runs through the symbols for events as if he were actually participating in the events. This leads to one-way (egocentric) thinking, as illustrated in the following example:

> A four-year-old subject is asked: "Do you have a brother?"
> He says, "Yes."
> "What's his name?"
> "Jim."
> "Does Jim have a brother?"
> "No." [Phillips, 1969, p. 61]

As can be seen, the preoperational child's thinking is not reversible. The child, however, is gaining skills that will eventually result in this new tool of thinking. While the sensorimotor child was "egocentric" in his or her overt actions, so the preoperational child shows symbolic egocentricity, or centration, while decentering actions. The preoperational child begins to show **classification skills** (being able to group events into concepts, or schemata), although the hierarchies thus generated may be very different from those of adults. In general, the categories tend to be more narrowly defined and broader in scope (having fewer defining attributes per category and having fewer categories). Though learning can now sometimes occur through cognitive mechanisms, these are primitive types of cognitive processes in which thought is dominated by environmental stimuli.

In the first (sensorimotor) period of Piaget's developmental system, the child progresses from unintentional exercise of reflexes, to discrimination learning and trial-and-error learning, to the beginnings of symbolic thinking and understanding of causality. In the second (preoperational) period, the child decenters actions and shows primitive conceptual behavior. Thinking is still egocentric or irreversible.

Concrete operations period (7-11 years)   During this period, the child's thinking becomes decentered and truly reversible. There is one important limitation to this ability; that is the child's need to see the operation or perform it in order to reverse it mentally. During this period, the basic logic of mathematics develops as a series of discrete logical schemata. Before the child has developed the fundamental concepts of number, he may memorize, say, $1 + 1 = 2$, through rote association mechanisms. This type of learning is considered to be isolated from mental structures, or schemata. Once the concepts of number are developed, the learning of $1 + 1 = 2$ becomes integrated with mathematical schemata, and learning with comprehension occurs (Wadsworth, 1978).

Another qualitative change in the child's logical abilities is the understanding that changing the appearance of something may not change its other properties **(conservation).** There are several types of conservations, and the child's skill in understanding each (and performing the correct acts) tends to appear in a sequence beginning with conservation of quantity and ending with conservation of volume. Conservation of quantity is shown in the water jar experiments in which two jars of equal appearance, containing equal amounts of fluid, are

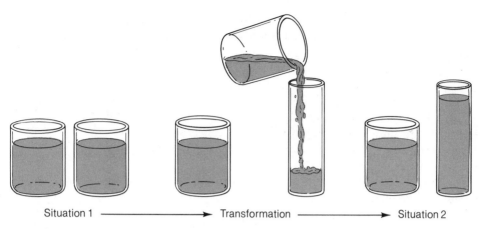

Situation 1 ⟶ Transformation ⟶ Situation 2

Figure 11.1 *Conservation of quantity with fluid. Situation 1 shows two containers of equal size, before the appearance of the fluid is transformed by pouring it into the tall, thin container. Situation 2 is after the pouring. A young child may watch the pouring and still give incorrect responses. If the water in the tall, thin container is then poured back into the wide container, the preoperational child will return to his Situation 1 response that "both have the same."*

presented to a child. The fluid from one jar is then poured into a tall, thin beaker or graduated cylinder and the child is asked which container now "contains more fluid." The preoperational child emits the surprising answer that the tall, thin container contains "more fluid." This illustrates irreversible thought. The operational child says, "The same, because if you poured them back they would look the same again." The experimental situation is shown in Figure 11.1.

Successful conservation of quantity is a prerequisite for the development of a true concept of number, which in turn is a prerequisite for learning arithmetic "with comprehension" (Wadsworth, 1978). This illustrates the principle that logical maturation is hierarchical (has a necessary sequence). While the child in the period of **concrete operations** may correctly solve conservation problems, his thinking is labeled concrete because it still requires direct sensory experience. If asked to identify the reason why the liquid is "still the same" after the transformation, the child will be unable to abstract the general principle. This ability will not appear until the final stage of logical development, or the period of formal operations.

Behaviorists and other non-Piagetian learning theorists have attempted to explain away the results of the conservation experiments by suggesting that motivational variables could be involved. When the experimenter asked a child, "Which glass has more now?" he or she may have been creating a demand in the child's mind to identify one glass as having "more." Since water is the fluid in the glasses in most of these experiments, the child did not really care about making a careful judgment and so reacted to the demand characteristics of the situation. The author, however, has seen the same results when a preoperational child is told that both containers contain lemonade or some other tasty fluid and that the child can drink the contents of the container holding "more."

Critics have also suggested that Piagetian researchers may have unconsciously shaped (guided) the childrens' responses. Sigel, Roeper, and Hooper (1965) have presented a summary of their attempts to shape conservation in preoperational children. They found that even though a child having the necessary prerequisite logical abilities could be trained to conserve, such training was ineffective with non-"transitional" children. In other words, motivational and training variables only work on children at a level of development very close to that at which they would naturally obtain conservation. They found that preliminary training of the prerequisite abilities (such as reversibility and decentration) aided in concept acquisition. This work essentially supported Piaget's developmental model. Other research showing that environmental variables can speed up the acquisition of specific conservations has been conducted by Wadsworth, Banks, and Kraemer (1975, reviewed in Wadsworth, 1978). They found that "disequilibrium training," which consisted of having the experimenter ask children to "review and reconsider" their erroneous results, was followed by significantly faster acquisition of conservation of length. In support of Piaget's view that development is ultimately dominant over direct teaching, however, a one-year followup uncovered no difference between trained and untrained (control) subjects.

During the third (concrete operations) period, the child begins to display signs of knowledge that operations which he or she sees changing the appearance of some substance or object can be reversed. This type of understanding is seen as qualitatively different from memorization of information and is best shown by conservation experiments. During this stage, direct sensory experience is necessary to solve the many types of conservation problems. Conservation depends upon maturation.

Formal operations period (11–15 years)   The final stage of logical development is that of **formal operations,** or the ability to use internalized abstract operations based on general principles or equations to predict the effects of operations upon objects. This ability appears in children between 11 and 15 years of age. Such a child is said to be fully operational. Also involved is a completion of the decentration process to the point that thinking and problem solving can take place in a purely abstract framework without ends of obtaining food or satisfying other needs (Bruner, Goodnow, and Austin, 1956). Because the teenager is able to formulate hypotheses about things which may not be available for manipulation, truly internal "trial and error" becomes possible, as well as more cognitive "reciprocal assimilations of schemata."

The differences in thinking among children in the three main periods of development (preoperational, concrete operations, formal operations) can be demonstrated by the "specific gravity problem." In this problem the child (or the adolescent) is presented with a series of objects (wood, iron, and other materials) and is asked why each either sinks or floats. A correct answer would be in terms of the volume of each object in relationship to its weight. Because the preoperational child's thinking is controlled by his representations of the world, he or she blithely invokes a special cause for each event. The child in the period of concrete operations, limited by his or her concern for organizing the data of his or her senses, will usually try to classify the objects from heavy things (iron bars which always sink), to somewhat heavy things (aluminum pan lids which sink only when filled with water), to light things (wood). New objects are then assimilated into these established categories (as keys sink because, "They must be iron also").

Though the thinking of the child in the period of concrete operations is orderly, it is based upon classification systems which incorporate only one physical dimension (weight, in this example). The child in the period of formal operations is able to coordinate information about two dimensions (weight and volume, as inferred by the volume of water displaced by the floating object) and to arrive at a conclusion about proportions. This type of thinking reflects the ability to think conceptually, or to perform operations on operations (which Piaget calls second-order operations), rather than just operations with objects.

Subjects in the period of formal operations formulate hypotheses about problems to fill in the gaps in their understanding. These subjects can manipulate one variable systematically while holding others constant, which is the classical method of experimental science. These interior manipulations of hypotheses represent internal tentative accommodation, or the forming of a series of schemata until a schema is formed which fits all the adolescent's data. Thus, the formal operations subject is able to depart from reality but in a lawful way which reflects his or her appreciation that direct sensory data is only a subset of a larger set of possibilities. This departure from reality allows this subject to form abstract laws which predict the properties of objects not yet encountered. Phillips (1969), however, notes that the formal operations subject may fail to distinguish between his or her hypotheses and the social or physical universe to which they are applied. This type of egocentric thinking may lead the adolescent to conclude that because his or her own ideas are logical, others should follow the same logic. This idealistic egocentrism is reflected in the types of moral judgments made by the formal operations subject. Because moral judgments illustrate the changes of thinking that occur over the periods, let us now briefly examine Piaget's developmental sequence for moral development.

During the fourth (formal operations) period, the person becomes capable of going beyond immediate sensory experience and can think abstractly, or perform operations on operations, to arrive at higher-order schemata, or general predictive hypotheses or laws.

Piaget's theory of moral development   Piaget has proposed that the two basic operations involved in the development of logic (reversibility and conservation) have their affective counterparts. Morality is defined as the system of rules that regulates interpersonal behavior on a reciprocal basis, or the conservation of feelings (as in reciprocating friendly behavior from another person). Preoperational children (those under seven years of age in most cases) are only able to think in one dimension; their thought patterns are self-centered or egocentric. Thus, they may classify people as behaving morally solely on the basis of persons behaving like themselves. The child in the stage of concrete operations is better able to use the data of his or her senses (what are his or her group's norms) and to think in two dimensions (how he or she feels about something and how he or she should behave towards others). This child has advanced beyond the selfish moral judgments of the preoperational child to making moral judgments based on his or her views interacting with peer-group and adult norms. In this stage, moral judgments are "conventional." In the last period of moral development, the person is able to make multidimensional moral judgments based on abstract principles* (or perform operations on operations) which may not conform to group norms. Moral thinking in this last period is similar to the logical thinking of the formal operations person (Biggs, in Varma and Williams, 1976).

The developmental system for moral judgments differs in two important respects from the developmental system for logic and thinking. First, progress is slower, with children in the period of concrete operations still showing egocentric, or preoperational, moral thinking and adolescents typically showing conventional, or concrete operations, moral thinking. Abstract, or "postconventional," moral thinking usually does not appear until the middle twenties and may never appear at all. Second, the type of moral judgments made are much more influenced by modeling and direct reinforcement than the more innately programmed sequence of development of logical thinking, in general. As Kohlberg has shown through research on his extension of Piaget's system, college-age students may show patterns of moral judgments ranging from very egocentric to very abstract (reviewed by Biggs, in Varma and Williams, 1976). He has also found that the speed with which persons progress through the sequence of moral development is influenced by other variables, such as social class and peer-group standards. This suggests that moral development is much more controlled by learning (not biological maturation) than is logical development.

Piaget has also proposed a developmental sequence for moral development, progressing from preconventional egocentric unidimensional moral concepts, to conventional sociometric bidimensional moral thinking, to postconventional abstract multidimensional moral schemata. This sequence is more variable and influenced by learning than is the sequence for the development of logic, in general.

Perspective

Piaget has developed a theory of learning and cognition stressing the epistemology, or structure, of logic. This theory includes the idea that innate factors, such as the functions of assimilation and accommodation, act together with environmental influences to change cognitive structures in qualitative ways, in accordance with an innately determined developmental order. This theory,

---

* Such as social justice.

then, is naturalistic, interactionist-maturationist, cognitive, and structuralist. Although Piaget's main audience among psychologists has been developmental psychologists, his theory that the mechanisms of learning depend upon developmental level and his suggestions for teaching and providing optimal learning environments* qualify his theory as a learning theory.

Taking seriously Piaget's opposition to "direct" teaching, on the grounds that lectures and reinforcement of selected behaviors develop cognitively isolated rote memory rather than integrated "knowledge," many teachers and some schools (Pacific Oaks experimental pre- and primary school in Pasadena, California is a good example) have tried to incorporate Piaget's ideas in their teaching programs. In part, this may reflect many educators' dislike of behaviorist approaches to education. A readable guide to Piagetian applications has been provided by Barry Wadsworth in his text *Piaget for the Classroom Teacher* (1978). Techniques of surprise (as in the disequilibrium training previously mentioned) and inquiry training (similar to the gestalt technique of discovery learning discussed in Chapter 5) have been found useful in motivating children to act on objects and events. This, of course, is the result of disconfirmation of the child's predictions.

Piagetians make a distinction between three types of knowledge: **physical knowledge** (which children learn through their activity with objects, such as unsuccessfully trying to burn stone), **logico-mathematical knowledge** (which comes from the child's actions imposed on objects, as when the child learns about number from counting collections of objects), and **social-arbitrary knowledge.** Only social-arbitrary knowledge should be taught and reinforced in the "didactic-lecture method" mode. The child is seen as being taught the first two types of knowledge by the objects themselves (much as Montessori's didactic materials were intended to be self-teaching and self-reinforcing). To interfere with the child's spontaneous activities is to retard his acquisition of true "knowledge" of the first two types. Letting the child be wrong in his predictions is seen as providing the motivation for accommodation.

Wadsworth (1978) also suggests that because the schemata of other children are more likely to be similar to a given child's logical structures, communication about logico-mathematical and social-arbitrary knowledge is often more efficient between children of the same developmental level than between children and adults. This suggests extensive use of "peer teaching" techniques. Wadsworth does concede that when rapid behavior change is necessary, behavior modification procedures may be appropriate, as long as the child is developmentally advanced enough to learn from them. He states that such behavior changes should not be confused with true knowledge or reasoning. This focus on the active, internally directed, organizing functions of learners is also to be found, in more mechanistic language, in the next theory to be reviewed.

---

* He suggests that every time a teacher teaches something, children are prevented from discovering it for themselves. Thus, classrooms should be full of opportunities for physical manipulation of objects, and teaching should be directed towards suggesting to children that they try to find out what would happen if something is changed or manipulated (Phillips, 1969).

Information-Processing Approaches
to Learning and Memory

The information-processing approach to learning originated from several sources. Ellis (1978) suggests an influence of the gestalt theory of memory, which states that the ways organisms actively organize their perceptions are reflected in how they organize their memories. Norman (1970) distinguishes three main influences reflected in current information-processing theories: (1) mathematical learning theories of the types first proposed by Estes, Hull, and Spence, (2) signal (attention) detection theories, which contributed the suggestion that learning is a multistage process beginning with selective attention and ending with long-term memory traces, and (3) computer models, which were highly indebted to the concept of cybernetics introduced by Norbert Wiener. Computer-model theorists contributed the idea that processing by peripheral processing devices precedes processing by the central computer, the idea that temporary working memories interact with more lasting core storage memories, and the idea that memorization is a function of the programs (or rules and strategies) involved. Thus, memory, for the information-processing theorists, is much more than just something that mediates between stimuli and responses.

We have already discussed the functionalist S-R association approach to human verbal learning characterized by a nonneurological environmentalist orientation in which memory is simply the consequence of the learning process. By contrast, information-processing theories often discuss possible neurological mechanisms (which will be explored further in the discussion of Pribram's neurological information-processing theory in Chapter 12) which may be involved at each of several of the stages of learning, or they suggest analogies with stages of computer information processing. As with computers, human learning involves three types of processes: encoding, storage, and retrieval (Ellis, 1978). Like the gestalt theorists, the information-processing theorists see perception, learning, and memory as reflecting a processing continuum unified by common organizational principles operating within actively organizing organisms. The portions of this continuum explored in depth by information-processing theorists include: attentional mechanisms (selective attention), storage at the level of the sense organs and lower brain areas (sensory information store, or SIS), working or immediate memory (short-term memory, or STM), mechanisms for transferring immediate memory into long-term storage (consolidation), and finally, mechanisms for retrieving information from long-term memory (LTM).

Like Spence and Bandura, and like the cognitive theorists, the information-processing theorists distinguish between what may be learned (defined as what is stored in permanent memory) and what will be performed (or retrieved) in tests of human memory. Failure to demonstrate stored knowledge in performance is seen as also involving a failure of retrieval mechanisms rather than forgetting, as postulated by the S-R associationists.

It is the explicit attempt to distinguish storage and retrieval using a conceptual language borrowed from computer technology that characterizes information-processing approaches. Retrieval, meaning the business of getting things out of storage, takes on a special importance for those psychologists who emphasize information-processing approaches. The focus is more on retrieval than on storage with these approaches because retrieval mechanisms are viewed as the key to unlocking memory. [Ellis, 1978, p. 80]

Let us now review each of the stages of learning as classified by Donald Norman (1970, 1976).

The Stages of Learning

Attention   The idea that attention is a vital part of the learning process has a long history. To aid orators in cultivating reliable memories, the Romans wrote a text (*Rhetorica ad Herennium*) on the subject of training memory. The first rule given in that ancient text was "Pay attention" (Norman, 1976)! First Pavlov (1960) and then Sokolov (1963) conducted research on the attention-related orienting reflex (OR) and concluded that conditioning was impossible until the OR had been elicited. The gestalt theory differentiating figure as what was attended to and learned, from ground, focused on **selective attention** as a primary variable in learning.

The problem of selective attention, rather than random responsiveness to environmental stimuli, is illustrated in the **cocktail party problem** investigated by E. Colin Cherry (in Norman, 1976). Consider the situation faced by someone at a large party. Several conversations may be taking place at the same time and yet each person is able, at will, to shift his attention to listen to any nearby single conversation which "interests" him. In the laboratory Cherry found that when his subjects were given two speeches (one presented through each side of a set of headphones), they could attend to either but not both. Some features of the nonattended speech, however, such as the introduction of non-human-originated sounds or a switch from a male to a female speaker, were noticed and reported. By switching that message to German without the subjects' being able to detect the change, Cherry demonstrated that attention to the "unattended" message did not extend to monitoring meaning.

Cherry also made extensive use of a technique called **shadowing,** which required the subject to repeat the attended message. Such repetitions were usually delivered in a monotone. It was found that when the subject was involved in generating such verbal responses, memory of the attended message was poorer than in the nonshadowing condition. Shadowing was most accurate when there was a time lag between hearing and repeating the message (phrase shadowing). This suggested that the message was being temporarily stored between stimulus and response, although most of this storage seemed to be temporary. It is almost as if a tape recorder were temporarily storing such verbal messages. The author has used such a very short-term storage mechanism when people have talked to him while his "mind was elsewhere." When asked if he is paying attention, he is usually able to repeat back the last few words of their conversation without being aware of their words when they spoke them.

At first it was thought that the selective attention mechanism was caused by the brain's blanking out most of the output of one ear. When both speeches are given to both ears, however, one message still is "heard" and the other attended to only minimally (Norman, 1976).

Anne Treisman (1964) suggested that some sort of partial sensory filters must be mediating between messages stored in this sensory information store, or SIS (as in the "tape recorder phenomenon" just discussed), and what is now called **short-term memory,** or **STM.** An example of STM is remembering a phone number you have just looked up long enough to dial it. Treisman postulated that the act of experiencing attention to something occurred after SIS storage had passed through the filters to the level of STM. She suggested that such filters only attenuated (weakened) the nonattended channels of information, rather than eliminating them. Because some messages were attended on the "nonattended" channels (such as hearing your own name), she suggested that there must be several filters, the first of which operates on the gross physical characteristics of the sounds received. Thus, even the matter of selective attention, which in turn determines what material is available for learning, may involve several stages. Norman (1976) suggests that there exist hierarchies of analyzers in which the output of the first analyzers of physical characteristics of stimuli become the input for meaning analyzers.

We pay attention to a few selected stimuli from a wide range of possible cues. This selective attention mechanism is based both on physical characteristics of the cues and on meaning variables. It has been suggested that a series of analyzers allows us to shadow one conversation while ignoring most features of others (cocktail party problem).

Processing modes for attended inputs   The type of initial processing may be in two basic modes. When looking for the friend who is to pick you up at an airport, you may think you recognize him or her in the crowd, only to find yourself in the embarrassing position of greeting a total stranger (a false positive, in signal detection jargon). The type of processing used when you have a concept or expectancy of what you are looking for (such as your friend's face) is called **conceptually driven,** or **top-down, processing** (Norman, 1976). The second mode of paying attention, or initial processing, is called **data-driven,** or **bottom-up, processing.** This involves tuning your attention to progressively more sophisticated aspects of the stimuli available in a situation where you are trying to make sense of the information available. In this mode of processing, the information passes through your hierarchy of analyzers, as when you seek to find a pattern or form a concept (for example, trying to understand and remember the central ideas from a lecture about a new and complex theory). In the first mode of processing (top-down), you begin processing with "preconceptions" about what you are experiencing. In the second mode (bottom-up), you begin with an open mind and try to form organized concepts. These two modes of processing may (and often do) occur simultaneously, as in the complex task of reading.

Most adults read faster than can be reasonably accounted for by data-driven processing. Norman (1976) says this occurs because grammatical and other contextual cues cause language to be so redundant that you can skip many individual letters and even words without losing much meaning. Of course, in tasks like reading highly technical material (data-dense material) or in proofreading, this "skimming," or high reliance on conceptually driven processing, may result in your missing important information.

That both processes are operating simultaneously may be shown by the phenomenon of reading rapidly, suddenly realizing that you did not understand a passage, and going back to read it slowly, word by word (data-driven processing). Norman suggests that speed-reading training forces a person to place increased reliance on conceptually driven processing, in which most central concepts are recognized (hopefully) and less important material is not attended to.

With all this attentional and sensory-store-level processing taking place before you become aware of perceptions and begin to put them in memory proper, it is hardly surprising that the central nervous system "performs substantial alterations of the physical image received by the sense organs" (Norman, 1976, p. 39). This conforms nicely to the gestalt theorists' ideas that perceptions are the end result of processing by active organisms rather than mirror images of environmental stimuli. In Norman's model, of course, the whole is less than the sum of its parts, in that only information passing through the filters is perceived or attended to at the level of consciousness.

Norman's theory of data-driven rather than conceptually driven attentional mechanisms has support from some of the verbal learning data. Miller (1962) found that when words were chunked (combined) into grammatical five-word sentences rather than being presented as individual words (which is assumed to require data-driven processing instead of using the concept information available in grammar), words in the sentences were correctly recognized more times than words presented individually. As "noise" (distraction) was increased, the advantage of having the words in sentences increased.

Another example of the interaction of the two types of processing can be seen in Figure 11.2. The rat can easily be recognized because it conforms to our concept pattern of "rat." Presented as parts of a puzzle, only fairly well-drawn features are recognized as rat ears, nose, and so on. Good caricaturists are able to suggest a well-known politician (of whom you have a strong concept) with a few pen strokes which often exaggerate dominant facial features. This also illustrates the gestalt principle of *Prägnanz*, which states that we tend to see and remember things in a way which is closer to their "ideal" form, or gestalt. Recognition of the whole rat illustrates conceptually driven processing; assembling a puzzle illustrates data-driven processing.

Because of the greater speed of conceptually driven processing in reading and other tasks of this nature, such processing tends to be dominant and interferes with data-driven processing. This is illustrated by the **Stroop** (1935) **phenomenon,** in which the word "blue" was printed in red ink on a card, the word

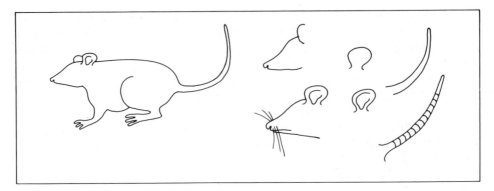

Figure 11.2   A poorly drawn whole rat; the same features with and without supporting detail. The rat is recognizable as such, but the parts of the same rat may not be recognized without enough detail to "cue off" the appropriate pattern recognition or concept of rat.

"green" in blue ink on another card, and so on. Subjects asked to name the color of the ink tended to respond instead with the word (incorrect) printed on the cards.

> Norman suggests that initial processing of information can take place in two modes. In conceptually driven, or top-down, processing, you begin with a concept of what you are looking for; this processing is very rapid. In data-driven, or bottom-up, processing, you try to assemble a concept from ambiguous information. Both types may operate simultaneously and may interfere with each other.

The influence of arousal level on attention   Levels of arousal also affect attention mechanisms. One of these effects is a shift from conceptually driven processing to data-driven processing as arousal increases. This creates the familiar inverted U curve of the relationship between performance and arousal, identified as the Yerkes-Dodson law (1908), shown in Figure 11.3. With very low arousal, subjects make quick guesses based on their concepts, and hence make many errors. As arousal increases, subjects tend to

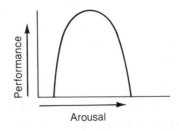

Figure 11.3   The inverted U curve shows that performance is highest with moderate levels of arousal.

focus their attention on details until, with very high arousal, the central task gets lost in details which may be irrelevant. Norman (1976) suggests this is the reason for panic reactions experienced under emergency situations. Maladaptive narrow focus in such situations can be overcome by **overtraining,** which reduces the number of cues that must be attended to by having each cue trigger a sequence of responses. This effect can be seen in learning to drive a car: At first, each individual skill (such as shifting) requires a great deal of attention (data-driven processing) until finally most driving responses become so automated that the driver can sing or talk while eating and driving. In a sense, the driving responses have been chunked into fewer and larger units.

The effects of level of arousal on the type of processing used suggests that the capacity of attention is limited—but that this limitation is based on the number of units attended to, rather than the amount of information available within each unit. Limitations on attention are of two basic types: the amount of resources available, such as intelligence or effort, and the amount of data available. You can have all the critical principles of learning available in one textbook, but if you cannot understand them or if you are unwilling to try to attend to them, you will learn little. Conversely, all the intelligence and effort in the world will be wasted if there is little data—as when you try to guess an absent person's true feelings towards you. In general, trying to do too many things at once strains attentional resources and nothing receives sufficient attention to get learned (for example, trying to skim highly technical material). Generally, high-priority tasks tend to be data limited; tasks of low importance (such as trying to study learning principles in the presence of a very attractive and seductive "friend") tend to be resource limited.

As arousal level increases, there is a shift from conceptually driven processing to data-driven processing. At first, this is adaptive, in terms of facilitating better learning and performance, but with very high arousal there is too much attention to detail (too much data) and performance deteriorates. Performance under conditions of high motivation tends to be limited by too little data; low-arousal tasks tend to be limited by the cognitive resources you are willing to apply.

Immediate true memory (short-term memory, or STM)   Although you may attend to or experience a great many things at one time in SIS, the number of such things that you can remember immediately, if asked, is rather small. The very act of being asked to tell what one experiences requires the act of coding the information which has passed the filters of attention; the end result of such coding is the first stage of real memory, or STM. Norman (1976) reviews the literature which suggests that the **channel capacity** of short-term, active, working memory is limited to about **seven ± two** units of information at any given time (Miller, 1956). Notwithstanding this limitation of immediate recollections, we are often aware that "we can see more than we can remember." Since the seven ± two limitation of STM is based on units of information rather than on basic yes/no **bits,** * the strategy of chunking several small units into a few larger units is a highly efficient way to get more information into STM in a given time.

For example, highly practiced typists think and type in whole words or short phrases rather than in individual letters. The basic technique of chunking is to group several items of information into a **chunk,** to name the group, and then to remember the name of the group. This illustrates the process of **coding** in information processing. Coding is a process which can occur in STM, in **long-term memory (LTM),** or in the transfer of information between the two types of memory.

This brings us to the question of the differences between STM and LTM. Norman views STM as a low-capacity storage unit for inputs, or as a **buffer memory system.** Since input levels are always fluctuating, STM serves to hold some of the inputs in consciousness during periods of high activity, until further processing can be effected. STM is then viewed as a fragile (a wide variety of influences can disrupt it), active (we are conscious of its contents; anything that disrupts active brain cell functioning obliterates STM) memory-trace system that holds a limited number of units of information. This memory-trace system may not only be disrupted by interference from new inputs, it also shows decay with time. A neuronal theory of these mechanisms will be discussed in the first section of Chapter 12.

Short-term memory (STM, or immediate memory) holds a limited amount (seven ± two units of information) for a short time for further processing (a buffer memory system). The units of information can be very small (bits) or large conceptual units (chunks). Unless protected by rehearsal, STM is easily interfered with by new inputs.

Consolidation—the process of transferring information from STM to LTM   Much of the material in immediate, experiential memory (STM) seems to vanish without a trace. Over time, however, we gradually accumulate information in the nonexperiential, relatively permanent form we call long-term memory, or LTM. This information, which can only be experienced after retrieval, is transferred from STM by the process (or processes) labeled **consolidation.** The primary mechanism for consolidation seems to be rehearsal, as when we try to learn something by repeating it to ourselves. Sometimes, as in trying to remember a phone number just long enough to reach a distant phone and dial it, the end result is nothing more than prolonging the STM, and no consolidation takes place. More commonly, we do succeed in consolidating at least part of the content of our STM. Norman (1976) suggests that the success of rehearsal in causing STM to translate into LTM partially depends upon a second process coming into play. This second process is coding. Coding can draw upon a strong

---

* "Bit" is the term used by computer people to designate the smallest possible unit of information that is either an active state (1) or an inactive state (0). These units constitute a binary (base 2) number system. More complex information is stored as combinations of bits (as when the number 5 is expressed in a base 2 number system as 101).

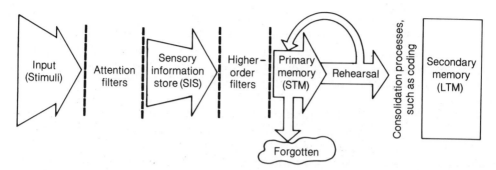

Figure 11.4   A summary schematic of the stages of learning in Norman's model of human information processing. Information is progressively lost in going from the great number of stimuli potentially available to that being attended to at the SIS level to the small number of units of information that can be held in STM at any given time. The capacity of LTM is presumed to be extremely large, but its content is, of course, slowly acquired over time through consolidation of material originally stored in STM.

preexisting association already in LTM, and it is more resistant to interference from distracting events than rehearsal. Therefore, the primary function of rehearsal is to hold input information* in STM (immediate memory) long enough for coding processes to be applied. The entire process of learning material (getting it into LTM) in Norman's information-processing theory is summarized in schematic form in Figure 11.4.

As we have seen, learning seems to occur more quickly with conceptually driven processing. This is partially a function of the relative contributions of rehearsal and coding in consolidating STM to LTM and may be experimentally manipulated. Restle (1964) found that giving subjects tasks and instructions designed to elicit strategy or concept-formation learning resulted in discontinuous learning or insightful-type rapid learning. Tasks and instructions which focused subjects' attention on the individual items to be learned resulted in continuous gradual learning. It is assumed that the coding operations in the first case were already present in LTM and the role of rehearsal was minimized. In the second case, considerable rehearsal was necessary for the subjects to hold the information in STM long enough to invent and perform coding operations. These results may explain why the types of learning tasks presented to subjects by behavioristically oriented researchers typically result in continuous learning curves, while the concept-formation tasks of the cognitive theorists are more likely to lead to discontinuous insight learning.

Both as a guide to understanding the concept of consolidation and as an introduction to the properties of the resulting LTMs, Norman (1976) classifies processing structures into two dichotomous types: fixed and flexible. Fixed processing structures are innately determined and consist of the central nervous system, the sensory apparatus, the mechanisms of sensory information store

---

* Much as information is held in a computer buffer storage system while awaiting processing.

(SIS), STM, LTM, and rehearsal mechanisms. These are analogous to computer "hardware" (computers and their input/output terminals). The second type of processing structures are flexible in that they are determined by the organism's experiences with its environment; they consist of controlling processes, such as rules and strategies (for attention and coding), and intentional control of rehearsal.

Flexible processing structures are analogous to the programs which specify how the computer hardware will actually process information. While fixed processing structures are very similar for all humans, flexible processing structures are much more variable. Most people, however, use some general principles of grouping and categorizing of information. For example, the names of the months are usually learned "chunked" into their seasons or through the rhyme, "30 days hath September . . ." Telephone numbers are learned as groups of digits rather than number by number, and the alphabet is learned in the form of the rhyme, "(ab-cd)–(ef-g)–(hi-jk)–(lmno-p). . . ." As can be seen in these examples, use of small numbers of chunks, which don't strain the capacity of STM, seems universal, and in many cases rhythm and rhyme cues act as supplemental contextual aids (which facilitates conceptually driven processing).

Transferring information from STM to LTM is called consolidation, and its primary mechanism is rehearsal. Coding STM in terms of existing associations increases resistance to interference. This occurs in conceptually driven processing. Coding strategies are flexible, learned processing procedures, such as grouping and categorizing information (analogous to computer programs).

Further characteristics of LTM   In the view of the gestalt theorists, permanent memory is not fixed, like words engraved on stone. Rather, they saw memories evolving towards better gestalts in accordance with gestalt laws. Since they saw these laws applying equally to perception, learning, and memory, their orientation was clearly a prelude to the information-processing theories, which see their processes (analogous to the gestalt laws) acting at every stage of the learning process (which begins with attention and perception, and concludes with long-term storage and retrieval mechanisms). Norman (1976) views processing of memories as not stopping with storage of the information in LTM. Newly arrived material, when retrieved, shows signs of having received less processing than older memories. Memories tend to get more and more "organized." Norman suggests viewing this as a hierarchy of processing steps leading to increasing "depth of processing." With time, memories get "hooked" to more and more associations and as a result become more persistent and more retrievable. Highly meaningful stimuli (which fit preexisting LTM structures) are more amenable to conceptually driven processing, leading to **deep processing** in less time. This is offered as an explanation of the tendency of seemingly more complex associated information to be learned faster and retained longer (or to be more retrievable). The possible brain mechanisms of LTM will be discussed in the next chapter.

LTM is not fixed but continues to be processed by organizing the information and hooking it to more and more associations. This activity, called deep processing, leads to longer retention (or easier retrieval).

The measurement of memory and the problem of retrieval   An enduring problem in the study of what is learned in either STM or more permanent memory is how to measure the extent of retention. Ellis (1978) discusses four basic measurement techniques, called **recall, recognition, savings,** and **reaction time,** respectively.

Recall may be the most obvious technique. Two types of recall procedures exist: free and aided. Free recall is simply being asked to tell what you remember of something you have just experienced (for measures of STM) or essay questions on tests (for measures of more permanent memory, or LTM). Aided recall involves remembering something when you are presented with contextual cues, such as previous words, in tests of serial learning. Since humans tend to create their own internal aids to memory (such as grouping the digits in series of numbers), what appears to be free recall may actually be aided recall.

The second technique, recognition, requires that you correctly identify items you have just seen (in tests of STM) or have previously experienced (for example, a multiple choice exam). Since strong arousal creates a tendency to "recognize" things never experienced, the general rule that recognition is more accurate than recall may not hold under conditions of overly high motivation (as in asking a rape victim to identify her attacker when she is at the peak of her anger).

The savings technique involves asking the person to relearn something experienced. Savings is a very sensitive measure of retention because a person may relearn something much more quickly than he or she originally learned it, even though he or she may fail recall and recognition tests.

Reaction time, finally, is a technique that tests recognition or recall of well-memorized items; it entails measuring the time between stimulus and response. This technique permits a detailed analysis of memory. Sternberg (1966) conducted research on the question of whether subjects examined items in memory one at a time **(serial processing)** or if all items were checked simultaneously **(parallel processing).** His subjects were given sets of digits having one to five numbers per set; later, they were presented with test digits and asked to report if the test digit was one of the numbers in a given set. If the subjects were using parallel processing, then they should have been able to check the test digit against the memorized sets of longer lists of digits in the same time required to check them against the shorter sets of digits. Sternberg found a linear relationship between the number of digits in the memorized sets and the time required for the comparison (about 38 milliseconds were required per digit, in the memorized sets). He interpreted these results as showing that memory scanning took place in the serial processing mode. Ellis (1978), however, notes that reading, in experienced readers, does not proceed in a letter-by-letter fashion but involves scanning groups of words and letters in a parallel processing fashion.

This parallel processing is analogous to the previously discussed conceptually driven processes that are dominant in experienced readers. Therefore, it might be concluded that serial processing would usually be used with less familiar material and parallel processing with highly familiar material.

Up to this point, we have discussed the information-processing theory of the stages and processes involved in learning. Theorists such as Norman have made other contributions to our attempts to understand learning (including mathematical models that are too complex to review here—consider yourself lucky). As we saw in the very beginning of this section, however, the general study of learning and memory has very ancient roots, and some of the results of these ancient studies have been influential in developing applications for improving your capacity to learn and memorize. In addition, modern theories may give us a way to better understand why the memory-enhancing methods of the ancients work as well as they do.

Four techniques have been developed to measure the extent of retention of memories: (1) recall (free and aided by contextual cues), (2) recognition (as in multiple choice tests), (3) savings (time required to relearn previously learned but apparently forgotten material), and (4) reaction time, which has been used to show that low-familiarity material seems to be associated with serial processing of memories rather than parallel processing (simultaneous scanning).

The techniques developed by the Greeks and Romans, called **mnemonic devices** today, illustrate the paradox that apparently complex material may be learned more easily than lists of simple words or nonsense syllables. Let us now turn to a discussion of these techniques.

Mnemonic devices, or plans for remembering and retrieving   Miller, Galanter, and Pribram (1960) suggest that the S-R "brute force" approach to memory followed by most of the associationists (behaviorists, or early functionalists) is simply unnatural when applied to human (or probably higher organisms') ways of remembering things under natural conditions. They even suggest that humans use plans, or strategies (coding systems), in the supposedly rote memorization of nonsense syllables. When Miller and colleagues (1960) asked (something not done by most behaviorists) subjects engaged in a task of "rote" memorization how they had learned the lists, all of the subjects who learned the lists reported using plans rather than sheer rehearsal. Some put the nonsense syllables into words; others used sheer drill but with rhythmic groupings (as in learning the alphabet) or imagined each syllable associated with a different part of the room or as part of an image or story. Moreover, when subjects were not told they would be asked to recall the lists, even hundreds of readings of the lists did not produce learning. This showed the critical importance of "intention variables" (resource allocation). The responses of the subjects seemed to show clearly that memorization was not the automatic process postulated by the behaviorists. It is of interest that all the techniques described by the subjects were mentioned in the ancient text on improving memory (*Rhetorica ad Herennium*) cited earlier.

The art (or science) of developing plans to aid memory is called mnemonics, named after the Greek goddess of memory, Mnemosyne. One of the several types of mnemonic devices described by Miller and colleagues (1960), called the **peg word technique,** may be useful for you to learn and use in memorizing lists of technical terms. You begin by thoroughly memorizing the following bits of doggerel (the numbers are the places in the list and the items mentioned are the "pegs"): One is a bun, Two is a shoe, Three is a tree, Four is a door, Five is a hive, Six are sticks, Seven is heaven, Eight is a gate, Nine is a line, Ten is a hen. The next step is to take the list of terms you wish to learn and form associations (usually in the form of visual images) between your terms and the peg words. As an example of "hanging your list of words to be memorized upon the pegs," consider the following numbered list of words: (1) ashtray, (2) firewood, (3) picture, (4) cigarette, (5) table, (6) matchbook, (7) glass, (8) lamp, (9) shoe, and (10) phonograph. You might begin by visualizing a bun of bread left on top of an ashtray, then setting wet shoes to dry beside a pile of just-ignited firewood, then a picture suspended from a tree or a photograph of a tree, and so on. If you carry out this exercise completely, you will be surprised at the ease with which the items can be learned, in order, and with excellent retention.

The role of imagery in facilitating learning and retention has been of interest to psychologists for a long time. This use of images as an associative technique has been investigated by Hasher, Riebman, and Wren (1976), who compared learning of pictures and concrete and abstract nouns under conditions of imagery, verbal, and standard free-recall instructions. Imagery was found to have facilitated learning, and concrete nouns (which could more easily be associated with images) were learned faster than abstract nouns. Subjects using imagery, however, did not have superior long-term retention of their material. In any case, if the use of imagery facilitates learning, then such conditions should have an indirect effect on retention, since new material which is learned more poorly would be less easy to recall.

Let us now turn to a second ancient method of aiding learning, the **method of loci,** which uses images of places or locations in a room as a mnemonic aid. Although this method is less used today, it is of interest because of the following story about how it was invented. In ancient Greece, the nobleman Scopas of Thessaly gave a great banquet and hired the poet Simonides of Ceos to chant a lyric poem in honor of his host. Simonides delivered the poem but included a passage in praise of the twin gods, Castor and Pollux. Egocentric Scopas was angered and told the poet that he would pay him only half the agreed-upon sum and that the poet should collect the rest from the twin gods. Just then a message arrived for Simonides telling him to leave the banquet hall to see two young men. The poet left but was unable to locate anyone outside. Before he could reenter the hall, the roof collapsed, killing everyone inside and smashing the bodies beyond recognition. The poet was able to identify all the guests for their relatives by visualizing the place occupied by each at the table and realized how his recall of names had been aided by his memory of locations. Speakers today may pay unknowing homage to Simonides' invention of the method of loci by beginning their speeches with the expression "in the first place." The first place in the method of loci was, of course, the mental image of a specific location in a building associated with the opening lines of speeches given by ancient Greek and Roman orators (in Norman, 1976).

Lindsay and Norman (1977) have suggested a modern version of the method of loci. In their version, a list of words to be remembered (such as a shopping list) is associated with a set of places lying along a path that is commonly used by the memorizer (in their example, the pathway leading to their university). The technique is to visualize the first item to be memorized in front of the door of the subject's house: in this example, a loaf of bread so huge it blocks the doorway. A similar procedure is followed with the other items on the list; the order of the items is linked to the order in which noticeable features of the pathway would be encountered. To recall the list, it is only necessary to imagine yourself going from your home to the final point on the path, looking at each location along the way and repicturing the objects placed there.

Norman notes that the problem with these mnemonic systems is the initial effort that must be expended to apply them. He gives four rules which relate these memory plans to modern theories of information processing: (1) the material must be divided into small basic units divisible into self-contained sections, consisting of four or five units per section; (2) the sections (chunks) should be internally organized into logical structures to facilitate conceptually driven processing, and sections should have names; (3) the material to be learned should be related to concepts already present (which could be peg words) in LTM to facilitate coding; (4) the speed with which processing depth increases can be improved by mental activities such as forming images, fitting material into stories or mental locations, or using rhythm or rhyme as unifying devices. The only problem with this last technique is that usually the whole rhyme must be given to remember items coming late in the lists. All these techniques conform to other aspects of information-processing theory in forcing full attention to the relevant material, forcing chunking, and providing structure to relate the chunks to one another and to previously learned material. Since memories so organized have received extensive processing, they are usually easily accessible from LTM. This brings up the final point, that most information-processing theorists assume that true forgetting (permanent loss of information) is a phenomenon associated only with STM. Inability to remember material that has reached LTM is assumed to reflect inadequate processing and is a failure of retrieval. Thus, the success of psychoanalysis in getting a patient back in touch with long-inaccessible memories is seen as caused by the fact that the sessions provide additional processing through free association.

Subjects using deliberate plans or strategies to aid them in memorizing material have been found to learn faster and retain more. Plans derived from ancient techniques for aiding memory are called mnemonic devices; the two reviewed here (peg word technique and method of loci) use the formation of images as an aid in learning. Imagery techniques have been found to aid learning but not retention.

Perspective

The stages of memory reviewed here are widely, but not universally, accepted. Some theorists postulate fewer or greater numbers of memories, and some even see SIS as simply the condition of fastest trace decay and LTM as the condition of slowest trace decay. Norman offers the following introspective exercise in defense of his theory: Although it is easy to recall immediately the last few words said by a conversation partner (and for some of us, even easier to parrot back those words), lasting verbatim recall requires considerable rehearsal of the material while it is still in STM.

In a sense, the information-processing approach represents a step backward for psychology. At the turn of the century, both James and Titchener discussed attentional mechanisms and types of memory corresponding to STM and LTM that they discovered through their "mentalistic" introspection method. Skinner (1974) dismisses information-processing theories as more of the same vague speculation about unobservable inner processes originally repudiated by the behaviorist revolution in psychology.

Chapter Perspective

The four approaches presented in this chapter differ almost as much from each other as they do from connectionist approaches. The type of approach represented by Saltz's theory is derived from the same experimentally oriented learning theory mainstream as the connectionist approaches, while the other three approaches all are derived from other traditions. Although information-processing theory is also closely tied to experimental psychology, its heavy use of computer terms and theory makes it a more esoteric branch of psychology. The other two approaches are not even derived from psychology as an academic discipline. Chomsky's theory has its roots in philosophy and linguistics; Piaget's theory originated in biology and today is more closely identified with developmental and educational psychology than with experimental psychology.

This diversity is reflected in the ways in which the data used in these theories has been collected. While the neofunctionalist and verbal learning theorists such as Saltz and the information-processing theorists have conducted much of their experimental work with college students, Piaget almost exclusively and Saltz to some extent have worked with small children. Chomsky's theory originated much more from his logical analysis of language than from experimental work per se, and Piaget has relied extensively on observational data rather than the results of controlled experiments. These theories are consequently focused on different learning phenomena than the theories tied to the learning psychology mainstream and are thus somewhat difficult to integrate with mainstream theories. Such an integration, if possible, would be desirable if the comprehensive learning theory of the future is ever to be developed. Hopefully, the diversity of modern cognitive approaches reviewed in this chapter will prove complementary to the ways in which the connectionist tradition is evolving.

Key Terms

accommodation

assimilation

attribute

base rule

bit

boundedness

buffer memory system

channel capacity

chunk

classification skill

coding

common response model

cocktail party problem

concept attainment

conceptually driven
(top-down) processing

concrete operations

conjunctive concept

conservation

consolidation

data-driven (bottom-up)
processing

decentration

deep processing

deep structure

dimension

disjunctive concept

egocentricity

equilibration

formal operations

function

generative grammar

integration

kernel sentence

linguistic competence

logico-mathematical
knowledge

long-term memory (LTM)

mediational facilitation

method of loci

mnemonic device

natural language

overtraining

parallel processing

particular grammar

partist strategy

peg word technique

phonological rule

physical knowledge

positive instance

preoperational

probabilistic concept

projection rule

reaction time

recall

recognition

savings

schemata

selective attention

serial processing

seven ± two

shadowing

short-term memory (STM)

simple concept

social-arbitrary knowl-
edge

Stroop phenomenon

structuralist

surface structure sentence

transformation

transformational rule

universal grammar

wholist strategy

Annotated Bibliography

A good introduction to the area of verbal learning and cognition in general is provided in E. Saltz, *The cognitive bases of human learning* (Homewood, Ill.: Dorsey Press, 1971). A classic text in the area is J. S. Bruner, J. J. Goodnow, and G. A. Austin, *A study of thinking* (New York: John Wiley & Sons, 1956). A much more recent text that provides a good overview of issues and research in cognitive learning theory is H. C. Ellis, *Fundamentals of human learning, memory, and cognition*, 2nd ed. (Dubuque, Iowa: William C. Brown, 1978).

Chomsky's theory of psycholinguistics and his critiques of Skinner's theory of language learning are given in N. Chomsky, *Language and mind*, enl. ed. (San

Francisco, Ca.: Harcourt Brace Jovanovich, 1972). A less idiosyncratic and more recent overview of psycholinguistics is D. S. Palermo, *Psychology of language* (Glenview, Ill.: Scott, Foresman, 1978).

An easy-to-read introduction to Piaget is his "How children form mathematical concepts" (*Scientific American,* 1953, 189, 74–79); a more recent and comprehensive work is his *Science of education and the psychology of the child* (New York: Viking Press, 1970). An informative collection of papers, including discussions of Piaget's theory of moral development, may be found in V. P. Varma and P. Williams (Eds.), *Piaget, psychology and education* (Itasca, Ill.: F. E. Peacock, 1976). Useful suggestions for applying Piagetian principles to the classroom are given in B. J. Wadsworth, *Piaget for the classroom teacher* (New York: Longman, 1978).

A very readable and comprehensive introduction to the area of information-processing theory is presented in D. A. Norman, *Memory and attention: An introduction to human information processing* (New York: John Wiley & Sons, 1976).

12

The Biological Boundaries of Learning

In the previous chapters on cognitive approaches to learning theory, we reviewed theorists (Montessori, Chomsky, Piaget, and others) who were not part of the mainstream of academic learning theory psychology. In this chapter, we will cover the contributions and ideas of theorists identified with comparative psychology, neuropsychology, and behavioral biology whose work adds another important dimension to our understanding of the learning process or processes. By relating learning phenomena to biological principles, such theorists have enriched our understanding in many ways.

As we have seen, two dominant trends seem to be emerging in our conceptualization of the learning process: (1) an increasing tendency to explain even such "simple" forms of learning as conditioning in terms of cognitive variables (awareness, predictive value of cues), and (2) an increased attention to biological variables. We shall explore the latter trend in this chapter. The biological variables we will examine are of two types: (1) those related to the neurophysiology and neuroanatomy of learning, and (2) those related to innate and "semiinnate" variables which reflect evolutionary pressures on the selection of adaptive modes of behavior.

Historically, most learning theories have been concerned with the effects of environmental cues on overt behavior. This position has taken its most extreme form in the radical behaviorist approach (now represented by the orthodox Skinnerians), which has deliberately tried to avoid speculations about events occurring within the "black box" of the brain. Even the cognitive behaviorists and the cognitive theorists have, for the most part, confined their speculations about internal processes to discussing internal variables in terms of "intervening variables" (hypothetical processes not related to neurophysiological or evolutionary data). Entities such as schemata, concepts, buffer memories, and S-R bonds, as well as processes such as bonding, equilibration, accommodation, and sensory filtering, are inherently unobservable. In part, this approach by learning theorists represents a residual reaction against the naive instinct theories and mentalisms of psychology's early history. In part, it may also reflect the repudiation of the primitive neurological models of learning developed by Pavlov and the gestalt theorists. Finally, it may reflect the woefully inadequate background in biological principles most American learning theorists possess. Whatever the reasons, the selective effects of evolution in preparing organisms to associate some cues more easily than others have largely been ignored. Both the "black box" (Skinnerian) and intervening variable approaches to understanding learning tell us little about the neurophysiology of learning. Almost every theorist reviewed in this text, however, would agree that learning is ultimately a function of the activities of the brain and its constituent neurons.

Before World War II, the techniques for investigating the functions of the brain were relatively primitive. Most research on the relationship of the brain to behavior was conducted by cutting out sections of brain (ablation) or damaging them (lesion). A host of more advanced methods have been developed since then, including electrical stimulation of, and recording from, selected brain areas; chemical stimulations; and much more precise lesion techniques (stereotaxic surgery). This entire line of research has greatly increased our knowledge of brain functioning and its relationship to learning. We will see how neuropsychological technology has advanced by comparing the pioneering contributions of Lashley and Hebb to the more recent comprehensive neurological model of learning and memory developed by Pribram. Pribram's theory will be explored in the most detail because it integrates many lines of physiologically oriented research on learning and memory, and because Pribram attempts to relate the processes postulated by Norman (in his information-processing theory) to neurological data and theory.

While the developing science of neuropsychology (a type of physiological psychology) has increased our understanding of what happens within the "black box" of the brain, advances in delineating the effects of evolutionary variables have come from two different scientific disciplines. One of these is the branch of behavioral biology known as **ethology,** which originated in Europe through the work of Konrad Lorenz, Niko Tinbergen, and others. The publication of Lorenz's book, *On Aggression* (1963), created considerable foment among environmentally biased American social scientists and rekindled the debate over instinct versus learning (nature/nurture). Ethology is characterized by a strong reliance on naturalistic observation in the field and by use of experimental procedures designed to approximate natural conditions in field and laboratory. An example of such an experiment would be to present various models of eggs outside the nest of a herring gull in order to determine which stimulus features of the models are most effective in eliciting the gull's instinctual response of egg retrieval. The ethologists suggested that many seemingly irrational human behaviors (such as war) reflect the same instinctual mechanisms (such as territory defense) mediating aggression in many lower animals. This view of human motivation as having instinctual components has recently been extended in the new (and very controversial) science of **sociobiology,** which will be briefly reviewed after we discuss the instinct theory of the ethologists. Another contribution of the ethologists has been the discovery of the phenomenon of **imprinting,** or the rapid learning of a very strong attachment to members of one's own species during a sensitive period of early development. This relatively (or sometimes totally) irreversible type of learning has characteristics of both learning and instinct.

The other scientific discipline which has contributed to our understanding of the effects of evolution on learning is the branch of American psychology known as **comparative psychology**. Although comparative psychology began very early in the history of psychology (in a sense, any psychologist who studies the behavior of more than one organism is a comparative psychologist), only recently has it focused on innate variables in behavior. Comparative psychology can be distinguished from ethology in the following ways: It tends to focus more on learning variables (rather than looking for examples of instinctual behaviors), and comparative psychologists make extensive use of laboratory experimentation on a relatively restricted number of species. Within this tradition, we will review the work of: (1) the Brelands, who discovered that learned behaviors similar to instinctual behaviors tended to "drift" towards becoming like the instinctual behaviors, (2) Bolles, who postulates that the behavior shown by animals during avoidance learning reflects "species-specific defense reactions," and (3) Garcia, Seligman, and others, who have found that organisms can easily associate some types of cues but may have great difficulty in associating other types. Garcia has related his results to innate "bait-shyness" mechanisms and suggests that all learning can be classified according to how innately prepared the organism is to learn a particular class of relationships. Seligman suggests that instinct and learning of such responses as bar-pressing by rats are only points on a preparedness continuum, with phenomena such as imprinting and learning of bait avoidance falling somewhere between instinct and unprepared learning, and contraprepared learning at the opposite end from instinct. All of these contributions suggest that it is necessary to take into account the evolutionary history of each organism studied. Thus, the principle of equipotentiality, which underlies the "laws of learning" described by most connectionist theorists, may only apply to "unprepared" responses, such as bar-pressing by rats. As evidence for the influence of genetic variables on learning, the chapter concludes with data concerning the differential learning abilities of strains of rats bred to be either "maze bright" or "maze dull."

As you read this material, you should try to learn: (1) where in the brain learning and storage of the different types of memory occur, (2) the probable physiology of the different types of memory first presented in the section of Chapter 11 covering the information-processing approach to learning, (3) how Pribram's holographic model of learning reconciles many different approaches to the neuropsychology of learning, (4) how different "learning" phenomena show how learning is related to instinct and the effects of evolution, and (5) what types of behavioral phenomena best illustrate biological influences on learning laws (such as imprinting, taste aversion, species-specific defense reactions, and so on).

The Neuropsychology of Learning and Memory
A Brief History of Neurophysiological Approaches to Learning and Memory
The search for the engram   Investigations of the relationship of the brain to learning and memory have been of two main types: (1) attempts to relate brain anatomy to the process of learning and to the storage sites of long-term memories **(engrams),** and (2) attempts to delineate the physiological processes

involved in learning and retrieval of memories. We shall first review the anatomical approach.

Historically, there have been two diametrically opposed views about the extent to which learning and memory can be related to specific brain areas. The extreme localizer (mosaic) view maintained that specific memories are stored in specific locations much as mail is stored in pigeonholes in a post office (in Gardner, 1974). This position was derived from the early successes of the great neuroanatomists, such as Paul Broca, in localizing cortical functions. A less extreme version of this view was advanced by Pavlov, who suggested that the cortical projection areas associated with USs act as dominant foci; when excited, they radiate electrical excitation which acts to attract the excitation produced by a CS, so that eventually the CS has the power to elicit the reflex. Thus, Pavlov saw classical conditioning as involving electrical connections between localized cortical projection areas (in Schneider and Tarshis, 1975). Opposed to this localizer view was the theory, advanced by the gestalt theorists, that the brain functions as a whole through electrical field forces generated by the brain during learning.

Karl Lashley, an American physiological psychologist, spent over 30 years trying to determine where, if anyplace, the engram might be localized. In his early work, he implanted insulating strips of mica between regions of the cortex to disrupt any possible field forces without effecting any losses of memory or learning. He made deep cuts between cortical regions to disrupt the kinds of connections between US-excited projection areas and CS-excited projection areas postulated by Pavlov—again, without losses of memory or learning ability. He then systematically removed various cortical regions from thousands of rats without destroying their ability to learn and remember, thereby disproving the localizer hypothesis.

Reviewing his research, Lashley concluded: "I sometimes feel, in reviewing the evidence on the localization of the memory trace, that the necessary conclusion is that learning just is not possible at all. Nevertheless, in spite of such evidence against it, learning does sometimes occur" (Lashley, 1950, p. 501). While Lashley found no evidence of localization of memory, memory deficits did appear in some of his subjects. The extent of such deficits, however, was related to the extent of the lesions—not to their location. From this data, Lashley (1963) advanced his **theory of mass action,** which stated that within functional regions (such as the visual association cortex), all parts of the region were equally effective in carrying out the function normally served by the entire cortical region. This mass function (within regions) compromise between strict localization theories and strict holistic theories has received clinical support. Observing brain-damaged World War I veterans, Kurt Goldstein (1963) noted that patients with damage in the association (thinking?) areas adjusted by accepting that their overall intellectual abilities had been reduced. Luria, the Russian cognitive-neuropsychologist whose work was discussed in Chapter 8, has also supported the mass function (mass action) concept by developing a series of testing strategies to evaluate the amount of intact function remaining within a damaged region (Luria and Majovski, 1977). If some intact function remains, the patient can be trained to compensate for behavioral deficits (showing plasticity, or flexibility, in brain functioning).

Testing both the holistic and the localizer views of brain functioning and memory, Lashley found memories to be represented diffusely throughout various regions of the cerebral cortex.

Following his studies of the effects of cortical lesions, Lashley rejected Pavlov's hypothesis that US-excited areas and CS-excited areas communicated through transcortical (horizontal) connections. He left open, however, the possibilities that either classical conditioning could be learned by subcortical centers or that cortical regions communicated indirectly through vertical connections to subcortical relay centers. Support for the first hypothesis was provided by Lashley himself when he found that rats could learn a light-dark discrimination after ablation of their visual cortex. This removal of the visual cortex, however, resulted in an almost complete loss of previously learned discriminations, suggesting that the conditioning was normally learned and stored at the cortical level. Further, this suggests that subcortical visual structures (the optic tectum) have the capacity to learn and store habits but do not do so as long as the visual cortex is intact. These results have been supported by the work of Doty (1961), who found horizontal cuts in the cortex of cats to have no effect, but vertical cuts (which interfere with subcortical connections) to impair, but not eliminate, classical conditioning. While teaching at Occidental College, the author and two of his students conducted a series of experiments which may also be interpreted as supporting the idea that learning is possible at either cortical or subcortical sites. They applied bits of paper soaked in potassium chloride (KCl) solution to the exposed membranes (the dura mater) of both cortical hemispheres of their experimental rats, and they applied saline solution to the exposed membranes of the "whole brain" control rats. (This procedure is supposed temporarily to shut off functioning of the KCl-treated cortices, or to create a "reversible lesion.") Both groups of rats were able to learn a black-white discrimination in the first experiment (Swenson and Goldwitz, 1972), with experimental animals learning almost as fast as saline-control rats. In the second experiment, the rats were required to run, alternately, into a white chamber and into a black chamber in successive trials. Before the beginning of each trial, a light was turned on over the entrance to the correct chamber. Both groups of rats learned this simple "concept" of alternating from chamber to chamber, although the KCl group (also called the cortical spreading depression, or CSD, group because KCl causes waves of depression of cortical functioning) took more trials to reach 90 percent accuracy (Swenson and Catania, 1973). When the status of the animals was reversed during testing of retention (the whole-brain control rats were tested after application of KCl and the experimental animals were tested without KCl), both groups showed retentional deficits. This suggests that the KCl rats learned through subcortical mechanisms and the whole-brain rats learned through cortical mechanisms. When their testing status was reversed, both groups showed effects that could be interpreted as resulting from interference between the two learning systems. In a further test, the guide lights were turned off and all animals were tested in their original training state (depressed or whole brain). Under these conditions, the KCl rats showed marked declines in accuracy, while the whole-brain controls were unaffected by the change. This final result (Swenson and Catania, 1974) suggests that the subcortical learning centers of the KCl rats learned primarily through the cues provided by the guide lights, while the rats with intact cortices learned a more flexible concept. It is, of course, not surprising, if one reviews the literature on classical conditioning of lower animals, to find that vestigial subcortical centers can be classically conditioned. Many animals with no cortex at all (and some without anything we would call a brain) can be classically conditioned (reviewed in Schneider and Tarshis, 1975).

If we conclude that learning is normally something that takes place at the cortical level in mammals, can we say anything further about localization of memories?* Diamond and Neff (1957) found that cats showed a loss of retention of an auditory discrimination after removal of their auditory cortex but were able to relearn the discrimination. This suggests that modality-specific learning (as auditory alone) is usually stored only in the appropriate region of the cortex, but that some other brain regions can store such information. Are there, then, any areas of the cortex that are particularly important for memory storage and learning? Penfield (1969) was able to evoke complex memories in the **temporal lobes** of patients awaiting surgical treatment for epilepsy. The complexity of the memory was proportional to the intensity of the electrical stimulation applied. Spinelli and Pribram (1966) found that stimulating the temporal lobes of monkeys through permanently connected electrodes (at low intensity) over a period of weeks resulted in faster learning of visual discrimination problems. Monkeys with temporal lobe lesions are not able to learn "learning sets," or general strategies for problem solving (Riopelle and Ades, 1951). This suggests that the temporal lobes have a special role in complex learning and memory. Penfield's results, however, could also be interpreted as showing that the temporal lobes are especially important for retrieval of memories rather than for their storage.

The focus on the temporal lobes is interesting because these lobes have embedded within them (below the temporal cortex) structures that are known to have an important role in the transfer of short-term memory to long-term memory (consolidation). Each temporal cortex has extensive connections with such a structure, known as the **hippocampus.** When the hippocampus is damaged in humans, they show severe **anterograde amnesias** (inability to form new permanent memories), although existing long-term memories remain intact. Such a person is forced to live in a world in which it is always a few hours or minutes after the accident that caused the injury (Milner, 1966). (We will further review the functions of the hippocampus in our discussion of Pribram's theory.) If the temporal cortex and the underlying hippocampus are especially implicated in learning and memory, is there any part of the cortex which may not store

---

* You may find it helpful at this point to turn ahead to Figure 12.3, which is a drawing of the brain showing areas involved in memory.

memories? The answer seems to be the frontal cortices, which, while they may be involved in reducing distractibility during learning, seem to have no storage functions. Tens of thousands of human patients have been subjected to removal of parts of the **frontal lobes** (and, in earlier days, to removal of the entire anterior portion), with few, if any, reports of memory loss (reviewed in Brown, 1976). These areas seem involved in abstract thinking rather than memory.

There is one more question we must try to answer before moving on with the history of the processes of learning. Do memories become localized in just one of our cerebral hemispheres, or does each hemisphere contain "carbon copies" of the memories of the other? In a series of animal studies, Sperry (1961) has shown that normally the engram formed by one surgically isolated hemisphere is transferred across the fiber bundles (corpus callosum and others) connecting the two hemispheres. Moreover, when these fiber bundles are cut in humans (for relief of the symptoms of major epilepsy), the person can be treated in such a way that independent memories are learned by each hemisphere (Gazzaniga, 1967). It has also been found (for right-handed persons, at least) that the left hemisphere is specialized for verbal functioning and the right hemisphere for spatial manipulation and recognition of temporal sequences, such as melodies. This may suggest that verbal and spatial memories do not completely transfer over to the right and left hemispheres, respectively, in adult humans. Gazzaniga (1967) has reported that when a split-brain subject (whose interhemispheric connections had been surgically severed) was shown a picture of a nude, projected so that it was only received by her right hemisphere, she denied seeing anything, but right-brain recognition was evidenced by her sly smile. This demonstrated that verbal labels were stored exclusively in her "blind" left hemisphere.

In summarizing the attempts to find an anatomical location for the engram, we can make the following points: (1) Memory in the intact mammal is stored throughout broad regions of the cerebral cortex except in the frontal lobes; (2) memories that are specific to one sensory modality are usually stored in that sensory receiving area, but other memory areas can store this type of information; (3) the temporal lobes are especially important for either the storage of complex memories or their retrieval; (4) the hippocampus, which lies in the medulla or white matter of the temporal lobes, is important in transferring complex short-term memories to long-term memories, and (5) memories "laid down" in one cerebral hemisphere transfer to the other hemisphere; such transfer, however, may be weak in the case of verbal information (which is stored in the left hemisphere of most people) and some types of spatial-temporal sequences (which are more strongly represented in the right hemisphere of most people).

It is clear that the strict localization theory of memory is invalid, although memories are not totally diffuse. Rather, they are somehow represented throughout large regions of the cortex. This suggests that individual memories must not be coded on individual neurons (cell bodies of nerves) but must instead be coded in patterns of cells. Since neurons form patterns by their

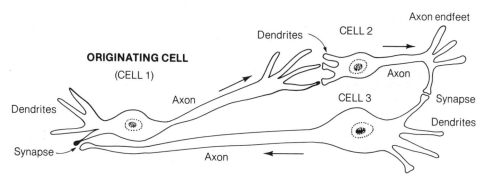

Figure 12.1   When the first cell is excited, it sends a message out its axon which synapses with the dendrites of Cell 2. Cell 2 then sends a message out its axon to Cell 3 (the message must cross the synaptic cleft between them) and Cell 3 reexcites Cell 1. This completes the first circuit of the loop. Cell 2 is then reexcited by Cell 1, and so on. The long arrows show the direction of the message.

connections to other neurons at their synapses (the gaps between the output of one neuron and the input areas of other neurons), alterations in synaptic structure or function have become the prime targets in the continuing search for the structural basis of long-term memory. We will now examine synaptic events and the processes of memory.

The processes of learning and memory   Donald Olding Hebb has been active in the investigation of brain functions and memory since the middle 1930s. He was one of the first physiological psychologists to develop a comprehensive multistage theory of learning, a theory which has influenced many cognitive and neurological theories of memory. The stages of memory described in the preceding chapter in the discussion of Donald Norman's information-processing theory of learning are very close to the stages described by Hebb. In turn, Karl Pribram's theory, to be described next, further develops many of the ideas advanced by Hebb.

Hebb first distinguishes between **immediate memory** (short-term memory, or STM) and long-term memory (LTM). He suggests that STM consists of active networks of nerve cells that repeatedly excite one another. These **reverberating loops** of cells can maintain a stimulus trace in the brain from a few seconds to many minutes. What makes the patterns of cells form into loops is that the cell which originally brings the sensory information into the cortex is hypothesized to receive onto its receiving processes **(dendrites)** inputs from cells further along in the loop. As the output processes **(axons)** of these cells stimulate the first cell, it then sends signals back to the next cells, which ultimately causes the first cell to be restimulated. The excitation in the loop, if fairly weak, finally dies down; the loop then "breaks" and the information is lost from the brain, or "forgotten." A simplified "loop" is shown in Figure 12.1.

Because loops are hypothesized to be dynamic electrical and chemical events (messages from dendrites to cell bodies to axons are electrical in nature; chemical substances called transmitters relay the messages across the synapses), they are fragile and prone to electrical and/or chemical disruption. For example, Hebb (1966) notes that when mental patients are scheduled to receive electroshock therapy, they can be asked to learn a series of nonsense syllables just before the treatment. After patients have recovered from the confusion that follows such shock treatments, they can be asked how many syllables they remember. When shock is given just after learning, the typical result is that no retention is evidenced. When there is a delay, some retention is found, and the subject shows considerable savings when relearning the list. This implies that short-term memory is susceptible to disruption in its initial stages but that it changes with time into a more durable form. This process of change is called consolidation; it is the process whereby the dynamic STM trace is converted into a structural LTM trace. Such a change clearly does not occur all at once. Hebb states that according to contiguity theory, when neuron A fires a neuron B, the A-B connection is strengthened. According to reinforcement theory, however, a reinforcement must occur just after the firing for the bond to be strengthened. In any case, the slow progress of consolidation shows that the synaptic change that strengthens the A-B connection is only begun by dynamic events. The full process of consolidation takes an hour or more. Hebb (1966) speculates that the consolidation process involves either a structural change at the synapse (such as growth in the synaptic knobs), or a narrowing of the synaptic cleft, or a biochemical change in the two neurons involved.

Hebb notes the effects of hippocampal damage in humans and compares these to animal studies. From this, he speculated that the hippocampus is only necessary for the consolidation of complex STM, and that simple S-R learning can be consolidated through some sort of biochemical effect of reinforcement which keeps the loops active long enough to "cement" the synapses involved. Thus, Hebb sees memory as involving a transition from a dynamic STM form (which involves activation traveling around loops) to a structural pattern of altered synapses (which occurs gradually in the process of consolidation). Since memory in this theory is stored in patterns and not in individual pigeonholes or nerve cells, it is reasonable to assume that memories are widely represented throughout functional regions of the brain rather than being stored separately in specific locations.

As noted, when mental patients are given electroshock therapy (also called **electroconvulsive therapy,** or ECT), they show a loss of memory for learning that occurred just before the shock **(retrograde amnesia).** This would seem to imply that disruptive electrical events stop the process of consolidation and hence prevent new STMs from ever becoming structural LTMs. There are some complications of ECT (called ECS, or electroconvulsive shock, when applied to animals, since no one pretends that shock is given to animals as therapy, or for their "own good"), however, that must be noted. Hines and Paolino (1970) found that while rats given ECS after learning a passive avoidance response show the expected amnesia for the avoidance response, their heart rates are accelerated in the test situation, showing some evidence of conditioned fear. This might be explained as either a function of fear conditioning that takes place in lower brain centers not affected by the shock, or as a sign that consolidation is faster for autonomic responses. Quartermain, McEwen, and Azmitia (1970) found that when animals trained to avoid shock were given ECS 1 second later (ECS is most effective if given very soon after the original learning), the expected loss of memory of the avoidance response resulted. But if the animals were given "reminder foot-shocks" outside the test situation, or if they were given repeated opportunities to display the "lost memory of the avoidance response," recovery from the apparent retrograde amnesia occurred. These results could be interpreted to mean that some consolidation had occurred almost immediately and the test procedures provided enough stimulation to allow these partially consolidated traces to complete the consolidation process, thus making it appear as though the memory "returned." Alternatively, it could be that ECS disrupts retrieval of the memory rather than blocking consolidation. This retrieval hypothesis has been supported by Meyer (1972). Another alternative to the "interference-with-consolidation" interpretation of the effects of ECS has been offered by Nielson (1968) and DeVietti and Larson (1971). These authors have suggested that since the ECS produces a change in brain state, material learned when the subject is in a normal brain state is not retrievable. Thus, retrieval is dependent upon the state of the animal's brain. DeVietti and Larson (1971) found that if the animals were tested four days after the ECS (presumably when their brains had returned to the same state as during the original learning), fear memories were again retrievable. This phenomenon, called **state-dependent learning,** could be offered as an alternative explanation of the results of the KCl (cortical spreading depression) studies presented earlier. That is, instead of proving the existence of subcortical learning, the results of these studies could be interpreted as demonstrating that the depressed animals tested in a nondepressed (whole-brain) state were unable to retrieve their memories of the alternation response because the state of their brains had been altered.

Most of ECS and human shock therapy studies, however, do support the "interference-with-consolidation" hypothesis, at least with responses mediated by the central nervous system. Many of the anomalies disappear if we think of consolidation as a process that begins immediately after the learning experience and then may take several hours to complete. Retrieval difficulties may reflect partially consolidated memories which can be more fully consolidated either by reminder cues or by time. State-dependent effects may be due to the fact that the cues (including the sensations induced by ECS) are part of the total experience of the subjects. One could hypothesize that since the memory is only weakened by ECS (assuming that some consolidation had occurred just prior to ECS), stimulus conditions unlike those of training would interfere with retrieval; on the other hand, cues associated with training (a non-ECS state) would facilitate retrieval.

For Hebb, the first stage of true (short-term, or immediate) memory consists of messages traveling around reverberating loops of neurons. STM is easily disrupted, or prevented from consolidating into LTM, by ECS, which produces a retrograde amnesia. This amnesia does not extend to primitive fear responses, may be at least partially reversible, and may reflect ECS stimulus properties or state-dependent learning.

Even if most evidence favors Hebb's contention that STM is a dynamic event which can be interfered with to prevent or weaken consolidation, what of his theory that LTM consists of altered synapses? Raisman (1969) has shown that synaptic connections have the ability to change (at least, in the septal nuclei of rat brains). Frazier, Angeletti, and Bradshaw (1972) have shown that new synapses can be formed by peripheral neurons (sprouting) in the presence of a naturally occurring substance (nerve growth factor). Rosenzweig and colleagues (1967) have shown that rats placed in enriched environments not only have much heavier brains than rats reared in stimulus-poor environments, they also show much faster learning. Morrell (1961) has demonstrated that treating one cortical hemisphere with aluminum hydroxide cream results in an irritative focus, with tangled and disordered nerve fibers. Interestingly, a similar "mirror focus" appears in the untreated hemisphere (presumably by transfer of information across the corpus callosum), indicating that patterns of neuronal synapses can be altered by dynamic factors (that is, by transfer of the "experiences" of the chemically treated hemisphere). Taken together, these results suggest that either changes in synapses or growth of new synapses can occur as the result of experiences and that these changes may represent the anatomical basis for consolidated, or long-term, memory.

This in turn leads one to speculate that perhaps the old popular belief that mental exercise strengthens the brain just as physical exercise strengthens the muscles might be correct after all. A few years ago, anyone suggesting that thinking and learning might make the brain grow would have been laughed right off the speaker's podium!

Several lines of evidence suggest that LTM could consist of altered synapses. It has been shown that dynamic events (such as those of STM) can alter synaptic connections and that high-stimulation environments lead to increases in cortical weight.

Morrell (1961) reported another interesting finding. He found that the ribonucleic acid (RNA) obtained from the "mirror focus" was considerably different from that found in normal brain tissue. This suggested that dynamic events in the brain could alter the kinds and amounts of RNA in the brain. RNA is the molecule that takes the instructions mapped onto DNA molecules (the genetic code) and uses them to direct protein synthesis. RNA molecules are very large; they consist of thousands of atoms arranged into four types of base substances and connectors. To those searching for a chemical substrate of memory, RNA is intriguing because its base substances can be arranged in many combinations; an impressive amount of information could be coded in sequences of such combinations. This great storage capacity is one of the reasons why many researchers have examined RNA as a possible element of learning and memory. The role of biochemical factors in memory can be viewed from two perspectives: (1) that memories are coded directly onto RNA or protein molecules and that somehow this coding is subsequently retranslated into altered patterns of specific neuronal activity, or (2) that

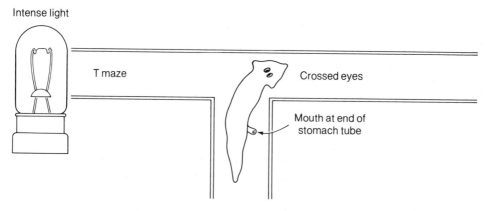

Intense light

T maze

Crossed eyes

Mouth at end of stomach tube

Figure 12.2   A flatworm (planaria) making up its mind in a T maze. Since most of the nervous system is posterior to the brain, this may be a difficult process. The worms do learn to choose one of the maze arms consistently, either because of the intense light (aversive US) or because of food rewards (instrumental learning?).

RNA or other macromolecules (such as proteins) are somehow involved in forming altered or new synapses. Let us examine the first perspective.

In 1964, Hyden and Egyhazi found that rats trained to use their nonpreferred paws to obtain food showed both higher amounts and different types of RNA in the half of their cortex that controlled that paw. Control animals who used their preferred paws (and hence required no new learning) showed no changes in RNA. Simply showing changes in RNA as the result of learning, however, does not explain whether the RNA molecules carry the memories, or if the changes in RNA reflect changes in structural characteristics of synapses or other brain elements. Dingman and Sporn (1964) found that injection of a chemical that inhibited RNA synthesis interfered with formation of new memories but had no effect on old memories. These results could be interpreted as either showing the production of RNA "memory molecules" to be necessary or as showing that RNA is somehow involved in structural changes during consolidation of STM to LTM. Again, we are unable to determine the exact role of RNA in memory. How, then, could it be shown that RNA is indeed the memory molecule? One method might be to transfer the memories of a task encoded on the RNA of one animal to another animal. If the second animal showed signs of "knowing" the solution to a task to which it had never been exposed, that would be solid evidence that RNA is a "memory molecule."

The first experiments to demonstrate this were conducted by James McConnell and his students, using flatworms (planarians). First, they classically conditioned their animals using shock as the US and a flash of light as the CS. The trained worms were then fed to untrained worms. The untrained worms exhibited the conditioned responses, indicating that "memory" had been transferred (McConnell, 1962). To prove that RNA was the critical element in the transfer, they then trained the planaria in a simple T maze (see Figure 12.2) and afterwards fed only the extracted RNA to untrained worms. Again, transfer of learning was implied by the superior performance of worms fed "trained RNA" when compared to the performance of worms fed "untrained RNA" (McConnell, 1966).

Though McConnell's results seemed to demonstrate that memories could be transferred by transferring RNA, criticisms were not long in coming. Hartry, Keith-Lee, and Morton (1964) found that RNA from worms given random shocks was just as effective in facilitating shock avoidance as that from worms trained to avoid shock. These results suggested that perhaps RNA simply produced a sensitization effect. McConnell (1968) replied to such criticisms by suggesting that the negative results represented methodological problems of rough handling procedures and failure to maximize motivation. In any case, attention then turned to attempts to replicate McConnell's transfer effects in mammals.

An early successful example of such transfer was performed by Jacobson in association with Babich and Bubash (in Jacobson and Schlecter, 1970). They trained rats to approach feeding places only when a light was on (a S_D). These donor rats were then sacrificed; their RNA was extracted and injected into the abdominal cavities of recipient rats, and these rats were, in turn, tested on a light and on a tone discrimination task. If the transfer effect was really sensitization, it would be expected that the recipients would approach the food cup during either tone or light presentation. The results were that the light-tested rats approached more during light flashes, offering strong support for the **RNA transfer hypothesis.** Another group of rats, trained to approach the food cup when a click was sounded, suffered a similar fate. The recipients of their RNA approached the food cup four times as often when a click was sounded as when a light was flashed. At this point, some of you are no doubt considering grinding up professors and extracting their (presumably) highly trained RNA as a shortcut to absorbing knowledge. But wait! As you should have suspected, numerous negative reports challenging these findings soon appeared (reviewed in Brown, 1976). In addition, Luttges and colleagues (1966), using radioactive tracers, found that most abdominally injected RNA was secreted before reaching the brain. In spite of many successful replications (over 50 are reviewed in an article by Byrne, 1970), the whole issue of transfer of memories through transfer of RNA is still in doubt. Chapoûthier (1973), reviewing the conflicting reports, concludes that the successful studies used a coarse RNA extract, while most unsuccessful attempts at replication used a pure RNA extract. This suggests that impurities (such as proteins) may actually have carried the memory information.

Some support for the **protein memory hypothesis** has come from the laboratory of Ungar (1966), who habituated two groups of rats to either a loud noise or a strong puff of air. Following habituation, the brains of the rats were homogenized and the resulting protein extracts were injected into naive recipients. The recipients habituated more rapidly to the stimulus to which the donor had been exposed. In 1970, Ungar reported the isolation of an extract obtained from the brains of mice that had learned to avoid shock by leaving a dark compartment. When injected into naive mice, it caused them to leave their normally preferred dark chambers, in the absence of experiences with aversive consequences. Ungar named this extract scotophobin (a Greek word meaning "fear of the dark"). Other support for the protein hypothesis came from the work of Barondes and Cohen (1966). They reported rapid forgetting of a maze habit in mice injected with puromycin (an antibiotic which inhibits protein synthesis). The same researchers, however, found no disruption of consolidation when cyclohexamide (also a protein synthesis inhibitor) was injected. Cohen, Ervin, and Barondes (1966) offered an explanation of this discrepency. Puromycin induces abnormal electrical activity in the hippocampus (which, as we have already seen, is involved in consolidation of complex memories), while cyclohexamide does not. Thus, the results of puromycin may reflect convulsion-inducing properties which act like ECS, rather than a direct interference with memories. The effects of puromycin can also be reversed by injections of saline solutions into the brains of the experimental animals (reviewed in Grossman, 1973). We are left with the conclusion that although protein formation may have some function in memory, its exact role is unclear and its status as the "site of engrams" is uncertain.

Another approach which examines the role of chemical factors in memory has concentrated on altered levels of **transmitter substances** (which carry messages from axons to dendrites). Deutsch and Deutsch (1973) have looked for the engram in altered mechanisms of transmitter substance storage and release at synapses. As the result of experience, these mechanisms might alter the efficiency of synapses, and hence make certain patterns of neurons better suited to conduct messages in the future. Drugs which block the action of transmitters were found to have selective amnesic effects. Scopolamine, which blocks the neurotransmitter acetylcholine (ACh), had no effect on memories of experiences occurring less than 30 minutes before the injection. As the time between training and drug injection increased, the amnesic effects increased, until almost complete amnesia was produced with one- to three-day training to injection intervals. If the injections were given two weeks after training, memory of the training was improved or unaffected. This was presumably because the drug acted to block more recent, interfering memories. Deutsch and Deutsch (1973) reported further: Drugs that blocked the enzymes (cholinesterases) that normally destroy ACh not only raised the levels of ACh but also had effects opposite to those of scopolamine. One- to three-day-old memories were unaffected, while one- to two-week-old memories were almost totally lost. With still older memories, the amnesic effects diminished. These results suggested that consolidation was a much slower process than indicated by the results of the ECS studies. Deutsch and Deutsch's findings may, however, reflect losses in ability to recall newly consolidated memories rather than interference with consolidation per se. These results do lend tangential support to the gestalt and information-processing view that memories continue to change and strengthen long after being learned.

Several types of macromolecules have been investigated in the search for the engram. It has been shown that increased and altered RNA is produced by learning, although the theory that memories can be directly transferred by

RNA injections is disputed. Drugs interfering with protein synthesis can apparently block consolidation, resulting in amnesia. Memory transfer by protein transfer is also disputed. Drugs interfering with transmitter substances cause amnesias—perhaps by blocking recall of newly formed memories.

Let us summarize the data presented thus far. The process of learning seems to begin with selective attention, which results in some dynamic activation of groups of neurons. In intact mammals, these are cortical neurons, and the activation consists of cells sending messages across their synapses to other neurons which, in turn, send messages onward in a chain of events that eventually reexcites the original neurons. This short-term memory trace is prone to disruption by electroconvulsive shock or by the waves of depression produced by KCl when it is applied to the surface of the membranes over the cortex. This pattern of activation stimulates the gradual formation of a structural representation of the memory, known as long-term memory or the engram. The transformation of STM to LTM, called consolidation, probably involves some changes in the synapses, just as Hebb predicted. During this process, altered RNA and new proteins are produced, and experimental manipulations which interfere with either RNA or protein production can produce amnesic effects. Some properties of memory may be coded on RNA or protein molecules, although the extent to which this occurs is debatable. Memories which are fairly well along in the process of consolidation may be blocked by agents which interfere with transmitter functions. Engrams seem to be diffusely represented throughout whole regions of the cortex, rather than being coded on individual neurons, and the hippocampus plays some vital role in the consolidation of complex information. Finally, we know that the total storage capacity of LTM is very large and that memories that appear to have been lost can, under certain conditions, be brought back.

Any theory that professes to be a comprehensive theory of memory must incorporate most of these ideas and research results. It must provide an explanation for the survival of engrams in the face of extensive cortical damage (recall the work of Lashley), and it must take into account the large storage capacity of LTM (Reynolds, 1974). One theory which is able to accomplish this is the **hologram* analogy theory** proposed by Karl Pribram (1971). This theory should not be interpreted as stating that we literally create holograms in our heads, but rather that learning and memory involve processes similar in function to those involved in the creation and depiction of holograms. Another advantage of the

---

* Holograms or holographs are the products of a special photographic process called holography in which laser beams (usually) are used to expose the photographic plate (the holograph). Unlike the photographs created in normal photography, holographs contain in each of their parts some information from each part of the scene photographed. Consequently, when viewed with normal light, holographs look like collections of wavy lines rather than pictures. If viewed under laser light, a three-dimensional image appears in front of the holograph; this image changes in appearance when viewed from different angles. When a holograph is cut in two, each half will show all the original scene, rather than half the scene, as when a conventional photograph is bisected. See the appendix to this chapter for a more detailed description of holography, or see Pribram's article in *Psychology Today* (1971b).

model of learning and memory developed by Pribram is that it provides neurophysiological explanations for the various stages of memory presented in the discussion of Norman's information-processing theory. To the extent that Pribram's theory accurately reflects the data on brain mechanisms during learning, it provides support for the multistage view of learning and memory.

Pribram's Theory of Learning and Memory: Holograms in the Head

As we saw in the discussion of Norman's information-processing theory, the first step in learning is paying attention, which is a highly selective process. A complex reflex correlated with paying attention is called the orienting reflex, or the "what-is-it?" reflex. Sokolov (1963) found that any change in a repeatedly presented stimulus configuration, including a reduction of intensity, could elicit this reflex. He concluded that the orienting reflex was triggered by a mismatch between incoming information and some patterned memory trace, or **neuronal model,** of a given situation. Thus, attention results from the simultaneous activation of an internal pattern and the effects of the incoming information. The interaction of these two sources of activation is the first step in forming new memory traces. Pribram (1971b) has noted that usually two laser beams (or two halves of one beam split by a mirror) are needed to create a hologram, or a holographic "memory," of the object exposed to the laser beams. The interaction between these two sources of "activation" creates a pattern, and all the information about the object viewed is coded in each part of this pattern. Why not, Pribram concludes, consider the two sources of activation eliciting the orienting reflex as analogous to the two laser beams?

Attention and Habituation

When a sensory input matches the internal neuronal model, no new learning occurs. Instead, the electrical responses recorded from the retina of the eye and from the visual relay stations show decrementing (decreasing) responses to monotonous visual stimulation (Pribram and McGuinness, 1975). Only changes in stimulation trigger increased responses from these sensory elements, and this may represent an initial stage of filtering sensory information store (SIS), a type of information storage in Norman's theory that occurs before true STM. This decrementing of sensory responses to repetitive stimuli is called **habituation;** it is the process by which we learn not to pay attention to redundant or irrelevant cues. Like other forms of learning, habituation begins with a STM phase and then progresses to a more permanent form of memory. Unlike normal LTM, however, habituation usually decays progressively over time periods as long as six months (Pribram, 1971b). Pribram and McGuinness (1975) also note that a more complex type of patterned habituation occurs in the visual cortex. In this type of habituation, some cells initially fire at higher rates (increment), while others fire at lower rates (decrement). These authors suggest that this complex pattern of changed firing rates to repetitive stimulation represents the initial, or STM, phase of forming a neuronal model of the ongoing environment. Eventually, this altered state of activity is consolidated into a more durable neuronal model. When reexposed to environments represented by the neuronal model, the organism again shows the behavior associated with habituation—that is, a lack of brain arousal and an absence of the orienting reflex. Paradoxically, even forms of mismatch with the neuronal model caused by removal of the repetitive stimuli or lowering of their intensity result in dishabituation and a return of the orienting reflex. Pribram (1971b) reports that when a very noisy elevated railway line in New York was torn down, people sleeping in apartments near the line suddenly awoke and called police to report "some strange occurrence." The calls coincided with the former schedule of the trains, and the strange occurrence was, of course, the deafening silence that had replaced the expected sounds of the trains. The fact that the people had learned to ignore the sounds of the trains illustrates a long-term form of complex habituation, and their arousal reactions to the lack of such sounds illustrates dishabituation. This suggests that the people's neuronal models of repetitive night sounds had even reflected the timing of the trains, and that the mismatch with that model caused by the closing down of the line had elicited the orienting reflex and arousal.

The types of habituation just discussed may be related to the stimulus filters responsible for selective attention effects. Recall the discussion of selective attention from the section on information-processing theory in the last chapter. We presented evidence that when a subject was exposed to two simultaneous messages, he or she was only able to report back the information contained in one of these messages. When the gross physical characteristics of the unattended message were changed radically (as from a male to a female voice), however, the subject was aroused by the change and able to report it. Somehow the subject had monitored the physical characteristics of the unattended message on an unaware level. For the subject to detect the change in type of stimuli, some part of the brain must have had a model of the general stimulus characteristics of the sound before the change. When the sound no longer matched this model, he or she began to pay attention to the sound on a conscious level. Norman suggests that lower-level filters reduce the intensity of such "unimportant messages," or attenuate them, so that without a radical change of the type just described they are not strong enough to lead to aware attention. This attenuation by Norman's "stimulus-characteristics filters" could be created by the decrementing of sensory responses to repetitive stimulation reported by Pribram and McGuinness (1975). It was also reported that when "highly meaningful" words (like the subject's name) were embedded in the unattended messages, the subject became aware of them. This "filter for meaning" process might be explained by Pribram's and McGuinness's patterned habituation, which they cite as evidence of the formation within the brain of a new neuronal model. This model of the present state of the person's environment, along with the altered state of the receptor processes, constitutes a memory system which operates on an unaware level and which inhibits the orienting reflex when the organism is exposed to conditions matching the neuronal model. Thus, habituation of the two types just described is a type of unaware learning of what not to pay attention to and what not to put into normal long-term memory. This learning occurs whenever the orienting reflex is not followed by unusual or consequential events and may involve the temporary arousal of some regions of the cortex while the appropriate neuronal model is being formed. This neuronal model then acts to inhibit the orienting reflex and conscious awareness while stimulus conditions remain unchanged.

In this model of selective attention, the subject monitors repetitive and/or meaningless stimulus events at an unconscious level. The process by which monitoring shifts from high-involvement aware attention to unconscious monitoring is habituation. The unconscious monitoring system scans incoming information and compares it to a relatively short-term model of the existing world. Whenever new information doesn't fit this neuronal model (either because of a radical change in stimulus characteristics or because of having a high "meaning value" through fitting existing long-term memories or predicting important events), the orienting reflex and conscious attention result. This mechanism has the result of ensuring that we spend most of our energy on important events and form new long-term memories only of such events. This protects us from filling our permanent memory banks with a multitude of trivial units of information.

Pribram suggests that our brain forms neuronal models of the world. When stimuli fit these models and do not lead to consequences, habituation occurs. Different types of habituation, analogous to the different stimulus filters in information processing, serve the same purpose—that of "tuning out" irrelevant information from aware attention of the type associated with the orienting reflex. Unaware scanning of habituated stimuli, however, continues until a mismatch is detected, causing dishabituation.

Pribram and McGuinness (1975) have tried to relate habituation and monitoring mechanisms to the functions of various parts of the brain. Habituation of the type that inhibits the orienting reflex seems to depend upon activities of the **amygdaloid nuclei** which lie deep in the temporal lobes between the hippocampus and the brainstem. When these nuclei are removed, the experimental animal shows an ever-continuing orienting reflex and cortical arousal which never habituates. During the orienting reflex, numerous body and visceral responses (such as increased heart rate) can be observed. These components of the orienting reflex can be abolished by lesions to the top and sides of the frontal lobes. Let us now review the functions of the frontal lobes in selective attention and learning.

Luria (1970) identifies the frontal lobes as the place where plans and strategies are first formed. These take the form of neuronal models "of the possible," or abstract thinking. These neuronal models, like other neuronal models discussed so far, are related to short-term memory in that they are assumed to consist of altered states of electrical activity originating in the functions of neurons. Miller (1972) reports that damage to the frontal lobes does not result in loss of memory of formerly learned abstract ideas (which are assumed to be stored in engrams or relatively permanent structural form in the back half of the cortex), but does prevent the learning of new abstractions. Pribram suggests that the frontal lobes are the place where ongoing events are compared to the highest types of neuronal models, which consist of expectancies about sequences of stimuli. Thus, they relate successive events to predicted sequences and coordinate different channels of information originating in different types of sensory cortex so that these different activated regions do not interfere with each other. An example of this functioning might be turning your head towards a sudden movement and being prepared to experience the sound associated with that movement. When events do not follow our expectancies, we experience surprise, which manifests itself in both arousal of other regions of the brain and in the physiological responses associated with the orienting reflex. This increased arousal, in turn, creates a state of aware attention and a readiness either to act or to memorize information about the unusual event.

We have already seen that damage to the frontal lobes of animals increases distractibility. When such animals are faced with tasks requiring delayed responses, they seem unable to prevent events occurring during the delay period from interfering with STM related to the original learning. Pribram (1971a) suggests that such animals can not form neuronal models which would predict that their original responses will still be successful after a delay. In other words, they do not discriminate the events occurring during the delay from events before (original training) and after (making the delayed response) because they have no neuronal model predicting the entire sequence of events. This is because they are unable to coordinate multiple channels of inputs (the inputs arising from the events of different parts of the entire sequence). For such animals, every event is a totally new event rather than part of an ongoing sequence and so every event calls for attention. This is the reason for the increased distractibility. Since every event is attended to, no one event stands out enough to call forth the body signs of the orienting reflex.

To conclude this discussion of Pribram's theory of the anatomy of learning and attention, one more area of the brain should be mentioned. The hypothalamus, which lies at the top of the brainstem, seems to coordinate most motivations and contains powerful "pleasure" and "pain" areas. This area becomes active during periods of uncertainty (mismatches between inputs and neuronal models) and may provide the motivation to reduce uncertainty. Pribram notes that damage to the part of the hypothalamus known as the mammillary bodies seems to reduce the incentive to recall previously learned material (1971a).

Pribram cites studies showing that the effects of these operations are exerted on central (higher) mechanisms controlling selective attention and not on sensory sensitivity or response mechanisms. These higher mechanisms, in turn, determine what gets registered as STM or, following the hologram analogy, what starts the operations of the neuronal equivalent of the laser beams which finally create a holograph.

Pribram summarizes data showing that when two input signals are separated by an interval, the first acts to start the formation of a neuronal model (similar to the first laser beam in holography) and the second determines what the organism will do (form a memory or make a response). Paying attention is

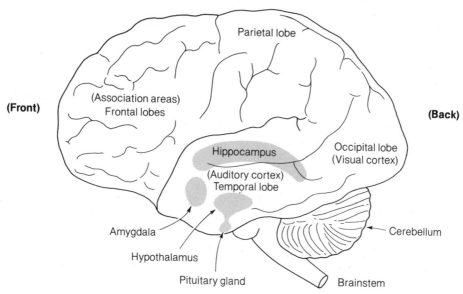

Figure 12.3   *An idealized side view of the human brain showing the locations of brain areas assumed to be vitally involved in memory functions. Deep structures are shown by dotted lines, and surface features by solid lines. Memory-involved structures are underlined, and the hypothalamus, which is in the center of the brain on top of the brainstem, is shown as lower than it would be in reality.*

reflected in slow changes in brain electrical activity called the **contingent negative variation** (CNV), which has been shown to correspond to expectancies or readiness to process information (Pribram and McGuinness, 1975). At the end of the CNV response, if and when the organism starts to do something, a sharp positive deflection is noted in the electrical recordings made from the cortex. If the actions do not confirm the expectancies, the hippocampus becomes active and the organism is ready to learn something new. This hippocampal activity is thus triggered by errors or mismatches between the neuronal models and the inputs. In a manner somewhat analogous to the actions of the second laser beam in forming a holograph, the hippocampal activity is involved in the process of consolidating the registered input into a new long-term memory. Pribram thus distinguishes between "registration in awareness," which is controlled by the amygdala circuits, and changes in the neuronal model, or learning, which is a "registration in memory" controlled by the activation of the hippocampus. As an aid to your processing of this information about the anatomy of the learning process, a simplified sketch of the human brain is presented in Figure 12.3.

To summarize: Stimulation activates the brainstem and is transmitted to the various areas of the sensory cortex to be compared to neuronal models (STM and/or LTM models) of past sensory events and to LTM models of expected sequences. Input is also compared to STM models of expected sequences in the frontal lobes, which also coordinate multiple inputs. If a mismatch between models and inputs is detected, the hypothalamus is activated and creates the motivation to resolve the mismatch. This motivation causes the excitatory circuits of the amygdala to trigger the orienting reflex and an aware and aroused cortex. If responding does not resolve the mismatch, the hippocampus inhibits overall arousal while facilitating the consolidation of STMs arising from other brain areas. If the new neuronal model (memory) resolves the mismatch, the inhibitory circuits of the amygdala facilitate patterned or complex habituation in the sensory cortex. Habituation to simple repetition of stimuli can occur at the brainstem level.

The Processing of Information

Pribram has attempted to explain the active processes (plans, strategies, and so on) first described by the cognitive theorists—and explain them in neurophysiological terms. He suggests that internally aroused "foci" in the brain are responsible for intentions, selective attention, and directing the eyes to scan for information congruent with existing neuronal models (stored as synaptic states).

Fitting inputs to existing patterns (neuronal models) enhances the coding and transmission of such inputs. This perceptual bias created by the brain is called **feedforward.** This bias may be responsible for the embarrassing situation created when you think you recognize someone (as in the example of concept-driven processing in Chapter 11) and greet him or her cheerfully, only to discover too late that you have addressed a total stranger by mistake. Since the brain seeks patterns, a visual source of information somewhat similar to your known acquaintance elicited the neuronal model corresponding to the known person. Thus, discrepancies between model and inputs were ignored (did not lead to aware attention) until the stranger's failure to respond to your greeting made your mistake painfully evident.

The reason that your brain saw a pattern is that uncertainty (mismatches) is a major reason for cortical arousal. To reduce that arousal, your brain selected the best-fitted neuronal model (memory) as a basis for designing your perception. Pribram describes the general mechanism for seeking complete or matching patterns as the **TOTE (test-operate-test-exit)** process. First, the brain acts to reduce mismatches between inputs and neuronal models by **testing** the incoming data against the existing models. If the patterns (assumed to reflect the relative states of arousal of regions of the synaptic microstructure) do not match, axons are activated and carry messages. Axons fire at a preset intensity when they become excited sufficiently over their firing thresholds. Since they either fire or do not fire, rather than becoming excited proportionately to the source of excitation as dendrites do, they operate by "1-0," or yes-no, digital logic. Their firing rates code the state of excitement of all associated dendrites and cell bodies. The messages carried by the axons can either **operate** to form new memories (new neuronal models) or to alter the environment through overt behavior. In any case, the brain then **tests** the state of affairs produced by the operations or, in other words, receives feedback on the success of its efforts. If the operation was successful, the arousal state ends **(exits).** Thus, both internal responses (cognitive restructurings) and external behaviors are tested to see if they have been successful. Of course, there may have to be several successive operates and tests before a difficult problem or a puzzling situation can be resolved. The same mechanism operates during attempts to recall difficult information. All of us have experienced the discomfort (from overarousal due to incomplete or mismatched patterns) occasioned by trying to recall a specific item and not being able to do it immediately. There is a very real sense of pleasure and relief in finally recalling the item (finding the appropriate model, or pattern) and terminating the cognitive process.

Pribram tries to relate active processes, such as plans, to active foci in the brain which create perceptual bias through a feedforward mechanism. He also presents a model of resolving mismatches called the TOTE model (test-operate-test-exit). The TOTE process functions through feedback mechanisms.

Learning on the Neuronal Level

As previously discussed, we must attend to stimuli before they can be registered in memory. Registration can occur for this reason: The stimuli are discrepant with existing neuronal models (which can result in emotional arousal) or because of arousal due to motivational variables. Pribram (1971b) suggests that both these phenomena can serve a function similar to one beam of the two laser beams used in making most holograms, with the sensory input analogous to the second laser beam. The two sources of excitation can be recorded as regions of altered electrical activity arising from the dense "feltworks" of synaptic connections within the brain. In the higher regions of the brain, each neuron has thousands of dendrites; while each has only one axon, this axon has thousands of "endfeet." Thus, every cortical neuron participates in thousands of connections or synapses (Pribram, 1969). These regions of altered electrical activity, generated by thousands of neurons, are the neurophysiological representatives of STM, in Pribram's theory, rather than impulses traveling from one neuron to another of a loop circuit, as in Hebb's theory. At every point where the active loci originating from internal attentional factors (such as previous memories, neuronal model mismatches, emotional reactions, and so on) intersect with the activation produced by the incoming perceptual information, an interference (interaction) effect is created. These interference patterns, created by the convergence of two sources of activation on synaptic connections, have been demonstrated to occur in the outer layer of the cerebellum (a part of the brain that integrates perception with motor coordination) and therefore are probably also present in the cerebral cortex (Pribram, 1971b). The interference patterns store information in a distributed form, which is congruent with Lashley's observations that localized lesions do not destroy specific memories. For these memories to be easily recollectable and clear, the intactness of wide areas of the pattern is required. The period of time in which the pattern is represented by the active neuronal processes of excitation and inhibition at the synapses and altered background levels of electrical potentials is the dynamic memory (STM) stage. If

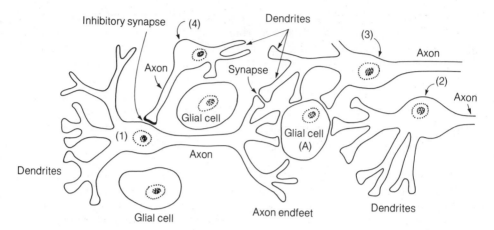

Stage I   As messages go from the axon endfeet of the neuron labeled as (1), in the form of transmitter substances which affect the dendrite of neuron (3), either transmitter substance or altered RNA builds up near glial cell (A). You will also note the inhibitory synapse between the axon of neuron (4) and the cell body of neuron (1).

Figure 12.4   Three stages in Pribram's model of how patterns of excitation (at synapses between dendrites and axons) and inhibition (at synapses between axons and cell bodies), which are the physical substrates for STM, are changed into physical patterns of new synaptic connections (the physical basis for LTM).

the inputs (from other brain areas and from sensory reception) which create the pattern are too weak, the STM traces will fade away (as more recent inputs interfere with their effects on synaptic connections).

If the altered synaptic patterns are maintained long enough, however, the neurons involved begin to respond to the altered chemical environments (created by the release of large amounts of transmitter substances and transmitter-destroying enzymes) by producing increased amounts and new types of RNA. This RNA may function as an inductor (a chemical-releasing factor that triggers cellular changes) for cell division of one type of glial cell. Under normal conditions, these glial cells surround all neurons and prevent them from forming new synaptic connections. Pribram suggests that the new types of RNA may also alter the characteristics of existing synapses by causing the axon "endfeet" to release still more transmitter substances into the synaptic clefts.

The end result is that either the increased transmitter substance or the new RNA triggers division of the glial cells. Pribram (1971a) has reviewed data showing that the number of glial cells in the cerebral cortex increases with age. When a glial cell divides, a space is left between the two daughter cells; through this space chemical substances can diffuse. These substances induce "sprouting" of the axon endfeet and/or dendritic endings adjacent to the new space. The

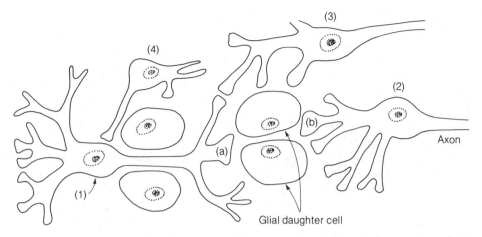

Stage II   The altered chemical environment of glial cell (A) induces it to divide into two daughter cells which opens a pathway for the formation of a new synapse between neuron (1) and neuron (2). This new space allows the diffusion of chemicals which induce axon (a) and dendrite (b) to "sprout."

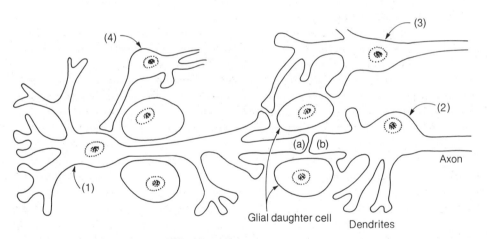

Stage III   Axon endfoot (a) and dendrite ending (b) have formed a new synapse. Until the endings are fully "mature," the amount of transmitter released by axon endfoot (a) is assumed to be relatively low.

sprouting is directed by chemical factors that attract the new nerve endings to grow towards each other through the space provided by the division of the glial cells (neurobiotaxis). When the sprouts stop growing at the point where their cell membranes are almost, but not quite, touching, a new synapse is formed. The new pattern of synaptic connections provides the structural basis of a new LTM. For the sprouting of the nerve cell endings to occur, new RNA must be produced to guide the production of new proteins. The new proteins are needed to construct the sprouts. This process is shown in Figure 12.4.

By postulating that consolidation is a complex multistage process, Pribram has provided us with a theory that can fit together much of the divergent data on factors involved in transforming STM into LTM. For example, we have noted that protein synthesis inhibitors (such as puromycin) normally create amnesic effects if injected within a few hours of learning new responses, and that such amnesia can be "undone" by procedures such as the injection of saline solutions into the brain. Pribram's theory would explain such effects in terms of the puromycin's preventing nerve-end sprouting but not preventing division of the glial cells. The injection of saline would then reverse the amnesia by triggering the nerve ends to resume growing towards each other through the space provided by division of the glial cells. When a new LTM is first forming, the new connections may be unable to generate large amounts of transmitter substances; hence, these new patterns are particularly sensitive to the effects of agents interfering with transmitter release or breakdown. We mentioned previously that agents affecting transmitter concentrations could create amnesic effects days after the original learning. This might be because these agents affect the last stage of the consolidation process, in which the new connections are gradually becoming more effective. Since Pribram's theory takes into account the processes of cell division and cell growth, it offers an explanation for the production of increased RNA and protein. You will (hopefully) be able to recall the information stored in your engrams concerning the data which showed that RNA production does seem to increase during learning and that injections of "trained" proteins may alter response characteristics of recipient animals. Pribram's theory would suggest that studies which seemed to show transfers of memories through injections of impure RNA or proteins may instead have demonstrated the transfer of substances conducive to glial cell division and nerve-end sprouting (and hence conducive to very rapid learning), rather than chemically coded memories per se.

Other virtues of Pribram's theory include a consideration of the potential for a very high storage capacity and a structural basis for the associative nature of memories. Because memories are stored in patterns, a given synapse could be part of many patterns, all of which could share the same general region of the cortex. Hence, the storage capacity of such a system of patterns is limited mainly by how many unique combinations could be created by an enormous number of synapses. The model might also predict, however, that if a very large number of patterns were stored in a particular region of the cortex, it might become harder and harder to retrieve a specific older memory. Newer memories, being more intimately associated with present events, should be easier to recall, as is indeed the case. Older memories might also have lost some of their constituent connections through normal neuron attrition. The model would predict, however, that as long as some of the pattern remains, the entire memory could be brought back. We have all experienced the recall of memories which we thought we had lost; often this recall occurs when we are again placed in situations similar to those in effect when the memory was formed; other times it is the product of deliberate, prolonged effort. This effort might begin by remembering events occurring near in time to the information you wish to recall. By beginning with strong memories and then mentally reviewing closely associated events, you can gradually work back to the difficult-to-recall material. Pribram explains the associative nature of memory by suggesting that associated patterns share some of the same connections. Recalling strong memories (such as the peg words of the mnemonists reviewed in Chapter 11) would result in activation of synapses common to both the strong memories and the associated material. This would enhance the activation of the rest of the pattern, where the weaker memory is stored. Similarly, learning new material in an associated context should be easier because you could use parts of existing patterns of connections rather than having to create a whole new pattern.

In Pribram's theory, arousal due to interaction of sensory inputs and internal factors results in regions of altered electrical characteristics (states) and increased production of transmitter substances, which induce production of RNA and cell division by glial cells. Division by glial cells makes room for the formation of new synapses, which require RNA and protein. This altered pattern of connections is the physical basis of LTM. At first, transmitter substance release is low, but this increases as the new patterns mature and become more resistant to disruption.

Perspective

The pace of research in the area of the neurophysiology of learning and memory has continued to increase, and many valuable insights into the processes within the brain have resulted. One attempt to integrate the seemingly chaotic (and sometimes conflicting) mass of data into a coherent theory has been made by Pribram. Such a theory allows us to see the relationships between different lines of research and serves to provoke future research aimed at either confirming or disconfirming the theory. Just as Norman's information-processing theory was based on analogies with computer processing, Pribram's theory is tied to analogies with holography. While such analogies do not tell us anything directly related to behavior, they can serve to generate predictions which, in turn, generate research. In addition, they can provide valuable guidance in our progress from vague speculations about the mechanisms of learning to the final goal of fully understanding such mechanisms. Let us now turn from our examination of neurological bases of learning and memory to an examination of the genetic factors interacting with learning.

The Biologically Determined Boundaries of Learning

Contributions by Ethology and Comparative Psychology to Understanding Learning

Ethology and the rebirth of instinct   Most American learning theorists have no difficulty accepting the idea that the anatomy and physiology of our brains are inherited and that the mechanisms of learning are therefore also inherited. What they have had trouble accepting is the idea that what can be learned, and even behaviors, may also be inherited. Learning, in higher organisms, has traditionally been thought to be determined merely by the environment's acting upon the highly developed mammalian brain (or bird brain, in the case of pigeons). Konrad Lorenz, a leading spokesman for the branch of behavioral biology known as ethology, has criticized psychology's neglect of the impact of selective evolution upon the behaviors of specific species:

> In retrospect it seems peculiar that psychologists have been so slow to pursue such clues to hereditary behavior. . . . Darwinian evolution quickly fired the imagination of biologists. Indeed, it swept through the scientific world with the speed characteristic of all long-overdue ideas. But somehow the new approach stopped short at the borders of psychology. The psychologists did not draw on Darwin's comparative method, or on his sense of the species as the protagonist of the evolutionary process. [Lorenz, 1958, p. 68]

The ethologists, by focusing on the evolution of **species-specific behaviors,** reintroduced the idea of instinct into the discussions of learning theorists. One of the central concepts of ethology, species-specific behavior refers to predispositions to behave in certain ways which are the product of the individual evolutionary history of each given species. Another central concept is the idea that such behaviors are elicited by a specific stimulus **(sign stimulus)** to which the species is innately programmed to respond by emitting an innately determined motor pattern **(fixed action pattern).** The mechanism connecting the sign stimulus and the fixed action pattern is called the **innate releasing mechanism.** For example, in the male stickleback fish, the sight of another fish with a red belly (which is the color of a male stickleback's belly in the breeding season) activates the innate releasing mechanism for the release of a stereotyped attack response. Selective attention factors are involved in instinctual behavior just as they are in learning. A wooden model of a fish that has a red belly but otherwise does not resemble a stickleback will be attacked, while a highly accurate model without the red belly does not provoke an attack (Tinbergen, 1951).

In the previous example, a fish was the experimental subject. Much of the ethologists' research was conducted with fish and birds. This is because the ethologists, while considering much mammalian behavior to be instinctual, also thought that instinctual behaviors in mammals were often masked by learned behaviors (Lorenz, 1958). They hoped that by studying instinctual behavior in fishes and birds, where such patterns were revealed with greater clarity, they could extract general principles that would also apply to higher mammals. Lorenz considered instinctual patterns to change slowly in the species, and to stubbornly resist learning in the individual. Further, he considered them to have a "peculiar spontaneity" (the emission of a fixed action pattern is considered to be reinforcing), and to be considerably independent of immediate sensory stimuli (except sign stimuli). Because the emission of fixed action patterns is reinforcing, the ethologists thought that animals would search for the appropriate sign stimuli and would learn the appropriate appetitive behaviors to gain access to the opportunity to emit the fixed action pattern. This model of the relationship of instinctual and learned behaviors is similar to the adaptive model proposed by Staddon and Simmelhag (1971), reviewed in Chapter 9. In both models, appetitive behaviors, though they can be learned, also reflect the process of selective evolution, and the tendency to emit such behaviors is inherited. Recently, Skinner (1969) has discussed the role of "phylogenic contingencies" which select for higher baseline rates of some operants than others when an animal is deprived of the opportunity to emit some consummatory response (such as chewing and swallowing food, which would be considered by the ethologists to be a fixed action pattern). Thus, most complex behavior involves an initial stage of variable appetitive behavior (which can be influenced to various degrees by inherited factors) and a final stage of stereotyped consummatory responses, which are almost completely or completely genetically determined (Burghardt, 1973). Which sets of appetitive behaviors are likely to be emitted in a particular situation are a function of the mood of the organism, which reflects changing internal variables such as deprivation states (Lorenz, 1963).

Moods can be transmitted from organism to organism by a process similar to imitative learning, or modeling. If the first rats in a pack (who are likely to be dominant animals) pass by an unknown food without eating any, no other rat pack member will eat any, either. When the first animals do not eat the food, they sprinkle it with their urine or feces. Since the first animals are usually the older rats in the group, they may have eaten (in the past) small amounts of poisoned food similar to that which they now mark. Through this behavior, knowledge about the probable safety of food is transmitted to younger rats, who may subsequently deposit feces on types of food marked by their elders. Subsequent generations of rats may imitate the marking behavior of these once-young rats, and thus experience is transmitted from generation to generation through "marking traditions." When marking is difficult in particular situations, the rats will still show considerable behavioral flexibility and expend considerable effort in attempting to mark (Lorenz, 1963).

The phenomena of mood transmission (transmission of a predisposition to emit certain classes of appetitive behaviors) can also account for the transmission of aggressive urges from a few individuals to all of the members of a human mob. Lorenz, who calls this group aggression in humans **militant enthusiasm,** regards it as the phylogenetically evolved behavior by which a group defends itself against anyone who appears different or who behaves in ways deviant from the group's norms. Thus, for Lorenz, aggressive behavior in humans is an instinctual behavior triggered by the sign stimuli of experiencing one's physical or psychological territory as being invaded, or of otherwise feeling threatened. The irrationality of human violence reflects the miscarriage in modern society of instinctual patterns that were adaptive in our early evolution. Since Lorenz sees aggression as innate and aggressive consummatory behaviors as self-reinforcing, he sees the answer to handling such impulses as one of providing channels for nonlethal expression of aggression through sports and other means. Other sign stimuli for the release of human aggression may include pain experienced in the presence of another member of your species and frustration (which may represent denial of access to important resources). Even in humans, some aggression in such circumstances may be adaptive, especially if through the expression of successful assertiveness one improves one's own chances of getting resources related to survival or success in mate selection.

Sociobiology and instinctually biased behavior in humans   This focus on the importance of genetically programmed behaviors in improving an organism's chances of surviving and passing on its genes is the subject matter of a new and controversial natural/social science called sociobiology. Its central premise is that much seemingly irrational human (and animal) behavior can best be understood as reflecting innate patterns that increase the chances of the survival of one's genes. In this context, altruism at the cost of one's own life is adaptive if it leads to the survival of enough of one's relatives (who carry many of one's genes).

Aggression, in this view, is seen as tending to occur only in those contexts where it improves the chances of the survival of your genes, either through your relatives or through your own efforts. Thus, human competition may lead to the acquisition of more material resources, and this in turn may make you more desirable as a mating partner. Killing members of groups unlike yourself may make more resources available for individuals who carry some of the same genes as yourself. In this model, nepotism, or a bias towards favoring your own relatives in hiring and other circumstances, is an adaptive, or "fit," behavior. Humans tend to favor their own kin in their wills, and relationships with relatives are very often more enduring than relationships with nonrelated friends. Selective factors related to innate biases towards selecting potential mates with "good genes" are seen as responsible for our "irrational behaviors" during courtship. Prejudices against people wearing glasses may partly reflect genetically determined avoidance of one who shows signs of bad genes for eyesight. Taking the sociobiological view to its extreme, love is nothing but DNA crying out for itself (and for a quality version of itself, at that)! Since males in most primate societies are the sexual aggressors, the continuance of such patterns in human societies in which most members are seeking to change traditional sex roles shows the resistance of inherited mechanisms to modification by learning. In general, the sociobiologists would maintain that we can best predict the actual behaviors of human beings in biologically relevant situations (competition, courtship, altruism) by examining their consequences in terms of gene selection and protection rather than through learning variables. "If we admit to the possibility that human behavior has been selected to maximize inclusive fitness, then our preoccupation with genetic relatedness and our responses to it are certainly no surprise"* (Barash, 1977, p. 310). That is, if our ancestors who survived were the ones who looked out after their kin and offspring, then whatever traits that were responsible for such behaviors would become more common in following generations.

The ethological and sociobiological assumption that many human behaviors

---

* "Inclusive fitness" refers to characteristics facilitating the survival of the individual carrying a specific set of genes.

are innately determined rather than learned has been given new support by recent studies of infants' imitations of adults' facial and manual gestures. Meltzoff and Moore (1977) found that infants as young as 60 minutes old were successfully able to imitate mouth opening, tongue protrusion, lip protrusion, and sequential finger movements. While rejecting the idea that each specific response modeled by the adults acted as a sign stimulus to release the corresponding fixed action pattern, the authors did conclude that imitation per se is an innate ability of humans. Its selective advantage would be that of increasing mother-infant interactions.

The ethologists say that some instinctual fixed action patterns of behavior are released by sign stimuli which "fit" into innate releasing mechanisms like a key into a lock. Consummatory responses are likely to be more stereotyped, innately determined, and self-reinforcing than appetitive behaviors. General behavioral tendencies, such as imitation and discrimination in mate selection, may have innate bases in humans.

Ethology and the phenomenon of imprinting   We have noted the ethological and sociobiological contributions to rekindling attention to instinctual determinants of behavior in higher mammals—and the ethologists' recognition of learning variables in appetitive behavior and in imitation. In this regard, the ethologists were much more open minded than even the functionalist school of American learning theorists. A major tenet of functionalism was that most apparent dichotomies actually represented extreme ends of common continua. One dichotomy not treated in this manner by the functionalists, however, was the learning versus instinct dichotomy. Rather than regarding most behavior of higher animals as learned, the functionalist could have tried to organize behaviors according to the extent to which they were determined by innate factors. If they had done this, they would have discovered several phenomena which have characteristics of both instinct and learning. The ethologists (and some modern learning theorists to be reviewed later in this chapter) have followed this approach. One such phenomenon explored by the ethologists is imprinting, or a young animal's acquisition of a very strong attachment to the first moving object presented during a restricted time period (critical or sensitive period). This phenomenon, in its pure form, is only found in animals able to following moving objects soon after they are hatched or born (precocial animals, such as ducks). Many features of this type of learning seem innately determined. For example, although ducklings will develop a strong attachment to any moving visual stimulus presented during their critical period for imprinting, imprinting is facilitated when duck calls are combined with the visual stimulus. Early in his scientific career, Konrad Lorenz imprinted ducklings by waddling in front of them and quacking, to the astonishment of the folks in his Austrian village (Lorenz, 1952). Hess (1972) has found that the apparent sign stimulus properties of duck calls are only partially prewired. Exposing duck eggs in an incubator to a recording of a human voice resulted in subsequent better imprinting to a visual stimulus combined with a human voice than to one combined with recordings of duck calls. Hess concludes that the mother duck may "preimprint" her duck-lings to her calls while they are still in the egg.

In addition, the development of imprinting is closely tied to maturational variables. Ducklings younger than 4 hours do not have the appropriate motor skills to follow objects moving with any considerable speed; at about 32 hours of age, the onset of an innate "fear of strange objects instinct" prevents following. You will recall that Maria Montessori also incorporated the idea of such critical (learning can only occur during a limited time period) or sensitive (learning occurs maximally during this limited time period) periods in her sensory-motor-maturational theory of learning (Chapter 5). Imprinting resembles in-stinct in another important way. Responses that are acquired during sensitive periods tend to resist extinction much more than other types of responses, and they tend to be relatively rigid in their expression. It is almost as if the organism to be imprinted is born with an almost completed instinct "wired in" its brain. All the early exposure to the moving object does is complete a small gap in the circuit. This flexibility ensures that under natural conditions the duckling will learn to follow its own parent (rather than all birds like itself) preferentially; although some following may occur to any conspecific (member of same species), the requirement for the fixed auditory component ensures that the bird will not follow prowling predators if they should pass near the nest before the parent bird(s) appear to become the normal imprinting stimuli.

Imprinting violates some learning principles which we have studied in previous chapters in ways other than showing maturational linkages and neg-ligible extinction. For example, punishing following responses (by shocking a duckling or placing hurdles in his pathway) increases the strength of the im-printing and the tendency to show the following response to artificial parents in a laboratory setting (Hess, 1972). A laboratory apparatus for the study of im-printing is shown in Figure 12.5.

If the bird is placed in a condition of sensory deprivation, the sensitive period may be extended (Sluckin, 1965) and the bird becomes progressively less fussy about adequate imprinting stimuli. Eventually, the innate urge to imprint may become so strong that the bird will imprint on a corner of a box!

Even though imprinting in the sense described by Lorenz, Tinbergen, and the other European ethologists is, strictly speaking, reserved for the type of very rapid development of attachments observed in precocial birds, many similar phenomena have been reported in altricial (born helpless) animals (Sluckin, 1970). Harlow's famous studies with monkey "mothers" made of cloth and wire have demonstrated that infant monkeys raised with a choice of cloth or wire "mother surrogates" show an innate preference for the cloth mothers and cling to them whenever frightened. This development of an abnormal attachment during the prolonged sensitive period of the altricial monkey works against the animals when they become adults. Harlow (1971) reports that such animals show missing or inappropriate social and sexual behaviors when grown up, indicating that normal patterns of species identification and attachment must be learned during the critical period or they may never be learned. Dennenberg (1973) has reviewed evidence that different patterns of early affectional relation-

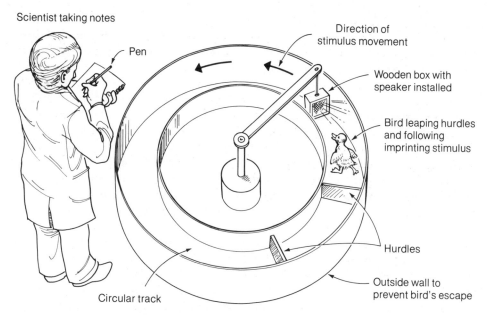

Scientist taking notes

Pen

Direction of
stimulus movement

Wooden box with
speaker installed

Bird leaping hurdles
and following
imprinting stimulus

Hurdles

Outside wall to
prevent bird's escape

Circular track

Figure 12.5   *A laboratory apparatus of the type used to produce and study imprinting. Speed of the imprinting stimulus and number and type of obstacles may be manipulated. After exposure to such a stimulus during its sensitive period, a duckling will follow such objects in the future and will even remain near them in preference to real birds in a choice situation!*

ships (as in communal kibbutzim in Israel) may lead to learning of very different patterns of adult affectional attachments. It is hardly unreasonable that so important a matter as learning appropriate affectional patterns should have a strong innate component.

The basic idea just presented is that learning of things related to an organism's chances of survival is a process which is affected by the selective effects of evolution. We will now turn to other phenomena which seem to show the influence of innate factors on learning. Such phenomena, which possess both learning and instinctlike properties, demonstrate the need to consider innate variables in controlling and predicting the behavior of organisms.

Imprinting is the development of a strong attachment to something experienced during a sensitive period of development. It is like both learning and instinct, extinguishes slowly if at all, and is strengthened by punishment experienced during acquisition.

The misbehavior of organisms   When Marian Breland (a former student of Skinner's) and her husband became comparative animal psychologists, they attempted to apply operant learning principles to earning money reinforcers for themselves. This they did by training animal acts for carnivals and advertising displays. One such display had a raccoon picking up coins and depositing them in a piggy bank for food reinforcement. Their subject quickly learned to pick up a coin and drop it through the slot in the bank, although the raccoon hesitated in letting go of the coin. When the task was made slightly more difficult, requiring the animal to pick up two coins, serious problems arose. Instead of depositing the two coins, the raccoon would pick them up, rub them together for a period of time (seconds, even minutes), dip them into the slot, and then pull them back out to rub them together again. The behavior of rubbing the coins together is, of course, similar to the "food-washing"* behavior shown by raccoons under natural conditions. With more trials (and nonreinforcement of the washing behavior), this interference by the strong instinctual pattern of food washing became stronger instead of being replaced by the "correct"† reinforced response of depositing the coins. Breland and Breland (1961) labeled this progressive interference of the instinctual behavior with the reinforced behavior **instinctual drift.** The "misbehavior" of the raccoon could not be controlled and predicted from the laws of operant conditioning. Breland and Breland (1961) suggested that the washing behavior was the normal food-related "species-specific behavior" of raccoons. Since the coin-handling behavior had been linked to food reinforcement, the food-related washing behavior was increasingly elicited by the stimuli of coins. The Brelands finally abandoned their project as it became clear that the "miserly behavior" of the raccoon would not be a good demonstration of saving money.

This demonstration of the tendency of natural food-related behaviors to be emitted in the context of food reinforcement fits nicely within the adaptive model developed by Staddon and Simmelhag (1971), which was presented in Chapter 9. You will recall that these authors reinterpreted Skinner's analysis of superstitious behavior by suggesting that the behaviors which Skinner saw as arising from the "blind" effects of reinforcement were, instead, natural responses related to the subject's "mood" when hungry and given food reinforcement. The tendency of behaviors related to the evolutionary history of a given species to be emitted in the appropriate motivational context has also been observed when the motivational state (or mood) is one elicited by aversive conditions.

The Brelands discovered that highly motivated animals began to show progressively more species-specific behaviors related to their motivational state. This instinctual drift interfered with reinforced new responses (operant conditioning).

Species-specific defense reactions   Bolles (1970) claims that avoidance reactions to aversive stimuli may be innate (rather than learned) defensive reactions related to a specific species' natural reactions to danger from predators. Because predators seldom permit repeated trials, learning would be too slow for a prey

---

* The author raised two raccoons while he was a student. Sometimes he would give them cookies and watch the cookies crumble in the raccoons' drinking water as they attempted to wash them. The otherwise intelligent animals never learned not to wash soluble food.

† Correct, of course, only from the perspective of the trainers. The raccoon probably "thought" that washing food-related objects was correct.

animal to acquire the necessary escape and avoidance behaviors. Thus, prey animals that had innate tendencies to emit appropriate defense behaviors were the only ones who survived to pass on their genes. The innate **species-specific defense reactions (SSDRs)** are elicited by any new, sudden, or aversive stimulus. All defense reactions are organized in a hierarchy. At the top of the hierarchy are the prepotent responses, which are innately organized. Next in the hierarchy come behaviors that can be learned with moderate ease once the innate responses are suppressed. Finally, at the bottom of the hierarchy, come behaviors that are alien or contrary to the species' natural defensive reactions. These can be learned only with great difficulty because of interference from the natural defensive reactions. Bolles (1975) presents data showing that while rats readily learn active avoidance responses when shocked (which is similar to fleeing from a predator and would be a response from the middle of Bolles's hierarchy), they have great difficulty in learning to bar-press to avoid shock. Some rats never learn this response at all, and those that do often perform inconsistently. Instead, some rats will continue to show the innate species-specific defense reaction of freezing when shocked if avoidance responses are ineffectual. Bolles suggests that freezing is the most prepotent, or innately determined, defensive reaction and that this reaction interferes with acquisition of the bar-pressing response. You have probably heard news stories about people who, when faced with a situation of acute danger (such as an oncoming train), panicked and froze instead of running away. Bolles's interpretation of avoidance behavior, like the Brelands' interpretation of the misbehavior of their subjects in food-related situations, suggests the necessity of considering the evolutionary history of a species in predicting its behavior under different motivational conditions. This, in turn, suggests that the ease with which particular responses or relationships of stimuli can be learned will vary as a function of the extent to which such learning is congruent with innate tendencies. In other words, evolution has prepared each species to learn some things easily and other things with difficulty or not at all. Difficulty in learning some things may be due to direct interference from instinctual response patterns. Smith, Gustavson, and Gregor (1972) used high-speed photography to compare the pigeon's innate response to unsignaled shock with key-pecking responses (it is difficult or impossible for pigeons to learn to key-peck to turn off shock). They found that the innate flexion of the pigeons' necks in response to shock was incompatible with key-pecking.

Bolles has also identified species-specific behaviors which interfere with learning in a conditioning situation. The species-specific defense reactions to shock, such as freezing, make it difficult for organisms to learn such operant responses as bar-pressing.

The preparedness continuum   We have seen how innate variables can influence the learning of different responses. Now let us examine the effects of innate mechanisms on learning different types of sensory relationships. You may remember the rats that passed on the tradition of fouling poisoned food. Rats have evolved in close proximity to man and his attempts to poison them. Given that evolution would be expected to take place relatively rapidly in a species as short-lived as rats, it would be logical to expect rats to have evolved other innate mechanisms to avoid unpleasant deaths from poisoning. Garcia and Koelling (1966) conducted research that demonstrated one such mechanism.

Two groups of thirsty rats were allowed to drink a saccharin-flavored solution, and a tone-light burst was presented with every lick. This "bright-noisy-taste" CS was then followed by a shock US for one group and an injection of lithium chloride for the other group. Lithium chloride induces nausea. The feelings associated with nausea were a second US. The results showed strong modality-specific effects. Rats that were shocked avoided water (flavored or unflavored) that was presented in the presence of the "bright-noisy" CS. Rats that had been poisoned with lithium chloride avoided saccharin-flavored water but drank plain water, regardless of the association of "bright-noise" with either liquid. These results support Lublin's suggestions for the choice of appropriate aversive USs to be used in aversive therapy with humans (Chapter 8). The important discovery that all CS-US combinations were not equally associable has been replicated numerous times. Garcia and colleagues (1968) found taste cues to be associated with nausea when the poisoning agent was X-irradiation and the external CS was the size of the food pellets. Both of these studies suggested that rats have an innate bias towards associating taste cues (which would be linked to foods in the natural environment) to nausea (which would result from the food's being poisoned or naturally poisonous in the natural environment). This effect has been labeled the **taste aversion** mechanism, bait shyness, and the **Garcia effect.**

The strength of bait avoidance conditioning is a function of the novelty of the taste presented. Novel tastes are much more easily associated with nausea. If a novel taste is present in combination with a familiar taste, and both are followed by sickness, the aversion develops only to the novel taste. If only a familiar taste is present, some aversion will develop to this taste. If two novel tastes are presented in sequence, this weakens the aversions developed to both tastes, compared to the aversion developed by single novel taste presentation (Revusky and Garcia, 1970). The adaptive significance of the greater power of novel tastes to evoke avoidance may lie in the fact that new foods are more likely to be poisonous than foods that have been tasted in the past without inducing nausea.

Gustavson and colleagues (1974) have capitalized on the bait shyness mechanism and demonstrated its existence in the coyote. Coyotes are difficult to control by trapping or shooting, and lethal poisons also kill other animals. Since coyotes may be predators on lambs, this presents major problems for sheepherders. Gustavson and colleagues (1974) injected sheep carcasses with lithium chloride and let coyotes feed on the treated meat. They reported that some of their captive subjects developed bait-avoidance responses so strong that the coyotes would subsequently run from live sheep! These authors advocate leaving injected carcasses out in areas where coyotes are major problems, in the hope that coyotes who had eaten the treated meat would confine their diet in the future to rodents. This method would be more humane than lethal poisons or shooting; if coyotes transmit knowledge of poisoned food like rats, it could also be more effective.

Similar effects occur in humans. Seligman (Seligman and Hager, 1972) reports the following incident: He went out to dinner and had filet mignon with sauce béarnaise. Some hours later, he became violently ill with stomach flu. When he attempted to eat sauce béarnaise later, he became nauseated by its presence or even the thought of eating it! This would seem to be a simple case of classical conditioning (Chapter 1) in which the US is nausea, the CS the taste of the sauce, and the response is throwing up. This learning, however, actually differs from the classical conditioning phenomena discussed in Chapters 1 and 8 in several ways. For one thing, strong learning occurred with an interval of about 6 hours between the taste (CS) and the sickness (US). For most types of classical conditioning, the strongest bonds are formed when the CS-US interval is around 30 seconds. It was noted in Chapter 8 that some types of autonomically mediated responses (such as the heart rate increases likely to be encountered in the CER paradigm) could be conditioned with CS-US intervals of up to 11 minutes. Perhaps taste aversion learning is simply a form of classical conditioning with very long maximal CS-US intervals. Second, temporal conditioning, mentioned in Chapter 1, also seems to involve very long CS-US intervals in some sense. Pavlov has stated, however, that this type of conditioning occurs very slowly. In Seligman's example, strong conditioning was obtained with a single learning trial, which is also relatively rare in classical conditioning. Third, the other environmental cues, such as his wife, the plate the food was served on, and more familiar tastes, did not become aversive to him. The laws of Pavlovian conditioning would predict that all these would be linked to the nausea. Fourth, the response persisted in spite of his knowledge that his nausea was caused by the stomach flu—thus violating the laws of the cognitive-behaviorists. Finally, the loathing of sauce béarnaise did not extinguish until over five years later. Most classical conditioning is not so robust (it has less resistance to extinction). This latter point is most easily explained away within the laws of traditional learning theories, as it could be suggested that avoidance of the aversive taste operantly reinforced avoidance and prevented the forced exposure that would have led to extinction. In any case, a close examination suggests that our laws of contiguity conditioning, while adequate for predicting learning that is less affected by innate variables, may need to be modified to predict the selective associations of cues found in learning of this type.

Data such as that reported by Garcia led Seligman to develop a theory to account for such selective association effects. This theory is based on the assumption that evolution makes some types of learning easier than others. Such predisposed learning is labeled **prepared learning.** On the other hand, making some types of associations might work against a species' chances for survival. In this case, animals having difficulty in making these associations would pass on the innate mechanisms responsible for this difficulty. This type of learning is called **contraprepared learning.** An example would be bar-pressing by a rat exposed to shock. If selection did not favor mechanisms responsible for either

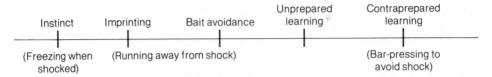

Figure 12.6   Different types of behavior are placed above the line representing the pre-paredness continuum. Bolles's classification of rats' responses to shock is shown below the line. Different laws may be needed to predict behavior at each place on the continuum.

the facilitation or the inhibition of making a particular type of connection, learning of these connections is **unprepared.** Such biologically unbiased learning is the type that can be predicted by the laws of conditioning, and it fits the assumptions of the equipotentiality doctrine. Thus, all types of learning can be fitted onto a **preparedness continuum.** This continuum would begin with totally prepared learning (instincts or species-specific defense reactions), and end with contraprepared learning. Imprinting would probably fit close to instinct, and bait-avoidance responses would fall somewhere between imprinting and unprepared learning (see Figure 12.6).

Preparedness-continuum theory relates the effects of selective evolution to different behavioral phenomena. This theory would predict that the various types of learning along the continuum would be related to the evolutionary history of each species. For rats, smell and taste would be predominant in food procurement. Other animals, such as quail, are primarily guided by their keen vision in making food choices. Wilcoxin, Dragoin, and Kral (1971) conducted a study using rats and quail in which these subjects became ill after drinking a blue sour solution. They were then given either blue water (tasteless) or colorless sour fluid. As expected, the rats avoided drinking the sour fluid and the quail avoided drinking the blue water.

Seligman and Hager (1972) further suggested that learning of food preferences, as well as food aversions, is learning of a prepared type. This mechanism could account for developing cravings for foods **(specific hungers)** having needed nutrients. Zahorik, Maier, and Pies (1974) maintained several groups of rats on a thiamine-deficient diet with access to quinine-flavored water. The taste of quinine, which was associated with the deficiency, became a cue for avoidance. Zahorik and colleagues (1974) then injected the rats with sufficient thiamine to produce recovery from the deficiency, while allowing them to drink water flavored with saccharin, anise, or vanilla. All groups of rats showed preferences for the flavor paired with recovery in their group. Humans may also show food preferences related to the associations of specific foods with specific needed nutrients. A child who is raised in a region where tomatoes are common but oranges are scarce would be expected to seek tomatoes, not oranges, when his/her vitamin C supplies are low. This could occur through previous eating of tomatoes when the child's vitamin C levels were low, resulting in an association of "tomato taste" and reductions in the internal cues related to a vitamin C deficiency.

In contrast to normal classical conditioning, learning of taste aversions or taste preferences seems to occur without awareness (remember the research by Biferno and Dawson presented in Chapter 8). Best and Zuckerman (1971) have shown such learning to be subcortically mediated, and Roll and Smith (1972) have demonstrated taste aversion learning in anesthetized rats. Kalat (1973) has carried this line of research to its illogical conclusion. In an article appearing in the *Worm Runner's Digest* (a tongue-in-cheek journal published by McConnell, who obtained fame by grinding up educated flatworms and feeding their RNA to their naive brethren), Kalat reported that rats that were killed after drinking a novel solution and poisoned while dead, showed a reduced intake of the novel solution. Since reduced intake is the normal criterion for demonstrating conditioned aversion, Kalat concluded that he had demonstrated the ultimate in learning without awareness.

Following Garcia's and others' demonstrations of the selective association of cues in taste aversion learning (Garcia effect), which was related to the dominant sensory modalities for food selection of the species involved, Seligman proposed his preparedness theory. This theory states that organisms are innately prepared to make some types of associations, contraprepared to make others, and have no innate bias for still others. This theory also accounts for taste preferences.

Clinical application of preparedness theory   Seligman (in Seligman and Hager, 1972) has suggested that preparedness variables apply to the learning of human phobias and have implications as well for producing "artificial phobias" through aversion therapy. In phobia learning, the authors suggest, inherited predispositions may be responsible for the greater frequency with which therapists are exposed to clients who have snake phobias than bee phobias, in spite of the fact that bees kill more people per years than snakes do. In addition, aversive experiences with bees are fairly common, while very few people are actually bitten by snakes. Seligman has stated that fears of such creatures as snakes, rats, and spiders are prepared phobic responses and easy to learn. According to this view, things that were dangerous to pretechnological man should have been associated with genetic selection for preparedness. To test this theory, Rachman and Seligman (1977) examined 69 phobic and 82 obsessional patients. They found that dangerousness of the object or situation feared by pretechnological man correlated r = .78 with the content of the phobias. Neither the extent to which phobic behavior was displayed, however, nor resistance to treatment was highly correlated with the preparedness dimension, giving only partial support to Seligman's hypothesis.

As for production of artificial phobias, Lamon, Wilson, and Leaf (1977) found that nausea-producing situations were more effective in producing aversions to selected beverages (including alcoholic beverages) than electric shock. This is directly parallel to the findings of Garcia and his associates that cues on related dimensions are more associable than cues on unrelated dimensions.

Perspective

This section has presented several lines of research directed towards delineating the biological boundaries of learning and behavior in general. This work suggests that considerations of the laws of learning should not be divorced from attention to the effects of selective evolution on the mechanisms of learning in each species studied. As we have noted in this and earlier chapters, even Skinner (1969, 1974) is now willing to consider the effects of evolution as "selecting for" innate biases in learning and behavior much like reinforcement "selects for" the reinforced responses.

As a general rule, then, evolution works much like learning in ensuring survivability. If inflexibility of responding to a particular cue is the pattern most linked to survivability, that totally prepared form of responding we call instinct becomes likely. If a small amount of flexibility is desirable, then a phenomenon like imprinting is selected for. Imprinting in ducks causes the learning of an attachment to any moving object to appear first within the critical/sensitive period, which is a highly prepared response-cue dimension.

Preparedness to learn specific types of tasks can also be experimentally manipulated by breeding. Tryon (1940) was able to breed strains of rats that were more prepared to learn complex mazes ("maze-bright rats") as well as strains that were less prepared to learn such mazes ("maze-dull rats").* More recently, Markowitz (Markowitz and Sorrells, 1969 and Markowitz and Becker, 1969) has demonstrated that these inherited differences in ability to learn mazes depend on the type of sensory cues that must be used (maze-dull rats do better on visually guided maze learning; maze-bright rats do better on spatial learning). Other presumably inherited differences in learning abilities between the two strains included better "hypothesis" learning in the maze-dull animals in a task in which they were required to learn a successive-reversal set[†] and differential responses to different types of reinforcers. When both strains were required to learn the reversal set with light cues under conditions of food reinforcement, the maze-dull rats were clearly superior. When shocked for incorrect choices in learning the same problem, only a slight superiority of the maze-dull rats was found. These studies provide some clues as to which particular underlying mechanisms may be responsible for demonstrated differences in specific learning abilities of different strains of rats or among different species. Such underlying mechanisms may eventually be tied to inherited differences in the anatomy and physiology of particular areas of the brain involved in learning. At this point, the research of the type presented in the first half of this chapter (neurophysiology and neuroanatomy of learning) would converge with the research presented in the second half (inherited variables influencing learning).

---

* Often called the Tryon effect.

† A successive reversal set is a simple concept of the "win-stay, lose-shift" type. In the Markowitz studies, for example, the light would be the first cue telling the rat which side of the maze was correct. As soon as the rat had learned always to go to the lighted side of the maze, the signal for correct (food reinforcement or absence of shock) was changed to darkness; responses to the lighted side would be nonreinforced or punished with shock. After several of these reversals, the rats would usually learn quickly to change which cue they followed as soon as a given response was either nonreinforced or shocked.

Chapter Perspective

Much as the varied cognitive approaches presented in Chapter 11 broaden the scope of learning theory by covering phenomena not usually investigated by connectionist theorists, so does the research reviewed in this chapter broaden the field of learning by relating learning to brain mechanisms and evolution. This connection makes it possible to relate the findings of learning psychologists to the data discovered by neurological and comparative biologists. It also provides a conceptual framework within which apparent anomalies such as the differing ease of conditioning of different types of stimuli and responses may be understood. By so doing, the types of research covered in this chapter help to make the field of learning part of the natural sciences as a whole rather than a specialized part of psychology. This should prove useful to the psychologist by making behavioral predictions and applications more specific and more precise.

Key Terms

anterograde amnesia	Garcia effect	RNA transfer hypothesis
amygdaloid nuclei	habituation	sign stimulus
axon	hippocampus	sociobiology
comparative psychology	hologram analogy theory	species-specific behavior
contingent negative variation (CNV)	immediate memory	species-specific defense reaction (SSDR)
	imprinting	
contraprepared learning	innate releasing mechanism	specific hunger
dendrite		state-dependent learning
electroconvulsive shock (ECS)	instinctual drift	synapse
	militant enthusiasm	taste aversion
electroconvulsive therapy (ECT)	neuronal model	temporal lobe
engram	prepared learning	theory of mass action
ethology	preparedness continuum	transmitter substances
feedforward	protein memory hypothesis	TOTE (test-operate-test-exit)
fixed action pattern	retrograde amnesia	unprepared learning
frontal lobe	reverberating loop	

Annotated Bibliography

For a good introduction to the area of the neurophysiology of learning and memory, I would recommend K. S. Lashley, *Brain mechanisms and intelligence* (New York: Dover, 1963); D. O. Hebb, *A textbook of psychology*, 2nd ed. (Philadelphia, Pa.: W. B. Saunders, 1966); and J. V. McConnell, "The modern search for the engram," in W. C. Corning and M. Balaban (Eds.), *The mind: Biological approaches to its functions* (New York: Wiley-Interscience, 1968). An easy introduction to Pribram's holographic theory of learning and memory is his "Holograms in the head" (*Psychology Today*, September 1971, 5, 44–48); a more advanced treatment of Pribram's ideas of brain mechanisms in attention and learning is K. H. Pribram and D. McGuinness, "Arousal, activation, and effort in the control of attention" (*Psychological Review*, 1975, 82, 116–149).

A short and readable introduction to ethology and Lorenz is K. Z. Lorenz, "The evolution of behavior" (*Scientific American*, December 1958, 199, 67–78), while a longer exposition of Lorenz's views in an equally readable form is his *On aggression* (New York: Harcourt, Brace & World, 1963). A further description of imprinting can be found in E. H. Hess, " 'Imprinting' in a natural laboratory" (*Scientific American*, 1972, 227, 24–31), while a general discussion of early learning is presented in W. Sluckin, *Early learning in man and animal* (Morristown, N.J.: Schenkman, 1970). For those wishing to become more familiar with the relatively new and provocative science of the genetic determinants of behavior called sociobiology, I would recommend D. P. Barash, *Sociobiology and behavior* (New York: Elsevier, 1977).

Approaches more closely allied with American learning theory approaches to the biological boundaries of learning can be sampled in: (1) K. Breland and M. Breland, "The misbehavior of organisms" (*American Psychologist*, 1961, 16, 681–684), a humorous description of genetic drift; (2) R. C. Bolles, *Learning theory* (New York: Holt, Rinehart and Winston, 1975), a well-written if limited learning text in which Bolles reports his research on species-specific defense reactions; and (3) M. E. P. Seligman and J. L. Hager, "Biological boundaries of learning (The sauce-béarnaise syndrome)" *Psychology Today*, August 1972, 6, 59–61, an amusing introduction to preparedness variables in learning.

APPENDIX TO CHAPTER 12

The Physical Hologram

Generally speaking, a hologram is the result of any photographic process which produces a three-dimensional image that retains most of the visual information of the object originally photographed. In this technique, a beam of coherent light (such as from a laser) is split by a beam splitter (see Figure 12.7). One beam is focused on the object to be photographed and the other is directed towards the photographic plate. Light bouncing off the object interacts with light reaching the photographic plate directly to create interference patterns. Each part of these patterns contains some information from each part of the object photographed, much like the blurred edges of objects viewed by an individual with uncorrected poor vision contain information from adjacent objects. The hologram (or holograph) that results from this process no more resembles the original object than an exposed view of our cortex would show the shapes of our visual memories. To reconstruct the image, a beam similar to the beam used to create the hologram is played over the surface of the hologram.

Holograms have several properties in common with memory. If a hologram is constructed by directing both beams at objects so that each beam is the reference beam for the other, both objects can be seen when only one is reilluminated. This is similar to associative recall of memories. Holograms are also resistant to damage, just as memories are. If half of a holograph is "lesioned" by

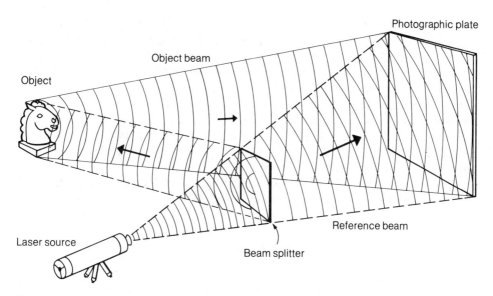

Figure 12.7a   *Making a hologram. Light (usually monochromatic, such as all green light of one wavelength) is directed so that some of it bounces off the beam splitter to hit the object to be photographed and some of it reaches the photographic plate directly. Light from the object beam and the reference beams interact to create interference patterns on the photographic plate. When the photograph (holograph) is developed, all that can be seen are swirls and areas of light and dark grays.*

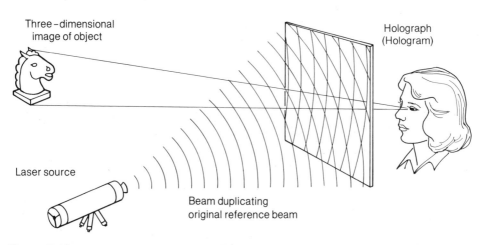

Figure 12.7b   *Viewing a hologram. Light from the duplicate of the original reference beam is diffused by the holograph in the same way that light from the original object was diffused by the photographic plate. The image has true three-dimensional perspective. By moving her head, the viewer could look around and behind the object in the picture just as if she were viewing the original object.*

removing it, the entire image can still be reconstructed by reilluminating the remaining half. Such an image is smaller than the image created from the intact hologram and, if enlarged to its original size, will be a little less distinct. Many memories, although widely distributed, become more difficult to recall after localized brain damage of cortical memory areas. Holograms also store enormous amounts of information, just as our LTMs do. By using different types of reference beams, many different interference patterns can be superimposed on one hologram (like multiple exposures of photographic film in ordinary photography). Up to 10 billion bits of information have been stored holographically in one cubic centimeter (Pribram, 1971b)!

Those of you who saw the movie *Star Wars* will remember the "ghostly" image of the princess projected from the robot R2-D2 which delivered the message requesting help. This was a simulated hologram very similar in appearance to an actual hologram. Other examples of holograms are the three-dimensional "ghostly" figures used in displays in some amusement parks.

So this is it—the end of this book and our exploration of the field of learning. We have followed four types of approaches to answering the questions of the hows, whats, and nature of learning. Researchers working within each of these traditions have advanced our knowledge about the many factors influencing what is learned and how it is learned. Many principles of learning have been discovered, although these principles may not apply to all species in all environments for all types of responses. It is generally accepted today that most learning in higher organisms involves some sort of meaning or cognitive units and that those types of learning least influenced by cognitive variables may involve the most innate factors. Learning principles have been related to the process of selective evolution and to brain mechanisms, resulting in a greater integration of biology and the psychology of learning. In spite of limited success in determining the processes underlying learning of the conditioning type, a wide range of successful applications has been developed and is being used. In spite of some areas of continued uncertainty, therefore, we may conclude that the exploration of learning has been a profitable endeavor in terms of increasing our knowledge about behavior. To reinforce this point, let us now summarize briefly, chapter by chapter, the major advances in knowledge contributed by the researchers reviewed in Part 2 of the text.

Chapter 8 began with a review of the contributions of Soviet psychologists and those of Gregory Razran (whose work is closely identified with the Soviet tradition) in extending the scope of the Pavlovian paradigm. One of these extensions was the development of techniques for classically conditioning the viscera (interoceptive conditioning). Another was the demonstration that the meaning, rather than the stimulus characteristics, of a CS could be the unit, or the "what," of learning (semantic conditioning). This phenomenon was found to be related to maturational factors and intelligence level (semantic conditioning does not occur in very young or retarded children). Also investigated was verbal conditioning, in which words were used as CSs or USs in combination with first signal system cues such as tones and shock. These studies demonstrated the extent to which a human being can direct his or her attention and speed up the process of conditioning. Because verbal cues are so powerful, they are usually dominant when combined with other types of cues (the rule of force). Similar control of a complex stimulus by one powerful cue, discovered in animal studies by American researchers, has been labeled overshadowing, or blocking. The CER, sensory preconditioning, and autoshaping phenomena have also been discovered by American researchers.

Aspects of the CER (and other features of classical conditioning) have been interpreted by Rescorla in terms of predictive variables. Rescorla's predictiveness hypothesis stated that organisms learn CS-US relationships because the CSs can be used to predict the occurrence of the US, rather than because of the contiguity relationship of the CS and the US. Although this hypothesis has generally been supported by fear-conditioning studies involving skeletal muscle responses, some contradictory results have been reported when responses mediated by the autonomic nervous system are conditioned.

Predictiveness variables are mediating variables similar to cognitive factors such as awareness. Some human research has been reported supporting the view that awareness is necessary for even autonomic nervous system controlled responses to be conditioned. Mediating variables complicate the task of discovering the "true" underlying process of classical conditioning. None of this uncertainty about process(es) has deterred efforts to apply classical conditioning paradigms in the real world.

Some of the procedures reviewed in Chapter 8 were the forced extinction techniques of flooding and implosive therapy (which are faster than systematic desensitization but may be less effective or have more side effects) and aversion therapy, used to condition fears of cues associated with unwanted behavior. The choice of cues used in this conditioning seems to be an important variable in predicting its effectiveness; cognitive variables also seem to be involved.

Chapter 9 reviewed both neo-Hullian and neo-Skinnerian contributions to reinforcement theory. Neo-Hullian approaches have become highly cognitive, with the introduction of variables such as frustration and the continued use of variables such as incentive motivation. In terms of principles to be applied, however, the neo-Skinnerian approach has been more productive. Within this orientation, three distinct groups of theorists can be distinguished. The first group—the theorists who have retained Skinner's emphasis on positive reinforcement (Premack, Terrace, Reynolds and colleagues)—have added the concept of superordinate stimulus, the Premack principle (reversibility of reinforcement), behavioral contrast, peak shift, and fading (errorless discrimination learning).

The second group of neo-Skinnerians—those who retain the basic Skinnerian framework but violate the dogma that punishment is an ineffectual technique of behavior control (Solomon, Azrin, and Sidman)—have mapped out the parameters of aversive control much as the first group of Skinnerians mapped out the parameters of control through positive contingencies. Some of their major principles describe the changing effects of punishment as a function of the effective strength of the aversive consequence. Phenomena described by these theorists include conditioned emotional responses (CER), conditioned facilitation, conditioned suppression (learned helplessness) and Sidman avoidance.

The third group of neo-Skinnerians—the liberals who deviate in many ways from the strict-connectionist views of the other two groups and whose best known spokesperson is Bandura—incorporate cognitive variables. Bandura's major new concept is modeling; other important contributions include the concept of vicarious reinforcement, an attention to attentional processes, and seeing reinforcement as linked to performance but not to learning. This school of theorists illustrates the tendency of many different theoretical approaches to develop variants which converge into a more middle-of-the-road position. For behaviorists, such convergence involves moving towards the cognitive position; for cognitive theorists, it involves moving towards acceptance of some behaviorist ideas. These convergences, of course, are also in the functionalist tradition. Bandura's work has led to a proliferation of modeling techniques for use in education and therapy, including: progressive modeling (a combination of modeling and systematic desensitization), symbolic modeling (using films or videotapes), participant-guided modeling, and self-modeling.

We also reviewed research which suggests that important modifications of our views about the effects of reinforcers are needed. Timberlake and Allison (1974) proposed a modification of Premack's theory of reinforcement in which the relative levels of deprivation of the opportunity to emit certain instrumental responses can be used to predict which responses will serve as reinforcers in a particular situation. This response deprivation model has important implications for development of behavioral modification methods. Dunham (1971) has proposed a new way of looking at the effects of punishment in which responses that predict the aversive event are actively inhibited and responses that predict the absence of the aversive event are actively excited. Staddon and Simmelhag (1971) have related behavior observed with the "superstition experiment paradigm" to natural instrumental behaviors which would be adaptive under natural conditions involving similar motive states. This adaptive model relates instrumental behavior to the effects of selective evolution, thus integrating learning and biological principles.

Both the operant principles presented in Chapter 4 and those reviewed in Chapter 9 have been widely applied to an impressive range of environments. These applications and the special techniques of behavioral modification of the operant type were discussed in Chapter 10, including a detailed analysis of the steps of specification, observation, and consequation and a review of the multiple baseline methodology (which provides a basis for the analysis of the effectiveness of a given contingency management procedure). Special procedures reviewed include training paraprofessionals to be the actual change agents (who administer the contingent consequences to the persons whose behaviors are to be modified—the triadic model of behavioral modification) and use of group contingency procedures (as in the good behavior game). Techniques, special considerations, and the probable future of biofeedback procedures were also reviewed.

A trend mentioned in the summary of Chapter 9 was the convergence of connectionism towards the cognitive view. This trend has also occurred on another plane: The cognitive position is moving towards acceptance of some aspects of behaviorist theory, a phenomenon illustrated in the theoretical position maintained by Saltz and discussed in Chapter 11.

Saltz did not suggest that all learning is cognitive. Instead, he presented evidence that either cognitive or connectionist types of learning may occur in a given situation and that attempts to use both types of learning together may create interference. He also suggested that it may be easier to explain conditioning in terms of cognitive variables rather than in the more conventional reverse order. The tortured complexity of behaviorists' formulations of concept learning in S-R terms would seem to support this viewpoint. Major concepts incorporated in Saltz's theory include concept growth, integration, and mediational facilitation.

Chomsky's theory retained Saltz's rejection of S-R explanations of concepts and of language. Chomsky, however, concentrated on language rather than on general problem solving, and he incorporated innate variables. Major terms in Chomsky's theory include: natural language, linguistic competence, surface and deep structures, universal grammar, generative grammar, and transformations.

Next, we examined a theory in the cognitive-maturationist mode first publicized by Maria Montessori. Like Montessori, Piaget was trained in biology and the method of natural observation. He postulated that more different logical processes are available to the child with a mature brain than are available for the younger child with an immature brain; he described the types of learning and thinking characteristic of each maturational stage. Major concepts, in addition to those directly tied to the developmental scheme, include: disconfirmation, assimilation, accommodation, schemata, equilibration, functions, decentration, operations, and conservations. Both Piaget and Chomsky have emphasized innate and structuralist variables more than Saltz, who maintains the environmentalist bias of the functionalist tradition in mainstream American psychology.

Finally, we reviewed Donald Norman's version of the information-processing approach to learning. This theory describes the various stages of learning (selective attention, sensory information store, short-term memory, long-term memory, and retrieval mechanisms) in terms of analogies with computer processing and signal detection theory. Norman discussed the difference between learning which begins with existing concepts (conceptually driven, or top-down, processing) and that applied to novel situations (data-driven, or bottom-up, processing), as well as research concerned with our ability to focus on one of two sources of information (the cocktail party problem). He noted that the channel capacity of short-term memory is limited to seven ± two pieces of information, and how this limitation could be bypassed by chunking bits of information into larger units. In his theory, the amount of learning that occurs is a function of the attention paid to the situation (resource-limited learning) as well as the information available (data-limited learning). Information stored in short-term memory (active memory) was seen as providing material for further processing, much like buffer memory systems in computer processing. Also discussed were various methods for determining the extent of learning and memory (recall, recognition, savings, and reaction time). He noted that several types of information may be processed simultaneously (parallel processing) or sequentially (serial processing). Finally, some of the techniques (mnemonic devices) used to improve memory abilities, such as the peg word technique and the method of loci, were presented to illustrate the importance of active plans for processing in facilitating the acquisition of information.

Chapter 12 reviewed the growing trend towards increasing the attention paid to biological factors in learning. The first half of this chapter began with a discussion of the anatomy of memory. Lashley's search for the engram (the physical trace of a memory) was reviewed. Lashley concluded that memories are distributed within specific broad regions of the cortex rather than being localized in specific groups of cells (the doctrine of mass action, or equipotentality of areas within one brain region). This was followed by a review of data on specific regions of the brain in relationship to memory. It is generally accepted that all cortical regions except the frontal lobes can store memories, although the temporal lobes may be particularly critical for storage of complex memories. A subcortical structure, the hippocampus, has also been implicated as vital to the process of consolidating complex short-term memories into long-term memories. Under normal conditions, duplicate copies of memories seem to be formed in each hemisphere of the cerebral cortex. This transfer phenomenon is absent when the connections between hemispheres are surgically "split." Evidence for subcortical memories was also presented.

Next was Donald Hebb's theory of the neuronal processes involved in short-term memory (reverberating loops) and the consolidation of these memories into long-term engrams (through changes in synaptic structures). Procedures (such as electroshock therapy) that cause amnesias by interfering with short-term memory were reviewed, and such anomalies as the return of "forgotten" information after reminder shocks were discussed. These data suggest that consolidation is a continuing process which begins immediately after exposure to the learning experience and continues for an hour or more. Hence, shock given after a few minutes have passed would prevent complete consolidation but leave intact the initial stage of consolidation. Data supporting Hebb's notion of structural changes in synapses as the basis of long-term memory (such as evidence for cortical growth following exposure to high-stimulus-value environments) were reviewed.

Research attempting to relate biochemical factors (RNA, proteins, transmitter substances) to learning was also presented. Although RNA does increase during learning, the results of studies showing transfer of memory by transferring RNA from trained to untrained animals have not been consistently replicated, and the view of RNA as a storage place for memories is still controversial. Similarly, the exact role of proteins is in doubt, with some researchers reporting transfer of memories through transfer of "trained" proteins and others disputing these claims. Interference with transmitter substances does cause apparent amnesias, but these effects are often reversible and may reflect recall rather than memory storage factors. At this point we concluded that all these biochemicals were involved in memory/recall in some way, but that their exact functions were as yet unknown.

Many of these contributions to understanding the neurophysiology of learning are integrated in Pribram's hologram analogy theory, which relates selective attention to activation of the amygdaloid nuclei and brainstem. Sensory information store is seen as patterns of activation of synaptic connections in receptors. Short-term memory is a state of altered electrical activity in cortical regions, which again reflects activity in dense networks of synaptic connections arising both from internal sources and as a product of sensory inputs carried into the brain by axons (operators). These two sources of activation interact or interfere with each other to cause changes in RNA and/or transmitter substance concentrations; such changes induce glial cells to divide. This allows dendritic and axonic endings to "sprout" through the openings left between divided glial cells, and patterns of the new synaptic connections thus formed provide the structural basis for the engram. A given memory is distributed throughout the pattern, so destruction of any part of the pattern does not mean loss of that memory. Since the "sprouting" process involves cell growth, protein is required, and protein synthesis inhibitors may act to block this growth while leaving potential spaces for later formation of new connections. It is reasonable to expect the new connections to be inefficient, and thus they may be more vulnerable to agents affecting transmitter substance levels.

In Pribram's theory, the brain is seen as forming memories from fragments of outside information, with the help of feedback and feedforward mechanisms (TOTE processes and plans and strategies). Thus, his is a cognitive neurological theory which is closely related to information-processing theories. Pribram uses the analogy of the hologram to explain distributed storage, associative recall, and enormous storage capacity in neurological memory systems.

The second half of Chapter 12 reviewed types of behavior that have a heavy "biological bias." Phenomena such as species-specific instinctual reactions, imprinting, innate defensive reactions, instinctual drift, and the development of food aversions and preferences show that the forces of evolution have caused some species to become better prepared to make some types of stimulus-response connections than others. This integration of the principles of evolution with behavior is reflected in the sociobiological view of highly motivated, or survival-critical, behaviors as having innate determinants, even in humans. Seligman's theory of the preparedness continuum (which suggests that different laws of learning may be necessary for types of learning differing in the degree to which they are "biased" by innate factors) provides a unifying framework which relates these phenomena to one another and to evolution. Preparedness theory and the Brelands' descriptions of the intrusion of instinctual responses (species-specific behaviors) into learned sequences of behavior (the phenomenon of instinctual drift) were both cited as evidence against strict equipotentiality doctrine. All this research reinforces the need to consider innate variables (also discussed in Chapter 9) in attempting to predict behaviors.

As you have seen in this part of the text, we are only a little closer to the development of the grand unifying unitheory than we were at the end of Part 1. The type of creative synthesis of neurological and cognitive learning data created by Pribram may be one fruitful approach. The greater tolerance of multiple types of learning by many theorists may be another, while the introduction of maturational, adaptive, and "preparedness dimension" variables may bridge the gap between nativists and environmentalists. One limited attempt to use such a multivariant approach was made by Hebb, Lambert, and Tucker (1973), who criticized both the neo-Skinnerians and Chomsky for their narrow positions on the language issue. Rather than assuming grammar to be innate if it does not follow the laws of operant conditioning, as Chomsky does, they suggested that it would be better to examine grammar in light of other types of learning mechanisms. Reflecting the idea that language learning is highly "prepared" learning and that there may be sensitive periods when language is most easily acquired, they suggested that grammar can be explained nicely by cognitive theories (Saltz's concept-growth theory would do the job). Most vocabulary learning, however, can be explained either through reinforcement principles or through associations of either classical conditioning or sensory preconditioning (from Chapter 9). If we accept the Russian work which demonstrated that meanings, not words as physical stimuli, are the units of classical conditioning of internal responses to words, then many of the examples cited by Chomsky in opposition to conditioning explanations of language lose their power. As noted, even Skinner is willing to accept "meaning" as a unit of learning in verbal learning.

In deference to the views of the Chomskians, Hebb, Lambert, and Tucker were willing to concede that the processes of auditory analysis necessary for language use and language learning are probably innate. They were also willing to incorporate active neuronal processes similar to those postulated by Pribram. These processes would account for the flexibility of language so strongly stressed by Chomsky. These theorists also pointed out that the universality of grammar is not necessarily proof of its innate origins; all human cultures, after all, share common features.

The concept of prepared learning can also be used to resolve some of the controversy about which processes are responsible for different types of learning. Any learning that does not have a strong innate component (even some types of classical conditioning) would be expected to be strongly influenced by processes related to higher brain activity. Since higher brain activity is assumed to be involved in awareness and expectancies related to the predictive values of cues, perhaps the studies showing awareness and expectancies to be related to classical conditioning are not surprising. Motivational variables (moods) might predispose organisms to emit certain classes of instrumental responses which have been selected by both evolutionary and reinforcement factors. Emission of these responses may be related to the organism's "expectancies" of gaining access to reinforcers or of predicting aversive events. Highly prepared modes of learning (such as imitation in primates or food taste aversion/preference in a range of species) might be expected to be less influenced by cognitive factors, if we assume that innate biases are largely controlled by older and more primitive regions of the brain. The study showing modeling without awareness (self-modeling), reviewed with the material on Bandura in Chapter 11, and the study on infant imitation (newborn infants have cortices that are not fully developed), reviewed in Chapter 12, support this view.

All this suggests that our general laws of learning must be modified to account for maturational levels and the effects of evolutionary forces on specific species. When the principles relating the laws developed from the study of unprepared learning in laboratory settings (in adult organisms) can be consistently integrated with maturational and innate factors, and when the extent to which cognitive variables are involved in different forms of learning is known, then we shall be almost to the point of developing unitheory. As we approach a fuller understanding of the underlying processes, both behavioral and neurological, of the different types of learning, then we will have our global (and probably very complex) theory of learning. From this theory, all the phenomena of learning will be predicted. Taking this optimistic view, we see that the present state of apparent confusion may only represent the building of the strong data base needed to understand learning fully. In this light, discoveries of new complexities about learning should be viewed not as cause for discouragement but as signs of hope.

Annotated Bibliography

An insight into attempts to reconcile behavioristic and cognitive explanations about the processes involved in learning can be gained by reading D. O. Hebb, W. E. Lambert, and G. R. Tucker, "A DMZ in the language war" *Psychology Today,* April 1973, 6, 54–63.

accommodation A process or function by which new information is absorbed only after existing schemata (concepts) are transformed or new schemata are formed.

accountability The responsibility of teachers and other professionals actually to produce the behavioral changes in their charges required of their jobs. In practice, this means evidence that these professionals are meeting their behavioral objectives for childrens' learning and improved in-class behavior.

active avoidance The paradigm in which an organism must make a response to prevent experiencing an aversive event.

adaptive model Timberlake's and Allison's model of the effects of response deprivation, which states that animals have needs to make responses that will get them in a position eventually to reach primary rewards (such as food) and that deprivation of the opportunity to emit a specific response can make that opportunity a powerful reinforcer.

amygdaloid nuclei Part of the basal ganglia in the brain buried within each cerebral hemisphere's white matter, heavily involved with emotional behavior related to choosing when to act on emotions. Part of the limbic system, they are tied to arousal mechanisms in response to important stimuli.

anterograde amnesia The loss of the ability to form new memories after a traumatic event (such as a serious head injury). Old (pretrauma) memories are not lost.

anticipatory responses Muscle responses conditioned to drive states that prepare the organism to make the responses (such as swallowing food) that actually reduce drive arousal.

approach-approach conflict The situation in which two separate goal-objects are desired at the same time. Once one goal becomes closer, the conflict vanishes.

approach-avoidance conflict The situation in which a goal has both attractive and fear/avoidance-arousing features. At a distance from the goal, approach is more powerful because approach gradients are less steep than avoidance gradients. As the subject gets closer to the goal, the strength of the avoidance tendency rises more rapidly than the strength of the tendency to approach the goal. The conflict arises at the point where the two tendencies are equal.

assertion training A type of counterconditioning procedure suggested by Wolpe together with the method of systematic desensitization. In assertion training, an assertive response is paired with a situation which formerly elicited anxiety. Eventually, the person can be assertive (which is incompatible with being timid) even in the presence of cues which formerly elicited strong anxiety.

assimilation   A process or function by which new information is absorbed into existing schemata (concepts) without altering those schemata.

associationist   A theorist who believes that mental elements or stimuli and/or responses become combined through contiguity, or their association in space and/or time.

associative inhibition   Guthrie's term for the process by which responses which do not lead to drive reduction are interfered with by increasing numbers of new responses (unlike responses that do lead to drive reduction, which are protected by the change in stimulus conditions drive reduction creates). Guthrie used this term to explain the process of forgetting.

associative shifting   See **law of associative shifting.**

attribute   A feature of a stimulus, utilized by organisms in discrimination and concept formation.

autonomic nervous system   The part of the nervous system other than the brain, spinal cord, and peripheral nerves. Divided into the sympathetic and parasympathetic systems, it controls emergency and relaxed state visceral and cardiovascular functioning, respectively. Normally, these regulatory functions proceed automatically, but they may be conditioned and controlled by the central nervous system (CNS), composed of the brain and spinal cord.

autoshaping   The development of a response (such as key-pecking in pigeons) which appears as a UR to USs (such as the appearance of food in front of a hungry organism) rather than through the operation of reinforcement variables. This phenomenon shows that responses which are normally considered to be influenced only by reinforcement contingencies can also be controlled by the classical conditioning contingencies of stimulus pairings.

aversion therapy   Treatments using aversive events (such as induction of nausea or use of shock) to try to prevent the occurrence of behaviors judged maladaptive (such as excessive alcohol consumption). The goal is to recondition the cues which formerly elicited the undesired behavior so that they come to elicit anxiety or nausea.

aversive stimulus   A stimulus that organisms avoid or do nothing to prolong (such as shock); roughly like the popular concept of a punisher.

avoidance-avoidance conflict   The situation in which two situations are to be avoided at the same time. Whichever goal situation is more feared is avoided first.

axon   The process of a neuron which carries messages away from the cell body toward other neuron's input processes (see **dendrite**) or toward other neurons' cell bodies.

backup system   Other reinforcement contingencies that are available in case mild consequences are ineffectual in modifying target behaviors; for example, money as a backup system for points earned.

backward conditioning   Conditioning in which the US precedes the CS, also known as **pseudoconditioning.** Such conditioning, hard to obtain, tends to be weak.

baselines 1 and 2   **Baseline 1** is the measurement period prior to intervention of a contingency management plan. **Baseline 2** is the measurement period after the contingency management plan has been implemented and then suspended in order to determine the extent of schedule control versus long-term changes in behavior.

base rule   One of many underlying deep structure/natural grammar rules governing syntax or the logical organization of language.

behavioral contrast   See **contrast.**

behavior modification Applications of conditioning learning principles to a wide range of behavior problems in fields ranging from psychotherapy to education.

behavioral objective An educational or therapeutic goal stated in terms of operationally defined, empirically measurable, observable behaviors (such as reading test scores or reduced rates of hitting other children).

behaviorist A theorist who believes that the proper unit of measurement for psychologists is behavior rather than verbal reports; usually a connectionist.

belongingness Thorndike's "organizational" factor, which he added to his theory as a concession to the gestalt theorists; the tendency of specific types of things to be perceived as belonging together.

biofeedback See **feedback.**

bit In computer and information processing terminology, the smallest possible unit of information. It consists of either a yes (on or 1) or no (off or 0) state or notation. Most computers code complex information as sequences of such bits.

blocking phenomenon The phenomenon that results when one component of a compound stimulus is made more salient or stronger through individual conditioning to a US. This results in the blocking of CR-eliciting properties of the other members of the compound or the overshadowing and diminishment of the influence of these weaker stimuli.

boundedness The limits of a concept, or how stimuli are assigned to a particular concept according to the rules specifying just what belongs to that concept.

branching program See **programmed learning.**

bridging stimulus A term used by operantly oriented animal trainers for a conditioned reinforcer used when it is impractical to deliver a primary reinforcer, to signal the animal that a behavior has been performed correctly. Also called a **bridging gap.**

buffer memory system A system that recycles information from short-term memory and back to it while the memory is being changed into long-term memory or while logical operations are being completed. This system preserves information until other parts of the brain are free to process it.

central nervous system (CNS) The brain and spinal cord.

cerebral cortex The six layers of neuron cell bodies which form the outer "bark" of the cerebrum (top brain) which is the most recently evolved region of mammalian brain and in humans is by far the largest part of the brain. It serves higher functions such as abstract thinking and complex memory.

change agent The teacher, therapist, paraprofessional, or other person responsible for modifying the behavior of the target person in a beneficial direction.

channel capacity An information-processing term signifying how much information can be decoded from a given sensory channel or logical processing modality; the carrying capacity of the sensory or other channel.

charting Keeping a graphic record of target behavior(s) over time, usually in the form of a cumulative graph. The feedback from a chart may sometimes influence rates of behavior without other reinforcers.

chunk In information-processing terminology, a large unit of information which consists of many bits of information. See **bit.**

classical conditioning The type of conditioning identified with Pavlov. Also called **type**

S (stimulus), **Pavlovian,** or **respondent conditioning,** it is a contiguity or association conditioning in which a new signal or cue (the conditional stimulus, or CS) is presented prior to a signal (the unconditional stimulus, or US), eliciting some response (the unconditioned response, or UR) which is usually of the type mediated by the autonomic nervous system. With sufficient pairings of the CS and US, the CS alone eventually elicits the response (now called the conditioned response, or CR).

classification skill A skill required to group stimuli into meaningful groups or concepts.

closure A principle introduced by the gestalt theorists which states that incomplete perceptual events tend to be seen and remembered as complete.

cocktail party problem The problem of understanding how a person exposed to multiple simultaneous conversations can still follow (selectively attend to) only one conversation while essentially ignoring all others.

coding Translating one kind of information into another kind. This may be done deliberately to facilitate memory and/or learning.

cognition Thoughts or ideas rather than stimulus-response chains; the basic unit of learning for the cognitive theorists. This unit is molar or large.

cognitive humanist The type of cognitive theorist who believes that humans are free to make real choices rather than being controlled by stimuli and reinforcers in the environment.

cognitive learning The learning of ideas, expectancies, or other complex mental entities rather than stimulus-response bonds or mechanical habits.

cognitive map A term introduced by Tolman to describe what a rat learns in a maze. A cognitive map is a gestalt or whole rather than a chain of stimulus-response associations.

common response model The behaviorist theory of how concepts are formed which suggests that several stimuli that lead to one response are learned as parts of one concept when only that one (of several possible) response is followed by consistent reinforcement. The common reinforced response unifies the concept and connects the various stimuli.

comparative psychology The branch of academic psychology which uses laboratory experimentation on a variety of species of animals to investigate both general trends in behavioral laws and problems which cannot be easily researched with humans. It is firmly rooted in the mainstream of American psychological tradition in contrast to the European ethologists (see **ethology**) who also study a wide range of animal species.

concept attainment How a concept is learned; the successful learning of a concept.

conceptually driven processing Attending and learning that is guided by a preexisting idea of what the subject looks for or wishes to learn.

concrete operations In Piaget's theory, the ability to do conservation tasks if the stimuli are physically present and the conserver is able physically to do and undo the transformations of the stimuli. It is also the name of the period of time in which most children learn to do these logical operations, which extends from 7 to 11 years of age.

conditional response (CR) Also conditioned response or conditioned reflex. See **classical conditioning.**

conditioned emotional response (CER) See **conditioned suppression.**

conditioned facilitation A phenomenon investigated in detail by Sidman in which an organism persists in making a response which once was effective in allowing the organism to avoid an aversive consequence even after such a response no longer has any effect on the rate or timing of the aversive consequence.

conditioned inhibition (S^{I}R)   A Pavlovian and Hullian term for a learned tendency not to respond, in which a formerly neutral cue acquires the power to prevent the elicitation of a specific response through classical conditioning. Hull called it S^{I}R.

conditioned neurosis   A maladaptive reaction produced experimentally which resembles a naturally occurring neurotic reaction. Usually (as in the "little Albert" experiment by Watson and Rayner) of a phobic avoidance type.

conditioned reinforcement   Also known as **secondary reinforcement.** A signal (CS) that acquires reinforcing properties through classical conditioning. The most powerful conditioned reinforcers are those associated with multiple unlearned reinforcers such as food, social approval, and so on. These CSs which have been paired with many USs are called **generalized secondary reinforcers.**

conditioned stimulus (CS)   A stimulus which has acquired the power to elicit a conditioned response or reflex through its prior association with an US. See **classical conditioning.**

conditioned suppression   The suppression of a response which occurs when the cues (discriminative stimuli) that normally set the occasion for its occurrence have been paired with aversive events. After such conditioning, these S$_D$s also elicit what appears to be a **conditioned emotional response** of fear **(CER).**

conjunctive concept   Saltz's term for a concept defined by multiple attributes occurring either together or in one subtype, by any of the several defining attributes.

connectionist   A theorist (usually a behaviorist) who states that the basic unit of learning is connections between stimuli and responses or between stimuli or between responses.

consequation   The third step in contingency management, in which reinforcers are delivered contingent upon the emission of target behaviors.

conservation   Piaget's term for the logical ability to see that although some aspect of the physical appearance of something is altered, the thing remains unchanged in other important ways.

consolidation   The usually gradual process by which dynamic short-term memories are transformed into structural long-term memories.

contiguity   The occurrence in the same time and/or space of two or more events. Contiguity theories postulate that learning occurs through such associations, and such theories are also called association theories (Pavlov, Watson, Guthrie). Also see **law of contiguity.**

contingency   Essentially the relation of two events in which, if the first event occurs, the second will occur: "If you do this, then I will . . . ." Extensively used by Skinnerians to describe response-reinforcement relationships, or the relationship between a behavior and its consequences.

contingency management   The art of controlling the relationships between selected behaviors and their consequences. A type of behavior modification approach derived from Skinnerian theory.

contingent negative variation (CNV)   A shift in the general electrical "tone" of the cortex which is correlated with expectancies or readinesses to respond.

continuity (common direction)   The tendency to continue a set or series of like elements and to see such a continuation as forming a coherent grouping or gestalt. This is a principle of gestalt theory.

contrast A change in response rates due to changes in reinforcement or schedule factors. **Behavioral contrast:** the tendency of rates of behavior in the presence of two cues signaling different reinforcement conditions to diverge from each other more than if the organism had encountered each cue independently.

positive contrast The increase in response rates associated with an increase in the amount of reward earned by a successful response. This effect is more difficult to demonstrate than negative contrast.

negative contrast The decrement in response rates observed when the amount of reinforcement for a successful response is reduced.

cortex (pl. cortices) See **cerebral cortex.**

counterconditioning A reconditioning process in which a cue acquires a new meaning for the organism and loses its old meaning (such as a CS for a fear response becoming conditioned to a relaxation response in the reciprocal inhibition paradigm).

covert desensitization The most common type of systematic desensitization used today, in which the fearful cues are imagined rather than actually experienced. See **systematic desensitization.**

CRF (continuous reinforcement) See **schedules of reinforcement.**

cybernetics Wiener's term for the study of guidance mechanisms for situations ranging from behavior to computers.

data-driven processing Attending and/or learning in which the subject has no idea of what to look for, forcing him or her to scan all existing possibilities to find some way to form the information into a pattern.

decentration Becoming less egocentric, either in logical processes or in moral judgments.

declining returns A Hullian description for the tendency for less strength to be added to habit strength with each succeeding response.

decremental reinforcement In Mowrer's system, the type of reinforcement that reduces the intensity of a drive. Eating food, for example, is decremental reinforcement and reduces the hunger drive.

deep processing Processing that occurs after information has already been consolidated into long-term memory. Such processing usually involves relating this information to concepts or otherwise making it easier to recall.

deep structure In Chomsky's theory, ideas formed in accordance with the rules of universal grammar. The words we speak are actually a translation from "natural language" deep structure coding of the basic idea to be communicated.

dendrite A nerve cell process (usually multiple) that carries information into the cell body. The strength of the electrical excitement carried by such processes varies according to the strength of the stimulation producing it and gets weaker (decremental conduction) as the electrical message gets further away from the synaptic point where stimulation originated.

dependent variable Outcome (response) variables.

didactic materials In Montessori's method, materials intended to teach or convey instruction.

dimension A physical aspect of stimuli, such as color, size, or meaning, which forms the basis of the organism's formation of discriminations.

discovery learning The teaching technique advocated by gestalt theorists in which the child is given materials and a question and directed to find his or her own solutions rather than being given formulas to memorize.

discriminated operant   An operant that is only emitted in the presence of a discriminative stimulus (S_D or $S+$). See **operant.**

discrimination   Also called **differentiation.** The process by which organisms tell cues and/or responses from each other (as in learning to respond in the presence of one cue and not another).

discriminative stimulus (S_D)   The term used by Skinnerians to denote the cue in whose presence the appearance of reinforcement is probable, usually the cue which signals the organism to respond. It is roughly the opposite of a S_Δ, which signifies nonreinforcement.

disinhibition   The removal of an inhibitory influence.

disjunctive concept   In cognitive theories such as Saltz's, this is a concept in which any single attribute (basic defining characteristic) of a concept found in an example qualifies that example as belonging to that concept. When several such attributes are found together in an example, however, that example may not belong to the concept.

docile   Tolman's term for teachable or flexible behavior.

double approach-avoidance conflict   The situation in which two goals are desired but both also arouse fear when approached too closely (the most common type of real-world conflict). An example might be wanting to study and wanting to talk to a friend. If you talk to the friend, you fear flunking; if you study, you fear hurting the feelings of the friend.

double blind   The experimental control procedure in which neither the target person nor the change agent is aware of which treatments (usually experimental versus control group) are being applied; only the professional supervising the whole procedure knows what is being tested.

drive (D)   An internal condition serving to energize and direct behavior (such as low blood sugar) resulting in producing specified sensations (hunger). Hull, who said that drive was necessary for learning to occur, did not specify its physiological basis.

drive, cue, response, reward   The four basic elements of any learning situation in the learning theory proposed by Miller and Dollard. For learning to occur, a **drive** must be aroused in the presence of a **cue** telling the organism which **response** to make to reduce the intensity of the drive, which acts as a **reward** and strengthens the learning.

eclectic theory   A theory borrowing ideas from other theories.

effect   See **law of.**

egocentricity   Seeing the outside world from the perspective of one's own self. Typical of immature thinking and moral judgments.

electroconvulsive shock (ECS) or (when used with humans) **electroconvulsive therapy/ ECT**   The application of a weak electrical current by two electrodes placed on either side of the head which induces convulsions and is followed by amnesia of varying degrees of completeness. ECS is an important research tool in investigating short-term memory in animals; ECT is an effective therapeutic technique for treating some types of depression in humans.

electromyographic potential (EMG)   The electrical potential recorded from the skin over skeletal muscles which indicates the level of tension in those muscles.

elicit   The power of a cue to draw forth a response from an organism. Cues in Pavlov's type of conditioning elicit responses; in Skinner's theory, however, responses are emitted and no cues are necessary for the response.

emit   In Skinner's theory, responses are given by the organism much as a lightbulb emits light. Cues guide responses but do not elicit, or pull them out.

empirical law of effect   A law that states that reinforcement increases the probability of a response's reoccurrence. This weak law draws no conclusion about the need for reinforcement or inner causes.

engram   The site where long-term memories are stored in the brain; the physical structures storing memories. See **long-term memory (LTM).**

equilibration   A need for a process by which new information is absorbed into existing concepts without creating imbalances or schemata-threatening inconsistencies. This need for balance with the environment and within the self Piaget assumes to be innate.

equipotentiality   The assumption that one set of laws of learning applies regardless of particular stimuli, responses, species, or reinforcers if they are compatible with the organism's capabilities.

errorless learning   Also known as **fading** or **vanishing** (Skinner's term). Terrace's method of beginning a discrimination with a positive cue so compelling that it elicits a response, then gradually fading out this cue or fading in a more vivid cue signaling nonreinforcement. Eventually, both cues are equally salient but the discrimination is maintained even though the S− was never responded to.

escape   The paradigm in which the organism experiences the aversive event and gets away from it by some type of response.

ethology   The branch of European-originated behavioral biology represented by Lorenz which reintroduced the concept of instinct to psychology. Relying heavily on field observations of a very wide range of animal species, today this discipline is drawing closer to the other main branch of the study of animal behavior, **comparative psychology.** These two disciplines have exerted a strong influence on each other and on psychology in general. Ethology has also been a strong influence on **sociobiology,** a new interdisciplinary science.

excitatory potential ($S^E R$)   The internal potential to perform a response actively. In Pavlov's theory, it results from electrical activation of cortical neurons. In Hull's theory, no neural basis is given but this construct is assumed to represent the force which would determine the occurrence or nonoccurrence of the response.

excitatory (+) reflex   An organism's reaction to stimuli which consists of an active response rather than stopping some response. See **inhibitory (−) reflex.**

exercise   See **law of exercise.**

experimental analysis of behavior   The method of examining behavior used by operant learning theorists and practitioners. It consists of examining the stimulus situation related to the occurrence of a given behavior and the reinforcement consequences of that behavior.

external inhibition   A Pavlovian term that describes events in the environment which act to block responding and/or learning (conditioning).

exteroceptive   Referring to cues applied outside the body (such as bells ringing) or to the surface of the body; stimulation that is not interoceptive.

extero-interoceptive conditioning   Classical conditioning in which the CS is external to the body and the US is applied to the viscera (such as the stomach lining). In most cases, this conditioning is slow to occur and slow to extinguish.

extinction The process by which organisms learn not to respond to cues that become associated with nonreinforcement. They must have had prior experience with the cue associated with reinforcement. See **reinforcement.**

fading See **errorless learning.**

feedback Information concerning the effectiveness of a response received by an organism following that response. Using machines to show failure or success in modifying internal physiological responses towards some externally set criterion level is called **biofeedback.**

> **negative feedback** Getting information about an action which indicates that the action has not been successful; the usual effect is to reduce the tendency or intensity of unsuccessful actions. This term is heavily used by cybernetic and information-processing theorists.

> **positive feedback** Information about an action that tells an organism or mechanism that the action was successful. The effects of positive feedback are usually to increase the frequency and/or intensity of the action.

feedforward Information about anticipated future events that influences present behavior.

figure The gestalt term for elements of a perceptual experience that stand out and are attended to and can be learned (in contrast to the **ground,** or background).

first signal system In Pavlov's theory, the system of nonverbal environmental cues such as the taste of meat powder, the sound of bells, shock, and so on.

fixed action pattern See **sign stimulus.**

fixed interval scallop See **schedules of reinforcement.**

flooding A forced extinction procedure for the removal of phobic symptoms that requires the client to have continued exposure to a graduated series of imagined stimuli that are fear CSs.

focal individual method Measuring the target behaviors emitted by only one selected target individual at a given time rather than trying to observe several persons' (or animals') behaviors simultaneously.

forced extinction The therapeutic modality in which a CS for an anxiety or/and phobic reaction is presented repeatedly without any aversive US being presented. Two behavioral modification procedures based on this means of extinguishing the anxiety/phobic response (CR) are **implosive therapy** and **flooding.**

formal operations In Piaget's theory, the ability to understand the rules underlying the essential stability of the properties of objects after transformations and to be able to express these rules verbally and/or as equations relating affected properties. Also the period of time in human development beginning about 12 years of age.

fractional anticipatory frustration In Amsel's theory, conditioned frustration attached to cues that predict frustrating situations. Since frustration has arousal properties, anticipatory frustration may increase drive towards a goal in those situations in which frustration has become a signal that the goal will soon be obtained.

fractional anticipatory goal reactions (r_G) A small response much like those made in the presence of a goal (drive reducer) but made at a distance from the goal. In Hull's theory, these "little r_Gs" serve to maintain and guide behavior.

frequency See **law of frequency.**

frontal lobe   The frontmost portion of the cerebral cortex, which is involved in anticipation, creativity, abstract thinking, and voluntary motor control. See **cerebral cortex.**

front loading   Giving high levels of points in a course early in the course to get students more involved at the beginning, to encourage early efforts, and to discourage "cramming" late in the course.

function   In Piaget's theory, an inherited process such as assimilation or accommodation.

functional behavior   Behavior (such as social skills and reading) that is effective in generating its own reinforcers.

functionalism   A school of thought among a loose aggregation of learning theorists unified in showing eclectic tendencies and in being interested in the purposes of behavior.

Garcia effect   The selective linking of taste to nausea or externally originated aversive stimuli such as shock to audiovisual stimuli. Taste aversion learning demonstrates the Garcia effect. (See **taste aversion.**)

generalization Also known as **irradiation**   The process by which an organism responds to cues similar to those formerly associated with reinforcement. In a sense, the opposite of discrimination.

generalized secondary reinforcer   A conditioned stimulus which has been associated with multiple primary reinforcers. Such a learned or conditioned reinforcer (such as money) is very powerful and resists extinction. See **secondary (conditioned) reinforcement.**

generative grammar   In Chomsky's theory, the grammar of transformations from deep to particular surface structure sentences.

gestalt   *Gestalt* is the German word for figure or form. Gestalt theorists, characterized by their belief that wholes are more than molecular components, attempted to analyze behavior as wholes rather than as discrete stimulus-response units.

goal response (R_G)   In Hull's theory, the response emitted in the actual presence of goal cues (such as salivation to the sight of food).

goal stimulus (S_G)   In Hull's theory, a stimulus related to the goal (such as the sight and smell of food).

gradient of generalization   The curve generated by plotting the number of responses made to stimuli that are similar in some specific way to a reinforced stimulus used in earlier training. As the new stimuli become more dissimilar from the training stimulus, less responses are made to them. For example, if responding to a green light is originally reinforced, the responder will usually make fewer responses to a greenish yellow light and still fewer to a yellow light.

gradients of approach and avoidance   The strength of the tendencies either to approach or to avoid a goal as a function of the distance in space or time from that goal. Gradients of avoidance are postulated to be steeper when drawn on a graph than gradients of approach, expressing the tendency of fear to increase more quickly than positive anticipations when a goal is approached closely.

ground   The gestalt theorists' term for backgrounds or aspects of the environment that are not attended to. See **figure.**

habit   Hull's basic molar (large-scale) unit of learning, a behavior pattern acquired through learning that shows itself through increased frequency or facility of performance.

habit-family hierarchy   A Hullian term derived from first-order principles which denotes the tendency first to try to solve a problem through the habit most often successful in the past and then to run through various other habits in the order of their previous successful associations with solving similar types of problems. When the entire list or hierarchy of habits is used up, the organism may begin again with the first habit.

habit strength ($S^H R$)   In Hull's theory, the result of the number of reinforced trials (those resulting in drive reduction). Habit strength is multiplied by intensity of drive (D) to predict an organism's tendency to perform a given response when confronted with a given stimulus. Spence modified this view by having habit strength add (rather than multiply) with drive to predict response tendencies. Habit strength is the measure of how well the habit was learned.

habituation   The process by which repeated exposure to some stimuli causes the organism to learn to ignore these stimuli with the conscious brain while lower-level unconscious brain mechanisms still monitor them.

hedonism   The psychological principle which states that organisms seek pleasure and avoid pain. In general, all reinforcement theories, and some cognitive theories which stress expectancies of reward, are hedonistic theories.

higher mental process   A cognitive or thinking process as opposed to an automatic conditioning process.

hippocampus   A region of primitive cortex hidden within the cerebrum which is highly involved in forming new complex memories and in habituation of tendencies to pay attention to repetitive stimuli. See **cerebral cortex, consolidation,** and **habituation.**

hologram analogy theory   Pribram's theory that the optical hologram (a method of recording, storing, and reproducing three-dimensional images) has many features in common with human memory and can explain such human processes by its example.

homeostatic   A system that resists change by actions which restore a condition existing before the change. A thermostat and our brain mechanisms regulating blood sugar concentrations are examples of homeostatic systems

imaginal aversion therapy   A form of aversive therapy in which the client imagines aversive consequences (such as becoming horribly ill in public) after performing the undesired behavior (such as overeating). In its use of imagined stimuli, this treatment is parallel to covert systematic desensitization.

imaginal system   Bandura's term for memories of observed behaviors which take the form of images of the actual actions.

immediate memory   See **short-term memory (STM).**

implosive therapy   A forced extinction procedure which exposes the client to imagined scenes derived from psychoanalytic assumptions about fearful and/or traumatic incidents likely to have occurred in early childhood.

imprinting   A rapid and sometimes irreversible type of learning that occurs mainly during a particular phase of early development in birds or mammals and is responsible for species identification in birds having the ability to locomote from the time of hatching. Very close to instinct, this type of learning was first examined by the European ethologists.

incentive motivation (K)   A Hullian variable representing the attractiveness of a given reward, which can be influenced by expectancies, previous learning, and costs of working for that reward.

incompatible response method   One of Guthrie's suggestions for getting rid of bad habits in which the subject is supposed to perform an act which is incompatible with the bad habit while in the presence of cues that would otherwise elicit the unwanted behavior.

incremental reinforcement A term used by Mowrer to describe the type of reinforcement that results in an increase in a drive, as in escaping from an aversive event (the better you are at getting away, the higher your urge to finish getting away).

independent variable The environmental variable which may be manipulated by a researcher.

induction A Pavlovian term derived from the electrical phenomenon of inducing a current from within one coil of wire by passing a current through another coil of wire. According to Pavlov, prolonged excitation in the brain induces a state of inhibition.

information-processing theories A branch of psychology which tries to trace how information gets into the nervous system by analogy to computer systems.

inhibitory (−) reflex A response to a cue that causes an ongoing reflex or response to stop. Novel cues in the environment tend to stop the expression of ongoing conditioned responses or inhibit the elicitation of such responses.

innate Present from birth and usually assumed to be due to the actions of genetic mechanisms. Innate factors are usually inherited, not learned, factors.

innate releasing mechanism See **sign stimuli.**

insight Seeing inside one's own head to derive a solution to a problem without overt trial and error. A type of one-trial learning described by the gestalt theorists as evidence against the connectionists' view that learning results from gradual strengthening of stimulus-response bonds.

instinctual drift The Brelands' term for the tendency of a learned behavior to "drift" towards an instinctual behavior pattern in spite of selective reinforcement only of the learned behavior. This effect occurs under conditions of strong motivation.

instrumental conditioning Operant or Skinnerian or reinforcement conditioning in which the organism's responses are "instrumental" in solving a problem or obtaining reinforcement. Also known as **type R** or **operant conditioning.**

integration Saltz's term for combining different stimuli into one cognitive unit or concept.

internal inhibition A Pavlovian term referring to the process by which responding and/or learning is blocked through internal mechanisms (such as in extinction).

interoceptive conditioning Conditioning in which either the CS or US or both are applied to the viscera, glandular systems, or cardiovascular system.

interresponse time (IRT) A Skinnerian term for the time between successive responses in a chain. These time units have cue properties. Short and long IRTs are differentially reinforced in ratio and interval schedules, respectively. See **schedules of reinforcement.**

intervening variable A logical construct used to bridge the gap between environmental (independent) variables and response (dependent) variables. Nothing is inferred about the physiological reality or nature of the construct.

interval method An observation method in which behavior is sampled at specified intervals (time sampling) rather than continuously.

introject A term used in gestalt therapy to describe material (such as values or morals) that is learned but not really incorporated into the person's other beliefs and motivations. Introjects are seen as foreign ideas originating in the ideas of significant others such as parents and teachers.

irradiation   See **generalization.**

Jacobson relaxation   Also called deep muscle relaxation or progressive relaxation. The method of tensing and relaxing the muscles of the body in sequence described by Jacobson and used in prepared childbirth training as well as in systematic desensitization.

kernel sentence   In Chomsky's theory, a deep structure sentence organized by universal grammar. Many **surface structure sentences** can be derived from one deep structure sentence.

Lamaze method   The method of psychoprophylaxis most used in the United States in preparing women for often drugless childbirth experiences. Based on Pavlovian concepts, it usually consists of six weeks of classes taught by a paraprofessional.

law of

    associative shifting   Thorndike's term for the mechanism for the transfer of stimulus control from one cue to another when the first cue is gradually transformed into the second.

    contiguity   Guthrie's one law of learning, which states that just the association of two stimuli is sufficient to account for the forming of a relationship between them as a memory trace.

    effect   Thorndike's central law, which follows the hedonistic tradition, stating that organisms tend to repeat activities associated with pleasure and to avoid or fail to prolong activities associated with annoyance.

    exercise   One of Thorndike's early laws stating that repetition can enhance learning. For Thorndike, this contiguity learning interacts with the law of effect and is not sufficient to produce learning when acting alone.

    frequency   One of Watson's early laws stating that the strength of a stimulus-response connection is a function of repetition.

    multiple response   Thorndike's law stating that if one response does not solve a problem, another response will be tried.

    prepotency of elements   Thorndike's law accounting for selective attention to particular stimuli in a stimuli array on the basis of some stimuli having the intrinsic power to direct attention.

    readiness   Thorndike's law related to the arousal state of hypothesized neural units. If a unit is ready, then conduction will be satisfying and nonconduction annoying; conduction in unready units is annoying.

    recency   Watson's early law stating that the strength of a connection between stimuli and responses is maximal when the events are close in time.

    response by analogy   Thorndike's law concerning the transfer of successful responses from one environment to a new environment.

    set or attitude   Thorndike's law of the effects of personal or cultural predispositions to behave in particular ways to particular situations.

learned helplessness   The phenomenon first investigated in detail by Seligman in which the organism learns that it can do nothing to alter when a US will be presented. When conditions are subsequently altered so that the organism can prevent the aversive US, the organism usually fails to learn this new contingency and persists in acting helpless. This is often accompanied by signs of emotional upset and depression.

learning set   Harlow's term for a strategy or plan for solving problems acquired through experience with previous problems of a similar type. Once a learning set is formed, learning shifts from trial and error to insight or rapid learning.

life space Lewin's term for a topological drawing or representation of an individual human's phenomenological reality or the world as he or she sees it. The various goals, forces, and barriers are used to predict or explain behavior.

linear program See **programmed learning.**

linguistic competence Chomsky's term for the ability to understand and generate meaningful language from basic ideas.

logico-mathematical knowledge In Piaget's theory, knowledge about abstract properties of things and of logical relationships. This knowledge is realized intuitively when a child at the appropriate stage of cognitive development is given access to relevant materials to manipulate.

long-term memory (LTM) Also called **permanent memory.** The high-capacity, permanent, or almost permanent storage of information in engrams.

maintaining stimuli Guthrie's term for stimuli generated by rewards or drive states. These are the stimuli that relate cues leading towards making a reinforcement-obtaining response and make the S-R bonds prior to getting a reward the most recent event and hence most likely to be repeated when the organism is again deprived. When the reward is obtained, reward-getting responses stop because the maintaining stimuli generated by the drive state are gone, not because of drive reduction.

mand Skinner's term for a child's primitive verbalized command or demand. Reinforcement following a mand makes the mand more likely to be produced in the future.

mechanistic Seeing learning as the result of environmentally determined or brain-mechanism-determined automatic processes rather than as a conscious effort by the learning organism.

mediational facilitation Using the assignment of arbitrary meanings to nonsense words to make them easier to learn.

method of loci A very ancient mnemonic device in which items to be remembered are associated with a sequence of well-remembered physical locations, such as areas of a house or cues associated with an often-followed pathway or road.

method of successive approximations See **shaping.**

militant enthusiasm Lorenz's term for the unconditioned arousing and reinforcing effects of a social species doing an activity in a group and imitating other group members in doing that behavior. Lorenz suggests that the militant enthusiasm response is responsible for seemingly irrational human actions such as mob behavior.

mnemonic devices Ancient and modern techniques developed by memory experts, which greatly help memorization of new lists of information. An example is associating the lists with nonsense jingles and/or lists of overlearned words (the **peg word technique**).

modeling Bandura's term for the process of vicarious learning, which is assumed to involve both reinforcement and cognitive elements. See **vicarious learning.**

molar Large-scale conceptual units (such as habits or concepts) rather than small units (such as bonds between individual stimuli and responses).

movement-produced stimulus In Guthrie's theory, cues resulting from activation of receptors of muscle movements. Such a stimulus serves to tell the organism what movement to make next, thus acting to glue together the various parts of complex sequences of responses.

multiple baseline   A method for evaluating the effectiveness of a behavioral modification procedure in which behavior is measured before, during the application of the procedure, and after that procedure is at least temporarily suspended. Sometimes several intervention (on-contingency) and nonintervention (off-contingency, or baseline) measurement periods are alternated.

multiple response   See **law of multiple response.**

multiple-response baseline procedure   Dunham's method for evaluating the effects of punishment by noting how several behaviors change from their baseline levels during the onset, offset, and between punishment time periods.

natural language   In Chomsky's theory, an inherited "base protolanguage" common to all human beings that is responsible for similarities between essential grammatical relationships of all human languages.

nature   The side of the nature/nurture debate that assumes that many or most of the causes of behavior are inherited rather than acquired.

negative feedback   See **feedback.**

negative practice paradigm   A therapeutic procedure for the removal or reduction of undesired behaviors that requires the client to perform the undesired behavior (such as smoking) at such high rates that these behaviors become aversive.

negative reinforcement   See **reinforcement.**

negative transfer   See **transfer.**

negative valence   See **valence.**

neuromuscular reeducation   A type of biofeedback procedure in which electrical signals from nerves that formerly were too weak to operate associated muscles are amplified; such signals are reinforced until they become strong enough to produce a return of muscle function. This is a variant of EMG biofeedback.

neuronal model   Pribram's term for memory, either short-term or long-term, stored in the brain and compared with incoming sensory information. Inputs matching the model are ignored on a conscious level; images not fitting the models lead to active processes of attention and/or learning.

nurture   The side of the nature/nurture debate that is based on the assumption that many or most of the causes of behavior depend upon learning by experience with the environment.

observation   The second step of contingency management, in which target behaviors are observed and recorded; an experimental analysis of behavior approach may be followed.

one-trial learning   Learning that appears at full strength following a single pairing of stimuli or stimuli and responses. This is contrasted with learning which continually grows in strength as a function of the number of learning trials. One-trial learning is also called discontinuous learning.

operant   A response made by an organism of sufficient strength to operate a device that will dispense reinforcers; a Skinnerian term applied to responses such as bar-pressing by rats.

operant conditioning   See **instrumental conditioning.**

operational definition   A definition stated in terms of the procedures used to measure the underlying construct, as in defining anger as hitting behavior to be counted by observers.

orienting reflex (OR)   The what-is-it reflex elicited by potentially important stimuli (new cues) that inhibits ongoing reflexes and that must come before learning. Stressed in Pavlovian conditioning and first described in depth by Sokolov.

oscillation function (S^OR)   Hull's "fudge" factor to account for intraorganism variation in performance, in which the organism's threshold for responding is believed to vary randomly over time as the organism's condition varies.

overlearning   Learning something to the point of 100 percent accuracy and then continuing to practice it. Overlearning increases memory retention.

overshadowing   The greater power of a stronger or more salient component of a compound stimulus to elicit a CR than weaker members of the compound. Similar to **rule of force.**

overtraining   Having a subject practice a task after he or she has already mastered it to the 100 percent (or close to it) criterion level. This results in superior retention and freedom from interference effects.

pain-aggression response   Aggression as an UR to the US of pain. Painful stimulation in the presence of a target usually leads to aggressive behavior.

paired associate procedure   A technique used by verbal learning researchers in which the subject, after learning pairs of words, must then supply the missing member of the pair when confronted with one of the words.

parallel processing   The information-processing theorists' term for a mode of processing information in which several features of a stimulus array or logical operation are processed by different brain areas simultaneously. This is a multiple information channel mode of processing; each channel carries less information than the single channel used in **serial processing.**

partial reinforcement effect   See **schedules of reinforcement.**

participant modeling   The modeling paradigm in which the client imitates each step of a progressive modeling sequence as soon as the model (live or symbolic) finishes acting out the desired behavior.

particular grammar   In Chomsky's theory, the grammar of an actual human language, such as Swedish.

partist strategy   Focusing on a single hypothesis at a time in learning to identify a concept and fully testing that hypothesis before accepting or discarding it. The opposite of **wholist strategy.**

passive avoidance   The paradigm in which the organism, in order to avoid experiencing an aversive event, must not make specified responses.

Pavlovian conditioning   See **classical conditioning.**

Pavlovian paradigm   The basic experimental arrangement used in producing simple classical conditioning with a CS presented prior to a US (a stimulus which elicits a response without known previous conditioning). After several such pairings of the US and CS, the CS is presented alone and, if conditioning is successful, will elicit the CR.

peak experiences   A sudden flash of joy or feeling of having achieved insight which, in the context of group therapy, usually involves experiences happening within the group. Peak experiences are seen as qualitatively better than normal types of happiness or understanding.

peak shift   The tendency for an organism confronted with both a S− (SΔ) and a S+ (S$_D$)

to respond maximally to cues most like the S_D and unlike the S− (SΔ). In other words, the peak of responding shifts away from the S−.

peg word technique   A commonly used mnemonic device in which a "peg word" list of ten images associated with the numbers 1 to 10 is remembered first. Subsequently, the first item of each new list of information to be remembered is associated with the "1" image of the peg word list, the second item of the new list with the second image, and so on.

permanent memory   See **long-term memory.**

personalized method of instruction (PSI)   The teaching method developed by Keller in which mastery criteria are substituted for performance criteria based on set time intervals. In the pure form of this system, students are allowed to have as much time as needed in individual study to master course objectives. Therefore, everyone can earn "A" grades, but some students will complete the course in much less time than other students.

phi phenomenon   The illusion of a moving light generated when a group of two or more light bulbs blink off and on out of sequence; used by the gestalt theorists as a demonstration that perceptual experiences are more than the sum of their stimulus events.

phobia   A strong aversion to a limited class of environmental events, often traceable to an early strong negative experience with the object of fear, which seems unreasonably strong and overgeneralized.

phobic avoidance   An unreasonable tendency to avoid some thing or situation; considered a form of neurotic behavior. See **phobia.**

phonological rules   Chomsky's term for the linguistic rules that determine how sounds can be combined in language.

physical knowledge   The Piagetian term for an understanding of the properties of objects obtained by manipulating those objects. This knowledge may be nonverbal, as in knowing how to mold clay.

placebo effect   The psychologically beneficial effect of substances or treatments that have no inherent therapeutic properties. Basically, suggestion effects that may make an ineffectual treatment effective with some clients.

positive feedback   See **feedback.**

positive instance   Concept learning jargon for guessing correctly which stimulus example belongs to a concept. This correct stimulus example and the trial in which it first is identified are both called positive instances.

positive reinforcement   See **reinforcement.**

positive transfer   See **transfer.**

positive valence   See **valence.**

post-reinforcement pause   A Skinnerian term for the break in responding noted on fixed interval and lean fixed ratio schedules. See **schedules of reinforcement.**

postulate   A proposition, taken as true, that is made the starting point in a chain of logic.

Prägnanz   The gestalt term for the tendency of perceptions and memories to seek "ideal form," much as a soap bubble returns to a sphere when a light distorting touch is removed.

predictiveness hypothesis   Rescorla's theory that the extent to which a CR allows the organism to predict when the US will occur is responsible for the extent to which such a CS will be effective in eliciting a CR such as a fear reaction in the CER paradigm (see **conditioned suppression**) and in subsequently facilitating or inhibiting a response which was linked to operant reinforcement.

Premack principle The theory that any high-probability response can be used to reinforce the emission of any low-probability response (or, roughly, eat your spinach and then you get ice cream).

preoperational In Piaget's theory, the developmental stage, or a child at that stage, in which conservation operations have not yet appeared. See **concrete operations.**

prepared learning Learning in which the nervous system seems innately designed to make certain types of associations easily that are very resistant to extinction. Examples include imprinting, species-specific defense reactions which are not fully instinctual (such as escape patterns), and taste aversions and preferences.

preparedness continuum A term introduced by Seligman referring to the extent to which behavior is influenced by inherited predispositions. This continuum extends from totally prepared behavior (instincts) through prepared learning, unprepared learning, and contra-prepared learning (learning or responding that is difficult or impossible because of inherited factors). See **prepared learning.**

prepotency of elements See **law of prepotency of elements.**

prepotent theory of reinforcement Premack's theory that if one response is more probable than another, the probable response can serve as a reinforcer to increase the rates of the less probable response.

proactive inhibition A negative transfer-of-training effect in which previously learned material interferes with the learning of new material.

probabilistic concept Saltz's term for a concept that is suggested but not completely defined by several attributes that have high correlations with the total concept.

programmed learning A term used to describe instructional materials where the information is arranged in a sequence with previous steps providing the information to answer questions asked during following steps and where the learner is asked to respond to questions following each major step of the program. Programmed material may be used in teaching machines or in programmed texts. If the sequence is fixed, the program is called a **linear program.** If a learner making errors is directed to specific remedial material and possibly an easier subprogram, the program is called a **branching program.**

progressive modeling The process in which a model gradually demonstrates closer and closer approaches to a feared object, organism, or situation.

projection A form of defense reaction in which the person assumes (usually falsely) that someone else has their motives and feelings. In gestalt therapy theory, this is seen as the result of inadequate discrimination of real self boundaries **(figure)** from those of others **(ground).**

prompt A hint or other contextual guide provided in programmed learning material to make a correct response easier to make. Such prompts are usually provided most liberally early in a program and gradually "faded out" in the final stages of the program.

protein memory hypothesis The theory that long-term memories are inscribed in altered protein molecules.

proximity A gestalt term for the tendency to perceive objects that are physically close as a unit or whole.

pseudoconditioning   See **backward conditioning.**

psychophysiology   The branch of psychology which alters stimulus conditions and then measures internal physiological reactions such as changes in EMG or blood pressure.

psychoprophylaxis   Using psychological methods to prevent pain, as in preventing the pain of childbirth.

punishment   A condition in which an aversive event is made contingent upon the emission of specified behavior (which is usually being maintained by positive reinforcement).

purposive   A term that describes behavior directed towards expected goals rather than mechanically guided by stimuli.

reaction time   Highly sensitive method for measuring poorly remembered material in which the subject is presented with previously learned cues and novel cues, with reaction times to respond to each measured. (Reaction times for responding to previously learned material are shorter than reaction times for unfamiliar cues.)

reactive inhibition (I_R)   Hull's term for the gradual tendency to stop making a response over continued trials; a tendency which operates much like fatigue.

readiness   See **law of readiness.**

recall   Remembering of stored information **(engrams).** Also a method of measuring the extent of learning by requiring the subject to produce a desired bit of information, as on short answer tests. Recall is usually the hardest test of memory.

recency   See **law of recency.**

reciprocal inhibition   A Pavlovian concept in which a CS formerly paired with a strong US is paired again with another strong US, which usually elicits a response incompatible with the response associated with the first US. The original US is usually also available but in sharply reduced intensity. The CS would then be associated with the second US-UR, an association which would reciprocally inhibit the expression of the first (original) association. An example would be pairing a cue for eating with a CS that was formerly associated with an US for fear. Reciprocal inhibition is a type of counterconditioning.

recognition   A method of testing the extent of learning/remembering in which the subject is given several alternatives and told to choose the one to which he or she had previously been exposed. It is an easier test of memory, in most cases, than recall.

reductionistic   A tendency to reduce variables at one level of explanation to variables of a more basic level of explanation, such as reducing neuronal functioning to chemical events or behavior to stimulus-response chains.

reflex   An automatic and usually inborn response to stimuli; stressed by Pavlov.

r_G-generated stimulus (s_G)   In Hull's theory (see **fractional anticipatory goal response**), the cues created by making responses similar to those at the actual goal serve to guide the organism through a long behavioral chain until the actual goal is reached.

reinforcement   In Pavlovian conditioning, the confirmation of a CS by the appearance of the associated US. In Skinner's theory, it is any event that can increase the probability of emission of a response that occurred just prior to the reinforcing event. In Hull's early model, it is something that reduces a drive. Roughly, a reward.

> **negative reinforcement**   The termination of an aversive event through emission of an active behavior, as in running into a shelter to avoid further soaking in a rainstorm.

positive reinforcement   The presentation of a specified positive reinforcer following a specified response.

reinforcer   Any thing or event which strengthens learning or increases a tendency to behave in a specified way.

negative reinforcer   Any thing or event whose removal or termination increases the probability of the reoccurrence of behavior which preceded such removal or termination. See **aversive stimuli.**

positive reinforcer   Any thing or event which increases the probability of the organism's repeating the acts which preceded the delivery of that thing or event; roughly like a reward but with no connotation of being deserved.

reminiscence effect   Remembering something better after the passage of a period of time than just after the material was learned.

resistance to punishment   The acquired insensitivity to the effects of an aversive consequence that results from beginning with a mild punisher and gradually increasing the intensity of the aversive stimulation as the organism learns to continue performing the unwanted behavior in spite of such punishers.

respondent conditioning   See **classical conditioning.**

response by analogy   See **law of response by analogy.**

response chain   A series of responses culminating in a reinforcing event.

response cost   The effort required to earn a given reinforcement.

response deprivation model   See **adaptive model.**

response generalization   The tendency not to make a response exactly the same from trial to trial. The resulting response variability makes the method of successive approximations **(shaping)** possible.

retroactive facilitation   A type of positive transfer of training in which learning a second set of responses or mental units aids in the recall of a previously learned set of responses or mental units.

retroactive inhibition   A type of negative transfer of training in which learning a second set of material leads to the interference with the recall of a set of material learned at an earlier time.

retrograde amnesia   A loss of memory of past events.

reverberating loop   Hebb speculated that short-term memory is stored in active circuits of neurons in which the first neuron in the loop is eventually restimulated by the neuron in the last position in the loop. See **short-term memory.**

reversal design   An experimental design used to measure the effects of contingency management programs consisting at least of a baseline 1, on-contingency, and baseline 2 sequence of measurement periods.

reversibility (transitivity) of reinforcement   Premack's notion that when an organism is deprived of the opportunity to emit a particular response, that response may become a powerful reinforcer even though that response previously had to be reinforced. For example, a rat deprived of access to exercise will drink to earn exercise.

RNA transfer hypothesis   The theory that RNA (ribonucleic acid) is the molecule upon which long-term memory is inscribed. By injecting RNA molecules from the brains of trained animals into the brains of untrained animals, according to this theory, the memories held by the trained RNA molecules will also be transferred.

rule of force   The tendency of the strongest component of a compound CS to dominate the combination and to overshadow the effects of previously conditioned (to other CRs) effects of weaker components (other cues). Normally, second signal system (verbal/thought) components of compound stimuli dominate over first signal system (physical) cues.

satiation   The termination or reduction in responding that results when the organism has received so many reinforcers that it seems to lose its motivation to work for these reinforcers.

savings   A method of measuring the extent to which material is remembered by having the subject relearn the material, noting the savings of time from original learning to relearning. Since relearning even of material subjects thought they had forgotten can be much faster than original learning, this method is much more sensitive to poorly remembered information than either recognition or recall testing methods.

schedules of reinforcement   The rules of specifying when reinforcers become available. Most of the schedules that follow were first described by Skinner and neo-Skinnerians.

> **concurrent**   A schedule in which an organism's behavior is controlled to some degree by each of several schedules operating simultaneously.
>
> **continuous reinforcement (CRF)**   The lowest fixed ratio schedule in which one reinforcement is delivered for every response. It is useful in shaping new responses but leads to rapid satiation. See **ratio** schedules.
>
> **differential reinforcement**   A schedule in which the organism must produce response rates within very narrow limits to gain reinforcements. If the level desired is low, the schedule is a **differential reinforcement of low levels (DRLL)**. If the level desired is high ("beat the clock"), the schedule is a **differential reinforcement of high rates (DRH)**. (A schedule in which any specified response other than an undesired one is reinforced is a **differential reinforcement of other responses (DRO)**.
>
> **full-session DRL**   A commonly used differential reinforcement of low levels procedure in which the target behavior is measured for a prolonged period (as a full class period in elementary school); the consequences are contingent upon the emission of the behavior within specified limits during that period. See **differential reinforcement** schedules.
>
> **interlocking**   Schedules in which the rules determining the availability of reinforcement are altered according to the experimenter's success in gaining the reinforcers. If success is followed by stiffening of the requirements, it is an **ascending interlocking schedule**. If failure is followed by reducing the requirements, it is a **descending interlocking schedule**.
>
> **intermittent reinforcement**   A schedule in which reinforcement is not available for every response; see **partial reinforcement effect**.
>
> **interval**   Schedules in which reinforcement is made available by time considerations. If the organism must respond within a specified time slot, the schedule is a **fixed interval (FI)**. If the time in which the response must be made is varied around a specified mean amount of time, the schedule is designated as a **variable interval (VI)**.
>
> **multiple**   Two or more schedules presented in sequence, each signaled by a characteristic cue. The subject must follow the rules of whatever schedule is in effect at a given time for reinforcement.

partial reinforcement effect In Amsel's theory, also known as **PRE**. The effect of intermittent schedules in leading to rates of behavior higher than those obtained with continuous reinforcement in many cases. Less reinforcement (especially with ratio schedules) often leads to more behavior. Also a feature of Tolman's theory, this effect presents a problem for some connectionists, in that animals extinguish more slowly under conditions of extinction following partial reinforcement than under conditions of extinction following continuous reinforcement. Cognitive theorists would interpret these results as reflecting the organism's uncertainty about when to expect the reinforcing event.

ratio A schedule in which the number of responses made by the respondent determines when reinforcement is available. The ratio may be fixed (**fixed ratio** or **FR**) or probabilistic (**variable ratio** or **VR**).

schemata In Piaget's theory, structural units of mind which correspond to concepts.

secondary (conditioned) reinforcement See **conditioned reinforcement, generalized secondary reinforcer.** Learned or conditioned reinforcement. The mechanism of conditioning is classical, where an environmental cue (as tokens) is paired with an unconditioned reinforcer (such as candy).

second-order conditioning The conditioning of a new CS to an existing CS that had become effective through its association with a US. This new CS is called a second-order or secondary CS; the response it elicits is a second-order conditioned response (CR). Second-order conditioning is weaker than primary (CS to US) conditioning.

second signal system The Pavlovian term for language, meanings, and thoughts which was supposed to obey the same rules as the first signal system of environmentally originated stimuli (such as meat powder, bells, and so on).

selective attention Attending to some features of a complex stimulus array and ignoring others, as the result of a deliberate process.

self-actualization A term used by humanistic and gestalt therapists to describe a person's growth into his or her maximum capacity; becoming the best person one's potential allows one to be.

self-modeling A modeling paradigm in which the participant is filmed performing a desired behavior and subsequently models his or her own earlier actions.

semantic conditioning Classical conditioning in which the meaning of words, not their sound or appearance, is the effective CS.

semantic transfer Generalization to new situations of the response-eliciting properties of words on a meaning dimension rather than a physical similarity dimension. An example would be eliciting a CR conditioned to a CS of the word "red" by the word "barn" rather than the word "read."

sensitive period In the theories of Montessori, Piaget, and the ethologists, a term that refers to each successive period of time in an organism's lifespan when it is most prepared to learn particular types of relationships. If the specified type of learning can *only* occur within a limited time span that time span is called a critical period.

sensitization The phenomenon related to classical conditioning in which strong stimuli make the nervous system and the receptors "supersensitive" so that strong responses may occur to new CSs which mimic true conditioning. Such responses, however, are totally indiscriminate.

sensory preconditioning The paradigm in which two cues (potential CSs) are paired with each other. Subsequently one of these cues is paired with a US. After this Pavlovian conditioning, the CS which was never paired with the US is found also to elicit the CR elicited by the CS which had been paired with the US.

sequential hypothesis   The theory which explains the PRE (see **schedules of reinforcement** and **partial reinforcement effect)** as the organism's learning that nonreinforced trials are only units in sequences of nonreinforced to reinforced responses.

serial learning   A technique used extensively by the functionalists to explore verbal learning. Essentially, learning a list of words or syllables.

serial processing   A mode of processing information in which the brain scans or processes each item in a list or group of stimuli in a sequential order and logical operations are performed in a sequential fashion.

seven ± two   The limit on how many concepts most higher organisms can hold in short-term memory or perceive simultaneously.

shadowing   The experimental procedure used in information-processing research in which a person pays attention to only one of two or more messages presented simultaneously (such as one message to each ear).

shaping   Also called the **method of successive approximations.** The Skinnerian technique in which new behavior is created by starting with existing behavior and gradually reinforcing only responses which become more and more like the final desired behavior.

short-term memory (STM)   Also called **immediate memory.** A transient type of true memory with a low holding capacity and low resistance to interference (such as an initial but fleeting memory of names of people following multiple introductions at a party).

Sidman avoidance   The experimental paradigm in which subjects are required to respond before the end of a preset time interval if they are to avoid shock. Their response resets the timer controlling the shock.

sign   In Tolman's theory, the general word for a stimulus attended to by the organism that carries meaning. Similar to **significate** and **sign-gestalt.**

signaled avoidance   The avoidance-learning paradigm in which a cue (usually a conditioned stimulus) signals that an aversive event will soon happen to subjects unless they perform some specified behavior such as bar-pressing or leaping over a hurdle separating two halves of a test chamber.

sign-gestalt   Tolman's term for the cue that tells an organism where key features of its environment are located after they have been internalized as a mental unit. Also called field expectancy.

significate   In Tolman's theory, a cue telling the organism what to expect (such as food or shock). Similar to **sign-gestalt.**

sign learning   Mowrer's term for classical conditioning of cues as acquired signals. These cues tell the organism what to expect in a situation.

sign stimulus   Environmental cue to which the organism is innately prepared to respond. Sign stimuli can elicit instinctual reflexes as complex as mating rituals in birds. The brain "prewiring" for this recognition is inherited.

similarity   The gestalt principle that things that are similar will be seen or experienced as belonging together.

simple concept   A concept defined by one attribute.

Skinner box   A test chamber of the type invented by Skinner, always equipped with a response device and a reinforcement device, that can be automatically triggered by operation of the response device (such as a rat lever). It may also be equipped with visual and/or audio cues for studies of discrimination.

social-arbitrary knowledge Piaget's term for knowledge that is the result of rote teaching or of the imposition of societal norms. This type of knowledge is seen as less integrated into the learner's basic cognitive structure than knowledge acquired through direct experience with objects and situations.

social learning theory The cognitive branch of the connectionist tradition typified by the cognitive behaviorism of Bandura.

sociobiology A very recent interdisciplinary science involving biologists, comparative psychologists (see **comparative psychology**), sociologists, and anthropologists, which assumes that much complex behavior in most higher species, including man, is at least partly controlled by instincts related to protecting each individual's genes (genetic blueprints stored on DNA molecules).

solution learning Mowrer's term for learning of responses or habits; a mechanism based on reinforcement principles.

species-specific behavior Behavior (usually innately determined) that is characteristic of a particular species (such as freezing to aversive stimulation in rats).

species-specific defense reaction (SSDR) Bolles's term for unconditioned responses (usually fixed action patterns) to aversive stimuli. In rats, these include freezing and, if a target animals is available (a sign of stimulus or US), an aggressive response.

specification The first step of contingency management, in which desired or undesired (target) behaviors, reinforcers, and contingencies are specified.

specific hunger Craving for a specific food and/or taste which has usually been associated in the past with reduction in dietary deficiency; thought to be a type of prepared learning. See **prepared learning.**

spontaneous recovery The phenomenon of an extinguished response's "bouncing back" following a rest period.

SQ3R method A method of improving retention during study of text materials. The student surveys or skims (S) material to derive questions (Q) to ask himself as he reads the material carefully (the first R). He then recites (the second R) back the answers to his questions; if he makes errors, he reviews the material (the third R).

state-dependent learning Learning during a particular state (such as drunk) that is not remembered well except when the conditions of the original learning are repeated.

stimulus intensity dynamism (V) Hull's term for the intensity of a stimulus or its power to elicit a response.

stimulus sampling theory Estes's theory which was based on the idea that each learning trial involves randomly sampling the "pool" of potential stimuli, with stimuli not leading to reinforcement returned to the pool following that unsuccessful trial.

straining the schedule The Skinnerian term for what happens when you try to get an organism to work for too few reinforcements. Essentially, schedule control is lost (straining the schedule) and the organism stops responding. This happens if the change from continuous reinforcement to leaner (more work for less reinforcements) ratio schedules is made too abruptly.

Stroop phenomenon A confusion between concepts and stimuli demonstrated by the Stroop experiment, in which subjects were shown stimuli of one color with the name of another color written on them and asked what color the stimuli were. Most responded with the word written on the card instead of the color.

structuralist   Behavioral scientists who seek to describe the "anatomy of the mind" or mental regions in terms of structural units (such as ego or schemata). Titchener, Piaget, Lewin, Freud, and the introspectionists in general were members of this school. Saltz, Chomsky, and most cognitive theorists have developed theories with some structuralist characteristics.

surface structure sentence   In Chomsky's theory, the sentence actually spoken, which represents a transformation of a kernel sentence.

superordinate stimulus   A stimulus that tells the organism which aspect of the stimulus array should be attended to.

superstitious conditioning   Skinner's term for regular effects on the behavior of an organism perceiving a contingency that does not exist in the environment. As the organism performs more and more of the behavior it "thinks" produces the reinforcement, some of the responses will coincide with reinforcements and the tendency to emit the behavior will increase.

surplus meaning   The problem of popular usage of terms having multiple meanings, many of which do not fit the definitions of the psychologist. (An example is using the term "reward," which can mean both reinforcement and moral judgment, in place of "reinforcement.")

symbolic modeling   Modeling demonstrated by film, videotape, or audio tape rather than by a live model.

symptom substitution   The replacement of one symptom by another as the result of a deep-seated cause not being affected by a treatment which removed only a symptom. This effect is predicted by Freudian theory when behavioral modification methods are used to treat phobias. Most research indicates such symptom substitution rarely occurs.

synapse   The junction between the **axon** of one neuron and the processes or cell body of another neuron. This junction or gap is bridged by transmitter chemicals released by the axon and is the place where messages are carried from one neuron to other neurons. See **axon.**

systematic desensitization   A method of treating phobias, popularized by Wolpe, which pairs Jacobson relaxation with weak versions of cues eliciting the phobic reactions. It is assumed that the formerly fearful cues become reconditioned to relaxation, after which no phobic reaction is experienced even as the patient experiences more and more intense cues from his or her "fear hierarchy."

tabula rasa   A Latin term meaning "blank slate," used in psychology to describe the radical environmentalist position of saying that we are all born without instincts, innately determined aptitudes, or inherited traits; therefore, all that we are is determined by our environment.

tact   Skinner's term for a word incorporated into a child's vocabulary through a process by which reinforcement attaches verbal behaviors to objects.

taste aversion   A type of **prepared learning** which links tastes experienced up to a few hours prior to nausea to a subsequent conditioned nausea and aversion to foods associated with that taste. It appears to be a type of classical conditioning in which the CS (taste) and US (nausea) intervals can be much longer than in other forms of classical conditioning and in which other potential CSs are not linked to the CR (conditioned nausea and aversion).

teaching machine   An instructional device that shares many common features with the Skinner box. It allows pupils to respond and be reinforced for correct answers almost immediately. Instructional materials, called programs, present the material in a highly organized sequential fashion.

token economy A system in which desired behaviors are reinforced with conditioned reinforcers (tokens), which may be physical objects, such as poker chips, or marks in a record book, that are redeemable in primary reinforcers. Token economies are usually employed in schools or mental institutions.

temporal conditioning A paradigm in which the cues associated with the passage of a specific amount of time act as CSs so that a CR occurs just before the US would have been presented.

temporal lobe The portion of the **cerebral cortex** lying roughly under the external ears that is highly involved in hearing and the storage of complex memories. Buried within this lobe is the **hippocampus,** which consolidates complex short-term memories. See **consolidation, short-term memory.**

text Skinner's term for learning reading following the reinforcement of appropriate verbal responses to words in printed form.

theorem An idea proposed as testable "truth." Derived from postulates, as in Hull's theory.

theory of mass action Lashley's theory that the effects of removal of sections of cerebral cortical tissue on memory are a function of the amount or mass of tissue destroyed and not of the location of the lesions.

threshold method One of Guthrie's methods for preventing undesirable behavior by presenting the cues that normally would have elicited that behavior at a strength below their effective threshold for eliciting such behavior. Subsequently, the cues would gradually be increased in intensity as the subject learned to associate the weak versions of the cues with not performing the unwanted behavior. Finally, even full-strength versions of the cues would become harmless.

time out A behavior modification procedure in which unwanted behavior is followed by removing the misbehaving child from the opportunity to obtain positive reinforcers for a specified period of time.

time sampling Measuring target behaviors intermittently rather than continuously.

token cost The system in which emission of undesired behavior or failure to emit desired behavior "costs" previously earned tokens.

topology A geometry of regions adapted by Lewin for use in his neo-gestalt cognitive learning theory to explain the structure of an individual's mind.

trace conditioning Conditioning which occurs to the trace presumed to be left in the brain by a US or CS which has occurred just previously, rather than directly to the US or CS. In this paradigm, the US or CS can be further removed in time from the new CS than is usually the case and may even have occurred prior to the new CS (so that the new CS still is presented prior to the disappearence of the internal neuronal trace).

transfer The process by which previous experiences and/or learning has an effect on later behavior, learning, or recall.

> **negative transfer** When previous learning interferes with learning new material or remembering previously learned material of another sort.

> **positive transfer** When previous learning facilitates learning of new material.

transformation The logical operation by which **kernel sentences** are translated into **surface structure** sentences.

transformational rules   The rules governing the translation of a kernel sentence into several possible surface structures (such as active and passive voices, different tenses, and so on).

transmitter substances   Biochemicals released from the endfeet of axons (the processes of neurons that carry messages away from neuron cell bodies) that float across the synaptic clefts separating neuron cell processes and cause excitation or inhibition on receiving dendrites or cell bodies.

triadic model   Also called the therapeutic pyramid. The situation in which mental health professionals teach paraprofessionals or others how to administer reinforcers (consequences) for target behaviors to the persons whose behavior is to be modified.

trial and error   Learning by making incorrect responses and gradually, over trials, eliminating errors; a blind and mechanical continuous mode of learning as opposed to sudden insightful learning.

truncated law of effect   Thorndike's later law of effect, in which learning is seen as depending almost entirely upon satisfiers with punishers having little effect. See **law of effect.**

two-factor theory   A theory which incorporates more than one mechanism by which learning occurs.

type R conditioning   Skinner's term for operant or reinforcement or instrumental conditioning.

type S conditioning   Skinner's term for respondent or classical or Pavlovian conditioning.

unconditioned response (UR or UCR)   An innately programmed or previously conditioned response in Pavlov's model of conditioning. It is elicited involuntarily by the unconditioned stimulus (US or UCS), which is either a sign stimulus or may have been previously conditioned long before the experimental sessions. In the Pavlovian context, unconditioned means independent of previous known conditioning processes.

unconditioned stimulus (US, UCS)   Also unconditional stimulus; see **unconditioned response.** In classical conditioning, the US becomes associated with a new cue presented just prior to its occurrence. This new cue is, of course, the conditional stimulus. A US requires no conditioning to be effective.

unitheory   The author's term for a hypothetical learning theory of the future that will incorporate all learning data, be accepted by almost all learning theorists, and will predict behavior far better than any existing theories. Such a theory might turn out to be so complex that only the unicomputer of the future could understand it.

universal grammar   In Chomsky's theory, the inherited tendency of the human brain to impose certain types of order on ideas, forming a grammatical "deep structure" that must be translated in the brain into the "particular grammars" of actual human languages.

unprepared learning   Learning with no significant innate component, which includes much of the behavior studied in conditioning studies (such as bar-pressing in rats); the opposite of **prepared learning.** Also the opposite of contraprepared learning, in which the organism is innately programmed not to learn specific types of associations (such as associating shock with taste).

valence   A Lewinian term borrowed from chemistry giving the strength of attractions **(positive valence)** or repulsions **(negative valence)** of various regions of the person's cognitive space.

vanishing   See **errorless learning.**

vector   A Lewinian term borrowed from the physics of mechanics referring to the strength and direction of mental forces pushing a person towards various goals.

verbal system   Bandura's term for coded memories of observed behaviors which are remembered as verbal thoughts.

vicarious extinction   Extinction that results from observing another subject's failure to be reinforced for performing the behavior specified.

vicarious learning   Learning by watching the experiences of others.

wholist strategy   Learning to identify concepts by focusing on the total gestalt of correct instances. The opposite of **partist strategy.**

Zeigarnik effect   The motivating effect of unfinished tasks first researched by Zeigarnik who was a student of Lewin's and associated with gestalt theory.

References

Introduction

Pavlov, I. *Conditioned reflexes*. Trans. 1927. New York: Dover, 1960.

Thorndike, E. L. Animal intelligence: An experimental study of the associative processes in animals. *Psychological Review Monographs Supplement*, 1898, 2, No. 8-7, 28–31.

Chapter 1

Asratyan, E. A. *I. P. Pavlov, His life and work*. Moscow: Foreign Languages Publishing House, 1953.

Babkin, B. P. *Pavlov, A biography*. Chicago: University of Chicago Press, 1949.

Cole, S. and Cole, M. Three giants of Soviet psychology, Conversations and sketches. *Psychology Today*, March 1971, 4, 43–98.

Grossman, S. P. *Essentials of physiological psychology*. New York: John Wiley & Sons, 1973.

Hall, J. F. *Classical conditioning and instrumental learning, A contemporary approach*. New York: J. B. Lippincott, 1976.

Hilgard, E. R. and Bower, G. H. *Theories of learning*. 4th ed. Englewood Cliffs, N.J.: Prentice-Hall, 1975.

Horton, D. L. and Turnage, T. W. *Human learning*. Englewood Cliffs, N.J.: Prentice-Hall, 1976.

Kanfer, F. H. and Phillips, J. S. *Learning foundations of behavior therapy*. New York: John Wiley & Sons, 1970.

Lorenz, K. *On aggression*. New York: Harcourt, Brace & World, 1963.

Pavlov, I. *Conditioned reflexes*. Trans. 1927. New York: Dover, 1960.

Schacter, S. Some extraordinary facts about obese humans and rats. *American Psychologist*, 1971, 26, 129–144.

Tarpy, R. M. *Basic principles of learning*. Glenview, Ill.: Scott, Foresman, 1975.

Chapter 2

Ayllon, T. Intensive treatment of psychotic behaviour by stimulus satiation and food reinforcement. *Behaviour Research and Therapy*, 1963, 1, 53–61.

Bolles, R. C. *Learning theory*. New York: Holt, Rinehart and Winston, 1975.

Estes, W. K. The statistical approach to learning theory. In S. Koch (Ed.), *Psychology: A study of a science*. Vol. 2. New York: McGraw-Hill, 1959.

Estes, W. K., The cognitive side of probability learning. *Psychological Review*, 1976, 83, 37–64.

Guthrie, E. R. *The psychology of learning.* New York: Harper & Row, 1935.

Guthrie, E. R. *The psychology of human conflict.* New York: Harper & Row, 1938.

Guthrie, E. R. Conditioning: A theory of learning in terms of stimulus, response, and association. In *Psychology of learning, 41st yearbook of the National Society for the Study of Education.* Part II. Chicago: University of Chicago Press, 1942, 17–60.

Guthrie, E. R. *The psychology of learning.* Rev. ed. New York: Harper & Row, 1952.

Guthrie, E. R. Association by contiguity. In S. Koch (Ed.), *Psychology: A study of a science.* Vol. 2. New York: McGraw-Hill, 1959.

Guthrie, E. R. and Horton, G. P. *Cats in a puzzle box.* New York: Rinehart Press, 1946.

Hall, J. F. *Classical conditioning and instrumental learning, A contemporary approach.* New York: J. B. Lippincott, 1976.

Hergenhahn, B. R. *An introduction to theories of learning.* Englewood Cliffs, N.J.: Prentice-Hall, 1976.

Hilgard, E. R. and Bower, G. H. *Theories of learning.* 4th ed. Englewood Cliffs, N.J.: Prentice-Hall, 1975.

Hill, W. F. *Learning; A survey of psychological interpretations.* Rev. ed. Scranton, Pa.: Chandler, 1971.

Hill, W. F. *Learning; A survey of psychological interpretations.* 3rd ed. New York: Thomas Y. Crowell, 1977.

Jones, M. C. The elimination of children's fears. *Journal of Experimental Psychology*, 1924, 7, 382–390.

Keen, S. Sing the body electric. *Psychology Today*, October 1970, 4, 56–58.

McGuigan, F. J. Electrical measurement of covert processes in an explanation of "higher mental events." In F. J. McGuigan and R. A. Schoonover (Eds.), *The psychophysiology of thinking.* New York: Academic Press, 1973.

O'Connor, N. Introduction. In N. O'Connor (Ed.), *Present-day Russian psychology.* New York: Pergamon Press, 1966.

Schultz, D. P. *A history of modern psychology.* New York: Academic Press, 1969.

Sheffield, F. D. and Roby, T. B. Reward value of a non-nutritive sweet taste. *Journal of Comparative and Physiological Psychology*, 1950, 43, 471–481.

Voeks, V. W. Postremity, recency, and frequency as bases for prediction in the maze situation. *Journal of Experimental Psychology*, 1948, 38, 495–510.

Voeks, V. W. Acquisition of S-R connections: A test of Hull's and Guthrie's theories. *Journal of Experimental Psychology*, 1954, 47, 137–147.

Watson, J. B. Psychology as a behaviorist views it. *Psychological Review*, 1913, 20, 158–177.

Watson, J. B. *Behavior, An introduction to comparative psychology.* New York: Holt, Rinehart and Winston, 1914.

Watson, J. B. The place of the conditioned reflex in psychology. *Psychological Review*, 1916, 23, 89–116.

Watson, J. B. *Behaviorism.* New York: Norton, 1924.

Watson, J. B. and Rayner, R. Conditioned emotional reactions. *Journal of Experimental Psychology,* 1920, 3, 1–14.

Chapter 3

Bolles, R. C. *Learning theory.* New York: Holt, Rinehart, and Winston, 1975.

Crespi, L. P. Quantitative variation of incentive and performance in the white rat. *American Journal of Psychology,* 1942, 55, 467–517.

Gleitman, H., Nachmias, J. and Neisser, U. The S-R reinforcement theory of extinction. *Psychological Review,* 1954, 61, 23–33.

Hergenhahn, B. R. *An introduction to theories of learning.* Englewood Cliffs, N.J.: Prentice-Hall, 1976.

Hilgard, E. R. and Bower, G. H. *Theories of learning.* 4th ed. Englewood Cliffs, N.J.: Prentice-Hall, 1975.

Hilgard, E. R. and Marquis, D. G. Acquisition, extinction, and retention of conditioned lid responses to light in dogs. *Journal of Comparative and Physiological Psychology,* 1935, 19, 29–58.

Hill, W. F. *Learning; A survey of psychological interpretation.* Rev. ed. Scranton, Pa.: Chandler, 1971.

Hull, C. L. Differential habituation to internal stimuli in the albino rat. *Journal of Comparative and Physiological Psychology,* 1933, 16, 255–273.

Hull, C. L. The conflicting psychologies of learning—A way out. *Psychological Review,* 1935, 42, 491–516.

Hull, C. L. *Principles of behavior.* New York: Appleton-Century-Crofts, 1943.

Hull, C. L. *A behavior system: An introduction to behavior theory concerning the individual organism.* New Haven, Conn.: Yale University Press, 1952.

Lefrancois, G. R. *Psychological theories and human learning: Kongor's report.* Belmont, Ca.: Wadsworth, 1972.

Pavlov, I. *Conditioned reflexes.* Trans. 1927. New York: Dover, 1960.

Sahakian, W. S. *Learning: Systems, models and theories.* 2nd ed. Chicago: Rand McNally, 1976.

Sheffield, F. D. and Roby, T. B. Reward value of a nonnutritive sweet taste. *Journal of Comparative and Physiological Psychology,* 1950, 43, 471–481.

Spence, K. W. The nature of discrimination learning in animals. *Psychological Review,* 1936, 43, 427–449.

Spence, K. W. The differential response in animals to stimuli varying within a single dimension. *Psychological Review,* 1937, 44, 430–444.

Spence, K. W. *Behavior theory and learning: Selected papers.* Englewood Cliffs, N.J.: Prentice-Hall, 1960.

Thorndike, E. L. Animal intelligence: An experimental study of the associative processes in animals. *Psychological Review Monographs Supplement,* 1898, 2, No. 8-7, 23–31.

Thorndike, E. L. *Educational psychology: The psychology of learning.* Vol. 2. New York: Teachers College, 1913.

Trowbridge, M. H. and Cason, H. An experimental study of Thorndike's theory of learning. *Journal of General Psychology,* 1932, 7, 245–252.

Chapter 4

Chomsky, N. The case against B. F. Skinner. *New York Review of Books,* December 30, 1971, 18–24.

Cook, J. O. Superstition in Skinnerians. *American Psychologist,* 1963, 18, 516–518.

Day, W. F. Radical behaviorism in reconciliation with phenomenology. *Journal of the Experimental Analysis of Behavior,* 1969, 12, 315–328.

Harris, G. T. The B. F. Skinner manifesto—An introduction. *Psychology Today,* August 1971, 5, 33–35.

Hilgard, E. R. and Bower, G. H. *Theories of learning.* 4th ed. Englewood Cliffs, N.J.: Prentice-Hall, 1975.

Kinkade, K. Commune: A Walden-Two experiment. *Psychology Today,* January 1973, 6, 35–42.

Miller, N. E. Learning of visceral and glandular responses. *Science,* 1969, 163, 434–445.

Mischel, W. Toward a cognitive social learning reconceptualization of personality. *Psychological Review,* 1973, 80, 252–283.

Repp, A. C. and Deitz, S. M. Reducing aggressive and self-injurious behavior of institutionalized retarded children through reinforcement of other behaviors. *Journal of Applied Behavior Analysis,* 1974, 7, 313–325.

Reynolds, G. S. *A primer of operant conditioning.* Revised ed. Glenview, Ill.: Scott, Foresman, 1975.

Sahakian, W. S. *Introduction to the psychology of learning.* Chicago: Rand McNally, 1976.

Skinner, B. F. *The behavior of organisms: An experimental analysis.* New York: Appleton-Century-Crofts, 1938.

Skinner, B. F. *Walden Two.* New York: Macmillan, 1948. (a)

Skinner, B. F., Superstition in the pigeon. *Journal of Experimental Psychology,* 1948, 38, 168–172. (b)

Skinner, B. F. *Science and human behavior.* New York: Macmillan, 1953.

Skinner, B. F. *Verbal behavior.* New York: Appleton-Century-Crofts, 1957.

Skinner, B. F. *The technology of teaching.* New York: Appleton-Century-Crofts, 1968.

Skinner, B. F. *Contingencies of reinforcement: A theoretical analysis.* New York: Appleton-Century-Crofts, 1969.

Skinner, B. F. *Beyond freedom and dignity.* New York: Alfred A. Knopf, 1971.

Skinner, B. F. Speech given at Royce Hall. University of California at Los Angeles, 1973.

Skinner, B. F. *About behaviorism.* New York: Alfred A. Knopf, 1974.

Solomon, R. L. Punishment. *American Psychologist,* 1964, 19, 239–253.

Chapter 5

Apter, M. J. *The computer simulation of behavior.* New York: Harper & Row, 1970.

Bolles, R. C. *Learning theory.* New York: Holt, Rinehart and Winston, 1975.

Feigenbaum, E. A. and Feldman, J. *Computers and thought.* New York: McGraw-Hill, 1963.

Hilgard, E. R. and Bower, G. H. *Theories of learning.* 4th ed. Englewood Cliffs, N.J.: Prentice-Hall, 1975.

Hill, W. F. *Learning; A survey of psychological interpretations.* Rev. ed. Scranton, Pa.: Chandler, 1971.

Hunt, J. McV. Revisiting Montessori. Introduction to *Maria Montessori; The Montessori method.* New York: Schocken Books, 1964.

Kaswan, J. Association of nonsense figures as a function of fittingness and intention to learn. *American Journal of Psychology,* 1957, 70, 447–450.

Koffka, K. *Principles of Gestalt psychology.* New York: Harcourt, Brace & World, 1935.

Kohlberg, L. Montessori with the culturally disadvantaged: A cognitive-developmental interpretation and some research findings. In R. D. Hess and R. M. Bear (Eds.), *Early education.* Chicago: Aldine, 105–118.

Köhler, W. *The mentality of apes.* Trans. E. Winter. New York: Harcourt, Brace & World, 1925.

Krechevsky, I. "Hypotheses" in rats. *Psychological Review,* 1932, 39, 516–532.

Laosa, L. M. and McNichols, J. P. Research on the Montessori Method: Review of findings and some methodological considerations. Paper presented at Western Psychological Association annual meeting, Sacramento, California, April, 1975.

Lewin, K. *Principles of topological psychology* Trans. F. Heider and G. M. Heider. New York: McGraw-Hill, 1936.

Lewin, K. Field theory and learning. In *The psychology of learning, yearbook of the National Society for the Study of Education,* 1942, Part II, 41, 215–242.

MacCorquodale, K. and Meehl, P. E. Preliminary suggestions as to a formalization of expectancy theory. *Psychological Review,* 1953, 60, 55–63.

MacCorquodale, K. and Meehl, P. E. Edward C. Tolman. In W. K. Estes, S. Koch, K. MacCorquodale, P. E. Meehl, C. G. Mueller, W. N. Schoenfeld, and W. S. Verplanck, *Modern learning theory.* New York: Appleton-Century-Crofts, 1954, 177–266.

Macfarlane, D. A. The role of kinesthesis in maze learning. *University of California Publications in Psychology,* 1930, 4, 277–305.

Montessori, M. *The Montessori method. Scientific pedagogy as applied to child education in "the children's houses" with additions and revisions by the author.* Trans. Anne E. George. 7th ed. New York: Frederick A. Stokes, 1912.

Rambusch, N. McC. *Learning how to learn; An American approach to Montessori.* Baltimore, Md.: Helican Press, 1962.

Sahakian, W. S. *Introduction to the psychology of learning.* Chicago: Rand McNally, 1976.

Spock, B. and Hathaway, M. L. Montessori and traditional American nursery schools— How they are different, how they are alike. In J. L. Frost (Ed.), *Early childhood education rediscovered.* New York: Holt, Rinehart and Winston, 1968.

Standing, E. M. *Maria Montessori, Her life and work.* Fresno, Ca.: Academy Guild Press, 1959.

Swenson, L. C. One versus two discrimination by whitenecked ravens (Corvus cryptoleucus) with non-number dimensions varied. *Animal Behavior,* 1970, 18, 454–460.

Tinklepaugh, O. L. An experimental study of representative factors in monkeys. *Journal of Comparative Psychology,* 1928, 8, 197–236.

Tolman, E. C. Prediction of vicarious trial and error by means of the schematic sowbug. *Psychological Review,* 1939, 46, 318–336.

Tolman, E. C. Cognitive maps in rats and men. *Psychological Review*, 1948, 55, 189–208.

Tolman, E. C. There is more than one kind of learning. *Psychological Review*, 1949, 56, 144–155.

Tolman, E. C. *Purposive behavior in animals and men*. New York: Appleton-Century-Crofts, 1967.

Tolman, E. C. and Honzik, C. H. Introduction and removal of reward, and maze performance in rats. *University of California Publications in Psychology*, 1930, 4, 257–275.

Tolman, E. C., Ritchie, B. F. and Kalish, D. Studies in spatial learning: I. Orientation and the short-cut. *Journal of Experimental Psychology*, 1946, 36, 13–24. (a)

Tolman, E. C., Ritchie, B. F. and Kalish, D. Studies in spatial learning: II. Place learning versus response learning. *Journal of Experimental Psychology*, 1946, 36, 221–229. (b)

Walter, W. G. *The living brain*. New York: Norton, 1953.

Ward, F. E. *The Montessori method and the American school*. New York: Macmillan, 1913.

Wertheimer, M. *Productive thinking*. Enl. ed. New York: Harper & Row, 1959.

Wiener, N. *Cybernetics*. New York: John Wiley & Sons, 1948.

Zeigarnik, B., Über das behalten von erledigten und unerledigten Handlungen. *Psychologische Forshung*, 1927. Abridged and translated in W. S. Sahakian (Ed.), *History of psychology: A source book in systematic psychology*. Itasca, Ill.: F. E. Peacock, 1968.

Chapter 6

Bandura, A. *Principles of behavior modification*. New York: Holt, Rinehart and Winston, 1969.

Bellack, A. S. and Herson, M. *Systematic desensitization*. Baltimore, Md.: Williams & Wilkins, 1977.

Breger, L. and McGaugh, J. L. Critique and reformulation of "learning theory" approaches to psychotherapy and neurosis. *Psychological Bulletin*, 1965, 63, 338–358.

Chertok, L. *Psychosomatic methods in painless childbirth; History, theory, and practice*. New York: Pergamon Press, 1959.

Crowder, N. A. and Martin, G. *Trigonometry*. Garden City, N.Y.: Doubleday, 1961.

Fox, L. Effecting the use of efficient study habits. *Journal of Mathetics*, 1962, 1, 75–86.

Goldstein, K. *Human nature in the light of psychopathology*. Cambridge, Mass.: Harvard University Press, 1963.

Holland, A. L. and Matthews, J. Teaching machine concepts in speech pathology and audiology. *American Speech and Hearing Association*, 1963, 3, 474–482.

Holland, J. G. Teaching machines: An application of principles from the laboratory. *Journal of the Experimental Analysis of Behavior*, 1960, 9, 65–78.

Jacobson, E. *Progressive relaxation*. Chicago: University of Chicago Press, 1938.

Jones, M. C. The elimination of children's fears. *Journal of Experimental Psychology*, 1924, 7, 382–390.

Krapfl, L. E. Differential ordering of stimulus presentation and semi-automated versus live treatment in the systematic desensitization of snake phobia. Unpublished Ph.D. dissertation, University of Missouri, 1967. Cited in D. C. Rimm and J. C. Masters, *Behavior therapy: Techniques and empirical findings*. New York: Academic Press, 1974.

Lang, P. J. and Lazovik, A. D. Experimental desensitization of a phobia. *Journal of Abnormal and Social Psychology*, 1963, 66, 519–525.

Lang, P. J., Lazovik, A. D. and Reynolds, D. J. Desensitization, suggestibility, and pseudotherapy. *Journal of Abnormal Psychology*, 1965, 70, 395–402.

Paul, G. L. *Insight versus desensitization in psychotherapy: An experiment in anxiety reduction*. Stanford, Ca.: Stanford University Press, 1966.

Paul, G. L. Behavior modification research: Design and tactics. In C. Franks (Ed.), *Behavior therapy: Appraisal and status*. New York: McGraw-Hill, 1969.

Pavlov, I. *Conditioned reflexes*. Trans. 1927. New York: Dover, 1960.

Persely, G. and Leventhal, D. B. The effects of therapeutically oriented instructions and of the pairing of anxiety, imagery, and relaxation in systematic desensitization. *Behavior Therapy*, 1972, 3, 417–424.

Polster, E. and Polster, M. *Gestalt therapy integrated, Contours of therapy and practice*. New York: Brunner/Mazel, 1973.

Rachman, S. *Phobias: Their nature and control*. Springfield, Ill.: Charles C. Thomas, 1968.

Rimm, D. C. and Masters, J. C. *Behavior therapy: Techniques and empirical findings*. New York: Academic Press, 1974.

Schubot, E. D. The influence of hypnotic and muscular relaxation in systematic desensitization of phobic behavior. Unpublished Ph.D. dissertation, Stanford University, 1966.

Schramm, W. *The research on programmed instruction: An annotated bibliography*. OE-34034. Washington D.C.: U.S. Office of Education, 1964.

Skinner, B. F. How to teach animals. *Scientific American*, December 1951, 185, 26–29.

Sloane, R. B., Staples, F. R., Cristol, A. H., Yorkston, N. J. and Whipple, K. *Psychotherapy versus behavior therapy*. Cambridge, Mass.: Harvard University Press, 1975.

Wertheimer, M. *Productive thinking*. Enl. ed. New York: Harper & Row, 1959.

Wolpe, J. *Psychotherapy by reciprocal inhibition*. Stanford, Ca.: Stanford University Press, 1958.

Woy, J. R. and Efran, J. S. Systematic desensitization and expectancy in the treatment of speaking anxiety. *Behavior Research and Therapy*, 1972, 10, 43–49.

Chapter 7

Bilodeau, I. M. and Schlosberg, H. Similarity in stimulating conditions as a variable in retroactive inhibition. *Journal of Experimental Psychology*, 1952, 42, 199–204.

Bolles, R. C. *Learning theory*. New York: Holt, Rinehart and Winston, 1975.

Breger, L. and McGaugh, J. L. Critique and reformulation of "learning theory" approaches to psychotherapy and neurosis. *Psychological Bulletin*, 1965, 63, 338–358.

CRM. *Educational psychology—A contemporary view*. Del Mar, Calif.: CRM, Inc., 1973.

DiCara, L. V. Learning in the autonomic nervous system. *Scientific American*, January 1970, 222, 30–39.

Dollard, J. and Miller, N. E. *Personality and psychotherapy*. New York: McGraw-Hill, 1950.

Harlow, H. F. The formation of learning sets. *Psychological Review*, 1949, 56, 51–65.

Harlow, H. F. Learning set and error factor theory. In S. Koch (Ed.), *Psychology: A study of a science*. Vol. 2. New York: McGraw-Hill, 1959, 492–537.

Harlow, H. F. *Learning to love.* San Francisco: Albion, 1971.

Hilgard, E. R. and Bower, G. H. *Theories of learning.* 4th ed. Englewood Cliffs, N.J.: Prentice-Hall, 1975.

Hill, W. F. *Learning: A survey of psychological interpretations.* 3rd ed. New York: Thomas Y. Crowell, 1977.

Hull, C. L. *A behavior system: An introduction to behavior theory concerning the individual organism.* New Haven, Conn.: Yale University Press, 1952.

Jenkins, J. C. and Dallenbach, K. M. Oblivescence during sleep and waking. *American Journal of Psychology,* 1924, 35, 605–612.

Keppel, G., Postman, L., and Zavortink, B. Studies of learning to learn: VIII. The influence of massive amounts of training upon the learning and retention of paired-associate lists. *Journal of Verbal Learning and Verbal Behavior,* 1968, 7, 790–796.

Koch, S. (Ed.). *Psychology: A study of a science.* Vol. 2. New York: McGraw-Hill, 1959.

Konorski, J. *Conditioned reflexes and neuron organization.* Cambridge: Cambridge University Press, 1948.

McGeoch, J. A. The influence of degree of learning upon retroactive inhibition. *American Journal of Psychology,* 1929, 41, 252–262.

Miller, N. E. Studies of fear as an acquired drive: I. Fear as motivation and fear-reduction as reinforcement in the learning of new responses. *Journal of Experimental Psychology,* 1948, 38, 89–101.

Miller, N. E. Liberalization of basic S-R concepts: Extensions to conflict behavior, motivation and social learning. In S. Koch (Ed.), *Psychology: A study of a science.* Vol. 2. New York: McGraw-Hill, 1959, 196–202.

Miller, N. E. and Dollard, J. *Social learning and imitation.* New Haven, Conn.: Yale University Press, 1941.

Mowrer, O. H. Two-factor learning theory reconsidered, with special reference to secondary reinforcement and the concept of habit. *Psychological Review,* 1956, 63, 114–128.

Osgood, C. E. The similarity paradox in human learning: A resolution. *Psychological Review,* 1949, 56, 132–143.

Sahakian, W. S. *Introduction to the psychology of learning.* Chicago: Rand McNally, 1976.

Shapiro, D. Presidential address, 1976: A monologue on biofeedback and psychophysiology. *Psychophysiology,* 1977, 14, 213–226.

Slamecka, N. J. Retroactive inhibition of connected discourse as a function of similarity of topic. *Journal of Experimental Psychology,* 1960, 60, 245–249.

Skinner, B. F. *About behaviorism.* New York: Alfred A. Knopf, 1974.

Tolman, E. C. There is more than one kind of learning. *Psychological Review,* 1949, 56, 144–155.

Thorndike, E. L. *Human learning.* New York: Appleton-Century-Crofts, 1931.

Underwood, B. J. Proactive inhibition as a function of time and degree of learning. *Journal of Experimental Psychology,* 1949, 39, 24–34.

Young, R. K. Tests of three hypotheses about the effective stimuli in serial learning. *Journal of Experimental Psychology,* 1962, 63, 307–313.

Part 1 Summary

Hilgard, E. R. and Bower, G. H. *Theories of learning.* 4th ed. Englewood Cliffs, N.J.: Prentice-Hall, 1975.

Skinner, B. F. *About behaviorism.* New York: Alfred A. Knopf, 1974.

Chapter 8

Airapetyantz, E. and Bykov, K. Physiological experiments and the psychology of the subconscious. *Philosophy and Phenomenological Research,* 1945, 5, 577–593.

Atnip, G. W. Stimulus-and response-reinforcer contingencies in autoshaping, operant, classical, and omission training procedures in rats. *Journal of the Experimental Analysis of Behavior,* 1977, 28, 59–69.

Barrett, C. L. Systematic desensitization versus implosive therapy. *Journal of Abnormal Psychology,* 1969, 74, 587–592.

Biferno, M. A. and Dawson, M. E. The onset of contingency awareness and electrodermal classical conditioning: An analysis of temporal relationships during acquisition and extinction. *Psychophysiology,* 1977, 14, 164–171.

Biferno, M. A. and Dawson, M. E. Elicitation of subjective uncertainty during vasomotor and electrodermal discrimination classical conditioning. *Psychophysiology,* 1978, 15, 1–8.

Bolles, R. C. *Learning theory.* New York: Holt, Rinehart and Winston, 1975.

Brickman, A. L. and Schneiderman, N. Classically conditioned blood pressure decreases induced by electrical stimulation of posterior lateral hypothalamus in rabbits. *Psychophysiology,* 1977, 14, 287–292.

Brogden, W. J. Sensory pre-conditioning. *Journal of Experimental Psychology,* 1939, 25, 323–332.

Brown, P. L. and Jenkins, H. M. Auto-shaping of the pigeon's key-peck. *Journal of the Experimental Analysis of Behavior,* 1968, 11, 1–8.

Cole, S. and Cole, M. Three giants of Soviet psychology, Conversations and sketches. *Psychology Today,* March 1971, 4, 43–98.

Davol, G. H., Steinhauer, G. D., and Lee, A. The role of preliminary magazine training in acquisition of the autoshaped key peck. *Journal of the Experimental Analysis of Behavior,* 1977, 28, 99–106.

Estes, W. K. and Skinner, B. F. Some quantitative properties of anxiety. *Journal of Experimental Psychology,* 1941, 29, 390–400.

Felberbaum, I. M. In Airapetyantz, E. S. and Felberbaum, I. M. A methodological contribution to the study of interoceptive conditioned reflexes: The uteral fistula. *Fiziologicheskii Zhurnall (London) SSSR,* 1951, 37, 240–243.

Feldman, M. P. and MacCulloch, M. J. The application of anticipatory avoidance learning to the treatment of homosexuality. *Behaviour Research and Therapy,* 1965, 2, 165–183.

Furedy, J. J. and Schiffmann, K. Concurrent measurement of autonomic and cognitive processes in a test of the traditional discriminative control procedure for Pavlovian electrodermal conditioning. *Journal of Experimental Psychology,* 1973, 100, 210–217.

Garskaya, G. B. The effect of EMG feedback on speech muscle afferentation under conditions of mental activity. *Vaproosy Psikhologü* [English Abstract], May-June, 1975.

Greenspoon, J. The reinforcing effect of two spoken sounds on the frequency of two responses. *American Journal of Psychology*, 1955, 68, 409–416.

Hall, J. F. *Classical conditioning and instrumental learning, A contemporary approach.* New York: J. B. Lippincott, 1976.

Hassett, J. *A primer of psychophysiology.* San Francisco: W. H. Freeman, 1978.

Hutton, R. A., Woods, S. C., and Makous, W. L. Conditioned hypoglycemia: Pseudoconditioning controls. *Journal of Comparative and Physiological Psychology*, 1970, 71, 198–201.

Jenkins, H. M. and Moore, B. A. The form of the auto-shaped response with food or water reinforcers. *Journal of the Experimental Analysis of Behavior*, 1973, 20, 163–181.

Jones, M. C. The elimination of children's fears. *Journal of Experimental Psychology*, 1924, 7, 382–390.

Kamin, L. J. Predictability, surprise, attention, and conditioning. In B. A. Campbell and R. M. Church (Eds.), *Punishment.* New York: Appleton-Century-Crofts, 1969.

Kaplan, H. S. *The new sex therapy: Active treatment of sexual dysfunctions.* New York: Brunner/Mazel, 1974.

Lang, P. J. The on-line computer in behavior therapy research. *American Psychologist*, 1969, 24, 236–239.

Lazarus, A. A. Has behavior therapy outlived its usefulness? *American Psychologist*, 1977, 32, 550–553.

Lublin, I. and Joslyn, L. Aversive conditioning of cigarette addiction. Paper presented at the American Psychological Association, annual meeting, San Francisco, September, 1968. (a)

Lublin, I. Principles governing the choice of unconditioned stimuli in aversive conditioning. In Frank Ruben and R. R. Ruben (Eds.), *Advances in behavior therapy.* New York: Academic Press, 1968. (b)

Luria, A. R. *The role of speech in the regulation of normal and abnormal behavior.* J. Tizard (Ed.). New York: Pergamon Press, 1961.

Mahoney, M. On the continuing resistance to thoughtful therapy. *Behavior Therapy*, 1977, 8, 673–677.

Malmo, R. B. *On emotions, needs, and our archaic brain.* New York: Holt, Rinehart and Winston, 1975.

Marx, M. H. and Bunch, M. E. *Fundamentals and applications of learning.* New York: Macmillan, 1977.

Mowrer, O. H. Preparatory set (Expectancy): A determinant in motivation and learning. *Psychological Review*, 1938, 45, 62–91.

O'Connor, N. (Ed.). *Present-day Russian psychology.* New York: Pergamon Press, 1966.

Pavlov, I. *Conditioned reflexes.* Trans. 1927. New York: Dover, 1960.

Powell, J. and Azrin, N. The effects of shock as a punisher for cigarette smoking. *Journal of Applied Behavior Analysis*, 1968, 1, 63–71.

Prewitt, E. P. Number of preconditioning trials in sensory preconditioning using CER training. *Journal of Comparative and Physiological Psychology*, 1967, 64, 360–362.

Prokasy, W. F. First interval skin conductance responses: Conditioned or orienting responses? *Psychophysiology*, 1977, 14, 360–367.

Rahmani, L. *Soviet psychology: Philosophical, theoretical and experimental issues.* New York: International Universities Press, 1973.

Raymond, M. J. The treatment of addiction by aversion conditioning with apomorphine. *Behavior Research and Therapy,* 1964, 1, 287–291.

Razran, G. A quantitative study of meaning by conditioned salivary technique (semantic conditioning). *Science,* 1939, 90, 89–91.

Razran, G. Soviet psychology and psychophysiology. *Science,* 1958, 128, 1187–1194.

Razran, G. The observable unconscious and the inferable conscious in current Soviet psychophysiology: Interoceptive conditioning, semantic conditioning, and the orienting reflex. *Psychological Review,* 1961, 54, 357–365.

Rescorla, R. A. Predictability and number of pairings in Pavlovian fear conditioning. *Psychonomic Science,* 1966, 4, 383–384.

Rescorla, R. A. Probability of shock in the presence and absence of CS in fear conditioning. *Journal of Comparative and Physiological Psychology,* 1968, 66, 1–5.

Rescorla, R. A. and Solomon, R. L. Two-process learning theory: Relationships between Pavlovian conditioning and instrumental conditioning. *Psychological Review,* 1967, 74, 151–182.

Rescorla, R. A. and Wagner, A. R. A theory of Pavlovian conditioning: Variations in the effectiveness of reinforcement and nonreinforcement. In A. Black and W. F. Prokasy (Eds.), *Classical conditioning II: Current theory and research.* New York: Appleton-Century-Crofts, 1972, 64–99.

Reynolds, G. S. *A primer of operant conditioning.* Rev. ed. Glenview, Ill.: Scott Foresman, 1975.

Rimm, D. C., Janda, L. H., Lancaster, D. W., Mahl, M., and Dittmar, K. An exploratory investigation of the origin and maintenance of phobias. *Behavior Research and Therapy,* 1977, 15, 231–238.

Rimm, D. C. and Masters, J. C. *Behavior therapy: Techniques and empirical findings.* New York: Academic Press, 1974.

Rudestam, K. E. and Bedrosian, R. An investigation of the effectiveness of desensitization and flooding with two types of phobias. *Behavior Research and Therapy,* 1977, 15, 23–30.

Schandler, S. L. and Grings, W. W. Comparison of progressive relaxation and EMG biofeedback procedures. Paper presented at Western Psychological Association annual meeting, San Francisco, April, 1975.

Seligman, M. E. P. *Helplessness: On depression, development, and death.* San Francisco: W. H. Freeman, 1975.

Solomon, R. L. and Wynne, L. C. Traumatic avoidance learning: The principles of anxiety conservation and partial irreversibility. *Psychological Review,* 1954, 61, 353–385.

Stampfl, T. G. and Lewis, D. J. Essentials of implosive therapy: A learning-theory-based psychodynamic behavioral therapy. *Journal of Abnormal Psychology,* 1967, 72, 496–503.

Tarpy, R. M. and Mayer, R. E. *Foundations of learning and memory.* Glenview, Ill.: Scott, Foresman, 1978.

Wasserman, E. A. Pavlovian conditioning with heat reinforcement produces stimulus-directed pecking in chicks. *Science,* 1973, 181, 875–877.

Whitehead, W. E., Lurie, E., and Blackwell, B. Classical conditioning of decreases in human systolic blood pressure. *Journal of Applied Behavior Analysis,* 1976, 9, 153–157.

Whitehead, W. E., Renault, P. F., and Goldiamond, I. Modification of human gastric acid secretion with operant-conditioning procedures. *Journal of Applied Behavior Analysis,* 1975, 8, 147–156.

Wilson, J. R., Simpson, C. W., DiCara, L. V. and Carroll, B. J. Adrenalectomy-produced facilitation of Pavlovian conditioned cardiodecelerations in immobilized rats. *Psychophysiology,* 1977, 14, 172–181.

Chapter 9

Amsel, A. The role of frustrative nonreward in noncontinuous reward situations. *Psychological Bulletin,* 1958, 55, 102–118.

Amsel, A. Partial reinforcement effects on vigor and persistence: Advances in frustration theory derived from a variety of within-subjects experiments. In K. W. Spence and J. T. Spence (Eds.), *The psychology of learning and motivation.* Vol. 1. New York: Academic Press, 1967.

Amsel, A., Hug, J. J., and Surridge, C. T. Number of food pellets, goal approaches, and the partial reinforcement effect after minimal acquisition. *Journal of Experimental Psychology,* 1968, 77, 530–534.

Azrin, N. H. Pain and aggression. *Psychology Today,* May 1967, 1, 27–33.

Azrin, N. H. and Holtz, W. C. Punishment. In W. K. Honig (Ed.), *Operant behavior: Areas of research and application.* New York: Appleton-Century-Crofts, 1966.

Azrin, N. H., Hutchinson, R. R., and Hake, D. F. Pain-inducing fighting in the squirrel monkey. *Journal of the Experimental Analysis of Behavior,* 1963, 6, 620.

Bandura, A. Social learning through imitation. In M. R. Jones (Ed.), *Nebraska Symposium on Motivation.* Lincoln: University of Nebraska Press, 1962.

Bandura, A. Behavioral psychotherapy. *Scientific American,* March 1967, 216, 78–86.

Bandura, A. *Principles of behavior modification.* New York: Holt, Rinehart and Winston, 1969.

Bandura, A. (Ed.). *Psychological modeling: Conflicting theories.* Chicago: Aldine-Atherton, 1971.

Bandura, A. *Social learning theory.* Englewood Cliffs, N.J.: Prentice-Hall, 1977.

Bandura, A., Grusec, J. E., and Menlove, F. L. Vicarious extinction of avoidance behavior. *Journal of Personality and Social Psychology,* 1967, 5, 16–23.

Bartlett, L. A. The effects of sex of model on task performance in young children. Paper presented at Western Psychological Association annual meeting, Seattle, April, 1977.

Bolles, R. C. and Riley, A. L. Freezing as an avoidance response: Another look at the operant-respondent distinction. *Learning and Motivation,* 1973, 4, 268–275.

Boren, J. J., Sidman, M., and Herrnstein, R. J. Avoidance, escape, and extinction as functions of shock intensity. *Journal of Comparative and Physiological Psychology,* 1959, 52, 420–425.

Breger, L. and McGaugh, J. L. Critique and reformulation of "learning theory" approaches to psychotherapy and neurosis. *Psychological Bulletin,* 1965, 63, 338–358.

Capaldi, E. J. The effect of different amounts of training on the resistance to extinction of different patterns of partially reinforced responses. *Journal of Comparative and Physiological Psychology,* 1958, 51, 367–371.

Capaldi, E. J. A sequential hypothesis of instrumental learning. In K. W. Spence and J. T. Spence (Eds.), *The psychology of learning and motivation.* Vol. 1. New York: Academic Press, 1967.

Capaldi, E. J. Memory and learning: A sequential viewpoint. In W. K. Honig and P. H. R. James (Eds.), *Animal memory.* New York: Academic Press, 1971.

Capaldi, E. J. and Wargo, P. Effect of transitions from nonreinforced to reinforced trials under spaced-trial conditions. *Journal of Experimental Psychology,* 1963, 65, 318–319.

Crespi, L. P. Quantitative variation of incentive and performance in the white rat. *American Journal of Psychology,* 1942, 55, 467–517.

Dunham, P. J. Punishment: Method and theory. *Psychological Review,* 1971, 78, 58–70.

Dunham, P. J. Some effects of punishment upon unpunished responding. *Journal of the Experimental Analysis of Behavior,* 1972, 17, 443–450.

Flaherty, C. F., Hamilton, L. W., Gandelman, R. J., and Spear, N. E. *Learning and memory.* Chicago: Rand McNally, 1977.

Hall, J. F. *Classical conditioning and instrumental learning: A contemporary approach.* Philadelphia: J. B. Lippincott, 1976.

Hanson, M. M. Stimulus generalization following three-stimulus discrimination training. *Journal of Comparative and Physiological Psychology,* 1961, 54, 181–185.

Herrnstein, R. J. Method and theory in the study of avoidance. *Psychological Review,* 1969, 76, 49–69.

Herrnstein, R. J. and Hineline, P. N. Negative reinforcement as shock-frequency reduction. *Journal of the Experimental Analysis of Behavior,* 1966, 9, 421–430.

Homme, L. E., DeBaca, P. C., Devine, J. V., Steinhorst, R., and Rickert, E. J. Use of the Premack principle in controlling the behavior of nursery school children. *Journal of the Experimental Analysis of Behavior,* 1963, 6, 544.

Hull, C. L. *A behavior system: An introduction to behavior theory concerning the individual organism.* New Haven, Conn.: Yale University Press, 1952.

Hutchinson, R. R. and Emley, G. S. Electric shock produced drinking in the squirrel monkey. *Journal of the Experimental Analysis of Behavior,* 1977, 28, 1–12.

Kanfer, F. H. and Phillips, J. S. *Learning foundations of behavior therapy.* New York: John Wiley & Sons, 1970.

Konorski, J. *Conditioned reflexes and neuron organization.* London: Cambridge University Press, 1948.

Logan, F. A. *Fundamentals of learning and motivation.* Dubuque, Iowa: William C. Brown, 1970.

Lovaas, I. After you hit a child, you can't just get up and leave him; You are hooked to that kid. (A conversation with P. Chance.) *Psychology Today,* January 1974, 7, 76–84.

Lovaas, O. I., Schaeffer, B., and Simmons, J. Q. Building social behavior in autistic children by use of electric shock. *Journal of Experimental Research in Personality,* 1965, 1, 99–109.

Martin, J. A. Generalizing the use of descriptive adjectives through modelling. *Journal of Applied Behavior Analysis,* 1975, 8, 203–209.

McKearney, J. W. Maintenance and suppression of responding under schedules of electric shock presentation. *Journal of the Experimental Analysis of Behavior*, 1972, 17, 425–432.

Miklich, D. R., Chida, T. L., and Danker-Brown, P. Behavioral modification by self-modeling without subject awareness. *Journal of Behavior Therapy and Experimental Psychiatry*, 1977, 8, 125–130.

Miller, N. E. and Dollard, J. *Social learning and imitation*. New Haven, Conn.: Yale University Press, 1941.

Mischel, W. Toward a cognitive social learning reconceptualization of personality. *Psychological Review*, 1973, 80, 252–283.

Nemetz, G. H., Craig, K. D., and Reith, G. Treatment of female sexual dysfunction through symbolic modeling. *Journal of Consulting and Clinical Psychology*, 1978, 46, 62–73.

Premack, D. Toward empirical behavioral laws: I. Positive reinforcement. *Psychological Review*, 1959, 66, 219–233.

Premack, D. Reversibility of the reinforcement relation. *Science*, 1962, 136, 255–257.

Rachlin, H. Response control with titration of punishment. *Journal of the Experimental Analysis of Behavior*, 1972, 17, 147–157.

Reynolds, G. S. *A primer of operant conditioning: Revised*. Glenview, Ill.: Scott Foresman, 1975.

Riess, D. Vicarious conditioned acceleration: Successful observational learning of an aversive Pavlovian stimulus contingency. *Journal of the Experimental Analysis of Behavior*, 1972, 18, 181–186.

Schusterman, R. J. Serial discrimination: Reversal learning with and without errors by the California sea lion. *Journal of the Experimental Analysis of Behavior*, 1966, 9, 593–600.

Seligman, M. E. P. *Helplessness: On depression, development, and death*. San Francisco: W. H. Freeman, 1975.

Seligman, M. E. P. and Johnston, J. C. A cognitive theory of avoidance learning. In F. J. McGuigan and D. B. Lumsden (Eds.), *Contemporary approaches to conditioning and learning*. Washington, D. C.: V. H. Winston & Sons, 1973.

Sidman, M. Some properties of the warning stimulus in avoidance learning. *Journal of Comparative and Physiological Psychology*, 1955, 48, 444–450.

Sidman, M. Normal sources of pathological behavior. *Science*, 1960, 132, 61–68.

Sidman, M. and Boren, J. J. The use of shock-contingent variations in response-shock intervals for the maintenance of avoidance behavior. *Journal of Comparative and Physiological Psychology*, 1957, 50, 558–562.

Skinner, B. F. "Superstition" in the pigeon. *Journal of Experimental Psychology*, 1948, 38, 168–172.

Skinner, B. F. *Science and human behavior*. New York: Macmillan, 1953.

Skinner, B. F. *The technology of teaching*. New York: Appleton-Century-Crofts, 1968.

Smith, G. P. and Coleman, R. E. Processes underlying generalization through participant modeling with self-directed practice. *Behavior Research and Therapy*, 1977, 15, 204–206.

Solomon, R. L. Punishment. *American Psychologist,* 1964, 19, 239–253.

Staddon, J. E. R. and Simmelhag, V. L. The "superstition" experiment: A reexamination of its implications for the principles of adaptive behavior. *Psychological Review,* 1971, 78, 3–43.

Swenson, L. C. A comparison of learning of an abstract concept under two types of fading procedure and a traditional control in inner city elementary school children. Unpublished Ph.D. dissertation, Wayne State University, 1969.

Terrace, H. S. Discrimination learning with and without "errors." *Journal of the Experimental Analysis of Behavior,* 1963, 6, 1–27. (a)

Terrace, H. S. Errorless transfer of a discrimination across two continua. *Journal of the Experimental Analysis of Behavior,* 1963, 6, 223–232. (b)

Timberlake, W. and Allison, J. Response deprivation: An empirical approach to instrumental performance. *Psychological Review,* 1974, 81, 146–164.

Todd, F. J. Coverant control of self-evaluative responses in the treatment of depression: A new use for an old principle. *Behavior Therapy,* 1972, 3, 91–94.

Wagner, A. R. Frustration and punishment. In R. N. Haber (Ed.), *Current research in motivation.* New York: Holt, Rinehart and Winston, 1966.

Waite, W. W. and Osborne, J. G. Sustained behavioral contrast in children. *Journal of the Experimental Analysis of Behavior,* 1972, 18, 113–117.

Chapter 10

Barrish, H. H., Saunders, M., and Wolf, M. M. Good behavior game: Effects of individual contingencies for group consequences on disruptive behavior in a classroom. *Journal of Applied Behavior Analysis,* 1969, 2, 119–124.

Bartlett, L. A. and Swenson, L. C. A contingency management system using positive reinforcement and peer pressure to reduce disruptive classroom behavior. Paper presented at Western Psychological Association annual meeting, Sacramento, California, April, 1975.

Bondy, A. S. and Erickson, M. T. Comparison of modelling and reinforcement procedures in increasing question-asking of mildly retarded children. *Journal of Applied Behavior Analysis,* 1976, 9, 108.

Bouchard, M. and Granger, L. The role of instructions versus instructions plus feedback in voluntary heart rate slowing. *Psychophysiology,* 1977, 14, 475–482.

Bufford, R. K. Evaluation of a reinforcement procedure for accelerating work rate in a self-paced course. *Journal of Applied Behavior Analysis,* 1976, 9, 208.

Chance, P. and Lovaas, I. After you hit a child, you can't just get up and leave him; You are hooked to that kid. *Psychology Today,* January 1974, 7, 76–84.

Chesney, M. A. and Shelton, J. L. A comparison of muscle relaxation and electromyogram biofeedback treatments for muscle contraction headache. *Journal of Behavior Therapy and Experimental Psychiatry,* 1976, 7, 221–225.

Chisholm, R. C., DeGood, D. E., and Hartz, M. A. Effects of alpha feedback training on occipital EEG, heart rate, and experiential reactivity to a laboratory stressor. *Psychophysiology,* 1977, 14, 157–163.

Cooke, T. P. and Apolloni, T. Developing positive social-emotional behaviors: A study of training and generalization effects. *Journal of Applied Behavior Analysis,* 1976, 9, 65–78.

Deitz, S. M. An analysis of programming DRL schedules in educational settings. *Behavior Research and Therapy*, 1976, 15, 103–111.

DuNann, D. H. and Fernald, P. S. An experimental comparison of a contingency managed course with large lecture method. *Journal of Applied Behavior Analysis*, 1976, 9, 373–374.

DuNann, D. H. and Weber, S. J. Short- and long-term effects of contingency managed instruction on low, medium, and high GPA students. *Journal of Applied Behavior Analysis*, 1976, 9, 375–376.

Epstein, L. H. and Abel, G. G. An analysis of biofeedback training effects for tension headache patients. *Behavior Therapy*, 1977, 8, 37–47.

Feallock, R. and Miller, L. K. The design and evaluation of a worksharing system for experimental group living. *Journal of Applied Behavior Analysis*, 9, 277–288.

Fichter, M. M., Wallace, C. J., Liberman, R. P., and Davis, J. R. Improved social interaction in a chronic psychotic using discriminated avoidance ("nagging"): Experimental analysis and generalization. *Journal of Applied Behavior Analysis*, 1976, 9, 377–386.

Glover, J. and Gary, A. L. Procedures to increase some aspects of creativity. *Journal of Applied Behavior Analysis*, 1976, 9, 79–84.

Goldiamond, I. Self-control procedures in personal behavior problems. *Psychological Reports*, 1965, 17, 851–868.

Haggerty, J. J. *Spinoff 1977, An annual report.* National Aeronautics and Space Administration Technology Utilization Office. Washington, D.C.: U.S. Government Printing Office, 1977.

Hall, J. N., Baker, R. D., and Hutchinson, K. A controlled evaluation of token economy procedures with chronic schizophrenic patients. *Behavior Research and Therapy*, 1977, 15, 261–283.

Harlow, H. F. Motivation as a factor in the acquisition of new responses. In *Current theory and research in motivation: A symposium.* Lincoln: University of Nebraska Press, 1953.

Harris, V. A., Katkin, E. S., Lick, J. R., and Habberfield, T. Paced respiration as a technique for the modification of autonomic responses to stress. *Psychophysiology*, 1976, 13, 386–391.

Hayes, S. C., Johnson, V. S., and Cone, J. D. The marked item technique: A practical procedure for litter control. *Journal of Applied Behavior Analysis*, 1975, 8, 381–386.

Hergenhahn, B. R. *An introduction to theories of learning.* Englewood Cliffs, N.J.: Prentice-Hall, 1976.

Hobbs, T. R. and Holt, M. M. The effects of token reinforcement on the behavior of delinquents in a cottage setting. *Journal of Applied Behavior Analysis*, 1976, 9, 189–198.

Holmes, T. H. and Rahe, R. H. The social readjustment rating scale. *Journal of Psychosomatic Research*, 1967, 11, 213–218.

Horne, A. M. and Matson, J. L. A comparison of modeling, desensitization, flooding, study skills, and control groups for reducing test anxiety. *Behavior Therapy*, 1977, 8, 1–8.

Hundert, J. The effectiveness of reinforcement, response cost, and mixed programs on classroom behaviors. *Journal of Applied Behavior Analysis*, 1976, 9, 107.

Hutchings, D. F. and Reinking, R. H. Tension headaches: What form of therapy is most effective? *Biofeedback and Self-Regulation,* 1976, 1, 183–190.

Inglis, J., Campbell, D., and Donald, M. W. Electromyographic biofeedback and neuromuscular rehabilitation. *Canadian Journal of Behavioral Science,* 1976, 8, 299–323.

Iwata, B. A., Bailey, J. S., Brown, K. M., Foshee, T. J., and Alpern, M. A. A performance-based lottery to improve residential care and training by institutional staff. *Journal of Applied Behavior Analysis,* 1976, 9, 417–431.

Kamiya, J., Barber, T. X., Miller, N. E., Shapiro, D., and Stoyva, J. (Eds.). *Biofeedback and self-control, 1976–77, An Aldine annual.* Chicago: Aldine, 1977.

Kantorowitz, D. A. A biofeedback approach to premature ejaculation in college students. Paper read at Western Psychological Association annual meeting, Seattle, April, 1977.

Kaplan, H. S. *The illustrated manual of sex therapy.* New York: Quadrangle/New York Times Book Co., 1975.

Keller, F. S. A personal course in psychology. In R. Ulrich, T. Stachnik, and J. Mabry (Eds.), *Control of Human Behavior.* Glenview, Ill.: Scott, Foresman, 1966.

Keller, F. S., Goodbye, teacher . . . *Journal of Applied Behavior Analysis,* 1968, 1, 69–89.

Kinkade, K. Commune: A Walden-two experiment. *Psychology Today,* January 1973, 6, 35–42.

Kleinman, K. M., Goldman, H., Snow, M. Y., and Korol, B. Relationship between essential hypertension and cognitive functioning II: Effects of biofeedback training generalize to non-laboratory environment. *Psychophysiology,* 1977, 14, 192–197.

Lubar, J. F. and Bahler, W. W. Behavioral management of epileptic seizures following EEG biofeedback training of the sensorimotor rhythm. *Biofeedback and Self-Regulation,* 1976, 1, 77–104.

Mahoney, M. On the continuing resistance to thoughtful therapy. *Behavior Therapy,* 1977, 8, 673–677.

Malott, R. *Contingency management in education; Or I've got blisters on my soul and other equally exciting places.* Rev. ed. Kalamazoo, Michigan: Behaviordelia, 1974.

Marholin, D. and Gray, D. Effects of group response-cost procedures on cash shortages in a small business. *Journal of Applied Behavior Analysis,* 1976, 9, 25–30.

Markowitz, H. New methods for increasing activity in zoo animals: Some results and proposals for the future. Paper presented at the Centennial symposium on science and research, Penrose Institute, Philadelphia, 1974.

Markowitz, H. In defense of unnatural acts between consenting animals. Paper presented at 51st annual American Association of Zoological Parks and Aquariums conference, Calgary, Alberta, 1975. (a)

Markowitz, H. Analysis and control of behavior in the zoo. *Research in Zoos and Aquariums,* 1975, National Academy of Sciences. (b)

Markowitz, H., Schmidt, M. J., and Moody, A. Behavioral engineering and animal health in the zoo. Paper presented at Western Psychological Association annual meeting, Seattle, April, 1977.

Miller, N. E. and DiCara, L. Instrumental learning of heart rate changes in curarized rats: Shaping, and specificity to discriminative stimulus. *Journal of Comparative and Physiological Psychology,* 1967, 63, 12–19.

Miller, K. L. and Weaver, H. F. A behavioral technology for producing concept formation in university students. *Journal of Applied Behavior Analysis,* 1976, 9, 289–300.

Ormund, J., Quintanella, A., and Swenson, L. C. A comparison of the effects of biofeedback and three control procedures on the output of fastwave EEG in male and female college students. Paper presented at Western Psychological Association annual meeting, San Francisco, April, 1978.

Powers, R. B., Osborne, J. G., and Anderson, E. G. Positive reinforcement of litter removal in the natural environment. *Journal of Applied Behavior Analysis,* 1973, 6, 579–586.

Robertson, S. J., DeReus, D. M., and Drabman, R. S. Peer and college-student tutoring as reinforcement in a token economy. *Journal of Applied Behavior Analysis,* 1976, 9, 169–177.

Rosen, R. C., Shapiro, D., and Schwartz, G. E. Voluntary control of penile tumescence. *Psychosomatic Medicine,* 1975, 37, 479–483.

Rosenthal, T. L., Hung, J. H., and Kelley, J. E. Therapeutic social influence; Sternly strike while the iron is hot. *Behavior Research and Therapy,* 1977, 15, 253–259.

Sakai, S. and Harkey, N. Scrotal temperature fluctuations in euspermic males. Paper presented at Western Psychological Association annual meeting, Anaheim, California, April, 1973.

Schandler, S. L. and Grings, W. W. An examination of methods for producing relaxation during short-term laboratory sessions. *Behaviour Research and Therapy,* 1976, 14, 419–426.

Seligman, M. E. P. Fall into helplessness. *Psychology Today,* June 1973, 7, 43–48.

Seymour, F. W. and Stokes, T. F. Self-recording in training girls to increase work and evoke staff praise in an institution for offenders. *Journal of Applied Behavior Analysis,* 1976, 9, 41–54.

Shapiro, D. Presidential address, 1976: A monologue on biofeedback and psychophysiology. *Psychophysiology,* 1977, 14, 213–226.

Shedivy, D. I. and Kleinman, K. M. Lack of correlation between frontalis EMG and either neck EMG or verbal ratings of tension. *Psychophysiology,* 1977, 14, 182–186.

Sheer, D. E. Biofeedback training of 40-Hz EEG and behavior. In I. Kamiya, T. X. Barber, N. E. Miller, D. Shapiro, and J. Stoyva (Eds.), *Biofeedback and self-control: 1976–77, An Aldine annual.* Chicago: Aldine, 1977.

Skinner, B. F. *Walden two.* New York: Macmillan, 1948.

Small, L. *Neuropsychodiagnosis in psychotherapy.* New York: Brunner/Mazel, 1973.

Swenson, L. C. Application of contingency management principles to the college classroom: The con game project. Paper presented at Western Psychological Association annual meeting, Anaheim, California, April, 1973.

Swenson, L. C. The effects of requiring charting on coursework output in college students enrolled in a point system based college course. Paper presented at Western Psychological Association annual meeting, Sacramento, California, April, 1975.

Tharp, R. G. and Wetzel, R. J. *Behavior modification in the natural environment.* New York: Academic Press, 1969.

Whitehead, W. E., Renault, P. F., and Goldiamond, I. Modification of human gastric acid secretion with operant-conditioning procedures. *Journal of Applied Behavior Analysis,* 1975, 8, 147–156.

Woolfolk, R. L., Carr-Kaffashan, L., McNulty, T. F., and Lehrer, P. M. Meditation training as a treatment for insomnia. *Behavior Therapy*, 1976, 7, 359–365.

Zlutnick, S., Mayville, W. J., and Moffat, S. Modification of seizure disorders: The interruption of behavioral chains. *Journal of Applied Behavior Analysis*, 1975, 8, 1–12.

Chapter 11

Asch, S. E. The doctrinal tyranny of associationism: Or what is wrong with rote learning. In T. R. Dixon and D. L. Horton (Eds.), *Verbal behavior and general behavior theory*. Englewood Cliffs, N.J.: Prentice-Hall, 1968.

Biferno, M. A. and Dawson, M. E. The onset of contingency awareness and electrodermal classical conditioning: An analysis of temporal relationships during acquisition and extinction. *Psychophysiology*, 1977, 14, 164–171.

Biferno, M. A. and Dawson, M. E. Elicitation of subjective uncertainty during vasomotor and electrodermal discrimination classical conditioning. *Psychophysiology*, 1978, 15, 1–8.

Biggs, J. B. Schooling and moral development. In V. P. Varma and P. Williams (Eds.), *Piaget, psychology and education*. Itasca, Ill.: F. E. Peacock, 1976.

Bourne, L. E., Jr. Knowing and using concepts. *Psychological Review*, 1970, 77, 546–556.

Bourne, L. E., Jr. An inference model for conceptual rule learning. In R. L. Solso (Ed.), *Theories in cognitive psychology: The Loyola symposium*. Potomac, Md.: Erlbaum, 1974.

Bower, G. H. and Trabasso, T. R. Reversal prior to solution in concept identification. *Journal of Experimental Psychology*, 1963, 66, 409–418.

Bruner, J. S., Goodnow, J. J., and Austin, G. A. *A study of thinking*. New York: John Wiley & Sons, 1956.

Chomsky, N. *Language and mind*. San Francisco: Harcourt Brace Jovanovich, 1968.

Chomsky, N. *Language and mind*. Enl. ed. San Francisco: Harcourt Brace Jovanovich, 1972.

Chomsky, N. Psychology and ideology. In T. G. Bever (Ed.), *Warner modular publication 65*. Andover, Mass.: Warner Modular Publications, 1973.

Ellis, H. C. *Fundamentals of human learning, memory, and cognition*. 2nd ed. Dubuque, Iowa: William C. Brown, 1978.

Freibergs, V. and Tulvig, E. The effect of practice on utilization of information from positive and negative instances in concept identification. *Canadian Journal of Psychology*, 1961, 15, 101–106.

Hasher, L., Reibman, B., and Wren, F. Imagery and the retention of free-recall learning. *Journal of Experimental Psychology: Human Learning and Memory*, 1976, 2, 172–181.

Hilgard, E. R. and Bower, G. H. *Theories of learning*. 4th ed. Englewood Cliffs, N.J.: Prentice-Hall, 1975.

Hill, W. F. *Learning: A survey of psychological interpretations*. 3rd ed. New York: Thomas Y. Crowell Company, 1977.

Horton, D. L. and Turnage, T. W. *Human learning*. Englewood Cliffs, N.J.: Prentice-Hall, 1976.

Houston, J. P. Verbal transfer and interlist similarities. *Psychological Review*, 1964, 71, 412–414.

Kendler, H. H. and Kendler, T. S. From discrimination learning to cognitive development: A neobehaviorist odyssey. In W. K. Estes (Ed.), *Handbook of learning and cognitive processes.* Vol. 1. Hillside, N.J.: Erlbaum, 1975.

Levine, M. Hypothesis behavior by humans during discrimination learning. *Journal of Experimental Psychology,* 1966, 71, 331–338.

Levine, M. Hypothesis theory and nonlearning despite ideal S-R reinforcement contingencies. *Psychological Review,* 1971, 78, 130–140.

Lindsay, P. H. and Norman, D. A. *Human information processing: An introduction to psychology.* New York: Academic Press, 1977.

Miller, G. A. The magical number seven, plus or minus two: Some limits on our capacity for processing information. *Psychological Review,* 1956, 63, 81–97.

Miller, G. A. Decision units in the perception of speech. *IRE Transactions on Information Theory,* 1962, IT-8, 81–83.

Miller, G. A., Galanter, E., and Pribram, K. *Plans and the structure of behavior.* New York: Holt, Rinehart and Winston, 1960.

Nelson, K. Concept, word, and sentence: Interrelations in acquisition and development. *Psychological Review,* 1974, 81, 267–285.

Norman, D. A. Introduction: Models of human memory. In D. A. Norman (Ed.), *Models of human memory.* New York: Academic Press, 1970.

Norman, D. A. *Memory and attention: An introduction to human information processing.* New York: John Wiley & Sons, 1976.

Norman, D. A. and Rumelhart, D. E. A system for perception and memory. In D. A. Norman (Ed.), *Models of human memory.* New York: Academic Press, 1970.

Osgood, C. E. *Method and theory in experimental psychology.* New York: Oxford University Press, 1953.

Palermo, D. S. *Psychology of language.* Glenview, Ill.: Scott, Foresman, 1978.

Pavlov, I. *Conditioned reflexes.* Trans. 1927. New York: Dover, 1960.

Phillips, J. L. *The origins of intellect: Piaget's theory.* San Francisco: W. H. Freeman, 1969.

Piaget, J. How children form mathematical concepts. *Scientific American,* May 1953, 189, 74–79.

Piaget, J. Development and learning. In R. Ripple and U. Rockcastle (Eds.), *Piaget rediscovered.* Ithaca, N.Y.: Cornell University Press, 1964, 7–20.

Piaget, J. *Science of education and the psychology of the child.* New York: Viking, 1970.

Reed, J. C. and Riach, W. The role of repetition and set in paired-associate learning. *American Journal of Psychology,* 1960, 53, 608–611.

Restle, F. Sources of difficulty in learning paired associates. In R. C. Atkinson (Ed.), *Studies in mathematical psychology.* Stanford, Ca.: Stanford University Press, 1964.

Saltz, E. *The cognitive bases of human learning.* Homewood, Ill.: Dorsey Press, 1971.

Saltz, E. Higher mental processes as the bases for the laws of conditioning. In F. J. McGuigen and D. B. Lumsden (Eds.), *Contemporary approaches to conditioning and learning.* Washington, D.C.: V. H. Winston & Sons, 1973.

Saltz, E. and Hamilton, H. Do lower IQ children attain concepts more slowly than children of higher IQ? *Psychonomic Science,* 1969, 17, 210–211.

Sigel, I. E., Roeper, A., and Hooper, A. A training procedure for acquisition of Piaget's conservation of quantity: A pilot study and its replication. Paper presented at New

Media in Education, Business, and Industry, conference, Wayne State University, January, 1965.

Silver, D. The role of awareness in learning and operant performance in the verbal operant situation. Unpublished master's thesis, Wayne State University, 1967.

Silver, D., Saltz, E., and Modigliani, V. Awareness and hypothesis testing in concept and operant learning. *Journal of Experimental Psychology,* 1970, 84, 198–203.

Skinner, B. F. *Contingencies of reinforcement: A theoretical analysis.* New York: Appleton-Century-Crofts, 1969.

Skinner, B. F. *About behaviorism.* New York: Alfred A. Knopf, 1974.

Sokolov, E. M. Higher nervous functions: The orienting reflex. *Annual Review of Physiology,* 1963, 25, 545–580.

Staats, C. K., Staats, A. W., and Biggs, J. B. Meaning of verbal stimuli changed by conditioning. *American Journal of Psychology,* 1958, 71, 429–431.

Sternberg, S. High-speed scanning in human memory. *Science,* 1966, 153, 652–654.

Stroop, J. R. Studies of interference in serial verbal reactions. *Journal of Experimental Psychology,* 1935, 18, 643–662.

Suppes, P. and Schlag-Rey, M. Observable changes in hypotheses under positive reinforcement. *Science,* 1965, 148, 661–662.

Tarpy, R. M. and Mayer, R. E. *Foundations of learning and memory.* Glenview, Ill.: Scott, Foresman, 1978.

Treisman, A. M. Verbal cues, language and meaning in selective attention. *American Journal of Psychology,* 1964, 25, 545–580.

Varma, V. P. and Williams, P. *Piaget, psychology and education.* Itasca, Ill.: F. E. Peacock, 1976.

Wadsworth, B. J. *Piaget for the classroom teacher.* New York: Longman, 1978.

Yerkes, R. M. and Dodson, J. D. The relation of strength of stimulus to rapidity of habit-formation. *Journal of Comparative Neurology of Psychology,* 1908, 18, 459–482.

Chapter 12

Barash, D. P. *Sociobiology and behavior.* New York: Elsevier North-Holland, 1977.

Barondes, S. H. and Cohen, H. D. Puromycin effect on successive phases of memory storage. *Science,* 1966, 151, 594–595.

Best, P. J. and Zuckerman, K. Subcortical mediation of learned taste aversion. *Physiology and Behavior,* 1971, 7, 317–320.

Bolles, R. C. Species-specific defense reactions and avoidance learning. *Psychological Review,* 1970, 71, 32–48.

Bolles, R. C. *Learning theory.* San Francisco: Holt, Rinehart and Winston, 1975.

Breland, K. and Breland, M. The misbehavior of organisms. *American Psychologist,* 1961, 16, 681–684.

Brown, H. *Brain and behavior.* New York: Oxford University Press, 1976.

Burghardt, G. M. Instinct and innate behavior: Toward an ethological psychology. In J. A. Nevin (Ed.), *The study of behavior—Learning, motivation, emotion, and instinct.* Glenview, Ill.: Scott, Foresman, 1973, 323–400.

Byrne, W. L. (Ed.). *Molecular approaches to learning and memory.* New York: Academic Press, 1970.

Chapouthier, G. Behavior studies of the molecular basis of memory. In J. A. Deutsch (Ed.), *The physiological basis of memory.* New York: Academic Press, 1973, 1–17.

Cohen, H. D., Erwin, F., and Barondes, S. H. Puromycin and cycloheximide: Different effects on hippocampal electrical activity. *Science,* 1966, 154, 1557–1558.

Dennenberg, V. H. (ed.). *Readings in the development of behavior.* Stanford, Conn.: Sinauer Associates, 1972.

Deutsch, J. A. and Deutsch, D. *Physiological psychology.* Rev. ed. Homewood, Ill.: Dorsey Press, 1973.

DeVietti, T. L. and Larson, R. C. ECS effects: Evidence supporting state-dependent learning in rats. *Journal of Comparative and Physiological Psychology,* 1971, 74, 407–415.

Diamond, I. T. and Neff, W. D. Ablation of the temporal cortex and discrimination of auditory patterns. *Journal of Neurophysiology,* 1957, 20, 300–315.

Dingman, W. and Sporn, M. B. Molecular theories of memory. *Science,* 1964, 144, 26–29.

Doty, R. W. Conditioned reflexes formed and evoked by brain stimulation. In D. E. Sheer (Ed.), *Electrical stimulation of the brain.* Austin, Texas: University of Texas Press, 1961, 397–412.

Frazier, W. A., Angeletti, R. H., and Bradshaw, R. A. Nerve growth factor and insulin. *Science,* 1972, 176, 482–488.

Gardner, H. *The shattered mind; The person after brain damage.* New York: Alfred A. Knopf, 1974.

Garcia, J. and Koelling, R. A. The relation of cue to consequence in avoidance learning. *Psychonomic Science,* 1966, 4, 123–124.

Garcia, J., McGowan, B. K., Ervin, F. R., and Koelling, R. A. Cues: Their relative effectiveness as a function of the reinforcer. *Science,* 1968, 160, 794–795.

Gazzaniga, M. S. The split brain in man. *Scientific American,* August 1967, 217, 24–29.

Goldstein, K. *Human nature in the light of psychopathology.* New York: Schocken Books, 1963.

Grossman, S. P. *Essentials of physiological psychology.* New York: John Wiley & Sons, 1973.

Gustavson, C. R., Garcia, J., Hankins, W. G., and Rusiniak, K. W. Coyote predation control by aversive conditioning. *Science,* 1974, Vol. 1843, 581–583.

Harlow, H. F. *Learning to love.* San Francisco: Albion, 1971.

Hartry, A. L., Keith-Lee, P., and Morton, W. D. Planaria: Memory transfer through cannibalism re-examined. *Science,* 1964, 146, 274–275.

Hebb, D. O. *A textbook of psychology.* 2nd ed. Philadelphia: W. B. Saunders, 1966.

Hess, E. H. "Imprinting" in a natural laboratory. *Scientific American,* August 1972, 227, 24–31.

Hines, B. and Paolino, R. M. Retrograde amnesia: Production of skeletal but not cardiac response gradients by electroconvulsive shocks. *Science,* 1970, 169, 1224–1226.

Hyden, H. and Egyhazi, E. Changes in RNA content and base composition in cortical neurons of rats in a learning experiment involving transfer of handedness. *Proceedings of the National Academy of Science: United States,* 1964, 52, 1030–1035.

Jacobsen, A. L. and Schlecter, J. M. Chemical transfer of training: Three years later. In K. H. Pribram and D. E. Broadbent (Eds.), *Biology of memory*. New York: Academic Press, 1970.

Kalat, J. W. Taste-aversion learning in dead rats. *Worm Runner's Digest*, 1973, 15, 59–60.

Lamon, S., Wilson, G. T., and Leaf, R. C. Human classical aversion conditioning: Nausea versus electric shock in the reduction of target beverage consumption. *Behavior Research and Therapy*, 1977, 15, 313–320.

Lashley, K. S. In search of the engram. *Symposium of the Society of Experimental Biology*, 1950, 4, 454–582.

Lashley, K. S. *Brain mechanisms and intelligence*. New York: Dover, 1963.

Lorenz, K. Z. *King Solomon's ring*. New York: Thomas Y. Crowell, 1952.

Lorenz, K. Z. The evolution of behavior. *Scientific American*, December 1958, 199, 67–78.

Lorenz, K. *On aggression*. New York: Harcourt, Brace & World, 1963.

Luria, A. R. The functional organization of the brain. *Scientific American*, March 1970, 222, 66–78.

Luria, A. R. and Majovski, L. V. Basic approaches used in American and Soviet clinical neuropsychology. *American Psychologist*, 1977, 32, 959–968.

Luttges, J., Johnson, T., Buck, C., Holland, J., and McGaugh, J. An examination of "transfer of learning" by nucleic acid. *Science*, 1966, 151, 834–837.

Markowitz, H. and Sorrells, J. M. Performance of "maze-bright" and "maze-dull" rats on an automated visual discrimination task. *Psychonomic Science*, 1969, 15, 171–172.

Markowitz, H. and Becker, C. J. Superiority of "maze-dull" animals on visual tasks in an automated maze. *Psychonomic Science*, 1969, 17, 257–258.

McConnell, J. V. Memory transfer through cannibalism in planarians. *Journal of Neuropsychiatry*, 1962, 3 (supplement 1), 542–548.

McConnell, J. V. New evidence for "transfer of training" effect in planarians. Symposium on the biological bases of memory traces, Eighth International Congress of Psychology, Moscow, 1966.

McConnell, J. V. The modern search for the engram. In W. C. Corning and M. Balaban (Eds.), *The mind: Biological approaches to its functions*. New York: Interscience, 1968, 49–68.

Meltzoff, A. N. and Moore, M. K. Imitation of facial and manual gestures by human neonates. *Science*, 1977, 198, 75–78.

Meyer, D. R. Access to engrams. *American Psychologist*, 1972, 27, 124–133.

Miller, E. *Clinical neuropsychology*. Baltimore, Md.: Penguin Books, 1972.

Milner, B. R. Amnesia following operation on temporal lobes. In C. W. N. Whitty and O. L. Zangwill (Eds.), *Amnesia*. London: Butterworths, 1966.

Morrell, F. Electrophysiological contributions to the neural basis of learning. *Physiological Review*, 1961, 41, 443–494.

Nielson, H. C. Evidence that electro-convulsive shock alters memory retrieval rather than memory consolidation. *Experimental Neurology*, 1968, 20, 3–20.

Penfield, W. Consciousness, memory and man's conditioned reflexes. In K. H. Pribram (Ed.), *On the biology of learning*. New York: Harcourt Brace Jovanovich, 1969, 127–168.

Pribram, K. H. On the neurophysiology of memory. *Scientific American,* January 1969, 220.

Pribram, K. H. *Languages of the brain: Experimental paradoxes and principles in neuropsychology.* Englewood Cliffs, N.J.: Prentice-Hall, 1971. (a)

Pribram, K. H. Holograms in the head. *Psychology Today,* September 1971, 5, 44–48. (b)

Pribram, K. H. and McGuinness, D. Arousal, activation, and effort in the control of attention. *Psychological Review,* 1975, 82, 116–149.

Quartermain, D., McEwen, B. S., and Azmitia, E. C. Amnesia produced by electroconvulsive shock or cycloheximide: Conditions for recovery. *Science,* 1970, 169, 683–686.

Rachman, P. de S. and Seligman, M. E. P. Prepared phobias and obsessions: Therapeutic outcome. *Behavior Research and Therapy,* 1977, 15, 65–77

Raisman, G. Neuronal plasticity in the septal nuclei of the adult rat. *Brain Research,* 1969, 14, 25–48.

Revusky, S. H. and Garcia, J. Learned associations over long delays. In G. H. Bower and J. T. Spence (Eds.), *The psychology of learning and motivation.* Vol. 4. New York: Academic Press, 1970.

Reynolds, D. V. The engram is not a hologram—at least not yet. Tutorial presented at Western Psychological Association annual meeting, San Francisco, April, 1974.

Riopelle, A. J. and Ades, H. W. Discrimination following deep temporal lesions. *American Psychologist,* 1951, 6, 261–262.

Roll, D. L. and Smith, J. C. Conditioned taste aversion in anesthetized rats. In M. E. P. Seligman and J. L. Hager (Eds.), *Biological boundaries of learning.* New York: Appleton-Century-Crofts, 1972.

Rosenzweig, M. R., Krech, D., Bennett, E. L., and Diamond, M. C. Effects of environmental complexity and training on brain chemistry and anatomy: A replication and extension. *Journal of Comparative and Physiological Psychology,* 1967, 55, 429–437.

Schneider, A. M. and Tarshis, B. *An introduction to physiological psychology.* New York: Random House, 1975.

Seligman, M. E. P. and Hager, J. L. Biological boundaries of learning (The sauce-Béarnaise syndrome). *Psychology Today,* August 1972, 6, 59–61.

Skinner, B. F. *Contingencies of reinforcement: A theoretical analysis.* New York: Appleton-Century-Crofts, 1969.

Skinner, B. F. *About behaviorism.* New York: Alfred A. Knopf, 1974.

Sluckin, W. *Imprinting and early learning.* Chicago: Aldine, 1965.

Sluckin, W. *Early learning in man and animal.* Morristown, N.J.: Schenkman, 1970.

Smith, R. F., Gustavson, C. R., and Gregor, G. L. Incompatibility between the pigeon's unconditioned response to shock and the conditioned key-peck response. *Journal of the Experimental Analysis of Behavior,* 1972, 18, 147–153.

Sokolov, E. N. *Perception and the conditioned reflex.* New York: Macmillan, 1963.

Sperry, R. W. Cerebral organization and behavior. *Science,* 1961, 133, 1749–1757.

Spinelli, D. N. and Pribram, K. H. Changes in visual recovery functions produced by temporal lobe stimulation in monkeys. *Electroencephlography and Clinical Neurophysiology,* 1966, 20, 44–49.

Staddon, J. E. R. and Simmelhag, V. L. The "superstition" experiment: A reexamination of its implications for the principles of adaptive behavior. *Psychological Review*, 1971, 78, 3–43.

Swenson, L. C. and Catania, J. Learning and transfer of a single alternation concept under conditions of cortical spreading depression in rats. *Physiology and Behavior*, 1973, 11, 319–322.

Swenson, L. C. and Catania, J. Reduced ability to cope with altered stimulus conditions in performance of a single alternation task under bilateral cortical spreading depression in rats. Paper presented at Western Psychological Association annual meeting, San Francisco, April, 1974.

Swenson, L. C. and Goldwitz, D. Learning of instrumental avoidance responses under conditions of bilateral spreading depression. *Psychonomic Science*, 1972, 29, 43–45.

Tinbergen, N. *The study of instinct.* Oxford: Oxford University Press, 1951.

Tryon, R. C. Genetic differences in maze-learning ability in rats. In G. M. Whipple (Ed.), *Yearbook of the national society for studies in education*, 1940, 39, 111–119.

Ungar, G. Chemical transfer of learning: Its stimulus specificity. *Federation Proceedings*, 1966, 25, 207.

Ungar, G., Ho, I. K., and Galvan, L. Isolation of a dark avoidance inducing brain peptide. *Federation Proceedings*, 1970, 29, 658.

Wilcoxin, H. C., Dragoin, W. B., and Kral, P. A. Illness-induced aversions in rat and quail: Relative salience of visual and gustatory cues. *Science*, 1971, 171, 826–828.

Zahorik, D. M., Maier, S. F., and Pies, R. W. Preferences for tastes paired with recovery from thiamine deficiency in rats: Appetitive conditioning or learned safety? *Journal of Comparative and Physiological Psychology*, 1974, 87, 1083–1091.

Part 2 Summary

Dunham, P. J. Punishment: Method and theory. *Psychological Review*, 1971, 78, 58–70.

Hebb, D. O., Lambert, W. E., and Tucker, G. R. A DMZ in the language war. *Psychology Today*, April 1973, 6, 54–63.

Staddon, J. E. R. and Simmelhag, V. L. The "superstition" experiment: A reexamination of its implications for the principles of adaptive behavior. *Psychological Review*, 1971, 78, 3–43.

Timberlake, W. and Allison, J. Response deprivation: An empirical approach to instrumental performance. *Psychological Review*, 1974, 81, 146–164.

SUBJECT INDEX   numbers in boldface indicate glossary entry